PSYCHOLOGICAL ANTHROPOLOGY

PSYCHOLOGICAL ANTHROPOLOGY

Edited by

FRANCIS L. K. HSU

NEW EDITION

SCHENKMAN PUBLISHING COMPANY, INC.

Cambridge, Massachusetts

Distributed by General Learning Press

Schenkman books are distributed by:
GENERAL LEARNING PRESS
250 James Street
Morristown, New Jersey 07960

CONTENTS

Contributors   vii

Preface   ix

INTRODUCTION

Psychological Anthropology in the Behavioral Sciences
Francis L. K. Hsu   1

PART I *Area*

CHAPTER ONE

Culture and Personality: The Japanese
Edward Norbeck and George DeVos   21

CHAPTER TWO

Africa   *Robert L. Munroe, Ruth H. Munroe,*
and Robert A. LeVine   71

CHAPTER THREE

North America   *John J. Honigmann*   121

CHAPTER FOUR

Oceania   *L. L. Langness and Thomas Gladwin*   167

CHAPTER FIVE

National Character and Modern Political Systems   *Alex Inkeles*   201

CHAPTER SIX

American Core Value and National Character   *Francis L. K. Hsu*   241

PART II *Methods and Techniques*

CHAPTER SEVEN

On the Use of Projective Tests for Research in Psychological
Anthropology   *David H. Spain*   267

CHAPTER EIGHT

An Experiment with TAT   *Blanche Watrous*
and Francis L. K. Hsu   309

CHAPTER NINE

Mental Illness, Biology and Culture   *Anthony F. C. Wallace*   363

CHAPTER TEN

Dreams and Altered States of Consciousness in Anthropological
Research   *Erika Bourguignon*   403

CHAPTER ELEVEN

The Mutual Methodological Relevance of Anthropology and
Psychology   *Donald T. Campbell and Raoul Naroll*   435

PART III *Socialization, Culture and Feedback*

CHAPTER TWELVE

Socialization Process and Personality   *Charles Harrington and
                                            John W. M. Whiting*   469

CHAPTER THIRTEEN

Kinship and Ways of Life: An Exploration   *Francis L. K. Hsu*   509

PART IV *Assessment*

CHAPTER FOURTEEN

An Overview and a Suggested Reorientation   *Melford E. Spiro*   573

A Supplementary Bibliography on Projective Testing
                                Compiled by David H. Spain   609

CONTRIBUTORS

ERIKA BOURGUIGNON, *Professor of Anthropology, Ohio State University*

DONALD T. CAMPBELL, *Professor of Psychology, Northwestern University*

GEORGE A. DEVOS, *Professor of Anthropology, University of California, Berkeley*

THOMAS GLADWIN, *Lecturer, University of Hawaii*

CHARLES HARRINGTON, *Associate Professor, Teachers College, Columbia University*

JOHN J. HONIGMANN, *Professor of Anthropology, University of North Carolina at Chapel Hill*

FRANCIS L. K. HSU, *Professor of Anthropology, Northwestern University*

ALEX INKELES, *Professor of Sociology, Stanford University*

LEWIS L. LANGNESS, *Associate Professor of Anthropology, University of Washington*

ROBERT A. LEVINE, *Professor of Anthropology, University of Chicago*

ROBERT L. MUNROE, *Associate Professor of Anthropology, Pitzer College*

RUTH H. MUNROE, *Associate Professor of Psychology, Pitzer College*

RAOUL NAROLL, *Professor of Anthropology, State University of New York at Buffalo*

EDWARD NORBECK, *Professor of Anthropology, Rice University*

DAVID H. SPAIN, *Assistant Professor of Anthropology, University of Washington*

MELFORD E. SPIRO, *Professor of Anthropology, University of California, San Diego*

ANTHONY F. C. WALLACE, *Professor of Anthropology, University of Pennsylvania*

BLANCHE G. WATROUS, *Professor of Anthropology, East Carolina University*

JOHN W. M. WHITING, *Professor of Anthropology, Department of Social Relations, Harvard University*

Preface to the Second Edition

Since publication of the first edition of the book, a number of anthropologists questioned the wisdom of devoting a large portion to division by geographical area. The editor and some of the contributors considered this problem, and we decided to keep this section as originally planned — partly because we also received a good deal of encouragement from others who found the arrangement very useful.

However, we have not only updated the chapters in this section by simply replacing some materials and adding others which appeared since 1961. We have amplified the summaries of the important studies in the various geographical areas covered so that the student can gain a far better panoramic picture. These summaries of studies are not intended as substitutes for the original full-length papers or monographs from which they have been abstracted. A consistent question from many an undergraduate or graduate student is: What are the major problems and how far have they been worked on? From my experiences these area chapters have saved many young men and women hours of search through mountainous amounts of material. Besides, the area approach is still important in our curriculum. Although I myself believe that the area approach must eventually be replaced by the comparative approach,[1] that is not yet a

[1] See Francis L. K. Hsu, THE STUDY OF LITERATE CIVILIZATIONS, 1969, New York, Holt, Rinehart and Winston. Pp. 52–56.

generally acknowledged reality. It is my hope that by simplifying the area results in this way, the student is more easily led or inspired into seeing the necessity or wisdom of true comparison.

Our Methods and Techniques section never was intended to be a systematic survey of all that has been conceived and used by psychological anthropologists. Instead it was and is designed to demonstrate how some major methodological considerations and tools have been employed to yield meaningful results. Toward this end we have added a new chapter detailing An Experiment with TAT (Chapter 8), which offers a way of utilizing this projective test never tried before by other workers. Some reviewers have raised the question as to whether Anthony F. C. Wallace's contribution on Mental Illness, Biology and Culture (Chapter 9) is in fact methodological and therefore should be moved to another part of the book. I think a new conceptual scheme for revealing the intricate matrix of mental illness, biology, and culture is methodological in the broad accepted sense of the term.

The reader will note that, other than having every chapter updated by the original author or by new authors, the general plan of the book has been maintained. From its inception, our emphasis was on balancing the more or less well-established materials with intellectual exploration. We did not intend to produce an orthodox and old-fashioned textbook. Hopefully our original thrust will continue to provide students with research leads and continue to fulfill the expectations of colleagues who used or will use this volume.

In the preparation of the manuscripts for publication and in the voluminous correspondence with the contributors, I am greatly indebted to the tireless assistance of Mrs. Adele Andelson and Mrs. Andrea Sherwin. In addition, Mrs. Andelson also compiled the two indexes.

F.L.K.H.

Psychological Anthropology in the Behavioral Sciences

FRANCIS L. K. HSU

At the beginning of our joint efforts the contributors[1] to this volume were of the opinion that attempts at delineating boundaries for culture-and-personality would do more harm than good. Too often precise boundaries have been used as excuses for lack of data, methods, and results. What we need in culture-and-personality is not orthodoxy but more specific research and discussion. Some opinions were milder than others but the direction of our comments was similar. One commented in the following vein:

> I feel that any area of study which is still as formative as ours can readily deal itself out of important areas of inquiry by a premature setting of limits. Anthropology itself supplies a classic example. The respective areas of study of archaeology, physical anthropology, and ethnology were so neatly defined and separated that it took years of effort and the pressure of great intellectual need to reconstitute the connective tissue which had been unthinkingly destroyed by the classificatory surgery once fashionable. We are not an exclusive society which needs entrance requirements for members.

[1] The contributors to the first edition of this book were: Aberle, Campbell, D'Andrade, DeVos, Gladwin, Honigmann, Inkeles, Kaplan, LeVine, Norbeck, Spiro, Wallace, and Whiting.

Others expressed themselves as follows:

My advice is not to worry about these demarcation problems but to go where our interests and talents lead us. Anthropology has always been distinguished by amoeba-like extensions into any discipline where its problems or interests have pushed it.

The virtues of anarchy and chaos are many — the pains of efforts to achieve unity are usually without compensatory gain.

Finally, I do not think we should repeat the errors of many in the standard academic disciplines by taking the boundaries of our field too seriously. A recent article begins with a comment that is relevant here: "It is perhaps a reflection of the intellectual insecurity of social scientists that they spend an inordinate amount of time and energy defining the boundaries of their respective fields as if these were holy lands which had to be defended against expansive, barbaric, and heathen invaders."

I received more reactions on this subject than I have reproduced here. They do not all state the point as strongly, but there is none which upholds the opposite view. In these circumstances it is natural that our ideas as to what should be the proper concern of culture-and-personality vary a good deal. As I scan our correspondence and the sometimes copious notes of our various meetings, I find the following general trends of thought:

1. A work of culture-and-personality is one by an anthropologist who has a good knowledge of psychological concepts or by the member of another discipline who has a good knowledge of anthropological concepts.
2. Any work that deals with the individual as the locus of culture.
3. Any work that gives serious recognition to culture as an independent or a dependent variable associated with personality.
4. Any work by an anthropologist which uses psychological concepts or techniques or by a scholar in a psychological discipline which provides directly pertinent data in forms which are useable by anthropologists.
5. The field of culture-and-personality is equivalent to the cross-cultural study of personality and sociocultural systems and includes such problems as (a) the relation of social structure and values to modal patterns of child rearing, (b) the relation of modal patterns of child rearing to modal personality structure as expressed in behavior, (c) the relation of modal personality structure to the role system and projective aspects of culture, and (d) the relation of all of the foregoing variables to deviant behavior patterns which vary from one

group to.another. The theories used and hypotheses tested can come from any of the behavioral sciences, but the characteristic mark of culture-and-personality research is the emphasis on natural group differences as the subject matter. Studies of individual differences are not, therefore, works of culture and personality. Nor are studies of the experimentally-produced group differences of many social psychologists. Studies of many role personalities within a particular society are on the borderline, but group differences within a society are, in my opinion, squarely within the culture-and-personality field. Thus Marvin Opler's studies of types of schizophrenia in two American ethnic groups are culture-and-personality work.

6. The conception of personality-culture as emergent from interaction is fruitful. To this it should be added that students of culture-and-personality are concerned with behavior always with reference to its antecedents and cannot be satisfied simply to describe its characteristics — as social psychologists are wont to do.

The possible differences between culture-and-personality and social psychology will be touched upon later. Our own lack of agreement is probably reflective of the perennial seesaw discussion among many anthropologists on culture. At one end is Kroeber's concept of the *Superorganic* and the perhaps more extreme position of Leslie A. White in his *Culturology*, which comes close to asserting that the march of history is independent of the birth of particular personalities and that cultures transcend the minds and bodies of the individuals living in them (Kroeber 1948:253–255 and White 1949). This view has been criticized on the ground that culture cannot exist without the individual, since "to objectify a phenomenon that can have no manifestation except in human thought and action is to argue a separate existence for something that actually exists only in the mind of the student" (Herskovits 1948:25). At the other end are students who note individual differences and cultural variation in each society. Herskovits shows how the same song, "John Crow," prevalent in the northwestern part of Jamaica, is rendered into many different versions by many different singers (Herskovits 1948:565–569). John Gillin demonstrates the intrasocietal differences among many nonliterate societies (Gillin 1939:681–702). Bert Kaplan has revealed similar differences in four American Indian cultures (Kaplan 1954). Hart perhaps pushed the importance of individual personality differences to a greater extent than most others (Hart 1954).

Needless to say, Kroeber was not unaware of the fact that cultures have to be expressed through individuals, for in his major textbook he did devote a whole chapter to "Cultural Psychology" (1948:572–621). On the other hand, it is equally obvious that no science of man is possible if we merely concentrate on individual differences. Perhaps it is to satisfy both extremes that Kluckhohn and Mowrer found it desirable to introduce an extensive analysis of all the components of personality, from the biological, the physical-environmental, the social, and the cultural, on the one hand, and the universal, the role, and the idiosyncratic on the other (Kluckhohn and Mowrer 1944:4).

In the 1948 edition of their anthology entitled *Personality in Nature, Society and Culture,* Kluckhohn and Murray reformulated the four determinants which were then designated as constitutional, group membership, role, and situational. The two editors concluded in the second edition of this book that "the differences observed in the personalities of human beings are due to variations in their biological equipment and in the total environment to which they must adjust, while the similarities are ascribable to biological-environmental regularities" (Kluckhohn and Murray 1953:65).

In a still later publication Kluckhohn leaned more strongly toward the cultural factor in human behavior, but modestly guarded himself by noting that the field structure-behavioral scientists have to deal with is complex, that the techniques at their command are as yet inadequate, and that they must for the time being be satisfied with "crude, first approximations." "If each specialist fully accepts the fact that his discipline can explain something but not everything, the results are not too bad." And he concluded with an interesting analogy:

> One may compare a game in which the high card or combination is crucial. Other cards in the hand have a value but a secondary importance for that deal. Some hands are dealt by science where the winning combination is certainly held by biology, others where psychology, sociology, geography, or anthropology can do the calling. So I shall here unashamedly concentrate upon the hands where, it seems to me, anthropology can bet high upon the significance of cultural factors for understanding and explanation (Kluckhohn 1954:3–4).

The Core of Culture-and-Personality

Though as a group we eschew boundaries, I think it is quite appropriate for the editor at least to offer some thoughts on the central concerns of culture-and-personality. In this venture I do not expect to settle anything. In such a fuzzy area no clarification is likely to meet with universal acceptance. What I shall try to do is to promote further discussion.

It is probably as trite to observe that all human behavior is mediated through the minds of individual human beings as it is to observe that all human individuals live in social groups each governed by a specific pattern of culture. All human behavior, except random movements and reflexes, is, therefore, at once psychological and social in nature. However, the same psychosocial data may be approached from different angles. The angle of approach would seem to be the primary difference between cultural anthropology and social anthropology, and between them and culture and personality.

Social anthropology began in Britain. The British view is that social anthropology is synonymous with anthropology and sociology combined. That is to say it deals with all aspects of human behavior from kinship and political organizations to economies and religions. The American definition is that social anthropology is confined to the study of social or political organizations. Therefore, some American students are surprised that E. E. Evans-Pritchard should have "left" his field to write a book on *Nuer Religion* (1954). There are perhaps two ways of seeing the real difference between them. First, the British social anthropologists really have distinguished themselves in the intensity of their field work and of analysis of the data, a trend first begun with Rivers and Williams in the Torres Straits and later Malinowski in the Trobriands. Thus Evans-Pritchard carried out his field work in the late twenties and spent the next thirty years publishing primarily on the two societies he studied. This is more or less true of other well-known British social anthropologists such as M. Fortes, R. Firth, and Max Gluckman, though most of them have studied more than one people. This contrasts with the less intensive pattern of field work among American anthropologists, characterized by shorter periods of sojourn, lack of emphasis on thorough familiarity with the native language, and even among many students of the Historical School, a relatively greater emphasis on problem orientation.

The other way is to see cultural anthropology as largely dealing with human behavior in terms of products (culture traits, rituals, dances, techniques, and so forth) while social anthropology deals in terms of relationships (such as kinship, inheritance, law, and government). According to this view cultural anthropology studies the end results — cultures, including their diffusion from area to area and their development from epoch to epoch; social anthropology studies the interpersonal mechanisms through which human beings learn, manipulate, and produce cultures.

Neither of these distinctions is complete in itself. The British and

American patterns of field work reflect no real difference in scope, only, with many obvious exceptions and to a certain extent, in thoroughness and depth. They are, in fact, complementary approaches to the same objective. The British way often leads the field worker into a displaced ethnocentrism in which Bongo ethnocentrism takes the place of English ethnocentrism. The American way sometimes leaves the field worker with many factual details but with possibly less sensitivity to the feelings and the views of the peoples he has studied. The product versus relationship distinction is equally without finality. For as the student intensifies his researches, his concern for the mechanisms will inevitably lead him to the end results and vice versa. Many anthropologists will probably deny the existence of either of these distinctions.

It is in this context that we must view culture-and-personality. Culture-and-personality deals with human behavior primarily in terms of the ideas which form the basis of the interrelationship between the individual and his society. On the one hand, it deals with ideas shared by a considerable portion of any society — the "shame" or "guilt" feelings among the Japanese, the belief in immanent justice among some children of Ghana, the anxiety about food in excess of the actual danger of going hungry among some Oceanic peoples, and even the world view of the Chinese; how these and other ideas held by the individuals are rooted in the diverse patterns of culture in which they grow up. On the other hand, culture-and-personality deals with characteristics of societies: patterns of reactions to conquest and disaster, internal or external impetuses to change, militarism and pacifism, democratic or authoritarian character, and so forth; and how such characteristics may be related to the aspirations, fears, and values held by a majority of the individuals in these societies.

With these thoughts on the central concerns of culture-and-personality, I would like to propose a new title for our subdiscipline: PSYCHOLOGICAL ANTHROPOLOGY.

For over twenty years culture-and-personality has retained its cumbersome title. I think the time has probably come for us to give it a less cumbersome and more logical title. The concept of personality, which anthropologists have borrowed from psychologists, leads to some difficulties. For example, some anthropologists, though resorting to psychological explanations at many crucial points of their arguments, tend to regard the personality concept either as indistinguishable from culture or as much deeper than what the anthropologist can usually deal with. In his book *The Foundations of Social Anthropology* Nadel expresses the following thoughts:

We may take it for granted that there is some connection between the make-up of a culture and the particular personality (or personalities) of its human carriers. Yet in taking this connection to be a simple and obvious one, so simple and obvious that one can be inferred from the other, we run the risk of arguing in a circle and of using the word "personality" in an ambiguous sense. For by "personality" we can mean two things. We can mean, first, the sum-total of the overt modes of behavior of an individual, in which we discern some integration and consistence, and which we thus understand to be facets or "traits" of that total, patterned entity. Or secondly, we can mean some basic mental make-up underlying the pattern of overt behavior and accounting for it in the sense of a "hidden machine" or a causally effective set of factors (Nadel 1951:405).

Nadel then refers to a distinction made by the psychologist, R. B. Cattell, between "surface traits" "which give us 'clusters' of intrinsically related characteristics of behavior observable in everyday life," and "source traits" or "factors," "which are extricated by analysis and have a causal significance, being possible explanations of how the actually existing cluster forms may have originated" (Cattell 1946:4). Nadel's reasoning goes as follows: if the anthropologist operates with the personality concept and wishes to ascertain the mental make-up of a group possessing a certain culture, he should resort only to tests and other techniques developed by psychology. If he wishes to "define the cultural patterns in terms of 'basic' psychological agencies," he "must examine them where they are ultimately rooted—in the individual" (Nadel 1951:407). But if the anthropologist approaches the personality merely from cultural observation, by means of direct inference, he can only reach the "surface traits." Even though he may infer the desires, motivations, and so forth, prompting the overt behavior he "penetrates, as it were, only a short distance beneath the surface;" for the desires and so forth are "simply implicit in the cultural mode of behavior," or "are merely its sustaining energies, and have no causal and explanatory significance" (Nadel 1951:405). Nadel concludes:

> As long as we are inferring personality types from cultural observation we cannot legitimately claim any explanatory value for the personality concept; if we did, we should be committing the cardinal sin in science, namely, of pronouncing upon invariant relations between facts which are not "demonstrably separate" (Nadel 1951:407).

I think Nadel is wrong here. Psychological constructs, by virtue of the fact that they have to be inferred from linguistic data or other indirect evidences supplied by the actors, are certainly "demonstrably separate" from behavior which can be directly observed. Furthermore, gravitation is inferred from falling apples, rises and falls of tides, and movements of the moon, earth, and other heavenly bodies. Gravitation can never be seen anywhere except in terms of what it does, through the behavior of the objects which it controls or influences. Similarly physical hunger can only be inferred by stomach contractions, nausea (if the hunger is severe enough), or malnutrition of the body (as a result of prolonged hunger). No one can see hunger except through these and other concrete expressions of it. I have yet to hear from a scientist who denies the usefulness of the concept of gravitation or hunger, and who insists that correlating certain movements of the heavenly bodies with gravitation, or correlating certain physiological phenomena with hunger, is equivalent to committing "the cardinal sin in science, namely, of pronouncing upon invariant relations between facts which are not demonstrably separate." As our knowledge progresses, we may conclude that the concept of gravitation or hunger is no longer adequate to account for certain phenomena, but we cannot deny that during a certain period of our scientific development these concepts have played crucial and organizing roles.

However, Nadel's arguments do point up one important matter, namely the personality which psychological anthropologists deal with is not the same as that of the individual psychologists. At least conceptually, the latter deal with the unique personality of the individual, while the former deal only with those characteristics of the individual's mind which are shared as part of a wider fabric of human minds. But the distinction has not been effectively dealt with scientifically by the use of such terms as "social personality" (Kaplan 1961:117), "model personality," "basic personality," or "status personality" (Linton 1945:129–130). For the term "personality" possesses connotations which lead the student to regard it as a complete entity in itself. Instead of seeing personality as a life-long process of interaction between the individual and his society and culture, he thinks of it as being some sort of reified end-product (of very early experiences according to orthodox Freudians, of somewhat later sociocultural forces according to many Neo-Freudians and social scientists), which is ready to act in this or that direction regardless of the sociocultural fields in which it has to operate continuously. It is true that the scholars have never quite said so in exact words. It is also true that the "field theory" of Kurt Lewin or the notion of "identity" seeking and maintenance central to the work of Erik Erikson have many advocates. But given the social scientist's individualist culture heritage of hero and martyr worship, and a

Judeo-Christian theological background of absolute conversion and final salvation, the one-sided finished-product view of personality would seem too "natural." Such a view must be resisted and the beginning of such a step is to eliminate the word personality from the title of our subdiscipline.

Some anthropologists may object to the new title of psychological anthropology on several grounds, though I see no insurmountable obstacles against it. One argument is that it may lead to proliferation of subdisciplines. But giving the subdiscipline a more logical name should not cause any more proliferation than culture-and-personality has done. In the second place, division of any large single discipline into subdisciplines is inevitable as our knowledge in that area grows. Seventy-five years or so ago it was as sufficient simply to be an anthropologist as it was to be a sinologist. But soon anthropology was divided into cultural anthropology, physical anthropology, and so forth, and we no longer find the term sinologist except in some ultraconservative academic pockets. The same phenomenon has occurred in biology, physics, chemistry, and even such subdisciplines as linguistics and geometry. The only caution that we must exercise in branching out is that we must make sure that the advances of knowledge are ahead of the subdivision and not vice versa.

Another argument against the new title is that it will turn out to be neither psychology nor anthropology, that it is a no man's land. This is not a fruitful argument. We have textbooks on physiological psychology, biochemistry, astrophysics, and psychosomatic medicine. There is not the slightest indication that the separate disciplines which have been so allied with each other have suffered intellectually. On the contrary psychosomatic medicine has enriched both psychology and medicine; and without biochemistry, biology and chemistry would both have been poorer. The psychological anthropologist should certainly make use of the results not only in psychology but also in psychoanalysis, sociology, and even experimental psychology and philosophy wherever these are relevant and applicable. This is the way all sciences grow, like so many amoebae which extend a pseudopodium here and another there, retracting them here and there while their nuclei remain more or less constant.[2]

Psychological Anthropology and Related Disciplines

To clarify our thoughts further, it may be advantageous to examine the relationship between psychological anthropology and a few other disci-

[2] Since the appearance of the first edition of this book the term Psychological Anthropology has gained considerable acceptance in the profession.

plines. In the short history of psychological anthropology as a subdiscipline the clinical sciences have figured largely. In fact the indebtedness of psychological anthropology to psychiatry and psychoanalysis is immeasurable. Anyone who knows anything about psychological anthropology can easily call to mind the significant roles of such clinicians as Abram Kardiner, Erik Erikson, Alexander Leighton, Karen Horney, Erich Fromm, Géza Roheim and associates, and of course the master himself, Sigmund Freud. These students have, either singly or in collaboration with anthropologists, helped to make psychological anthropology grow immensely in stature, concepts, and volume of research.

However, psychological anthropology is not a clinical science and, though it has benefited from the clinical sciences, it has its own ways. In objectives, psychological anthropology is concerned with large numbers of individuals who are normal and functioning members of their societies. In methods of approach psychological anthropology follows the usually accepted scientific procedure of hypothesis formation, testing of hypothesis, cross-cultural validation of the result, and further refinement of the hypothesis. In this it must first be emphasized that psychological anthropology is not simply the psychology of the individual, and it must shun psychoanalysis of whole cultures in the manner of some of Freud's disciples — for example, Roheim (1950) and Wilbur and Muensterberger (1951).

To begin with, the psychic materials which psychological anthropology deals with are (a) the conscious or unconscious ideas shared by a majority of individuals in a given society as *individuals* (which are what some students hope to subsume under the term modal personality) and (b) the conscious or unconscious psychic materials governing the action patterns of many individuals as a *group* (aspects of which are variously described by such terms as group psychology, mob psychology, collective consciousness, or basic personality). Both of these are different from the unique psychology of the individual. It is not maintained that the ideas underlying the life pattern of a group and those of the actions of an individual are two distinct entities. They must be seen in terms of a continuum. There is much evidence to indicate that many individuals evaluate national or international affairs in terms of their own personal likes and dislikes, anxieties, or aspirations. But before the psychological anthropologist can conclude that one is rooted in the other, he must make sure that he is not arguing merely from analogy, that he has made sure he is not confusing broad trends of cultural development, which may be psychologically propelled, with specific institutional details, which are usually historically determined. For the purpose of finding a balanced and scientifically realistic link between individual psyche and the pattern of society and culture the concept of Psychosocial Homeostasis (PSH) may in time become highly useful for the future of our subdiscipline (Hsu 1971).

The damage to psychological anthropology by the failure to differentiate the normal from the abnormal is great. Admittedly the demarcation line between the normal and the abnormal is not clear. Nevertheless, even after allowing cultural variations, there is still undeniable evidence for certain core differences between them (Hsu 1952:238–248). The extension of the abnormal psychology of the individual into the normal pattern of the group was, I think, responsible for Freud's lopsided emphasis on the death instinct, and its continued lopsided emphasis by modern Freudians of many hues. That all human beings die is as indisputable as the fact that all human beings live. The extent to which some human beings apparently seek self-destruction in wars, suicides, alcoholism, and psychotic behavior, and the possible psychological mechanisms underlying such patterns of action are not unknown (see Masserman 1955:647–649).

However, while the evidence in support of the universality of the life instinct among humans and animals is overwhelming, the evidence in support of the death "instinct" comes chiefly from the relatively abnormal. This is why the self-destructive tendencies are uncommon among the majority of any society. Furthermore, the incidence of suicide and homicide no less than delinquency and adventure vary from culture to culture. Clearly another type of explanation than a universal postulate of death instinct is indicated. It will probably be well for psychological anthropologists to be on guard against generalizing from the psychology of a minority of the relatively abnormal to that of a majority of the relatively normal when they make use of the psychiatrically derived resources, insights, and data.

Among all the behavioral sciences, psychological anthropology and social psychology have the future potentiality of developing the closest and most mutually enriching relationship with each other. Both disciplines deal with society and both deal with psychology, but they have been separated from each other so far in significant ways. We have seen that two of the points made in the preliminary discussions among the contributors to this volume were: (a) that the characteristic mark of research in psychological anthropology is the emphasis on natural group differences along ethnic or societal lines as the subject matter, whereas social psychology usually deals with experimentally produced group differences;

and (b) that psychological anthropologists are concerned with behavior always with reference to its antecedents, while social psychologists are satisfied simply to describe its characteristics. I do not think the second distinction to be valid, for many studies in social psychology are attempts to discover the antecedents of behavior; and I think the first distinction is only partially valid, since psychological characteristics due to role, sex, and occupational affiliations are also problems of psychological anthropology.

What have so far differentiated psychological anthropologists from the social psychologists are found in three areas. First, psychological anthropology is cross-cultural in approach from its inception while social psychology has traditionally drawn its data from Western societies. Second, social psychology is quantitative and even, to a certain extent, experimental in orientation, while psychological anthropology has paid little attention to research designs and only lately awakened to the need for rigor in the matter of hypothesis formation and of verification.

In both of these connections the distance between the two disciplines is narrowing, and rightly so. Social psychologists have become increasingly more interested in cross-cultural validity of their generalizations. This anthropological contribution to psychology is well recognized by Campbell, a social psychologist, in Chapter 11 of this volume.[3] A comparison of the earlier and later editions of many texts on social psychology shows far greater use of cross-cultural data in the later than in the earlier works, though some such as Klineberg (1940 and 1954) have always led among the pioneers in interdisciplinary thinking and research, while others such as Bogardus (1950) are less inclined in that direction. In fact, it is a rare social psychology text today which does not contain at least references to the work of some anthropologists. Psychological anthropologists, on their part, have become increasingly more sensitive to the importance of sophistication in research designs and quantification. The chapters by Wallace, Whiting and Harrington, Bourguignon, and Spain in this volume and the works of Kluckhohn, D'Andrade, Goodenough, Naroll, R. Cohen, and many others are, in different ways, objective evidence in this new direction. The psychological anthropologist may not agree with (or may not be able to do much about it at the moment even if he does agree with) some of the methodological points raised by Campbell and Naroll in Chapter 11, but there is no doubt about the importance of such thinking to psychological anthropology. Psychological anthropology has already

[3] Co-authored with Naroll in the second edition.

derived no small part of its methodological inspiration from social psychology and, as time goes on, its indebtedness to social psychology is likely to be even greater than its previous indebtedness to the clinical disciplines.

The third area in which psychological anthropology differs from social psychology thus far is that it deals not only with the effect of society and culture on psychic characteristics of individuals (a basic concern of social psychology) but also with the role of personality characteristics in the maintenance, development, and change of culture and society. Chapters 6, 7, 8, 12, and 13 of the present volume touch upon this in different ways. But the core of Spiro's Chapter 14 is especially relevant to this process. He shows how potentially disruptive individual drives are transmuted into powerful forces, at least for the maintenance of the social organization and culture pattern of the society. A sound theory which aims at explaining the relationship between man and culture must not only account for the origin of psychological characteristics as they are molded by the patterns of child rearing, social institutions, and ideologies but must also account for the maintenance, development, and change in the child-rearing practices, institutions, and ideologies. It is a well-known fact that societies and cultures do change, often slowly but sometimes drastically. Since human beings are not so many helpless creatures simply being pushed by external forces such as geographical conditions, ecological limitations, foreign conquests, fate, gods, or the unaccountable vicissitudes of some superorganic, we must at least find part of the explanations for cultural and social changes in the interaction between the human minds and the societies and cultures in which they operate. Different peoples even vary in their respective reactions to similar disasters and conquests. This is fully one half of the task of our subdiscipline which most psychological anthropologists have left untouched to this day (Barnouw 1963; Honigmann 1967; and Wallace 1970).

However, over and above the question of similarities and differences between our subdiscipline and its related disciplines, there is one problem anthropologists in general and psychological anthropologists in particular have yet to face: our failure wholeheartedly and systematically to include the large literate societies and cultures in our intellectual deliberations. This points is alluded to by Spiro in Chapter 14. It is true that a number of psychological anthropologists have studied some literate societies. The impressive results on Japan summarized in Chapter 1 by Norbeck and DeVos bear witness to this, But what has occurred so far is still well constricted by the conservative conceptual boundaries of traditional anthropology. As a result, in spite of lip service to the effect that the term "primitive" is indefensible and that "primitive" societies and cultures are really diverse, the term "primitive" is still very much in use (Hsu 1968). As another result, even most of those who venture into literate societies such as Japan, China, India, and the United States have generally eschewed the comparative approach — comparing India with the United States, or Japan with some African tribes. They have simply retained the one-tribe-only approach to the large literate societies by concentrating on single villages (Hsu 1969). This is a state of affairs sorely needing correction, a cause which I hope psychological anthropologists will not be too slow to espouse (see Chapters 5, 6, 13 and 14).

At the beginning of this attempt at clarifying our thoughts on psychological anthropology, I noted the difficulties besetting it. What I hoped to do was not to close the discussion but to keep it going. Furthermore, just as no hard and fast line separates cultural anthropology from social anthropology, neither is psychological anthropology from its related disciplines. For example, a cultural anthropologist will ultimately come to analyze the ideas behind the diffusion of certain cultural traits and complexes; a social anthropologist will ultimately look at the material wealth involved in the different forms of social organization, exactly as the psychological anthropologist will ultimately relate the conscious or unconscious ideas to both particular cultural end results and particular human relationships. It is probably desirable, however, for the student from one viewpoint to hold on to his particular viewpoint as he probes deeper and deeper into his data, or else he may be hopelessly enmeshed in them without guideposts to go forward or backward. The significance of such a viewpoint to the field worker is comparable to that of the "ego" to the maker of a kinship chart. As the maker of a kinship chart cannot change the "ego" in it without getting lost, the field worker who shifts from one viewpoint to another, or has no viewpoint at all, is likely to bring back little that is of coherent significance.

BIBLIOGRAPHY

BARNOUW, VICTOR. 1963. Culture and Personality. Homewood, Ill., Dorsey Press.
BOGARDUS, E. E. 1950. Fundamentals of social psychology. New York, Appleton-Century-Crofts.

CATTELL, R. B. 1946. Description and measurement of personality. Yonkers, N.Y., World Book Co.

EVANS-PRITCHARD, E. E. 1954. Nuer religion. London, Oxford University Press.

GILLIN, JOHN. 1939. Personality in preliterate societies. American Sociological Review 4:681–702.

HART, C. W. M. 1954. The sons of Turimpi. American Anthropologist 54(2):242–261.

HERSKOVITS, M. J. 1948. Man and his works. New York, Alfred Knopf.

HONIGMANN, JOHN J. 1967. Personality in Culture. New York, Harper & Row.

HSU, F. L. K. 1952. Anthropology or psychiatry: A definition of objectives and their implications. Southwestern Journal of Anthropology 8:227–250.

———. 1968. Rethinking the Concept 'Primitive'. Reprinted in Ashley Montagu (ed.), The Concept of the 'Primitive'. Glencoe, Ill., Free Press.

———. 1969. The Study of Literate Civilizations. New York, Holt, Rinehart and Winston.

———. 1971. Psychosocial homeostasis and *Jen:* A new conceptual tool for advancing psychological anthropology. American Anthropologist 73(1):23–44.

KAPLAN, BERT. 1954. A study of Rorschach responses in four culture. Papers of Peabody Museum of Archaeology and Ethnology, Harvard University, Vol. 42, No. 2.

KLINEBERG, OTTO. 1954. Social psychology. New York, Henry Holt (1st edition, 1940).

KLUCKHOHN, CLYDE. 1954. Culture and behavior. In Handbook of Social Psychology, Gardner Lindzey, ed. Cambridge, Mass., Addison-Wesley Press.

KLUCKHOHN, CLYDE AND O. H. MOWRER. 1944. Culture and personality: A conceptual scheme. American Anthropologist 46:4.

KLUCKHOHN, CLYDE, HENRY A. MURRAY, AND DAVID SCHNEIDER. 1953. Personality in nature, society, and culture (2nd edition). New York, Alfred Knopf.

KROEBER, A. L. 1948. Anthropology. New York, Harcourt Brace & Co.

LINTON, R. 1945. Cultural background of personality. New York, D. Appleton Century Co.

MASSERMAN, JULES. 1955. Dynamic psychiatry. Philadelphia: W. B. Saunders Co.

NADEL, S. F. 1951. Foundations of social anthropology. Glencoe, Ill.: Free Press.

ROHEIM, GÉZA. 1950. Psychoanalysis and Anthropology. New York, International Universities Press.

WHITE, LESLIE A. 1949. The science of culture. New York, Farrar, Strauss & Co.

WILBUR, GEORGE B. AND WARNER MUENSTERBERGER. 1951. Psychoanalysis and culture. New York, International Universities Press.

Area

The treatment of the subject matter of psychological anthropology by area presents some difficulties. Differences in culture and in behavior tendencies between tribal groups and national groups within these large areas are sometimes so great that the contributors will either have to generalize on a relatively superficial level or else have to confine themselves to a few selected studies which already possess some intensity and depth.

There is no adequate answer to these difficulties. In a work of this scope it is simply not possible to gain the intensity and depth attainable in a field report on a single tribe or community. A general picture of the psychology of a region like North America or even Japan is bound to contain fewer details than a monograph on the culture and behavior tendencies of Polish peasants inhabiting a village in Ruthenia. The contributors themselves are keenly aware of the danger of overgeneralization, or generalization based on scanty data. Munroe, Munroe and LeVine indicate, with reference to Africa, a clear example of overgeneralization. Norbeck and DeVos point out that more recent works on Japan tend to be constricted in scope because "no interpretation of (Japanese) national character is acceptable." Langness and Gladwin seem more impressed by the diversity of cultures even in the New Guinea Highlands alone than by the similarities between Polynesia and Micronesia.

On the other hand, Honigmann, after viewing the literature on North American Indians, seems to agree that there is "a high degree of psychological homogeneity" which "characterizes the American Indian." Similarly Munroe, Munroe, and LeVine give us a list of twelve "African" cultural characteristics "which have demonstrable or potential relevance to psychological variables." Although they do not deal directly with the generalizations on African kinship and ways of life discussed by the editor in Chapter 12, the reader will find some possible links between the two chapters: for example, the infant precocity, followed by a slump after about age 10, or the lack of sharp male-female differences in perception, noted in Chapter 2 related to a kinship content with a high degree of rivalry. There are many social and cultural mechanisms which, on closer inspection, make for psychological standardization of large communities. Communal, tribal, or national myths are some of these. Communication and diffusion processes are others. The authors of at least two chapters (2 and 4) deal with the possible effects of common ecological factors.

However, even in this section of the book our interest is only partially areal. The areal arrangement is convenient in providing the reader with a panorama of the most significant works of psychological anthropology in the area of his curiosity. But a problem orientation is also the concern in this section of the book, as in the subsequent sections. Norbeck and DeVos discuss personality factors affecting differential Japanese acculturation on different continents. Munroe, Munroe, and LeVine deal with the link between childhood and adolescent experiences on the one hand and cognitive development and achievement motivation on the other. They also deal with the problem of differential incidence and types of mental illness. Honigmann treats the problems (amongst others) of values and of model personality. Langness and Gladwin analyse the theoretical contributions of a variety of scholars from those of Mead, Linton, and Malinowski to Lawrence, Ritchie, and Salisbury. In these and other materials the problem-minded reader will find much that is informative and stimulating.

The last two chapters deal with some composite psychological characteristics of large, modern, and complex societies, relating the individual aspirations, anxieties, and fears to the over-all thought and action patterns of each group. They, along with Chapter 13 in a later section of the book, indicate to the reader something about the difficulties but also the possibilities in arriving at generalizations on huge societies. Too often national character studies have been attacked on *a priori* grounds, that it is "impossible" to gauge the psychological characteristics underlying complex civilizations, with hundreds of millions of individuals living in them. But the basic problem is surely one of level of generalization. If we look for individual differences, there is no shortage of data which compels us to observe that no two individuals are identical. But if we raise our sights to a different level, we shall at once see that millions of human beings interact with each other, voluntarily or involuntarily, in any large society on any one day, often sight unseen, apparently without any significant difficulties. This relatively smooth interaction among strangers in any large, modern society is a remarkable reality, which will be impossible without some high degree of cognitive and affective uniformity, not merely in externally visible laws, customs, procedures, and usages but also in externally invisible ideas, emotions, expectations, and faiths.

Inkeles (Chapter 5) deals with the "relation of personality patterns to the development and maintenance of political systems." He reviews and assesses all the significant works based on more or less hardnosed methodology, including the use of psychiatric interviews and projective instruments, which bear on this problem. In particular his interests center in the differences in personality characteristics in "democratic" societies as distinguished from "authoritarian" societies. He does not find adequate evidence for the contrast, but believes nevertheless that prolonged democratic regimes and authoritarian regimes are linked with psychological characteristics respectively commensurate with them.

On the other hand, Hsu (Chapter 6), reviewing the facts as a long time participant-observer of United States society, a society with a long history of democracy in Inkeles' terms, has come to a very different conclusion. He finds extremism, which according to Inkeles is an authoritarian characteristic, to be common in democratic United States. This seeming contradiction is also evident in connection with church affiliation: church members tend to exhibit more prejudice than those with no church affiliation. Is this due to the differences in point of view of the two authors? Is this due to differences in the kinds of fact upon which the two authors based their generalizations? Are the two papers products of different levels of abstraction? Or are they evidence that we must employ more precise methods?

CHAPTER ONE

Culture and Personality: The Japanese

EDWARD NORBECK AND GEORGE DEVOS

A decade has passed since the authors wrote the original review of which the present chapter is a revised version. We have made substantial changes here, but these, we wish to note, are principally expansions and additions that do not greatly alter the conclusions of the original version. Various passages of the first writing are appropriate today, and we have included them with little change. As before, the objectives are to review and appraise research from the standpoint of the contribution it has made to theory and the promises of future contributions that it holds.[1]

Anthropological interest in Japan and the Japanese is old, but until World War II it was left principally to native Japanese scholars, whose publications rarely reached the Western world. For decades before the war both Western and native writers had made impressionistic observations on the character of the Japanese, but writings on this subject by scholars trained in psychology, sociology, and anthropology are almost entirely postwar. Entry of the United States into the war served in several ways to direct the attention of American social scientists to Japanese culture, and it is during the war years that research on Japan using modern techniques

[1] For other reviews of this subject with various aims, see the following: Sofue, 1960; Norbeck and DeVos, 1961; Silberman, 1962; Shimada, 1963; Yamamoto, 1964; Hamaguchi, 1965; Moore, ed., 1967; Japanese Society of Ethnology, 1968; Wagatsuma, 1969, 1970; Caudill, 1970; and Bennett, 1970.

22   *Area*

of personality and culture began, principally under the sponsorship of the United States government. The first published studies are papers by Gorer (1942, 1943), LaBarre (1945), and others which attempt to describe the Japanese personality and relate it to cultural institutions of child training. As is well known, Ruth Benedict's *The Chrysanthemum and the Sword* also sprang from research conducted during the war under governmental subsidy.

Since the end of the war, the number of American social scientists engaged in research on Japan has grown, and scholarly writings on Japanese culture have correspondingly increased. A list compiled in 1969 of Western scholars concerned with the study of Japan in the fields of social and cultural anthropology, social psychology, and sociology contains the names of 71 persons, of whom nearly all are citizens of the United States.[2] About two-thirds of these scholars are anthropologists, and only a small handful are psychologists. Although only a small number are specialists in the subject of Japanese personality, the research of all is relevant to this topic. As a result of studies conducted since World War II, we have become aware of many regional distinctions in Japanese culture and differences along lines of occupation and social class that relate to personality. Western students of Japan have also become increasingly aware that Japanese culture is in a state of rapid change so that observations made at any one point in time are often quickly outdated.

Research on Japan concerned with the relationship between personality and culture began with American scholars. Soon after the end of the war, the behavioral sciences saw their first substantial development in Japan, and trained Japanese scholars in these fields included personality among their subjects of study. Social psychology developed in Japan at this time as an importation from the United States; in 1966 the membership of the Japanese Society of Social Psychology had grown to 435 persons (Wagatsuma, 1969a:37). Other branches of psychology, especially educational psychology, grew much larger than social psychology, and the number of professional Japanese psychologists in 1969 exceeded 3,000 persons (Wagatsuma, 1969a:37-38). The fields of anthropology and sociology in Japan also expanded greatly. In 1969, the membership of the Japanese Society of Ethnology was about 800 persons (Sofue, 1969:17), and the number of sociologists in the various sociological societies of the nation was probably several times greater than this figure. Japanese scholars in the behavioral

[2] Compiled in connection with the conference on Japan in the behavioral sciences described further in note 4.

sciences today thus total several thousand persons. It is particularly noteworthy that most Japanese scholars in these fields limit their study to their own society and culture. As a result, although only a small proportion of research has focused directly on culture and personality, a vast and growing body of published data useful to the specialist in this subject is available, principally in the Japanese language. An outstanding Japanese project of research is a statistical study of regional cultural variation that contains information on 1100 communities and makes some use of projective tests (Izumi et al., 1963; Nagashima, 1964). The combined results of research of Japanese and foreign scholars published in the English language are also impressive in quantity, and Japan is probably unique in the field of personality and culture in being the focus of fairly extensive study by both natives and foreigners.

We shall here review both Western and Japanese research that has been completed and discuss some projects now under way. Since most of our readers are interested in works in the English language, emphasis will be given to them. As a matter of convenience, we have classified these studies under several major headings, indicating either subjects of study or approaches, which are not mutually exclusive:

1. National Character and Regional Variations in Personality
2. Content Analyses of Forms of Expressive Behavior
3. Studies using Projective Techniques
4. Early Socialization
5. Achievement Motivation
6. Deviancy and Social Problems
7. The Japanese Overseas

Judgment as to the kind of research and the specific studies to include has been made in part arbitrarily. We have not limited ourselves to research conducted by anthropologists, but have included publications in social, clinical, and child psychology, psychiatry, sociology, and in other fields when these studies have dealt with questions of the relationship between culture and personality. No attempt will be made to review all writings relevant to Japanese culture and personality. Many publications, especially in the fields of psychology and psychiatry, have been omitted or mentioned only in passing because they make no attempt to relate traits of personality to cultural determinants. For lack of space, a very large group of studies of Japanese culture prepared by ethnologists, sociologists, historians, economists, and political scientists, both Japanese and Western, are given no discussion. Omission is made with full awareness that these publications are relevant to an understanding of Japanese culture and personality as they provide vital information on such matters as differences in culture by region and class, and trends of cultural change.

1. National Character and Regional Variations in Personality

Ruth Benedict's *The Chrysanthemum and the Sword* is the only major Western publication on Japan that consensus would place under the heading of studies of national character. The impact of this pioneering work upon both the scholarly world and the general public of Japan was surprisingly great. Translated into Japanese, it was widely read and served as a strong stimulus to Japanese scholarly interest in personality and culture, an interest that seemed often to be subjective. Benedict's work became the topic of a series of seminars, well-publicized in scholarly circles, in which prominent Japanese scholars participated. An English summary of the Japanese critique of Benedict's methodology and conclusions is available (Bennett and Nagai, 1953), and we shall mention here only the chief criticisms that her study presents a static picture of ideal patterns of a time long gone by, and ignores distinctions by social class and changes through time. Jean Stoetzel's postwar study of attitudes and values, *Without the Chrysanthemum and the Sword*, also indicated that much of what Benedict describes did not apply to at least youthful Japanese of the mid-1950's.

Benedict's work not only stimulated interest in Japanese character but also led to field research by Japanese scholars, notably T. Kawashima (1951a,b), on modes and differences in conceptions of the values in interpersonal relations (*chū, on, giri*) with which her study had dealt. This research brought out clearly the existence of regional and class differences in Japanese attitudes, which many later studies further describe. Benedict's interpretation stands out also from the standpoint of methodology. As one of the earliest studies of "culture at a distance," it points out the potentialities of this approach. As a result of subsequent field research in Japan and the critique of her study by Japanese scholars, we are given a better idea of its limitations. Benedict's work remains worthwhile, however, and discusses many attitudes and values that do not appear to be wholly obsolete. In a recent review of Western and Japanese writings on Japan of the nineteenth and twentieth centuries by authors of highly diverse backgrounds, William Caudill (in press) extracts the following common themes relating to Japanese character, nearly all of which appear in Benedict's work:

1. A sense of the group or communality as being of central importance.
2. A strong sense of obligation and gratitude.
3. A sense of sympathy and compassion (*ninjō*) for others.
4. A strong sense of "we" versus "they."
5. An underlying emotionality and excitability which is controlled by a somewhat compulsive attention to details, plans, and rules.
6. A willingness to work hard, and to persevere toward long-range goals.
7. Devotion to parents, and an especially strong and long-enduring tie to the mother persisting in almost its childhood form.
8. An emphasis on self-effacement and a tendency to avoid taking responsibility for the actions of oneself or others.
9. A tendency toward understatement and an emphasis on nonverbal communication.
10. A great pleasure in the simple things of life, such as being in beautiful surroundings, playing with children, bathing, drinking, eating, and sex.

Since the publication of *The Chrysanthemum and the Sword*, several projects of research have been conducted, principally by Japanese scholars, with aims of understanding Japanese national character. The largest project was conducted over a period of nearly ten years beginnning in 1953 by the Human Relations Research Group, an interdisciplinary research team under the direction of Tsuneo Muramatsu, a psychiatrist at Nagoya National University, a team which included one American scholar, George A. DeVos. The principal aims of this project were to determine both national modes and regional differences in cultural values as these are related to types of personality. Through the efforts of nearly 80 researchers, a total of over 3,000 persons in three rural communities and two cities of southwestern Japan were subjected to a battery of psychological tests and interviews. Principal test instruments used were the F Scale of authoritarian personality; two opinion scales devised to test attitudes toward familial relations and "liberal-traditional" attitudes toward Japanese values, the Rorschach test; the Thematic Apperception Test modified by Japanese culture; a problem situation test; figure drawings; a "child-parent problem" test, and questionnaires on customs of child training. This research has resulted in a number of short publications on restricted aspects of personality or socialization, which will later be discussed, and one major work (Muramatsu, 1962) in the Japanese language, the title of which may be translated as *The Japanese, An Empirical Study of Culture and Personality*. Despite its title, this publication offers no complete or rounded account of national character, although it does present a substantial quantity of data useful in the understanding of personality.

Other noteworthy empirical research relating directly to national character completed to date leans heavily toward attitude surveys. Many of these surveys have been conducted by sociologists and others by statisticians. Sponsoring organizations have sometimes been governmental bureaus and even newspapers with large national circulations. The usefulness of the surveys expectably varies. Most outstanding among these is a series conducted under the auspices of a Japanese governmental agency, the National Institute of Statistical Research (*Tōkei Sūri Kenkyūjo*), by a research committee named, in English translation, Committee for the Study of National Character. Three national surveys of attitudes, conducted at intervals of five years, have been completed by this research organization. The resulting publications (*Tōkei Sūri Kenkyūjo*, 1961, 1964) provide useful information, especially on changing attitudes toward traditional values concerning inter-personal relations, but provide no integrated account of national or regional modes of personality. Like various other studies of much smaller scale, this research reflects a trend of thought and emphasis common to various social sciences in Japan for some years after World War II and particularly strong in sociology. This was an attempt to delineate and eradicate traditional social values and traits of character regarded as "feudal," as these were generally regarded as inimical to the welfare of the nation under modern conditions of life. Other attempts by Japanese scholars to deal with national character are impressionistic accounts of doubtful value that make essentially no use of modern methods and instruments of research (e.g., Sera, 1963).

Numerous studies of much smaller scale by Japanese scholars may be described as attempts to depict regional Japanese types of personality. These include extensive publications on modal personality in rural communities, many of which are impressionistic, making little or no use of psychological tests or of information on practices of rearing children. Among these are a series of publications by the social psychologist Kenzō Tsukishima (e.g. Tsukishima, 1954, 1961). Certain projects of research concerning individual communities or segments of Japanese societies, comparing types of communities, or dealing with aspects of Japanese character are methodologically on a sounder base, and these will be discussed under topics that follow (e.g., Fujioka, 1957, Konishi, 1963, and publications by Sofue and Wagatsuma).

One of the greatest deficiencies of studies of national character or regional types of personality, especially of the studies done by Japanese scholars, is the lack of cross-cultural comparison, a deficiency that may be said to characterize studies of national character elsewhere and doubtless reflects the lack of firmly delineated modal types for any nation. One Japanese attempt at cross-cultural comparison, based upon limited secondary sources available at the time, sought to compare the national characters of Japan, the United States, England, Germany, and France (Sofue and Wagatsuma, 1959). Although not intended to depict national character, two essays by the late, distinguished ethnologist Eiichiro Ishida are of more than casual interest to the student of Japanese personality. One essay (Ishida, 1961) discusses perceptively fundamental differences between the cultures of Japan and of Western societies, and the second (Ishida, 1964) is a subjective account of the author's reactions to Japanese people and culture upon his return to Japan after a sojourn in the West. This account is informative about the values and attitudes of Japanese who have had considerable direct contact with Western culture, and includes a subjective account of feelings of inferiority.

No synthetic study of national character approaching the scope of Benedict's work has since appeared, but the objective of an overall characterization has not been entirely set aside. Native and foreign scholars today appear generally to be well aware that no interpretation of national character so far offered is acceptable and that presently available information on regional variations and trends of change render very difficult or impossible the formulation of an accurate and viable delineation. Comparative studies completed in the last decade, or now under way, concern lesser aspects of the whole. These include a study of socialization processes in Japan, India, and various Western nations (Hoshino, Nishimura, and Hasegawa, 1966); comparisons of conformity among Americans and Japanese (e.g., Kikuchi, 1964, Frager, 1969, 1970); a comparison of values and attitudes of Japanese and Chinese in relation to the forms and functions of the family (Hsu, 1971); and a comparison of traits of Japanese and American students (Abate and Berrien, 1967). Frager (1970) sees student uprisings in Japan as negative conformity rather than true independence. In demanding "democratic" reforms but acting in totalitarian ways, they and also many American students are held to be negatively reacting against authority rather than seeking new, independently formulated goals.

Other research relating to national character includes studies of patterns of emotions in Japan (Caudill, 1962, Caudill and Doi, 1963) and various additional studies of values as related to cultural change (e.g., Caudill and Scarr, 1962) will be discussed later under other headings. A number of additional studies by Japanese and foreign scholars, some of which are discussed below, touch in varying but lesser degrees upon the subject of national character or modal personality.

2. Content Analyses of Forms of Expressive Behavior

Postwar publications by Japanese social psychologists for a number of years included a group of content analyses of Japanese movies, popular songs, life-counseling columns in newspapers, novels, and common folk-sayings, attempting to determine the values which stand out most strongly in these forms of expressive behavior. Some of these studies have been published in English translation (Kato, ed., 1959). The technique was American derived, and in some instances the Japanese interpreters made comparisons with similar research in the United States. Although none of these studies attempted to be comprehensive in the manner of Benedict and the whole genre is regarded today as less reliable and valuable than research using other approaches, all of these studies have bearing on the subject of Japanese personality. We shall here present only a sample of the conclusions of these reports.

The most ambitious of these impressionistic studies is Hiroshi Minami's *Nihonjin no Shinri* (Psychology of the Japanese), which attempts to outline "those modes of feeling, thinking, and expressing which are peculiar to the Japanese." Minami uses in a highly intuitive way popular songs, ideas expressed in fiction, common sayings, writings on army life, essays by successful men, and similar non-scholarly sources to deduce a number of themes or motifs. His study seems questionable from the standpoint of method; one wonders whether the themes are in fact inferred or whether the raw data are used to buttress preformulated themes. The work nevertheless contains observations that seem apt and, like others of its kind, provides information and interpretations that might serve as starting points for future research. In a rather lengthy discussion of conceptions of happiness and unhappiness, for example, Minami observes that the Japanese seldom express happiness. Words conveying this idea are few, and when they are used the turn of expression sounds awkward. The

Japanese vocabulary is, however, rich in words denoting unhappiness. Many aphorisms, songs, writings, and personal philosophies of life contain as their central theme ways to cope with unhappiness, and attempts are made to justify unhappiness on the grounds that it serves a useful purpose, as in ensuring the proper ordering of familial relations. Other major sections of Minami's work are entitled The Conception of the Self, Rationality and Irrationality; Spiritualism versus Sensualism, and Patterns of Human Relationships. No attempt is made to present a systematic characterization of the Japanese.

An analysis of life-counseling columns in newspapers (Kato, ed., 1959) reports that letters from the lovelorn are much fewer than is characteristic of similar columns in American papers. Letters are placed under three classifications: those concerned with group or international situations; those which center on human relations with one other individual; and those expressing concern with height, weight, looks and other physical features of the individual. Among adults the greatest source of distress is interpersonal relations in the family. Letters concerning relations between two individuals are principally between a young male and a young female. Among young girls the greatest concern is expressed over their own physical features. A majority of letters from mature adults consist of complaints made against persons of higher social status than the writers. Wives complain more about husbands than husbands do about wives. This observation, it may be noted, seems contrary to the stereotype of the uncomplainingly submissive Japanese woman.

An analysis of the lyrics of 61 post-war songs (Kato, ed., 1959) judged to be the most popular on the basis of sales of phonograph records reports that the majority are sentimental, sometimes telling of love but never expressing happy sentimentality. The authors find in the songs four prevailing motifs: pessimism, fatalism, "existentialism" (explained as unexpressed feelings of loneliness and helplessness), and "pre-modern humanism" (feudal values in interpersonal relationships).

Most of the attitudes and values reported in this group of studies seem curiously obsolete today, and the principal value of these publications in the future may be as data relevant to the study of cultural change. The observations about happiness and unhappiness, for example, do not appear to fit the modern scene. For some years now, many observers of Japan have remarked upon a change in attitudes toward approving or even recommending the pursuit of happiness as a worthwhile goal of life. For example, an extremely popular song of the mid-1960's is entitled

"Shiawase-san," translatable as "Mr. Happiness" or "Mr. Good Fortune," and the pursuit of happiness is a stated goal of the religious sect Sōka Gakkai.

3. Studies Using Projective Techniques

Japanese scholars of personality have made considerable use of projective tests.[3] Foreign scholars of personality have also made extensive use of these tests, but the number of such scholars has been few. Unfortunately, analysis in much of the early Japanese research was confined to interpretation of the tests themselves with little or no attempt to relate findings to elements of culture. Results of most of the early studies using the Rorschach, for example, are relatively crude statistics on the types of responses, giving means and percentages of color, movement, animal content and whole responses. During World War II and shortly afterward a number of studies were conducted by Japanese scholars with a Rorschach in which certain standard blots were modified and new ones added. It is, of course, highly doubtful that the results of these studies can be directly comparable with those based upon the standard Rorschach. For lack of other opportunity to learn, many Japanese researchers using the Rorschach and other projective tests in normative, non-clinical studies were self-taught from reading American publications, and their interpretations often indicated a lack of familiarity with the potentials and limitations of the techniques. It must be added that these scholars were sometimes emulating the manner of use of projective tests followed by a number of American anthropologists some years ago.

A continuing weakness of Japanese scholars employing projective tests has been a general reluctance to interpret findings of the tests. When interpretation is made, the basis for the conclusions presented is seldom clearly stated. Thus, although a number of studies attempt to depict modal personalities for individual villages or occupational groups, and many others describe types of responses, until about ten years ago these were generally of little value except insofar as they might constitute acceptable

[3] Formosan natives were given Rorschach tests by a Japanese psychologist in 1930. This is said to constitute the earliest trial of the Rorschach on a primitive people. A fairly extensive program of psychological testing of Formosan aborigines was conducted from that time until World War II. Projective tests have also recently been given to the Ainu by Japanese researchers. In recent years research by Japanese social scientists has again expanded into areas outside Japan, and projective tests have been used on native populations of Nepal, Thailand, Brazil, Peru, and several other countries. Analyses of many of these data have not as yet been made or have not been published.

raw data. Research using projective tests has become more promising as the years have passed, and we have already noted two large projects employing them (Izumi et al., 1963; Muramatsu, 1962), one of which (Muramatsu) began in 1953. This research by the Human Relations Research group at Nagoya University is remarkable in the field of culture and personality because of the number of its respondents to Rorschach tests, and also because it uses a large number of projective and non-projective techniques and is the first large sample of its kind that cuts across occupational groups and social classes of a culturally advanced, large nation. One other sizeable normative study of Japanese Rorschach responses is available (Murakami, 1959). Other smaller studies of note that concern modal personalities and make use of Rorschach tests include the early testing of a sample of Tokyo residents (Kodama, 1953); various studies sampling small communities and comparing responses of residents of communities economically based upon different occupations, such as farming, fishing, pottery making, and forestry-farming ("mountain villages"), and other studies that compare groups differing in age or other characteristics (e.g., Fujioka, 1952, 1957, 1958, 1959a, 1959b; Fujioka et al., 1956; Imanishi et al., 1955; Sofue, 1954). Various other works by foreign and native scholars are discussed in the pages that precede and follow.

Reviewing the results of these various reports, we may conclude that Japanese responses to the Rorschach indicate characteristics markedly different from those regarded as general for the population of the United States. The findings may be summarized briefly as follows:

The number of responses is low in all social groups. Rejections are very high (from 20 to 25 per cent) on colored cards 1 and 9, and black and white cards 6 and 7. There is a relatively high rate of rejection of card 10, which seems related to an inability or reluctance to use the details on this complex card. Difficulty in handling color freely and other indications attest to difficulty with spontaneous affect. Although markedly lower among urban residents than among rural residents, personal rigidity is generally very high in comparison with norms for the United States. A great deal of organizational drive in the use of intellectual functions is indicated; the Japanese subjects are prone to push for complex, integrated whole responses. The sense of reality is generally very adequate. Although sometimes imaginative, responses include little fantasy of an extreme sort in directions considered primitive or psychopathological. The form level is characteristically quite high. Labile color responses are usually perceptually tolerated when they are incorporated in some complex overall concept. Pure color by itself is almost completely lacking. These and other signs attest to the effectiveness of ego control that appears to be characteristic throughout the population.

Although less commonly used than the Rorschach until recently, various other projective tests have been employed to interpret Japanese values and attitudes as well as personality dynamics, and they have yielded interesting results. Basing his arguments principally on responses to the Thematic Apperception Test and a problem-situation test, DeVos (1960a) argues against the widely held view that Japanese culture may best be regarded as a "shame" culture in a guilt-shame dichotomy. He holds that the strong achievement drive so often noted among the Japanese — a subject that we shall later discuss separately — is not to be understood solely in terms of shame-oriented concern with community standards but is also linked with a deep undercurrent of guilt. The Japanese seem to suffer from guilt which is not associated with any complex of supernatural sanctions, but is instead derived from the system of loyalties which cements the structure of their traditional society. Guilt among Japanese is hidden from Western observation because we do not understand Japanese familial relationships, and because conscious emphasis on external sanctions helps to disguise the underlying feelings of guilt which, severely repressed, are not obvious to the Japanese themselves. The keystone toward understanding Japanese guilt is held to be the nature of interpersonal relationships within the Japanese family, particularly the relations of children with the mother. (For further discussion of this subject, see *Achievement Motivation*.)

Another study based upon responses to the Thematic Apperception Test (DeVos and Wagatsuma, 1959) reports a high incidence of concern over dealth and illness, which the authors interpret as introjection of guilt. Death and illness of parents, as seen in cards of the Thematic Apperception Test by respondents, is very often related by them to failure of a child to comply with parental wishes in entering an arranged marriage or in meeting other standards of behavior and achievement. Another recurrent theme found in responses is that of expiation; achievement of honor or success on the part of a child atones for egocentric or profligate behavior.

Research on Japanese attitudes toward arranged marriages in a farming community and a fishing community (Wagatsuma, 1959; DeVos, 1961; Wagatsuma and DeVos, 1962) analyzes responses to the Thematic Apperception Test and compares them with data derived by techniques eliciting more consciously controlled attitudes. Although current public opinion in Japan is increasingly lenient toward love marriage, as opposed to the traditional arranged marriage, individuals who have contracted love marriages are often reported to feel considerable guilt and inner restriction. Dependent upon the level of consciousness involved, attitudes and emotional reactions toward the two forms of marriage differ. A phenomenon labeled "psychological lag" appears to exist. In responses to the Thematic Apperception Test many respondents give clear evidence of strong internalized feelings against love marriage although, as revealed by opinion surveys and direct interviews, when speaking on a conscious level these individuals express approval of this form of union.

The results of the Thematic Apperception Tests used in this study also indicated differences in attitudes between occupational and social groups that conform with and amplify observations made by ethnologists using traditional techniques of interviewing and observation. A farm community, in which the so-called "traditional" Japanese pattern of hierarchical authority according to age, sex, order of birth, and status in the household is well established, is compared with a fishing community, where social relationships within the family do not follow such a strict hierarchy. Responses to tests indicate markedly less rigidity, freer expression of aggression between the sexes, and less guilt in connection with intra-familial relations in the fishing community.

Projective tests have also been put to use in the study of Japanese communities abroad, and, to a lesser extent, in research on child training and deviancy. Discussion of these studies follows. One unpublished study of regional variations in Japanese personality conducted by Takao Sofue in the mid-1960's is based on the Sentence Completion Test. During recent years, the use of projective tests by Japanese scholars has declined somewhat, as is also the circumstance among American scholars in personality and culture.

4. Early Socialization

Japanese customs of rearing and socializing children have been the focus of more research in the field of personality and culture than any other subject. Perhaps the most outstanding feature of published accounts resulting from this research has been conflict of opinion, especially during the postwar period until about 1960. As might be expected in a rapidly changing society, sharp contrasts were reported between rural and urban life, and in studies made at different points in time. For some years after the end of World War II, the principal controversy in the entire field of Japanese culture and personality revolved about interpretations of the influence of practices of child rearing and the adult personality. Early wartime studies, conducted in the United States, influenced by psychoanalytic ideas, emphasized customs of toilet training and weaning, and contended that Japanese practices, particularly in toilet training, were harsh and strongly influenced the adult personality. In this as well as other instances where interpretations have conflicted, differences by region and class and differences accounted for by the rapid cultural change which Japan has been undergoing were often overlooked or ignored. The pioneer studies of Gorer and LaBarre, long looked upon with question, were based upon information drawn from a limited number of informants residing in the United States, who appear to have held middle-class ideas of child training current at that time. The results of an early postwar investigation of practices of toilet training among Hawaiian Japanese (Sikkema, 1947) were the first to present conflicting data, which cast further doubt on the idea that severity of toilet training was contributing to compulsive personality traits in Japanese. The sample in this instance was composed of individuals stemming principally from rural Japan, who had presumably been exposed to American ideas.

Betty Lanham later (1956) reported the results of fairly extensive investigations in a community of southwestern Japan of practices of weaning, toilet training, and forms of sanctions used to discipline children. Her statements agree with unquantified observations made by Margaret and Edward Norbeck (1956) in a fishing community approximately 200 miles from Lanham's community. Lanham concluded that although there are a number of sharp differences between Japan and the United States in other customs of child training, practices of toilet training differ little.

As a result of these various studies, the conclusions of the early inadequately empirical studies were generally set aside as unacceptable, but other minor controversies continued for some time. For example, Lanham's report was criticized by Japanese scholars, who reported different findings, especially in practices of weaning (e.g., Hoshino, Sofue, and others, 1958). The Japanese contended that weaning began and ended earlier than Lanham had reported. Much of the argument here hinged upon the definition of weaning. The Japanese scholars held the view that weaning begins with the introduction of supplementary "solid" foods; thus, the span of time from the beginning of "weaning" until the child ceases to nurse may be long. Improved communication between Western and native scholars subsequently helped to clarify problems of interpretation of this kind.

Subsequent studies by Japanese and American scholars have covered a widening but nevertheless spotty range of subjects relating to childhood socialization and in some expectable degree reflect general trends of research in those fields. An early shift, implied in foregoing paragraphs, was away from rather sweeping generalizations concerning early childhood training to empirical research that emphasized the who, what, and when of socialization and noted regional and subcultural differences in these customs. Today, highly variable amounts of quantified data are available on a wide variety of subjects that include customs of toilet training, nursing, weaning, sleeping and eating; the age, sex and other characteristics of the adult socializers; sibling and other familial relations; and the nature of social sanctions. For the most part, these accounts are fairly consistent, and the greatest disparities they have reported reflect differences according to social class, urban and rural residence, and trends of change in child management following the increasing urbanization of Japan. Certain characteristics of Japanese customs of early socialization have been frequently noted. After selecting for discussion a sample of studies to illustrate the range of the studies and their conclusions, we shall take special note of these traits that stand out as foci of scholarly attention.

One of the early studies that took cognizance of differences by social class (Ishiguro, 1955) may be regarded as fairly representative of research on this subject, although later reports have not agreed with it in all details. Practices of child training in three social strata called "old middle class," "new middle class," and "lower class," are compared with practices reported in the United States. As Lanham also notes, the nursing period in Japan is reported to be longer than in the United States and nursing tends to be on demand rather than on a fixed time schedule. Toilet training begins and ends earlier in Japan, but unlike circumstances in the United States, control over urination precedes bowel control. In both countries weaning is abrupt in only approximately 20 per cent of the cases reported. Practices of the American lower class are reported to resemble most those of the Japanese "old middle class," and practices of the American middle class are most similar to those of the Japanese "new middle class" and "newer lower class." Although this study recognizes that change has occurred in customs of child training (the category "new middle class" is composed of salaried men in industry, commerce, and public service, a relatively new social group in Japan), data used in the study depended upon the recall of the mothers who served as informants, and are thus subject to distortion — probably in the direction of modern trends of change in these practices.

Other research by Western scholars concerns the children of suburban salaried workers of Tokyo (Vogel, 1963, Ch. 12); children in the small provincial city of Wakayama in central Japan (Lanham, 1962); research on parent-child sleeping partners (Caudill and Plath, 1966; Morioka, 1968); a study of values, attitudes and social concepts of Japanese and American children as related to vocational aspirations (Goodman, 1957); investigations of mother-child relationships (DeVos, 1966; Lanham, 1956; Caudill and Weinstein, 1969); a study of inter- and intra-generational differences in maternal attitudes toward child rearing (Kitano, 1964); and various studies by DeVos and Wagatsuma (summarized in DeVos, 1968a) concerning child rearing, and other studies of social problems and deviancy that will be discussed later.

Studies by Japanese scholars with varying relevance to the subject of personality and culture are much more abundant, especially in the field of educational psychology. These include various publications by the Institute for the Study of Child Rearing in Japan (*Nihon Jidō Kenkyūsho*). Noteworthy studies by Japanese scholars, published in the Japanese language, include the subjects of family relationships and personality formation (Eguchi, 1965); birth order (Fukazu and Yoda, 1962–67; Takahashi et al., 1968a); forms of childhood discipline (Kodama et al., 1964; Tsuru, 1963); a study of mothers' expectations concerning the independent behavior of children (Miyake, 1961); sources used by mothers in rural and urban communities in learning methods of child rearing (Takahashi et al., 1968a, 1968b); parental attitudes toward child rearing (Niwa and Yamauchi, 1960; Tanaka, 1967); dependency (Tsumori and Inage, 1960, 1961; Harada, 1962); a study of urban kindergarten children (Yoda and Takuma, 1961); a series of studies of children of an isolated mountain community whose parents are migrant laborers (Miyawaki, 1960, 1962–67); and a report on practices of child rearing in a rural community of Nagano Prefecture (Sue, 1960). An unusual custom of rural Japan aroused research interest for a time and resulted in a number of publications (e.g., Sofue et al., 1958). This is the use of the *ejiko*, a type of cradle for children, usually made of straw and bowl-shaped. When the child must be left unattended, it is placed in a squatting position within the cradle, wrapped in a quilt and tied by a rope so that hardly any movement is possible. Conclusions concerning the effects of this practice as evident in the adult personality are admitted to be difficult to draw because of lack of knowledge of the number and relative influence of other factors relating to the formation of personality.

Although the results of these and other studies are not always in accord with each other, several trends of congruence in both emphases of study and reported results are evident. For the most part, the studies have implicitly or explicitly concerned the relationship of rearing practices to adult behavior, although they seldom present firm conclusions about these relationships. They have also described regional variations, which are pronounced between rural and urban communities. They present clear evidence of changing attitudes toward child training and consequent changing practices of doing so. The description we have presented, drawn from the account in 1955 by Ishiguro, is still fairly representative, but, it must be noted, data available today on early socialization do not permit the assured formulation of a modal description. Certain themes nevertheless stand out in the various accounts, particularly in those by Western scholars. One of these is the contention that young Japanese children are reared with great permissiveness, and that this permissiveness declines progressively after children reach school age. An associated trait upon which there is general agreement is that a high degree of dependency exists between children and parents, especially between children and their mothers (see, for example, Vogel, 1963; DeVos, 1968a; Lanham, 1956; Caudill and Weinstein, 1969). A modern trend of change from emphasis on the parent-child relationship toward increased emphasis on the husband-wife relationship (Dore, 1958) has not been interpreted as generally weakening bonds of dependency. Caudill and Weinstein compare American and Japanese infants, observing that the Japanese child has much greater physical contact with its mother than does the American, a circumstance that favors the growth of dependency. Basing his statements on responses to a picture test similar to the Thematic Apperception Test used in a study on impulse gratification that is relevant to dependency, Caudill (1959c) compares Japanese and American mothers in feelings of sensual gratification derived from nursing infants. He states that such gratification is consciously acceptable to the Japanese mother but is generally repressed by the American mother. Long continued dependence upon the mother is also described by Caudill as being psychologically acceptable to the Japanese; a young man may remain dependent upon his mother for many satisfactions long past the age that would be appropriate in the United States.

Although they have wider significance, a group of unique papers by the Japanese psychologist L. Takeo Doi (1956, 1958, 1960) relate very directly to dependency and indirectly to child training. Doi calls attention to

Japanese words and concepts as illustrative of Japanese psychology, and states that terms referring to the emotions and interpersonal relationships often have no suitable equivalents. He cites as an example the noun *amae*, derived from the verb *amaeru*, which he defines in English as *to depend and presume upon another's love or indulge in another's kindness*, a meaning which refers to needs of dependency. To Japanese minds, the word usually means what a child feels about or how he acts toward his parents, particularly his mother, and thus it relates to the nursing period. Thinking in terms of this very familiar Japanese concept, Doi states, easily led Japanese psychoanalysts to formulate theories about the importance of oral dependency in the formation of neuroses, an interpretation that arose only later in Western psychoanalysis.

The subject of dependency has for several years been the major focus of psychocultural studies of Japan because it appears to offer keys to understanding Japanese traits that have long been puzzling. The importance of dependency or interdependency may be easily inferred by examination of various Japanese values and features of Japanese social organization which have been described and discussed in contexts having no direct bearing on the study of personality. The tendency frequently noted among the Japanese — in the business world, religious sects, academic circles, the underworld, and elsewhere — to form small, exclusive groups with strong attachments to other members is congruent with, and perhaps explained by, a condition of strong dependency created in infancy and childhood by the circumstances of rearing. The socialization of dependency — and mutual interdepency in the formation of small groups and in the continuing interpersonal ties that result — may be seen as an important contributing factor in the rapid industrialization and modernization of Japan. Modernization in Japan, rather than stressing individualistic behavior, was accomplished by using rather than prohibiting personalized bonds of relationship, as is examplified by the paternalism that exists in the Japanese world of commerce and industry. Dependency is also seen as one of the important factors contributing to the success of certain postwar religious sects that have risen to great size and wealth (Norbeck, 1970) and also as an important component of the Japanese analogue of the Protestant ethic, a subject that will later be further pursued.

Various other projects of research bear upon but are more or less peripheral to the subject of child rearing. Among these are a number of studies of social problems and deviancy, and increased studies of the Japanese overseas, subjects to be discussed separately. Certain reports on child rearing which we have discussed compare Japan and the United States, but cross-cultural comparison ordinarily does not extend beyond these two societies. An exception is an interesting and useful film on child rearing (National Film Board of Canada, 1959) which gives a visual comparison of Japanese, Hindu, French, and Canadian customs. The Japanese section, prepared with the advice of William Caudill, depicts the events of a day in the life of an infant girl, 10 months of age, from a farming family of the Kantō Plain, near Tokyo.

5. Achievement Motivation

The remarkable speed and success with which Japan transformed itself from a technologically undeveloped feudal state into an industrialized, international power have long piqued the interest of Western scholars, an interest that was intensified by Japan's astoundingly swift economic recovery from the devastation of World War II. Western observers have seen, as one contributing factor, a counterpart in Japan of the Protestant ethic of northern Europe and the United States. The Japanese are seen characteristically to place high value on industriousness, thrift, self-sacrifice, and achievement. Until recent years, attempts to explain the rapid modernization of Japan have, however, scarecely considered the matter of motivation. Robert Bellah's study of Tokugawa religion (1957) is exceptional. Following the line of thought of Max Weber's views of the Protestant ethic, Bellah saw in Tokugawa religion, especially in quasi-religious Confucian ideals of interpersonal relations, a strong reinforcement for the Japanese drive to achieve. Other interpretations of reasons for the speed and success of modernization in Japan characteristically dealt with economic factors, such as the supply of labor, or features of social organization, such as the familial nature of Japanese society and the congruent familial nature of Japanese industry. With the exception of some passages in Benedict's *The Chrysanthemum and the Sword*, none of the early studies approached the subject from a psychocultural viewpoint.

Since the late 1950's, however, achievement motivation has been increasingly a focus of study among scholars of Japanese culture and personality, a focus that began with American scholars and has extended to the Japanese scholarly world (e.g., Hayashi and Yamauchi, 1964; Maruyama, 1965; Doi, 1967). Many additional projects of research with goals other than gaining an understanding of motivation toward achievement have had important bearing on this subject, and these have perhaps been heuristic spurs toward its study. Certain early studies of Americans of Japanese descent (cf. *The Japanese Overseas*) directly concerned the subject of achievement, seeing a congruence of American and Japanese values as an explanation of the successful adjustment of Japanese migrants and their descendants to life in the United States. The current trend of studies centered on achievement motivation is to consider both precognitive and cognitive drives in the social contexts that implant and reinforce the drives. Explanations are couched in terms of "need achievement" (Atkinson, ed., 1958; McClelland, 1961), affiliative needs, authoritarianism and rigidity, and certain dominant cognitive values such as the emphasis in Japanese society upon particularism as opposed to universalism (e.g., Kiefer, in press). These traits are considered in the context of the Japanese social groups in which the drives and values are acquired and maintained and include consideration of the sanctions involved.

The greatest emphasis in these studies has been upon needs of dependency and affiliation, especially upon bonds within the family. As we have earlier noted in discussing dependency, this subject is one on which there is general scholarly agreement; dependency is strong, as are related and congruent affiliative needs, and these needs in turn are seen to be related to need for achievement, which is also strong. Certain studies, such as the Caudill and Weinstein (1959) research on maternal care and infant behavior, point to conditions that foster feelings of dependency beginning in early childhood. Other studies that are not directed toward the subject of achievement motivation in one way or another provide support for the contention that dependency and affiliative needs are strong. Goodman (1959), for example, reports that vocational aspirations of children are influenced by parental wishes more strongly among Japanese than among American children. (See also our earlier discussion of guilt and expiation.) DeVos (1968a) has summarized much of his own research and that of other scholars on this subject in an interpretation which gives greatest emphasis to the mother-child relationship and especially to the relationship between mother and son. Our earlier discussion regarding guilt and shame and related affective bonds between mother and child is again relevant here. DeVos sees in the Japanese mother a particularly forceful agency for implanting and fortifying achievement needs. The mother, without conscious intent, has perfected techniques of inducing guilt in her children by such means as quiet suffering. She takes the burden of responsibility for their behavior, and, as also with bad conduct on the part of her husband, will often manifest self-reproach if her children conduct themselves badly or in any other way fail to meet the standards of success set for the community. If one fails to meet social expectations, he thereby hurts his mother and he also hurts other familial members; as a result, he suffers unhappiness and feelings of guilt. Also important to the achievement syndrome of the Japanese is a psychological tendency to delay gratification that is congruent with long-range goals. We may note in passing that no information is available on the historic depth of such close bonds between mother and child, but they are presumably fairly ancient. We may note also the very recent development of a seeming apogee of Japanese motherhood, the "education mama" (*kyōiku mama*), who compulsively drives her children toward success in school as the key toward success in adult life.

Much work remains to be done on the subject of achievement motivation in Japan, particularly on the means by which ideals of achievement become established, but it is reasonable to state that research completed to date has contributed to knowledge by making clear that the cultural, social, and psychological factors involved in the formation and perpetuation of drives toward achievement analogous with the Protestant ethic are not everywhere the same. The idea of Hagen (1962) that economic development may spring from feelings of deprivation of minority groups of a population that foster compensatory forms of innovation resulting in national economic development does not describe the circumstances in Japan, as research on the *Tokushu Burakumin*, the pariah class of Japan, attests (DeVos and Wagatsuma, 1966). McClelland's interpretation (1961) of achievement motivation in the United States as depending importantly upon early training in independence is similarly inapplicable to Japan. From economic, ethnological, and sociological researches on the modernization of Japan as well as from research in Japanese personality and culture it has become increasingly apparent that the social, cultural, and psychocultural routes to modernization of non-Western societies may diverge farther than scholarly thought once held from the patterns of the West. The foregoing statement does not deny that similarities exist — there is, for example, a curious resemblance between the Japanese and the Jewish mother. We would expect that ultimately achievement motivation in all societies will be understood through statements of general principles, qualified by peculiar individual circumstances.

6. Deviancy and Social Problems

Until recent years, the subjects of deviancy and related social problems were left almost entirely to Japanese scholars. To be sure, American studies during World War II and immediate postwar years often concerned supposed pathological traits of the enemy Japanese. These studies did not, however, concern social problems or deviancy as these are seen by the Japanese or, after Japan lost its status as an enemy, by foreign scholars.

Japanese study of these subjects has been principally postwar, American-derived, sociological, and centering upon crime, juvenile delinquency, poverty, and family welfare (cf. Iga, 1970). Suicide and problems of the aged have been lesser foci of study. In general, Japanese scholars have shied away from study of their own minority groups; university or college courses on social problems are very rare; and, as compared with conditions in the United States, scholarly concern with social problems is not intense. Japanese scholars of these subjects, especially sociologists, have nevertheless produced an abundance of raw data that are potentially valuable to students of personality and culture. Iga (1970) observes that two underlying characteristics appear eminent in Japanese studies of social problems including some psychiatric studies, characteristics which he reasonably contends are reflections of general Japanese values of emphasizing the group over the individual: 1) Individual deviance is dealt with as a problem of social maladaptation rather than as an individual psychological problem, and 2) Other social problems are analyzed from "ideological" points of view — that is, the pros and cons of governmental welfare policy and other views of welfare policy in general — and not from the standpoint of the experiences of the individuals concerned.

American social scientists have done little systematic work on the full range of Japanese social problems, and, expectably the research which they have done does not concern medico-social problems such as those relating to public health or physically based mental handicaps. The American research which has been conducted on subjects that may involve hereditary factors, such as psychosis and suicide, has been from a psychocultural viewpoint centering on cultural factors involved. Despite spottiness of coverage, this body of research has contributed to knowledge of the Japanese and, in a broader sense, to an understanding of the human problems involved. We shall review this research under several headings, including in our discussion certain studies by Japanese scholars that seem particularly relevant.

Problems of the Urban Ecological Environment. Research on the subject of urban ecology may be described as having only begun, but there is growing scholarly realization that the progressive urbanization of Japan has, perforce, made the city the vital subject of study. Our discussion here points to no single contributions of major significance, but is instead intended to inform of the state of research with a second aim of encouraging the development of much additional study.

The urbanization of Japan has been the subject of sociological and ethnological studies by foreign scholars that deal more or less incidentally with social problems (e.g., Dore, 1958; Vogel, 1963) in the rapidly changing Japanese society. In particular, these studies have dealt with tensions resulting from changes in institutions and customs, such as family structure and familial relations, modes of arranging marriage, and conditions of life associated with residence in large modern *danchi*, governmentally subsidized housing developments consisting of complexes of small apartments (e.g., Nakano, 1962; Yamane and Nonoyama, 1967; Blood, 1967; Kiefer, 1968). Various studies tell us of lingering pre-modern patterns of paternalism in urban industries marginal to the main currents of Japanese industry (e.g., Bennett and Ishino, 1963). Two remarkable studies concern the bottom-most social strata of the modern Japanese city, a study of the residents of urban flophouses (Caldarola, MS), and a study of a community of rag pickers in Tokyo (Taira, MS). Other research under way includes a study of familial life of a lower class ward in Tokyo (DeVos and Wagatsuma) and of the adjustments of rural migrants to urban life in southwestern Japan (Erwin Johnson).

Culture and Mental Health. We shall note in passing that Japanese research in clinical psychology and psychotherapy has made extensive use of Western therapeutic techniques as well as the Rorschach test and other diagnostic tests. These have been somewhat altered in adaptation to the Japanese circumstances, but it is clear that the tests and techniques are valid and useful in Japan (see DeVos, Murakami, and Murase, 1964). A recent application of the California Psychological Inventory to Japanese juvenile delinquents has been equally successful (DeVos and Mizushima, 1967; Gough, DeVos and Mizushima, 1968). Studies of the relationship between culture and mental health in Japan by Western or Western-oriented scholars commonly compare circumstances with those in the United States, showing general similarities but also certain noteworthy differences (see Kāto, 1969). A substantial group of studies has concerned symptoms and treatment of psychosis (e.g., Caudill and Doi, 1963; Caudill and Schooler, 1969), showing that symptoms are generally milder among Japanese patients and that care and treatment of patients is differently conceived (Caudill, 1959a, 1959b, 1961). Caudill has also reported differences in mental illness that relate to birth order in the family (Caudill, 1964).

The subject of dependency has been the focus of various studies of psycnological adjustment, and these point to maladjustive features as well as to the adjustive features of social and economic relevance that we have previously discussed. Various writings of Doi, some of which we have already discussed, concern mental health as related to child rearing and later socialization. Doi (1956, 1962, 1963, 1969) describes dependency as a major factor in the problems of psychological self-realization and maturation faced by many Japanese under conditions of modern life, which have come to favor autonomy and indivualism more than in the past.

Many studies concerning psychological problems of the Japanese relate directly to the subject of mental health but are presented in other contexts. Among these are the studies of the psychological tensions of guilt and shame, previously cited, and various studies, to be discussed later, of psychological traits of Japanese abroad, some of which compare Japanese nationals and American Japanese. Various studies of authoritarianism also relate to mental health, and these may be summarized as reporting a high correlation between rigidity and authoritarianism (e.g., DeVos and Wagatsuma, 1959, 1964) and generally high scores in authoritarianism in Japan (Niyekawa, 1966).

Problems of self-identity and alienation and the features of socialization which foster these problems, especially as they are related to the high incidence of suicide among young Japanese, have been the subject of several studies (Lifton, 1962; DeVos, 1962, 1964, 1967b; Burg, 1961; Iga, 1961, 1968; Bennett, Passin and McKnight, 1958; Wagatsuma, 1969b). The rate of suicide among young Japanese is by far the highest recorded in the world, and these various studies offer interpretations of this phenomenon with reference to dependency, individualization, and commitment that show youth as a highly critical period psychologically. Other related studies of psychological stress among Japanese youth include research on the stresses imposed by modern demands for achievement in education imposed by mothers and other family members and the society at large (Vogel, 1962; Kiefer, 1968), and includes a study of psychological problems of Tokyo college students (Sofue, 1964).

Juvenile Delinquency, Crime and Prostitution. One of the concomitants of the modernization and urbanization of Japan has been a great rise in the incidence of juvenile delinquency and crime, especially criminal assault. A great quantity of variably useful sociological and psychological research on these subjects has been done by Japanese scholars but this remains essentially unknown outside of Japan. A summary and review of these studies is now being prepared in English (DeVos, Mizushima and Hunn). Studies by foreign scholars have been few but these have pointed out certain features that are illuminative of Japanese personality and contrast with conditions in the United States. These features may be summarized briefly. Juvenile delinquency differs in beginning a few years earlier (DeVos, 1967a). (As in the United States, delinquency rates are highest among members of the minority groups.) Japanese criminals are remarkable in preserving longer than in other sectors of the society traditional family-like forms of social relations that formerly characterized Japanese society in general, including the *oyabun-kobun*, a form of ritual or fictive kinship after the model of parent-child relationships of ordinary life (Mizushima and DeVos, 1967c; Bennett and Ishino, 1963). In postwar times, prostitution legally became a crime in Japan, and it has since tended to become an enterprise of organized criminal groups, which also exercise political influence by support of candidates for public office (Iga, 1968; Mizushima and DeVos, 1962). Despite their official designation as criminals, Japanese prostitutes are described as generally being psychologically normal women (Iga, 1968), mostly married, divorced, or separated, and often the mother of children. They are older than their American counterparts and have taken up their professions primarily as a means of gaining a livelihood for themselves and their dependents.

Problems of Minority Groups. As we have noted, Japanese scholars have given little attention to the study of their nation's minority groups. Only two groups are ordinarily regarded as minority groups, Koreans, who number about 600,000 persons, and the native Japanese outcast class of *Tokushu Burakumin* (customarily called by the abbreviation *Burakumin*, a term which has displaced the earlier and highly pejorative name *Eta*), whose number is variously estimated as between one and three million persons. Some reportorial research, notably a study by Mitchell (1967), concerns the Koreans, but no psychocultural research has been conducted on this group except insofar as Koreans have been included in studies of crime, juvenile delinquency, and the like. The few remaining Ainu are ordinarily omitted from consideration in conceptions of minority group status, and they have not been the subject of modern studies of social or psychological problems. A small group that has been the subject of some studies by Japanese scholars consists of the offspring of Japanese women and American soldiers of the military occupation, many of whom were Negroes. This group is reported as being subjected to strong discrimination.

Only one minority group, the *Burakumin,* has been the focus of substantial research by foreign scholars (Passin, 1955; Donoghue, 1957; Cornell, 1961, 1967; Iga, 1967; DeVos, 1965; Wagatsuma, 1967a; Devos and Wagatsuma, 1967). This research and also a little Japanese research on the subject are summarized and incorporated by DeVos and Wagatsuma in the work *Japan's Invisible Race* (1966). The sociocultural circumstances surrounding Burakumin status are shown to be essentially like those associated with racial prejudice elsewhere in the world; a signal difference is that the Burakumin do not differ in physical characteristics from the dominant population.

7. The Japanese Overseas

A group of studies which gives promise of being particularly useful for comparative study in culture and personality is that conducted on Japanese immigrants to non-Asian countries and their descendants. Most of the approximately half-million Japanese emigrants settled in Hawaii, the continental United States, and Brazil. Smaller groups of Japanese migrated to Peru and other countries of South America, sometimes by remigration from Brazil, and other relatively small groups settled in Mexico, Cuba, and Canada.

Historians, sociologists, educational psychologists, anthropologists, and scholars in various additional fields have long engaged in research on these Japanese and their descendants. A vast accumulation of published studies now exists on the Japanese in Hawaii and the continental United States and Brazil, but few or no similar studies have been made on the Japanese of the other nations. Most of the accounts are historic, ethnographic, or sociological studies that have no direct relevance to the study of personality. These have been competently reviewed by Cornell and Smith (1970), and we shall limit our discussion of them to a few passing remarks and give our attention to works that relate to personality. Many of the publications on Brazil were written by Brazilians in the Portuguese language and are historic accounts or concern the Japanese development of small-farm agriculture. Studies of the Japanese in the United States lean much more heavily to consideration of social problems. A recent trend of research has been toward study of South American Japanese by non-native scholars; that is, some substantial research on the Japanese in Brazil and Peru has been done by Americans and Japanese from Japan. It is also noteworthy that *Issei* and *Nisei* have long been regarded as culturally distinct groups even by scholars whose primary interests have been history.

One of the earliest studies of interest to the concerns of this chapter was an investigation by educational psychologists of the school behavior of Nisei children on the Pacific coast of the United States. A summary of these studies (Strong, 1934) compares Caucasian-American and Japanese-American grade school and high school children in intellectual functioning and related features of personality. The studies make no explicit use of the concept of culture and for this reason appear naive in the light of present-day theory and knowledge in the social sciences. They bring out distinctly, however, a number of traits that characterize the *Nisei*. Psychological tests indicated no differences in the intellectual functioning of *Nisei* and Caucasian-American children, although they did indicate different artistic sensibilities. Other traits noted are of greater interest. One of these is close conformance with middle-class American norms of behavior. Behavior of the *Nisei* children in the schools is described as characteristically docile, patient, and respectful and obedient to the teachers. Motivation to achievement is strong, and it is clear that parents of the *Nisei* exerted strong pressure to inculcate in their children the idea that meeting American standards of achievement and other norms of behavior is desirable. *Nisei* students tended to earn higher grades for school work than others and to receive greater recognition from teachers for exemplary conduct.

Interest in the Japanese of the Pacific coast and elsewhere in the United States was heightened during World War II, when many were sent to relocation centers. A number of published accounts deal with the adjustment of the Japanese to life in these camps and the new surroundings to which they moved when the war ended and the camps were closed, Among these studies, Alexander Leighton's *The Governing of Man*, although not a study in culture and personality, is especially noteworthy for the incisive comments it makes on characteristic Japanese reactions to stress.

Postwar interdisciplinary research on the acculturation of Japanese in the Chicago area has yielded publications on acculturative changes in personality and on the nature of psychological conflicts which the bridging of Japanese and American cultures has produced among the Japanese-Americans. Among these is Caudill's (1952) extensive analysis of psychological aspects of the drive toward achievement and other value-attitudes of the *Nisei*. A study, based on Rorschach tests, of acculturative changes in structural aspects of personality of *Issei* and *Nisei* (DeVos, 1955) reports a high level of rigidity and certain indications of maladjustment among the *Issei*. *Nisei* were much lower in rigidity, and displayed fewer indications of maladjustment. Comparison with data on Japanese in Japan of the same social backgrounds (i.e., rural residents) revealed equally high rigidity, but indications of severe maladjustment were found only among the American *Issei* and appear to be related to stress in adjusting to the alien American culture.

A focus of continuing interest in the study of the Japanese in America has been attempts to analyze their drive toward achievement. The question has been asked why *Issei* and *Nisei* have adopted the attitudes, and values, including the strong motivation to achievement, of the American middle class when certain other immigrant groups under comparable circumstances have not done so to the same degree (see, for example, Norbeck, 1959). Scholars have also asked why the Japanese have made such apparently successful adjustments to life in the United States when other minority groups, some of them suffering less social discrimination, have failed to do so. Similarities and compatibilities in certain American and native Japanese values and attitudes have been offered in partial explanation (Caudill and DeVos, 1956). Japanese are described as extremely sensitive to stimuli from the outer world and as having a superego structure that depends strongly on external sanctions for reinforcement. Cultural values are internalized in a socialization process that emphasizes long-range goals, perseverance, obedience to authority, and a sense of obligation to parents. This socialization takes place within the family, but the drive to achievement is satisfied by conforming with expectations of the outer society. (This observation, it may be noted, is in keeping with opinions expressed by numerous other scholars describing Japanese in Japan and elsewhere. For example, a study comparing the vocational aspirations of American and Japanese schoolchildren (Goodman, 1957) describes the Americans as "self-oriented" (egocentric) and the Japanese as "others-oriented.") Attitudes and community values to which the *Nisei*, as a minority group, are most strongly exposed in extra-familial contacts, and which the *Nisei* internalize, are those of the American middle class. Thus native Japanese and American attitudes of valuing conformance and achievement and stressing long-range goals reinforce each other. Success for the *Nisei* differs from success for the non-Japanese American, however, in being closely related to the fulfillment of filial obligations. The feeling of necessity to succeed as a means of satisfying obligations to parents is brought out in clinical studies of individual *Nisei* (e.g., Babcock and Caudill, 1958). A tendency toward psychological depression among *Nisei* is well documented in a collection of papers on culture conflict related to psychiatric problems of the *Nisei* (Georgine Seward, ed., 1958), which includes a particularly pertinent paper by Marvin Opler on psychological stress as related to filial obligations in the case history of an individual *Kibei*.

An indication of the multiplicity of factors involved in the formation of the adult personality is provided by the results of a psychological testing of *Kibei*, American-born Japanese who, after spending their early childhood in the United States, are taken to Japan for a number of years for schooling, and then return to the United States (DeVos, 1955). From the standpoints of personality rigidity and maladjustment, the *Kibei* were generally intermediate to the *Issei* and *Nisei*. If the earliest practices of socialization are in fact the most powerful, little difference should of course be found between *Kibei* and *Nisei* as they appear to have been exposed to essentially identical practices of training in infancy and early childhood.

A study which compares acculturating Arabs in Algeria and other minority groups with Japanese-Americans reports that certain indications of intra-psychic stress appear in the Rorschach record of all groups except the *Nisei*, and concludes that the stress is connected with acculturation or status as members of minority groups because the indications do not appear in the records of individuals of the majority groups of the nations in question (DeVos, in Kaplan, ed., 1961).

Data on immigrant and South American-born Japanese in Peru and Brazil that allow comparison with studies in the United States were collected in the 1950's by Japanese scholars under the direction of Seiichi Izumi of Tokyo University, and a part of the findings have been published (Izumi and Saito, 1954; Izumi, ed., 1957). Results of Rorschach, Thematic Apperception Tests and problem situation tests in Peru differ from those obtained in Brazil, the United States, and Japan (Hiroshi Wagatsuma, personal communication). Japanese-Peruvians appear to be less strongly motivated toward personal achievement than Japanese-Brazilians, Japanese-American, or Japanese in Japan, and, as indicated by the Rorschach, to be more pragmatic, presenting less emphasis on the integrated conceptions characteristic of the Japanese in the United States and at home. Research conducted more recently in Brazil by John B. Cornell and Robert J. Smith (report in preparation), P. S. Staniford (1967), and various studies by Japanese scholars add substantially to information useful for comparative purposes although these studies do not center on personality.

The Ryukyu Islands are not "overseas" in the same sense as North and

South America, but research in personality and culture on Japanese of these islands is of significance for comparison in the same way as data on Japanese in faraway lands. Although the islands were a part of Japan for many centuries before the end of World War II, because of their isolated geographic position they escaped or were only lightly affected by many cultural innovations that swept Japan proper. In a short article on the island of Amami Ōshima, Douglas Haring (1954a) describes the islanders as having more "open" personalities than the residents of Japan proper. He suggests that the lack of sustained direct contact with Japan proper prevented the spread to this small island of attitudes and values which permeated the principal islands during the Tokugawa era (1603–1868). The modern Amami Ōshima islanders, more impulsively labile and directly expressive of emotions than modern mainland Japanese, may represent a type of personality that characterized the whole nation before Tokugawa times.

J. Moloney's controversial writings (e.g., 1954) on the Okinawans describe them as relatively free of conflict and assert that as a result of permissive practices of nursing there is little mental illness among them. A carefully executed study of child rearing practices in an Okinawan community by T. W. Maretzki (1957) casts much doubt on the statements of Moloney. Maretzki's research centered on dependence-independence, aggression, and internalization of values with the objective of relating measures of children's personality to antecedent factors of socialization. He observes that both adults and children indulge in a great deal of verbal aggression, and he reports many traits that differ from observations made on Japanese from the main islands. Notable among these is a low drive to achievement. Tightly knit social relationships throughout the whole community, encouraged by customs of community endogamy, are tied in with the high sociability, low dominance, and lack of competitiveness which characterize the children. Outstanding features in Okinawan socialization include an emphasis on nurturance, a high diffusion of caretakers of children, and the importance of the role of peers in every stage of child development. The community as a whole is almost an extension of the household environment. Later research by Maretzki (1964) on personality in rural Okinawa supports earlier findings, and also provides information on suicide (Maretzki, 1966) useful for comparative purposes. Additional data on Ryukyuan practices of child rearing, including mechanisms of social control, are provided by reports of field research by Allan H. Smith (1960) and Trude Smith (1961). A summary of research on the Ryukyu Islands that gives additional ethnographic references is provided by William P. Lebra (1970), whose own studies have centered on Okinawan religion.

Pertinent investigations that fall outside the classifications we have used here but are worthy of notice include linguistic research on perception and cognition (e.g., Niyekawa-Howard, 1968), and writings following the line of thought in Doi's treatment of the word *amae*, which offer interpretations of the psychological significance of certain "untranslatable" Japanese words (Doi, 1956; Wagatsuma, in press). Also relevant are recent publications concerning the Japanese view of themselves, the tendency to view their own physical attributes as inferior to those of Westerners (Wagatsuma, 1967; Norbeck, 1969; see also earlier references to works by Ishida).

Summary and Conclusions

In the decade since the original version of this chapter was written the number of Western scholars whose work at least indirectly concerns the subject of our interest has grown somewhat and the number of Japanese scholars similarly engaged has grown far more. The absolute number of foreign and native scholars who specialize in the study of Japanese personality and culture is still not great, but no other foreign culture has been the subject of study by so many individuals. The total of relevant published studies, especially works in the Japanese language, was impressive in volume a decade ago. It has since grown very greatly, but it continues to be weak or deficient in a number of respects, some of which we have noted. The techniques and theories of modern culture and personality research have still had no adequate testing in Japan — but it is extremely doubtful that they have had adequate testing in any other culture. Certain new subjects of investigations have been added in the past decade, and considerable progress has been made in determining differences in culture and traits of personality according to region and social class in Japan. Much more continues to be required before generalizations on the nation may be made with assurance.

Study completed to date continues to have strengths and weaknesses. Some of these are continuations from the past; others were not obvious to the authors a decade ago. A failing of Japanese scholars has been a strong, and traditional, scholarly encystment into small specialized groups that have little communication with other groups, a circumstance that does not foster the interdisciplinary research vital to the study of culture and personality. Communication between foreign and Japanese scholars has improved greatly, but it is still hampered by the language barrier. Both Japanese and foreign scholars are now professionally more sophisticated, but the Japanese tend as before to concern themselves with minute scholarly problems and to avoid studies that go beyond description. Notable exceptions exist, and we believe we have called attention to them in the foregoing pages. One general trend of change among both Japanese and foreign scholars has been a shift in emphasis from rural to urban Japan, a shift that rather tardily reflects demographic changes of the Japanese nation.

Foreign scholars continue to be principally citizens of the United States, whose command of the Japanese language is variably imperfect, and who undoubtedly bring to their research the various species of cultural biases peculiar to Americans. Japanese scholarship in all of the social sciences is strongly influenced by the United States, and no important indigenous developments of theory or methodology relevant to the study of culture and personality are evident in Japan.

A conspicuous failing of both Japanese and American scholarship has been a scarcity of comparative studies in all aspects of research in personality and culture. The Japanese, by preference, usually study only Japan and Japanese. Americans most frequently compare Japan with the United States, often implicitly. We believe that this procedure has been useful, but a broader scope of comparison seems to us highly desirable. This criticism, we realize, may be applied to the entire field of culture and personality.

The preceding observations and opinions about progress and problems differ somewhat from our conclusions a decade ago, principally reflecting a new awareness on our part of problems that exist. We reproduce below in very slightly edited form several paragraphs from the conclusions offered ten years ago concerning positive contributions. These statements seem to us applicable today.

> Despite our negative comments, research in Japanese culture and personality has not been merely a spotty repetition of techniques and interpretations borrowed from scholars of the United States and Europe. It has made its own contributions of theoretical significance and it holds unusually great promise of making future contributions. Subjects of research have been examined in such a way that their conclusions concern and shed light on issues of general interest in the field of culture and personality and the social sciences as a whole. Past or present research in Japanese culture and personality has special relevance to the following subjects of general interest:
>
> 1. The nature of human drives to achievement.
> 2. Variations in the cultural conditioning of basic psychological mechanisms:

shame versus guilt as motivating forces; different uses of introjection and projection.

3. Processes of acculturation: factors involved in making acculturation easy and successful or difficult and unsuccessful; the relationship between acculturation and psychic stress.

Motivation toward achievement has long been a subject of scholarly interest, and the practical value of an understanding of factors that inhibit and encourage the growth of drives to achievement is obvious. Explanations have been sought through examination of religiously sanctioned ideals of behavior and in many other ways. The eagerness and speed with which Japan assimilated Western culture, the startling rapidity with which it emerged from cultural backwardness to a position as a major international power, and the remarkable recovery of the nation after devastating defeat and economic collapse in World War II have stimulated much curiosity and theorizing. Historians have pointed to the long-established receptiveness of the Japanese to items of foreign culture and their equally long record of successful adaptation of borrowed items. Other scholars have held that the hierarchical ordering of Japanese society, especially the former tight control of ruler over subject, has made the industrialization and "modernization" of Japan easy. Robert Bellah's interesting *Tokugawa Religion* (1957) approaches the problem sociologically after the manner of Max Weber. He concludes that an equivalent of the Protestant ethic, evident in Tokugawa times, served as a spur to Japanese economic growth. T. C. Smith (1959) has argued effectively that the road to industrialization was paved by indigenous developments during Tokugawa times.

All of these studies leave off where culture and personality begins. The pattern of psychological integration of the personality that encourages diligence and self-denial for the purpose of attaining long-range goals is of particular interest in understanding the achievements of Japan as a nation. It is here that research in culture and personality can be very helpful. As we have noted, much evidence from studies in culture and personality indicates that strong motivation toward success exists among the Japanese of Japan and Japanese-Americans. Other research has suggested the means by which motivation is inculcated and reinforced. Research under way on intra-familial relations gives promise of telling us more about motivation as it is related to Japanese social structure as well as contributing to our understanding of psychological stress arising from social living. These theoretical matters are, of course, highly relevant to the problem of understanding other Asian countries where economic developments have followed quite different courses and to the understanding of motivation and achievement for all mankind.

In connection with the problem of understanding the drive to achievement of the Japanese, published studies in personality and culture have presented hypotheses that should stimulate re-examination of theories of the relationships between superego and ego ideal as these are related to guilt and shame. Perhaps all scholars working in the field of personality and culture would agree that theorizing on the subject of guilt versus shame has often been oversimplified. Certainly, the Japanese studies suggest strongly that shame and guilt are not necessarily antithetical or mutually incompatible. The question of the relative weight of the sanction of shame versus that of guilt in any society cannot be investigated satisfactorily without consideration of several other related subjects, including the mechanisms of introjection and projection. Research on Japan on this latter subject points up the necessity of reexamination of theories and of further cross-cultural comparison.

Perhaps the most promising avenue of research in Japanese personality and culture bears on the subject of acculturation. The fact that Japanese citizens of similar backgrounds have migrated to several nations with quite different cultures provides a unique opportunity for cross-cultural comparison of processes of acculturation. Research completed to date indicates that the Japanese of the United States differ considerably in traits of personality from those who have settled in South America. Studies of the Japanese in these areas suggest that compatibility rather than duplication of values between the minority and majority group are necessary for successful acculturation, and that quite different patterns of psychological reinforcement of values may yield results that are similar. Delineation of the values as well as interpretation of associated psychological mechanisms are problems which appear to yield best results when approached through the methods of personality and culture.

Research conducted to date on the Japanese also indicates that projective tests are useful instruments for detecting intra-psychic stress arising from difficulties of acculturation. Further comparison with data on Chinese-Americans, American Negroes, Puerto Ricans, Filipinos and other minority groups and acculturating peoples in the United States in this and other matters should be extremely fruitful.

The promise which future research holds seems particularly great. Japan is a large and culturally complex society with many social strata representing subcultures, and many regional differences. This circumstance provides an unusually fine opportunity for comparison to aid in gaining understanding of many questions concerned with personality and culture. The Japanese abroad offer another useful avenue of comparison. Japan is, moreover, a highly literate society with much recorded history. During the past century it has undergone tremendous cultural change, proceeding at an accelerated rate since the end of World War II, and much of the change is well documented. In these respects, Japan offers an exceptional opportunity for observation of sociocultural change and its relationship to personality. In all of these matters, the prospect of future contributions to knowledge is particularly favored by the fact that both native and foreign scholars in several disciplines are engaged in research directed toward solving the same problems.

The preceding paragraphs require change only to take cognizance of progress. A decade ago we discussed achievement motivation, but did not classify it as a separate topic, as we have felt to be appropriate here. Research completed during the past decade on achievement motivation has contributed to general understanding of this subject, in part by serving as a check against scholarly ethnocentrism that is prone to generalize for all nations on the basis of circumstances in the United States. It is increasingly clear that the psychocultural dynamics of achievement in the two societies are different and in some respects involve opposing forms of behavior.

Research on psychological mechanisms of guilt-shame, introjection-projection, and psychocultural aspects of acculturation has similarly expanded, amplifying earlier interpretations but making no fundamental changes in them. Forthcoming interpretations of acculturation among Japanese in South American promise to be particularly valuable in extending the base of comparison beyond the United States.

The past ten years has also seen an expansion of research into fields and subjects previously untouched or scarcely touched. The study of deviancy and social problems, a new development, has shed light on the subjects of achievement motivation, the dynamics of guilt and shame, introjection and projection, and problems of acculturation. This research has also contributed to an understanding of the genesis and nature of human stress and its attendant social problems. As contributions to knowledge in the social sciences, research on two subjects directly and indirectly connected with the study of social problems has had outstanding value, although the results of the research appear as yet not to have been communicated widely to the scholarly world:

1. *Dependency and Affiliative Needs.* Psychocultural studies of dependency in Japan combined with non-psychologically oriented studies of social units such as kin groups, common-interest associations, and underworld gangs, have relevance to many subjects of scholarly investigation in addition to the topics of achievement, deviancy, and social problems which we have discussed at some length. These include questions about the industrialization and modernization of Japan such as patterns of authority and other organizational features of industrial concerns that distinguish them from industrial concerns of the West; student unrest in the colleges of Japan and other nations; and the acculturation of Japanese overseas. The relevance of research on these topics for cross-cultural comparison and the furthering of knowledge in the social sciences seems obvious.

2. Minority group status and racial prejudice. Research on the outcasts of Japan has contributed to an understanding of pariah status and racial prejudice, and it is uniquely valuable in being a substantial body of works on a minority group that is physically indistinguishable from the dominant population, which regards and treats it in ways that elsewhere in the world, where racial differences do in fact exist, are called racial prejudice.

In conclusion, we are happy to be able to state that we regard the future optimistically. Many problems remain unsolved, of which the largest is perhaps simply lack of personnel to handle adequately the questions of investigation that are current today in the social sciences. An omen hopeful for the future of research in personality and culture was an interdisciplinary conference on the study of Japan in the behavioral sciences conducted in 1969 as part of a series of conferences aiming to appraise the current state of Japanese studies. Attended by Western and Japanese scholars in social and cultural anthropology, social psychology, and sociology, this conference was the first interdisciplinary conference of substantial size (41 persons) of the disciplines in question, all of which relate directly or indirectly to the study of culture and personality.[4] New questions and approaches continue to rise, especially as interdisciplinary communication increases. We would expect, for example, that ten years from now an account of this sort would appropriately include research on cognition, perception, and psycholinguistics, subjects that we have here mentioned only tangentially and which have as yet had little development. The general expansion of the social sciences, in trained personnel, theoretical formulations, and in methods, fortunately shows no signs of coming to an end.

BIBLIOGRAPHY

ABATE, MARIO AND F. K. BERRIEN. 1967. Validation of stereotypes: Japanese versus American students. Journal of Personality and Social Psychology 7:435–438.

ATKINSON, J., ED. 1958. Motives in fantasy, action and society. Princeton, Van Nostrand.

BABCOCK, CHARLOTTE, AND WILLIAM CAUDILL. 1958. Personal and cultural factors in treating a nisei man. *In* Clinical studies in culture conflict, Georgene Seward, ed. New York, Ronald Press.

[4]Conducted April 11–12, 1969 at Rice University, under the auspices of the Social Science Research Council and the American Council of Learned Societies. Most of the papers presented at the conference have been published (Norbeck and Parman, eds., 1970).

BELLAH, ROBERT N. 1957. Tokugawa religion; the values of pre-industrial Japan. Glencoe, Free Press.

BENEDICT, RUTH. 1946. The chrysanthemum and the sword: patterns of Japanese culture. Boston, Houghton Mifflin.

BENNETT, JOHN W. 1970. Some observations on behavioral science research on Japan: with special reference to anthropology. *In* The study of Japan in the behavioral sciences, Edward Norbeck and Susan Parman, eds., Rice University Studies, Vol. 56, No. 4.

BENNETT, JOHN W. AND IWAO ISHINO. 1963. Paternalism in the Japanese economy: anthropological studies of *oyabun-kobun* patterns. Minneapolis, University of Minnesota Press.

BENNETT, J. W. AND MICHIO NAGAI. 1953. Echoes: reactions to American anthropology — Japanese critique of the methodology of Benedict's "Chrysanthemum and the sword." American Anthropologist 55:404–411.

BENNETT, JOHN W., HERBERT PASSIN, AND ROBERT McKNIGHT. 1958. In search of identity: the Japanese overseas scholar in America and Japan. Minneapolis, The University of Minnesota Press.

BLOOD, ROBERT O., JR. 1967. Love match and arranged marriage, a Tokyo-Detroit comparison. New York, Free Press.

BUCHANAN, D. C. 1954. Japanese character and personality as revealed in their culture. *In* Understanding other cultures, William A. Parker, ed. Washington, American Council of Learned Societies.

BURG, MOSES. 1961. A psychocultural analysis and theoretical integration of the dynamics of Japanese parent-child suicide. Department of Sociology Bulletin No. 2. University of Tokyo.

CALDAROLA, CARLO. MS. The Japanese *Doya-Gai*. Unpublished paper.

CAUDILL, WILLIAM. 1952. Japanese-American personality and acculturation. Genetic Psychology Monographs 45. Provincetown, Mass., Journal Press.

———. 1959a. The relationship of anthropology to psychiatry in the study of culture and personality. Seishin Bunseki Kenkyū (The Japanese Journal of Psychoanalysis) 6:57–65.

———. 1959b. Similarities and differences in psychiatric illness and its treatment in the United States and Japan. Nagoya University, Seishin Eisei (Mental Hygiene) 61/62:15–26.

———. 1959c. *Watakushi no pikuchā intabyū gijutsu* (The use of a "Picture Interview" technique in the study of impulse gratification and restraint). Yokohama, Hiyoshi Byoin, Seishinbunsekigaku no Susume 3:1–13.

———. 1961. Around the clock patient care in Japanese psychiatric hospitals: the role of the tsukisoi. American Sociological Review 26:204–214.

———. 1962. Patterns of emotion in modern Japan. *In* Japanese culture: its development and characteristics, Robert J. Smith and Richard K. Beardsley, eds. Chicago, Aldine Publishing Co.

―――. 1964. Sibling rank and style of life among Japanese psychiatric patients. *In* Proceedings of the joint meeting of the Japanese society of psychiatry and neurology and the American Psychiatric Association, Haruo Akimoto, ed. Published as Supplement No. 7 of Folia Psychiatrica et Neurologica: 35–40.

―――. 1970. The psychological study of Japan. *In* The study of Japan in the behavioral sciences, Edward Norbeck and Susan Parman, eds., Rice University Studies, Vol. 56, No. 4.

CAUDILL, WILLIAM AND GEORGE DEVOS. 1956. Achievement, culture and personality: the case of Japanese Americans. American Anthropologist 58:1102–1126.

CAUDILL, WILLIAM AND L. TAKEO DOI. 1963. Interrelations of psychiatry, culture, and emotion in Japan. *In* Man's image in medicine and anthropology, Iago Galdston, ed. New York, International Universities Press.

CAUDILL, WILLIAM AND DAVID W. PLATH. 1966. Who sleeps by whom? Parent-child involvement in urban Japanese families. Psychiatry 29:344–366.

CAUDILL, WILLIAM AND HARRY A. SCARR. 1962. Japanese value orientations and culture change. Ethnology 1:53–91.

CAUDILL, WILLIAM AND CARMI SCHOOLER. 1969. Symptom patterns among Japanese psychiatric patients. *In* Mental health research in Asia and the Pacific, William Caudill and Tsung-yi-Lin, eds. Honolulu, East-West Center Press.

CAUDILL, WILLIAM AND HELEN WEINSTEIN. 1969. Maternal care and infant behavior in Japan and America. Journal for the Study of Interpersonal Processes 32, No. 1:12–43.

COLTON, H. A., JR. AND F. G. EBAUGH. 1946. Japanese neuropsychiatry. American Journal of Psychiatry 103:342–348.

CORNELL, JOHN B. 1961. Outcaste relations in a Japanese village. American Anthropologist 63:286–296.

―――. 1967. Individual mobility and group membership—the case of the burakumin. Paper prepared for the Second Conference on the Modernization of Japan, organized by R. P. Dore.

CORNELL, JOHN B. AND ROBERT J. SMITH. 1970. The Japanese abroad. *In* The study of Japan in the behavioral sciences, Edward Norbeck and Susan Parman, eds., Rice University Studies, Vol. 56, No. 4.

DENING, WALTER. 1891. Mental characteristics of the Japanese people. Trans. and Proc. of the Japan Society, old series, 19(1):17–36.

DEVOS, GEORGE. 1954. A comparison of the personality differences in two generations of Japanese Americans by means of the Rorschach test. Nagoya Journal of Medical Science 17(3):153–265.

―――. 1955. A quantitative Rorschach assessment of maladjustment and rigidity in acculturating Japanese Americans. Genetic Psychology Monographs 52 (First Half):51–87. Provincetown, Mass., Journal Press.

———. 1960a. The relation of guilt toward parents to achievement and arranged marriage among the Japanese. Psychiatry: Journal for the Study of Interpersonal Processes, Vol. 23, No. 3.

———. 1960b. Psycho-cultural attitudes toward primary relationships in Japanese delinquents—a study on progress. Seishin Eisci (Mental Hygiene), No. 66.

———. 1961. Symbolic analysis in the cross-cultural study of personality. *In* Studying personality cross-culturally, Bert Kaplan, ed., Evanston and White Plains, Row Peterson.

———. 1962. Deviancy and social change: a psychocultural evaluation of trends in Japanese delinquency and suicide. *In* Japanese culture: its development and characteristics, R. J. Smith and R. K. Beardsley, eds. Chicago, Aldine Publishing Company.

———. 1964. The legendary yakuza: a functional analysis. California Monthly 74:8–11.

———. Assimilation and social self-identity in the Japanese former outcaste group. *In* Mobility and mental health, Mildred Kantor, ed. Springfield, Charles C. Thomas.

———. 1967a. The Japanese adolescent delinquent in a period of social change. East-West Center Review 4:35–53.

———. 1967b. The psychology of purity and pollution as related to social self-identity and caste. *In* Ciba Foundation symposium on caste and race: comparative approaches, A. V. S. de Reuck and Julie Knight, eds. London, J. & A. Churchill.

———. 1968a. Achievement and innovation in culture and personality. *In* Norbeck, Edward, Douglass Price-Williams, and William M. McCord, The study of personality: an interdisciplinary appraisal, 348–370. New York, Holt, Rinehart and Winston.

———. 1968b. Suicide in cross-cultural perspective. *In* Suicidal Behaviors, H. L. P. Resnik, ed. Boston, Little, Brown and Company.

DeVos, George and Keiichi Mizushima. 1962. The school and delinquency: perspectives from Japan. Teacher's College Record 63:626–638.

———. 1967. Organization and social function of Japanese gangs. *In* Aspects of Social Change in Modern Japan, R. P. Dore, ed. Princeton, N. J., Princeton University Press.

DeVos, George, Eiji Murakami and Takao Murase. 1964. Recent research, psychodiagnosis and therapy in Japan. *In* Progress in clinical psychology (Vol. 6), Lawrence E. Abt and Bernard F. Riess, eds. New York, Grune and Stratton.

DeVos, George and Hiroshi Wagatsuma. 1959. Psychocultural significance of concern over death and illness among rural Japanese. International Journal of Social Psychiatry 5:5–19.

————. 1961. Variations in traditional value attitudes toward status and role behavior of women in two Japanese villages. American Anthropologist 63:1204–1230.

————. 1964. Alienation and the author, a triptych on social conformity and deviancy in the Japanese intellectuals. Unpublished paper presented at the National Meeting of the Association for Asian Studies, Philadelphia.

————. 1966. Japan's invisible race — caste in culture and personality. Berkeley and Los Angeles, University of California Press.

————. 1967. The outcaste tradition in modern Japan: a problem in social self-identity. *In* Aspects of Social Change in Modern Japan, R. P. Dore, ed. Princeton, N.J., Princeton University Press.

Doi, Takeo. 1956. Japanese language as an expression of Japanese psychology. Western Speech 20:90–96.

————. 1958. *Shinkeishitsu no seishinbyori* (Psychopathology of *"shinkeishitsu"*). Seishinshinkeigaku Zasshi (Psychiatria et Neurologia Japonica) 60:733–744 (English abstract).

————. 1960. *Jibun to amae no seishinbyori* (Psychopathology of *"jibun"* and *"amae"*). Seishinshinkeigaku Zasshi (Psychiatria et Neurologia Japonica) 62:149–162 (English abstract).

————. 1962. *Amae:* a key concept for understanding Japanese personality structure. *In* Japanese culture: its development and characteristics, R. J. Smith and R. K. Beardsley, eds. Chicago, Aldine Publishing Company.

————. 1963. Some thoughts on helplessness and the desire to be loved. Psychiatry 26:266–272.

————. 1967. *Giri-ninjo:* an interpretation. *In* Aspects of social change in modern Japan, R. P. Dore, ed. Princeton, N.J., Princeton University Press.

————. 1969. Japanese psychology, dependency need and mental health. *In* Mental health in Asia and the Pacific, William Caudill and Tsung-yi-Lin, eds. Honolulu, East-West Center Press.

Donoghue, John D. 1957. An *Eta* community in Japan: the social persistence of outcaste groups. American Anthropologist 59:1000–1017.

Dore, R. P. 1958. City life in Japan. London, Routledge and Kegan Paul.

Eguchi, Keika. 1965. *Kazoku kankei to jinkaku keisei* (Family relationships and personality formation). Nihon Jidō Kenkyūsho (Institute for the Study of Child Rearing in Japan) 4.

Fischer, J. L. and Teigo Yoshida. 1970. Some issues in the study of Japanese modal personality. *In* The study of Japan in the behavioral sciences, Edward Norbeck and Susan Parman, eds., Rice University Studies, Vol. 56, No. 4.

FRAGER, ROBERT. 1969. *Dento-shugi to confuomitei.* Archives of Japanese Social Psychology.

――. 1970. Social conformity: studies in cross-cultural social psychology. *In* The study of Japan in the behavioral sciences, Edward Norbeck and Susan Parman, eds., Rice University Studies, Vol. 56, No. 4.

FUJIOKA, Y. 1952. Rorschach test *ni yoru* personality *no chosa* (1) — *Nara-ken, Seiki-gun, Hirano-mura no baai* (An investigation of personality by means of the Rorschach test, 1, Hirano Village, Seiki-gun, Nara Prefecture). Kyōto Daigaku Jimbun Kagaku Kenkyūsho Chōsa Hōkoku (Social Survey Report of The Research Institute for Humanistic Studies, Kyoto University), 8.

――. 1957. A statistical approach to group comparison based on the distribution of Rorschach responses. Memoire of The Research Institute for Humanistic Studies, Kyoto University.

――. 1958. *Jinruigaku ni okeru* personality *no mondai* — Rorschach test *ni yoru hikaku kenkyū* (Some problems of personality studies in anthropology — comparative research by means of the Rorschach test). Shisō 412:34–44.

――. 1959a. Rorschach *hannō no sūgakuteki bumpu ni yoru* group *hikaku no kokoromi* (An attempt to compare groups by means of the mathematical distribution of Rorschach responses). Shinrigaku Hyōron (Psychological Review) 1:35–49.

――. 1959b. Rorschach *hannōshū* — *Nihon nōsanson dansei shotaishu no baai* (Tables of Rorschach responses of male house-holders in Japanese farming and mountain communities). Kyōto Daigaku Jimbun Kagaku Kenkyūsho Chōsa Hōkoku (Social Survey Report of the Research Institute for Humanistic Studies, Kyoto University), 18.

FUJIOKA, Y., Y. MAKI, T. IKEDA, AND M. OKANO. 1956. Rorschach test *ni yoru* personality *no chōsa* (III) — *Nara-ken, Yoshino-gun, Totsugawa-mura no baai* (An investigation of personality by means of the Rorschach test, III, Totsugawa Village, Yoshino-gun, Nara Prefecture). Kyōto Kaigaku Jimbun Kagaku Kenkyūsho Chōsa Hōkoku (Social Survey Report of The Research Institute for Humanistic Studies, Kyoto University), 14.

FUKAZU, CHIKAKO AND AKIRA YODA. 1962-7. *Kyōdai no ichi to seikaku* (Birth order and personality). *In* summary article of Annual Report of Japanese Educational Psychology.

GOODMAN, M. E. 1957. Values, attitudes and social concepts of Japanese and American children. American Anthropologist 59:979–999.

GORER, GEOFFREY. 1942. Japanese character structure and propaganda: a preliminary survey. Prepared for the Committee on National Morale and the Council on Human Relations. Yale University (mimeo).

――. 1943. Themes in Japanese culture. Trans. New York Academy of Sciences, Series II, 5:106–124.

GOUGH, HARRISON G., GEORGE DEVOS, AND KEIICHI MIZUSHIMA. 1968. Japanese validation of the CPI social maturity index. Psychological Reports 2:143–146.

HAGEN, E. E. 1962. On the theory of social change. Homewood, Illinois, The Dorsey Press.

HAMAGUCHI, ESYUN. 1965. A bibliographic overview in the postwar studies of Japanese culture. Psychologia 8:50–62.

HARADA, ATSUKO. 1962. *Shogakusei no izonsei ni tsuite no Ichiken-kyu* (A study of dependency among elementary school children). Paper presented at the 4th Convention of Nihon Kyōikushinri Gakkai (Japanese Association of Educational Psychology).

HARING, D. G. 1943. Comment on Japanese personal character. *Excerpts from* Blood on the rising sun, by D. G. Haring. *Reprinted in* Personal character and cultural milieu, D. G. Haring, ed. Syracuse, Syracuse University Press.

———. 1946. Aspects of personal character in Japan. Far Eastern Quarterly 6:12–22.

———. 1949. Japan and the Japanese. *In* Most of the world, Ralph Linton, ed. New York, Columbia University Press.

———. 1953. Japanese national character; cultural anthropology, psychoanalysis and history. The Yale Review 42:375–402.

———. 1954a. Comment on field techniques in ethnography; illustrated by a survey of Amami Ōshima. Trans. New York Academy of Sciences 16:271–276.

———. 1954b. Comment on field techniques in ethnography; illustrated by a survey of the Ryukyu Islands. Southwestern Journal of Anthropology 10:255–267.

HAYASHI, T. AND K. YAMAUCHI. 1964. The relation of children's need for achievement to their parents' home discipline in regard to independence and mastery. Bulletin, Kyoto Gakugei University 25:31–40.

HOSHINO, AKIRA, HARUO NISHIMURA AND KŌICHI HASEGAWA. 1966. *Jidō seito no shakai-ka katei ni kansuru rakka-koku kyōdō kenkyū-chūkan hōkoku* (Cooperative studies of socialization processes of school children in six countries — interim report). Tokyo: International Christian University (mimeo).

HOSHINO, AKIRA, TAKAO SOFUE, HIROKO SUE, AND YOSHIKAZU IMAI. 1958. *Ikuji yōshiki to paasonaritei* (Infant training and personality) (I), International Christian University, Kyōiku Kenkyū 5:148–216.

HSIAO, H. H. 1939. Mentality of the Chinese and Japanese. Journal of Applied Psychology 13:9–31.

HSU, F. L. K. 1949. Suppression versus repression: a limited psychological interpretation of four cultures. Psychiatry 12:223–242.

———. 1971. Japanese Kinship and Iemoto. Chapters 11, 12 and 13 in *Hikaku bunmei shakai ron* (Japanese translation of Clan, Caste and Club [Princeton: Van Nostrand, 1963] by Keiichi Sakuda and Esyun Hamaguchi). These three chapters are new additions to the Japanese translation.

IGA, MAMORU. 1961. Cultural factors and suicide of Japanese youth with a focus on personality. Sociology and Social Research 46:75–90.

——. 1967. Functions of *Eta* prejudice in Japan. Unpublished paper.

——. 1968. Sociocultural factors in Japanese prostitution and the 'Prostitution Prevention Law.' Journal of Sex Research 4:127–146.

——. 1970. Studies of social problems by Japanese scholars. *In* The study of Japan in the behavioral sciences, Edward Norbeck and Susan Parman, eds., Rice University Studies, Vol. 56, No. 4.

IMANISHI, K. 1952. *Mura to ningen* (Villages and people). Tokyo, Shinhyōronsha.

IMANISHI, K., Y. MAKI, AND Y. FUJIOKA. 1955. Rorschach test *ni yoru* personality *chōsa* (A study of personality by means of the Rorschach test). *In Tachikuiyō no kenkyū — gijutsu, seikatsu, ningen* (Studies on a pottery-making village, Tachikui — technology, way of life, the people), K. Yabuuchi, ed. Tokyo, Kōseisha Kōseikaku.

ISHIDA, EIICHIRO. 1961. A culture of love and hate. Japan Quarterly 8:394–402.

——. 1964. Japan rediscovered. Japan Quarterly 12:276–282.

ISHIGURO, TAIGI. 1955. *Haha-ko kankei no shinrigakuteki kenkyū (sonoichi) — Nyūyōji-ki no shitsukekata no jittai* (Psychological study on mother-child relations (1) — actual circumstances in child training). Nagoya Daigaku Kyōiku Gakubu Kiyō (Bulletin of the Faculty of Education, Nagoya University) 1:74–86 (English abstract).

IZUMI, SEIICHI, ED. 1957. *Imin: Burajiru imin no jittai chōsa* (An empirical study of migrants to Brazil). Tokyo, Kokon Shoin.

IZUMI, SEIICHI AND HIROSHI SAITO. 1954. *Amazon: sono fūdo to Nihonjin* (The Amazon, its natural features and the Japanese). Tokyo, Kokon Shoin.

IZUMI, SEIICHI, ET. AL. 1963. *Nippon bunka no chiiki ruikei* (Regional patterning of Japanese culture). Jinrui Kagaku 15:105–131.

JAPANESE SOCIETY OF ETHNOLOGY, ED. 1968. Ethnology in Japan: historical review. Tokyo, K. Shibusawa Memorial Foundation for Ethnology.

KAPLAN, BERT, ED. 1961. Studying personality cross-culturally. Evanston and White Plains, Row Peterson.

KATO, SEIICHI. 1956. Suicide. *In* Annual Report of Mental Health of the National Institute of Mental Health, Chapter IV, Section 22. Tokyo.

KATO, HIDETOSHI, ED. AND TRANS. 1959. Japanese popular culture. Tokyo and Rutland, Vt., Charles E. Tuttle.

KATO, MASAAKI. 1969. An analysis of psychiatric epidemiological surveys in Japan. *In* Mental health in Asia and the Pacific, William Caudill and Tsung-yi-Lin, eds. Honolulu, East-West Center Press.

KAWASHIMA, TAKEYOSHI. 1951a. *Giri no kannen ni tsuite* (On the concept of *giri*). Shisō, Sept., 21–28.

————. 1951b. *On no ishiki no jittai* (The nature of the concept of *on*). Chuō Kōron 56:119–129.

————. 1957. *Ideorogii to shite no kazoku seidō* (The family system as ideology). Tokyo, Iwanami Shoten.

KERLINGER, F. N. 1953. Behavior and personality in Japan: a critique of three studies of Japanese personality. Social Forces 31:250–258.

KIDA, MINORU. 1956. *Nihonbunka no kontei ni hisomumono* (What lies at the bottom of Japanese culture). Tokyo, Kōdansha.

KIEFER, C. W. 1968. Personality and social change in a Japanese danchi. Unpublished Ph.D. dissertation, University of California, Berkeley.

————. 1970. Motivation for social and economic change in Japan. *In* The study of Japan in the behavioral sciences, Edward Norbeck and Susan Parman, eds., Rice University Studies, Vol. 56, No. 4.

KIKUCHI, AKIO. 1964. *Nihon-jin no taijin kankei — Gordon, L. V. no SIV shiryō o chūshin ni shite* (Survey of the Japanese interpersonal values centered on Gordon's Survey of Interpersonal Values). Nenpō 5:161–177.

KITANO, HARRY H. L. 1964. Inter- and Intragenerational differences in maternal attitudes towards child rearing. The Journal of Social Psychology 63:215–220.

KODAMA, HABUKU. 1953. *Nihonjin no ryōrushyakku hannō no kenkyū* (A study of Rorschach responses of Japanese). Shinrigaku Kōza 7:1–92.

KODAMA, MAKOTO, FUMIKO SHIBATA, YŌKO SUZUKI AND MICHIKO YAMAMOTO. 1964. *Shitsuke ni tsuite; shitsuke no ruikei* (Types of Discipline). Study Report of Himeji Junior College 1:25–36.

KONISHI, T. 1963. *Nōsōn to gyoson ni okeru kazoku kankei o chūshin to suru kōdō yōshiki no sai* (Differences between two farming villages and a fishing village in behavioral patterns in regard to family relationships). Kōnan University, Bungaku Kai Ronshū 20:10–28.

KYŪGAKKAI RENGŌ TSUSHIMA KYŌDŌ CHŌSA IINKAI. 1954. *Tsushima no shizen to bunka* (Nature and culture in Tsushima). Sōgō Kenkyu Hōkoku, 2. Tokyo, Kokinshoin.

LaBARRE, WESTON. 1945. Some observations on character structure in the Orient: the Japanese. Psychiatry 8:319–342.

LANHAM, BETTY B. 1956. Aspects of child care in Japan: preliminary report. *In* Personal character and cultural milieu, D. G. Haring, ed. Syracuse, Syracuse University Press.

————. 1962. Aspects of child rearing in Kainan, Japan. Unpublished doctoral dissertation, Syracuse University.

LEBRA, WILLIAM P. 1970. The Ryukyu Islands. *In* The study of Japan in the behavioral sciences, Edward Norbeck and Susan Parman, eds., Rice University Studies, Vol. 56, No. 4.

LEIGHTON, ALEXANDER H. 1945. The governing of men; general principles and recommendations based on experience at a Japanese relocation camp. Princeton, Princeton University Press.

LIFTON, ROBERT JAY. 1962. Youth and history: individual change in postwar Japan. Daedalus 91:172–197.

MARETZKI, T. W. 1957. Child rearing in an Okinawan community. Yale University, Ph.D. dissertation.

———. 1964. Personality in rural Okinawa: a survey. *In* Ryukyuan culture and society, A. E. Smith, ed. Honolulu.

———. 1965. Suicide in Okinawa. International Journal of Social Psychiatry: 11:256–263.

MARUYAMA, M. 1965. Patterns of individuation and the case of Japan: a conceptual scheme. *In* Changing Japanese attitudes toward modernization, M. B. Jansen, ed. Princeton, N.J., Princeton University Press.

McCLELLAND, D. C. 1961. The achieving society. Princeton, Van Nostrand.

MINAMI, HIROSHI. 1954. *Nihonjin no shinri* (Psychology of the Japanese). Tokyo, Mainichi Shimbunsha.

MITCHELL, RICHARD H. 1967. The Korean minority in Japan. Berkeley, University of California Press.

MIYAKE, KAZUO. 1961. *Yōji no jiritsukōdō ni taisuru hahaoya no kitaide* (Mother's expectations toward children's independent behavior). Proceedings of the 25th Convention of Japan Psychological Association.

MIYAWAKI, JIRO. 1960. *Hekichi jidōseito no shinrigakuteki kenkyū* (III); *Hida sanson jidō no jittai chōsa* (Psychological study of children in an isolated area (III); empirical research in the mountain village Hida). Paper presented at the Convention of Nihon Oyoshinri Gakkai (Japanese Association of Applied Psychology).

———. 1962–67. *Hekichi jidōseito no shinrigakuteki kenkyū* (II); *Dekasegi buraku ni okeru oyako kankeī* (Psychological study of children in an isolated area (II); parent-child relationship in a hamlet of migrant laborers). *In* summary article of Annual Report of Japanese Educational Psychology.

MOLONEY, J. C. 1954. Understanding the Japanese mind. New York, Philosophical Library.

MOORE, CHARLES A., ED. 1967. The Japanese mind. Honolulu, East-West Center Press.

MORI, SHIGETOSHI AND TADASHI MIWA. 1958. *Okinoerabutō-tōmin no paasonaritei* (Personality of Okinoerabutō Islanders). Jinruikagaku, 10.

MORIOKA, KIYOMI. 1968. *Dare to dare ga issho ni neru ka.* Seishin 1, No. 2:18–23.

MURAKAMI, E. 1959. A normative study of Japanese Rorschach responses. Rorschach Kenkyū-Rorschachiana Japonica 2:39–85.

MURAMATSU, TSUNEO, ED. 1962. *Nihon-jin-Bunka to pāsonariū no jisshō-teki Kenkyū* (The Japanese — an empirical study in culture and personality). Tokyo: Reimei Shobō.

NAGASHIMA, N. 1964. *Nippon bunka no chiikiteki sai: sonraku shakai ni kansuru tōkei-teki kenkyū* (Regional differences within the Japanese culture: a statistical study of village society). Jinrui Kagaku 16:87–103.

NAKANO, TAKASHI. 1962. Recent studies of change in the Japanese family. International Social Science Journal, S. Friedman, ed.

NATIONAL FILM BOARD OF CANADA. 1959. Four families (film on practices of child rearing). Box 6100, Montreal, Quebec.

NIWA, YOSHIKO AND SHIGERU YAMAUCHI. 1960. *Yōikutaido no kenkyū; toku ni nyujiki o chūshin ni shite* (Study of attitudes toward child-rearing; especially in infancy). Presented at the 27th convention of Nihon Oyoshinri Gakkai (Japanese Association of Applied Psychology).

NIYEKAWA, AGNES M. 1966. Authoritarianism in an authoritarian culture: the case of Japan. The International Journal of Social Psychiatry 12:283–288.

NIYEKAWA-HOWARD, AGNES M. 1968. A psycholinguistic study of the Whorfian hypothesis based on the Japanese passive. Education Research and Development Center, University of Hawaii (mimeo).

NORBECK, EDWARD. 1959. Pineapple town — Hawaii. Berkeley, University of California Press.

――――. 1969. Biosocial influences on culture — a neglected category. *In* Proceedings, VIIIth International Congress of Anthropological and Ethnological Sciences, Tokyo, 1968.

――――. In press. Religion and society in modern Japan, continuity and change. Houston, Tourmaline Press.

NORBECK, EDWARD AND GEORGE DEVOS. 1961. Japan. *In* Psychological anthropology, Francis L. K. Hsu, ed. Homewood, Illinois, Dorsey Press.

NORBECK, EDWARD AND MARGARET. 1956. Child training in a Japanese fishing community. *In* Personal character and cultural milieu, D. G. Haring, ed. Syracuse, Syracuse University Press.

NORBECK, EDWARD AND SUSAN PARMAN, EDS. 1970. The study of Japan in the behavioral sciences. Rice University Studies, Vol. 56, No. 4.

ORANO, M. 1956. *Shūdan kōzō to* personality (Group structure and personality). Shinrigaku Kenkyū (Japanese Journal of Psychology) 27:8–14.

PASSIN, HERBERT. 1955. Untouchability in the Far East. Monumenta Nipponica 2:27–47.

SELIGMAN, C. G. 1930. Japanese temperament and character. Trans. and Proc. of the Japan Society. London. 28:123–142.

SERA, MASATOSHI. 1963. *Nihon-jin no pāsonariū* (Japanese personality). Tokyo: Kinokuniya Shoten.

SEWARD, G. H., ED. 1958. Clinical studies and cultural conflict. New York, Ronald

Press. [Chapters pertaining to Japan]: C. G. Babcock and W. Caudill, Personal and cultural factors in the treatment of a nisei man; T. E. Bessent, An aging Nisei anticipates rejection; N. L. Farberow and E. S. Schneidman, A Nisei woman attacks by suicide; L. B. Olinger and V. S. Summers, The dividing path: psychocultural neurosis in a Nisei man; and M. K. Opler, Cultural dilemma of a Kibei youth.

SHIMADA, KAZUO. 1963. *Nihonjin no pāsonariti kenkyū no gaikan.* Nenpō Shakai Shinrigaku 3:61–78.

SIKKEMA, MILDRED. 1947. Observations on Japanese early training. Psychiatry 10:423–432.

SILBERFENNIG, JUDITH. 1945. Psychological aspects of current Japanese and German paradoxa. Psychoanalytic Review 32:73–85.

SILBERMAN, BERNARD S., ED. 1962. Japanese character and culture. Tucson, University of Arizona Press.

SMITH, ALLEN H. 1960. The culture of Kabira, southern Ryukyu Islands. Proceedings of the American Philosophical Society 104:134–171.

SMITH, T. C. 1959. The agrarian origins of modern Japan. Stanford, Stanford University Press.

SMITH, TRUDE. 1961. Social control in a southern Ryukyuan village. Research Studies 29:51–76, 151–174, 175–209.

SOFUE, TAKAO. 1954. Patterns of the Japanese personality indicated by the Rorschach test. Japanese Journal of Projective Techniques, 1.

———. 1958. *Ejiko ni tsuite — sono bumpu to jinruigakuteki igi* (Ejiko: its distribution and anthropological significance). Shōnika Shinryo (Journal for Pediatric Practice), 21.

———. 1960. Japanese studies by American anthropologists: review and evaluation. American Anthropologist 62:306–317.

———. 1964. *Tokyo no daigakusei ni okeru tekiō no ichi bunseki* (An analysis of the degree of adjustment of Tokyo college students). Nempo Shakai Shinrigaku 5:133–160.

———. 1965. *Nihonjin pāsonariti no chiikisa: bunshō kanseiho tesuto ni yoru bunseki* (Regional variations of the Japanese personality: an analysis by the aid of the Sentence Completion Test). Paper read at the 20th Joint Annual meeting of the Anthropological Society of Nippon and the Japanese Society of Ethnology, Sendai.

———. 1969. Social anthropology in Japan. The American Behavioral Scientist, January-February:15–35.

SOFUE, TAKAO, HIROKO SUE AND TAIJI MURAKAMI. 1958. *Ejiko ni kansuru bunkajinruigakuteki kenkyū — bumpu oyobi chiikiteki heni ni tsuite* (Anthropological study of the Ejiko, a Japanese cradle for child: its distribution and areal varieties). Jinruigaku Zasshi (Journal of the Anthropological Society of Nippon) 66:77–91 (English abstract).

Sofue, Takao and Hiroshi Wagatsuma. 1959. *Kokumin no shinri — Nihonjin to Ōbeijin* (National character — Japanese, Americans, and Europeans). Tokyo, Kōdansha.

Spitzer, H. M. 1947. Psychoanalytic approaches to the Japanese character. *In* Psychoanalysis and the social sciences, Vol. 1, G. Roheim, ed. New York, International Universities Press.

Staniford, Philip S. 1967. Political organization in a north Brazilian community. Unpublished doctoral dissertation, London School of Economics.

Stoetzel, Jean. 1955. Without the chrysanthemum and the sword; a study of the attitudes of youth in post-war Japan. New York, Columbia University Press.

Strong, E. K. 1934. The second-generation Japanese problem. Stanford, Stanford University Press.

Sue, Hiroko. 1958. *Ejiko ni kansuru bunkajinruigakuteki kenkyū — Miyagi-ken no ejiko shiyō chiiki ni okeru chōsa* (Anthropology study of *ejiko* (cradle) — intensive study of an *ejiko*-using community in Miyagi Prefecture). Jinruigaku Zasshi (Journal of the Anthropological Society of Nippon) 66:128–136 (English abstract).

————. 1960. *Nihon ni okeru ikuji-yōshiki no kenkyū; Nagano-ken k-mura no ikuji-yōshiki ni tsuite* (A study of child training in Japan; practices in a village of Nagano Prefecture). Japanese Journal of Ethnology 24:267–274.

Taira, Koji. MS. Ragpickers and anti-poverty community action: 'Ants Villa' in Tokyo. Unpublished paper.

Takahashi, Keiko, Sachiko Ishikawa and Takado Shioda. 1986a. *Yōiku kōdō ni okeru hahaoya no jōhōgen:* II; *chiiki oyobi shusseijuni ni yoru chigai ni tsuite* (Sources used by mothers in determining child rearing methods according to geographical area and birth order of child). Nihon Jidō Kenkyūsho (Institute for the Study of Child Rearing in Japan) 10.

————. 1968b. *Yōiku kōdō ni okeru hahaoya no jōhōgen:* III; *toshi to hekichoi no chigai ni tsuite* (Sources used by mothers in determining child rearing methods: differences for rural and urban areas). Nihon Jidō Kenkyūsho (Institute for the Study of Child Rearing in Japan) 11.

Tanaka, Kunio. 1967. *Yōikutaido no jittaichōsa* (An empirical investigation of attitudes on child rearing). *In* MCC Baby Test, Yukiyoshi Koga, ed. Tokyo, Dōbunshoin.

Tōkei Sūri Kenkyūjo. 1961. *Nihon-jin no kokumin-sei* (National character of the Japanese). Tokyo: Shiseidō.

————. 1964. *Kokuminsei no kenkyū, daisanji zenkoku chōsa ni tsuite* (Study of national character, third national investigation). Tokyo: Tōkei Sūri Kenkyūjo.

Tsukishima, Kenzō. 1954. *Nōmin no paasonaritei — Kitakami-gawa chūryūiki no nōson no baai* (The personality of farmers, as seen in the farming villages of the middle reaches of the Kitakami River). Tokyo University, Tōyō Bunka Kenkyūsho Kiyō (The Memoirs of the Institute for Oriental Culture) 5:1–76.

————. 1955. *Gyomin no paasonaritei — Nanao-wangan no gyoson no baai* (The personality of fishermen, as seen in the fishing villages of Nanao Bay). Tokyo University, Tōyō Bunka Kenkyūsho Kiyō (The Memoirs of the Institute for Oriental Culture) 7:147–190.

————. 1957. *Nihon kōzan buraku no ningenkankei ni kansuru bunka shinrigakuteki chōsa hōkoku* (A study of human relations in Japanese mining communities from the standpoint of cultural psychology). Tokyo University, Tōyō Bunka Kenkyūsho Kiyō (The Memoirs of the Institute for Oriental Culture) 13:149–188.

————. 1961. *Hamo mura jūmin no pāsonariti* (Personality of Hamo villagers). Jinrui Kagaku (Anthropological Science) 14.

TSUMORI, MAKOTO AND KYOKO INAGE. 1960. *Yōji no izonsei ni kansuru kenkyū; izonsei to oya no yōikutaido oyobi jyūjunsei no sōkankankei ni tsuite* (Study of dependency in children; correlations among dependency, parental attitudes, and obedience). Kyōikushinrigaku Kenkyū (Japanese Journal of Educational Psychology) 7:210–220.

————. 1961. *Yōji no* personality *hattatsu no tsuizui kenkyū* (Follow-up study on the development of children's personality). Paper presented at the 25th Convention of Nihon Shinrigakkai (Japanese Psychological Association).

TSURU, HIROSHI. 1963. *Shitsuke ni okeru shikarikata to homekata* (Methods of scolding and praising in child-rearing). Jidōshinri (Child Study) 17:30–39.

VOGEL, EZRA F. 1962. Entrance examinations and emotional disturbances in Japan's 'New Middle Class.' *In* Japanese culture: its development and characteristics, R. J. Smith and R. K. Beardsley, eds. Chicago, Aldine Publishing Company.

————. 1963. Japan's new middle class: the salary man and his family in a Tokyo suburb. Berkeley, University of California Press.

WAGATSUMA, HIROSHI. 1959. *Kekkon, renai, fujin no yakuwari nado ni kansuru nihon nōmin to gyomin no taido no sai ni tsuite* (On some differences in attitudes between Japanese farmers and fishermen concerning love, marriage and women's role). Shakai Jinruigaku (Social Anthropologist) 2, No. 1:15–29.

————. 1967a. The pariah caste in Japan: history and present self image. *In* Ciba Foundation symposium on caste and race: comparative approaches, A. V. S. de Reuck and Julie Knight, eds. London, J. & A. Churchill.

————. 1967b. Social perception of skin color in Japan. Daedelus, spring.

————. 1969a. Major trends in social psychology in Japan. The American Behavioral Scientist, January-February:36–45.

————. 1969b. A psychoanalytic study of Ishiwara Shintaro's early novels and its implications for the understanding of Japanese male psychology. Unpublished paper.

————. 1970. The psychological study of Japan. *In* The study of Japan in the behavioral sciences, Edward Norbeck and Susan Parman, eds., Rice University Studies, Vol. 56, No. 4.

WAGATSUMA, HIROSHI AND GEORGE DEVOS. 1962. Recent attitudes toward arranged marriage in rural Japan. Human Organization 21, No. 3:187–200.

YAMAMOTO, TATSURO. 1964. Recent studies in the Japanese national character. *In* Cross-cultural understandings: epistemology in anthropology, F. S. C. Northrop and Helen H. Livingston, eds. New York, Harper and Row.

YAMANE, TSUNEO AND HISAYA NONOYAMA. 1967. Isolation of the nuclear family and kinship organization in Japan: a hypothetical approach to the relationships between the family and society. Journal of Marriage and the Family:783–796.

YODA, AKIRA AND TAKETOSHI TAKUMA. 1961. *Yōji no seikaku to bunkateki wakagumi; toshi-yochienji no odanteki kenkyū* (Children's personality and cultural milieu; study of urban kindergarten children). Nihon Kyōikushinrigakkai (Japanese Journal of Educational Psychology) 9:75–83.

CHAPTER TWO

Africa*

Robert L. Munroe, Ruth H. Munroe, *and* Robert A. LeVine

Introduction

Subsaharan Africa has hundreds of peoples, and its ethnographic
literature is vast. Yet until recent years, the number of culture and
personality studies was probably smaller in Africa than in any major area
of the world. Most of the psychocultural work there was carried out by
missionaries, educators and psychiatrists untrained in scholarly research.
The overgeneralizing and ethnocentric flavor of much of this work is
illustrated in statements like the following from a psychiatrist.

> The native African in his culture is remarkably like the lobotomized Western
> European and in some ways like the traditional psychopath in his inability to
> see individual acts as part of a whole situation, in his frenzied anxiety and in the
> relative lack of mental ills (Carothers 1951:47).
>
> If one scans the faces of the passers-by in any town in Western Europe it is
> clear that most of the people observed are impelled by some continuing inner

*This chapter is a revised version of LeVine's article which appeared in the first edition of
Psychological Anthropology. Material from the original has been incorporated in the present
chapter. The authors are indebted to Miss Carol Flint and Mr. Gordon Ahlschwede for
invaluable bibliographical assistance. Preparation of the chapter was aided by Ford
Foundation funds granted by the Research and Development Committee of Pitzer College.
The chapter covers the literature through mid-1969.

purpose and yet are also alert to the events around them. If one leaves the ship for a moment at any African port, it is equally clear that most of the faces observed express either exclusive interest in some immediate affair or complete apathy (Carothers 1953:108).

Although many British social anthropologists specializing in Africa have observed what Richards has called a "psychology taboo" (1958:118), their field reports contain much data of interest to the student of psychological anthropology, particularly on family relationships, sexual behavior, the life cycle of the individual, and religion. That they have so rarely availed themselves of psychological theory in the analysis of their data is perhaps attributable to the persistence of a tradition concerning the separation of social and psychological facts. However, recent anthropological work in Africa often has been more interdisciplinary in character than the earlier research, and in many cases psychological variables have come to occupy an important place in the interpretation of data. Furthermore, some large-scale projects in psychocultural research have been undertaken, notably part of the Six-Cultures Study, which includes an African society (B. Whiting 1963; Minturn, Lambert *et al.* 1964; Whiting *et al.* 1966), and a major aspect of the Culture and Ecology project in East Africa (Goldschmidt 1965; Edgerton 1965).

In psychology, relatively few African studies were carried out until the past decade or so, and in many of these little attention was paid to the culturally diverse backgrounds of samples drawn from, say, university students or city dwellers or mine workers. Now, however, a number of psychologists with greater cultural sophistication have begun to produce culture-personality research. These studies, besides emphasizing methodological rigor and formal hypothesis testing more often than do anthropological works in culture and personality, frequently display an interest in topics seldom pursued systematically by anthropologists, e.g., perception, cognition, attitudes, and conformity. The studies in Africa, like those being carried out today in other parts of the world, are not only adding to the fund of psychocultural investigations but are also making it possible to ascertain the cross-cultural validity of psychological findings hitherto established solely within the West.

The quality of research among nonanthropologists has been rising markedly as a result of growing awareness of the great cultural variation in Africa. But assumptions about "African Culture" continue to be made in many studies, and it remains necessary to emphasize the fact of variability. At the same time, it may be pointed out that there are numerous cultural characteristics which, though neither limited to Africa nor universally present there, may be seen as distinctively African. For purposes of comparison with other areas of the world, a list is presented of some distinctively African cultural characteristics which have demonstrable or potential relevance to psychological variables: (1) pastoralism; (2) highly developed prestige economy and acquisitive culture patterns; (3) centralized political institutions and institutionalized leadership; (4) unilineal descent groups; (5) polygyny and the mother-child household; (6) initiation rites and genital operations; (7) bridewealth; (8) witchcraft and sorcery; (9) ancestor cults; (10) structural peculiarities of certain languages (Doob 1965); (11) importance of proverbs in folklore; (12) separatist offshoots of Christian churches.

In addition, certain other psychologically relevant conditions, some imposed from the outside, may be noted as having wide distribution in Africa: (1) both extremely high and extremely low population densities; (2) a high malnutrition rate (Doob 1965); (3) societies arbitrarily divided by Europeans, and subjected to different colonial rules, with the arbitrary boundaries retained after independence (Doob 1965); (4) rapid emergence of elites (Doob 1965).

In this paper, a review is made of African studies of psychological anthropology under the headings of infancy, childhood and adolescence, adult psychological characteristics, sociocultural change, and mental illness. The review is not exhaustive; primary emphasis is placed on studies which fit into a coherent body of findings or which seem to possess some likelihood of being generalizable. Although some French studies have been included, a systematic search of the French literature has not been undertaken. A representative sampling of French psychocultural research in Africa may be found in Wickert (1967). Considerations of space have led to the exclusion or abbreviated treatment of some clearly relevant materials. Two pieces of work involving African data, F. L. K. Hsu's (1961) delineation of kinship and ways of life, and J. W. M. Whiting's (1961) interpretation of male initiation rites, are discussed in other chapters in this volume. Research in child health and nutrition (e.g., Jelliffe *et al.* 1963), important for work in child development, is not discussed. The large body of data on ritual and witchcraft and the rapidly accumulating literature on urbanization have received only the briefest mention. African psychiatric work, discussed only briefly in this chapter, is covered in two journals, *Transcultural Psychiatric Research* and *Psychopathol-* ogie *Africaine.* A review of research on African intelligence may be found in

Doob (1965), and a comprehensive bibliography on psychological research in Africa may be found in Irvine (in manuscript). Of particular relevance to the present chapter, Evans (1970) has reviewed major African child-rearing and child-life studies.

Infancy

Much of what has been written on early childhood in Africa by researchers and casual observers has emphasized the closeness of the mother-child relationship, the prolonged indulgence of infants, and the traumatic character of weaning. Paradoxically, while some recent work has shown that these patterns are not nearly so common in Africa as formerly believed, other research has suggested that in African societies where these practices do occur the consequences may be important for development.

Aspects of the supposed close mother-infant relationship include direct and prolonged physical contact, exclusive care of the infant by the mother, demand feeding, and the assertion, or implication, that these factors lead to intense emotional involvement of the mother with the infant. One writer notes that "Whatever the mother's other duties, the infant, almost from the start, is carried on her back — often in contact with her body — and, at the least whimper, is put to the breast" (Carothers 1953:4). Although any casual observer could note both close mother-infant physical contact and demand feeding upon occasion in many parts of Africa, two questions arise: the degree to which this mother-infant contact is constant and exclusive, and the degree to which this contact may be assumed to imply intensive positive affect. On the latter of these questions, no systematic data are available. (Cf. LeVine [1963] for the view that the mother lacks emotional intensity in several important contacts with her infant.) On the former question, however, data from several sources indicate that the mother-infant relationship is not necessarily either physically close for long periods of time or exclusive with regard to caretaking. In the Six-Cultures Study carried out by the Whitings and their associates among societies in Africa, India, Mexico, Okinawa, the Philippines, and the United States, it was found that the African Gusii mothers were least likely among the six societies to be sole caretakers of their infants (Minturn, Lambert, *et al.* 1964). Similarly, from Zulu case histories presented by Albino and Thompson (1956), three of the sixteen mothers of young infants are described as away a great deal, three others are noted as sometimes away (with caretakers designated), and half of all

babies are noted as having child nurses. Finally, although Geber
(1958a:520) refers to the Ganda mother-infant relationship in the child's
first year as being almost a "symbiose mère-enfant," Ainsworth (1967)
reports a high frequency of other caretakers for the Ganda. In a short-term
longitudinal study of twenty-eight babies, Ainsworth (1967:96) found that
"only five babies were looked after exclusively by their mothers. In all
other instances, the mother shared her duties to some extent with other
figures—other adults or older children in the household or neighbors."
These data, from relatively systematic studies, do not support the generalization that the mother-infant relationship is marked by constant physical
contact and exclusive mother caretaking.

On the question of general indulgence of infants, Doob (1965) has made
a geographical breakdown of the cross-cultural survey of socialization
practices carried out by Bacon, Barry and Child (1955). Area-sorting was
made for Africa, Oceania, North America, and a residual "remainder"
category. The result was unexpected.

> Contrary to its reputation among certain scholars and investigators, *Africa* . . .
> is rated not higher but lower in indulgence towards infants than are *Oceania* and
> *North America* [as well as the 'remainder' category], but the differences are not
> statistically significant and may be a function of sampling fluctuations. This
> mean of 9.7 for Africa, moreover, is derived from ratings which range from a low
> of 7 for five societies (Chaga, Fon, Swazi, Thonga, and Zulu) to a high of 13 for
> two of them (Bena, Turkana) (1965:400).

Not only is the indulgence "average" for Africa surprisingly low, but the
very concept of an average carries little meaning in the face of the
variability from one society to another. However, the apparent absence of
a typically African level of infant indulgence does not remove the issue of
the determinants and effects of particular degrees of indulgence in given
African societies. There are some studies relevant to this question.

Whiting (1961) has shown, on the cross-cultural level, that societies with
households having many adults tend to treat infants indulgently, presumably because of the number of caretakers available. The cross-cultural
finding has been replicated on a small sample at the level of the individual
household among the Logoli of Kenya (Munroe and Munroe, 1971).
Although the Logoli household, usually being nuclear or mother-child,
does not vary much by number of adults, the total membership fluctuates
according to the number of children. Since Logoli children as well as
adults act as caretakers of infants, the question was asked as to whether
the total number of persons residing in a house was a factor influencing

infant care. Repeated observations were made of several aspects of caretaking for twelve children between the ages of seven and thirteen months (and ten of the same children three months later). Despite the small sample, there was a significant relationship between the number of persons in the home and the frequency with which the infant was held. Additionally, a strong relationship obtained between number of household members and the delay in responding to a child's crying: the more people who lived in the house, the more quickly the child received attention when he cried. To take the largest and smallest households as an example, in the home with ten members (besides the infant), the average latency of response to the child's crying was only 14 seconds, while in the home with two members, the average latency was 78 seconds.

Ainsworth's (1967) major study of the psychosocial development of Ganda infants offers another example of the possible influence of household membership on the child. The twenty-eight babies were classified into three categories on the basis of the degree of attachment displayed toward the mother: *secure-attached,* in which the infant cried little and was especially content when with the mother; *insecure-attached,* in which the infant showed attachment to the mother but was insecure about it and cried frequently; *non-attached,* in which the infant did not show any differential attachment to the mother in relation to others. Ainsworth found three variables significantly related to the degree of mother-attachment displayed by the infant: mother's reported amount of care, mother's reported enjoyment of breastfeeding, and mother's excellence as an informant. These antecedents were interpreted as reflecting more important underlying variables, such as the mother's positive attitude toward the child, and her interest in and attention to it. Although these factors in all probability do influence the infant's attachment to the mother, a re-analysis of Ainsworth's published data indicates that the degree of attachment also has a rather strong inverse relationship to the number of persons in the home (rank-order correlation coefficient = -.49, $p < .01$, $N = 27$, one case excluded due to incomplete information). That is to say, the more people in the home, the less attached to the mother is the infant. Thus again the sheer number of persons with whom the infant regularly interacts may be a significant factor in development.

In addition to the purported effects of positive care reported in Ainsworth, striking findings by Geber of precocity in Ganda infants, to be described below, were attributed in the main to "affection" and the "loving and warm behavior of the mothers" (1958b:194) toward the baby.

Although there is definite variability in Ganda caretakers and attitudes of mothers, a case could nevertheless be made for considering the Ganda baby highly indulged in comparison to infants in the Western world, where the child is kept in a crib much of the time and where there is less holding and carrying. For example, Ainsworth's Ganda mothers, though differing in interest and attention to children, were characterized as warm and affectionate in all but two cases. "The typical Ganda baby is indulged in the sense that he gets what he wants when he wants it and is frequently picked up and held" (Ainsworth 1967:452).

The effects of the positive attitude and the high level of care, according to Geber, are a precocity in the child's sensorimotor attainment[1] and social-intellectual capacities. Geber and Dean (1957a, 1957b, 1958; Geber 1956, 1958a, 1958b, 1960, 1961) report on Gesell tests conducted on 252 infants. (Although most of these infants are Ganda, "nearly all" of one group of sixty-eight infants examined were members of other Uganda groups.) The results of the examinations indicated that all babies under six months of age were above the European average (Gesell Developmental Quotient of 100), as were 95% of those between six and twelve months, and 75% of those between twelve and twenty-four months (Geber 1960:110). Although motor precocity contributed heavily to the achievement of high developmental quotients, the infants showed similar precocity in areas of development such as language and personal-social behavior (Geber and Dean 1957b). In home observations and interviews with Ganda mothers, Ainsworth (1967) found supportive evidence for Geber's testing in the clinic. Precocity among infants of other African groups has been reported as well (Geber 1958b, 1960, 1961; Biesheuvel 1959a). The specific hypothesis that this precocity is a product of a particular type of mother-infant relationship has not been investigated. Other hypotheses have been put forward, e.g., that the pattern of child rearing may contribute to rapid maturation by placing the infant in a setting in which he is constantly subjected to a wide variety of sensory input (see Casler 1961).

[1] Ainsworth (1967) emphasizes as well the interaction of freedom of movement and social stimulation in bringing about precocious locomotor development. In a study of American Negro infants, Williams and Scott (1953) found motor precocity among infants from "permissive-accepting" homes. Infants from homes rated as "rigid-rejecting" did not differ from norms obtained on U.S. white samples. Bayley (1965) found motor precocity among U.S. Negro infants (as compared with white and U.S. Puerto Rican infants) for 6 of the first 12 months of life. Educational differences among the parents (as a measure of socioeconomic status and indicator of child-rearing practices) failed to account for differences in motor development, leading Bayley to skepticism concerning the environmental explanation for these differences.

Other findings made by Geber and Dean (Geber 1958b, 1960, 1961; Geber and Dean 1957a) raise a problem for the interpretation of precocity in terms of early infant experiences. Examination of 107 primarily hospital-born infants (60 Ganda, 47 other) within the first eight days after birth disclosed that the neonates were undoubtedly advanced.[2] In discussing the differences between results obtained from "typical" European infants and the African infants, 77% of whom were examined within forty-eight hours after birth, the authors note that

> Much of the activity [observed in the African infants] corresponded to an age of 4–6 weeks [for European infants]. Some was even more precocious: for example, the raising of the chin and the scratching of the fingers on the table, when the children were placed on their bellies, might be expected at 6–8 weeks, and so might the maintenance of the head in the mid-position when they were on their backs (1957a:125).

The precocity closely after birth is suggested to have a genetic basis in one discussion (Geber and Dean 1958), but in other papers the authors suggest that it may be an outcome of a highly positive prenatal attitude on the part of the mother. The anxiety-free pregnancy is hypothesized to create an excellent prenatal environment which in turn allows a high level of development (Geber 1958b; Geber and Dean 1958). As yet, however, the degree to which a "happy acceptance of motherhood" is typical for the Ganda is unknown. For the Ganda, as for other groups, a jump has been made from the cultural value on human fertility to the individual mother's "happy and eager waiting-period" (Biesheuvel 1959a:8). One summary of student-conducted interviews in Ghana suggests that an individual acceptance is not reported by all females of all tribes despite the evidence of similar values on human fertility (Kaye 1962). Among the Ila of Zambia, Arthur Tuden (verbal communication) reports that young married women induce abortions so that they can go on with their marital and extramarital sexual lives.

The precocity found at birth is maintained for the next few years in the children tested by Geber and Dean. However, sometime around the age of

[2] Preliminary results of behavioral assessments of twenty-four West African neonates (majority Hausa) indicate support for Geber's finding that motor precocity is present among infants shortly after birth. For example, almost all of the one- to two-day old West African neonates showed "unusual strength as exemplified by the ability to hold up the head when pulled to a sitting position." In other areas of development, e.g., temperament, sensory development, social interest and response, no immediately striking differences between the African neonates and previously tested groups of European-American and Chinese-American neonates are apparent (personal communication, Daniel G. Freedman, Committee on Human Development, University of Chicago).

three, the test achievements of these children fall below the European norms (Geber and Dean 1958; Geber 1960, 1961). This is interpreted to be the result of an abrupt and traumatic weaning, followed by a great decrease in mother-child interaction and exchange of affection, and often accompanied by physical separation as the child may be sent to live with the mother's mother or other kinsmen. Geber cites the case of a group of children (some of whom were Ganda) who attended a nursery school and showed much less decline in their third and fourth years than did children who had not attended nursery school (Geber and Dean 1957b, 1958; Geber 1960). In a later cross-sectional study of sixty Ganda children from acculturated homes, Geber (1958a) reports both little deviation from European standards during the first year and no evidence for a period of decline around the age of two or three. Tables indicate, however, that these children are somewhat precocious under the age of six months, and that *all* sample children of all but one age group (one to two year olds) achieve Gesell scores over 100 through age five (Geber 1960). For both the sample of children attending nursery school and the sample of children from acculturated homes, the authors indicate that there was no severe weaning experience to bring on a negative emotional reaction and consequent interruption in development.

Once more, just as with the generalizations about mother-infant closeness and infant indulgence, statements about traumatic weaning in Africa must be carefully scrutinized. Geber based her Ganda statements on inadequately documented beliefs which were widespread among Europeans, and apparently extended these beliefs to include other tribal groups represented in the Uganda sample. Ainsworth (1967) found that an abrupt method of weaning was actually used in only one case of the total of eleven infants who were weaned during her observation-interview period. Furthermore, "inquiries about weaning plans yielded the information that abrupt weaning was *not* customary among the Ganda, contrary to the impression that Europeans commonly had gained ... " (1967:4). Nonetheless, Ainsworth found weaning to be upsetting for demand-fed children. The overall impression received is that the decline in development may well be contingent in some way upon weaning and post-weaning changes in the mother-child relationship, but the present data do not admit of an adequate interpretation.

A study which does deal with the immediate consequences of abrupt weaning was carried out among the Zulu, who wean suddenly, on a day set in advance (Albino and Thompson 1956). Sixteen infants, ranging in age from fifteen to twenty-four months, were studied through the use of interviews, observations and selected developmental test items from the Gesell battery. Dietary supplements and physician's examinations provided assurance that any changes were not due to nutritional deficiencies. Behavior ratings from the week before weaning, the day of weaning, and post-weaning (up to seven weeks after the day of weaning) were available for comparisons. Data from the developmental test, administered the day before weaning, the day after weaning, and one week after weaning indicated that, during this brief period, there was no change in the child's level of performance. Behavior ratings made during the testing, however, did indicate that the newly weaned children displayed more uncooperative behavior than they had prior to weaning; no similar alteration was observed among a group of control infants who were given the same retesting schedule but who were not, at the time, in the process of being weaned.

From the interviews and observations, the authors identified a patterned disturbance in the mother-infant relationship (typical of ten of the sixteen infants). This pattern, beginning on the day of weaning, included: (1) a period during which the infant alternately attacked and ignored the mother, (2) a period during which the child attempted to be near the mother and to gain her attention, and (3) a period of increasing independence from the mother during which the mother was neither the object of many direct positive overtures nor the object of anger. This latter stage, considered along with an increasing helpfulness and increasing imitation of adult behavior, led the authors to the conclusion that sudden weaning, although temporarily disturbing and permanently influential in altering the mother-infant relationship, is facilitating in the formation of self-reliance. An increase in aggressive behavior directed toward siblings and family members other than the mother, although highly associated with an increase in "naughty" behavior, was seen by the authors as socially useful in that the child, through the use of such behavior, was better able to satisfy his own needs and wishes.

A salient feature of the Zulu weaning process is the mother's apparent expectation of mature behavior from the newly weaned infant. This altered expectation is interpreted as facilitating the development of both helpfulness and imitation of adult behavior. Although Geber stresses the significance of weaning as a "negative emotional experience" among the Ganda, it is also mentioned that the Ganda mother has as a goal "to help [the child] separate himself and become quickly independent of her"

(Geber 1961:58). Data from both the Zulu and the Ganda, then, tend to support the conclusion that weaning places the young child in a very new position, one for which his pre-weaning experience may have provided little preparation. The changed expectation, coupled with a paucity of both direct tuition and stimulating material for learning, may be as significant as the emotional experience in explaining the lowered rate of development after weaning.

One other caution might be added to any interpretation: the developmental tests used are Western tests with Western norms. Although the tests for neonates and very young infants are probably fairly appropriate cross-culturally, the items are more directly related to Western culture as the child progresses in chronological age. The language-acquisition items on the Gesell scale would need alteration for use in societies which differ greatly from the West in the typical amount of verbalization in family life. The "lag" in development reached by Geber's sample around the age of three may reflect more about the test items than any change in developmental pace. For example, Geber notes that children of twenty to twenty-six months have reached the point at which "no further progress in movement remains to be made; the child can run, walk up and down stairs, put 10 pellets into the small bottle in less than 10 seconds (the performance of a 6 year old), catch and throw a ball" (1961:55). The effect of reaching a ceiling early in a developmental test is, of course, that of decreasing the overall score as chronological age increases. Geber and Dean have urged the development of tests which are more appropriate to the populations tested.

The studies reviewed in this section indicate the need for questioning some of the general statements about the pervasiveness of close mother-infant ties, high infant indulgence, and traumatic weaning, and, on the other hand, they demonstrate that these remain fruitful variables for investigation. The evidence for early precocity is convincing while the data on a later slow-down in development need further support using more appropriate instruments. The studies nearly all point to the need for a combination of intensive ethnographic investigation and measurement of individual variation.

Childhood and Adolescence

Adequate descriptive data on childhood and adolescence are available for relatively few African societies. An ethnography of socialization and child behavior for the Gusii was produced as part of the Six-Cultures project (LeVine and LeVine 1966). Raum (1940) graphically describes the punitive discipline of Chaga parents. Simmons (1960) has provided a brief but careful description of childhood and adolescence among the Efik. A survey of child training practices in Ghana was carried out by interviewing university students about customs in their home areas (Kaye 1962). Autobiographical sketches from one individual in each of the Idakho, Kamba and Acholi groups in East Africa are presented in Fox (1967), and, in a work of literary merit, a Malinke of Guinea (Laye 1954) describes his early experiences, including initiation.

Going a step beyond straight descriptive materials, several accounts show the congruence between socialization practices and adult role expectations, either within a single society or in two contrasted groups. Fortes (1939) emphasizes how much the Tallensi child learns by observation without instruction by adults, and how strong and early identification develops which results in spontaneous imitation of adult sex role behavior. Read (1960), in an analysis of Ngoni childhood, sees values as determinants of child training practices, operating through an "ideal personality" which the Ngoni aristocrats with whom she worked hold up to their children as a standard. Socialization is viewed as a conscious attempt to shape children's behavior in the direction of cultural ideals. In the concluding section of the Gusii ethnography, LeVine and LeVine (1966) show how the immediate interpersonal environment of the child molds motives, values, and habits into distinctive features of adult Gusii cultural behavior. Enlarging on part of that analysis, LeVine (1960) has contrasted the aggression training and subsequent political role requirements of the Gusii and Nuer. The Nuer encourage children to fight for themselves, while the Gusii train their young to report quarrels and attacks to adult authority. The difference is seen as related to the greater tendency of the contemporary Nuer to settle quarrels by the feud, and of Gusii to resolve them in litigation. In a brief comparison, Biesheuvel (1959b) shows that two closely related Bantu groups, the Pedi and Lovedu in the Northern Transvaal, differ in the requirements of their social systems. The Pedi are warlike, group oriented, and accord a low place in society to women. The Lovedu are peace loving and individualistic, with women having high status in their society. Child training among the Pedi involves "frequent and severe corporal punishment," with the education of boys being "directed towards the development of aggressive virtues," while the Lovedu consider corporal punishment an "insult to personality."

Are there any typically African child-rearing variables? As with infant care, Doob (1965) sorted other cross-cultural socialization data (from

Bacon, Barry and Child 1955) by geographical areas. It was found that African societies differ significantly from other areas of the world in stressing the learning of obedience and responsibility. This is not an isolated relationship. The responsibility-obedience emphasis in African socialization is an important theme around which a number of findings revolve.

Sociocultural factors producing responsibility and obedience training were delineated in a cross-cultural study by Barry, Child and Bacon (1959). Predicting that "the emphasis in child training will be toward the development of kinds of behavior especially useful for the adult economy," they found that socialization pressures toward responsibility and obedience — together termed "compliance" — tend to be used in societies in which food has to be accumulated and cared for, i.e., in herding societies and, to a lesser extent, agricultural societies. Conversely, socialization pressures toward "assertion" tend to be used in societies in which development of individual skills and initiative seem to be useful, i.e., in societies with hunting and fishing as important activities. In a high-accumulation economy,

> Pressure toward obedience and responsibility should tend to make children into the obedient and responsible adults who can best ensure the continuing welfare of a society . . . whose food supply must be protected and developed gradually throughout the year (1959:62).

High-accumulation economies are widespread in Africa. Of the nineteen African societies in the Barry, Child and Bacon sample, sixteen emphasize animal husbandry as an important activity, thus falling into the highest accumulation grouping, and the remaining three emphasize agriculture, thus falling into the second highest grouping. As the analysis by Doob indicated, the pressure toward child-rearing compliance in Africa is particularly strong, and eighteen of the nineteen societies are stronger on compliance than assertion socialization pressures.

Evidence from the Six-Cultures project supports the findings and implications of the cross-cultural surveys, both for socialization practices and for child behavior. Among the mothers of the six cultures, the East African Gusii mothers' interviews report high expectation of prompt obedience — in fact, 100% have this expectation whereas no more than 77% and as few as 17% of the mothers in the other societies expect prompt obedience (Minturn, Lambert et al. 1964). The Gusii mothers are also more likely to be punitive when their children become angry with them than are any other group of mothers. With respect to training in responsibility behavior, the Gusii children are highest in the total frequency of chores. Investigating further the implications of herding for the socialization of boys, Whiting and Whiting (1968) find, in analyzing standardized observations of normal activities, that boys in the six cultures who were observed to spend time herding—the majority of those being Gusii boys—were issued commands and suggestions by their mothers at a higher rate than boys who did not herd. Also, boys who herded were reported to be punished physically more frequently than nonherders. As the authors interpret this,

> Assuming that physical punishment for disobedience represents a stronger pressure than less expressive forms of punishment, this finding confirms the cross-cultural results that herd boys are under strong demands to be obedient (Whiting and Whiting 1968:12–13).

Finally, boys in Gusii society were observed to show prosocial dominance and to make responsible suggestions more than boys in any of the other societies.

Although the strongest emphasis on compliance is expected in societies with animal husbandry, agricultural societies are also expected, as noted above, to produce a higher level of compliance than hunting and fishing tribes, in which individual assertion is thought more likely to be rewarded. An investigation of this hypothesized difference was carried out by measuring the degree of conformity displayed by adult individuals among the agricultural Temne of Sierra Leone and the hunting and fishing Baffin Island Eskimo (Berry 1967). Ethnographic evidence was consistent with theoretical expectations: among the Temne, food accumulation is high, with an annual rice crop being stored for daily use, and socialization practices tend to discourage the assertion of individuality; whereas among the Eskimo, there is little food accumulation, socialization discipline is "lenient," and adults, according to numerous ethnographic reports, are independent and individualistic. To test whether Temne individuals would in fact conform more highly than Eskimo, an Asch (1956) type task was administered. An individual was shown a sheet with a standard line at the top and eight lines of systematically shortening lengths beneath it. The experimenter, pointing to the line five positions below the correct match, told the subjects that most members of the society said this was the "matching" line. Then the subject, having been shown the supposed societal norm, was asked which line he thought to be the same as the standard. Conformity was measured by the magnitude of the subject's shift from the correct line toward the reported societal norm line. As hypothesized, the Temne shifted much more strongly than the Eskimo. Though reactions to the test were not solicited, one Temne spontaneously commented: " 'When Temne people choose a thing, we must all agree with the decision — this is what we call cooperation' " (Berry 1967:417).

Though little hard evidence is available, some speculative suggestions may be made about other possible effects of the generally strong level of compliance training in many African societies. In schooling, for example, a prior training in obedience might well lead to a lack of initiative or creativity, which is sometimes remarked for students in parts of Africa (cf. Whiting and Whiting 1968). At the same time, the low level of juvenile delinquency for much of subsaharan Africa could conceivably also be in part a function of the early learning of compliance with authority.

Stimulated by the work of Piaget, numerous studies dealing with cognitive development have been carried out in Africa in recent years. Though Piaget has acknowledged that experience influences cognitive development, the work done by him and his associates in Geneva has in fact tended to show little interest in the effects of experiential factors, and has focused instead on careful analysis of the "stages" of thought and the sequence of their emergence. In contrast, much of the work done by others in Europe and the United States has been concerned, first, with "operationalizing" Piaget by defining his stages of thought in terms of some of the measurable tasks given children in the original Genevan work, and, second, with ascertaining the generality of the sequence of stages. Much of the Piagetian research in Africa has had these latter characteristics and, in addition, has often attempted to ascertain the role of experience in cognitive maturation. At this point in time, the gist of the African research may be stated as follows: (1) Insofar as certain operationally defined stages of abstract thought are attained in various societies, they do seem to follow the sequence outlined by Piaget; however, (2) some stages of cognitive functioning evidently are not reached by most, or perhaps all, individuals in some societies, and (3) performance on measures has been found to vary significantly with several experiential variables. Some of the evidence for each of these general statements may be examined.

The sequence of stages postulated by Piaget is based on research findings that an older child shows a level of understanding that he did not show when younger. Operationally, the level of understanding has been judged by the ability of the child to perform and explain tasks which, at an earlier age, he could not perform. All the African research thus far on Piagetian tasks has corroborated the sequence in the sense that the younger children in any sample do not outperform a comparable group of older children. If superior performance is shown within a sample of children comparable except for age, it is the older children who display the superiority. Before examples are given, two points should be emphasized. First, in many cases there is no superior performance by any group because the sample as a whole fails to reach some criterion. Second, in several studies younger children have outperformed either older children or adults because the groups were not comparable in some important respect. An example showing age effects can be given for each of the two areas of cognitive development most studied in Africa: conservation and concept formation.

In a typical conservation study, Price-Williams (1961) showed forty-five Tiv children, ages five to eight, two glasses each three-quarters filled with fine earth. With the child watching, the contents of one glass were poured into two identical tall containers, while the contents of the other glass were poured into two identical short containers. The child was asked whether one set of the containers held more than, less than, or the same quantity of dirt as the other set of containers. The ability of the children to understand that the change in levels did not change the quantity of dirt was a direct function of age: Prior to 6½ years, none of the 18 children tested gave a "same" response; between 6½ and 7½, 6 of 18 gave the conservation response; and between 7½ and 8, all 9 children responded that the quantity had not changed. Several other experiments with the same children yielded similar results. The switch from what is often called a *per*ceptual to *con*ceptual level of response is similar in its distribution to that found in the West, with but a slight lag in age for the Tiv.

Greenfield (Bruner, Olver, Greenfield *et al.* 1966) carried out a study of concept formation among the Wolof. Thirty unschooled children from six to sixteen years were shown objects found in an African market. The array of objects included four articles of clothing, four round objects, and four red things, so that grouping of objects could be made by function, form, or color. Children were asked to show the experimenter the things that were "alike." Practically all the children of all ages used color as a basis for sorting, but the younger subjects tended to choose only pairs of objects as groups while the older children exhaustively applied the rule of sorting to all four members of the group. Older children seem to have achieved a "true" or superordinate concept, whose presence "is indicated by the correct recognition of its particular instances" (1966:285).

Although studies indicate growth with age, there are findings indicating that many members of some societies may never attain some of the stages (or, at least, that these levels of functioning are not properly tapped by the tasks thus far employed). This should not be too surprising in view of the fact that part of at least one stage, that of formal operations or "scientific thinking," has been found lacking in a majority of junior and senior high-school students in a U.S. sample (Elkind 1961). Among the Wolof, Greenfield (Bruner *et al.* 1966) found that the proportion of unschooled Wolof children achieving the concept of conservation rose to almost half at about the age of eight, then levelled off so that little further change occurred, even among unschooled adults. Also among unschooled Wolof, Greenfield (Bruner *et al.* 1966) asked children to group three pictures into pairs, the pairs being sortable on the basis of color, form, and function. Even successful children were able to sort on only one principle, almost always color, and no child made a functional grouping. Suchman (1966) found no tendency among 119 Hausa children, aged 3–15, to move from color to form preferences as typically occurs in the West (e.g., Kagan and Lemkin 1961). In a learning experiment, Evans and Segall (1969) found that of twenty-eight Ganda adults who had had less than four years of schooling, none learned to sort by function whereas all but two learned to sort by color.

Findings like those listed above of course do not indicate some irreversible deficit in cognitive capacities. Practice may produce large differences in performance (cf. Jahoda 1956). A small sample of Hausa schoolchildren performed poorly on tasks involving the Kohs blocks, but careful observation of the kinds of mistakes they made enabled D'Andrade (1967) to design "programmed instruction" which led to rapid and striking improvement. Furthermore, there are instances in which children of traditional societies outperform Western subjects, as among the Kpelle of Liberia (Gay and Cole 1967), who were better than American subjects at solving a problem using the logical connective of disjunction.

The Kpelle data lead directly to a consideration of experiential factors influencing cognitive development. The superior Kpelle performance on the disjunction problem is attributed by Gay and Cole (1967) to a linguistic factor: The Kpelle language is more precise with respect to disjunction than is English. Another factor related to cognitive abilities is environmental experience (Munroe and Munroe 1971). Among the Logoli, systematic observations showed that children found to be farther from home in their free time (usually boys) were also superior on a spatial-conceptual task.

Mentioned in several studies is the apparent relationship between poor performance and the habitual, unthinking obedience of children to adults. Despite Kpelle performance in some areas, Gay and Cole (1967) feel that an unquestioning acceptance of authority is a stumbling block in school progress. This recalls the set of findings reported above on the compliance syndrome in African socialization practices. Bruner *et al.* (1966) found implicit evidence in support of such an interpretation when the un-schooled Wolof children showed marked improvement in attainment of conservation if directed to perform the experimental manipulations themselves. It is most revealing to find that the Tiv children, who achieved conservation very early in comparison to other African societies studied, were reported by Price-Williams (1961) to have *spontaneously* performed the experimental operations themselves. Indeed, the Bacon, Barry and Child (1955) ratings for compliance and assertion show that Tiv males (no ratings available for Tiv females) have more pressure exerted toward assertion (vis-à-vis compliance) than any other group of males in the entire sample of African societies.

Beyond the sociocultural factors discussed, there is abundant evidence that schooling plays a highly significant part in cognitive maturation. Comparing the Wolof findings with those made in other areas in a large scale cross-cultural study, Greenfield and Bruner (1969:652) evaluate the effects of schooling: "Wolof children who have been to school are more different intellectually from unschooled children living in the same bush village than they are from city children in the same country or from Mexico City, Anchorage, Alaska or Brookline, Massachusetts." Bruner and his associates argue that the school gives the child practice in using language "outside a context in which his reference is supported either by pointing or by the structure of the situation" (Bruner *et al.* 1966:323). More specifically still, it is thought to be the *written* form that carries this non-contextual use of language to a degree which greatly promotes cognitive growth. Other interpretations might well be given to the relationship, and some African studies have failed to find any effect for schooling (e.g., Price-Williams 1962; Serpell 1966), but the overall indica-tion is that educational experience does change conceptual functioning in important ways. Finally, it should be noted that the degree of urbanism also has been shown to have an effect on cognitive growth (Bruner *et al.* 1966; Evans and Segall 1969).

A different aspect of Piaget's work was investigated by Jahoda (1958a, 1958b, 1958c), who found that with increasing age there was a decline in animistic thinking and belief in immanent justice among 120 Ghanaian schoolchildren (cultural groups unspecified). The findings generally paralleled those made by Piaget (1929, 1932) but were at odds with results obtained in other non-Western societies. Jahoda points out some of the methodological problems involved in the study of concepts like animism and immanent justice, and suggests that these difficulties may account for the discrepancy between his findings and those of other investigators. (Cf. Greenfield and Bruner [1969] for a different view of animism.)

A few other scattered studies have explicitly linked an experiential variable to some carefully measured outcome in child or adolescent behavior. Jahoda (1954) showed that cultural expectations can produce aggressive traits in individuals. Ashanti children are named for the day of the week on which they are born. It is believed that a boy born on a Monday will be quiet and peaceful, while a Wednesday boy will be quick-tempered and aggressive. A check of juvenile court records showed that Monday children were underrepresented among delinquents and that Wednesday children were highly overrepresented in cases of "offence against the person," presumably a rather direct measure of an aggressive disposition. Lloyd (1968) found that social structural emphases on sex differences among the Gusii and age seniority among the Yoruba were mirrored in the choices of children six to fourteen years old in a Pretend Game. Gusii children chose more often to "be" same-sex statuses whereas Yoruba children more often chose in accordance with an age principle. In a study using systematic behavioral observations of thirty-six five to eight year old Gusii children, Nerlove (1969) found that the degree of proximity to others was different for boys and girls but that variations from this typical proximity were associated with the chores being performed. For example, boys and girls were found to be similar with respect to proximity while playing the role of caretaker. Aside from the significance of the findings themselves, these studies demonstrate the usefulness of a wide variety of methods in cross-cultural child study, ranging here from use of official records to standardized testing to systematic observations.

The provocative interpretation of male initiation ceremonies by J. W. M. Whiting (Whiting 1961; Burton and Whiting 1961), though of interest because of the wide occurrence of male initiation in Africa, is treated elsewhere in this volume and is therefore not considered in the present chapter.

Adult Psychological Characteristics

The term "psychological characteristics," though somewhat awkward, is used in the heading to convey the fact that investigators in Africa have generally shifted away from global accounts of culture and overall "personality." Research tends now to focus either on some specific aspect of personality, e.g., achievement motivation, or on some psychological process which falls below the threshold of the usual definition of personality, e.g., perception. Despite the narrowed emphasis, much of this research attempts to link some aspect of psychological functioning, however specific, to social, cultural, or ecological variables.

To begin with the more specialized work, Segall, Campbell and Herskovits (1966) hypothesized that cultural differences in susceptibility to visual illusions could be explained in terms of environmental experiences. They argued that the organism develops visual inference habits through experience with the environment, that these habits are functional in general but not in every specific instance, and that an optical illusion marks an instance in which the organism may misjudge visual cues due to the illusion's "ecological unrepresentativeness." Thus environmental differences, including the man-made parts, ought to lead to visual-inference differences, and thence to differences in susceptibility to visual illusions. Relying on anthropologists in the field to gather most of the data, Segall *et al.* had sets of five geometric illusions presented to 1878 subjects in fifteen societies, of which twelve were African. Among the illusions was the well-known Müller-Lyer, on which W. H. R. Rivers had early found non-Western samples less susceptible than an English sample. The same results were expected in the modern groups, the prediction being based on the following reasoning. The Western world is replete with rectangular objects. Although these objects are projected on the retina as obtuse and acute angles (except when line of sight is normal to an object), the individual learns to interpret them as right angles extended into space. When a person from this "carpentered world" is shown the two Müller-Lyer figures, he can be expected unconsciously to interpret the diagonal lines as representations of partial rectangles extended into the third dimension. Given this interpretation by the subject, one of the figures is structured in such a way as to seem farther away in perspective, and thus should be perceived as longer. The prediction was strongly supported by the test data, with the American samples being more susceptible than any others to the illusion. Then for another illusion, the horizontal-vertical, a different set of environmental factors was predicated as producing susceptibility, and the Western samples were not expected to be either very high or very low. This expectation was upheld.

Going beyond the general support found for the hypotheses, the authors attempted to specify, in terms of ecological unrepresentativeness of the illusions, the precise position of susceptibility which should have been occupied by each of the societies. Of particular interest here is the possibility of closely accounting for the illusion susceptibility of the many African societies in the total sample. This effort, however, was only partially successful. For example, the Bushmen, who live in the least carpentered environment of the sample, were extremely low on susceptibility, as predicted. The Bété of the Ivory Coast, however, were reported to live in a moderately carpentered environment yet also showed very low susceptibility to the Müller-Lyer illusion. The Bété, in fact, anomalously ranked at or near the bottom on all illusions. It is to the point to observe that the paucity of sociocultural and environmental data in the study hindered the author's attempts to interpret exceptional cases. As a further problem, increasing age, which indicates greater environmental experience, should have led to increased illusion susceptibility but did not do so in most of the societies sampled. In spite of these difficulties, the study offers strong evidence to support the thesis of cultural differences in perception and takes the important step of identifying possible environmental parameters which produce the differences. Subsequent African research seeking to replicate the findings has on the whole yielded positive if partial confirmation but, at the same time, has raised a number of methodological questions (cf. Jahoda 1966).

Another study involving perceptual skills and environmental factors was carried out by Berry (1966) among the Sierra Leone Temne and the Eskimo, whose performance on a conformity measure was discussed in the preceding section. The hypothesis was

> . . . that differences in visual perceptual skills would exist between societies with differing ecological and cultural characteristics and that these perceptual differences . . . might be predicted from an analysis of the ecological requirements and cultural practices of each group (1966:208).

First, ecologically, Berry contrasts the varied visual stimulation of Temne vegetation with the bleak Eskimo environment, and the settled village life of the Temne with the far-ranging hunting and trapping life of the Eskimo. With these environmental and economic differences, the Temne would not seem to require certain of the perceptual skills needed by the Eskimo. The Eskimo, for effective hunting, must be alert to minute detail and, for effective navigation, must be able to use these small details in locating position. Moving from the ecological to the cultural level, Berry finds three other factors which ought also to lead to stronger perceptual-spatial skills among the Eskimo: language — the Eskimo make more geometrical-spatial distinctions than the Temne; arts and crafts—the Eskimo use more elaboration and intricate detail; socialization practices —the Eskimo are lenient and the Temne strict and limiting in discipline, which practices are associated in Western culture with spatial-perceptual ability (Witkin *et al.* 1962), "limiting" socialization having a depressing effect. Ecological and cultural variables, therefore, led jointly to prediction of superior Eskimo spatial and perceptual skills. The prediction was strongly borne out. Four tests of spatial skills were administered, and the Eskimo scored substantially higher than the Temne on all of them. As to "awareness of minute detail," on a closure task administered tachistoscopically the Eskimo saw more gaps and smaller gaps than the Temne. Berry concludes that perceptual skills have been shown to "vary predictably as the demands of the land and the cultural characteristics vary." He notes, however, that the study does not allow any untangling of the respective contributions of the ecological demands and the "cultural aids." It should also be noted that many other differences in cultural characteristics may contribute to the level of perceptual skills attained by members of two such disparate groups.

Temne spatial-perceptual skills were also compared with those of another Sierra Leone group, the Mende, in terms of hypotheses drawn in part from Witkin's (1962) Western culture findings (Dawson 1967). On the basis of descriptive material on child-rearing practices and retrospective ratings made by subjects about parental harshness, both of which agreed in evaluating Temne childhood as a period of greater strictness than Mende childhood, it was hypothesized that the spatial and perceptual skills of the Temne would be less developed than those of the Mende. A series of measures administered to young adult males confirmed the prediction.

Witkin (1967:234) conceives Berry and Dawson's research as supportive cross-cultural evidence for differential "cognitive styles," i.e., "characteristic self-consistent modes of functioning found pervasively throughout an individual's cognitive, that is, perceptual and intellectual, activities." He says further that cognitive styles speak on more than cognition, being manifestations of still broader dimensions of personal functioning. The differences among the Temne, Mende and Eskimo are pronounced enough to indicate the possibility of speaking meaningfully not simply about individual cognitive styles but also about strong modal tendencies within populations. (Nadel's [1937] work contrasting the Yoruba systematizing style and the Nupe emphasis on "situational facts and connexions of time and place" in story-recall methods is an earlier example.) The Temne performance on spatial-perceptual tasks is typical of what, at the individual level, has been termed a "field-dependent" cognitive style (Witkin *et al.* 1962), which is typified by attention to the entire stimulus field rather than its individual parts and, as a social extension of this mode, greater sensitivity to group norms rather than more autonomous functioning. The relationship between high field dependence and socialization practices emphasizing the child's compliance, found in the Berry and Dawson work, may have a fairly wide range of application in Africa since, on the one hand, strong socialization compliance pressures occur in many societies and, on the other, "Various investigations in different parts of Africa have accumulated data showing the difficulties Africans experience in manipulating spatial relations and perceiving complex shapes" (Jahoda 1956:241). It should be stressed, however, that the childhood antecedents of spatial-perceptual skills among the Temne and Mende are highly inferential, being based not on the longitudinal study of children but on adult reports of their childhood and somewhat general descriptive data. Also to be made clear is the fact that although the concept of field dependence may be broadly useful, there is no implication here of a pan-African cognitive style: The Mende and Temne are significantly different as noted, Beveridge (1939) found a group of Ghanaians to be more field independent than a European group, and Wober (1967) found a sample of Nigerians to perform better on a field-independence task than American subjects.

Ecological variables, related thus far to perceptual-spatial skills, are tied to more general personality variables in the Culture and Ecology project carried out in East Africa by Goldschmidt, Edgerton, and their associates. The theoretical orientation of the study is stated by Goldschmidt (1965:403):

> We treat environment as the independent variable; then, assuming a repertoire of techniques available, the pattern of economic exploitation becomes the intermediate variable, while the institutions of society, cultural attitudes and behavior patterns, become the dependent variables.

The specific point of investigation was the contrast between the two basic economic life modes in subsaharan Africa, cattle pastoralism and hoe farming, not only in their ecological requirements but in their hypothesized differential sociocultural and psychological concomitants. Four cases were selected in which a single tribe contained both a highland farming community and a lowland pastoral community, thus giving a total community sample of eight. The tribal groups were the Hehe, Kamba, Pokot and Sebei, each studied by an anthropologist.

Edgerton carried out the psychological portion of the project with all tribes. A series of hypotheses was formulated as a general orientation around which data could be assembled, but "data collection was permitted to range over both a wide array of expected and unexpected differentia" (Edgerton:in manuscript) in the hope of discovering unanticipated differences as well. After extensive pretesting and consultation with the ethnographers working within the sample societies, an interview schedule was constructed which contained eighty-five questions covering various subject areas, ten Rorschach plates, nine values-pictures, and twenty-two color slides. Within each of the eight selected communities, a sample of at least 30 men and 30 women was drawn, with a total sample of 505. Interviews were standardized and conducted in private in the native language through use of an interpreter. Following the interview sessions in each group, Edgerton conducted "verification" sessions with key informants in an effort to ascertain possible areas of misunderstanding or deception. A validating procedure of this kind might be recommended for any researcher carrying out interviewing in multiple-sample cross-cultural work.

The findings in this comparative study are impressive in number, largely consistent with each other, and convincing in light of ethnographic knowledge of East Africa. Only a few of the results can be reviewed here. The most important theoretical comparison, between farmers and pastoralists, reveals the following contrasts among many: the farmers show high hostility, high concern with avoiding conflict, strong emotional constraint, impulsive aggression; whereas the pastoralists exhibit high self-control, show strong respect for authority, and value independent action. The latter two findings, both strong, are somewhat puzzling when juxtaposed. Yet "respect for authority" corroborates expectations about reponsibility and obedience training among pastoralists as discussed above, and "independent action" is a trait often mentioned by anthropologists as characterizing pastoral peoples. Lack of space precludes discussion of this problem.

Other analyses in the study indicate that age and sex have surprisingly little effect, that over and above the pastoral-farming findings each culture possesses a response pattern unique to it, and that the linguistically related tribes — two are Kalenjin speaking, two Bantu speaking — have distinctive patterns. One of the language-group differences is a high valuation of cattle by the Kalenjin speakers and a high valuation of land by the Bantu speakers. The land-cattle value difference has been shown elsewhere to have an effect on perception of the size of coins among Logoli (Bantu) and Kipsigis (Kalenjin) children (Munroe, Munroe and Daniels 1969). Logoli children, whose fathers' status depends on land holdings, reflected the status by estimating an East African shilling to be small when the father possessed large land holdings and large when the father possessed little or no land. Among the Kalenjin-speaking Kipsigis, on the other hand, the child's coin-size estimation was inversely related not to the father's land but to the number of cattle the father possessed. As well as supporting the land-cattle value difference found in the Culture and Ecology project, the finding is another instance of cultural influence on perception.

There are two studies of personality variables which use dreams as a source of data and employ the concept of "psychocultural lag" in the analysis. In one of the studies the content of the dreams is investigated in an exploratory fashion, and in the other the variable of interest is defined beforehand and the content predicted. In the first, Lee (1958) analyzed the effects of sex and age roles on the dreams of the Zulu. Dreams were collected from 600 men and women, and an intensive study was made of another 120 women who were interviewed and given the TAT. A general finding was that "dream content, for the particular sex, is derived almost exclusively from areas of social experience permitted by the culture *in the indigenous system of sanctions*, of some 50 to 100 years ago" (1958:270, italics in original). Thus women, "acting under a traditionally very strong cultural imperative," dreamed of babies and children but not cattle, while men dreamed more often of cattle, their chief economic goal and source of prestige. This is significant since Zulu women were formerly prohibited from handling cattle, but with husbands being away at migratory labor, now do so more than men. More males also dream directly of fighting, which Lee interprets as related to the traditional warrior role of men. In his intensive study of females, Lee found that traditional imagery and folklore were more accurate in dreams than in TAT responses. He tentatively concludes that "the unconscious minds of individuals are very stable repositories of the past . . . " (1958:280). The cultural lag of the unconscious is attributed to its being acquired in childhood, while living in comparatively traditional circumstances and before exposure to European culture. This is similar to E. Bruner's finding in his study (1956) of acculturation in an American Indian group.

The second study involving the use of data from dreams and the concept of "time lagging" was carried out among three Nigerian ethnic groups, the Ibo, Yoruba and Hausa. LeVine (1966a) predicted that differing characteristics of the traditional status mobility systems of the three groups would be reflected in differential frequencies of achievement motivation. Among the Ibo "the status mobility system was occupationally oriented — that is, rising was dependent on individual achievement in pecuniary activity . . . Social incentives favored enterprise, diligence, and independent effort on a man's own behalf" (LeVine 1966a:41). The Ibo system, in a word, favored the development of individuals with high achievement motivation. This was less true for the Yoruba, and still less for the Hausa, among whom social incentives favored "the subservient follower." Although the traditional systems are no longer functioning today, it was suggested, following Lee's (1958) reasoning, that structural changes would not lead to immediate changes in the personality characteristics of the adult population. Therefore, the contemporary level of achievement motivation might be expected to reflect the status mobility system of a generation or more earlier.

To measure the achievement motive, LeVine had male secondary school students from the three ethnic groups write descriptions of dreams. Available evidence indicates that social motives are expressed in the manifest content of dreams in a way resembling TAT stories, which are the usual means of measuring achievement motivation. Results were in accord with the prediction, the only discrepancy being that the Ibo-Yoruba difference, though in the right direction, did not reach an acceptable level of significance. In addition, the students wrote essays on "success," and these were scored according to achievement and obedience-social-compliance motifs. Although achievement themes did not differ significantly among the groups, the Ibo were lowest on obedience-social-compliance, which conceptually seems to be inversely related to the need for achievement. Furthermore, a nation-wide public opinion survey of Nigerian adults indicated that the Ibo were more likely than the other groups to mention self-development or improvement as a leading personal aspiration.

A problem with the Ibo-Yoruba results was that not only their dream-scores but all their differences on the various measures were directionally correct without reaching statistical significance. Another study (Hare and Hare 1968) found no difference between the Ibo and Yoruba on a measure of autonomy, a dimension conceptually close to achievement. Taken overall, however, the weight of the findings supports the hypothesis. Further, the well-known entrepreneurial activities and high receptivity to change of the Ibo (cf. Ottenberg 1958) in modern Nigeria (prior to the outbreak of the civil war) are positive evidence for the contention that achievement motivation can be a significant factor in economic development (McClelland 1961).

At the broad institutional level, only brief mention can be made of ritual and magico-religious phenomena like witchcraft and sorcery. For many years ethnographers have been describing culture patterns which allow the occasional expression of feelings usually kept strictly in check. (See Norbeck [1963] for a discussion of the literature.) Most commonly these institutions involve the expression of political hostility or antagonism between the sexes. In both cases, the form is frequently one of status reversal: the subject or vassal reprimands his chief or lord; the submissive female dons male clothes, swaggers, insults men. Many anthropologists view the expression of ordinarily suppressed emotions as a safety valve, functional for the maintenance of institutions which require restraint of individuals. The relevance of psychoanalytic concepts is clear, and numerous writers have used phrases like "repression and outlet" and "canalizing of neuroses and psychopathic fantasies" in their interpretations of "socially institutionalized release" (Herskovits 1934:77). The anthropological view that witchcraft and sorcery accusations "reflect areas of tension within the local community" (Middleton 1968:1205) has proved a fruitful point of departure in African analyses. Various aspects of social structure are seen as generating or directing the hostilities of incumbents of certain social positions. Thus among the Nupe, female economic dominance together with an ideal of masculine domination may account for the fact that accusations of witchcraft are directed only toward women and not toward men (Nadel 1952).

Finally, attention may be drawn to several promising psychological variables whose covariation with specific sociocultural phenomena — beyond education and acculturation — is still largely undetermined: (1) alpha rhythm frequencies in the electroencephalogram (Mundy-Castle, McKiever and Prinsloo 1953; Reader 1963); (2) pictorial depth perception (Hudson 1967; Mundy-Castle 1966; Kilbride and Robbins 1969); (3) eidetic imagery (Doob 1966).

Sociocultural Change

A large number of psychological studies of sociocultural change have been carried out in Africa, but many investigations using acculturation as a variable have ignored differences in traditional culture in the samples being surveyed or tested. There are, nonetheless, some findings of interest. Two kinds of studies are treated herein: first, those which deal with factors affecting the processes of culture contact in some important way, and second, those which deal with effects of sociocultural change. (Cf. Doob's [1960] terms "causal" and "sequential" in his work on the psychology of acculturation.)

Among the general factors affecting the processes of contact are the duration and intensity of Western influence. One of the numerous hypotheses tested in an acculturation study by Doob (1957) concerned the relation between amount of Western education and deviation from traditional beliefs and practices concerning the family. Differences between responses of more and less educated groups were strong for the Zulu (.01 level of significance), weak for the Ganda (.10 level), and nonexistent for the Luo. The degree of difference parallels the degree of Western influence in the areas in which these three cultural groups are located, with Western influence deemed highest in Natal, South Africa (Zulu), and lowest in Central Nyanza, Kenya (Luo).

Doob states that another important factor may be the age at which exposure to Western influence occurs:

> Psychologically ... the person [African] who is like a European in many respects because during or since adolescence he has learned European ways may resemble only superficially the person who was raised like a European in the same respects by his somewhat acculturated parents (1957:156).

This statement is given indirect confirmation in two studies of the changing values of African students. Powdermaker (1956) analyzed the imagery in essays written by students of the Northern Rhodesia (now Zambia) copperbelt; Lystad (1960a) analyzed the favorite stories recounted by students in a secondary school outside Accra, Ghana. In both cases, many of the students had been born in rural areas, and the predominance of traditional themes and values over urbanized Western ones was a major finding in both studies, as it was in Lystad's (1960b) analysis of paintings by Ashanti schoolboys. (Cultural affiliation was not specified in either the copperbelt or Accra samples.) Thus, as in many acculturation studies outside Africa, childhood experience is seen as a crucial factor leaving persistent marks on the individual's response patterns. This view is consistent with both theoretical and empirical considerations from psychology (e.g., McClelland 1958; Hunt 1961; Hess and Bear 1969).

Certain groups are thought to possess psychological characteristics which make them especially open to acculturative influences. Just as the Ibo were argued in the preceding section to be particularly receptive to change, so too other groups, e.g., "the Kikuyu in Kenya, the Chagga in Tanganyika [now Tanzania], the Ewe in Ghana, the Bamileke in Cameroun . . . are examples of groups noted for their opportunism and industry in response to the new situation created by Western institutions in this century" (LeVine 1966a:2). (See Ostheimer [1969] for primarily negative evidence on the applicability of psychological concepts to Chagga economic development.) Whether the strivings of such groups can be understood through psychological concepts or through sociocultural concepts, or both (cf. Oliver 1965), is a matter for research to determine, but the explanation poses a set of significant problems.

The psychological effects of sociocultural change in Africa have been extensive, and may be seen in aspects of life as diverse as land shortage, urban living, and socialization practices. On land shortage, it is true, as Bohannan (1964:78) has put it, that in Africa "the people are probably less thick on the ground than anywhere in the world save the Amazon basin and the Australian outback," but the use of an average population density masks the great variation found over the continent. The drawing of fixed tribal boundaries has put an end, in many areas, to migration and expansion, the traditional solutions to population pressure. In numerous places the situation has become as serious as among the Iraqw of Tanzania, of whom Winter and Molyneaux (1963:505) say: "If the Iraqw continue to increase at their present rate . . . it is inconceivable that such a population [as is projected for 1990] can support itself by means of the techniques presently utilized by the Iraqw for the exploitation of their environment." In Kenya, three highland groups, the Logoli, Gusii and Kipsigis, have all experienced increases in density, but the Logoli have grown from about 70 per square mile in the nineteenth century to a highly crowded 1440 per square mile as of 1962. The Gusii density is just under 700 per square mile, while Kipsigis density is less than 300 per square mile. Although ethnographic materials indicated that the Logoli seemed to be manifesting greater concerns about food than the Gusii and Kipsigis, documentation of the difference was attempted by gathering systematic and comparable data from the three groups (Munroe, Munroe, Nerlove and Daniels 1969). Folktales were collected and scored for references to food, and the Logoli tales averaged more than twice as many food references as the Gusii stories and almost three times as many as the Kipsigis. On a short-term memory task given secondary-school students, the Logoli remembered a higher proportion of food items than students from the other two groups. Again the Gusii were above the Kipsigis. Other measures gave similar results.

A degree of relief from population pressures has often resulted from migratory labor and urbanization, which are common features in much of modern Africa. Yet these can have their own effects as well. Scotch (1960) has shown that urban Zulu have a higher frequency of elevated blood pressure than rural Zulu. Also, the urban-rural differential in blood pressure is less for men than for women, who have a less clearly defined role in the city. Essential work identifying and describing critical elements in the emerging African social urban environment is being conducted by anthropologists, sociologists, political scientists and geographers. The progress in this important area is remarkable, and will provide necessary background material to studies of individual variation within the urban setting.[3]

Economic changes in Nigeria have enabled women in certain groups to expand their traditional marketing role, allowing wives to attain independent and sometimes greater incomes than their husbands, and thereby undercutting the ideal of male domination. An investigator of this pattern concludes that "the men in these societies experience intense relative deprivation which results in their hostility to women, feelings of sexual inadequacy, and envy of women, all of which have cultural expressions" (LeVine 1966b:192). This analysis is regarded by the investigator as tentative, but is thought testable in systematic research.

In the sphere of religious change, missionary activity has had far-reaching effects. Occasional data seem to give at least weak support to Weber's (1930) hypothesis, and McClelland's (1961) elaboration of it, concerning the Protestant Ethic and the entrepreneurial spirit. Hare and Hare (1968) found Protestant Ibo to be significantly stronger on autonomy than Catholic Ibo, but the relationship did not hold for the Yoruba. Doob (1960) found for the Ganda that Protestants were more numerous than Catholics among better educated individuals. Evidence of strong achievement concern exists for the Quaker Logoli vis-à-vis the non-Quaker Gusii and Kipsigis. A promising set of psychocultural research problems may also be found in the separatist movements which have sprung from various Christian churches (cf. Fernandez 1964).

To pursue a point made above in the section on childhood and adolescence, the introduction of formal education may have widespread effects which tend to override the peculiarities of given sociocultural

[3] Recent compilations of works of some of the leading contributors to this research include Miner (1967), P. Lloyd (1966), Kuper (1965) and van den Berghe (1965).

systems. For example, some of the proposed cultural "consequences of literacy" (Goody and Watt 1963) are context-independent thought, greater abstraction of thought, and awareness of alternatives. These, in their turn, are believed to have psychological correlates like greater individualization of personal experience, a greater degree of detachment, and a more critical awareness (Goody and Watt 1963; Greenfield and Bruner 1969; Horton 1967; Hsu 1969; Powdermaker 1962). Careful comparative investigations of the psychological effects of reading and writing are possible in Africa, where different societies and even sub-groups of the same society range all along the literacy continuum. The hypothesized effects of literacy may not be automatic, however, and might be inhibited in certain sociocultural settings. Thus the Kpelle schoolchild is

> ... unwilling, or finds it extremely difficult, to relinquish rote memory and imitation, stemming undoubtedly from the long-ingrained traditional Kpelle method of learning.... It is obvious that the instruction he receives in school dismays and confuses without enlightening him (Gay and Cole 1967:93).

A general trend toward westernization is often accompanied by changes in child rearing practices, particularly in the urban setting. A group of "educated elite" urban Yoruba families, when compared to more traditional urban Yoruba families, displayed a decreased emphasis on "getting along with everyone" (Lloyd 1966:179), an increased tolerance of the child's aggression, both toward the father and other children, and a more intimate and affectionate father-child relationship, oriented toward the raising of fewer, more self-directed children (LeVine, Klein and Owen 1967; LeVine:in press). Comparing two ethnic groups, the Abure and the Bété of the Ivory Coast, Clignet (1967) found that several aspects of family life were more westernized for both groups in the urban setting, e.g., later age of marriage, earlier age of weaning. Differences which were not in the direction of westernization (e.g., a higher use of physical punishment among urban *vs.* rural Abure mothers) were interpreted in terms of traditional culture, with special emphasis on social structure. Changes in practices are not clearly preceded or accompanied by changes in ideology; the more permissive atmosphere surrounding the child in the "educated elite" Yoruba family may be due to either an ideological shift toward egalitarianism or a general decline in social distance between the father and other members of the nuclear family (LeVine, Klein and Owen 1967). The greater pressure put upon mothers in an urban environment may account for the changes in some of the practices, e.g., earlier weaning (Clignet 1967). The urban environment in Africa will continue to provide a laboratory for the study of socialization, not only in its function as the means by which tradition is transmitted, but also as a "process promoting the cumulation of individual change over generations" (LeVine, Klein and Owen 1967:216).

Mental Illness

There is a body of psychiatric literature on Africans, much of it authored by psychiatrists who have carried out almost all their work with hospital and clinic patients and who have failed to distinguish one African cultural group from another. Recent studies with an interdisciplinary orientation bring evidence to bear on two salient features of the strictly psychiatric work. First, psychiatrists in Africa have employed the concepts of European psychiatry. As Doob (1965:393) points out, this "might be interpreted to mean that Africans by and large exhibit the same types of mental abnormality as Europeans." And in fact such statements are frequently made (e.g., Tooth 1950; Forster 1962). However, since "psychiatrists virtually without exception have been trained in the European tradition, and inevitably they must employ the medical paraphernalia they have thus acquired" (Doob 1965:393), the applicability of the concepts to African patients must be demonstrated. The second feature of the psychiatric work is the very common statement that, despite the similarities in types of mental disorder, there is a differential incidence in types: In Africa, "depressive" conditions are said to be rare in comparison to Europe and the United States.

A large-scale survey of psychiatric disorder among the Yoruba (Leighton, Lambo *et al.* 1963) produced evidence on the validity of standard psychiatric concepts in African settings. The psychiatric classifications and Yoruba classifications of disorder differ in certain important respects, such as the Yoruba linking of symptoms and causal ideas (particularly supernaturalistic ideas) in ways that have no counterpart in psychiatry. But the Yoruba also group symptoms together that are commonly found associated in patients in the West. According to the authors, "if attention is limited to the comparison of symptom patterns, rather than diagnostic categories, a great part of the cross-cultural obstacle disappears . . . " (1963:117).

Even stronger in its conclusions is the study of psychosis undertaken in four East African societies as part of the Culture and Ecology project (Edgerton 1966). Not only is the general symptom pattern seen to be highly similar for all four tribes, but in addition

... the symptom picture given by over 500 respondents in 4 different tribes is quite similar to the clinical picture seen in mental hospitals throughout East Africa. Contrary to the contention that hospital admissions ... reflect only those behaviors that lead to major law violation in the European legal system, it is apparent that the same behaviors that lead to hospitalization are the basis for native conceptions of psychosis ... they do not produce symptoms which are understandable as psychotic only within the context of their own cultures. What is psychotic for them would be psychotic for us (1966:415).

Despite the strong finding that the catalogue of behaviors constitutive of psychosis was "not markedly at variance with Western symptomatology," Edgerton emphasizes that the question of the transcultural similarity of mental illness cannot be answered until more data are available. He points out that even within the four samples studied, there were enough differences among the tribes and enough divergence from the Euro-American pattern that a case could be made for relativism. Account must also be taken of patterns like the "malignant anxiety" described by Lambo (1962). Nonetheless, it can be said that recent interdisciplinary work tends to support earlier psychiatric conclusions insofar as the behaviors comprising relatively severe psychosis are concerned.

Cultural conceptions of mental illness and curing have received further attention in recent ethnopsychiatric research (e.g., Kiev 1964). One of the more intriguing aspects of such work in Africa is the oftnoted parallel between many indigenous belief systems and psychoanalytic concepts. African ethnographic work shows that among the beliefs of various peoples are included the following concepts: conflicting psychic agencies within an individual, conflicts between personal impulses and social prohibitions, the pathological damming-up of affects that can be therapeutically released in cathartic or abreactive therapy, and defense mechanisms such as displacement, projection, identification with the aggressor, and ego-restriction.

Horton (1961) presents the psychoanalytic parallel explicitly for the Kalabari Ijaw of Nigeria. In Kalabari thought, the human personality has two sections. One of these, the *biomgbo,* is the agency associated with the feelings, desires and thoughts of which the individual is aware, and corresponds closely to what in the West would be called the "conscious mind." The second section, the *teme,* brings about everything that happens in the *biomgbo.* The *teme* is conceived by the Kalabari as the steersman of the personality. Yet "many of the activities and experiences of the *teme* are inaccessible to the *biomgbo:* they are, in other words, unconscious"

(1961:113). In some individuals the desires of the *teme* are in conflict with the contents of consciousness. A man who is attempting to succeed but consistently failing may have a *teme* which refuses to attempt success for fear of failing as it has done in a previous incarnation. A person afflicted in this way will eventually go to a diviner, who diagnoses the words spoken by the man's *teme*. The diviner finally makes the individual reject the exposed wishes of the *teme* in a dramatic rite. After this, the individual should in theory recover. Horton (1961:113) says that this is "the whole cycle of neurotic conflict and its resolution conceptualized in virtually Freudian terms": first, the experience of frustration of some powerful desire, then unconscious fear and avoidance of pursuing the desire, and finally the dragging out of unconscious fears by an expert and the presentation of them to the victim. "Underlying all this is the Freudian vision of the individual as an unhappily enforced association of several distinct and warring personalities" (1961:113).

Also along Freudian lines, some recent major attempts have been made to carry out psychoanalytic work among the Dogon of Mali (Parin, Morgenthaler and Parin-Matthèy 1963; Parin and Morgenthaler 1964; Morgenthaler and Parin 1964) and among the Senegalese (Ortigues and Ortigues 1966). Both of the studies cited here give a wealth of clinical data, and make numerous useful comments about methodological problems encountered in the attempt to employ the analytic technique in non-Western settings.

The validity of the second feature of African psychiatric work, the repeated statements of low incidence of depression in Africa, has been called into question by recent research. Field (1960) carried out a study of mental illness among the rural Ashanti. Utilizing her previous experience as an ethnographer, Field returned to the Ashanti as a psychiatrist and set herself up near a shrine where troubled people came to receive help from a deity whose priest becomes possessed and communicates advice from the god. It was possible for her to observe and obtain case histories on those supplicants who were mentally ill, and she conducted some local surveys as well. For the most part, standard diagnostic categories are used, and the emphasis is on similarities between behavior patterns observed in the field and those found among Europeans. Her findings on depression are very different from those of standard psychiatric work. She states:

> Depression is the commonest mental illness of Akan rural women and nearly all such patients come to the shrines with spontaneous self-accusations of witchcraft. . . . The depressive personality is, in sickness and health, self-effacing

and is seldom a disturbing nuisance. She is therefore the last type of patient who would ever find her way to any kind of European hospital unless she had some concurrent and conspicuous physical trouble. . . . It is not surprising therefore that psychiatrists and other doctors who see patients only in hospitals and clinics should have the idea that depression in Africa hardly exists (1960:149).

Depressive disorders are adequately documented in the case histories, but there is no discussion of the psychocultural determinants of guilt in Akan individuals. (Prince [1962] holds that the self-denigration of many of Field's melancholics may be situation determined, i.e., due to confession's being a part of the "healing shrines" ritual rather than an integral part of the illness.) Field appears to regard the guilt and depression as a tendency not produced by the conditions of Akan culture but occurring equally among all peoples who actively believe in witchcraft. She claims that only the confessions of depressives can keep such beliefs alive in a group; the fantasies of paranoids are not sufficient. This is contrary to fact, for there are numerous African societies in which witchcraft is a major preoccupation but no one ever confesses to being a witch. Field does not take into account the variation in witch beliefs among African societies, and this leads her away from investigating the particular conditions in Ashanti which make confession a pronounced pattern. However, the study presents psychotic behavior in cultural context, and clearly delineates the element of supernatural belief, which is so important in these disorders. The etiology of the psychoses described is considered as being outside the limits of the study.

The Yoruba study cited above (Leighton, Lambo *et al.* 1963) also found cases of depressive illness to occur. (Cf. Savage and Prince [1967] on depression among the Yoruba.) In addition, the authors refer to other recent research with similar findings. In discussing their data, they point to some of the difficulties in identification which may have misled psychiatrists in the past:

> The symptom pattern of depression as such . . . was not volunteered by our informants and when described to them was not accepted immediately as something familiar. On the other hand, many of the component symptoms of depression came up in one context or another. . . . There is linguistic difficulty in finding Yoruba words with which to describe the subjective feeling meant by the term [depression]. It is likely that these circumstances could have a distorting influence from the psychiatric point of view on the responses obtained from patients and their families in the course of examination and history taking (1963:112).

Investigation of factors affecting the incidence or prevalence rates of psychiatric disorder has hardly begun. The most careful study thus far, the Yoruba work by Leighton, Lambo *et al.*, was based on the methods, theory and findings of the North American Stirling County Study, and had as a theoretical focus the question of whether sociocultural disintegration is a critical factor in psychiatric disorder. In measuring psychiatric problems, the researchers used an interview which relied on symptom patterns rather than on diagnostic entities. Individuals in fifteen villages were chosen for the main part of the study. Social disintegration, after an inital classification, was defined in terms of various indicators, the most useful being poverty, secularization, family instability and weak leadership, and poorly developed associations and recreational institutions. The data for the social-disintegration measure came from observations, interviews with key informants, and questionnaire interviews from a sub-sample of the subjects interviewed on the psychiatric questionnaire.

The expectation that the degree of sociocultural disintegration would be related to mental health was upheld for females but not males. The interpretation of this finding was that in integrated villages the females live in an environment which is steady and has little uncertainty, confusion, disorientation or role conflict. In a disintegrated village, females are exposed to these noxious features. Men, because of the nature of the male role, are thoroughly exposed to the change going on in West Africa as a whole, even when they live in the highly integrated villages. The authors feel that "this effect is sufficiently strong and pervasive to render the sociocultural environment of men not drastically different as one moves along the range from integrated . . . to disintegrated villages" (1963:237–238).

The degree-of-integration categories were not meant to be measures of sociocultural change. When the villages were categorized as "changing" or "traditional," no overall effect on mental health was discerned. The authors conclude that "disintegration . . . is a common but not a necessary accompaniment of cultural change and modernization" (1963:279). A few other findings can be mentioned. The prevalence of psychiatric disorder was greater among men than among women in the Yoruba group, though in the Stirling County Study the prevalence had been greater among women. Yoruba respondents with psychoneurotic symptoms were apt also to have physiologic discomforts. Concern with supernatural forces was strongly related to the presence of psychiatric symptoms. The authors feel that in a culture in which troubles are often believed supernaturally caused, supernatural phenomena "are the things people worry about when they develop psychiatric disorder — they are not the cause in any primary sense" (1963:148).

Although the relationship found between sociocultural disintegration and psychiatric disorder among the Yoruba is enhanced by the fact that it was also found in the Stirling County work, a certain amount of caution must be expressed about the Yoruba study. The total number of village subjects, though over 200, was too small to register numerically infrequent but important patterns such as schizophrenic behavior. Another problem is that the absence of statistical tests of significance makes evaluation of the findings very difficult. Finally, the investigators had both to pre-select a sample of villages which ranged from socially disintegrated through socially integrated and to test the validity of indicators of social integration using data from these same villages. The pre-selection obviously involved pre-judgments by the same set of investigators who gathered data on the indicators: the circularity was complete with the assessment of these indicators against this initial judgment.

Lee has carried out an extensive set of studies (e.g., 1950, 1962, in press, in manuscript) on Zulu disorders. Among the disorders are a crying fit (termed *umHayizo*) and a highly structured possession-state (termed *ukuthwasa*) which, if followed by appropriate treatment, leads to membership in a cult of diviners. Both problems are found among females more than males and tend to be mutually exclusive. The more common crying fits are reported by half of the 1,000 Zulu women interviewed by Lee. The tendency for cryers not to experience *ukuthwasa* possession is interpreted in terms of the more traditionally feminine, passive desires which cryers exhibited in answers to questions, desires which are antithetical to the active, "masculine" behaviors necessary to successful divination. The one exception to the generally low level of conversion hysteria symptoms displayed by cryers was in cases of pseudocyesis, nearly all of which occurred among cryers. Such women, in the great majority of cases, had not borne their expected first child, they dreamt far more of babies than did other women, they responded in answer to a question that they wanted a baby more than anything else, and they were more apt than other women to report a common hallucination of seeing a small baby. Because women who have crying fits are much more likely to have "blood relatives" with *ukuthwasa* possession than women who have not experienced a crying fit, Lee feels that a constitutional predisposition to neurotic disorder may exist. Among possible social causes of crying, it was found that fits occurred not among women who had changed maximally but among those "who had just, in most social contexts, been dislodged from the traditional rut" (1962:17–18). In this instance, "a relatively small amount of change is the wrong amount."

Other studies have also looked into the possible effects of sociocultural change on mental disorder. Fortes and Mayer (1966) find a large increase in psychosis among the Tallensi since the time of Fortes' field work in the 1930's. The evidence indicates that "there is more psychosis among persons who have been exposed to the conditions of life in the alien and largely urban environment of South Ghana than among those who have remained in their traditional social environment" (1966:40).

Tooth (1950) found that in areas of the Gold Coast (now Ghana) with more European contact the insane tended to identify with the Western, anthropomorphic God. Nadel (1946) proposed, on the basis of data from the Nuba mountains, that shamanistic groups may be able to cope with the general psychological disturbance resulting from acculturation without a higher incidence of mental disease. The shamans are seen as providing an institutionalized catharsis to the group, thus reducing a psychopathic incidence which otherwise might be much larger. Suicide was found to *decrease* among the Basoga of Uganda with the breaking down of traditional institutions (Fallers and Fallers 1960).

Psychocultural research in mental illness is a promising area which appears to be growing in sophistication. Systematic observations of psychotic behavior in the field setting, the heightening of observer-subject agreement through the use of symptomatology rather than diagnostic categories, the use of multi-sample comparative data, the full-scale replication of a previous major work — all these recent approaches have been productive of significant research.

Conclusions

The studies cited in this chapter have found numerous relationships between culture and psychological functioning. In many of the investigations, quantifiable data on the psychological variables were gathered under fairly standard conditions. The same care, however, was seldom devoted to ascertaining the validity of statements concerning sociocultural characteristics, despite the fact that these characteristics were often inferred to be causal. In one case stereotypes rather than first-hand observations were used as a basis for a cultural statement; in other cases observations made in a setting such as a hospital were assumed to be valid for all settings; and in still another, part of the ethnographic material covering one part of a large tribal group was applied to another sub-unit of the tribe without prior checking (Leighton, Lambo *et al.* 1963). Short-cut assumptions about sociocultural patterns often lead to serious errors. Ideally, of course, detailed ethnographic data on the specific sociocultural variable of interest would be obtained within the sample unit which is being used for the collection of psychological data. When a sociocultural characteristic is used as a primary variable in a study, evaluation of findings must rest on a principle of ethnographic plausibility, and it behooves the investigator to present a careful and detailed case.

Of the many promising topics reviewed, there are three which seem particularly likely to produce a high research yield in the African setting. The first is the phenomenon of infant precocity, found mainly among the Ganda thus far. That the precocity exists there can be little doubt, but the factors producing it are obscure at this point. Also, the later "slump" which the child supposedly falls into seems to be documented, though not as well as could be wished, and again the factors behind the pattern remain unclear. Infant behavior differences between ethnic groups have been found in other parts of the world as well (Caudill and Weinstein 1966), so comparative possibilities are increasing. The possible environmental, socialization, genetic, and nutritional variables associated with early infant behavior all need assessment.

The "compliance" syndrome in the socialization practices of many African societies, and its possible connections with habitual deference patterns and with relatively passive cognitive styles, constitutes a second area to which research might very fruitfully be directed. In societies with strong emphasis on compliance, schooling has been shown to change cognitive functioning in the direction of Western norms, but the change is usually only partial and does not involve any modification of the traditional deference patterns (cf. Klingelhofer 1971). In school, the teacher-student relationship is based on the traditional expectation of full, unquestioning acceptance of the teacher's authority, and out of school the child still is likely to be punished for asking "Why?" when given a chore. But such patterns may be undergoing a good deal of change in the westernizing portions of Africa. As was seen in modern urban elite Yoruba families, the child is allowed to display more aggression toward the father and toward playmates than in traditional families. In this regard, a relevant finding in a study of acculturation was that students in more acculturated areas in East Africa attributed annoyances to frustration by authority more frequently than did less acculturated students (Ainsworth and Ainsworth 1962). The "active-mastery" approach to cognitive tasks typically displayed by Euro-American children may be in part a function of the generally aggressive approach to the full socio-physical environment which is encouraged, or at least tolerated, in the urban-industrial world (cf. Peterson and Migliorino 1967). Juvenile delinquency also tends to emerge in the modern setting (DeVos and Hippler 1969), and its hitherto low incidence in many parts of Africa may change. These points raise a whole series of questions for African research on interrelations among socialization practices, authority patterns, schooling, westernization, and delinquency.

The third area of particular interest is ecology. In recent years, ecological relationships have begun to receive increased attention from archaeology, primatology, and social anthropology, and this growing interest has been augmented by the use of ecological analyses in psycho-cultural research. In the studies described in this chapter, environmental variables — the physical environment, material culture, mode of subsistence (shading here into the cultural), population density — have been suggested to affect a wide range of psychological factors, e.g., perception, memory, cognitive style, values. In addition, child training practices such as the indulgence of infants and the compliance pressures placed on children have been seen as possible effects of environmental factors.

Investigations seeking effects of ecological variables are generally working within a framework of adaptive functionalism. The survival relevance of some of the psychological characteristics is clear. (Cf. LeVine 1969.) Conversely, the *un*developed character of certain psychological factors in environments where they are unnecessary is the other side of the adaptive fit between conditions and response. As Berry has said of the West African Temne, whose spatial-perceptual skills stay approximately constant from the age of ten:

> This peculiarity is considered to reflect the lack of any need to develop these skills; the basic ability to produce a score on the tests apparently exists from the age of ten onwards, and there is little later development through lack of demand by the environment or the society for this particular skill (1966:227).

A framework employing ecological analysis may be more useful in Africa than in many other parts of the world because numerous indigenous sociocultural systems are still relatively intact and therefore more nearly integrated. As acculturation proceeds, many of the psychological characteristics developed in response to ecological factors — as well as to socio-cultural factors, of course — will prove to be maladaptive to Western institutions and will undergo a series of gradual changes toward adaptation to new requirements. Some of the urban socialization changes referred to above may be occurring partially in response to new ecological demands. The assumption made here is not one of perfect adaptive fit but rather of a strain toward consistency with ecological pressures playing an important role. (Cf. Murdock [1949] and Driver [1967] on the limits of functional integration in social organization.) An example of the overriding of ecological-functional variables by stronger historical-traditional factors is the high valuation of cattle by Kalenjin speakers and high valuation of land by Bantu speakers. This relationship was even stronger than the expected functional relationship between cattle-valuation for pastoralists and land-valuation for farmers (Edgerton:in manuscript).

Each of the three topics discussed has been the subject of a number of studies. Many other investigations cited in the present chapter can and should be followed up with further work. This is an important procedure to follow if a research tradition with established methods and a cumulative set of findings are to be built up in psychocultural study. The one-shot investigation is not likely to produce a large research payoff: field experiments may be seen not as producing definitive solutions but as part of a process of progressive refinement of research studies and their findings. Long-term projects within a single community, longitudinal data on children within that community, interproject comparability, all can be used to achieve a secure body of knowledge. An approach of this kind, though it would mean the testing of pre-selected hypotheses and the use of a fairly standard methodology, would not stultify efforts to carry out creative or exploratory research. Leighton, Lambo *et al.* (1963), in their well planned study, made a useful distinction between minimum objectives, which were carefully defined, and additional objectives, "in which serendipity and unexpected opportunity were given a place." Such a procedure would seem to have much to recommend it for future African research in psychological anthropology.

BIBLIOGRAPHY

AINSWORTH, MARY D. SALTER. 1967. Infancy in Uganda. Baltimore, The Johns Hopkins Press.

112   *Area*

AINSWORTH, MARY D. AND LEONARD H. AINSWORTH. 1962. Acculturation in East Africa. II. Frustration and aggression. Journal of Social Psychology 57:401–407.

ALBINO, RONALD C. AND V. J. THOMPSON. 1956. The effects of sudden weaning on Zulu children. British Journal of Medical Psychology 29:177–210.

ASCH, S. E. 1956. Studies of independence and conformity: I. A minority of one against a unanimous majority. Psychological Monographs 70:1–70.

BACON, MARGARET K., HERBERT BARRY III, AND IRVIN L. CHILD. 1955. Cross-cultural ratings of certain socialization practices. Mimeographed. Published as: Barry, Herbert III, Margaret K. Bacon, and Irvin L. Child. 1967. Definitions, ratings and bibliographic sources for child-training practices of 110 cultures. *In* Cross-cultural approaches, Clellan S. Ford, ed., New Haven, HRAF Press.

BARRY, HERBERT III, IRVIN L. CHILD, AND MARGARET K. BACON. 1959. Relation of child training to subsistence economy. American Anthropologist 61:51–63.

BAYLEY, NANCY. 1965. Comparisons of mental and motor test scores for ages 1–15 months by sex, birth order, race, geographical location, and education of parents. Child Development 36:379–411.

BERRY, J. W. 1966. Temne and Eskimo perceptual skills. International Journal of Psychology 1:207–229.

———. 1967. Independence and conformity in subsistence level societies. Journal of Personality and Social Psychology 7:415–418.

BEVERIDGE, W. M. 1939. Some racial differences in perception. British Journal of Psychology 30:57–64.

BIESHEUVEL, SIMON. 1959a. Report of the CSA meeting of specialists on the basic psychological structures of African and Madagascan populations. Commission for Technical Co-operation in Africa South of Sahara, Scientific Council for Africa South of the Sahara, Publication No. 51.

———. 1959b. Race, culture, and personality: The Hoernle Memorial Lecture. Johannesburg, South African Institute of Race Relations.

BOHANNAN, PAUL. 1964. Africa and Africans. Garden City, The Natural History Press.

BRUNER, EDWARD M. 1956. Cultural transmission and cultural change. Southwestern Journal of Anthropology 12:191–199.

BRUNER, JEROME S., ROSE R. OLVER, AND PATRICIA M. GREENFIELD, ET AL. 1966. Studies in cognitive growth. New York, John Wiley.

BURTON, ROGER V. AND JOHN W. M. WHITING. 1961. The absent father and cross-sex identity. Merrill-Palmer Quarterly of Behavior and Development 7:85–95.

CAROTHERS, J. C. 1951. Frontal lobe function and the African. Journal of Mental Science 97:12–48.

———. 1953. The African mind in health and disease, a study in ethno-psychiatry. Geneva, World Health Organization Monograph Series, No. 17.

CASLER, L. 1961. Maternal deprivation: A critical review of the literature. Monographs of the Society for Research in Child Development, 26, No. 2.

CAUDILL, W. AND HELEN WEINSTEIN. 1966. Maternal care and infant behavior in Japanese and American urban middle class families. *In* Yearbook of the International Sociological Association, Rene Konig and Reuben Hill, eds.

CLIGNET, REMI. 1967. Environmental change, types of descent, and child rearing practices. *In* The city in modern Africa, Horace Miner, ed., New York, Frederick A. Praeger, Publishers.

D'ANDRADE, ROY G. 1967. Testing and training procedures at Bassawa. Paper 4, Institute of Education, Ahmadu Bello University. Mimeographed.

DAWSON, J. L. M. 1967. Cultural and physiological influences upon spatial-perceptual processes in West Africa: Part I. International Journal of Psychology 2:115–128.

DEVOS, GEORGE A. AND ARTHUR A. HIPPLER. 1969. Cultural psychology: comparative studies of human behavior. *In* The handbook of social psychology (2nd edition), G. Lindzey and E. Aronson, eds. Reading, Massachusetts, Addison-Wesley Publishing Co. Vol. IV.

DOOB, LEONARD W. 1957. An introduction to the psychology of acculturation. Journal of Social Psychology 45:143–160.

———. 1960. Becoming more civilized. New Haven, Yale University Press.

———. 1965. Psychology. *In* The African world, R. A. Lystad, ed. London, Pall Mall Press.

———. 1966. Eidetic imagery: a cross-cultural will-o'-the wisp? Journal of Psychology 63:13–34.

DRIVER, HAROLD E. 1967. An integration of functional, evolutionary, and historical theory by means of correlations. *In* Cross-cultural approaches, Clellan S. Ford, ed., New Haven, HRAF Press.

EDGERTON, ROBERT B. 1965. "Cultural" vs. "ecological" factors in the expression of values, attitudes, and personality characteristics. American Anthropologist 67:442–447.

———. 1966. Conceptions of psychosis in four East African societies. American Anthropologist 68:408–425.

———. (n.d.). Pastoralists and farmers: a comparison of four East African societies. In manuscript.

ELKIND, DAVID. 1961. Quantity conceptions in junior and senior high school students. Child Development 32:551–560.

EVANS, JUDITH. 1970. Children in Africa: A review of psychological research. New York, Institute of International Studies, Teacher's College, Columbia University Press.

EVANS, JUDITH L. AND MARSHALL H. SEGALL. 1969. Learning to classify by color and by function: a study of concept-discovery by Ganda children. Journal of Social Psychology 77:35–53.

FALLERS, L. A. AND M. C. FALLERS. 1960. Homicide and suicide in Busoga. *In* African homicide and suicide, Paul Bohannan, ed., Princeton, Princeton University Press.

FERNANDEZ, JAMES W. 1964. African religious movements — types and dynamics. Modern African Studies 2:531–549.

FIELD, M. J. 1960. Search for security: an ethno-psychiatric study of rural Ghana. Evanston, Northwestern University Press.

FORSTER, E. B. 1962. The theory and practice of psychiatry in Ghana. American Journal of Psychotherapy 16:7–51.

FORTES, MEYER. 1939. Social and psychological aspects of education in Taleland. London, International African Institute Memorandum. XVII.

FORTES, MEYER AND DORIS Y. MAYER. 1966. Psychosis and social change among the Tallensi of northern Ghana. Cahiers d'etudes Africaines VI:5–40.

FOX, LORENE K. (ED.). 1967. East African childhood: three versions. Nairobi, Oxford University Press.

GAY, J. H. AND M. COLE. 1967. The new mathematics and an old culture: a study of learning among the Kpelle. New York, Holt, Rinehart and Winston.

GEBER, MARCELLE. 1956. Developpement psychomoteur de l'enfant africain. Courrier 6:17–28.

———. 1958a. L'enfant africain occidentalise et de niveau social superieur en Ouganda. Courrier 8:517–523.

———. 1958b. The psycho-motor development of African children in the first year, and the influence of maternal behavior. Journal of Social Psychology 47:185–195.

———. 1960. Problemes poses par le developpement du jeune enfant africain en fonction de son mileau social. Le Travail Humain 23:97–111.

———. 1961. Longitudinal study of psychomotor development among the Baganda children. Proceedings of the 14th International Congress of Applied Psychology.

GEBER, MARCELLE AND R. F. A. DEAN. 1957a. Precocious development of newborn African infants. Lancet 1:1216–1219. Reprinted *in* Behavior in infancy and early childhood, Yvonne Brackbill and George G. Thompson, eds., 1967, New York, The Free Press.

———. 1957b. Gesell tests on African children. Pediatrics 20:1055–1065.

———. 1958. Psychomotor development in African children: the effects of social class and the need for improved tests. World Health Organization Bulletin 18:471–476.

GOLDSCHMIDT, WALTER. 1965. Theory and strategy in the study of cultural adaptability. American Anthropologist 67:402–408.

GOODY, JACK AND IAN WATT. 1963. The consequences of literacy. Comparative Studies in Society and History 5:304–345.

GREENFIELD, PATRICIA MARKS AND JEROME BRUNER. 1969. Culture and cognitive growth. *In* Handbook of socialization theory and research, David A. Goslin, ed., Chicago, Rand McNally and Co.

HARE, RACHEL T. AND PAUL A. HARE. 1968. Social correlates of autonomy for Nigerian university students. Journal of Social Psychology 76:163–168.

HERSKOVITS, MELVILLE J. 1934. Freudian mechanisms in primitive Negro psychology. *In* E. E. Evans-Pritchard, Raymond Firth, Bronislaw Malinowski, and Isaac Schapera, Essays presented to C. G. Seligman. London, Kegan, Paul, Trench, Trubner and Co.

HESS, ROBERT D. AND ROBERTA MEYER BEAR. 1969. Early education. Chicago, Aldine Publishing Co.

HORTON, ROBIN. 1961. Destiny and the unconscious in West Africa. Africa 31:110–116.

———. 1967. African traditional thought and Western science: II. The 'closed' and 'open' predicaments. Africa 37:155–187.

HSU, FRANCIS L. K. 1961. Kinship and ways of life: an exploration. *In* Psychological anthropology, Francis L. K. Hsu, ed., Homewood, The Dorsey Press.

———. 1969. The study of literate civilizations. New York, Holt, Rinehart and Winston.

HUDSON, WILLIAM. 1967. The study of the problem of pictorial perception among unacculturated groups. International Journal of Psychology 2:89–107.

HUNT, J. McV. 1961. Intelligence and experience. New York, The Ronald Press Co.

IRVINE, S. H. (n.d.). Bibliography on human behaviour in Africa. In manuscript.

JAHODA, GUSTAV. 1954. A note on Ashanti names and their relationship to personality. British Journal of Psychology 45:192–195.

———. 1956. Assessment of abstract behavior in a non-Western culture. Journal of Abnormal and Social Psychology 53:237–243.

———. 1958a. Child animism: I. A critical survey of cross-cultural research. Journal of Social Psychology 47:197–212.

———. 1958b. Child animism: II. A study in West Africa. Journal of Social Psychology 47:213–222.

———. 1958c. Immanent justice among West African children. Journal of Social Psychology 47:241–248.

————. 1966. Geometric illusions and environment: a study in Ghana. British Journal of Psychology 57:193–195.

JELLIFFE, D. B. ET AL. 1963. Custom and child health in Buganda. Parts I–V. Tropical and Geographical Medicine 15:121–157.

KAGAN, JEROME AND S. LEMKIN. 1961. Form, color and size in children's conceptual behavior. Child Development 32:25–28.

KAYE, BARRINGTON. 1962. Bringing up children in Ghana. London, Allen and Unwin.

KIEV, ARI (ED.). 1964. Magic, faith, and healing. New York, The Free Press.

KILBRIDE, PHILIP L. AND MICHAEL C. ROBBINS. 1969. Pictorial depth perception and acculturation among the Baganda. American Anthropologist 71:293–301.

KLINGELHOFER, E. L. 1971. What Tanzanian secondary school students plan to teach their children. Journal of Cross-Cultural Psychology 2:189–195.

KUPER, HILDA (ED.). 1965. Urbanization and migration in West Africa. Berkeley and Los Angeles, University of California Press.

LAMBO, T. ADEOYE. 1962. Malignant anxiety: a syndrome associated with criminal conduct in Africans. Journal of Mental Science 108:256–264.

LAYE, CAMARA. 1954. The African child. Great Britain, Fontana Books.

LEE, S. G. 1950. Some Zulu concepts of psychogenic disorder. Journal for Social Research, Pretoria, I:9–18.

————. 1958. Social influences in Zulu dreaming. Journal of Social Psychology 47:265–283.

————. 1962. Stress and adaptation. Leicester, Leicester University Press.

————. (in press). Spirit possession among the Zulu. In Spirit mediumship and society in Africa, J. Middleton and J. H. M. Beattie, eds., London, Routledge and Kegan Paul.

————. (n.d.). Culture change and psychological adjustment among the southeastern Bantu. In manuscript.

LEIGHTON, ALEXANDER H., T. ADEOYE LAMBO, CHARLES C. HUGHES, DOROTHEA C. LEIGHTON, JOHN M. MURPHY, AND DAVID B. MACKLIN. 1963. Psychiatric disorder among the Yoruba. Ithaca, Cornell University Press.

LEVINE, ROBERT A. 1960. The internalization of political values in stateless societies. Human Organization 19:51–58.

————. 1963. Child rearing in sub-Saharan Africa: an interim report. Bulletin of the Menninger Clinic 27:245–256.

————. 1966a. Dreams and deeds: achievement motivation in Nigeria. Chicago, University of Chicago Press.

————. 1966b. Sex roles and economic change in Africa. Ethnology 5:186–193.

————. 1969. Culture, personality, and socialization: an evolutionary view. In

Handbook of socialization theory and research, David A. Goslin, ed., Chicago, Rand McNally and Co.

LeVine, Robert A. and Barbara B. LeVine. 1966. Nyansongo: A Gusii community in Kenya. New York, John Wiley and Sons.

LeVine, Robert A., Nancy H. Klein, and Constance R. Owen. 1967. Father-child relationships and changing life-styles in Ibadan, Nigeria. *In* The city in modern Africa, Horace Miner, ed., New York, Frederick A. Praeger, Publishers.

Lloyd, Barbara B. 1966. Education and family life in the development of class identification among the Yoruba. *In* The new elites of tropical Africa, P. C. Lloyd, ed., London, Oxford University Press.

———. 1968. Choice behavior and social structure: a comparison of two African societies. Journal of Social Psychology 74:3–12.

Lloyd, Peter C. (ed.). 1966. The new elites of tropical Africa. London, Oxford University Press.

Lystad, Mary Hanemann. 1960a. Traditional values of Ghanaian children. American Anthropologist 62:454–464.

———. 1960b. Paintings of Ghanaian children. Africa 30:238–242.

McClelland, David C. 1958. The importance of early learning in the formation of motives. *In* Motives in fantasy, action, and society, John W. Atkinson, ed., Princeton, D. Van Nostrand Co.

———. 1961. The achieving society. New York, The Free Press.

Middleton, John. 1968. Review of Witchcraft and Sorcery in Rhodesia by J. R. Crawford. American Anthropologist 70:1205–1206.

Miner, Horace (ed.). 1967. The city in modern Africa. New York, Frederick A. Praeger, Publishers.

Minturn, Leigh and William W. Lambert et al. 1964. Mothers of six cultures: antecedents of child rearing. New York, John Wiley and Sons.

Morgenthaler, Fritz and Paul Parin. 1964. Typical forms of transference among West Africans. International Journal of Psychoanalysis 45:446–449.

Mundy-Castle, Alastair C. 1966. Pictorial depth perception in Ghanaian children. International Journal of Psychology 1:289–300.

Mundy-Castle, Alastair C., B. L. McKiever and T. Prinsloo. 1953. A comparative study of the electroencephalograms of normal Africans and Europeans of Southern Africa. Electroencephalography and Clinical Neurophysiology 5:533–543.

Munroe, Robert L. and Ruth H. Munroe. 1971. Effect of environmental experience on spatial ability in an East African society. Journal of Social Psychology 83:15–22.

Munroe, Robert L., Ruth H. Munroe, and Robert E. Daniels. 1969. Effect of status and values on estimation of coin size in two East African societies. Journal of Social Psychology 77:25–34.

MUNROE, ROBERT L., RUTH H. MUNROE, SARA B. NERLOVE, AND ROBERT E. DANIELS. 1969. Effects of population density on food concerns in three East African societies. Journal of Health and Social Behavior 10:161–171.

MUNROE, RUTH H. AND ROBERT L. MUNROE. 1971. Household density and infant care in an East African society. Journal of Social Psychology 83:3–13.

MURDOCK, GEORGE PETER. 1949. Social structure. New York, The Macmillan Co.

NADEL, S. F. 1937. A field experiment in racial psychology. British Journal of Psychology 28:195–211.

———. 1946. A study of shamanism in the Nuba mountains. Journal of the Royal Anthropological Institute 76:25–37.

———. 1952. Witchcraft in four African societies: an essay in comparison. American Anthropologist 54:18–29.

NERLOVE, SARA B. 1969. Trait dispositions and situational determinants of behavior among Gusii children of southwestern Kenya. Unpublished Ph.D. dissertation, Stanford University.

NORBECK, EDWARD. 1963. African rituals of conflict. American Anthropologist 65:1254–1279.

OLIVER, SYMMES C. 1965. Individuality, freedom of choice, and cultural flexibility of the Kamba. American Anthropologist 67:421–428.

ORTIGUES, MARIE-CECILE AND EDMOND ORTIGUES. 1966. Oedipe africain. Paris, Plon.

OSTHEIMER, JOHN M. 1969. Measuring achievement motivation among the Chagga of Tanzania. Journal of Social Psychology 78:17–30.

OTTENBERG, SIMON. 1958. Ibo receptivity to change. *In* Continuity and change in African cultures, W. R. Bascom and M. J. Herskovits, eds., Chicago, University of Chicago Press.

PARIN, PAUL AND FRITZ MORGENTHALER. 1964. Ego and orality in the analysis of West Africans. *In* The psychoanalytic study of society, Volume III, W. Muensterberger and S. Axelrad, eds., New York, International Universities Press, Inc.

PARIN, PAUL, FRITZ MORGENTHALER, AND GOLDY PARIN-MATTHÈY. 1963. Die Weissen denken zuviel. Zürich, Atlantis Verlag.

PETERSON, DONALD R. AND GUISEPPE MIGLIORINO. 1967. The uses and limitations of factor analysis in cross-cultural research on socialization. International Journal of Psychology 2:215–220.

PIAGET, JEAN. 1929. The child's conception of the world. London, Kegan Paul.

———. 1932. The moral judgment of the child. London, Routledge and Kegan Paul, Ltd.

POWDERMAKER, HORTENSE. 1956. Social change through imagery and values of teen-age Africans in Northern Rhodesia. American Anthropologist 58:783–813.

———. 1962. Copper town: changing Africa. New York, Harper and Row.

PRICE-WILLIAMS, D. R. 1961. A study concerning concepts of conservation of quantity among primitive children. Acta Psychologica 18:297–305.

———. 1962. Abstract and concrete modes of classification in a primitve society. British Journal of Educational Psychology 32:50–61.

PRINCE, R. 1962. Frequency of depressions in African natives (comments on M. J. Field's book, *Search for Security*). Review and Newsletter, Transcultural Research in Mental Health Problems 13:42–50.

RAUM, O. F. 1940. Chaga childhood. London, Oxford University Press.

READ, MARGARET. 1960. Children of their fathers: growing up among the Ngoni of Nyasaland. New Haven, Yale University Press.

READER, D. H. 1963. African and Afro-European research: a summary of previously unpublished findings in the National Institute for Personnel Research. Psychologia Africana 10:1–18.

RICHARDS, AUDREY I. 1958. Review of Custom and Conflict in Africa by Max Gluckman. Man 58:117–118.

SAVAGE, CHARLES AND RAYMOND PRINCE. 1967. Depression among the Yoruba. *In* The psychoanalytic study of society, W. Muensterberger and S. Axelrad, eds. Vol. IV. New York, International Universities Press, Inc.

SCOTCH, NORMAN A. 1960. A preliminary report on the relation of sociocultural factors to hypertension among the Zulu. Annals of the New York Academy of Sciences 84:1000–1009.

SEGALL, MARSHALL H., DONALD T. CAMPBELL, AND MELVILLE J. HERSKOVITS. 1966. The influence of culture on visual perception. Indianapolis, The Bobbs-Merrill Co.

SERPELL, R. 1966. Selective attention in children. Lusaka, Bulletin No. 1, Inst. Social Research, University of Zambia.

SIMMONS, DONALD C. 1960. Sexual life, marriage, and childhood among the Efik. Africa 30:153–165.

SUCHMAN, ROSSLYN GAINES. 1966. Cultural differences in children's color and form preferences. Journal of Social Psychology 70:3–10.

TOOTH, GEOFFREY. 1950. Studies in mental illness in the Gold Coast. London, His Majesty's Stationery Office, Colonial Research Publication No. 6.

VAN DEN BERGHE, P. L. (ED.). 1965. Africa: social problems of change and conflict. San Francisco, Chandler.

WEBER, MAX. 1930. The Protestant ethic and the spirit of capitalism. 1904. (translated by T. Parsons), New York, Scribner.

WHITING, BEATRICE B. (ED.). 1963. Six cultures: studies of child rearing. New York, John Wiley and Sons.

WHITING, BEATRICE B. AND JOHN W. M. WHITING. 1968. Task assignment and personality: a consideration of the effect of herding on boys. Paper presented at the University of East Africa Social Sciences Conference, Dar-es-Salaam.

WHITING, JOHN W. M. 1961. Socialization process and personality. *In* Psychological anthropology, Francis L. K. Hsu, ed., Homewood, The Dorsey Press.

WHITING, JOHN W. M. ET AL. 1966. Field guide for a study of socialization. New York, John Wiley and Sons.

WICKERT, FREDERIC R. (ED.). 1967. Readings in African psychology from French language sources. East Lansing, African Studies Center, Michigan State University.

WILLIAMS, JUDITH AND R. B. SCOTT. 1953. Growth and development of Negro infants: IV. Motor development and its relationship to child rearing practices in two groups of Negro infants. Child Development 24:103–121.

WINTER, EDWARD H. AND LAMBERT MOLYNEAUX. 1963. Population patterns and problems among the Iraqw. Ethnology 2:490–506.

WITKIN, H. A. 1967. A cognitive-style approach to cross-cultural research. International Journal of Psychology 2:233–250.

WITKIN, H. A., R. B. DYK, H. F. FATERSON, D. R. GOODENOUGH, AND S. A. KARP. 1962. Psychological differentiation. New York, John Wiley and Sons.

WOBER, MALLORY. 1967. Adapting Witkin's field independence theory to accommodate new information from Africa. British Journal of Psychology 58:29–38.

CHAPTER THREE

North America

JOHN J. HONIGMANN

Introduction

The distinction between ethnology and that specialty of anthropology, psychological anthropology or culture and personality, rests on which of two ideally distinct points of view an observer adopts. Paraphrasing Sapir (1932; cf. Kluckhohn 1944:602–604), an ethnologist looks at a segment of behavior as a culture pattern, while the psychological anthropologist studies the same segment from the standpoint of the persons whom it directly involves. The behavior has "person-defining value." Using other words, in culture and personality an observer focuses on culture as experienced or manifested by a composite (or typical) individual — *the* Hopi child, *the* Sioux Indian, or *the* U.S. American. Or an observer studies a real individual or categories of people to see how they experience a way of life. Culture and personality implies sustained concentration on the explicit and implicit meanings which cultural traits (artifacts, ceremonies, legal norms, or epic poems) possess for *persons* in the community. Culture itself is the personality of its carriers writ large. True, all cultural anthropology gives attention to persons, meanings, and to the subjective. In psychological anthropology there is simply more emphatic recognition of the social actor as a person, often to the relative exclusion of social structure, technology, and ideological systems. In a work of culture and personality, whether it is a record of children's development, a life history, or an interpretation of Rorschach tests, the individual as a system of behavior looms very large.

My object in this chapter is primarily to review culture-and-personality research which has been conducted in native North America and, somewhat more incidentally, below the border and in South America. But I will also refer methodological matters that the literature presents. My coverage is selective; I have sought work that reveals new interests, techniques, or levels of sophistication and that indicates directions which psychological anthropology has taken.

Indian Personality and Life on the Reservation

Aboriginally North America was a continent of varied lifeways, traces of which still remain. Practically all over the continent, however, missions, schools, traders, and government administrators have churned up culture change. The displacement of war, hunting, and many ceremonies brought about a profound alteration in the traditional roles of men and women and in all other interaction patterns. The socially standardized milieux in which children were aboriginally socialized have been substantially transformed. In the United States, as well as in southern Canada, Indians cluster on reserves and occupy a special status as far as the larger society is concerned. Someone might regard these conditions as evidence that the American Indians, with a few exceptions, no longer possess truly exotic cultures. He might believe that the Indians could hardly be worth studying in order to learn something about the diverse systems of personality that occur under differing cultural conditions. He might believe that, while the Indians who live under reservation conditions might at best reveal traumatized personalities, casualties of culture change, they will not provide the kinds of insights that it is possible to obtain, say, in parts of Africa and the Southwest Pacific. One could conceivably interpret some of the works to be reviewed in this chapter as supporting such extreme expectations. Anthropologists have indeed found some Indian social personalities to be laden with conflict and uncertainty. But it is worth remembering that the theoretical point from which much research in psychological anthropology departs has been heavily oriented toward discovering *pathology* in people's world- and self-views. Anthropologists have mostly employed a crisis-oriented approach when they studied personality and consequently have been much more responsive to evidence of conflict and stress than to behavior that indicates personal wellness (Honigmann 1967:38, 111; Maslow 1950). Acculturation or, to be more exact about what is probably crucial, uneven culture change (*cf.* Mead 1956), undoubtedly encourages personal stress, but stress is also evident in American Indian personality as it became known in very early contact times (Hallowell 1946).

How far anthropologists' accounts of contemporary American Indians have been influenced by factors such as reservation life and many Indian tribes' marginal status in society remains debatable. There are anthropologists who believe that poverty and related social conditions are responsible for personality traits, like deep-rooted suspiciousness of neighbors and government, low achievement drive, and a "lower-class value system," found among some Indians and Indian Métis (James 1961; Witthoft 1961:76; French 1967). As a result of their marginal social existence, those observers maintain, the personality structure of American Indians is only superficially like that which prevailed at the time of European colonization. Whether their theory be true or not, modern American Indian culture and personality can still reward anthropological study. For someone psychologically trained and clinically sensitive, even a single summer of field research in the United States, Canada, or Central America will reveal distinctively contoured overt and covert facets of behavior. I am not claiming a few months of casual observation to be enough. The longer a trained inquirer devotes to developing rapport with specific individuals seen from day to day in their natural social environment, to learning their language, and to closely sharing their lives so as to penetrate below the veneer of mass-produced ubiquitous cultural trappings, the richer will be the insights and understanding that can develop. These rules of anthropological method, of course, hold not only for studying Indians but any people.

Personal Documents

Some of the earliest interest in studying individual configurations of behavior began with the collection of personal documents, a category in which I include autobiographies, biographies, and psychological analyses such as *Gregorio, The Hand-Trembler* (Leighton and Leighton 1949), or Devereux's (1951) account of a psychoanalysis. American Indians have provided some notable personal documents, including Radin's (1920) account of Crashing Thunder, Dyk's story of Son of Old Man Hat (1938),

Simmon's (1942) rendering of Sun Chief's own life, and Ford's *Smoke from Their Fires* (1941). However, the exploitation of this channel to present "person-defining" behavior has not been very widely pursued. Rarely have we more than one first-rate life history per culture. Nor have many innovations appeared within the life-history approach. Oscar Lewis (1959; 1961) is responsible for a new departure in his portrayal of family cultures in Mexico, though his approach departs somewhat from the strictly personal document. Life histories, as Kluckhohn (1945) points out, are valuable for the insight they provide into the meaning which social forms possess for the members of a given community. But anthropologists are ultimately interested in more than a specific individual's experiences. They note Sun Chief's attitudes toward sex not merely as one individual's way of handling a universal situation, but for what they tell us about how that aspect of Hopi culture is generally experienced on a personal level — hence, the importance of accumulating personal documents from a number of people who occupy different statuses in a particular community.

The Era of Edward Sapir and Ruth Benedict

To understand how anthropologists came to apply theories from child development, psychology, and psychiatry in the study of culture, we must note the emergence at the end of the nineteenth century of psychology as a science. Twentieth century psychologists developed increasing interest in the relationship of personality development (including the breakdown of personality organization) to social conditions (Honigmann 1968). Meanwhile, anthropologists noted that culture after all is manifested only through individuals. This conclusion occurred to Franz Boas, for example, though he did little to pursue it. He did, however, transmit his interest to a number of his students who were to become extremely influential in the new movement that came to be called culture and personality (*cf.* Kluckhohn 1944:596; Mead 1959:14).

Among those students was Edward Sapir, who, in his paper "Culture, Genuine and Spurious" (1924), distinguished between the concept of culture as applied to man's whole material and spiritual social heritage and to "those general attitudes, views of life, and specific manifestations of civilization that give a particular people its distinctive place in the world." Sapir was offering a new version of an orientation that had long interested certain historians, like those of the *Volksgeist* group in nineteenth century Germany. In subsequent papers (for example, "Cultural Anthropology and Psychiatry," 1932), Sapir advanced the germ of the definition of psychological anthropology which I have offered at the start of this chapter. Cultural anthropology, he said, emphasizes the group and its traditions but pays little regard to the individuals who make up the group and who actualize its traditions in individual variations of behavior. Anthropology might also focus on persons and see culture in its "true locus," namely, "in the interactions of specific individuals and, on the subjective side, in the world of meanings which each one of these individuals may unconsciously abstract for himself from his participation in these interactions" — in much the same way as psychiatry focuses on a whole individual and observes him in his world of social relationships.

If I had to date the actual beginning of field research conducted in this spirit, I would choose the year 1928, when Margaret Mead — a student of Boas — published *Coming of Age in Samoa*. However, we are concerned with American Indians. Here the signal event emerged from Ruth Benedict's (1928, 1932, 1934) preoccupation with characterizing cultures in psychological terms. In 1934 this brilliant student of Boas published *Patterns of Culture*. The book attempts to interpret several cultures in terms of their distinctive psychological orientations. One chapter of the book, in which she compares the Indians of the Great Plains with the Pueblo people (Zuni) of the Southwest, will illustrate Benedict's approach.

The Plains Indian way of life reveals a Dionysian quality. In personal experience the Plains Indians seek to press beyond the commonplace toward excess in order to achieve a certain psychological state. The Pueblo Indians in contrast are Apollonian, meaning that they distrust excess, prefer to keep to the middle of the road, and avoid meddling with disruptive psychological states. Benedict saw Plains and Pueblo cultures as two configurations. The Dionysian and Apollonian emphases reveal themselves in many parts of the configuration, for example, in response to death. The Plains Indians give way to uninhibited grief when a kinsman dies; mourning is prolonged, and some people even mutilate their bodies to properly express grief. The Appollonian Pueblos also react to death with sorrow, but people seek to make as little, rather than as much, of the event as possible. In each culture area the ideal personality type reflects the dominant psychological emphasis. The Plains value the self-reliant man. By showing initiative in war or hunting, such a man achieves honor. The Pueblos have a different ideal. They value the mild-mannered and affable man who acts in moderate rather than in grandiose or spectacular terms.

In another chapter of her book, Benedict describes the Kwakiutl Indians of the North Pacific Coast. She views them not only as Dionysian, but characterizes them as obsessed by megalomaniac ideas of grandeur, ideas which express themselves in furious competitive feats (potlatches) and in the way chiefs seek to gain the best of one another through boasting and mutual ridicule.

The inspiration for Benedict's brand of configurationalism came not from a school of psychology that was already current, Gestalt psychology, but from a historian, Oswald Spengler (1926). Benedict's interpretations of cultures in psychological terms omits intensive, firsthand study of the people whose behavior she describes. The Plains and Kwakuitl ways of life which she characterizes had long vanished, and Benedict relied on ethnographers' earlier accounts. Culture and personality rarely again followed this method but instead put great reliance on firsthand field work. For if personality is interpreted solely from ethnographic materials which describe a culture, there will be no empirical clinical data by which to know the people who live that culture. Explanation will be circular: the cultural datum — people behave peaceably and co-operatively — will be ascribed to underlying peaceful and co-operative motivations. This danger is inherent in Benedict's approach, though mostly she avoids falling into circularity because she does not essay a direct account of personality. She tends to say people act *as if* they had such motives. The safe position in the absence of independent validating information is never to assume that overt peaceableness or any other cultural trait is motivated by a similar state, like absence of hostility. It may or may not be. The point is that the existence of motives cannot be directly inferred from the outward form of behavior alone. Motives must be assessed through studying living individuals in depth. That is the clinical method.

How shall *Patterns of Culture* be evaluated? Some anthropologists have condemned the book as subjective and unscientific. In some instances such condemnation is motivated by anthropologists' unwillingness to admit that their discipline includes a strong humanistic tradition. Benedict, however, clearly thought of her work as scientific. One reason why she may have identified with science is that in her day, as in ours, categorizing a piece of research as scientific surrounds it with greater authority. Debating whether something is scientific is jejune. The proper question is what contribution does a work make in the discipline and for the period to which it belongs. *Patterns of Culture* represents an extraordinary accomplishment in early twentieth century anthropology. Inspired by the historian,

Spengler, Benedict showed that the first-order facts of a culture, the details which had solely preoccupied anthropologists, could be transcended by finding abstract qualities linking domains of life like war, menstruation, death, puberty, and others. The abstractions thus created could, like the first-order facts themselves, be discussed and compared. This method gave anthropology a new maturity and opened the way for other bases of interpretation using, for example, psychoanalytic theory to find new meaning in familiar cultural forms. Naturally critics asked whether Benedict's abstractions could be replicated and whether they adequately accounted for all that there is to see in Pueblo, Plains, and Kwakiutl culture. The critics found her work incomplete and charged her with having ignored some instances of behavior that were incongruent with the dominant qualities she abstracted and ascribed to the cultures (Codere 1956). A paper written by John Bennett (1946) reviews disagreements over the interpretation of Zuni and adjacent Pueblo cultures and raises methodological implications that go quite beyond the field of psychological anthropology. Bennett examines the similar interpretations of Pueblo life made by Benedict and others and sets them in opposition to a radically different view of Pueblo culture and personality, the "repressed" approach that emphasizes hostility, anxiety, and other traits less exalted than peaceableness and co-operation. He concludes that in each case values to a certain extent necessarily govern the way an anthropologist structures his data. We cannot, he adds, determine on empirical grounds once and for all which point of view is right.

Despite disagreements, *Patterns of Culture* remains timelessly important in the same way that a judicious historian's work remains viable even after subsequent works are written that contain more complete evidence or interpretations more acceptable to the discipline as it has become. Is the book true? Truth in any discipline is never stable and as controversy indicates, agreement on what is true may be nearly impossible to attain. Perhaps for that reason Gjessing (1968:427) exclaims that "the word 'truth' is so ambiguous that it should possibly be barred from scientific usage." *Patterns of Culture* is true in an existential sense. Benedict presumably responsibly checked her interpretations against her experience. That is the only way verification can occur in a discipline like anthropology in which often individual researchers by themselves for prolonged periods of time conceptualize, collect, and in their own minds process or integrate countless bits of experience that are their data. Given such a method the test of truth by replication, as occurs in the experimental sciences, remains impossible. In short *Patterns of Culture* is true to the degree that Benedict at some time in its production believed it to be true.

Psychological Persistence Among Ojibwa Indians

The publications that appeared in the latter part of the thirties and in the forties reveal that actual field research was already under way when *Patterns of Culture* appeared. In 1937 came the first of Landes' reports on the Ojibwa (1937, 1938a, 1938b) and Hallowell's (1936, 1937; also see 1942, 1951) work on another branch of the same ethnic group. Hallowell generated considerable excitement by findings showing that, although personality development is undoubtedly influenced by cultural change, in some respects the personality system is also highly autonomous and persists. In eastern North America, his evidence indicates, the fundamental organization of personality persisted through two centuries of culture contact. Hallowell's (1946, 1952) method was to compare the reports of seventeenth and eighteenth century missionaries and explorers with the people as he knew them. In the early period Europeans characterized the Indians as emotionally restrained, stoical, strongly inhibited in the expression of aggression, mild in the face of provocation to anger, and suppressive of open criticism. In other terms, Hallowell finds in the reports evidence that the northeastern Indian was anxious lest he fail to maintain the required standards of fortitude, express anger and resentment, or provoke the anger of others. Essentially the same characteristics still existed in relatively unassimilated Ojibwa Indians whom Hallowell observed along the upper banks of the Berens River which flows into Lake Winnipeg and even in more assimilated Ojibwa who live farther down the river. Indians who had been in more intense contact with Euro-Canadians did differ in some respects from their more isolated contemporaries. For example, they were more extroverted. But the personality core, Hallowell found when he scored responses to the Rorschach test given by both Berens River groups, was fundamentally the same. No radical psychological shift had occurred in the course of acculturation. Later Hallowell shifted his attention to the still more acculturated Lac du Flambeau Indians in northern Wisconsin, another branch belonging to the Ojibwa. Here, in spite of heavy culture change and cross breeding between Indians and whites, he found that the Lac du Flambeau people remained psychologically Indians. Consequently they were having a difficult time adjusting to their social environment. Characterologically they were in another cultural world, says Hallowell, anticipating one of the main conclusions of the U.S. Indian Education Research Project which will be described more fully below.

No full or satisfactory explanation exists of how the traditional character structure has managed to be transmitted from one generation to another for 300 years or more. James (1961) denies that there has in fact been any persistence. He argues that depressed conditions among some modern Ojibwa groups sustain traits resembling the psychological features reported by explorers and discovered by Hallowell. Against his view two counter arguments can be mustered. First, independent support exists for the possibility that psychological features can persist in a population despite a changing cultural context (Inkeles, Hanfmann, and Beier 1958). Second, support for the antiquity of certain Ojibwa personality traits comes from the widespread distribution of similar characteristics among other North American Indians (Spindler and Spindler, 1957). Interpreting that distribution with reference to the age-area principle (Kroeber 1948:561–564) suggests a respectable age for the traits, though why they occur so widely and how they are perpetuated remain crucial questions for which anthropology needs a theory.

Culture Change and Personality

Certain methodological aspects of Hallowell's work deserve special note. In effect he applied to his three communities a variant of the experimental method — actually the only kind of experimental method that can be applied in studying living groups of people (Chapin 1947). His groups illustrate three levels of acculturation. On Level One were the least acculturated, pagan inland Ojibwa of Berens River. Then came the Christian lakeside people, among whom aboriginal dwellings had disappeared along with the old songs and ceremonies. About 20 per cent of this group were of mixed racial ancestry. On Level Three we find the highly acculturated Lac du Flambeau Indians of Wisconsin, 80 per cent of whom were racially mixed and all spoke some English. The Lac du Flambeau children attend school, their families have radios, and in general the people maintain a close association with whites. However, at Lac du Flambeau the Midewewin ceremony has been carried over from precontact times.

The Rorschach test offered Hallowell a common device to apply in each group to measure differences in response. He tested over 200 people with this instrument, recognizing, of course, that it had never been fully validated for cross-cultural use (Hallowell 1951). One of his findings we have already stated: persistence of personality independent of degree of assimilation to Euro-Canadian culture. Another finding comes from counting the number of signs of adjustment that appear in the Rorschach responses of each group. Differences in adjustment are not significant when the two Berens River communities are compared to one another, but there is a significant increase in personal maladjustment in the records of Lac du Flambeau. For example, 9 per cent of the Level One records show signs of bad integration compared to 18 per cent of the Lac du Flambeau subjects.[1]

Hallowell revealed new possibilities in using ethnohistorical method to reconstruct aboriginal personality. One other example of this method may be mentioned, Esther Goldfrank's (1943) work on the Teton Dakota. She shows how aspects of Dakota interpersonal behavior — notably aggression — altered in pace with other changes in the way of life. Before 1850 the Dakota were horse-mounted buffalo hunters and warriors. Ingroup violence was fairly common and sprang partly from ingroup rivalries. The rich competed with displays of wealth. The introduction of liquor by early fur traders intensified violence toward the end of this early period. Between 1850 and 1877 increasing contact occurred with the white man and there was a growing decimation of the wild buffalo, the Indian's mainstay. Aggression was turned outward as wars broke out between the Indians and Euro-Americans over the latters' encroachment on the land and on account of broken treaties. When the Indians' aggressive energies began to be deflected against enemies, a need for increased responsibility and ingroup co-operation arose. It is largely for this reason that ingroup aggression began to decline, though competitive displays of wealth by the rich continued. What pressures were used to alter behavior with respect to aggression? The chiefs, whose position had grown stronger, gave sermons on the importance of ingroup co-operation. Blood money rather than blood revenge was used to settle murder. To borrow terms which Anthony F. C. Wallace (1959) has introduced, the periodic expression of impulses normally suppressed gave way to an emphasis on the *lasting* suppression of incongruent motives and behavior. For a time the Dakota managed to release aggression outward, against rival tribes and the United States' troops, but their power to do so was broken following Custer's massacre. Between 1877 and 1885 the Indian was "crushed." In this third period the buffalo disappeared and the old economy was wrecked. Most of the horses had been taken by the victorious army. With the external threat removed, internal aggression again broke forth. The chiefs' injunctions were ignored. But now a strong, foreign, legal system was on hand to curb the disruptive

[1] For other research on Ojibwa personality see Caudill 1949, Barnouw 1950, and Boggs 1956, 1958.

trends that had almost free play prior to 1850. From 1885 onward the people reluctantly turned to making a living as farmers and also to religion. Chiefs entered the ministry and became pastors of their people. The Indians eagerly adopted one feature of Christianity, the blessedness of giving. Religion and law restored ingroup peace and generosity became an ideal.[2]

Goldfrank's work exhibits the same difficulty that we saw in the method followed by Ruth Benedict: it fails to provide clinical access to motivation. The available data force the student to deal largely with the overt features of personality or interpersonal relations.

Use of Psychoanalytic Theory

For many early workers the dominant aim in psychological anthropology research has been to throw light on motives and feeling states which underlie overt behavior. One cannot infer covert phenomena from outward forms without theory, the purpose of which is to specify how to proceed with interpreting in covert terms what people say, do, make, or write. The Rorschach test is based on one such theory but some form of the psychoanalytic theory (usually not in its most extreme, orthodox form) has been even more widely employed in culture-and-personality research, though the utility of the theory for cross-cultural research has been questioned at certain points, for example, concerning the universal existence of an Oedipus complex. However, with regard to unconscious motivation, defense mechanisms, the importance of childhood in personality formation, the overdetermined nature of behavior, the motivated nature of dreams, and other subjects, psychoanalytic theory has been confidently and productively utilized.

I shall not trace the early history of that theory. The psychoanalytic approach in anthropology came to maturity with the publication of *The Individual and His Society*, a book written by Abram Kardiner, psychoanalyst, in collaboration with Ralph Linton, anthropologist (Kardiner 1939). *The Individual and His Society* is not based on deliberately organized field work in North America, although the authors do briefly examine the Zuni and Kwakiutl Indians and also the Eskimo in terms of their theory. The book grew out of a seminar jointly conducted at Columbia University by Kardiner and, Linton and was based on analysis of already collected cultural materials, once again without benefit of clinical study. The

[2] For other studies of Dakota (Sioux) personality see Erikson 1939, 1963:Ch. 3, and Macgregor 1946.

seminar continued and provided Kardiner with material for a second volume, *The Psychological Frontiers of Society* (1945). In this book one American Indian group, the Comanche, receives intensive consideration though no fresh data were collected for the purpose of this analysis.

Since a comprehensive statement of Kardiner's theory is given by Thomas Gladwin in another chapter of this book (Chapter 5) I need not do so here. We should, however, recognize the emphasis which most schools of psychoanalysis put on the early years of life. Childhood is the period when the meanings in terms of which individuals carry out other aspects of their culture — war, religion, child rearing, and many other activities — are established in personality. Ideally, psychoanalytic theory aims to predict the way an adult will regard his world and himself in terms of the way he was reared. But it is doubtful if an adult social personality can really be predicted in this way except in very general and not very useful terms. What customarily happens is that the adult covert personality — what Kardiner calls the "basic personality type" — is interpreted using knowledge of how children are currently being socialized and drawing simultaneous inferences from adult activity. Instead of really predicting, the researcher attempts to develop a plausible explanation which will tie into a neat package both certain events of early life and certain selected features revealed by adults' overt behavior (Honigmann 1963:307).

In 1945 I was enough impressed with the potentialities inherent in Kardiner's work and Karen Horney's (1939, 1945) version of psychoanalytic theory to apply this approach to the Kaska Indians who live in northern British Columbia and southern Yukon Territory (Honigmann 1949). My intentions among the Kaska were to identify the emotional qualities which people revealed as they acted their cultural roles and account for such qualities in terms of underlying motivations. I also hoped to explore the conditions of early life under which the motivations are learned.[3]

Dominant Motivations of Kaska Indians

Kaska social personality is characterized by seven, very much interrelated, dominant motivations, each of which must be understood in terms of its context and not by other definitions which the terms may have. The first of these motives is egocentricity, defined here as a high evaluation of personal independence in which interests are self-centered rather than

[3] For a study of Aymara Indians of Peru which employs a similar approach see Tschopik 1951.

group-centered. This motivation colors the way Kaska Indians resist direction from sources outside the family. It enters into the positive evaluation of work, which guarantees independence and self-sufficiency in this trapping-hunting economy, and also into the masculine striving of women, some of whom appear to be in part dissatisfied with their sex role.

A second dominant motivation is utilitarianism, a concept that refers to a practical and resourceful attitude toward the problems of living, an interest in concrete rather than abstract thinking. The Kaska are present-oriented and little concerned with a remote future. Deference is a third guiding tendency in Kaska social personality. The word denotes an attempt to maintain frictionless human relationships and a concern lest one becomes disliked and rejected. In conformity with this orientation, people make requests obliquely, thereby not risking open rejection and also not pressing on other people too aggressively. More directly, deference is expressed by avoidance of face-to-face quarrels. Hostility is, however, expressed indirectly and covertly through gossip. In other words, hostility is not lacking in Kaska social personality. Evidence for it appears in dreams and more overtly in how some people act when they are intoxicated, for example, threatening others and themselves with violence. The normal suppression of interpersonal hostility is very useful for people who live in an atomistic social system, one without strong social controls.

The next dominant motivation, flexibility, is difficult to define positively. It denotes a state of mind in which external necessity, duty, and hurry are subordinated to personal inclination. This state reveals itself in an absence of rigidity and in tolerant, even indecisive, attitudes toward the demands of living. The absence of hurry or of rigorous timetables, the people's easy conscience, the non-compulsive way in which children are reared and dogs trained, and the lack of obsessiveness all express this motive. In certain crisis situations flexibility combines with dependence, another dominant motivation, to produce procrastination and hesitation. As a result of these behaviors, the critical state that confronts the individual may grow worse instead of being resolved. The dominant motivation of dependence needs little explanation, though it should be noted that this tendency in character structure is at variance with the emphasis also placed on egocentricity and resourcefulness. It is quite possible for a social personality to reveal inconsistent trends which people themselves occasionally have difficulty reconciling in their day-to-day living.

Finally there is emotional isolation, perhaps the most dominant note in Kaska Indian social personality. The concept includes a strong desire to maintain aloofness from emotional experience and emotional involvement as well as a tendency to suppress strong feeling, including affection. Egocentricity is quite congruent with a social organization in which for much of the year families engaged in trapping live in relative isolation from one another in the bush and under a social system that is without superordinate authorities. Sexual constriction is one specific mode in which emotional isolation is expressed in interpersonal behavior. It shows up in the ambivalence that marks relations of men and women, in the absence of public display of affection between couples, in the reluctance to marry (that is, to enter a strong emotional — even dependent — relationship), and, most dramatically, in the behavior accompanying premarital sexual relations. Premarital sexuality includes considerable preliminary teasing that culminates in a chase, capture, struggle, and, finally, coitus. Such a sequence, I discovered when I lived among the Indians, is often difficult to distinguish from actual rape. Girls and also married women conceive of the sex act as a hostile encounter, a perception they reveal in dreams and in associations spontaneously given to dreams. The promiscuity of adults, since it offers opportunity for sexual satisfaction without risk of emotional involvement, also reveals emotional isolation.

In general the Kaska world-view wavers between the idea that experience is manageable and the idea that life is difficult as well as uncertain. The self-view also comprises two conflicting attitudes: value placed on self-reliance and a tendency to abandon striving and revert to passivity. In each case the former is far more conscious, and much more acceptable, than the second. Passivity manifests itself in crises, when there is eager reaching out for help (cloaked, of course, by virtue of the tendency called emotional isolation) and surrender of active striving.

Emotional isolation is the motivation whose grounding in early socialization is easiest to perceive. This orientation is rooted in the way a Kaska mother withdraws emotionally from her child when the youngster is between two and three years old. She does not outrightly reject the child but spontaneously withdraws show of warmth and affection. The mother becomes more impersonal, more concerned with herself, or more preoccupied with a younger sibling. She shows herself less patient and indulgent to the youngster. In this situation the child unconsciously makes a decision never again to invest strong affection in others. The significance of growing up and spending all one's life with relatively affectless people who serve as role models must not be ignored in understanding how the Kaska style of life is acquired.

Psychoanalytic theory suggests that the striving for independence, which forms so conspicuous a part of Kaska social personality, is founded on indulgent care of infants. In this highly favorable period of life, the Kaska baby develops an unverbalized attitude of confidence in himself and hopeful expectations toward the world. These expectations are only loosely entrenched, however. They are contradicted by the emotional withdrawal that comes as an early shock. The passivity of Kaska personality in certain crisis situations can be explained as it derives from this traumatic episode and also as it reflects the hold which the passive-receptive state of infancy continues to exert in the personality.

The major test of truth that can be applied to this kind of interpretation is the test of consistency. Is the explanation sufficient, reasonable, clear? Does the explanation offered explain the facts in noncontradictory fashion? Does the evidence hold together sensibly? Are contradictions between facts, if they occur, adequately accounted for in terms of the theory that is being used?

Conclusions whose validity can only be assessed by applying rules of consistency and reasonableness, without help from controlling part of the data and administering clearcut tests to another part in order to see if the anticipated correlates also appear in that part, are not confined to cultural anthropology or to research on personality. This method of proof pervades the discipline of history and also operates productively in other social science fields. What varies in the method is degree of preoccupation with variables or processes that remain hidden from empirical gaze and are not identified by visible indicators. Psychoanalysis tended to keep research preoccupied with the complex hidden world of personality dynamics. As the hold of that discipline on anthropology lifted, proportionately more attention was devoted to dealing with observable behavioral phenomena whose correlation or interaction different observers can reliably follow. Such phenomena, for example, responses given to the Rorschach test, are in turn referred back to a hidden theoretical factor by which they are interpreted to give them their meaning.

Psychogenetic Development of Hopi Indian Children

Culture-and-personality studies directed to the American scene thrived in the forties. One development that added to our knowledge of American Indians as persons began in 1941 with the start of the Indian Education Research Project (also called the Indian Personality and Administration project). In that co-operative venture the Committee on Human Development of the University of Chicago was allied with the United States Office of Indian Affairs where John Collier was Commissioner (Havighurst and Neugarten 1955:v–vi; Thompson 1951:12). Their general purpose was to examine the whole development of Indian children in six American Indian tribes in order to derive practical, useful lessons for Indian education. What was happening to the personalities of Indians under the impact of American civilization? An answer to this question, it was believed, would help to define the "real needs" and resources of American Indians and would serve as a guide for administrators. In other words, although the results of the project were expected to contribute substantially to general knowledge, the project was designed as action research or applied anthropology. Indian Service personnel, mainly teachers, nurses, and school administrators, were enlisted to do much of the field work, but professional anthropologists were also assigned to the six groups selected for intensive study. In addition to anthropologists the project was carried through psychologists, psychiatrists, public administrators, linguists, and other specialists. The groups for which monographs of findings have been published are the Hopi (Thompson and Joseph 1944), Sioux (Macgregor 1946), Navaho (Leighton and Kluckhohn 1947; Kluckhohn and Leighton 1946), Papago Indians (Joseph, Spicer, and Chesky 1949), and Zuni (Leighton and Adair 1966). The report on Zia Pueblo has unfortunately never appeared.

The approach which these works follow may be called psychogenetic or developmental. With a variety of methodological aids (Emotional Response, Moral Ideology, Rorschach, Thematic Apperception, and other tests) as well as direct observation, the intellectual and emotional development of children is followed from birth to adolescence. The underlying theory draws from psychoanalysis, but the various workers are concerned with more than the earliest years of life and base interpretations on experiences that occur considerably later than feeding, toilet training, or early sexual training.

Fair evaluation of this ambitious project is difficult, for clear evidence concerning how the results of the research entered into the administration of the United States' Indians is hard to come by. Laura Thompson (1951) has written on the significance of the project for which she co-ordinated research activities. Six years of field work, she says, were required before a general solution of the welfare problem peculiar to each tribe could be formulated. The research involved far more than the relationship of personality to culture change. Other variables also had to be taken into

account: ecology, health, social organization, language, arts, crafts, ceremonies, and the core values of the people. The main findings were, first,
that a program of administration which was oriented primarily to
assimilating the Indians into the general American population was highly
detrimental to the welfare of Indian communities and Indian personality.
Second, a substantial increase in costly schools, health services, and
technological aid will not bring about rapid assimilation of the Indians
into the general population. Thompson writes: "We may predict with
assurance that the current Indian Bureau policy of rapid assimilation and
'liquidation,' in so far as it is effectively implemented at the reservation
and the community levels, will be detrimental to Indian personality
development and community welfare." On the other hand, her findings
support the wisdom of the Indian Reorganization Policy which had been
adopted under the early administration of Commissioner Collier.

Perhaps the best way to give some conception of this research is to take
a specific tribe and describe findings which are relevant to culture and
personality there. For this purpose I have selected the Hopi Indians
(Thompson and Joseph 1944; Thompson 1950).

The birth of the Hopi child occurs in the mother's home. Shortly
thereafter rites introduce the newborn individual to his father and to the
Sun and also initiate a life-long series of gift exchanges between the child
and his father's clanspeople. The infant spends practically all of the first
three months of life in a supine position on a cradleboard. After this time
the cradle is used only as a place to sleep until it finally becomes discarded
between six months and a year. The cradle, it is suggested, probably
contributes to the baby's feeling of security and also conditions the
newborn individual to expect restriction. But many other, less physical
restrictions will appear as the child matures. Weaning occurs with little
difficulty, usually around the age of two years. Cleanliness training is
introduced gradually, without shock. Up until the age of six in boys and
throughout youth in girls the mother and other females of the matrilocal
household act as the primary agents of socialization. The mother's brother
is a source of stricter discipline. Though the general character of early life
is permissive, the freedom of the youngster is firmly limited in the interests
of his physical safety. From such limitation every Hopi probably gains an
early conception of how hazardous the environment is in his village.
Adjustment is more difficult for boys than for girls, a generalization
revealed in boys' behavior problems, like thumbsucking, temper tantrums,
and stealing. The explanation lies in the fact that girls grow up in a house

where they are expected to remain even after marriage. Boys, already by the age of four or five, begin to break away from the family group and spend more and more time in the kiva (a religious structure) or in the fields and on the range. Eventually a young man will marry into a strange house and there assume a very marginal position. Actually, the boy gains freedom by breaking away from his family around the age of five. In contrast, the girl's role remains restricted. She must stay close to home and help her mother, and she too experiences conflicts that show up in temper tantrums, stealing, and fighting. Psychological tests show that five-year-olds among the Hopi are more relaxed and spontaneous than older Hopi children. For one thing, they are not yet fully disciplined. The girl's inner life at this age is simpler than the boy's; he is already quite introverted and shows a pervasive, vague anxiety.

Initiation into the Kachina cult marks the transition from childhood to youth. The ceremony introduces the child to the Kachinas, his ancestors, who send rain and food in exchange for prescribed ritual behavior. Initiation means a ceremonial whipping for some children, depending on the sodality into which they are initiated. Naughty boys, it is said, are usually initiated into the sodality that calls for the more severe whippings. The boy is whipped while he is stripped naked, but a girl initiate wears her clothes and is beaten less severely. Following initiation, public opinion to a considerable extent replaces the matrilocal household as the main control over the child's behavior. The father remains a source of happiness to youngsters but, tests show, the larger community becomes a source of fear, punishment, anger, and shame. The tests also reveal the child's conception of his family as a source of reward and praise. Economic responsibilities increase for the initiated boy so that now both sexes must fulfill household duties that force them to restrict their play to the evening. From six to twelve youngsters attend day school, an experience that girls particularly welcome because it liberates them from the house. At fourteen some boys go on to boarding school. As is seen in psychological tests, the period from eight to ten is a time when outside contacts increase for both sexes. Girls are finally aroused from their simple, unquestioning, walled-in existence; their imagination develops; their personality becomes more complex, more like the boy's. Just before puberty, however, boys and girls reveal a tendency to withdraw into themselves and much of their earlier spontaneous responsiveness to outside impressions disappears.

The transition to adulthood in Hopi life is not clearcut, though marriage marks a profound change in role. Tests probe below the surface to reveal what happens in adolescence as the sexual impulse rises in consciousness. However vaguely sex is defined by the young person, it is not perceived as evil. The force of the maturing sex impulse halts the introversive trends so apparent at the threshold of puberty so that an easier acceptance of outside contacts takes place. Boys achieve sex indulgence more easily than girls. Hopi girls are not allowed to roam around and must avoid showing themselves to be boy-crazy. Hence, girls continue to demonstrate more emotional withdrawal than boys.

The Hopi and other Indian samples of children were compared to a Midwest, white sample in order to establish differences (Havighurst and Neugarten 1955). In contrast to the latter, Hopi children derive little happiness from personal achievement. This is understandable for they have been taught to avoid any demonstration of achievement. Yet the Hopi youngsters are consciously proud of being praised and respected. Tests show that aggression makes Hopi children anxious, perhaps because of the enormous pressure that the community exerts against fighting. Work is important in their young lives; in how well or poorly he performs it, an individual demonstrates whether he is of good or evil character. Conscience is reflected through belief in immanent justice — belief that morality is sanctioned by an all-knowing, unchangeable, and unchallengeable external moral power. Belief in immanent justice in Hopi children does not decline with age as it does in Midwest children. In fact, it increases with age and belief in animism decreases more slowly among the Hopi than in the Midwest sample.

The Rorschach test reveals near-adolescent Hopi children to possess a deeply disciplined character structure. These youngsters are carefully selective with regard to their emotions; they are cautious and restrained. Yet they recognize pleasurable aspects of the world, though these must be accorded their due place. Exuberance is toned down. The children have average good imagination but it is seldom richly fluid, lively, or vivacious. Here again appears the all-pervasive note of restraint. (Compare how closely these findings correspond to Ruth Benedict's [1934] characterization of the Pueblo Indians as Apollonian. Remember, Benedict achieved her insight without the benefit of gathering her data clinically.) Instead of being primarily concerned with the emotional aspects of impressions and events, Hopi children approach the world intellectually and imaginatively, though without abandoning themselves to fantasy. The Hopi child is cautious, especially in his approach to a new situation. He does not become confused by something new. He rather firmly accepts or declines what is offered; such behavior sometimes makes the Hopi youngster appear stubborn or unshakeable to his teachers. The personality reveals a vague, free-floating anxiety which is unattached to definite, fear-provoking objects. In this character structure we see reflected the "price" that the Hopi child pays in order to survive in an environment which he has been taught is filled with potential danger and one which for these desert farmers is actually perilous. The Hopi adapts by limiting his desires, emotions, and ambitions. Limitation in turn generates an "inside pressure" that lacks any definite outlet. The child feels discomfort and fear without understanding that the source of the disturbing force is his own overdisciplined self. Such fear is expected in the Hopi community and is socially "normal." One area of personality remains unaffected by discipline, the area of the instinctual (including sexual) urges — the id. These impulses remain unusually vivid and spontaneous.

Adult Hopi are much given to malicious gossip and frequently suspect one another of witchcraft, behavior that probably originates from hostility and anxiety. Whence do hostility and anxiety arise? They arise from social relations carried on in a small, town-dwelling group, a group that is vulnerable to danger of famine and epidemics and whose pressure directed against the individual is a source of anger, shame, and punishment. The role of the mother plays a part. As a disciplinarian she too is a source of anger, shame, and discipline — more to the boy than to the girl. Hostility and anxiety are also rooted in the inability of the child to form deep, emotional attachments with anybody, except the mother, a person with whom his relationship is ambivalent.

Critical Notice and Other Signs of Maturity

Two further developments that brought psychological anthropology to maturity in the forties must be mentioned. First, criticism began to be leveled against the new movement. Particularly did critics object because, they thought, too much was being claimed for the formative years of childhood in the process of personality formation. Anthropologists doing such research, themselves deplored the excessive weight that, under the inspiration of psychoanalytic theory, was sometimes given to early disciplines (Goldfrank 1945; Underwood and Honigmann 1947). But this was only one controversial feature of the vigorous, new approach. Others too received a full, frank, and sometimes hostile airing. In her review of "Recent Trends in American Ethnology" Betty J. Meggers (1946:186) looked with alarm at the way Sapir had been heeded and attention was being diverted from cultural to psychological problems. Censure, Meggers claimed, was being met by anthropologists who chose to study culture. "That this trend will continue for some time to dominate anthropology cannot be doubted," she wrote. "In the meantime, however, the province of culture is being neglected."

Critical notice was not the only indication of the maturity which psychological anthropology had achieved. A second was the appearance of two collections of readings (Haring 1948; Kluckhohn and Murray 1948). These, naturally, did not limit themselves to data from North America. Both quickly went into new editions and were joined by a textbook (Honigmann 1954), the first of several (e.g., Weinberg 1958; Wallace 1961; Barnouw 1963).

The new decade opened with two contributions from Latin America which marked new levels of development. Holmberg's (1950) study of the Siriono is essentially ethnographic, but the underlying problem derives from psychological theory. Where a sparse and insecure food supply exists, do frustrations and anxieties centering around the hunger drive have major repercussions on behavior? Holmberg found overwhelming evidence for strong anxiety responses toward food among the Siriono and traced their development back to Siriono childhood. In the other work, John Gillin (1951) examined cultural sources of threat and security affecting Indians and Ladinos in a Guatemalan community. Rorschach analyses had already appeared comparing those two populations and had also examined the motivational makeup of six village "witch doctors" (Billig, Gillin, and Davidson 1947–48). In the same year as Gillin's publication, Oscar Lewis (1951) published his research on Tepoztlan, a book important as much for the questions it poses pertaining to the re-examination of already studied cultures as for being a meticulous approach to personality conceived of largely as manifesting itself in interpersonal relations.

One major development of the fifties transcends the North American culture area. This is a comparative approach that utilizes statistical techniques to test *cross-culturally* the relationship between aspects of child rearing (the antecedent variables) and subsequent personality or cultural variables. The pioneer work of this type is Whiting and Child's (1953) *Child Training and Personality: A Cross-Cultural Study.* Since the major figure who has employed the cross-cultural method in psychological anthropology, John W. M. Whiting, has written a chapter for this volume (Chapter 12), I will not deal with it beyond pointing out that it offers anthropology a means to overcome serious limitations that some people perceive in the evidential method. Where the latter remains tied solely to rational proof of relationships linking variables (either in a single culture or in human culture generally), the cross-cultural method in an experimental manner employs statistical procedures, applying them to a comparatively large number of cultures in order to test whether particular variables are indeed dependably connected.

In Pursuit of Objectivity

The introduction of cross-cultural testing did not still criticism directed against what is sometimes called the "excesses" of culture and personality studies. Orlansky's (1949) literature search had already assembled much material showing that, contrary to psychoanalytical theory, no consistent or meaningful relationship linked early forms of nursing and personality traits in later childhood. In the next year, further searching questions were asked by an anthropologist, psychologist, and two sociologists (Goldman 1950; Farber 1950; Lindesmith and Strauss 1950), not to speak of Roheim's (1950) strictures directed against members of the "culturalist school" for rejecting pure Freudian theory as being too biological! Against this background criticism let us examine briefly some methodological innovations in North American research, particularly those introduced by the Harvard Values Project (Kluckhohn 1951); by George Spindler (1952, 1955) in his careful research design for studying personality variation as correlated with differential assimilation of a foreign culture among the Menomini, and by Wallace (1952), who demonstrates how the Rorschach test can help in deriving a true modal personality type. All of these works pay little heed to childhood antecedents of adult personality traits thereby perhaps revealing their authors' sense of the difficulty into which extreme reliance on a psychogenetic approach had led anthropology.

We begin with the study of values. Research on values is not always equally concerned with studying personality. For example, Northrop's (1946) and Albert's (1956) interests hardly seem to be. But the Harvard Values Project has tended to keep its focus on individuals, and Clyde Kluckhohn (1954:691) said that the work of his colleagues is partly in the field of culture and personality.

Vogt's (1951) work among the Navaho is an example of the contribution that the values approach makes to understanding people. Some Navaho men who served in the U.S. Armed Forces significantly shifted their value orientations (*cf.* Florence Kluckhohn 1950), for example, dropping the Navaho view of man being subjugated to nature and adopting the position that man controls nature. Some veterans also adopted a future outlook in place of being primarily oriented to the present. All veterans, however, did not assimilate Euro-American values. Vogt shows that sociocultural variables, like disruption of a man's family of orientation as well as the size and structure of that family, are conditions which governed the veterans' acculturation. Large extended families, to take another specific instance, tended to conserve Navaho values, exerting a negative influence on assimilation. The individual's personality adjustment also governed his readiness to alter his values. Those Navahos who accepted white values tended to be characterized by stronger personal conflicts and insecurity.[4]

George Spindler's (1955) methodological innovation applied to the Menomini Indians on a Wisconsin reservation notably advanced the method that Hallowell pioneered when he compared personality adjustment between groups of Ojibwa Indians who had reached different degrees of acculturation. Like Hallowell, Spindler relied on the Rorschach test. To control degree of assimilation or type of acculturation he graded a sample of 68 male Indians (all at least half Indian in ancestry). At one extreme of his five-point continuum are the native-oriented population, people who obtain subsistence from wage work but also continue with hunting and fishing. They consciously maintain kinship ties and traditional ceremonies. All persons in this category speak Menomini. In character structure they show a passive but not hopeless orientation toward life unmarked by strong threat. This narrowly defined personality is hardly suited to competitive struggle or to the expression of aggression. They keep a damper on emotional expressiveness.

Next come the peyotists, members of the peyote ritual group who practice a ceremony that is not traditional and in which visions are a key feature. They are people over whom the old culture maintains a substantial hold although they do not fully endorse its traditions. Characterologically they reveal a quality of hopeless, passive soul searching that expresses individual anxiety.

Then come the reservation's transitional people who have no overt ties with the old culture and have in considerable measure adopted the new way of life. On a deeper level, however, nostalgia for the past reveals itself even while they identify with Euro-American culture. Transitionalists are less passive and more aggressive than the native-oriented population. They

---

[4] For comparative material on values among five groups of people who live adjacent to one another, including the Navaho, see Vogt and Albert 1966.

do not deal with anxiety through hopeless soul searching. In them aggression sometimes takes explosive forms.

In fourth place are the lower-ranking, assimilated Indians who obtain their living from lumbering and belong to the Catholic Church. People on this level of assimilation are no longer passively oriented but the character structure is deeply disturbed.

Most assimilated are the elite-assimilated Menomini, Spindler's fifth category of reservation people. The men hold supervisory jobs in lumbering and other fields and also belong to the Catholic Church. Personality reveals a quality of ready emotionality. There are no signs of disturbance as in the previous group and little evidence of passivity.

Spindler's study is notable for several things. It confirms and amplifies the thesis that acculturation has been detrimental for some American Indians. Instead of speaking globally of all Menomini men, it divides the population into categories based on degree of assimilation and demonstrates meaningful psychological differences between the categories. This represents a degree of refinement in culture and personality research. Principally, Spindler's work is meritorious for its precision and objectivity, qualities it has not been possible to demonstrate adequately in this small summary. The almost complete reliance on the Rorschach test is unfortunate in one respect. Good clinicians do not rely exclusively on one test. There are characteristics of behavior that the Rorschach cannot pick up but which a sensitive observer could bring out. The loss in objectivity would to my way of thinking be balanced by the enriched picture of personality produced.[5]

Anthony Wallace (1952) has demonstrated how the Rorschach test and appropriate statistical procedures allow a strictly modal-personality type to be contructed. The term "modal personality," of course, was used before Wallace but there is a substantial difference between usages. The usual constructs of so-called modal personality (for example, by Honigmann 1949; DuBois 1944) or of what Kardiner calls "basic personality" are really ideal types and not constellations of traits most frequently (modally) appearing together in a community (*cf.* Aberle 1954:669). Among the New York State Tuscarora Indians Wallace deals with true modal types. Without going into details of his method (for a summary see Honigmann 1967:118–119) let me hurry to his main results. He found that 26 out of his sample of 70 adult subjects fell into the modal class. This amounts to about one third of the Tuscarora whom he tested. An additional 16

---

[5] Louise Spindler (1962) in her work with Menomini women augmented use of the Rorschach with expressive autobiographical interviews designed to elicit values.

individuals came so close to the mode on the Rorschach items to which he paid special attention that they too could be described as belonging to the modal group. This procedure left him with 28 statistical "deviants," persons who fell within or close to the modal class on only a few Rorschach test items. Wallace now proceeded to treat the 26 Rorschach records of his modal class as if they belonged to a single individual's test protocol. He interpreted the psychological features of the group, some of which may sound familiar. " . . . one might describe the Tuscarora modal personality type as displaying: (1) on a basic but presumably largely unconscious level, a strong urge to be allowed to become passive and dependent; (2) a fear of rejection and punishment by the environment and by the self for these demands; (3) a compensatory drive to be hyper-independent, aggressive, self-sufficient; (4) an ultimate incapacity to feel, to adapt, to evaluate the environment realistically, and a concomitant dependence upon categories, stereotypes, and deductive logic" (Wallace 1952:75).

The noteworthy feature linking values research, use of the Rorschach test, and employment of statistics to formulate a modal personality lies in the way those developments contributed to forging a tradition in psychological anthropology. All three developments reduce subjectivity and heighten reliability — in the case of the Rorschach as far as test protocols, not interpretations, are concerned. George Spindler (1955:122–123) sharply separates his interpretation of Rorschach scores from the scored responses themselves which he analyzes statistically in order to formulate his conclusions. His first and main proof of personality differences existing between categories of people lies in the objective and statistically defensible test scores. Wallace's modal personality, too, is first constructed out of test scores; interpretation — to which the problem of validity attaches — comes as an apparently less important second step. While echoes of psychoanalytic preoccupation with covert processes remain in the three developments, each puts emphasis on highly specific, fully objective, observable empirical indicators whose strength, distribution, and interrelations in a population are accorded the highest importance. Interest in the Rorschach test and other projective tools would in a short time diminish in anthropology but insistence on dealing with clear-cut empirical data, regardless of the abstract underlying theoretical propositions guiding research, would remain.

Theory of Personality Resynthesis

As we come closer to the present it is hard to gauge the long-range significance of a given piece of work. But the good sense that Anthony F.

C. Wallace (1956a, 1956b) makes out of certain of the ethnohistorical data pertaining to North American Indian acculturation impresses many anthropologists. He introduces the concept of "revitalization" to designate the psychological processes that operate in persons during certain kinds of nativistic and messianic movements. Such movements he interprets in psychological terms. The sequence of a typical revitalization movement, according to Wallace, begins with a period of constantly mounting stress. Over the years people look for a way out, for some way to restore a more satisfactory culture. Some people "succeed" in effecting rather narrow-base, personal "solutions" for their stress through such behaviors as alcoholism or neurosis. War and changes in political leadership are also tried, and new economic doctrines are advanced, but generally without much success. At one point a prophetic leader appears. He announces a solution that came to him, perhaps from a divine source. At this point, assuming that the leader is indeed heeded, revitalization sets in as order is restored in the community's world of meanings. People become more satisfied and hopeful; the stressful conditions of their existence are alleviated, at least for a time. The prophet shows an intense concern for cultural reforms. The changes he prescribes range from minor ritual innovations to institutional rearrangements that add up to a substantially new culture. Wallace focuses on the prophet and tries to account dynamically for his behavior. Typically prophets are disturbed people exposed to intense personal and social stress. Wallace looks to the level of physiological functioning for much of the explanation of the prophets' personality resynthesis. When the prophet's stress reaches a critical point "the physiochemical milieu for resynthesis is automatically established." A convulsive effort to redesign his perception of the situation occurs and becomes the basis of his teaching. Of course, what message the prophet hears as he hallucinates and what lines of action he recommends cannot be explained physiologically. They depend on his prior experience and intelligence.

Wallace's work is notable for the way it fuses social and physiological levels of analysis. True he opens himself to the charge of being reductionistic, that is, of explaining phenomena on one level by phenomena belonging to another, but for some people such criticism carries little weight, provided that the explanation which is offered illuminates what is being studied. His explanation, of course, is hypothetical, and we may not know for a long time, if ever, whether physiochemical changes are indeed associated with prophetic inspiration.[6]

Eskimo Myths and Personality

The prevailing tendency in psychological anthropology, I said, is to observe with the aid of appropriate theory and clinical directness living people in their normal environment. But we also noted that Benedict, Goldfrank, Hallowell, and Wallace sometimes utilized published or historical data as a substitute for direct observation in fieldwork. Margaret Lantis (1953, 1959) demonstrates how clinical field techniques may be combined with published materials (some of which she collected and published herself) to learn about psychological processes. She uses Nunivak Eskimo myths for her purpose, justifying use of the rich mythology by saying that myths bring out people's objective view of reality and offer insight into their subjective perception of what that reality means to them. The sharing of myths in a community offers all members an opportunity to standardize their views of human behavior and the natural world. Myths, in other words, constitute an amalgamated body of science, philosophy, and religion through which people give structure to reality.

Elimination, sex, intercourse, and other bodily functions are referred to very casually in Nunivak Eskimo myths. Their relative de-emphasis may, of course, be due to repression, but such an interpretation is not confirmed by other evidence (for example, extant cultural patterns). Apart from sex, myths indicate that the relationship of men and women is quite a complex problem for the Eskimo. Men pursue in women an idealized mother image. Yet the terms in which the myths portray women suggest that men are often disappointed in their quest.

Nunivak Eskimo individuals seem to possess a firm idea of what they want to be and a clear image of the world in which they realistically strive to attain desired ends. The characters in the myths are persistent; usually they are cautious and judicious observers, rational beings, willing to admit defeat while at the same time trying to overcome it. They are responsible, diligent, and methodical beings who in most cases prove to be effective in their goal-oriented behavior. All these traits, says Lantis, indicate that the Eskimo himself has a "good orientation to reality." Yet, on the ego level of functioning the Eskimo personality, judging from the myths, is not quite

[6] For a related view of American Indians' response to Euro-American civilization see Voget (1956), though he does not write primarily from a psychological point of view.

what at first glance it seems to be. The readiness of the people in the stories to accede to others' desires and the tendency to be submissive suggest a restricted ego. Particulary does ego restriction reveal itself in the way the individual in myths is unable to be aggressive when he has to further his competitive ambition or satisfy some other desire. Toward some interpersonal problems the characters maintain a laissez-faire attitude; they are afraid of impinging on others and therefore restrict their own area of assertive activity. Close examination of the stories makes it clear that the characters obtain objectives not solely by their own efforts but also through magic. When a defense is needed against a feeling of inferiority or against real ineffectiveness in a tough stiuation, the people in the stories resort to supernatural power. In psychological terms, this suggests that the feeling of inadequacy that the Eskimo experiences in some situations motivates him to objectify his wishes and to rely on relatively passive forms of coping. Such a readiness to inhibit vigorous self-assertion may be acquired early in life, Lantis suggests, explaining that her evidence for this hunch comes not from the myths but from observation of child rearing among the Nunivak people. Submissiveness and only the gentlest signs of physical assertion suffice to bring the child satisfying rewards.

We have looked briefly at the id and ego, and now come to material from myths bearing on the superego level of the Eskimo personality. A strong superego is evident in phenomena such as repression, subconscious compulsion, and other defenses that appear in mythology. Furthermore, restraint on a person's physical drives is made into an acceptable positive value. Hostility is often expressed deviously, that is, by magical means, rather than through direct aggression. More clues to superego functioning come from examining the many emotional threats that confront the characters. One, especially, is significant: being bitten or eaten. Lantis finds an explanation for this anxiety in the guilt and fear of retaliation that Eskimo probably feel for killing and eating the soul-bearing animals on which their life depends. Lantis reasons cogently in order to support this interpretation:

> . . . these people who are among the world's most effective hunters, that is, among the greatest human predators against animals, feel continuous guilt for this very effectiveness and so must enter into the myriad small rituals, must observe the tabus, load themselves down with amulets, rush to confess what seem trivial offenses, practice the magic, in order to reduce their anxiety . . . The hunter must have sensed his own deep hostility against these creatures that so often eluded and frustrated him.

The myths reveal a large stock of defenses that presumably also operate in Eskimo personality, including wish fulfillment, avoidance, denial of reality, projection, rejection, displacement, undoing, and others. Yet, in her final assessment, Lantis finds this personality not to be a morbid one. Destructive forces in the myths are after all combated successfully. The death of a protagonist is rare and so, too, are unhappy endings. The myths show "an objective and effective people, much too busy meeting the world to think about the emotional conflicts within themselves."

Lantis reports a brief analysis of thirty-two Rorschach records from Nunivak Eskimo men and women that at many points corroborates interpretations derived from the myths. Subjects who took the Rorschach are shown to be of "high average" intelligence and given to careful, meticulous observation, almost to the point of compulsiveness. They reveal high energy, persistence, and extroversion. There is a manifest tendency to conform but no direct evidence of submissiveness. The subjects are preoccupied with sex but without conflict or guilt (preoccupation seems to be concentrated in the Rorschach records of adolescents). The test records reveal signs of frustrated aggression, dependence, and oral aggression (for example, revealed by biting and eating). Repression, too, is shown to be a fairly common defense. Lantis's work, unusual for the systematic way it combines published and clinical material, is further noteworthy because it is one of the few apparaisals we have of Eskimo social personality.[7]

Researching Deviance

American Indian studies have naturally been affected by anthropology's preoccupation with adaptive difficulties signalled, for example, by anxiety, by other morbid personality states, and by deviant behavior, especially as it involves use of alcohol. A number of tribes have encountered serious problems through heavy drinking, but reasons why Indians often find it hard to confine drinking within limits of moderation remain elusive. For the Kaska (Honigmann and Honigmann 1945) I tried to treat even excessive and reckless use of alcohol relativistically, that is, to see it as a normal culture pattern for the Kaska which if it gave them trouble did so in about the same way that automobiles cost lives and maim people in our communities. Such relativistic conceptions are no longer acceptable in anthropology which, following the example of psychiatry and medicine, applies universal standards in determining what is deviant. Writing on

[7] For personality interpretations of other Eskimo groups see Honigmann and Honigmann 1959, 1965 and Ferguson 1962.

alcohol among Northwest Coast Indians, Edwin M. Lemert (1954:381) struck an interesting note when he branded as spurious the idea that alcohol can promote social integration when it does so at the cost of considerable guilt to the individual, particularly where the culture provides no effective way for expiating the guilt. However, when the potential consequence of drunkenness is shame, then the integration promoted by alcohol need not be held spurious. In shame-oriented cultures people will be able pragmatically to write off shame that accumulates from the consequences of drinking. The distinction between shame and guilt cultures has not held up well enough to satisfy anthropologists, but the distinction between two outcomes of drunken behavior possesses merit quite apart from whether or not there are two comparatively independent modes of personal control. Lemert recognizes that drunkenness on the Northwest Coast carries dysfunctional consequences but notes that some Indian groups have built "normal" social roles around the legal and illegal use of alcohol, roles by which they assert Indian identity in society. I believe that endowing a style of alcohol use with identificatory meaning and weaving the heavy use of alcohol firmly into the culture pattern — as indeed the Kaska also did — are not uncommon among present-day U.S. and Canadian Indians and Eskimo (Honigmann and Honigmann 1968).

Studies of excessive drinking and other deviance appear in *Society, Personality, and Deviant Behavior,* by an interdisciplinary team in which Theodore D. Graves represents anthropology (Jessor *et al.* 1968; Graves 1967). The team worked in a small tri-ethnic community of southwestern Colorado that included an Indian reservation. The principal research tool was a field theory which, as the name implies, traces behavior not solely to personality or external situational variables but to the joint action of both. The community comprised in addition to 20 percent Indians, 46 percent Anglo Americans and 34 percent Spanish Americans. Information gained about Indians receives heightened significance through being compared to similar information about the other two ethnic groups. The method of data collection was exceptional for anthropology (though it would be considered commonplace in sociology). The chief field technique consisted of interviewing a stratified random sample of informants with schedules, the questions of which were deductive, based on the guiding theory. This theory prescribed what the investigators must know if they were to be able to explain the circumstances under which deviance occurs. In a manner of speaking, the researchers already knew the explanation of deviance before they started research, thanks to accumulated knowledge in other social sciences. Consequently their data served primarily to test the theory. However to the degree that empirical data supported the theory, our understanding of behavior would be advanced, and this actually is what the tri-ethnic study accomplished. Deliberately the authors expose their mammoth underpinning of theory so that the reader may know the rationale of the research and of the measures devised and built into the interview schedules. Only by knowing the theory, to which I come in a moment, can we understand the point of a specific question like this: "Think about your family for a minute. How sure do you feel that things can work out the way you want them as far as your family or family life is concerned? (3) very sure (2) pretty sure (1) not too sure (0) not sure at all." Several similar questions also sought to measure how strongly persons expect to realize certain important goals in life. Parenthetical weights attached to possible answers indicate that responses will be scored, each interviewee receiving an "expectation score" based on all questions bearing on the same theme.

Deviant behavior is identified by the fact that it departs from shared norms and expectations and in doing so is likely to evoke a corrective social response from the community — not merely the ethnic group — wherein it occurs. This definition implies that no discrepancy exists between what is wrong according to the norms of Indians, say, and the norms of Anglo Americans, though the ethnic groups may indeed differ in their readiness to conform to the norms they presumably share. The assumption of shared norms has proven to be useful in studying stratified communities but I think it remains debatable. Insistence that all those who fail to acknowledge moral authority in the norms do in fact share them smacks of middle-class and perhaps white "imperialism." With that attitude we will fail to perceive when social norms are in process of being dumped by some members of the stratified society and rather than appraising such action as constructive, we will as long as possible assess it as purely destructive.

The authors visualize three "systems" jointly involved in producing deviant or conforming behavior: the sociocultural environment, the internalized personality, and the socialization process whereby what was initially "outside" the individual comes to influence what is "inside" the person. Direct training, parental beliefs and values, and behavioral models are instrumentalities through which socialization occurs in the family. I will limit my summary of the theory to how the sociocultural and personality systems lead an individual to deviant behavior.

Each of these systems contains component "structures" that bear somewhat formidable names. For example, the sociocultural system is differentiated into an opportunity, normative, and social control structure. The task of such names is to epitomize three key conditions that exist externally to an individual and affect his behavior. While they add to the jargon that a discipline carries and perhaps limit the number of people who will read a research report, they economically express a large amount of information that it would be wearisome to restate periodically in more extensive form. To return to the theory, a person's simultaneous location in each of the three sociocultural structures accounts for his likelihood to engage in deviant behavior. Thus Indians, Anglos, and Spanish figuratively speaking stand at different points in the community's opportunity structure, meaning that each group has unequal access to legitimate channels for achieving goals valued in American culture. As elsewhere in American Indian and other societies, in this tri-ethnic community people of the lowest socioeconomic status have the poorest access to the good things of life (as defined by American culture). Hence, theory predicts, they will experience the strongest pressure toward deviance of any group in the opportunity structure. If their position in other structures and systems is equally unfavorable, then they will disproportionately often commit deviant acts as defined by the dominant members of society. Many ingenious means were used to ascertain individuals' locations in the opportunity and other structures. Indians occupy the most disadvantageous positions in nearly all structures, the Anglos the most advantageous, with the Spanish in between. But in terms of having access to culturally valued goals (as a result of age under 40, present job possessing higher status than father's job, and being "Old-Line Protestant" in religion — all considered to advantage people), Indians occupy a somewhat better location in the opportunity structure than the Spanish, though below that of Anglos. The tribal bureaucratic structure, the opportunities it offers for employment, leadership, and status, as well as per capita payments that augment Indian income are responsible for bolstering the Indian's economic resources and widening his opportunities for prestige. The Spanish lack such support which chiefly derives from the Indian's special status in American society and his membership in Indian reservations.

The opportunity structure operates in conjunction with the other structures in the sociocultural system. Individuals also have locations in the normative structure. That is, they differ in the extent to which they share norms and attach moral authority to norms that are supposed to govern the means used to attain culturally desirable goals. Anomie, a word that sums up normative dissension, is a cultural condition conducive to deviance because it encourages the choice of illicit means. Anomie is especially powerful in conjunction with a location in the opportunity structure where one lacks legitimate channels giving access to desirable goals. Under such circumstances, recourse to illegitimate means becomes easy.

Before reporting on the extent to which Indians, Spanish, and Anglos engage in deviant behavior, we have to examine the personality system that also helps to account for conformity or its lack. Personality includes, first, the individual's perception of his location in the opportunity structure; second, his personal beliefs about being able to influence his future through his own actions or, conversely, his belief that luck or fate determines what happens, and, finally, his conscience, tolerance for deviance, and expectation that he will be punished if he acts deviantly. Using the authors' terms, the personality system contains a perceived opportunity, a personal belief, and a personal control structure. In each of these structures individuals and groups have different locations, some locations being more likely than others to foster deviance. For example, when a gap exists between a goal that an individual values and his expectation of being able to reach it, a condition is created that favors the selection of deviant means of overcoming the disjunction. The Indians and Spanish are similar in the wide disjunction they report between their goals and expectations. The three ethnic groups differ little in the degree to which they believe a person can influence the outcomes of behavior — none is heavily fatalistic, but a strong contrast shows up between the Indian adults and members of the other ethnic groups with regard to tolerance of deviant behavior. Indians are far more permissive than the Spanish or Anglos.

Generally the Anglos have the greatest perception of opportunity; they are also the least alienated in their personal beliefs, that is, least beset by feelings of powerlessness over their lives, and they have the strongest internalized personal controls governing behavior. Indians tend to hold the most deviance-prone position in the three structures of the personality system, and the Spanish are in between, though not consistently so. Two independent studies, one dealing with a sample of over two hundred adults and the other with one hundred percent of the adolescents of high school age, give closely similar results with regard to locations of the three ethnic groups in the personality and sociocultural systems.

When the three groups are compared with the aid of several measures of deviance, including excessive use of alcohol, the prediction that Indians will be most deviant is fulfilled. A higher percentage of Indians occurs on every one of nine criteria of deviance; the Spanish are between the other two groups but closer to Indians than to Anglos. In one test the researchers split the adults of their sample into a deviant and nondeviant group. An individual was put into the former category if he reported when interviewed that he had been drunk 15 or more times during the previous yeaı, that he had encountered drinking-related problem behavior, or that he had engaged in at least one instance of serious other deviance. The investigators also searched court records, and any instance of a conviction during the previous ten years sufficed to put an individual in the deviant category. Note that these patterns of behavior are regarded as deviant because the researchers and other members of the dominant portion of society believe they are. How, for example, the Indians conceive drunkenness or the role it plays in their lives makes no difference. By this test, 24 percent of the Anglos in the sample were classed as deviant, 30 percent of the Spanish, and 75 percent of the Indians. On a similar measure applied to high school students (using teacher and peer ratings, however, rather than self-reported deviance), 29 percent of the Anglos were grouped as deviant, 42 percent of the Spanish, and 45 percent of the Indians.

Results support the theory with which the authors began, though closer examination of the results might show that Indian adults differ more from the Spanish in rates of deviance than they differ from the latter in their locations within the personality and sociocultural systems. They seem to run a higher risk of deviance simply because they are Indians and not because they occupy a proportionately less advantaged position in society. Deviance, according to the theory, is explicable as not merely the outcome of specific environmental conditions that produce pressure to depart from norms. It is also produced by anomie, alienation, learning, and failure to endow deviant acts with danger or moral disapproval. Indians who are highly likely to behave deviantly in terms of norms held by the larger community are not only victims of social inequities but are agents who choose their own behavior on the basis of whatever information they possess. Whether the behavioral outcomes of such choice should always be called deviance simply because it contradicts communal norms, regardless of the role it may play in the Indian's scheme of things, is questionable. Unfortunately the study, although admitting that deviance may be functional, doesn't tell us what role the deviant behaviors play in Indian culture and personality.

Of several limitations that inhere in research of this type, the chief arises from the impersonal, nonnaturalistic[8] framework in which it is carried out and in which the people being studied must confine what they reveal of themselves. We get one glimpse of how individuals organize their beliefs, expectations, norms, and roles through the stark skeleton of the theory and the three structures that it imposes on Indians, Spanish, and Anglos alike. However since these structures are the same for everybody in the world, they possess no particular person-defining value as far as the Colorado Indians are concerned. We get another glimpse of personality through the long questions that cover certain situations in which people find themselves. But those questions were constructed by the university researchers; they don't reflect the subjects' phrasings of their lived experience. The subjects are forced to confine their answers to a few stated alternatives, the only kind of responses that the researchers, constrained by their schedules, are prepared to heed. The approach places minimal value on what life is like in the subjects' phenomenological experience, the kind of experience to which anthropology has usually given heavy emphasis. I make the same criticism of other recent nonnaturalistic approaches containing a psychological bent, formal semantic analysis (cf. Wallace 1965). When Indians are constrained to break experience into categories or ethnographers do so on the basis of components recognized in kin terms, the results are usually elegant tours de force and demonstrate impressive analytical skills. Nevertheless the very strengths of the methods entail an ineradicable limitation, for precision means that the practitioner must sacrifice many features looming large in his informants' experience that he isn't prepared to hear about.

General Assessment

U.S. anthropologists working in their own back yards have done practically all the psychological anthropology that deals with North American Indians (and, for that matter, with Latin American Indians as well). The researchers have worked with a variety of theories, approaches, and techniques. Like any vigorous, growing discipline anthropology

[8] The term "naturalism" is used by sociologists to describe "an insistence upon concreteness and dense and detailed description: disposition to depict subject matter in its own terms" (Lofland 1967:46). By this definition anthropology is frequently naturalistic in its treatment of culture and personality and so are authors like Emile Zola and John O'Hara.

encourages methodological innovation and experimentation in an effort to achieve more satisfactory work. The investigators have primarily been seeking more objective data and more acceptable conclusions. Inevitably, new departures that carry advantages for their enthusiastic practitioners usually alarm other members of the profession who can't reconcile themselves to the unavoidable disadvantages that follow. The social sciences find it hard to achieve consensus regarding what type of work is most satisfactory.

Almost forty years of field work gave time to try many approaches, but they have scarcely been sufficient (considering the available manpower) to investigate more than a small fraction of the indigenous New World population. A few culture areas are well represented in culture and personality literature but for many our knowledge is spotty indeed. The Southwest has been well studied, but all tribes have not received the same amount of attention (Kluckhohn 1954:689). People like the Navaho and Hopi have been repeatedly visited and are our best laboratories for future problem-oriented research. Considerably less thoroughly studied in the Southwest are groups like the Papago and Apache. California, the Great Basin, Plateau, and North Pacific Coast have been briefly sampled but only exceptionally by more than one field worker. Enough work has been done on the Plains for Gladwin (1957) to suggest that the cultural unity of the area may not be accompanied by much homogeneity of basic personality. Ethnohistorical data pertaining to New York State Iroquois Indians have been intensively utilized for research and anthropologists have also looked at the Iroquoian-speaking Cherokee Indians of North Carolina (Gulick 1960:Ch. 8–9; Holzinger 1961). In the far North the situation is striking: a number of excellent Algonkian studies (mostly of Ojibwa-Chippewa communties), one detailed Athapaskan monograph, and, apart from Lantis's work, little concerning the popular Eskimo. For Latin America the total picture is far more spotty.

Just as culture areas have been spottily covered and with varying degrees of intensity so methodology has been divergent from one group to another. If we are really to compare the Navaho, Hopi, and Ojibwa, don't we have to do among the Hopi and Ojibwa what has been done among the Navaho and apply to the Navaho some of the questions asked in the other groups? Against this suggestion runs the preference to approach each new piece of work with a fresh mind (Mead and Wolfenstein 1955:5). This brings up the value of revisits, preferably by different anthropologists, to communities that were studied some time ago. Indications are that tremendous theoretical advances will come in anthropology when research workers with different methods and approaches or at any rate a healthy skepticism concerning some of their predecessors' findings, systematically re-examine already studied communities.

Having complained about spotty coverage in North America, let us admit that we know enough to begin to develop wider generalizations and comparisons (*cf.* Kluckhohn 1954:693). A number of reports, for example, suggest quite convincingly that a high degree of psychological homogeneity characterizes the American Indian. A portion of the available data has been assembled by George D. and Louise S. Spindler (1957). The psychological features which they discovered to be most widely exhibited among Indians are: "nondemonstrative emotionality and reserve" accompanied by a high degree of control over in-group aggression; autonomy of the individual; ability to stoically endure deprivation and frustration; high value on bravery; "a generalized fear of the world as dangerous"; a proclivity for practical joking; "attention to the concrete realities of the present" (in Rorschach argot, the large D approach), and dependence on supernatural power that one strives purposefully to obtain. The picture of homogeneity is even more clear cut if we limit ourselves to northern forest people, Algonkians and Athapaskans. Emotional restraint, for example, appears to be a highly reliable characterization of these Indians. Other common traits include a high value placed on deference in interpersonal relationships, personal resourcefulness, and individualism. People do not attempt to tell others what to do. Authoritarian attitudes and leadership behavior are suppressed.

Another line of constructive synthesis for which the cross-cultural method is best suited is to relate particular personality syndromes to technology, social structure, and other segments of cuture. Hallowell and I have suggested a relationship between the relatively atomistic social systems of northern hunters and their personality. He also perceives consistency between the inhibition of overt aggression and use of sorcery. Laura Thompson (1948) relates Indian world-views to bases of subsistence. In the hunting world-view, man conceives of himself as a helpless supplicant for power on which he depends for success. It comes to him from a universal power pool through disparate nonhuman entities, chiefly animals, whom he obtains as personal guardians. This world-view persists even among agriculturalists in North America but there it is altered. Where people develop a more systematic control of the food supply, they no longer conceive of themselves as helpless supplicants of power which derives from disparate power sources. They become power entities in their own right and the power source also becomes more clearly structured.

Not many years ago some anthropologists wrote off psychological anthropology as dead or at least moribund. Research (though not teaching) interest in the relations of culture and personality diminished considerably between 1950 and 1960. Since then, however, a fresh wave of interest came about accompanying the rapid expansion of American anthropology during the past decade. Regular reviews of the literature attest to a vigorous lease on life.[9] The nature of research has changed from what it was in the thirties and forties; for example, hardly ever do we see reports concerned with the "personality of the so-and-so." Instead psychological concepts and personality mechanisms are isolated with the purpose of explicating the motivational and cognitive sources of religion, culture change, deviance, and other topics (Honigmann 1969). Or else the impacts of cultural phenomena and adaptive stress are traced in personality. Occasionally the cross-cultural method is employed to secure general knowledge. The words "psychological" or "personality" may not appear in the titles of such research, but the point of view is psychologically informed. Psychological concepts and associated theory are used eclectically. Objectivity is maintained by clearly specifying empirical correlates of covert psychological states, thereby making as public as possible the data of analysis, as well as by faithfully reporting the reasoning through which conclusions are reached. Aesthetic elements — meaning the investigator's opinions and feelings about the people, culture, and behavior he is studying, his view, admittedly hard to document and hard to teach, of the meaning their life holds for them and us, the culture's satisfyingness or its traps — find little or no place in most modern anthropological accounts of culture and personality. An aesthetic approach as conspicuous, say, as appears in *Patterns of Culture* or Erikson's (1963:Ch. 3–4) accounts of the Sioux and Yurok (I refer not to the psychological theory he employs but to the fruits of his theoretically informed experience with those cultures) would be regarded as improper by many, no doubt in part because of the controversy such perspectives unleash. Yet some writers who maintain admirable levels of empirical analysis and manage to suppress sensitivity (except when it is aroused by the elegance or disappointing imprecision of their techniques), apologize for omitting a humanistic dimension. The final word in *Society, Personality, and Deviant Behavior* (Jessor *et al.* 1968:420–421) explains that "the path we chose to follow was an abstract one. . . . and the data generated have given us a beginning sense of understanding." But, the authors admit, "Our work has captured, obviously, neither the quality of daily life nor the succession of events which pattern the course of life in the community; that task belongs to the sensitive ethnographer." In how many graduate departments, one wonders, is sensitive ethnography being encouraged in those students who show corresponding talent and inclination.

[9] Such reviews appear in the *Biennial Review of Anthropology* edited by Bernard Siegel.

BIBLIOGRAPHY

ABERLE, D. F. 1954. Comments. *In* Southwestern studies of culture and personality, by Clyde Kluckhohn. American Anthropologist 56:697–700.

ALBERT, E. M. 1956. The classification of values: a method and illustration. American Anthropologist 58:221–248.

BARNOUW, V. 1950. Acculturation and personality among the Wisconsin Chippewa. Memoirs of the American Anthropological Association No. 72.

———. 1963. Culture and personality. Homewood, Ill., The Dorsey Press.

BENEDICT, R. 1928. Psychological types in the cultures of the southwest. Proceedings of the International Congress of Americanists 23:572–581.

———. 1932. Configurations of culture in North America. American Anthropologist 34:1–27.

———. 1934. Patterns of culture. Boston, Houghton Mifflin Co.

BENNETT, J. 1946. The interpretation of Pueblo culture: a question of values. Southwestern Journal of Anthropology 2:361–374.

BILLIG, O., J. GILLIN, AND W. DAVIDSON. 1947–48. Aspects of personality and culture in a Guatemalan community: ethnological and Rorschach approaches. Journal of Personality 16:153–187, 326–368.

BOGGS, S. T. 1956. An interactional study of Ojibwa socialization. American Sociological Review 21:191–198.

———. 1958. Culture change and the personality of Ojibwa children. American Anthropologist 60:47–58.

CAUDILL, W. A. 1949. Psychological characteristics of acculturated Wisconsin Ojibwa children. American Anthropologist 51:409–427.

CHAPIN, F. S. 1947. Experimental designs in sociological research. New York, Harper & Bros.

CODERE, H. 1956. The amiable side of Kwakiutl life: the potlatch and the play potlatch. American Anthropologist 58:334–351.

DEVEREUX, G. 1951. Reality and dream: psychotherapy of a Plains Indian. New York, International Universities Press.

DU BOIS, C. 1944. The people of Alor. Minneapolis, University of Minnesota Press.

DYK, W. 1938. Son of Old Man Hat. New York, Harcourt, Brace & Co.

ERIKSON, E. H. 1939. Observations on Sioux education. Journal of Psychology 7:101–156.

――――. 1963. Childhood and society. Second edition. New York: W. W. Norton.

FARBER, M. L. 1950. The problem of national character: a methodological analysis. Journal of Psychology 30:307–316.

FERGUSON, F. N. 1962. Great Whale River Eskimo personality as revealed by Rorschach protocols. *In* Social networks in Great Whale River, by John J. Honigmann. National Museum of Canada, Bulletin 178.

FORD, C. S. 1941. Smoke from their fires. New Haven, Yale University Press.

FRENCH, C. L. 1967. Social class and motivation among Metis, Indians, and Whites in Alberta. *In* A. K. Davis, ed., A northern dilemma. Two volumes. Bellingham, Wash., Western Washington State College.

FRIEDL, E. 1956. Persistence in Chippewa culture and personality. American Anthropologist 58:814–825.

GILLIN, J. 1951. The culture of security in San Carlos. Middle American Research Institute, Publication 16.

GJESSING, G. 1968. Comment. Current Anthropology, 9:427–428.

GLADWIN, T. 1957. Personality structure in the Plains. Anthropological Quarterly 30:111–124.

GOLDFRANK, E. S. 1943. Historic change and social character: a study of the Teton Dakota. American Anthropologist 45:67–83.

――――. 1945. Socialization, personality, and the structure of the Pueblo society (with particular reference to Hopi and Zuni). American Anthropologist 47:516–539.

GOLDMAN, I. 1950. Psychiatric interpretation of Russian history: a reply to Geoffrey Gorer. The American Slavic and East European Review 9:151–161.

GRAVES, T. D. 1967. Acculturation, access, and alcohol in a tri-ethnic community. American Anthropologist 69:306–321.

GULICK, J. 1960. Cherokees at the crossroads. Chapel Hill, Institute for Research in Social Science, University of North Carolina.

HALLOWELL, A. I. 1936. Psychic stresses and cultural patterns. American Journal of Psychiatry. 92:1291–1310.

――――. 1937. Temporal orientation in western civilization and in a preliterate society. American Anthropologist 39:647–670.

————. 1942. Acculturation processes and personality changes as indicated by the Rorschach technique. Rorschach Research Exchange 6:42–50.

————. 1946. Some psychological characteristics of the northeastern Indians. *In* Man in northeastern North America, F. Johnson, ed. Papers of the Robert S. Peabody Foundation for Archaeology, 3.

————. 1951. The use of projective techniques in the study of the socio-psychological aspects of acculturation. Journal of Projective Techniques 15:27–44.

————. 1952. Ojibwa personality and acculturation. *In* Acculturation in the Americas, proceedings and selected papers of the XXIXth International Congress of Americanists, Sol Tax, ed. Chicago, University of Chicago Press.

HARING, D. G. (ED.). 1948. Personal character and cultural milieu. Syracuse, University of Syracuse Press.

HAVIGHURST, R. J. AND B. L. NEUGARTEN. 1955. American Indian and white children: a sociopsychological investigation. Chicago, University of Chicago Press.

HOLMBERG, A. R. 1950. Nomads of the long bow. The Siriono of Eastern Bolivia. Smithsonian Institution, Institute of Social Anthropology, Publication No. 10.

HOLZINGER, C. H. 1961. Some observations on the persistence of aboriginal Cherokee personality traits. *In* Symposium on Cherokee and Iroquois culture, W. N. Fenton and J. Gulick, eds. Bureau of American Ethnology, Bulletin 180.

HONIGMANN, J. 1949. Culture and ethos of Kaska society. Yale University Publications in Anthropology, No. 40.

————. 1954. Culture and personality. New York, Harper & Row.

————. 1963. Understanding culture. New York, Harper & Row.

————. 1967. Personality in culture. New York, Harper & Row.

————. 1968. The study of personality in primitive societies. *In* The study of personality: an interdisciplinary appraisal. E. Norbeck, D. Price-Williams, and W. M. McCord, eds. New York, Holt, Rinehart & Winston.

————. 1969. Psychological anthropology. Annals of the American Academy of Political and Social Science 383:145–158.

HONIGMANN, J. J. AND I. HONIGMANN. 1945. Drinking in an Indian-White community. Quarterly Journal of Studies on Alcohol 5:575–619.

————. 1959. Notes on Great Whale River ethos. Anthropologica n.s. 1:106–121,

————. 1965. Eskimo townsmen. Ottawa, Canadian Research Centre for Anthropology, University of St. Paul.

————. 1968. Alcohol in a Canadian northern town. Paper prepared for the 1968 meeting of the Canadian Sociology and Anthropology Association.

162   *Area*

HORNEY, K. 1939. New ways in psychoanalysis. New York, W. W. Norton & Co., Inc.

————. 1945. Our inner conflicts. New York, W. W. Norton & Co., Inc.

INKELES, A., E. HANFMANN, AND H. BEIER. 1958. Modal personality and adjustment to the Soviet socio-political system. Human Relations 11:3–22.

INKELES, A. AND D. J. LEVINSON. 1954. National character: the study of modal personality and sociocultural systems. *In* Handbook of social psychology, G. Lindzey, ed. Two volumes. Cambridge, Mass., Addison-Wesley Publishing Co.

JAMES, B. 1961. Social-psychological dimensions of Ojibwa acculturation. American Anthropologist 63:721–746.

JESSOR, R., T. D. GRAVES, C. HANSON, AND L. JESSOR. 1968. Society, personality, and deviant behavior. New York, Holt, Rhinehart, & Winston.

JOSEPH, A., R. B. SPICER, AND J. CHESKY. 1949. The desert people: a study of the Papago Indians of southern Arizona. Chicago, University of Chicago Press.

KARDINER, A. 1939. The individual and his society. New York, Columbia University Press.

————. 1945. The psychological frontiers of society. New York, Columbia University Press.

KLUCKHOHN, C. 1944. The influence of psychiatry on anthropology in America during the last 100 years. *In* One hundred years of American psychiatry, J. K. Hall, G. Zilboorg, H. A. Bunker, eds. New York, Columbia University Press.

————. 1945. The personal document in anthropological science. *In* The use of personal documents in history, anthropology and sociology, L. Gottschalk, C. Kluckhohn, and R. Angell, eds. Social Science Research Council Bulletin 53.

————. 1951. A comparative study of values in five cultures. *In* Navaho veterans: a study of changing values, by E. Z. Vogt. Papers of the Peabody Museum of American Archaeology and Ethnology, Vol. 41, No. 1.

————. 1954. Southwestern studies of culture and personality. American Anthropologist 56:685–697.

KLUCKHOHN, C. AND D. LEIGHTON. 1946. The Navaho. Cambridge, Harvard University Press.

KLUCKHOHN, C. AND H. A. MURRAY (EDS.). 1948. Personality in nature, society, and culture. New York, Henry A. Knopf.

KLUCKHOHN, F. 1950. Dominant and substitute profiles of cultural orientations. Social Forces 28:376–393.

KROEBER, A. L. 1948. Anthropology, New York, Harcourt, Brace and Co.

LANDES, R. 1937. The personality of the Ojibwa. Character and Personality 6:51–60.

————. 1938a. The abnormal among the Ojibwa Indians. Journal of Abnormal and Social Psychology 33:14–33.

———. 1938b. The Ojibwa woman. Columbia University Publications in Anthropology, No. 31.

LANTIS, M. 1953. Nunivak Eskimo personality as revealed in the mythology. Anthropological papers of the University of Alaska 2:109–174.

———. 1959. Alaskan Eskimo cultural values. Polar Notes 1:35–48.

LEIGHTON, A. H. AND D. C. LEIGHTON. 1949. Gregorio, the hand-trembler: a psychobiological personality study of a Navaho Indian. Papers of the Peabody Museum of American Archaeology and Ethnology, Vol. 40, No. 1.

LEIGHTON, D. C. AND J. ADAIR. 1966. People of the Middle Place. New Haven, Behavior Science Monographs.

LEIGHTON, D. C. AND C. KLUCKHOHN. 1947. Children of the people. Cambridge, Harvard University Press.

LEMERT, E. M. 1954. Alcohol and the Northwest Coast Indians. University of California Publications in Culture and Society 2:303–406.

LEWIS, O. 1951. Life in a Mexican village: Tepoztlan restudied. Urbana, University of Illinois Press.

———. 1959. Five families: Mexican case studies in the culture of poverty. New York, Basic Books, Inc.

———. 1961. The children of Sanchez. New York, Random House.

LINDESMITH, A. R. AND A. L. STRAUSS. 1950. Critique of culture-personality writings. American Sociological Review 15:587–600.

LOFLAND, J. 1967. Notes on naturalism in sociology. Kansas Journal of Sociology, Vol. 3, No. 2, 45–61.

MACGREGOR, G. 1946. Warriors without weapons. Chicago, University of Chicago Press.

MASLOW, A. H. 1950. Self-actualizing people: a study of psychological health. Personality Symposium 1:11–34.

MEAD, M. 1928. Coming of age in Samoa. New York, William Morrow & Co.

———. 1956. New lives for old. New York, William Morrow & Co.

———. 1959. An anthropologist at work: writings of Ruth Benedict. Boston, Houghton Mifflin.

MEAD, M. AND M. WOLFENSTEIN (EDS.). 1955. Childhood in contemporary cultures. Chicago, University of Chicago Press.

MEGGERS, B. J. 1946. Recent trends in American ethnology: American Anthropologist 48:176–214.

NORTHROP, F. S. C. 1946. The meeting of east and west. New York, The Macmillan Co.

ORLANSKY, H. 1949. Infant care and personality. Psychological Bulletin 46:1–48.

RADIN, P. 1920. The autobiography of a Winnebago Indian. University of California Publications in American Archaeology and Ethnology 16:381–473.

ROHEIM, G. 1950. Psychoanalysis and anthropology. New York, International Universities Press.

SAPIR, E. 1924. Culture, genuine and spurious. American Journal of Sociology 29:401–429.

———. 1932. Cultural anthropology and psychiatry. Journal of Abnormal and Social Psychology 27:229–242.

SIMMONS, L. (ED.). 1942. Sun Chief, the autobiography of a Hopi Indian. New Haven, Yale University Press.

SPENGLER, O. 1926. The decline of the west. Two volumes. New York, Alfred A. Knopf.

SPINDLER, G. D. 1952. Personality and peyotism in Menomini Indian acculturation. Psychiatry 15:151–160.

———. 1955. Sociocultural and psychological processes in Menomini acculturation. University of California Publications in Culture and Society, No. 5.

SPINDLER, G. D. AND L. S. SPINDLER. 1957. American Indian personality types and their sociocultural roots. Annals of the American Academy of Political and Social Science 311:147–157.

SPINDLER, L. S. 1962. Menomini women and culture change. Memoirs of the American Anthropological Association, No. 91.

THOMPSON, L. 1948. Attitudes and acculturation. American Anthropologist 50:200–215.

———. 1950. Culture in crisis. New York, Harper & Row.

———. 1951. Personality and government. Mexico, D.F., Ediciones del Instituto Indigenista Interamericano.

THOMPSON, L. AND A. JOSEPH. 1944. The Hopi way. Chicago, University of Chicago Press.

TSCHOPIK, H., JR. 1951. The Aymara of Chucuito, Peru. 1. Magic. Anthropological Papers of the American Museum of Natural History, Vol. 44, Pt. 2.

UNDERWOOD, F. AND I. HONIGMANN. 1947. A comparison of socialization and personality in two simple societies. American Anthropologist 49:557–577.

VOGET, F. W. 1956. The American Indian in transition: reformation and accommodation. American Anthropologist 58:249–263.

VOGT, E. Z. 1951. Navaho veterans: a study of changing values. Papers of the Peabody Museum of American Archaeology and Ethnology, Vol. 41, No. 1.

VOGT, E. Z., AND E. M. ALBERT. 1966. People of Rimrock. Cambridge, Harvard University Press.

WALLACE, A. F. C. 1952. The modal personality structure of the Tuscarora Indians as revealed by the Rorschach test. Bureau of American Ethnology, Bulletin 150.

————. 1956a. Mazeway resynthesis: a biocultural theory of religious inspiration. Transactions of the New York Academy of Sciences n.s. 18:626–638.

————. 1956b. Revitalization movements: some theoretical considerations for their comparative study. American Anthropologist 58:264–281.

————. 1959. The institutionalization of cathartic and control strategies in Iroquois religious psychotherapy. *In* Culture and mental health, M. K. Opler, ed. New York, The Macmillan Co.

————. 1961. Culture and personality. New York, Random House.

————. 1965. The problem of the psychological validity of componential analysis. *In* Formal semantic analysis, E . A. Hammel, ed. Special Publication of the American Anthropologist, Vol. 67, Pt. 2.

WEINBERG, S. K. 1958. Culture and personality. Washington, D.C., Annals of American Sociology, Public Affairs Press.

WHITING, J. W. M. AND I. L. CHILD. 1953. Child training and personality. New Haven, Yale University Press.

WITTHOFT, J. 1961. Eastern woodlands community typology and acculturation. *In* Symposium on Cherokee and Iroquois culture, W. N. Fenton and J. Gulick, Eds. Bureau of American Ethnology, Bulletin 180.

CHAPTER FOUR

Oceania

L. L. LANGNESS* and THOMAS GLADWIN

Introduction

Much of Oceania is comprised of small, tropical islands separated from adjacent land by wide, sometimes vast, stretches of ocean. Obvious exceptions are the great land mass of the Australian continent and the islands of New Guinea and New Zealand. Those who have worked on the smaller tropical islands have met inevitable limitations and challenges not encountered by those who have worked in New Guinea or New Zealand.

In all areas, however, severe limitations have been encountered due to the thinness of the archaeological record. This can be ascribed, in part, to the high rates of oxidation and biotic decay characteristic of warm climates, heavy rainfall, and proximity of the sea. In recent years there has been a substantial increase in archaeological research, particularly in Polynesia and Melanesia. There has also been an increase in studies of comparative linguistics and culture history in general, so that we now have

*The original version (1961) of this paper was prepared by Thomas Gladwin. The revision was prepared by L. L. Langness with the concurrence of Gladwin. Langness wishes to acknowledge the assistance of the Social Science Research Institute (NIMH Grant MH09243) and the East-West Center at the University of Hawaii in preparation of this paper.

the possibility of adding a crucial developmental perspective to what have heretofore been studies primarily of the here and now.

The islands of the Pacific provide the challenge of a nearly ideal research setting. The physical anthropologist can find a relatively stable, isolated, and homogenous breeding population on which to base his studies. Cultural homogeneity within an island can bring similar clarity to the study of social structure and cultural dynamics. Further, the small size and isolation of many island communities permit the detailed description of the totality of a finite population. Within a setting of this sort, it is often possible to define and examine *all* of the interpersonal and intergroup relationships which determine the relevant social environment of an individual.

Disregarding, for the moment, the large masses of New Zealand, Australia, and New Guinea, the ecology and basic economy of the smaller islands of Polynesia, Micronesia, and Melanesia have many common, almost uniform attributes. They are tropical, with abundant rainfall at least part of the year, and are favored with trade winds. In all three areas, there are islands which are clustered together and some which are widely scattered and isolated. There are flat, sandy coral islands or atolls ("low" islands), and steeper, usually larger, volcanic ("high") islands. On all of them the soil is relatively poor, favoring principal reliance on root and tree crops, and discouraging domestication of animals for meat. This leaves the ocean as a primary source of protein. Metal is generally lacking. While this is only a partial list of shared characteristics, it could be extended to include technology, health conditions, transportation, etc. On this common ecological base, one finds a wide range of social and political organizations, value systems, and personality types. A special opportunity thus exists for comparisons between one group and another, with a number of variables fairly well controlled.

Similar comparative studies are possible in the larger land areas as well. In the New Guinea Highlands, for example, it is possible to find ecologically and economically similar societies only a few miles apart, one of which has homosexuality and one of which does not; or societies which attribute all illness to ghosts while others attribute it only to sorcery; or where cannibalism was present in one valley and absent in the next, and so on. But the large land areas offer, in addition, the possibility of comparing roughly similar groups in different ecological settings. It is an ethnographic laboratory probably without peer.

Fruitful comparisons are also possible with respect to the responses of these various peoples to foreign, especially European, contact. Valentine (1963) has shown, for example, that although the circumstances of culture contact were roughly similar in Melanesia and in Polynesia-Micronesia, there were quite different native responses. Valentine's analysis does not deal directly with psychological variables but makes strong suggestions and opens the way for such comparisons. Clearly such things as cargo cults —a peculiar Melanesian response to contact—cannot be explained without a consideration of the psychological factors involved, nor can the complex factors of prejudice and "blackbirding" (Oliver, 1961).

A more recent and specifically psychologically-oriented study tends to justify Valentine's earlier lumping together of Micronesia and Polynesia in this way. Levy, surveying the psychologically-oriented literature on Polynesia and Micronesia, reports a "striking picture of similarities in the [psychological] forms reported throughout the area, and of an apparent persistence in these forms throughout time" (1969:45). He recognizes, however, that "the reported similarities are partially a matter of simplicity of description" (1969:47) and that "the models of 'personality' or 'psychological structure' presented are really very simple ones ... and do not differentiate possible significant smaller classes which might be sensitive to the evident ecological, and culture-historical variables in the area" (1969:47). Oceania, just as it invites other comparative work, is also an unusually inviting area in which to make systematic, comparative studies of culture change, including its psychological dimensions.

In evaluating the work done to date in this area of the world, we must bear in mind the history of anthropological research in various parts of the Pacific as well as the multitude of environmental settings. It is legitimate to ask what real contributions to our understanding of personality (as well as of culture) have emerged from Oceania. We return to this question in the assessment and conclusions.

For convenience, we will review the literature for Melanesia, Micronesia, and Polynesia in that order. Australia is only incidentally included here and will be mentioned with Melanesia. This review cannot be taken as encyclopedic but deals, rather, with the major landmarks. The supporting bibliography is selective rather than complete.[1] Finally, we do not dwell upon those studies which, while developing data potentially useful

[1] For bibliographies of the area see Howard, Vinacke and Maretzki (1963) and Taylor (1965). There is also *An Ethnographic Bibliography of New Guinea* (1968) published by the Department of Anthropology and Sociology. Australian National University.

for the elucidation of personality dynamics, have not been developed in this way either by the authors or by others. The monograph of the Berndts (1951) on sexual behavior in Western Arnhem Land or Warner's *Black Civilization* (1937) would be cases in point.

Obviously, inclusion in this survey is based on the locus of field work, not on the nationality of the researcher. With the exception of Ernest Beaglehole of Victoria University and his students, and possibly some of the people at the University of Hawaii, none of the researchers discussed are residents of the area under consideration.

Melanesia

Melanesia can claim a twenty-year head start on the rest of the world in the history of psychological anthropology. It was the locus of the first systematic field work among non-European peoples designed to enrich the interpretation of ethnology by the insights of psychology. This was one of the explicit aims of A. C. Haddon in organizing the Cambridge Anthropological Expedition to the Torres Straits. The published report (Myers and McDougall, 1903) deals almost entirely with the sensory modalities and would not now be included within the purvey of culture and personality as the field has evolved. But its undeniable historical significance rests on the fact that Haddon sought, as collaborators, Rivers (who was himself trained in psychophysiology) and Seligman, two psychologists who were felt to be competent in the most fruitful procedures of the scientific psychology of the day. However, at the time the Torres Straits Expedition was in the field in 1898, Sigmund Freud was at work on the manuscript of *The Interpretation of Dreams*. It is an historical fact, but not necessarily a stroke of undiluted good fortune, that the study of culture and personality came to depend almost exclusively upon the line of inquiry being initiated sixty years ago by Freud rather than that envisioned by Haddon.

Certainly considerable credit for determining this trend is due to Géza Roheim, the most orthodox and loyal of Freudian psychoanalysts to concern himself with non-European personality. In 1913, Freud had completed his first major work on religion, *Totem and Taboo*. This drew heavily upon the ethnographic data on Australian aborigines assembled up to that time by such notables as Sir James G. Frazer and Robertson Smith. These data, like most ethnographic data of the period, were piecemeal and secondhand. They emphasized both totemism and primitiveness as characteristic of Australian aborigines. Freud used them to argue for an equation of tabooed-totem-animal with father, thus explaining the origin of religion in universal Oedipal conflict. Roheim, much to his credit, but also after having first published a book entitled *Australian Totemism: a Psychoanalytical Study in Anthropology* (1925), determined to see for himself. He undertook field studies in several parts of the world (Roheim, 1932), but spent the largest time with the Aranda of Central Australia, where he explored, at first hand, questions of totemism and conflict. Furthermore, because Malinowski had denied the existence of Oedipal conflicts in matrilineal societies (see below), Roheim also went to matrilineal Normandy Island near Malinowski's Trobriands, gathering evidence in an attempt to refute Malinowski (cf. Roheim, 1950). Although he was willing to test his beliefs under field conditions, Roheim's psychoanalytic excesses in attributing symbolic and historical significance to cultural facts eventually alienated his audience. In spite of his real contributions, and in spite of his acknowledged influence on many distinguished members of the profession, many anthropologists still find it difficult to take his work seriously (Lessa, 1956).

The first monograph which undertook to systematically examine a hypothesis of personality dynamics through the use of solid ethnographic data, and in accordance with acceptable standards of interpretation, was Bronislaw Malinowski's *Sex and Repression in Savage Society* (1927). Malinowski drew upon his extensive data from the Trobriand Islands to re-examine some aspects of *Totem and Taboo*. As noted above, he rejected the universality of the father-son Oedipal conflict, essentially on the ground that, in the Trobriands at least, discipline is in the hands of the mother's brother and not the father. He also discussed Freud's more anthropologically acceptable development of the psychological and social dynamics which support exogamy and the incest taboo. This excursion into psychoanalytic theory extablished a precedent for anthropologists — it was, in effect, the first anthropologically "respectable" substantive study in culture and personality. Malinowski, virtually ridiculed by Roheim and Ernest Jones, also became the first of many anthropologists to be criticized for a failure to understand the implications of psychoanalytic theory (cf. LaBarre, 1958).

Malinowski's theoretical position, based as it was on a system of primary, secondary and derived needs, however crude it may appear now, was an important development in anthropology and is much more in the tradition of psychological anthropology than the functionalism of A. R. Radcliffe-Brown. In addition, Malinowski's encyclopedic and highly literate ethnographic accounts of the Trobriander Islanders (1922, 1929,

1935) have also made important contributions to culture and personality studies through their use by others in developing new lines of analysis. As we shall note later, Kardiner started with these materials (as summarized by Du Bois) in developing his particular approach (Kardiner, 1939). More recently, Dorothy Lee (1950) made a valuable contribution to cognitive theory and psycholinguistics in her paper, "Lineal and Nonlineal Codifications of Reality," based entirely on Malinowski's published accounts of the Trobriands.

In 1929, Seligman made his unfortunate claim that "psychoses" did not occur among "primitives" living in their uncontacted environment. During the same decade, Margaret Mead came to the area — first to Samoa and then to New Guinea. She has continued her research to the present time. Her contribution to the psychological anthropology of Melanesia (and in general) has been enormous: her first monograph, on Manus, appeared in 1931, to be followed, in 1935, by a book describing and comparing personality in three contrasting New Guinea cultures — Arapesh, Mundugumor, and Tchambuli (the three monographs appeared together in 1939). Accompanying most of her books on personality were solid ethnographic works as well.

Reo Fortune's *Sorcerers of Dobu* appeared at this same time (1932). Fortune was trained as a psychologist and strongly influenced by Freud and W. H. R. Rivers, especially the latter's *Conflict and Dream* (1923). Before going to Dobu, a Melanesian island near the Trobriands, Fortune himself had published a book on dream interpretation, *The Mind in Sleep* (1927). In spite of this background, Fortune did not systematically address himself to personality as such, although he did pay consistent attention to psychologically relevant aspects of Dobuan culture. His psychodynamic orientation, and the influence of Mead on the work, made his work highly appropriate for use by Ruth Benedict in counterpoint to Zuni and Kwakiutl in *Patterns of Culture* (1934). It is, in fact, in the latter context that the Dobuans have become most widely publicized.

Gregory Bateson in *Naven* (1958), although well ahead of his time, did not attempt a full descriptive ethnography, concentrating instead on exploring the implications of several ceremonies, especially the *naven* ceremony, among the Iatmul of New Guinea. His analysis of these ceremonies led to the formulation of two important new constructs. One of these, *eidos,* will be discussed later in this chapter. The other is *schizmogenesis.* Schizmogenesis describes those forces in society which are centrifugal: that is, which increase the social distance between individuals or groups. Schizmogenesis can be complementary, as in dominance-submission relationships, or symmetrical, as in rivalry. The centrifugal effect of schizmogenesis derives both from social dynamics and from personality. Both of these factors are culturally determined. Marriage in Iatmul, for example, is socially defined as a dominance-submission relationship (complementary schizmogenesis). It also brings together two people with culturally-defined male and female personalities. Yet these marriages persist (sometimes) in spite of the forces which tend to drive the couple apart. However, where in Iatmul schizmogenic forces are strong enough to make any equilibrium precarious, a comparable analysis of Bali (Bateson, 1949) revealed that stabilizing forces are so effective that schizmogenic sequences can never get started. Bateson then became interested in those counterforces which keep centrifugal tendencies from going to the extreme of destroying all social relationships. This led him to seek controlling and stabilizing mechanisms which would return the social system to balance. In collaboration with a number of persons in various fields, he turned to theories of mechanics, physics, and mathematics, concerned with feedback and other mechanisms responsible for maintaining systems in a steady state of dynamic equilibrium. This field of inquiry is now referred to as cybernetics. The concept of schizmogenesis would also seem to be the precursor of the "double-bind" theory of schizophrenia, and led Bateson into the area of communications research in general. His collaboration with people in fields so exotic to anthropology seems to have created a lack of communication between Bateson and all but a handful of anthropologists. If this is true, it is unfortunate indeed. Anthropologists who are content merely to feed their cultural data into equations provided for them ready-made by personality psychologists can remain union members in good standing, but why should someone who reaches out to develop radically new equations of human behavior move beyond the pale of anthropological discourse?

Another "first" in the study of personality falls in the area of intelligence and cognition. In 1929, Stanley D. Porteus, a clinical psychologist trained in Australia but with most of his professional career in the United States, undertook field work with the Arunta in Central Australia, and more limited work in Northwest Australia (Porteus, 1931). He administered, primarily to children, a variety of intelligence and performance tests, principal among these being his own Maze Test. This test, as its name implies, consists of a series of mazes on paper which the subject is asked to trace. Porteus later did comparable work among the Bushmen of the

Kalahari Desert in South Africa (Porteus, 1937), and also extensively utilized the test in obtaining comparative data among the various ethnic groups available to him at the University of Hawaii. Of all the tests of mental ability thus far generally available for use in cross-cultural settings, there is some reason to feel that the Porteus Maze is the "fairest" in the sense that it appears to be the least strange and confusing to non-Europeans (cf. Masland, Sarason, and Gladwin, 1958).

As a result of this work, Porteus was able to formulate a formidable list of cautions to be observed by anyone attempting cross-cultural intelligence measurement; cautions which, despite later elaboration by Klineberg and others, were more often than not ignored. Porteus also devoted considerable thought to the nature of mental ability and its measurement. He concluded that any test designed to measure the kinds of mental ability valued in our culture would fail to tap those intellectual resources which would be useful to a person in another culture where the approach to thinking and problem solving might take different directions. This applies as much to the Maze as to any other test. However, he also made an important but usually overlooked distinction with respect to the purposes of measurement: if one is concerned with making comparisons between the essential intelligence of two groups in an absolute sense, a test built around the concepts of thinking taught in one culture cannot be used validly in another. But if one is interested in identifying those persons in another culture with the greatest potential for being trained to think in *our* way, for example in recruiting for schooling, a test devised for our culture might be useful. Furthermore, in the latter context, it becomes crucial to minimize the degree of strangeness which the test and the testing situation evoke among people who are unfamiliar both with the materials used and with the whole idea of a test. The Porteus Maze perhaps best meets this latter criterion. It would appear useful for anthropologists interested in cognitive development to explore whether this is really so and to develop further the potentialities of this approach. Thus far the Maze has received only passing attention from anthropologists.

Another study of significance identified with the 1930's was John W. M. Whiting's *Becoming a Kwoma* (1941). This came out of a ferment of interest at Yale in the anthropological implications of the theories of learning and behavior developed by Clark Hull and his students (cf. Miller and Dollard, 1941), based largely on learning experiments with rats. Whiting wrote a standard ethnography of the Kwoma, a mountain tribe in the Sepik River area of New Guinea, with considerable attention devoted to personality development. He then re-analysed his material in terms of drive, cue, response, and reward, as an exercise in the application of Hull's theory of learning to concrete ethnographic data. A brief example will suffice to illustrate the mode of analysis:

> In adolescence a boy learns to carry on secret love affairs with adolescent girls. The drives are sex, sex appetite, and anxiety (sex impels him to seek girls, sex appetite leads him to choose a girl culturally defined as attractive, and anxiety impels him to do so secretly); the response is the complex of behavior which leads to and includes sexual intercourse in the bush; the cues are the sight of an attractive girl, verbal permission from her, the environmental scene which has both public and secluded spots, etc.; the reward is sexual orgasm, satisfaction of sex appetite, and anxiety reduction. (pp. 176–177).

Whiting's literal application of Hull's concepts to the Kwoma study was so exhaustive, the exercise has not been repeated by others. It was, however, an instructive undertaking and undoubtedly contributed to the explicit and scrupulous approach to theory which has been characteristic of Whiting and his students. It also served to refine and make more effective the use of Hull's theory in culture and personality studies.

After this early period of relatively intensive work in psychological anthropology, there was an hiatus partly caused by World War II, and partly by the premature death of S. F. Nadel and the rise of a new generation (in the 1950's) of field workers with markedly different interests. Nadel was Professor of Anthropology at the Australian National University, and had also been trained as a psychologist. He attempted to start an ambitious program of research in New Guinea, including psychological testing, but the program was abandoned when he died.[2]

Nonetheless, there were studies done during the 1950's which deserve mention. K. E. Read, one of the first anthropologists in the New Guinea Highlands, although not working in the tradition of psychological anthropology, gave us some valuable psychological descriptions and insights (1952/53, 1954/55, 1959, 1965). The same is true of Marie Reay (1959). James B. Watson administered the first Thematic Apperception Tests in New Guinea in 1953, using a slightly modified version of the Murray. A survey of mental health (Sinclair, 1957) also was done during this period which, although quite inadequate, resulted in the appointment of a psychiatrist to the governmental administration of Melanesia, and thus

---

[2] We are indebted to Professors Ian Hogbin and James B. Watson for information on this period although we elected not to pursue it further here.

helped direct attention to problems of personality and culture as well as psychopathology (Burton-Bradley, 1967, 1968, 1969).

The 1960's witnessed an increase in the number of field workers visiting all parts of Melanesia. Many had specific interests in the psychological dimensions of culture. At least five investigators repeated the TAT series first used by Watson. Charles Valentine did a long paper on Lalakai ethnopsychology (1963); Leonard Glick published on cognition (1963, 1964, 1967); and Madeline Leininger did a comparison of personality in two different Gadsup villages (1966). Several investigators have published on disturbed behavior (Glick, 1968; Langness, 1965, 1967, 1969; Newman, 1964; Reay, 1960/61; and Salisbury, 1966, 1966a, 1967, 1969); and brief life history materials have been furnished by Watson (1960, 1967) and Glasse (1959). Mervyn Meggitt has published on dream interpretation (1962). Meggitt (1964) and Langness (1967a) have written on hostility and antagonism between the sexes, and a more recently published book on New Guinea marriage (Glasse and Meggitt, 1969) pursues this and related topics more fully. The limited work done on Melanesian religion (Lawrence and Meggitt, 1965; Newman, 1962, 1964a), and the more extensive work on cargo cults (Burridge, 1960, 1969; Lawrence, 1964; Worsley, 1957), also offer some psychological clues.

Thus while there has ben a long history of interest in psychological problems in Melanesia and, although during the 1940's and 1950's this interest slackened, it has been somewhat revived. As further published materials become available, it is quite likely they will be psychologically better informed.

Micronesia[3]

Micronesia is not represented in culture and personality research until the 1940's, but during this decade the Coordinated Investigation of Micronesian Anthropology (CIMA), sponsored by the Pacific Science Board of the National Research Council, put a large number of anthropologists (and related scientists) into the field. Among these were four persons primarily interested in the study of culture and personality: Joseph and Murray on Saipan, Spiro on Ifaluk, and Gladwin on Truk. In addition, Lessa on Ulithi, had a strong secondary interest in the field.

Alice Joseph and Veronica Murray (1951) undertook to see how much

[3] A very good survey of both Micronesia and Polynesia was done by Robert I. Levy in 1969. This section and the one to follow draw considerably on Levy's work. We take this opportunity to express our appreciation to him.

useful information could be derived from a relatively short study of Chamorro and Carolinian children (and a few adults) on Saipan. Although both are physicians, Joseph in particular was already well known to anthropologists for her work with the Hopi. In this study, primary reliance was placed on projective and performance tests administered to one hundred children of each of the two ethnic groups. The Bender-Gestalt test was interpreted by its author, Lauretta Bender. The Rorschach, Arthur Point Performance Scale II, and the Porteus Maze were treated exclusively by Joseph and Murray using conventional scoring and interpretive procedures. This study did not, therefore, make any new contributions to methodology, nor can it be said to have validated a field procedure for economical personality delineation. Numerous subsequent studies, in which ethnographic and projective interpretations have been compared for cross-validation, show the clear danger of accepting projective test results at face value. In fact, Joseph and Murray's own findings tend to confirm this danger. They conclude their discussion of the Rorschach results with the prediction that "either large scale antisocial behavior with unconscious self-destructive aims or death-like apathy might be expected from the younger generation" (p. 202). Bender found that the normal Saipanese Gestalt patterns corresponded to those found in confusional states elsewhere, and speculated whether "environmental influences can, in a people with strong primitive tendencies, produce a state of intellectual perplexity and disorientation which will manifest itself in a disturbance of Gestalt function similar to that produced by toxic influences" (p. 142). As of this writing, the children so delineated now range in age from 27 to 39 years and thus far show no external evidence of crippling psychopathology. It is quite plausible to conclude that differences in perceptual orientation and in style of cognitive thinking were responsible for the response patterns the authors found so bizarre. Certainly this possibility must be considered rather than merely accepting at face value conclusions based on interpretive criteria developed with European and American subjects.

Joseph and Murray made further contributions to the literature on non-western "psychotic" personalities, giving ten short summaries and a brief coverage of disorders of other kinds. Again, the unfortunate imposition of western nosological categories renders their account much less useful than it might have been.

The Truk study, undertaken by Gladwin and Seymour Sarason, a clinical psychologist (Gladwin and Sarason, 1953), was also intended to develop a relatively quick method of personality assessment, aided in this case by the presence of other anthropologists on the team who covered areas not directly relevant to personality development. The method was an evolution of that used by Du Bois (1944) on Alor. Rorschachs and TAT's were used in conjunction with life histories and dreams of 23 individuals selected to include both "average" and deviant persons. These data were combined with a standard ethnography. "Blind" interpretations of the Rorschachs and TAT's were undertaken by Sarason, using a clinical mode of interpretation rather than placing reliance, as is more customary in such studies, on scoring categories and frequencies. It was felt that a clinical interpretation, while admittedly more subjective, permitted fuller exploitation of the material produced by the subjects. This procedure also made possible explicit examination of the ways in which culturally determined perceptual modes affected the response pattern in all subjects, a factor which is obscured in interpretations based upon the scoring of responses. The interpetations in this study appeared to have considerable face validity. The methodology used here was perhaps more rigorous and self-conscious than that usually found in culture and personality studies — at least those which attempt to collate a variety of kinds of data. But very little in this monograph was new methodologically or theoretically. Subsequently, some of these data were re-analysed in an attempt to define the cognitive structure of Trukese thinking (Gladwin, 1960).

On Ulithi, William Lessa undertook an even more abbreviated method than those described above (Lessa and Spiegelman, 1954). He administered the Thematic Apperception Test to 99 persons well distributed in age and sex, and scored the resulting stories in accordance with procedures developed by William E. Henry. His psychologist-collaborator, Marvin Spiegelman, then interpreted the results solely on the basis of the comparative frequencies of different responses in the various age and sex groups. This was the first time the TAT had been used in this way, and Lessa found a quite satisfying congruence between Spiegelman's conclusions and those based on the ethnographic data. This congruence held throughout a wide range of behaviors, including general motivational structure, handling of aggression, attitudes toward sex, food anxieties, etc. This does not necessarily mean that the TAT can be assumed to yield valid personality measures when used as a basis for quantitative interpretation in a culture other than Ulithi. However, an accumulation of similar evidence might encourage those anthropologists who are still interested in using projective tests to shift their emphasis away from the Rorschach.

Interpretation of the Rorschach in any setting necessarily requires more inference than the TAT because the Rorschach presents a less structured stimulus, and its interpretation rests on a larger series of assumptions about unconscious psychological processes derived from our own culture than does the TAT.

Melford Spiro's study of Ifaluk was undertaken in conjunction with the late Edwin Burrows. A number of projective and attitudinal measures were used, coupled with a full ethnography and psychological interpretations of individual and group behavior. Spiro has written a number of papers based upon this field work which consider fundamental problems of culture and personality. He was an early contributor to the literature on non-western mental illness (1950, 1959), pointing to the relationship between institutional forms, personal tensions, and tension reduction. He was particularly interested in Ifaluk ghost beliefs which, he believed, were intimately related to Ifaluk child-rearing practices, and operated to reduce in-group hostility and tension (1952, 1953). There is little doubt that this early Micronesian experience influenced Spiro's theoretical position (1961, 1961a, 1967, 1968).

Barnett (1949) and Mahoney (1950) worked together on Palau, with the latter concentrating upon the use of the Rorschach and the TAT to uncover data on personality and culture change. Mahoney was interested in the effects of rapid acculturation upon "basic personality" but appears to have concluded there was a "surprising amount of continuity in both cultural institutions and personality structure" (Levy, 1969:43). Barnett's theoretical development, like Spiro's, seems to have been stimulated by this experience (1953), and he subsequently integrated Mahoney's test results with his own views of Palauan personality (1960).

Since the late 1940's and early 1950's there has been little psychological work done in Micronesia, but John Fischer has written a series of papers, mostly on folktales, which are of importance to the psychologically-oriented (1956, 1957, 1958, 1963, 1966). Roland and Maryanne Force have done a study similar in emphasis (1961). Marc Swartz, working on Truk, has written on sexuality and aggression (1958), and has done a psychological analysis of the Trukese reaction to outside political control (1965). Gladwin has continued his interest in Micronesia and in cognitive processes (1964). He has most recently demonstrated (1970) through an analysis of Puluwat navigation, that Trukese thinking contains both abstract and concrete modes, can involve heuristics and innovation when necessary, and is a perfectly acceptable problem-solving cognitive style.

Stimulated and directed by Homer Barnett, there have been intensive studies done with Micronesians living as "displaced persons." Hopefully, as more materials become available from these investigations, they will tell us something of the psychology of such an experience (Kiste, 1968; Knudson, 1964; Larson, 1966; Lieber, 1968; Lundsgaard, 1966, 1966a; Schwimmer, 1969; Tonkinson, 1968; White, 1965).

The overall paucity of anthropological work in Micronesia is regrettable, especially now, because the people of the area are entering a period of unprecedented change and acculturation. And although Micronesia may tell us much about these problems, provided we pursue them, that which it *might* have told us more about, a more stable human condition, will be lost.

Polynesia

Psychological anthropology in Polynesia began with Margaret Mead's work in the 1920's. Publication of *Coming of Age in Samoa* (1928), a landmark in culture and personality research, set forth now accepted ideas which were, however, not widely held at that time. She examined, among other things, questions of cognition and maturation which were well ahead of their time. Ralph Linton was in the Marquesas in 1920–1922, but he was interested in material culture and did not become interested in psychological questions until much later.

In the late 1930's, Ernest Beaglehole began a series of field researches in Oceania which, through his and his students' efforts, have continued to the present. Although primarily trained in his native New Zealand and in London as a psychologist, Beaglehole studied with Sapir and others at Yale in 1931–34, and became a well-qualified anthropologist. In 1936, he returned to the Pacific, first to the University of Hawaii and then to the Victoria at Wellington, where he initiated a series of ethnographic and culture and personality studies in Polynesian societies including: Pukapuka (Beaglehole and Beaglehole, 1938, 1941); native Hawaiians (Beaglehole, 1939); Tonga (Beaglehole, 1940, 1941); Maori in New Zealand (Beaglehole and Beaglehole, 1946); Rarotonga, and Aitutaki (Beaglehole, 1957). In addition, he published a number of important theoretical papers in culture and personality. He has directed a group of his students in a large-scale interdisciplinary study of personality development in Rakau, a Maori community in somewhat different circumstances than Kowhai, the New Zealand community studied by the Beagleholes themselves. The Rakau study is notable for its extensive experimentation with various methodological approaches to the use of projective tests (Beaglehole and Ritchie, 1958).

Beaglehole's contribution to culture and personality in Polynesia would be notable for the sheer quantity of solid, insightful research he has contributed to the literature, but he has also made a number of clarifying theoretical observations, expecially his 1944 paper on "Character Structure." In it, he considered the cultural directives governing interpersonal behavior and their relationship to individual personality and behavior deviation, observing that when a person

> . . . is acting according to the major directives, he is really acting according to a personal organization or structure of his own needs, emotions and thoughts which is in congruence with the emphasis of the major directives themselves. In other words, the person has developed a character structure in response to the specific pressures of his own culture. When a person acts idiographically, he is determined by a personal variant on this character structure, that is, by the specific drives of unique personality. A person's integrations can be predicted when it is known that his personality corresponds rather exactly to the character structure of the group. One is often at a loss to predict the course of a person's integrations when how different or how alike his personality is to this character structure is not known. (p. 148).

This position is in many respects similar to that of Mead; in each case, attention is directed to the shaping of personality by the totality of expectations and pressures exerted on and communicated to a person by other persons sharing the same culture. Explanatory concepts must then emphasize the conditions under which behaviors, attitudes, and feelings are learned by living with other who already share such attributes. This is contrasted by explanations which stress individual emotional reactions to a succession of experiences shared with others in childhood.

Beaglehole has also gone considerably deeper than most psychologists or anthropologists into questions of cognitive structure raised by the administration of intelligence and other tests to non-European people. The following discussion of his findings on Aitutaki bears on this.

> In the cross-cultural measurement of intellectual capacity, the psychologist's skill and techniques do not yet appear to be adequate to measure differences in quantitative amounts of latent intelligence. But test results are still valuable insofar as they can be used to indicate the existence of cross-cultural qualitative differences in intellectual or cognitive organization. Two aspects of Aitutaki cognitive organization seem to be suggested by the present results. The first concerns the fact that the culture itself does not place value on problem-solving.

In its technological aspect Aitutaki culture is extremely simple. Results are achieved by the simple application of rules traditionally inherited. This is not to say that judgment is not required of the successful fisherman or cultivator, but the number of variables within his control are so few that complicated judgments are hardly ever required. Success in farming and fishing or even in many aspects of social life is more likely to be achieved by the application of rules learned by rote, rather than by the use of principles applied by reason. Cognitive organization, therefore, is likely to be rather simple in structure and largely formed by experience derived through the rote learning of repeated lessons (1957:221).

The second characteristic aspects of Aitutaki thinking is the fact that it functions mainly at a perceptual, rarely at an abstract level, and at a perceptual level which may be significantly different from the perceptual level thinking of the Western European. . . . The way perceptual relations are noticed will be a function of a given culture. How the relations, once noticed, will be abstracted and generalized about will also depend on the interests and training available in the culture concerned. The children of Aitutaki have plenty of experience of coloured objects or variously shaped objects, but their culture teaches them to be interested mainly in the objects and not in their abstracted shapes, colours and patterns. Therefore, the quality of their thinking will reflect this perceptual orientation, and imaginative thinking either of a controlled or a free fantasy type will be rare. This quality of Aitutaki thought again receives confirmation from the limited use of imagination in Rorschach records. (1957:222-223).

We shall return to the discussion of cognitive process and problem-solving in the final portion of this chapter. For the present, we will say only that whereas Porteus and others went no further than to note factors in the tests which interfere with the performance of non-Europeans, Beaglehole's discussion goes beyond to consider the differences in learning and thinking which actually create differences in performance. He is also concerned with how these are related to the demands of the culture. There is a further question, however, about the meaning of "rote learning" which is at best an oversimplification.

Beaglehole's 1957 study, *Social Change in the South Pacific,* combined historical documentation with observation and psychological testing, and attempted to demonstrate that while change had certainly occurred in the Cook islands, there had been little or no change in "basic" personality. It is a study of more than passing interest since it appears to have set a pattern for studies that followed (Levy, 1969:13).

The Beagleholes' study of Maori character (1946) was similarly influential. It emphasized a theme of parental rejection after the age of two or three which has been widely used as a "crucial interactional theme" by subsequent investigators in both Micronesia and Polynesia (Levy, 1969:16).

A number of others, all stimulated by Beaglehole, have worked on questions of Maori personality. James E. Ritchie set forth a developmental sequence of adult Maori personality (1956) which he later modified somewhat and developed in detail (1963). On the basis of his psychological test results, he also had much to say on questions of Maori cognitive organization and modal personality.

John Williams, working with Ritchie, studied achievement motivation and attempted to link this to "types of Maoriness" (1960). Margaret J. Earle studied Maori children (1958) and D. G. Mulligan concentrated on Maori adolescence (1957). Jane Ritchie, working in the same area, wrote on Maori children (1957) and more recently on Maori families (1964). Intensive study of "Rakau," the Maori community on which the above studies are based, is continuing, but the emphasis seems now to be shifting more to the psychology of acculturation and problems of urbanization (Levy, 1969:23). Questions of acculturative stress and the problems of Maori youth have already been asked by David Ausubel (1960, 1965).

Abram Kardiner's *The Individual and His Society* (1939), was another significant point in the history of culture and personality studies. It deserves mention here because of Kardiner's early dependence upon Oceanic data. Ralph Linton was a collaborator in Kardiner's seminar at Columbia University at the time this and subsequent studies developed (e.g., Kardiner *et al.*, 1945; Du Bois, 1944; West, 1945). He contributed ethnological reports based on his own earlier field work on the Marquesas, as well as in Madagascar. Since preliminary exploration of Kardiner's method was worked out using Malinowski's Trobriand material, the debt to Oceania is obvious. The high point of this collaboration was the study of the village of Atimelang on Alor, an island in eastern Indonesia, by Cora Du Bois (1944). This was the first anthropological field work explicitly designed to employ an array of personality assessment techniques of psychologists in a non-European culture. These included the Rorschach, the Porteus Maze, word associations, children's drawings, autobiographies, and systematic observation of behavior sequences. Most of these techniques had been used singly by earlier investigators, but their coordinated use was a distinct milestone and helped Kardiner and his associates to speak with authority during the formative years of culture and personality. Indeed, this work became a methodological model for many subsequent studies in spite of recognized inadequacies in the theoretical underpinnings and the overwhelming emphasis on psychoanalytic theory. Kardiner's books (1939, 1945) and Du Bois' *The People of Alor* (1944) were available at the time, shortly after the war, when clinical psychologists in large numbers became interested in cultural differences. Undoubtedly Kardiner's work spurred this trend, but its real impetus derived from the participation of psychologists in wartime intelligence analysis and psychological warfare. When psychologists then began to collaborate with and train anthropologists, they found Kardiner's tools were the ones with which they were themselves familiar. Kardiner was not the first to use any of these tools, but he brought them together in a persuasive and effective manner.

Psychologists were also comfortable in accepting Kardiner's assumption of the primacy in personality development of the individual's intrapsychic integration of emotional experience. However, while citing Kardiner to legitimize their focus on emotional determinants of behavior, the psychologists and their anthropological colleagues disregarded the one solid tie to culture in Kardiner's scheme — his concept of primary and secondary institutions. The latter concept may or may not be useful, but the effect was, for a time, the uncritical acceptance by many of both the theory and the tools of clinical psychology in culture and personality studies (Hsu 1952, 1955), an acceptance that seems to have hindered further theoretical developments for a time.

In spite of his psychoanalytic orientation, Kardiner recognized cultural reality and cultural imperatives. Briefly, his logical analysis began with primary institutions — the cultural systems devoted to meeting essential needs. Adaptation and socialization in accordance with the dictates of the primary institutions requires the control of natural impulses. This control leads to frustration, and then to reactions to frustration, especially the formation of aggressive tendencies. The anxieties so created give rise to secondary institutions, which are projections of anxiety in a variety of forms. The working out of anxiety is examined primarily at the level of the ego and of the superego in people, and also through the analysis of projective systems in culture.

This thumbnail summary obviously does not do justice to Kardiner's conceptual scheme, but it is sufficient to make clear the difference in emphasis in his approach from that adopted by Mead or Beaglehole. Both Mead and Beaglehole treat personality development in the broader framework of the learning of culture and its appropriate behaviors. Mead adds constitutional temperament and the effect of biological changes in maturation. Kardiner, in contrast, accounts for the same phenomena primarily in terms of psychological response to emotionally important experiences. In Kardiner's scheme, the observable congruence in adult personality necessarily requires the assumption that each individual who shares a culturally determined socialization experience will respond to it in substantially the same fashion as his fellows. Similar anxieties in large numbers of people will then give rise to projective systems which serve to comfort all. This is an extremely crucial assumption and exceedingly difficult to demonstrate.

For the present, without raising questions regarding the usefulness of either mode of analysis, the difference between Kardiner's approach and the emphasis partially shared by Mead and Beaglehole can perhaps be exemplified by parallel examples. Each deals with a culture in which older children have extensive responsibility for the care of their younger siblings during the day. The cultural behavior, and the reason for its existence, are highly comparable in both instances, but the significance seen in it differs sharply.

First, Kardiner's discussion of Alor (Kardiner, *et al.,* 1945, p. 155):

> In late childhood . . . both sexes are prematurely inducted into the role of taking care of their younger siblings. The performance of this role is undoubtedly subject to much variation. In general, however, a child who is robbed of the care essential for growth and development will not bestow such care upon a younger claimant without resentment. The result is that the older child, who is now the mother-surrogate, is no more dependable than the mother herself. So the situation for the younger child is not greatly ameliorated by this institution. On the other hand, the older sibling is likely to be given attributes which were prevented expression toward the mother by the strong ambivalence to her. This attitude is furthermore facilitated by both older and younger sibling having a common claim. This is a factor which in some would tend to ameliorate the situations of sibling rivalry and render the hatred toward the parent still greater. In others it might terminate in intensified sibling rivalry and hatred.

Contrast this with the view of James Ritchie, a student of Beaglehole, of essentially the same behavior in Rakau (Ritchie, 1956:47):

> The Maori child is typing himself against an older sibling's concept of the adult world. His perceptions of adult behavior and adult roles are being strained through the perceptions of his older sibling. The latter will only be approximate varying in their degree of conformity according to the age, sex, intelligence and experience variables of the older child. In this transmission of percepts from a

child's view of the world, the value structure is thrown into sharp relief. The limited comprehension of the older child requires that the values he sees around him be used in modifying the behaviour of younger children; he cannot, therefore, make do with a tentative approximation but must resolve his percepts into a formal structure from which he is able to direct and instruct younger children.

Originality departs. The value-structure sets hard, prematurely, and the child enters onto a plateau in value-learning. The organized model with which he has been presented will do for all situations right up to the time he assumes direct adult behaviour and even then a rigid conformity based on the simplicity and absolutism of the middle years will be a ready source of certainty in conflicting or incipiently dangerous social situations.

Although Beaglehole and his students are not always consistent in viewing personality as learned rather than as shaped by emotional response, they are carrying forward and developing an approach which, like Mead's, is more concerned with when and from whom a person learns his culture, than with the more restrictive psychoanalytically-bound questions of Kardiner.

The only other early work of relevance was that of P. H. Cook who did considerable Rorschach-testing in Samoa, and attempted, on the basis of his test results, to say something about both cross-cultural variables in testing and Samoan personality (1941–42, 1942).

Beaglehole's early work in Hawaii (1939) contrasted the Hawaiian experience with that of the Maori, and pointed out many of the more difficult adaptive problems of the former. As the problems seem to have intensified in recent years, Hawaii has been the scene of considerable research activity. The Bishop Museum has sponsored a program of research since 1965, directed by Alan Howard. This has involved an intensive community study, much work on Hawaiian child-rearing practices and family life, and an investigation of school problems among other things (Howard, 1967; Gallimore and Howard, 1968). Interdisciplinary attempts have not always been as successful as this one promises to be. It has demonstrated, with some clarity, the effects of culture on various dimensions of personality, and the effects of specifically Hawaiian personality on attempts to cope with new cultural demands. As Levy points out (1969:28), this study is especially interesting when contrasted with the experiences of Japanese and Chinese-Hawaiians, whose cultural backgrounds appear to have fitted them for a much more successful transition.

Other recent activity in psychological anthropology has centered in the

Society Islands of French Polynesia. Douglas Oliver and several others, including Robert Levy, have worked over a ten-year period (1954–1964) in eight different Tahitian communities graded roughly in "amount of contact." Levy studied a fairly "traditional" village, doing intensive psychological research. He has published on Tahitian drinking behavior (1969), "psychotherapy" (1967), the Tahitian family and how it manages children (1968), and on getting angry in Tahiti (1969). In addition to the remarkable psychological depth of Levy's work (he is a psychiatrist as well as an anthropologist), it also has the advantage of an unusually thorough historical background.[4]

Other work in Polynesia in recent years has included that done on cognition by E. P. Torrance (1962, 1967) and R. T. Johnson (1962); Alan Howard's study of Rotumans on Fiji (1966), which contrasts their achievement levels with that of native Fijians; and the work of Raymond Firth, which spans forty years, and although not psychological by design, is an exceedingly rich source of psychologically relevant materials (1959, 1967; Firth and Spillius, 1963).

Assessment

The history of culture and personality studies in Oceania is very similar to the history of such studies in general. First there was an interest in ethnic differences related to beliefs and assumptions about race and racial inferiorities. These were predicated on further assumptions about the nature of human nature which were drawn almost exclusively from biology. Then there was Margaret Mead's articulate and convincing demonstrations that facts of personality or human nature were not simply the result of some inevitable biological process similar in human beings wherever found and predetermined by heredity alone. The thesis of Freud, given impetus by Roheim, and the antithesis of Malinowski which, however much of a dead issue now, were crucial in bringing about the modifications of classical psychoanalytic theory that followed. The Rousseauian claims of Seligman, with their implicit theory of society, did much to stimulate research on non-western mental illness. Subsequently came the development and testing of new instruments for studying personality cross-culturally, and the more systematic use and elaboration of older instruments. There were repeated attempts to try out new concepts and conceptual frameworks and the creation of entirely new concepts. In the

[4] See Levy, 1969, for a summary of his work to 1969 and also for references to his unpublished materials.

early years, the few pioneers were followed by a period of excitement, then more intense activity by greater numbers, and now the current situation, which some claim is only the last stage of a disappearing fad. Before accepting this conclusion, however, a more careful examination is in order.

Oceania, as noted at the beginning of this chapter, held vast opportunities for students of culture and personality. The challenge was well met. Much pioneering work was done. Out of this has come many genuine contributions to anthropology but, of course, not everything attempted proved to be of lasting value.

Considerable time and energy was spent on psychological testing and on methods for efficiently measuring personality variables cross-culturally. Although this had an important effect on psychological testing in general, the tests are now only rarely used by anthropologists, and the methods did not prove as useful as we might have wished. Likewise, the elaborate conceptual framework and methodology of Kardiner and associates, except for those portions distilled out and used by Whiting and his students, has not stood the test of time. The same thing is true of Hull's learning theory which, in Whiting's first attempt to apply it to human beings and cultural descriptions, was tried and found wanting. Bateson's concept of schizmogenesis as such, appears not to have stimulated the interest it deserved, although it probably was the building-block for much subsequent research on communication and disturbed communication. Also, the notions of *eidos* and *ethos* have not taken hold as one might have expected. What, then, can we point positively to from the seventy years of Oceanic research?

One pioneer example of Mead's has always received too little attention and comes quickly to mind, especially in view of the current surge of interest in the work of Piaget. A primary purpose of Mead's 1928–29 field work in Manus (Mead, 1932) was to examine the assumptions of Piaget (and of Levy-Bruhl) that the less "logical" (by European standards) thought of children was a function of their immaturity, and that the thought processes of primitive people were analagous to those of children in our society. Using a variety of ingenious psychological measures, she found that Manus children actually analysed situations in a far more matter-of-fact ("logical") fashion than characterized the animistic reasoning of their elders. She offered several possible explanations and then arrived at the well-documented conclusion that, Piaget and Levy-Bruhl to the contrary, "Animistic thought cannot be explained in terms of intellectual immaturity." This early study of cognitive processes is all the more significant when it is realized that cognitive development was otherwise ignored by culture and personality researchers until approximately the 1940's. When anthropology did come into this field of inquiry, it entered largely through linguistics. But much of the work on cultural differences in logical processes and cognition, following Mead, has been done in Oceania (Bateson, 1942, 1958; Beaglehole, 1957; Gladwin, 1960, 1964, 1970; Glick, 1964, 1967; Lee, 1950; and Porteus, 1931, 1937).

Bateson's early emphasis on the distinctness and importance of cognitive processes must be mentioned here also. In 1936, in the first edition of *Naven*, he characterized the usual grist for the culture and personality mill as *ethos*, "the expression of a culturally standardized system of the organization of the instincts and emotions of... individuals" (1958:118). But he also went on to speak for the first time of *eidos*, "a standardization [and expression in cultural behavior] of the cognitive aspects of the personality of individuals" (1958:220). *Eidos* embraces such matters as the nature of memory, the perception and structuring of external reality, the possibility of a positive valuation of intellectuality (e.g., expert knowledge of genealogy or folklore), and preferred strategies in problem solving. Subsequently, he carried *eidos* one step further, evolving the concept of *deutero-learning*, or learning how to learn, referring to the context or intellectual tools of learning (Bateson, 1942). In neither instance did Bateson carry through with a full review of his ethnographic material to demonstrate the potentialities of an analysis in these terms. His concepts, however, were important in that they pointed to culturally determined differences in the basic intellectual tools available to persons reared in different societies. It would appear that the current higher standards of field work and the so-called "new ethnography" are not unrelated to this tradition. Nor are current developments in research on poverty, cultural deprivation, thinking styles, and educational methods unrelated (Ausubel, 1965; Gallimore and Howard, 1968; Gladwin, 1970; Valentine, 1968).

The ultimate effects of the work of Malinowski, Mead, Bateson, Beaglehole, etc., on views of human nature and culture should not be underestimated, although these effects might be seen more as slow and indirect than as quick and direct. This is especially true of Mead's early work on adolescence and animistic thinking. It was a result of efforts of this kind that the foundations of psychoanalytic theory were shaken and culture was added to biology as a determinant of personality.[5] Now that it is commonly accepted that culture is, in some sense, a determinant of behavior; now that the tenacity of Orthodox Freudianism has at last been overcome; and now that we can see a newer, more comprehensive theory of behavior beginning to emerge, we can also see that culture and personality studies, including those done in Oceania, were vital ingredients.

We do not mean to imply, however, that having enjoyed its heyday, psychological anthropology is now disappearing. This is clearly not the case. Anthony F. C. Wallace, since the first edition of this book, has spoken of "The New Culture and Personality" (1962); and Melford Spiro in that edition spoke of a "re-orientation of culture and personality" (1961*a*) which clearly seems to be underway. There remain several very active programs in psychological anthropology, and recently new ones have been started. A journal devoted to the subject is about to be inaugurated. In addition to the impact of culture and personality research on studies of learning and cognition, and hence on the poverty program and "urban problems" in general, there now exists an Association for Anthropology and Education, and a Society for Medical Anthropology, both of which can be traced more readily to the tradition of psychological anthropology than to anything else.

More important, in addition to these visible signs of good health as a distinct subject-matter, the basic tenets of psychological anthropology have been incorporated into American anthropology. There are few who would argue any longer that psychology has no place in anthropology, motivation is an insignificant variable for anthropologists to be concerned with, or that individuals are irrelevant to the study of culture and so on. There are few, also, no matter how ecological or materialistic their orientation, who would deny that "human ecology," as contrasted to ecology, is quite a different thing — different precisely because of facts of human nature and personality. Indeed, it is in the union of cultural materialism and culture and personality studies that some of the most exciting and productive work in anthropology is now being done.[6] We suspect that many have mistaken this incorporation for disappearance.

In addition to what might be considered as mere fads in social science, there are different demands placed on the profession from time to time. The demands of the moment have to do with such things as poverty, prejudice, dehumanization, alienation, and other such things, all related to urbanization and rapid technological change — that is, to the complex

[5] For an account of the crucial theoretical significance of this see Chapter 2, "The Recapitulation Theory and Culture," in A. I. Hallowell's, *Culture and Experience* (1955).

[6] We cannot pursue this here but see Barry, Bacon and Child (1959), Harris (1968), Whiting (1961, 1964), Wallace (1961), and Young (1962).

system of feedback between nature, personality, and culture that we call evolution and try to pretend has either stopped entirely or is under human control.[7] Some areas of the world, including most of Oceania, have not experienced the full impact of such changes yet, but the process, as Levy sums it up for Polynesia, is going on now, and not without the attendant problems:

> In recent years a different kind of change has affected these various island communities, and new and severe adaptational problems are once again being presented to the stabilized cultures. These are essentially *modernization* rather than *acculturative* changes. They consist of successive shifts from partial subsistence economies to market and, finally, wage economies; of progressive urbanization of centrally located island towns with the creation of hinterlands and of peasant conditions; of the development of an active labor market and the creation of a town proletariat; and of the development of widespread, low-cost communication networks, on the one hand bringing in masses of tourists, and on the other allowing opportunities for the islanders to travel and to seek work in various "developed" countries. . . . Consideration of these modernization changes is just beginning in the most recent psychologically oriented studies in Polynesia (Levy, 1969:7).

It is clear that this is true of all of Oceania. And it is equally clear that just as Oceania played an important part in the history of psychological anthropology, so will it continue as a critical area for further research in the future.

Bibliography

Australian National University. 1968. An ethnographic bibliography of New Guinea. Department of Anthropology and Sociology, Australian National University, Canberra.

Ausubel, David P. 1960. Acculturative stress in modern Maori adolescence. Child Development 31:617–31.

——. 1965. Maori youth: a psychoethnological study of cultural deprivation. New York, Holt, Rinehart and Winston.

Barnett, Homer B. 1949. Palauan society: a study of contemporary native life in the Palau islands. Eugene, Oregon, University of Oregon Press.

——. 1953. Innovation: the basis of cultural change. New York, McGraw-Hill.

---

[7] Behavioral evolution is probably a better term for what we have in mind although not widely in use as yet. See Hallowell (1968) and Roe and Simpson (1958).

————. 1960. Being a Palauan. New York, Henry Holt and Company.

BARRY, H., BACON, M. K., AND CHILD, I. L. 1959. Relation of child training to subsistence economy. American Anthropologist, 61:51–63.

BATESON, GREGORY. 1942. Social planning and the concept of "Deutero-learning." Conference on Science, Philosophy and Religion, Second Symposium. New York, Harper and Brothers.

————. 1949. Bali: the value system of a steady state. *In* Social structure: studies presented to A. R. Radcliffe-Brown. Meyer Fortes, ed. Oxford, Clarendon Press. pp. 35–53.

————. 1958. Naven. 2nd edition. Stanford University Press, Stanford, California.

BEAGLEHOLE, ERNEST. 1939. Some modern Hawaiians. University of Hawaii Research Publications, 19.

————. 1940. Psychic stress in a Tongan village. Proceedings of the Sixth Pacific Science Congress. Berkeley, University of California Press, 4:43–52.

————. 1941. Pangai village in Tonga. Memoirs of the Polynesian Society, 18.

————. 1944. Character structure: its role in the analysis of interpersonal relations. Psychiatry, 7:145–162.

————. 1957. Social change in the South Pacific: Rarotonga and Aitutaki. New York, MacMillan.

BEAGLEHOLE, ERNEST AND PEARL. 1938. Ethnology of Pukapuka. Bulletin of the Bernice P. Bishop Museum, 150:1–470.

————. 1941. Personality development in Pukapukan children. *In* Language, culture and personality. Leslie Spier, A. Irving Hallowell, and Stanley S. Newman, eds., pp. 282–298. Menasha, Sapir Memorial Publication Fund.

————. 1946. Some modern Maoris. New Zealand Council for Educational Research. Wellington, Whitcombe and Tombs.

BEAGLEHOLE, ERNEST AND JAMES E. RITCHIE. 1958. The Rakau Maori studies. Journal of the Polynesian Society, 67:132–54.

BENEDICT, RUTH. 1934. Patterns of culture. New York, Houghton Mifflin.

BERNDT, R. M. AND CATHERINE H. 1951. Sexual behavior in Western Arnhem land. Viking Fund Publications in Anthropology No. 16. New York, Wenner-Gren Foundation for Anthropological Research, Inc.

BURRIDGE, KENELM O. L. 1960. Mambu: a Melanesian millenium. London: Methuan.

————. 1969. New heaven, new earth: a study of millenarium activities. Oxford, Blackwell.

BURTON-BRADLEY, B. G. 1967. Some aspects of South Pacific ethnopsychiatry. Technical Paper No. 156, South Pacific Commission, Noumea, New Caledonia.

————. 1968. Mixed race society in Port Moresby, New Guinea Research Bulletin, No. 23, Port Moresby, New Guinea.

————. 1969. Papuan and New Guinea transcultural psychiatry. Australian and New Zealand Journal of Psychiatry, 3:124–129, 130–136.

Cook, P. H. 1941–42. Mental structure and the psychological field: some Samoan observations. Character and Personality, 10:296–308.

————. 1942 The application of the Rorschach test to a Samoan group. Rorschach Research Exchange, 6:51–60.

Du Bois, Cora. 1944. The people of Alor: a social psychological study of an East Indian island. Minneapolis, University of Minnesota Press.

Earle, Margaret Jane. 1958. Rakau children: from six to thirteen years. Wellington, Victoria University of Wellington Publications in Psychology 11. (Monographs on Maori Social Life and Personality 4).

Firth, Raymond. 1959. Social change in Tikopia. New York, The MacMillan Company.

————. 1967. Tikopia ritual and belief. Boston, Beacon Press.

Firth, Raymond and James Spillius. 1963. A study in ritual modification. Occasional Paper No. 19. London, Royal Anthropological Institute of Great Britain and Ireland.

Fischer, John L. 1956. The position of men and women in Truk and Ponape: a comparative analysis of kinship terminology and folktales. Journal of American Folklore, 69:55–62.

————. 1957. Totemism on Truk and Ponape. American Anthropologist, 59:260–65.

————. 1958. Folktales, social structure, and environment in two Polynesian outliers. The Journal of the Polynesian Society, 67:11–36.

————. 1963. The sociopsychological analysis of folktales. Current Anthropology, 4:235–295.

————. 1966. A Ponapean oedipus tale: structural and sociopsychological analysis. Journal of American Folklore, 79:109–129.

Force, Roland W. and Maryanne. 1961. Keys to cultural understanding. Science, 133:1202–1206.

Fortune, Reo. 1927. The mind in sleep. London, Kegan Paul.

————. 1932. Sorcerers of Dobu: the social anthropology of the Dobu islanders of the Western Pacific. New York, Dutton.

Gallimore, Ronald and Alan Howard. 1968. Studies in a Hawaiian community: Na Makamaka O Nanakuli. Pacific Anthropological Records No. 1, Bernice P. Bishop Museum, Honolulu.

Gladwin, Thomas. 1960. The need: better ways of teaching children to think. *In* Freeing Capacity to Learn: Papers and Reports from the Fourth ASCD Research Insitute, pp. 23–39. Washington, National Educational Association.

————. 1964. Culture and logical process. *In* Explorations in Cultural Anthropology, Ward H. Goodenough, ed., New York, McGraw-Hill. pp. 167–77.

————. 1970. East is a big bird: Navigation and Logic on Puluwat Atoll. Cambridge, Harvard University Press.

GLADWIN, THOMAS AND SEYMOUR B. SARASON. 1953. Truk: man in paradise. Viking Fund Publications in Anthropology No. 20. New York, Wenner-Gren Foundation for Anthropological Research, Inc.

GLASSE, ROBERT M. 1959. Revenge and redress among the Huli; a preliminary account. Mankind, 5:273–88.

GLASSE, ROBERT M. AND MERVYN MEGGITT (EDS.). 1969. Pigs, pearlshells and women. New York, Prentice-Hall.

GLICK, LEONARD B. 1963. Foundations of a primitive medical system: the Gimi of the New Guinea Highlands. Ph.D. thesis, Department of Anthropology, University of Pennsylvania.

————. 1964. Categories and relations to Gimi natural science. American Anthropologist, Part 2, 66:273–280.

————. 1967. Medicine as an ethnographic category: the Gimi of the New Guinea Highlands. Ethnology, 6:31–56.

————. 1968. Possession in the New Guinea Highlands, L. B. Glick comments in news and views. Transcultural Psychiatric Research Review, pp. 200–205.

HALLOWELL, A. I. 1955. The recapitulation theory and culture. *In* Culture and Experience, Philadelphia, University of Pennsylvania Press.

————. 1968. Self, society, and culture in phylogenetic perspective. *In* Culture: Man's Adaptive Dimension, ed. M. F. Ashley Montagu, Oxford University Press, pp. 197–261.

HARRIS, MARVIN. 1968. The rise of anthropological theory. Thomas Y. Crowell Co., New York.

HOWARD, ALAN. 1966. Plasticity, achievement and adaptation in developing economies, Human Organization, 25:265–272.

————. 1967. Bishop Museum community research program: a progress report. Mimeographed, 19 pages. Honolulu, Bernice P. Bishop Museum.

HOWARD, IRWIN, W. E. VINACKE AND T. MARETZKI. 1963. Culture and personality in the Pacific Islands: a bibliography. Honolulu, Anthropological Society of Hawaii.

HSU, FRANCIS L. K. 1952. Anthropology or psychiatry: a definition of objectives and their implications. Southwestern Journal of Anthropology, 8:227–250.

————. 1955. An anthropologist's views of the future of personality studies. Psychiatric Research Reports, 2:155–168.

JOHNSON, R. T. 1962. Observations on Western Samoa culture and education. (Unpublished manuscript. Minneapolis, University of Minnesota, Bureau of Educational Research).

JOSEPH, ALICE AND VERONICA F. MURRAY. 1951. Chamorros and Carolinians of Saipan, personality studies. Cambridge, Harvard University Press.

KARDINER, ABRAM. 1939. The individual and his society: the psychodynamics of primitive social organization. New York, Columbia University Press.

KARDINER, ABRAM ET AL. 1945. The psychological frontiers of society. New York, Columbia University Press.

KISTE, ROBERT C. 1968. Kili Island: a study of the relocation of the ex-Bikini Marshallese. Eugene, Oregon, Department of Anthropology, University of Oregon.

KNUDSON, K. E. 1964. Titiana: a Gilbertese community in the Solomon Islands. Eugene, Oregon. Department of Anthropology, University of Oregon.

KOCH, KLAUS-FRIEDRICH. 1968. On "possession" behavior in New Guinea. The Journal of the Polynesian Society, 77:135–146.

LABARRE, WESTON. 1958. The influence of Freud on anthropology. American Imago, 15:275–328.

LANGNESS, L. L. 1965. Hysterical psychosis in the New Guinea Highlands: a Bena Bena example. Psychiatry, 28:258–77.

———. 1967. Rejoinder to R. Salisbury. Transcultural Psychiatric Research, IV, 125–129.

———. 1967a. Sexual antagonism in the New Guinea Highlands: a Bena Bena example. Oceania, 37:161–77.

———. 1969. Possession in the New Guinea Highlands. Transcultural Psychiatric Research Review, pp. 95–100.

LARSON, ERIC H. 1966. Nukufero: a Tikopian colony in the Russell Islands. Eugene, Oregon, Department of Anthropology, University of Oregon.

LAWRENCE, PETER. 1964. Road belong cargo. Manchester, England, Manchester University Press.

LAWRENCE, PETER AND MERVYN MEGGITT (EDS.). 1965. Gods, ghosts and men in Melanesia. Melbourne, Oxford University Press.

LEE, DOROTHY M. 1950. Lineal and nonlineal codifications of reality. Psychosomatic Medicine, 12:89–97.

LEININGER, MADELINE. 1966. Convergence and divergence of human behavior: an ethnopsychological comparative study of two Gadsup villages in the Eastern Highlands of New Guinea. Ph.D. dissertation, Department of Anthropology, University of Washington, Seattle, Washington.

LESSA, WILLIAM A. 1956. Oedipus-type tales in Oceania. Journal of American Folklore, 69:63–73.

LESSA, WILLIAM A. AND MARVIN SPIEGELMAN. 1954. Ulithian personality as seen through ethnological materials and thematic test analysis. University of California Publications in Culture and Society, 2:243–301.

LEVY, ROBERT I. 1966. Ma'ohi drinking patterns in the Society Islands. The Journal of the Polynesian Society, 75:304–320.

――――. 1967. Tahitian folk psychotherapy. International Mental Health Research Newsletter, Vol. 9, winter.

――――. 1968. Child management structure and its implications in a Tahitian Family. *In* A Modern Introduction to the Family, Ezra Vogel and Normal Bell, eds. New York, Free Press.

――――. 1968a. Tahiti observed: early European impressions of Tahitian personal style. Journal of the Polynesian Society, 77:33–42.

――――. 1969. Personality studies in Polynesia and Micronesia: stability and change. Working Paper Number 8, Social Science Research Institute, University of Hawaii, Honolulu.

――――. 1969a. On getting angry in the Society Islands. *In* Mental Health Research in Asia and the Pacific, William Caudill and Tsung-Yi Lin, eds., Honolulu, East-West Center Press.

LIEBER, MICHAEL D. 1968. Porakiet: a Kapingamarangi colony on Ponape. Eugene, Oregon, Department of Anthropology, University of Oregon.

LUNDSGAARD, HENRY P. 1966. Cultural adaptation in the Southern Gilbert Islands. Eugene, Oregon, Department of Anthropology, University of Oregon.

――――. 1966a. Social change in the Southern Gilbert Islands. Eugene, Oregon, Department of Anthropology, University of Oregon.

MAHONEY, FRANCIS B. 1950. Projective psychological findings in Palau personality. M.A. Thesis, University of Chicago, Chicago.

MALINOWSKI, BRONISLAW. 1922. Argonauts of the Western Pacific, an account of native enterprise and adventure in the Archipelagoes of Melanesian New Guinea. London, Routledge.

――――. 1927. Sex and repression in savage society. London, Kegan Paul.

――――. 1929. The sexual life of savages in North-Western Melanesia. New York, Halcyon.

――――. 1935. Coral gardens and their magic, a study of the methods of tilling the soil and of agricultural rites in the Trobriand Islands. New York, American Book, 2 vols.

MASLAND, RICHARD L., SEYMOUR B. SARASON AND THOMAS GLADWIN. 1958. Mental subnormality: biological, psychological, and cultural factors. New York, Basic Books.

MEAD, MARGARET. 1928. Coming of age in Samoa. New York, William Morrow and Company.

————. 1931. Growing up in New Guinea. London, G. Routledge and Sons.

————. 1932. An investigation of the thought of primitive children, with special reference to animism. Journal of the Royal Anthropological Institute, 62:173–190.

————. 1935. Sex and temperament in three primitive societies. New York, William Morrow and Company.

————. 1939. From the South Seas: studies of adolescence and sex in primitive societies. New York, Morrow. (Comprises reprints of Coming of Age in Samoa, 1928; Growing up in New Guinea, 1930; Sex and Temperament in Three Primitive Societies, 1935).

————. 1954. Research on primitive children. *In* Manual of Child Psychology, Leonard Carmichael, ed., 2nd ed., pp. 735–80. New York, John Wiley.

————. 1956. New lives for old, cultural transformation: Manus 1928–53. New York, William Morrow and Company.

MEAD, MARGARET AND THEODORE SCHWARTZ. 1960. The cult as a condensed social process. *In* Group Processes: Transactions of the Fifth Conference, October 12, 13, 14 and 15, 1958, Princeton, New Jersey. Bertram Schaffner, ed., New York. Josiah Macy, Jr., Foundation, pp. 85–187.

MEGGITT, MERVYN. 1962. Dream interpretation among the Mae Enga of New Guinea. Southwestern Journal of Anthropology, 18:216–29.

————. 1964. Male-female relationships in the Highlands of Australian New Guinea. American Anthropologist, Part 2, 66:204–24.

MILLER, NEAL E. AND JOHN DOLLARD. 1941. Social learning and imitation. New Haven, Yale University Press.

MULLIGAN, D. G. 1957. Maori adolescence in Rakau. Wellington, Victoria University College Publications in Psychology 9. (Monographs on Maori Social Life and Personality 2.)

MYERS, CHARLES J. AND W. McDOUGALL. 1903. Reports of the Cambridge anthropological expedition to Torres Straits II, physiology and psychology. Part 2. Cambridge, Cambridge University Press.

NEWMAN, PHILIP. 1962. Supernaturalism and ritual among the Gururumba. Ph.D. dissertation, Department of Anthropology, University of Washington, Seattle, Washington.

————. 1964. "Wild man" behavior in a New Guinea Highlands community. American Anthropologist, 66:1–19.

————. 1964a. Religious belief and ritual in a New Guinea Society. American Anthropologist, Part 2, 66:257–72.

————. 1965. Knowing the Gururumba. Holt, Rinehart and Winston, New York.

OLIVER, DOUGLAS. 1961. The Pacific Islands. Natural History Library, New York.

PORTEUS, S. D. 1931. The psychology of a primitive people: a study of the Australian Aborigine. New York, Longmans, Green.

———. 1937. Primitive intelligence and environment. New York, MacMillan.

READ, K. E. 1952/53. Nama cult of the Central Highlands, New Guinea. Oceania, 23:1–25.

———. 1954/55. Morality and the concept of the person among the Gahuku-Gama, Eastern Highlands, New Guinea. Oceania, 25:233–82.

———. 1959. Leadership and concensus in a New Guinea Society. American Anthropologist, 61:425–36.

———. 1965. The High Valley. New York, Scribner and Sons.

REAY, MARIE. 1959. The Kuma. Melbourne, Australia, Melbourne University Press.

———. 1960/61. "Mushroom madness" in the New Guinea Highlands. Oceania, 31:137–39.

RITCHIE, JAMES E. 1956. Basic personality in Rakau. Wellington, Victoria University College Publications in Psychology 8. (Monographs on Maori Social Life and Personality I).

———. 1963. The making of a Maori. Publications on Psychology, No. 15. Wellington, New Zealand, Victoria University of Wellington, A. H. and A. W. Reed.

RITCHIE, JANE. 1957. Childhood in Rakau: the first five years of life. Wellington, Victoria University College Publications in Psychology 10. (Monographs on Maori Social Life and Personality 3).

———. 1964. Maori families. Publications in Psychology, No. 18. Wellington, New Zealand, Victoria University of Wellington.

RIVERS, W. H. R. 1923. Conflict and dream. New York, Harcourt, Brace.

ROE, ANNE AND SIMPSON, GEORGE GAYLORD (EDS.). 1958. Behavior and evolution. New Haven, Yale University Press.

ROHEIM, GÉZA. 1925. Australian totemism: a psycho-analytical study in anthropology. London, Allen and Unwin.

———. 1932. The psychoanalysis of primitive cultural types. International Journal of Psychoanalysis, 13:1–224.

———. 1950. Psychoanalysis and anthropology. New York, International Universities Press.

SALISBURY, RICHARD. 1966. Possession in the New Guinea Highlands: review of literature. Transcultural Psychiatric Research, III, 103–108.

———. 1966a. Possession among the Siane (New Guinea). Transcultural Psychiatric Research, III:108–116.

————. 1967. R. Salisbury replies. Transcultural Psychiatric Research, IV:130–134.

————. 1969. Possession in the New Guinea Highlands. Transcultural Psychiatric Research Review, pp. 100–102.

Schwimmer, Eric G. 1969. Cultural consequences of a volcanic eruption experienced by the Mt. Lamington Orokaiva. Eugene, Oregon. Department of Anthropology, University of Oregon.

Seligman, C. G. 1929. Temperament, conflict and psychosis in a stone-age population. Medical Psychology, IX:187–202.

Sinclair, Alex. 1957. Field and clinical survey report of the mental health of the indigenes of the territory of Papua and New Guinea. Port Moresby: W. S. Nichols, Government Printer.

Spiro, Melford. 1950. A psychotic personality of the South Seas. Psychiatry, 13:189–204.

————. 1952. Ghosts, Ifaluk, and teleological functionalism. American Anthropologist, 54:497–503.

————. 1953. Ghosts: an anthropological inquiry into learning and perception. The Journal of Abnormal and Social Psychology, 48:376–82.

————. 1959. Cultural heritage, personal tensions, and mental illness in a South Sea culture. *In* Culture and Mental Health, Marvin K. Opler, editor. New York, The MacMillan Company.

————. 1961. Social systems, personality, and functional analysis. *In* Studying Personality Cross-Culturally, (ed. Bert Kaplan), pp. 93–128. New York, Harper and Row.

————. 1961a. An overview and a suggested reorientation. *In* F. L. K. Hsu (ed.), Psychological Anthropology, 1st edition, Homewood, Illinois, The Dorsey Press, pp. 459–492.

————. 1965. Religious systems as culturally constituted defense mechanisms. *In* M. Spiro (ed.), Context and Meaning in Cultural Anthropology. Glencoe, The Free Press.

————. 1967. Burmese supernaturalism. Englewood Cliffs, Prentice-Hall, Inc.

————. 1968. Virgin birth, parthenogenesis and physiological paternity: an essay in cultural interpretation. Man, 3:242–261.

Swartz, Marc. 1958. Sexuality and aggression on Romonom, Truk. American Anthropologist, 60:467–486.

————. 1965. Personality and structure: political acquiescence in Truk. *In* Induced Political Change in the Pacific, Roland Force, ed., Honolulu, Bishop Museum Press.

Taylor, C. R. H. 1965. A Pacific bibliography. London, Oxford University Press.

Tonkinson, Robert. 1968. Maat village, Efate: a relocated community in the New Hebrides. Eugene, Oregon. Department of Anthropology, University of Oregon.

Torrance, E. Paul. 1962. Cultural discontinuities and the development originality of thinking. Exceptional Children, 29:2–13.

———. 1967. Understanding the fourth grade slump in creative thinking. Washington, D.C., Office of Education, Bureau of Research, U.S. Department of Health, Education and Welfare.

Valentine, C. A. 1963. Social status, political power, and native responses to European influence in Oceania. Anthropological Forum, Vol. I, No. 1, pp. 3–55.

———. 1963a. Men of anger and men of shame: Lakalai ethnopsychology and its implications for sociopsychological theory. Ethnology, 2:441–77.

———. 1968. Culture and poverty; critique and counterproposals. Chicago, University of Chicago Press.

Wallace, Anthony F. C. 1961. Mental illness, biology, and culture. *In* Psychological Anthropology, F. L. K. Hsu, ed., Dorsey Press, Homewood, Illinois, pp. 255–94.

———. 1962. The new culture-and-personality. *In* T. Gladwin and W. Sturtevant, eds., Anthropology and Human Behavior, Washington, Anthropological Society of Washington 1–12.

Warner, W. Lloyd. 1937. A black civilization: a social study of an Australian tribe. New York and London, Harper and Brothers.

Watson, James B. 1960. A New Guinea "opening man." *In* J. B. Casagrande (ed.), In The Company of Man, New York, Harper and Brothers, pp. 127–73.

———. 1967. Tairora: the politics of despotism in a small society. Anthropological Forum, Vol. II, pp. 53–104.

West, James. 1945. Plainville, U.S.A. New York, Columbia University Press.

White, G. M. 1965. Kioa: an Ellice community in Fiji. Eugene, Oregon, Department of Anthropology, University of Oregon.

Whiting, John W. M. 1941. Becoming a Kwoma: teaching and learning in a New Guinea tribe. New Haven, Yale University Press.

———. 1961. Socialization process and personality. *In* Psychological Anthropology, F. L. K. Hsu, ed., Dorsey Press, Homewood, Illinois, 1st ed., pp. 355–80.

———. 1964. Effects of climate on certain cultural practices. *In* Explorations in Cultural Anthropology, McGraw-Hill, New York, pp. 511–44, Ward Goodenough, ed.

Williams, John Smith. 1960. Maori achievement motivation. Wellington, Victoria University of Wellington Publications in Psychology 13. (Monographs on Maori Social Life and Personality 5.)

Worsley, Peter. 1957. The trumpet shall sound. London: MacGibbon and Kee.

Young, F. W. 1962. The function of male initiation ceremonies: a cross-cultural test of an alternative hypothesis. American Journal of Sociology, 67:379–396.

CHAPTER FIVE

National Character and Modern Political Systems*

ALEX INKELES

The method of analysis which yields studies in psychological anthropology when applied to "primitive" peoples has its analogue among studies of large-scale societies in a varied assortment of investigations on what is called national character. If, under this heading, we allow impressionistic, introspective, and loosely evaluative works to qualify, then for the United States alone — from De Tocqueville to Brogan and Gorer — the articles and books depicting the American character will be numbered in the hundreds (Commager 1947). Were we to extend our coverage to the major nations of Europe and Asia, the number of relevant studies would be in the thousands. To review even the most important of these would strain the limits of our allotted space even while permitting only the driest catalogue of their contents. Yet if we were to insist on the more rigorous standards of empirical social science, and were to consider only more systematic investigations based on representative samples and utilizing standard psychological tests, then not more than two or three studies in the relevant literature could qualify. There is a third alternative. By selecting

*Revised and expanded version of a paper read at the Fourth World Congress of Sociology, Stresa-Milan, 1959. The aid of the Social Science Research Council is gratefully acknowledged, as well as the support of the Russian Research Center at Harvard. Professors S. N. Eisenstadt and Daniel J. Levinson were kind enough to offer numerous excellent suggestions.

a specific problem focus we may simultaneously escape the boundlessness of a general review and the confining restrictions forced on us through the adoption of a rigorous methodological canon. A topic suitable to our purpose, one of interest and importance, is the relation of national character to the political systems found in modern national states, and more specifically, to the establishment and maintenance of democracy. Before we examine this relationship, we must clarify the meaning of our concepts.

What Is National Character and How Can It Be Measured?

Problems of Definition

The confusion about the term *national character* is pervasive and enduring. Yet arguing about what a concept *should* mean can be utterly sterile. What is important is that we designate some empirical phenomenon which has concrete reference, which can be effectively distinguished from other phenomena, and which can conceivably be investigated by standard replicable, reliable, and valid methods. For purposes of this discussion I will adopt the definition of national character presented in the *Handbook of Social-Psychology* (Inkeles and Levinson 1954) which, I believe, is now widely accepted: "National character refers to relatively enduring personality characteristics and patterns that are modal among the adult members of a society."

The other meanings given to national character, and related terms such as people's character, folk character, national (or "racial" or popular) psychology, are almost as numerous as the roster of political essayists from Plato to Pareto and from Pareto to Potter. Some treat national character as simply "the sum total" of all the values, institutions, cultural traditions, ways of acting, and history of a people. However useful this idea may be for popular discourse, it is sadly lacking for purposes of scientific analysis, since the failure to differentiate the elements of the phenomenon makes an impossible task of measurement, obfuscates issues of cause and effect, and precludes systematic study of the relations between elements. With most other definitions we have no quarrel, so long as those using the different terms are appropriately aware that each has a special and restricted meaning, and that no one of these concepts exhaustively describes the phenomenon under investigation. The following main types of definition may be discerned (*cf.* Herz 1944, and Klineberg 1944):

National Character as Institutional Pattern.   In this approach, most common among political scientists, the national character is epitomized by the dominant, or typical and representative, institutions, particularly those concerned with politics and economics. The choice between dominant as against typical or representative institutions as the basis for characterizing a nation is a difficult one, and has led to much confusion in those studies in which the distinction was not precisely made or rigorously adhered to. Outstanding examples of the genre are to be found among numerous studies of the American character, such as those by Andre Siegfried (1927) or D. W. Brogan (1933, 1944).

National Character as Culture Theme.   Broadly similar to the preceding approach, this genre gives prime emphasis not to political and economic institutions but to the family, friendship, the local community, and to values, attitudes, philosophy of life, religion and the like. Themes are often selected as cutting across or as infusing these and other social realms. Most common among anthropologists, this approach is also typical for many historians, political scientists, and essayists who speak in terms of spirit or *folkgeist*, world outlook, life-ways, and similar themes. Perhaps the best known of the more or less modern efforts of this type woud be de Madariaga's *Englishmen, Frenchmen, Spaniards* (1929) and the most impressive of the recent statements, Ruth Benedict's *The Chrysanthemum and the Sword* (1946).

National Character as Action.   In this approach stress is placed on behavior and its consequences, with special reference to political and economic *action*. In this view both formal institutional patterns and informal cultural norms, in and of themselves, are not regarded as very reliable guides to a nation's "character." Those adopting this approach stress particularly the history of peoples or societies, and on this basis may characterize them as warlike or peaceful, enterprising or backward, trustworthy or deceptive, pragmatic and industrious, or idealistic and impractical. Germany is a case often discussed in this context. Many have emphasized the contrast between Germany's outstanding institutional creations and cultural achievements on the one hand, and on the other its historic role in Europe in the first half of the twentieth century. Hearnshaw's *Germany the Aggressor Throughout the Ages* (1940) may serve as an example. This mode of analysis should not be confused with a more sophisticated type in which national character is recognized to be a property of persons, and is treated as an independent variable contributing to an explanation of some form of political action considered as a dependent variable. An outstanding example is Gabriel Almond's (1950) use of material on the American character to explain certain persistent tendencies in the conduct of foreign policy by the United States.

National Character in Terms of a Combination.   Here the emphasis is put on diverse aspects of society and culture, including all three of the above: institutional pattern, theme and action. In this approach all of these are seen as possible manifestations of some core axiom governing interpersonal relationships in each culture. The anthropologist centrally concerned with this all-embracing approach is Francis L. K. Hsu (*Americans and Chinese: Two Ways of Life* [1953]; *Americans and Chinese: Purpose and Fulfillment in Great Civilizations* [1970]; *Clan, Caste and Club* [1963]).

Hsu shows, for example, a fundamental difference between the Chinese and Euro-Americans as regards emigration. With their basic *situation-centered* orientation the Chinese tend to be centripetal toward their kinsmen and local ties. Therefore, instead of finding solutions for their problems by expanding into new frontiers or revolutionary breaks with the past, the Chinese by and large expanded their human bonds through kinship and intensified their linkage with the past through the cult of ancestors. They achieved a highly developed ethics centered in filial piety. They institutionalized a highly familist political structure and system of law — the philosophy of "that which governed least governed best." They produced a huge body of literature extolling the virtue of never forgetting one's roots. Throughout history the Chinese have known practically no instance of large scale polarization based on irreconcilable religious, political or economic conflicts.

The result is that, historically, few Chinese followed their imperial leaders' military conquests outside of Chinese borders. A very tiny minority of Chinese, nearly all from the two provinces of Kwangtung (of which Canton is the capital) and Fukien (opposite Formosa), settled in the South Seas and in the Western world. Very few Chinese ever became explorers and no Chinese, either on their own or at the command of their rulers, went to foreign lands to spread the Chinese way of life or Chinese religion. All of these are in sharp contrast to *individual-centered,* centrifugal ways of Euro-Americans (Hsu 1970: 243–252; 288–289; 375–379).[1]

National Character as Racial Psychology.   The identification of national character with the allegedly "inborn" and presumably biological characteristics (generally defined as superior or inferior) of a group is one of the

[1] Since 1949 the new leaders of mainland China, pursuing a Western ideology, have been trying to make some fundamental changes in the Chinese orientation with as yet indifferent success (Hsu 1968).

oldest and most common approaches, and in modern social science the one most severely criticized if not actively abhorred (*cf.* Benedict 1945). A typical illustration, by no means the most extreme, may be found in Jaensch's (1938) study, published under Hitler, in which he asserted that the French were usually erratic and unreliable, the German consistent and stable.

The belief in racial psychology is by no means restricted to racist theoreticians. As tolerant and democratic a man as Andre Siegfried (1951), for example, attributes one of the two main qualities he finds in the French mind—its being "extremely practical and matter of fact"—to a Celtic heritage which he says is found wherever "Celtic blood prevails," including places as widely separated as northern Spain and the west of the British Isles. And Brickner's (1943) analysis of the German character as one essentially paranoid struck many students of the problem as verging on racism in psychology, even though it certainly did not suggest that the allegedly typical paranoid behavior was biological in origin. Although the pendulum may have swung too far in the opposite direction, there is today general agreement that the biologically given properties of what are in any event extraordinarily mixed national populations are *not* a significant influence in shaping the institutions, culture, or behavior of those national populations. Yet the altogether proper discrediting of racial psychology has perhaps had the unfortunate unintended effect of discouraging serious scientific research on a basic question of social science.

In most of the better known general essays on national character, such as those by Sforza (1942) on Italy, Siegfried (1930) on France, and Ortega y Gasset (1937) on Spain, more than one of these definitions or approaches will be used simultaneously and generally without any special note being taken of this fact. Typically, no distinction is made between character as something already formed and acting, and those forces such as climate and geography, history, biology, or child rearing which may be designated as the causes or consequences of the observed national character. If progress is to be made in the field, we need to make our investigations more systematic. There is no one line of development which can do full justice to the complexities of the problem. We feel, however, that great advantages inhere in the concentration on *modal adult personality* characteristics as a central problem in national character study. We therefore pose the question: whether produced by common heritage, common upbringing, the sharing of common culture, the exposure to common institutional pressures, or other causes, are there in fact any clearly demonstrated important differences in the psychological characteristics of the populations who make up modern national states? The question is more difficult to answer with confidence than many imagine it to be.

The Problem of Measurement

No matter how we conceive of national character, a scientific approach to it must face the problem of its assessment — or to use a less evasive word, its measurement. This subject generates as much confusion and malaise as does the issue of definition. The different approaches to national character based on institutional structure, and on national action or behavior, involve virtually no common understanding, standard techniques, regular procedures, or canons of reliability and validity. The situation is only slightly less variable in the racial psychology and the culture-pattern approaches. Each study proceeds almost entirely independently of all others, utilizes unique perspectives, draws on distinctive materials, follows idiosyncratic rules of evidence, and observes only its own standards of reliability and validity. The result is, if not intellectual chaos or anarchy, at least a great buzzing, blooming confusion which defies representation. Under the circumstances, a systematic comparative perspective is almost impossible.

It is argued by some, not without cogency, that institutional arrangements are so varied, culture patterns so unique, national psychologies so distinctive, that no common or standard language can hope to encompass this infinite diversity. Under these circumstances, it is said, we cannot do justice to the unique character of any people unless we develop a special battery of concepts and a new glossary of terms to describe them. This claim may be somewhat exaggerated. In any event it suggests that systematic analysis of national character as a field of scientific investigation is blocked. The same basic difficulty does not, at least in equal degree, attend efforts to deal with national character as modal personality patterns. There is good reason to believe that the range of variation in human personality, however great, can be adequately encompassed by a conceptual scheme, with a sufficiently limited set of terms to make for manageable research designs without sacrifice of essential richness or variety. We also maintain that, despite the many methodological and conceptual problems involved, this scheme and its measuring instruments can be developed so as to permit reliable and valid applications across national lines.

Harold Lasswell once claimed it would be an exaggeration to say that in two thousand years of studying politics we had made no advances whatsoever beyond Plato and Aristotle. Perhaps an exaggeration, but not a great one. At least so it seems when we recognize that the genius of political analysis has gone mainly into the invention of new terms for old ideas which were never made operational, never tested, and therefore never developed. For how else is one to choose between Plato's theory of the desiring, spirited, and reasoning parts, Pareto's "residues of combination" and "residues of persistence of aggregates," Spranger's six types of men, or Thomas and Znaniecki's Philistine, Bohemian, and Creative Man. These approaches must meet the criticism, as Spranger acknowledged, that they "abandon the concrete ground of experience and reduce psychology to mere speculation" (1928:xi).

As Harold Lasswell went on to say, however, our chief contemporary advantage over Plato and Aristotle lies "in the invention and adaptation of procedures by which specific individuals and groups, operating in specific historic and cultural settings, can be understood. . . . In a word, the modern approach is toward the building of scientific knowledge by perfecting the instrumentalities of inquiry" (1951:468–459). For the first time in the history of the study of politics we actually have within our grasp the means for systematic study of such conceptions as those developed by Plato, Pareto, and Spranger. I refer, of course, to the great strides made in this century in our understanding of personality dynamics and in the means for personality testing, measurement, and assessment. However, the concepts of Plato and others must first be clarified. They must be made operational, that is, transformed into possible research procedures of testing and measurement.

In some cases this has already been attempted, and it has been found possible and useful to devise formal measures of these classic typologies. Spranger's types, for example, were an important influence in shaping the widely used Allport-Vernon Scale of Values. In the process the old concepts may be found wanting. For example, Lurie's (1937) factor analysis to ascertain which generalized attitude clusters, if any, conform to Spranger's types, located several fitting Spranger's definition fairly closely — the theoretical, the religious, the social, and the economic-political. Several others, however, could not be empirically distinguished. As we test and perhaps discard some of these "classic" concepts, they will be replaced by others which are proving important in our study of personality and have obvious relevance to politics, such as: the needs for power, affiliation, and achievement; the authoritarian and ethnocentric syndrome; dominance drives; alienation and anomie; dogmatism and rigidity; tough- and tender-mindedness. It is in the nature of science and the inevitable path of its advance that concepts are replaced as empirical research advances. If for sentimental reasons we are unable to abandon the old familiar concepts, we may do ourselves honor as classicists, but we disqualify ourselves as scientists.

Political Systems as Objects of Study

The definition and classification of political systems is a more familiar and less ambiguous task, although it too has its vicissitudes. The sturdy old distinctions among political forms such as democracy, oligarchy, and tyranny which come down from Plato and Aristotle still serve us well today, although some may prefer a more contemporary classification, such as that proposed by Gabriel Almond (1956) who identifies the Anglo-American, the Continental European, the pre- or partially industrial, and the totalitarian political systems. Whatever scheme we might choose, we would probably not have great difficulty in agreeing on the defining characteristics of each type and could probably attain fair agreement in classifying particular societies.

Such classifications are, however, deceptively easy, and for many purposes they may be misleading. We generally accept the Greek city-state as the epitome of the democratic political system, but we should not forget that internally it rested squarely on a large slave class, and in external affairs was characterized by almost continuous intercity warfare motivated by nothing more noble than the desire for power and gain. Tsarist Russia was perhaps the most absolute autocracy in Europe in the eighteenth and nineteenth centuries, yet the village *mir* was a self-governing community observing some of the purest principles of egalitarian democracy. Germany was an outstanding example of relatively absolute monarchy before World War I, although intellectually and spiritually one of the freest nations in Europe. The Weimar Republic which followed represented the embodiment of the most advanced democratic principles, but it was succeeded by one of the blackest of totalitarian regimes — which again is followed by a West German Republic which seems one of the stablest and most genuine of Europe's democracies. The rule of Ataturk in Turkey was a dictatorship, yet he used his dictatorial power to foster democratic institutions against the resistance of the traditional religious oligarchy and the peasant masses. Soviet Russia under

Stalin had what was nominally the most democratic constitution in the world, while in fact it closely approximated a regime of absolute totalitarian terror.

The obvious point is that we must differentiate the components of political systems just as we must distinguish the diverse elements in, and the different bearers of, national character. As a minimum we must make a distinction between: the relatively enduring and the more fleeting or transitional features of a nation's political system (*cf.* Lipset 1960 on stable and unstable democracies); the formal, exoteric system from the informal, esoteric, operational patterns (*cf.* Leites 1951 on the *Politburo*); the politics of central government from that which characterizes vital institutions such as the local community, the church, trade union, or family (*cf.* Michels 1949 on the iron law of oligarchy); the principles embodied in constitutions and other venerated documents and those commonly held by the populace (*cf.* Stouffer 1955 on civil liberties in the United States); the political orientation of the elite as against that of the rank and file of the population (*cf.* Stouffer 1955 and Mills 1956 on the power elite).

Only if we recognize both politics and national character as highly differentiated systems of variables can we hope to do any justice to the complex phenomena we are studying. Unfortunately many, indeed most, studies which seek to relate character to political systems fail to make these necessary distinctions. They treat political systems as undifferentiated and more or less unchanging units rather than as complex variables.

Review of Systematic Empirical Studies

Despite the efflorescence of the field of culture and personality during the last three decades,[2] and a parallel growth of interest in the empirical study of modern political systems, we can point to very few systematic empirical studies of the relations between personality patterns, or psychological factors in general, and the rise, functioning, and change of political systems. As usual the history of intellectual disciplines reveals much of the story. Modern studies of the relations between personality and sociocultur-

---

[2] The point at which a new field of exploration begins can as a rule be designated only on an essentially arbitrary basis. Most authorities acknowledge Franz Boas as the father of this movement (see especially Boas 1910), and many date its formal beginning with the publication in 1934 of Ruth Benedict's *Patterns of Culture*. Ruth Benedict and Margaret Mead were, of course, students in the seminars on Individual and Society which Boas gave at Columbia in the late twenties. Boas himself gave great credit to Theodore Waitz, of whose *Anthropolgie der Naturvolker* he said "[this] great work is an inquiry into whether there are any fundamental differences between the mental make-up of mankind the world over, racially as well as socially."

al systems have been developed almost exclusively by cultural anthropologists. Perhaps because most nonliterate (or primitive) people rarely have a formal or specialized political organization, all but a few cultural anthropologists have shown little interest in political structure. In this respect, at least, the students of personality and culture have followed the dominant pattern in their discipline. Benedict's book on Japan (1946) and Hsu's comparison of the Chinese and American culture (1953) each give a chapter or more to politics and government, and Mead (1957) devoted an entire book to Soviet attitudes toward authority, particularly political authority. But these are outstanding exceptions. The early editions of the two standard and massive American collections of articles on culture and personality do not contain a single item which deals directly with the relation of personality patterns to the political system.[3] Similarly, the standard anthropological textbook in the field contains a chapter on psychiatric disorders and one on "personality in class, caste, region and occupation," but none on politics.[4] Linton's (1945) little classic on *The Cultural Background of Personality* makes no mention of government or politics. The same may be said of the works of Abram Kardiner (1939, 1945) which have done so much to shape the field. Geoffrey Gorer's study of the English character has chapters on "friends and neighbors," on "people and homes," on "religion," and on "marriage," but none on attitudes about those political institutions such as parliaments, elections, local government, civil liberties, and personal rights which most people regard as the truly distinctive political features of English society.[5]

---

[3] Clyde Kluckhohn and Henry Murray (1953); Douglas Haring (1948). The former did contain an article on personality under the Nazis, but rather than having a political focus it was designed only to show that personality remained unchanged despite changes in the individual's political security. The latter had an article on the armaments race, but only as illustrating a type of mechanism in interpersonal relations. Later editions gave somewhat, but not much more, attention to the political process. The later edition of the Kluckhohn, Murray (and Schneider) volume (1956) included a new article by R. Bauer, "Psychology of the Soviet Middle Elite." In addition, the third edition of the Haring volume (1956) included materials on the role of character in postwar Japanese sociopolitical development and one by Gorer which, while not explicitly dealing with political structure, discussed the role of the police in the apparent modifications of the English character in modern times.

[4] John Honigmann (1954). The index does call attention, under the heading "political relations," to two pages which discuss the evidence that organizational atomism in a community is related to the degree of ingroup sorcery, and two pages on the relations of family patterns to political structure.

[5] Gorer's (1955) book does contain a chapter on "law and order," but it deals exclusively with two questions: the popular image of the police and the attitude toward "fiddling," a term used to describe minor infractions of the rationing regulations.

These comments are, of course, not meant to ignore the substantial contribution of the British anthropologists to our understanding of primitive political systems, but in this case the hiatus is complementary to that found in the culture and personality studies. In their exceptionally fine work on African political systems Fortes, Evans-Pritchard, and their associates (1940) say virtually nothing about the characterological qualities which may be important to the development and maintenance of stable political orders in these important underdeveloped regions.

Unfortunately the situation is not markedly changed when we consider the work of political scientists, to whom one might appropriately assign greater responsibility for this line of work. Although Plato and Aristotle both stressed the role of character in shaping political forms and processes, the person tends periodically to disappear from political theory. Early in this century Graham Wallas made a plea for a return to the study of human nature in politics. He deplored the books by American university professors as useless, because the writers "dealt with abstract men, formed on assumptions of which they were unaware and which they had never tested either by experience or by study" (1908:10). Very little was done to take up the challenge. More than two decades later Charles E. Merriam (1925) was still pleading the same needs, but in a more focused and hopeful manner with emphasis on personality measurement, large-scale statistical studies, and correlational analysis of the relations between political conduct and psychological characteristics of the political man. In the same year Henry Moore (1925) published a pioneering study of psychological factors associated with holding radical and conservative political opinions. Moore's analysis, utilizing tests for resistance to majority opinion and of readiness to break old habits, anticipated much of the recent research on personality and politics. Unfortunately it failed to become the start of an active research tradition in psychology.

Merriam's role in fostering the application of psychology to politics is comparable to that played by Franz Boas in the development of culture and personality studies. It was under Merriam's influence that Harold Lasswell wrote what was probably the first modern, systematic, and broad application of psychology to contemporary politics. In *Psychopathology and Politics* (1930) Lasswell broke new ground in going beyond the usual hypothetical classification of political types to develop the detailed study of life histories. Guided by psychoanalytic theory, he showed quite explicitly and empirically the connection between personality traits and the choice and style of political roles such as the agitator, the propagandist, and the administrator. In the same volume he sketched one of the first systematic schemes for describing personality in politically relevant terms. Although he worked mainly with the individual case study, Lasswell was not unaware of the implications of this mode of analysis for the study of political patterns characteristic of classes and national populations. "What matters to the student of culture," he said, "is not the subjective similarities of the species but the subjective differences among the members of the same and similar cultures" (1930:261). He did not, however, follow through to undertake the systematic research this statement implied.

A decade elapsed before the next really major event in the field occurred with the publication of Erich Fromm's *Escape from Freedom* (1941). Fromm took the step that Lasswell had anticipated but failed to make himself. He held that the typical character types prevalent at any given time were different, that these differences varied systematically with changes in the socioeconomic system, and that character types could serve either as a cement holding the system together or as an explosive tearing it apart, depending on the degree to which a given character type fit the demands of the system and found satisfaction in it. He traced this interaction through the history of medieval Europe and the Reformation, sought to explain the appeal of Hitler by the widespread prevalence of the authoritarian character in Germany, and sketched some of the forces in democratic society — such as the sense of aloneness, the loss of individuality and spontaneity — which he saw as inducing an "escape from freedom."

Fromm's theory has been extraordinarily stimulating to all concerned with the study of personality and politics. We should appreciate his theoretical sophistication, his clinical intuition, and his clear recognition of the most vital problems. His use of historical documents and contemporary sources, such as political speeches and party platforms, represented a commendable improvement over the efforts of those who were content to rely more or less exclusively on their clinical experience with psychoanalytic patients. Nevertheless, many students of the problem would insist that Fromm's analysis did not present more than suggestive hypotheses. It was yet to be demonstrated by objectively verified testing based on adequate samples that the modal personality types in different socioeconomic systems were significantly different from each other, or that within any nation the form and content of political action varied according to the personality traits typical for any group.

Considering that the conflict of political principles played so central a role among the issues in World War II, it is rather striking that the series of books on national character which anthropologists contributed to the war effort gave such incidental, indeed almost casual, treatment to the relations between national character and democratic government. There are important limitations on the justice with which this characterization can be applied in one or another case, yet it fairly well fits the work of Gorer on Japan (1943), Russia (1950), and the United States (1948), Mead on the United States (1942), and Benedict on Japan (1946). Insofar as they did deal with governments, they did not with any rigor specify the personality traits of politically active adults which might conduce them to support democratic or autocratic government. Instead, their method was to highlight the analogy between the political system and other features of the culture, most notably the family. Thus Gorer notes the characteristic division of power in the United States as contrasted with greater centralization in European governments, then points to the typical American nuclear family council, and concludes that "to a certain extent the pattern of authority in the state is reflected in the family" (1948:44–45). Similarly, Benedict notes that the Japanese father is not a martinet, but rather exercises his authority as the representative of the larger family. The attitude thus "learned by the child in his earliest experiences with his father" is then invoked to explain why in Japanese governmental affairs "the officials who head the hierarchy do not typically exercize the actual authority" (1946:301).

These are undoubtedly important insights. Nevertheless, to conceive of the family as the mirror of the state, and of the state as a reflection of the pattern of relations in the family, establishes a circle without any suggestion as to how change can and does come about. In the case of the Japanese, Benedict sought to meet this challenge by stressing the Japanese "ethic of alternatives." But what of the Germans and Russians who presumably do not have such an ethic? Are they doomed to perpetual authoritarian government as the cycles of family and state patterns ever renew themselves?

The basic difficulty with this approach, one pervasive in the psychological anthropology literature, is its failure to take adequate account of the differentiation within large national populations. It emphasizes the central tendency, the existence of which it presumes but does not prove, and neglects the range of variation within and around the average or typical. Once we begin to deal with distributions, with variation and range, we must recognize that a second weakness of this approach is that its descriptive language, the technical terms on which it is based, does not easily permit the precise measurement and quantitative expression necessary to the study of a distributive phenomenon. These deficiencies were largely remedied in another set of the wartime studies, particularly those by Henry Dicks (1950) and David Levy (1951), which represent an important landmark in the development of our understanding of how personality relates to political action.

Dicks' work was in the main line of culture and personality studies in that it considered personality in psychoanalytic terms and was based on a general model of the German personality drawn from a variety of cultural sources. In his case, however, what is generally the conclusion of many studies was only the starting point. He went beyond previous studies in three important respects: (1) the personality of each subject was explicitly scored on clearly specified and carefully defined variables; (2) the political orientation of each person was also carefully measured in concrete terms; and (3) the personality measures and the indices of political orientation were systematically related to each other by standard statistical procedures. All this was done with clinical sensitivity, with use of general theory, and without loss of contact with the more traditional but impressionistic description of the German national character.

Dicks worked with a sample of 138 German soldiers taken as prisoners of war between 1942 and 1944. On the basis of *politically* focused interviews each man was classified on a five-point scale running from "fanatical, wholehearted Nazi" to "active, convinced anti-Nazi." In addition, on the basis of nominally free but in fact highly focused *psychiatrically* oriented interviews, each man was rated on 15 different psychosociological variables ranging from degree of religiosity to presence or absence of schizoid features. Relationships attaining a high degree of statistical significance (at the .01 level or better) were obtained between Nazism and six of the fifteen psychosocial variables. For example, those high on the scale of Naziism showed a marked taboo against tenderness, were more sadistic or antisocial, and were much more likely to engage in projection.

It is important to recognize that Dicks did not prove these or any other characteristics to be *generally* present in German nationals. He proved only that Nazis and near-Nazis were different from non-Nazi Germans in a number of important respects. This is not to say that Dicks did not attempt a general characterization of the German personality. He could hardly have undertaken his study without some such hypothetical model which, he assumed, the Nazi "embodied in more exaggerated or concentrated form." The typical German he described as having "an ambivalent, compulsive character structure with the emphasis on submissive dominant conformity, a strong counter-cathexis of the virtues of duty, of 'control' by the self, especially buttressed by re-projected 'external' super-ego sym-, bols." Even though such individuals might be highly susceptible to the propaganda themes and the style of leadership offered by the Nazis, it is also apparent that this character type could freely support any one of a number of different sociopolitical orders. Dicks' study is of particular value, therefore, in keeping before us the awareness that in any national population there is likely to be substantial variation in modal personality patterns, even though for any given nation this variation may cover only a narrow part of the world-wide range. Dicks' study also suggests that the extreme political positions are those which are most likely to be attractive to the extremes on the personality continuum. If the extremists seize power, the resulting political forms may or may not be congruent with the dominant personality tendencies in the population at large. It seems likely that this congruence was greater in Hitlerite Germany than in Stalinist Russia.

Inkeles, Hanfmann, and Beier (1958) administered a battery of tests including the Rorschach, TAT, sentence-completion test, and others to a small sample (51 cases) of refugees from Soviet Russia who departed during and just after World War II (*cf.* Dicks 1952). On this basis they constructed a composite national character portrait, differentiating a main modal pattern, a variant on it, and a residual group. The subjects were also divided into four social classes. The authors did not, unfortunately, relate the personality characteristics of each individual directly to his mode of political orientation. For the group as a whole, however, they related its adjustment to the Soviet political system to each element of the modal personality pattern — which included a strong need for affiliation, marked dependency needs, emotional expressiveness and responsiveness, and resistance to being shamed for failures in impersonal performance. The authors found, for example, that the persistent shortages of food, shelter, and clothing which characterized Soviet life under Stalin, aggra- vated the anxieties about oral deprivation which were frequently mani- fested in the Russian character. In general, they concluded, "there was a high degree of incongruence between the central personality modes and dispositions of many Russians and . . . the behavior of the regime." This was most marked, however, for those who represented the basic personality mode, and was much less true for those whose personality reflected a substantial departure from the modal pattern common to the mass of peasants and workers.

Postwar Developments

Research in the period after World War II has been characterized by two important developments: (1) improvements in the methods for assessing personality on a large scale and (2) the application of such methods on a cross-national or comparative basis.

If we require that national character studies be based on systematic and objective study of personality, that they represent all the diverse elements of national populations, and that they permit meaningful comparison with results from other studies, we are in effect calling for a transformation of the standard methodology of the field. Such a demand made before 1940 would have been perhaps not visionary, but hardly reasonable as a practical matter. The postwar period, however, has seen the development and application of means for the assessment of personality which enable us to measure it with relative ease, and to do so with large representative samples. There is reason to believe that at least some of these instruments may be effectively used cross-nationally.

The effort to measure with some precision the personality traits of entire national groups has a longer history than many suppose. One of the earliest ventures in the use of a standard psychological test to assess personality trends in a significantly large population was the Bleulers' (1935) application of the Rorschach Ink-Blot test to Moroccans in the thirties. The Bluelers administered the Rorschach to an unspecified number of "simple country folk" (half Arab, half Berber) living in the vast plains of West Morocco. Their characterization, based on the Rorschach records as measured against their experience with the test in Europe, is full of comments of the following order: the Moroccan lacks the typical European "tendency to abstractive generalization"; his extroversion emerges mainly in "a marked enthusiasm under the influence of momentary events . . . but he lacks the systematic, energetic, and persevering striving after outward success."

Of course we will wonder whether we can safely generalize these comments to other Moroccans, and how much these patterns reflect not Moroccan culture but rather the low level of education and the relative isolation of these people. But more important for our purposes is the question of the relevance of such qualities of character for the ability to act as a good citizen in a stable political order of a national state. The

Bleulers' description typically makes no mention of images of authority, civic consciousness, or other traits of obvious political relevance, and we do not have the knowledge to judge whether the lack of a tendency to abstractive generalization is conducive to good democratic citizenship or not. That these defects of the typical Rorschach analysis of group personality are relatively persistent may be observed by comparing the Bleulers' study with later ventures, such as the study of the Chinese by Abel and Hsu (1949). Indeed, the Rorschach has come into serious question as an instrument for systematic research into group traits (Carstairs, Payne, and Whitaker 1960).

Probably the greatest influence on our thinking and practice in the measurement of personality dimensions relevant to politics is exerted by the now classic study of the authoritarian personality by the Frankfurt Institut fur Sozialforschung (Horkheimer 1936). Erich Fromm played a major role in this group's development of the concept of the authoritarian personality, which Adorno (1950) and his associates carried forward in the United States both theoretically and methodologically. The main fruit of the California group's investigation was the isolation, definition, and measurement of a particular personality type, but the conception of that type was initially derived from ideas about the distinctive psychological coloration of authoritarian political creeds and movements. Although the F scale[6] has been severely criticized because it can distinguish right authoritarians but permits left authoritarians to escape notice (Christie 1954), there can be no serious question but that the psychological syndrome thus isolated is highly correlated with extreme right-wing political attitudes.

The semipsychiatric interview which Dicks used requires special talent to conduct, is difficult and expensive to code or score, and must therefore be restricted to very small samples. By contrast the F scale has the special virtue of great simplicity as a test instrument, something unusual in the earlier efforts to measure personality variables of theoretical interest and proved clinical significance. The F scale thus made possible for the first time the simultaneous collection of data on personality and on political orientations from a fully representative national sample. Using a modified version of the F scale, Janowitz and Marvick found that in the United

[6] The letter F was used with the scale to designate "susceptibility to Fascism." This sounds more like a specifically political than a psychological measure, although the authors intended it mainly as a measure of personality. This use of the term Fascism for the scale unfortunately clouded the issue by seeming to prejudge the relation between measures of personality and those of political orientation, or worse, to suggest they were perhaps one and the same thing.

States those whose personality tended more toward authoritarianism were also more markedly isolationist in foreign affairs (*cf.* Levinson 1957). The more authoritarian also revealed a sense of political ineffectiveness, that is, they believed themselves powerless to influence government action. The conclusion reached by Janowitz and Marvick is particularly noteworthy: "Personality tendencies measured by [an] authoritarian scale served to explain political behavior at least as well as those factors [such as age, education, and class] traditionally included in political and voting behavior studies." (1953:201; also see Lane 1955.)

In addition to the F scale, there are other personality measures suitable for administration to large samples and relevant to political orientations, such as Rokeach's (1956) dogmatism scale and Eysenck's (1954) classification of the tender minded and tough minded. In their study of American automobile workers, Arthur Kornhauser (1956) and his associates utilized measures not only of authoritarianism but also of life satisfaction and social alienation or "anomie." Those characterized by anomie showed little interest in politics, and were much less likely to vote. When they did vote, they tended to vote contrary to the prevailing sentiment among their fellow workers. Among numerous important findings in this rich and interesting study was the discovery that authoritarianism is related to political extremism *whether of the right or left.* This assumption gains support from a study of political orientations in Iran. Despite their fundamental differences in political position, the extreme rightists and extreme leftists were more like each other in many social and behavioral characteristics — such as "level of social detachment" and "breadth of social horizons" — than they were like the more moderate groups of the political center (Ringer and Sills 1953).

In summarizing their detailed results, Kornhauser and his associates reach a conclusion which accords well with the requirements of our model of the democratic personality. They say: "The problem of democracy . . . is partly the problem of maintaining an adequate proportion of members who are capable of engaging in the market place of proposals and counter-proposals, immune from the feeling that 'the leader knows best' and from the temptation to condone, or to resort to, desperate measures in times of social and political crisis" (1956:249–250).

Perhaps the most systematic effort to relate personality to political inclinations is to be found in the pioneering study by Herbert McClosky (1953) in which he sought to define the personality characteristics of those taking positions along the continuum from conservative to liberal politics.

He unfortunately defines conservatism not by party affiliation, but on the basis of agreement with a set of normative propositions drawn from the works of leading, modern, conservative spokesmen. These statements include items such as: you can't change human nature; no matter what people think, a few people will always run things anyway; duties are more important than rights. Using a rich battery of personality scales developed at the University of Minnesota and elsewhere, he finds that the extreme conservatives are sharply differentiated from both the "liberals" and "moderate liberals" in being more submissive, anomic, alienated, pessimistic, guilty, hostile, rigid, paranoid obsessive, intolerant of human frailty, and extremely ego-defensive. It will be immediately apparent that the personality traits of the extreme conservative or "reactionary" bear a very close relation to those of the authoritarian personality, and at every point are polar to the qualities described below in our model of the democratic personality.

It is unfortunately characteristic of McClosky's study, and many others in this field, that they are not comparative. This necessarily leaves us in doubt as to whether in other countries or environments the same traits of personality would also be associated with the same kinds of political orientation. For example, Dicks' (1950) study raises at once a question as to the uniqueness of the Nazi pattern and the degree to which we can generalize his findings. Since all of Dicks' comparisons were made within the German sample, he is quite justified in saying that in Germany certain individual characteristics are more associated with fascist political leanings than others. But his assumption that the Nazis are only extreme variants of a more general or typical German character cannot be taken as proved. On the basis of his sample he could hardly establish what the average or typical German is like, if he exists at all. In any study restricted to one sample, we may easily be led into assuming that the response which fits our preconception of the group is distinctive to it, when in fact that response is quite common in other populations as well. For example, we would have much more confidence in Schaffner's (1948) finding of extreme authoritarianism in the typical German conception of the family had he given his sentence completion test to at least one other comparable national group.

This defect was remedied in a number of studies conducted after World War II. Indeed the postwar period is outstanding for the development of more systematic comparative research. For example, D. V. McGranahan (1946) put a number of questions on basic issues — such as obedience to authority under duress, and freedom of the press even when not "for the good of the people" — to comparable samples of American and German boys. In the latter case he made a distinction by political orientation between Nazis, neutrals, and anti-Nazis. The German youth distinctly favored obedience to authority more often than the Americans, showed less faith in the common man, and were more admiring of people with political or military power. In general these findings fit our expectation with regard to the greater emphasis on democratic values in American as against German society. But it is crucial to note that *within* the German group, those classified as anti-Nazi were on some questions closer to the Americans than to their Nazi-oriented compatriots.

Of course, no simple conclusions can be drawn from one such study standing alone. For example, when the same questions were given by Stoodley (1957) to a more or less comparable group of youths from the Philippines, he found that on some dimensions they were closer to the Germans, on others, to the Americans, thus yielding a distinctive national profile. Unfortunately, he did not inquire into the relation of these attitudes to political orientation, which would have enabled us to judge whether the same value orientations which made for Nazism in Germany made for comparable antidemocratic leanings in the Philippines.

Gillespie and Allport (1955) studied hopes for the future among college students in several countries. Although they did not inquire directly into political beliefs, several of the topics they dealt with are clearly relevant to an evaluation of the strength of tendencies toward various forms of active "citizenship." They reported the Japanese to be outstanding in their "sense of obligation to the social group in which they live." The Japanese were, for example, first among all countries in saying they would seek to inculcate in their children such qualities as good citizenship, social usefulness, and service to society (*cf.* Stoetzel 1955). On this and similar questions Americans were near the bottom of the list. They "emphasized their rights rather than their duties and in all presented a picture of individuality, separation from the social context of living, and privatization of values and personal plans" (1955:29). The New Zealanders presented a profile quite similar to that of the Americans, but we cannot say whether this results from their common Anglo-Saxon heritage, the common experience of settling a new continent, or some combination of these and similar influences. These findings are well in accord with the conclusions of earlier, more impressionistic studies of American and

Japanese character. They are none the less welcome for providing firm confirmation of these hypotheses.

Despite such promising starts there seems to be great hesitation to undertake systematic comparative studies. The hesitation to apply methods of personality testing cross-nationally arises not merely from the magnitude and cost of the task, admittedly substantial, but in large part from resistance, skepticism, and outright rejection of the possibility of reliable and valid cross- national testing of opinions, values, and personality traits. We should not minimize the substantial technical difficulties facing any such effort. But the objections often offered to such attempts seem exaggerated, and in any event the appropriate response is to accept the challenge and attempt the necessary methodological innovation. By way of encouragement we may note that a number of studies have shown that certain tests can be used cross-nationally with a high degree of reliability. In a study of UNESCO (Cantril and Buchanan 1953) conducted in nine countries it was found that most questions had the same meaning in all the countries studied, and that the opinions related to each other in one setting were similarly correlated in the others. For example, in each country those who believed human nature can be changed were also more likely to believe that national characteristics arise from the way in which people are brought up. Indeed the same syndrome, or complex pattern of attitudes, was represented in all countries. One group in each country, who might be called the optimists, believed human nature perfectible, national character pliable, world peace attainable, and world organization desirable. The pessimists, or fatalists, believed there would always be wars, human nature cannot be changed, and that efforts at improving the international situation are bound to fail.

The UNESCO study, of course, dealt more with opinions than with deeper lying attitudes and facets of personality, but we are not limited to that level. In an important study of values which Charles Morris (1956) conducted in the United States, India, and China, he discovered that in each country the ratings of individual questions were made along the same common value dimensions and that "there is thus revealed an underlying value structure (or value space) which is very much the same in the culturally diverse groups of students." In addition, the relation of the value factors to other issues was much the same in each culturally distinct group. For example, those individuals whose values centered on receptivity to and sympathetic concern for others tended, in all three countries, to dislike or reject the operative values of the political world, as measured by the Allport-Vernon scale.

Morris's comparative study was limited to student samples. While recognizing that this might yield an exaggeratedly homogeneous picture, he nevertheless concluded that there were substantial national differences. Using the four basic factors which emerged from the factor-analytic study of his "paths of life" value test, he developed comparable profiles for the several national groups. Thus, the American students emerged as "the most activistic and self-indulgent, less subject to social restraint and less open to receptivity than any of the four other groups and second lowest in inwardness." By contrast, the Indians had a very high score on the factor on which the Americans scored lowest. They were characterized by strong emphasis on social restraint and self-control, stood second highest on the factor which measured withdrawal and self-sufficiency, and in the same rank on that which measured receptivity and sympathetic concern. The other student groups from Japan, China and Norway each, in turn, produced its own distinctive pattern on the four-factor profile. Morris' findings, though not some of his interpretations, found support in Hsu's comparative study of India, China and the United States (Hsu 1963:237–240).

Comparable evidence of the cross-national relevance of personality tests and of cross-national regularity in the relation of personality to political orientation is reported in the use of a personality test which presumably taps deeper-lying strata of the personality. In a comparative study of teachers in seven European countries it was found that the same items of the F scale designed to test authoritarianism tended to cohere and form a pattern in all of the countries studied.[7] In addition, the research uncovered high consistency in the way in which orientations toward threatening situations in both domestic and international politics were patterned in the several countries. But at the same time the authors offer us some sobering words of caution regarding the difficulties facing such comparative studies. They found "many of the relationships vary in size, direction and significance in different countries . . . modified by specific national and international situational factors — by the historically given structures of political forces, by the dominant policies, by majority-minority relations, by the ongoing communication processes in the mass media and in the larger organizations" (Aubert et al. 1954:38).

[7] Personal Communication from Drs. D. J. Levinson and Stein Rokkan. They were collected in the study reported in Aubert, 1954.

Development in the 60's

Although there were many important differences among the typical studies of national character completed before 1955, they shared certain significant similarities. Generally, they sought to encompass in more or less its totality the modal personality of a major group. Their task was descriptive rather than analytical. The groups were selected to be studied not because some theory required that group, but rather because of their intrinsic interest or because they represented some major culture area. The measures used were mostly of the projective variety. The findings were woven together with other materials, and with impressions based on origin or residence, to yield a complex and essentially clinical-interpretative, general portrait of the modal type. The personality patterns of other groups were either not considered simultaneously, or were used mainly as a standard permitting clearer and sharper delineation of the character of the group under study. There was no great interest in systematic comparison in its own right. Finally, the modal personality delineated in these studies was generally related to the culture as a whole, or to a variety of its features, rather than to some specific substructure such as the polity.

Alongside continuing studies representing an earlier tradition, there appeared in the decade after 1960 a substantial number of studies done in an almost entirely new style. Rather than attempt a general portrait, they usually focused on a single trait or complex. They usually eschewed impressionistic, informal observation in favor of systematic testing. The projective psychological test was fairly consistently replaced by the public-opinion poll. No longer focused on a single nation or group, these studies generally dealt with a set of nations at one time in an explicitly comparative design. The small, special, and often markedly unrepresentative samples of the past were replaced by large and often representative samples drawn from the entire national population. And rather than relate their findings about personality modes to the culture or society as whole, the authors of these new studies generally restricted their discussion to a limited segment of the social structure, to a particular set of roles, or even to a single status such as that of entrepreneur. As LeVine (1963) summed up the trend, studies in "group" personality became now "virtually a residual category." "In the newer studies," he continued, "it is the *relationship* between personality and some other variables which is the focus of analysis rather than the characterization of the group personality itself." (p. 123)

Daniel Lerner's (1958) exploration of the modernization of six countries of the Middle East stressed the increasing and ever more widely diffused *rationality,* in which "ways of thinking and acting are instruments of intention not articles of faith." His study of several countries in the Arab world used a scale of *empathy,* defined by Lerner as the ability to put oneself in the role of the other, particularly in the role of leading political figures. Though all the countries shared broadly the same religious and cultural heritage, there were marked differences in degree of empathic ability in the different national groups.

The samples for this study of six Middle Eastern nations were chosen not primarily to represent their respective populations, but rather to represent certain social groups selected mainly on grounds of communication behavior. Nevertheless, if we assume that the group low in education, rural in residence, and little exposed to the mass media — whom Lerner called the "traditionals" — is most typical of each country and broadly comparable from nation to nation, then the classification of his respondents permits systematic cross-national comparisons. The Turks consistently emerged as more modern than the citizens of Iran; they less often show a sense of "personal impotence" and more commonly have "empathic" ability.[8]

Almond and Verba (1963) refer to the subject of their investigations as "political culture" but they are using culture in the sense of "psychological orientation." They say: "When we speak of the political culture we refer to the political system as internalized in the cognitions, feelings, and evaluation of its population" (p. 14). They use this term rather than "national character" or "modal personality" mainly in order to distinguish between political and nonpolitical attitudes. The political culture is expressed in the prevalence of certain types of orientation, which they term *participant, subject* and *parochial..* An individual or group is classified as

[8] In contrasting the Chinese and American attitudes toward their respective governments and leaders, Hsu characterizes them as follows: "Fundamentally, however, the various levels of officials and the American people maintain a level of communication and a degree of unity of outlook that, in their constancy and extent, differ greatly from the relationship of the Chinese and their government. If we characterize the Chinese attitude toward government as checking it through respect and distance, we must note in contrast that the American attitude toward government is to control it through equality and identification" (Hsu 1970:194). Obviously what Hsu notes as "equality and identification" is very close to Lerner's "empathic" ability. If so the Chinese would have rated very low in modernity while the Americans would rate very high. However, following Hsu's analysis, the American *individual-centered* orientation, which forms the basis of this American high rating in modernity, is also the root of many American problems, such as generation gaps and racial violence (Hsu 1970:325–341)

one or another type on the basis of answers to such questions as: "What knowledge does he have of his nation and political system (and) how does he perceive of himself as a member of his political system?"

Almond and Verba also develop the concept of *subjective competence,* which is the belief that an individual has that he can influence the political process, or the perception of his ability to exert political influence. This idea is clearly related to Lerner's (1958) concept of "personal impotency": the *feeling* that you cannot do something about a personal or communal problem linked to the *idea* that you cannot go against fate or religion. Lerner sees this quality as opposed to "an expectation that what one does or says will matter in the world" (pp. 100–101). Studying the "civic culture" of six countries, Almond and Verba devised an index to measure the sense of civic competence, the feeling that one understands local politics and can effectively do something about it. The countries with the more formal and long-term democratic tradition, England and the United States, had the highest proportion of citizens with a strong sense of civic competence. Other studies attempting similar national comparisons are being conducted by Cantril (1965) on hopes and fears for the future, and Inkeles (1966a, 1969) and Smith (1966) on the modernization of attitudes in developing countries.

Though these new-style studies did not in most cases set out to describe group personality patterns, they in fact constitute a major resource for doing precisely that. In using them we must accept their self-imposed restriction of paying attention mainly to one particular aspect of personality selected according to their theoretical interest in some selected element of social structure. It by no means follows, however, that an approach to personality shaped by an interest in some specific social problem must necessarily yield a thin or impoverished description of modal personality. For example, Almond and Verba (1963) produced the following complex portrait of the Italian character (pp: 402–403):

> The picture of the Italian political culture that has emerged from our data is one of relatively unrelieved political alienation and of social isolation and distrust. The Italians are particularly low in national pride, in moderate and open partisanship, in the acknowledgement of the obligation to take an active part in local community affairs, in the sense of competence to join with others in situations of political stress, in their choice of social forms of leisure-time activity, and in their confidence in the social environment . . . Italian national and political alienation rests on social alienation. If our data are correct, most Italians view the social environment as full of threat and danger.

Whatever the description of modal personality in these studies may lack in depth or complexity is compensated for by the greater precision of measurement, by the larger, more representative samples studied, and, perhaps most important, by the opportunity for a strictly comparative analysis which permits us to see the characteristics of one national or ethnic group in relation to others.

Toward the Delineation of the Democratic Character

It is apparent that we have made at least a modest beginning in studying the relation of personality patterns to the development and maintenance of political systems. There is substantial and rather compelling evidence of a regular and intimate connection between personality and the mode of political participation by individuals and groups within any one political system. In many different institutional settings and in many parts of the world, those who adhere to the more extreme political positions have distinctive personality traits separating them from those taking more moderate positions in the same setting. The formal or explicit "content" of one's political orientation — left or right, conservative or radical, pro- or antilabor — may be determined mainly by more "extrinsic" characteristics such as education and social class; but the form or style of political expression — favoring force or persuasion, compromise or arbitrary dictation, being tolerant or narrowly prejudiced, flexible in policy or rigidly dogmatic — is apparently largely determined by personality. At least this seems clear with regard to the political extremes. It is not yet certain whether the same characteristics make for extremism in all national groups and institutional settings, but that also seems highly likely.

Prominent among the traits which make for extremism appear to be the following: exaggerated faith in powerful leaders and insistence on absolute obedience to them; hatred of outsiders and deviates; excessive projection of guilt and hostility; extreme cynicism; a sense of powerlessness and ineffectiveness (alienation and anomie); suspicion and distrust of others; and dogmatism and rigidity. Some of these terms have been or will be shown to be merely alternative designations of the same phenomenon, but some such general syndrome of authoritarianism, dogmatism, and alienation undoubtedly is the psychological root of that political extremism which makes this type actively or potentially disruptive to democratic systems.

If political extremism is indeed an accompaniment — and even more a product — of a certain personality syndrone, and if this syndrome produces the equivalent extremism in all national populations and subgroups, that fact poses a considerable challenge to the student of national character in its relation to political systems. At once we face this question: Are the societies which have a long history of democracy peopled by a majority of individuals who possess a personality conducive to democracy? Alternatively, are societies which have experienced recurrent or prolonged authoritarian, dictatorial, or totalitarian government inhabited by a proportionately large number of individuals with the personality traits we have seen to be associated with extremism? In other words, can we move from the individual and group level, to generalize about the relations of personality and political system at the societal level?

Almost all the modern students of national character are convinced that the answer to this question is in the affirmative. Systematic empirical evidence for this faith is unfortunately lacking. To prove the point we would be required to show that the qualities of personality presumably supportive or less destructive of democracy are more widely prevalent in stable democracies such as the United States, England, Switzerland, or Sweden than in Germany, Japan, Italy, or Russia. At the present time we cannot offer such proof. We will continue to be unable to settle this question until we undertake nation-wide studies of modal personality patterns — such as we do of literacy or per capita income — and test their relation to the forms of political organization in various countries. Before we undertake such studies we must have some conception of the character types for which we are looking.

The problem of defining anything as broad as "the democratic character" may be much like the problem of locating the Manchester economists' "economic man" who Unamuno somewhere described as "a man neither of here nor there, neither this age nor another, who has neither sex nor country, who is, in brief, merely an idea — that is to say, a 'no-man.'"

The danger of excessive generality in defining the democratic character is not greater than the danger of "misplaced concreteness," that is, defining the characterological requirements of *any* democracy as identical with those of some particular people who have a strong democratic tradition. For example, it has been true of the great majority of commentaries on the people of the United States, going back to its earliest days, that "practicality" and "emphasis on religion" have been consistently cited as American traits (Coleman 1941). Yet it would be difficult to argue that either quality is a sufficient or even a necessary requirement for effective citizenship in a democracy. The same may be said of other traits frequently cited as characterizing the American people, such as valuing success and achievement, which are also strongly emphasized in Japanese culture, or the marked emphasis on activity and work, which is also commonly cited as typifying the German character.

While observing these cautions, we should not avoid postulating certain qualities which are probably indispensable to the long-run maintenance of a democratic political order. In holding this view we do no more than did De Tocqueville. De Tocqueville weighed the role of geography and climate, of religion and political institutions, and finally of what he called "manners," meaning thereby "various notions and opinions current among men . . . the mass of those ideas which constitute their character of mind . . . the whole moral and intellectual condition of a people." Comparing Mexico, South America, and the United States in these terms, he concluded: "The manners [character] of the Americans of the United States are the *real* cause which renders it the only one of the American nations that is able to support a democratic government . . . I should say that the physical circumstances are less efficient than the laws, and the laws very subordinate to the manners [character] of the people" (1947:213).

De Tocqueville's insistence that the maintenance of democracy depends upon the primacy of certain popular values, and what we would today call character traits, has often been reaffirmed since by numerous authorities including men as widely separated in formal philosophical allegiance as Sidney Hook and Jacques Maritain.[9] What specific qualities do we then require in a people as a necessary condition for the maintenance of a democratic political order? Even a casual content analysis of any sampling of opinion on the democratic society reveals an extraordinary degree of agreement about the values, attitudes, opinion and traits of character which are important to its maintenance. The various formulations may be summed up by reference to conceptions about others, about the self, about authority, and about community and society.

Values about the Self.   All authorities are agreed that democratic societies require widespread belief in what Maritain calls the "inalienable rights of

[9] Hook has said, for example, "Democracy is an affirmation of certain attitudes and values which are more important than any particular set of institutions" (1950:294). Maritain argues that "the democratic impulse burst forth in history as a temporal manifestation of the gospel" and says directly that the democratic ideal "is the secular name for the ideal of Christianity" (1944:65). It does not seem necessary or desirable to clutter the text in the remainder of this section with source and page citations for each of the numerous quotations. In addition to the cited works of Hook and Maritain the main sources are Lasswell (1951) and De Tocqueville (1947).

the person," and Hook "the belief that every individual should be regarded as possessing intrinsic worth or dignity." "Where low estimates of the self are permitted to develop," says Harold Lasswell, "there the democratic character cannot develop."

Orientation toward Others. The basic dignity not only of the self but of all others is an essential ingredient cited by virtually every theory on the democratic character. This particularly manifests itself in the concept of equality, under which Hook includes recognition "that equal opportunities of development should be provided for the realization of individual talents and capacities." To hold this view one must have a basic acceptance of other people. In Lasswell's words: "The democratic attitude toward other human beings is warm rather than frigid, inclusive and expanding rather than exclusive and constricting . . . an underlying personality structure which is capable of 'friendship' as Aristotle put it, and which is unalienated from humanity." Underlying these attitudes is a fundamental conception of the perfectibility of man, which De Tocqueville phrased as the belief "that a man will be led to do what is just and good by following his own interest rightly understood."

Orientation toward Authority. At the core of the democratic personality lies a stress on personal autonomy and a certain distance from, if not distrust of, powerful authority, or, to put it negatively, an absence of the need to dominate or submit such as is found in the authoritarian personality. As Sidney Hook phrased it: "a positive requirement of a working democracy is an intelligent distrust of its leadership, a skepticism stubborn but not blind, of all demands for the enlargement of power, and an emphasis upon critical method in every phase of social life . . . Where skepticism is replaced by uncritical enthusiasm . . . a fertile soil for dictatorship has been prepared." Almost identical language is used by Maritain. Maritain described the democratic philosophy as one insisting on the "political rights of the people whose consent is implied by any political regime, and whose rulers rule as vicars of the people . . . it denies to the rulers the right to consider themselves and be considered a superior race and wills nevertheless that their authority be respected on a juridical basis. It does not admit that the state is a transcendent power incorporating within itself all authority and imposed from above upon life . . . " The same idea is stressed by Lasswell who says: "the democratic character is multi-valued rather than single valued . . . disposed to share rather than to monopolize. In particular, little significance is attached to the exercise of power as a scope value . . . [for] when the demand for respect is the consuming passion, other values are sacrificed for the sake of receiving symbolic acknowledgments of eminence."

Attitudes toward the Community. Although overweaning authority may be controlled, there is always the danger of that tyranny of the majority which De Tocqueville early warned might undo democracy. This realization has repeatedly led those who sought to define the democratic character to stress the importance of openness, ready acceptance of differences, and willingness to compromise and change. De Tocqueville early anticipated this point, as he did so many others. Stressing the belief "that every man is born of the right of self-government, and that no one has the right of constraining his fellow creatures to be happy," he went on to say we must recognize "society as a body in a state of improvement, [and] humanity as a changing scene in which nothing is or ought to be permanent." Hook also speaks of the importance of "a belief in the value of differences, variety, and uniqueness in a democracy [where] differences of interest and achievement must not be merely suffered, they must be encouraged." According to Hook this requires that the ultimate commitment of a democracy must be in some method by which value conflicts are to be resolved, which in turn means that policies must be treated as hypotheses, not dogmas, and customary practices as generalizations rather than as God-given truths.

It will be apparent from this extremely brief review that there is substantial agreement about the core personal beliefs and values which have been frequently identified as important to the maintenance of a democratic order. The relevant "themes" can, of course, be integrated into the personality at different levels. They may reflect opinions publicly held, but not vitally important to the person. They may represent basic attitudes or central values in the belief system, typical "ideologies" to which the individual has deep allegiance. Or they may be even more "deeply" embedded in the personality at the level of character traits and modes of psychodynamic functioning. Most of the outstanding writers on the democratic character do not trouble to distinguish these "levels." I have not attempted above to sort them out, and merely note here that most of the characterizations given above are statements at the level of ideology. We can, however, translate or transform the classic portrait of the democratic character to present it in the language of clinical psychology, expressed in terms of character traits, defenses, ways of dealing with wishes and feelings, and the like. In those terms, the democratic character emerges at the opposite pole from the authoritarian personality syndrome.

The citizen of a democracy should be accepting of others rather than alienated and harshly rejecting; open to new experience, to ideas and impulses rather than excessively timid, fearful, or extremely conventional with regard to new ideas and ways of acting; able to be responsible with constituted authority even though always watchful, rather than blindly submissive to or hostilely rejecting of all authority; tolerant of differences and of ambiguity, rather than rigid and inflexible; able to recognize, control, and channel his emotions, rather than immaturely projecting hostility and other impulses on to others.

This model of the democratic personality represents only a very rough first approximation. Although it is based on a great deal of philosophical wisdom and historical experience, by the standards of modern social science it rests on an extremely narrow and uncertain base of empirical research. Indeed, it might be argued that at the present moment there is no relevant evidence which meets the standards set by contemporary social science research. It is largely to the future that we must look for refinement of the model, and for testing of its actual relevance for political systems and popular participation in them. No doubt some elements in the model will be discarded, others added. It may even be discovered that some one element is critical, all the others incidental or even irrelevant. In the present stage of our work it is important to avoid premature closure through the exclusive concentration on one conceptual scheme for analyzing personality. It is true that earlier efforts which accepted publicly offered opinions, attitudes, and values as guides to the individual's probable political action were often naive and misleading. Nevertheless, an analysis couched exclusively in terms of psychodynamic depth psychology, of defenses, projective tendencies, and the like may also leave out much which is of great significance in shaping the pattern of political life. We cannot be satisfied with a scheme of personality analysis which is insensitive to themes such as self-centeredness or "privatism" which Gillespie and Allport (1955) found so important in distinguishing the students from different countries in their study. Nor can we be content with an analysis of the "compulsive" German character (Kecskemeti 1947) if it leads us to neglect the feelings of obligation to self and society (McClelland 1958).

Whatever the defects of the available scheme, the use of some explicit model is essential to focus our studies in this area. It is also a necessary condition for the meaningful comparison of different studies, and particularly for our efforts to cumulate the results in ever firmer generalizations or conclusions. We must particularly regret, therefore, that so few of the empirical investigations into the relations of character and political systems have sought systematically to test the model of the democratic character presented above, or, for that matter, any other explicit model.

Some Problems and Prospects

With very few exceptions, the available studies of modal or group personality unfortunately suffer from several defects which make them poor evidence in support of *any* systematic proposition. As a rule they are not designed to test any theory or validate any model. They are usually based on very small and haphazardly selected samples, making it extremely difficult to generalize with any confidence beyond the sample itself or the narrow circle from which it is drawn. In addition, the analysis is usually based on the total sample, without basic differentiation of the characteristics of subgroups, whether deviant or merely variant. More serious for our purposes is the fact that the description of personality is generally cast in clinical or psychodynamic terms which are difficult to relate to social structure. Even in the rare cases when a study has given attention to the more politically relevant realms of personality such as attitude toward authority, tolerance of ambiguity, acceptance of differences, and the need for power, it generally fails to record information on the political attitudes and opinions, the party affiliation, or other political characteristics of the subjects. Most of these studies, therefore, are obviously of limited usefulness to the student of politics. Only in the last few years have we attained the first, limited personality inventory of a representative sample of the national population of the United States — and this applies only to the F scale, as we have already noted, and more recently to the TAT variables of n affiliation, achievement, and power.[10] There are apparently no comparable results on these or any other dimensions for any other modern nation, and it will undoubtedly be many years before we have such results for a number of major nations simultaneously.

Even when we attain good data on the distribution of personality traits in a number of national populations, a great many questions will remain. For example, we will need to understand better the relation between personality dispositions in the rank and file of a population, and their orientation to different kinds of leadership. The decisive factor affecting

[10] The test was administered in connection with the national survey sponsored by the Joint Commission on Mental Illness and Health and conducted by the Survey Research Center of the University of Michigan. Reports on this material are in preparation by Gerald Gurin, Joseph Veroff, and John Atkinson.

the chances of preserving democracy may not be the prevalence of one or another undemocratic personality type, but rather the relation between the typical or average personality and that of the leaders. It is highly unlikely that any character type will be found to be invariably associated with a single form of political system. Nevertheless, certain personality types may indeed be more responsive to one than to another form of government. Their character, then, may be an important determinant of their susceptibility to certain kinds of influence. Thus, Dicks does not argue for the propensity toward authoritarian government *per se* in the German character. The typical German character delineated by Dicks was a type highly susceptible to the style of leadership the Hitler movement offered and extremely vulnerable to the kind of propaganda appeals it utilized. Much the same conclusion is suggested by Erikson's (1950) analysis of the German character and Hitler's appeal to it. Neither analysis should be interpreted as suggesting that the German character, as described, could not under any circumstances adjust to or function in *any* democratic political order. McClelland's analysis (1958) of the distinctive structure of obligations to self and society in Germany and the United States is particularly interesting for the light it throws on this question.

Whatever the distribution of personality types, including leaders, in any population, we will want to know what produces the types. This enormously complex problem is one I have been obliged by limits of space to ignore almost entirely, although it is one of the most fundamental facing the field. The predominant opinion among students of national character is that these types arise mainly out of the socialization process, and that in democratic societies the family structure is one which generates individuals adapted to life in a democracy. The typical argument was forcefully stated by Ralph Linton when he declared: "Nations with authoritarian family structure inevitably seem to develop authoritarian governments, no matter what the official government forms may be. Latin American countries with their excellent democratic constitutions and actual dictatorships would be a case in point" (1951:146).

Linton's opinion is not uniformly held. On the basis of a thorough review of a great deal of relevant empirical research, Herbert Hyman (1959) poses a formidable challenge to this assumption and suggests a number of other factors — particularly experiences in adulthood — which may account for the political orientations we observe in certain groups. Even after we secure data on the distribution of personality characteristics in large populations, there will be much work to be done in discovering

what produces the propensity to extremism, how it operates, and what —
if anything — changes or modifies it.

Another problem we must face is the relation between personality
factors and other forces which affect the political process (*cf.* Levinson
1958). To analyze political participation and political structures through
a study of personality and its statistical distribution is, of course, only one
of the possible avenues of approach to the problem. Clearly, political
institutions and political action cannot be comprehended exclusively or
even predominantly by reference to attitudes and values. The history of a
people obviously plays a major role in shaping the basic structure of their
political institutions. And institutional frameworks, once established, may
have an endurance much greater than the formal allegiance to their
principles would have indicated. Indeed, once firmly established, institutions have the capacity to develop or generate support among those whose
early disposition would hardly have led them to move spontaneously in
that direction.

A recent extensive comparative study by S. M. Lipset (1959) of the
relation between a complex of factors including industrialization, urbanization, literacy, education, and wealth, reveals that they are highly
correlated not only with each other, but also with the existence of stable
democratic systems.[11] None of these factors cited by Lipset is at all
psychological or attitudinal, but it is interesting to note that in seeking to
understand why these factors play such a role, Lipset had to fall back from
these more "objective" to more subjective causes, in particular to such
concepts as the "effectiveness" and the "legitimacy" of a political system
in the eyes of its constituents. By effectiveness he means the capacity to
satisfy the basic interests of most members of society, or of the most
important groups in it, and by legitimacy "the capacity of a political
system to engender and maintain the belief that existing political institutions are the most appropriate or proper ones for the society" (1960:77).
Surely the tolerance of ambiguity, the readiness for compromise, the level
of projectivity characteristic of a people or important subgroups, will play
a major role in shaping the "effectiveness" of the political system and even
its freedom of action *to be* effective. The value placed on autonomy versus

[11] De Tocqueville made the same point: "Their ancestors gave [the people of the United
States] the love of equality and of freedom, but God himself gave them the means of
remaining equal and free by placing them on a boundless continent ... When the people
rules it must be rendered happy or it will overthrow the state, and misery is apt to stimulate
it to those excesses to which ambition rouses kings" (1947:185).

control and direction, the strength of needs for power or achievement, the wish for dominance or subordination, the orientation toward authority figures, will all clearly play an important part in determining whether a particular political system is felt by people to be legitimate or not.

Although further refinements are needed, it is not likely that we will make any further unusual leaps along the line of analysis which Lipset has so diligently pursued. By contrast, the role of psychological factors — of attitudes, values, and character traits — in influencing the political process is an almost virgin field which promises a rich harvest. To secure it we must overcome imposing but by no means insuperable obstacles. We need to clarify our concepts, isolating or delineating those personal characteristics which, on theoretical grounds, seem to have the greatest relevance for the development and functioning of the political system. We must also refine our analysis of the political system, so that our descriptive categories are maximally analytical and conducive to comparative study. Our next step must be to assess systematically the distribution of these qualities in different national populations and in important subgroups of those populations. This poses one of the most difficult methodological problems, since the meaning of important terms, the pattern of response to tests, and the interpretation of those responses are highly variable as we move from country to country. On this base we can then proceed to correlational and causal analyses of the relations between opinions, values, and personality on the one hand, and the quality of political participation and the stability of political structures on the other. We may thus develop a comparative social psychology of the political process to support and supplement our traditional study of politics.

Bibliography

Abel, Theodora M. and Francis L. K. Hsu. 1949. Some aspects of personality of Chinese as revealed by the Rorschach test. Rorschach Research Exchange and Journal of Projective Techniques 13:285–301.

Adorno, T. W., E. Frenkel-Brunswik, D. J. Levinson and R. N. Sanford. 1950. The authoritarian personality. New York, Harper and Bros.

Almond, Gabriel A. 1950. The American people and foreign policy. New York, Harcourt Brace.

———. 1956. Comparative political systems. The Journal of Politics 18:391–409.

ALMOND, GABRIEL A., AND SIDNEY VERBA. 1963. Civic culture: political attitudes and democracy in five nations. Boston, Little, Brown.

AUBERT, VILLEM, B. R. FISHER AND STEIN ROKKAN. 1954. A comparative study of teachers' attitudes to international problems and policies. Journal of Social Issues 10:25–39.

BAUER, RAYMOND A. 1953. Psychology of the Soviet middle elite. *In* Personality in nature, society, and culture, Kluckhohn, Murray, and Schneider, eds. New York, Alfred Knopf.

BENEDICT, RUTH. 1934. Patterns of culture. Boston, Houghton Mifflin.

———. 1943. Race: science and politics (rev. ed.). New York, Viking Press.

———. 1946. The chrysanthemum and the sword. Boston, Houghton Mifflin.

BLEULER, M. AND R. 1935. Rorschach's ink-blot test and racial psychology: mental peculiarites of Moroccans. Character and Personality 4:97–114.

BOAS, FRANZ. 1910. Psychological problems in anthropology. American Journal of Psychiatry 21:371–384.

BRICKNER, RICHARD M. 1943. Is Germany incurable? Philadelphia, J. B. Lippincott.

BROGAN, D. W. 1933. Government of the people, a study in the American political system. New York, Harper and Bros.

———. 1944. The American character. New York, Alfred Knopf.

BUCHANAN, W. AND H. CANTRIL. 1953. How nations see each other, a study in public opinion. Urbana, Ill., University of Illinois Press.

CAMPBELL, ANGUS, G. GURIN AND W. E. MILLER. 1954. The voter decides. Evanston, Ill., Row, Peterson.

CANTRIL, HADLEY. 1965. The pattern of human concerns. New Brunswick, N.J., Rutgers University Press.

CARSTAIRS, G.M., R. W. PAYNE AND S. WHITAKER. 1960. Rorschach responses of Hindus and Bhils. Journal of Social Psychology 51:217–227.

CHRISTIE, RICHARD AND M. JAHODA, EDS. 1954. The authoritarian personality: studies in continuities in social research. Glencoe, Ill., Free Press.

COLEMAN, LEE. 1941. What is American: a study of alleged American traits. Social Forces 19:492–499.

COMMAGER, HENRY STEELE, ED. 1947. America in perspective, the United States through foreign eyes. New York, Random House.

DAVIES, JAMES C. 1954. Charisma in the 1952 campaign. American Political Science Review 48:1083–1102.

DICKS, HENRY V. 1950. Personality traits and national socialist ideology, a wartime study of German prisoners of war. Human Relations 3:111–154.

———. 1952. Observations on contemporary Russian behavior. Human Relations 5:111–175.

EYSENCK, H. J. 1954. The psychology of politics. London, Routledge and Kegan Paul.

FORTES, MEYER AND E. E. EVANS-PRITCHARD, EDS. 1940. African political systems. London and New York, Oxford University Press.

FROMM, ERICH. 1941. Escape from freedom. New York, Farrar and Rinehart.

GILLESPIE, JAMES M. AND GORDON W. ALLPORT. 1955. Youth's outlook on the future: a cross-national study. Garden City, New York, Doubleday.

GORER, GEOFFREY. 1943. Themes in Japanese culture. Transactions of the New York Academy of Sciences Ser. II, 5, 106–124.

———. 1948. The American people, a study in national character. New York, W. W. Norton.

———. 1955. Exploring English character. London, Cresset Press.

GORER, GEOFFREY AND JOHN RICKMAN. 1949. The people of Great Russia, a psychological study. London, Cresset Press.

HARING, DOUGLAS G. 1948. Personal character and cultural milieu. Syracuse, N.Y., Syracuse University Press. (3d ed. 1956.)

HEARNSHAW, F. J. C. 1940. Germany, the aggressor throughout the ages. London, W. and R. Chambers.

HERZ, FREDERICK. 1944. Nationality in history and politics. London, Routledge and Kegan Paul.

HONIGMANN, JOHN J. 1954. Culture and personality. New York, Harper and Bros.

HOOK, SIDNEY. 1950. Reason, social myths, and democracy. New York, Humanities Press.

HORKHEIMER, MAX, ED. 1936. Studien uber authorität und familie. Paris, Alcan.

HSU, FRANCIS L. K. 1953. Americans and Chinese: Two Ways of Life. New York, Schuman

———. 1963. Clan, Caste and Club. Princeton, N.J., Van Nostrand

———. 1968. Chinese Kinship and Chinese Behavior. *In* Ping-ti Ho and Tang Tsou (eds.), China in Crisis, Vol. I, Chicago, University of Chicago Press, pp. 579–608.

———. 1970. Americans and Chinese: Purpose and Fulfillment in Great Civilizations. New York, Doubleday and Natural History Press.

INKELES, ALEX. 1966. The modernization of man. *In* M. Weiner (ed.), Modernization. New York, Basic Books, pp. 138–151.

———. 1969. Making men modern: on the causes and consequences of individual change in six developing countries. American Journal of Sociology 75:208–225.

INKELES, ALEX AND D. J. LEVINSON. 1954. National character: the study of modal personality and sociocultural systems. *In* Handbook of social psychology, vol. II, G. Lindzey, ed. Cambridge, Mass., Addison-Wesley.

INKELES, ALEX, EUGENIA HANFMANN AND HELEN BEIER. 1958. Modal personality and adjustment to the Soviet socio-economic system. Human Relations 11:1–22.

JAENSCH, ERICH R. 1938. Der gegentypus. Leipzig, Barth.

JANOWITZ, MORRIS AND D. MARVICK. 1953. Authoritarianism and political behavior. Public Opinion Quarterly 17:185–201.

KARDINER, ABRAM. 1945. The psychological frontiers of society. New York, Columbia University Press.

KARDINER, ABRAM AND L. OVESEY. 1951. The mark of oppression: a psychosocial study of the American Negro. New York, W. W. Norton.

KECSKEMETI, PAUL AND NATHAN LEITES. 1947. Some psychological hypotheses on Nazi Germany. Journal of Social Psychology, I 1947 26:141–183; II 1948 27:91–117; III 1948 27:241–270; IV 1948 28:141–164.

KLINEBERG, OTTO. 1944. A science of national character. Journal of Social Problems 19:147–162.

———. 1951. Psychological aspects of international relations. *In* Personality and political crisis, Alfred H. Stanton and Stewart E. Perry, eds. Glencoe, Ill., Free Press.

KLUCKHOHN, CLYDE AND HENRY MURRAY. 1953. Personality in nature, society, and culture. New York, Alfred Knopf. (Rev. ed., with David Schneider, 1956.)

KORNHAUSER, ARTHUR, H. L. SHEPPARD AND A. J. MAYER. 1956. When labor votes, a study of auto workers. New York, University Books.

KORNHAUSER, WILLIAM. 1959. The politics of mass society. Glencoe, Ill., Free Press.

KROUT, MAURICE H. AND ROSS STAGNER. 1939. Personality development in radicals: a comparative study. Sociometry 2:31–46.

LANE, R. E. 1955. Political personality and electoral choice. American Political Science Review 49:173–190.

LASSWELL, HAROLD D. 1930. Psychopathology and politics. *In* The political writings of Harold D. Lasswell. Glencoe, Ill., Free Press, 1951.

———. 1951. Democratic character. *In* The political writings of Harold D. Lasswell. Glencoe, Ill., Free Press.

———. 1959. Political constitution and character. Psychoanalysis and the Psychoanalytic Review 46:3–18.

LEITES, NATHAN C. 1948. Psychocultural hypotheses about political acts. World Politics 1:102–119.

———. 1951. The operational code of the politburo. New York, McGraw-Hill.

LERNER, DANIEL. 1958. The passing of traditional society; modernizing the Middle East. Glencoe, Ill., Free Press.

LEVINE, ROBERT. 1963. Culture and personality. Biennial Review of Anthropology 107–146.

Levinson, Daniel J. 1957. Authoritarian personality and foreign policy. Conflict Resolution 1:37–47.

———. 1958. The relevance of personality for political participation. Public Opinion Quarterly 22:3–10.

Levy, David M. 1951. Anti-Nazis: criteria of differentiation. *In* Personality and political crisis, Alfred H. Stanton and Stewart E. Perry, eds. Glencoe, Ill., Free Press.

Linton, Ralph. 1945. The cultural background of personality. New York, D. Appleton-Century.

———. 1951. The concept of national character. *In* Personality and political crisis, Alfred H. Stanton and Stewart E. Perry, eds. Glencoe, Illinois, Free Press.

Lipset, S. M. 1959. Some social requisites of democracy: economic development and political legitimacy: American Political Science Review 53:69–105.

———. 1960. Political man: the social bases of politics. Garden City, New York, Doubleday.

Lurie, Walter A. 1937. A study of Spranger's value-types by the method of factor analysis. Journal of Abnormal and Social Psychology 8:17–37.

Madariaga, Salvador de. 1929. Englishmen, Frenchmen, Spaniards: an essay in comparative psychology. London, Oxford University Press.

Mannheim, Karl. 1950. Freedom, power and democratic planning. New York, Oxford University Press.

Maritain, Jacques. 1944. Christianity and democracy. New York, Scribners.

McClelland, David, J. F. Sturr, R. H. Knapp and H. W. Wendt. 1958. Obligations to self and society in the United States and Germany. Journal of Abnormal and Social Psychology 56:245–255.

McCloskey, Herbert. 1953. Conservatism and personality. American Political Science Review 52:27–45.

McGranahan, Donald V. 1946. A comparison of social attitudes among American and German youth. Journal of Abnormal and Social Psychology 41:245–257.

McGranahan, Donald V. and I. Wayne. 1948. German and American traits reflected in popular drama. Human Relations 1:429–455.

Mead, Margaret. 1942. And keep your powder dry. New York, William Morrow.

———. 1951. Soviet attitudes toward authority. New York, McGraw-Hill

Merriam, Charles E. 1925. New aspects of politics. Chicago, University of Chicago Press, Selections reprinted in H. Eulau, S. J. Eldersveld and M. Janowitz, Political behavior. Glencoe, Ill., Free Press, 1956.

Michels, Robert. 1949. Political parties. Translated by Eden and A. Paul. Glencoe, Ill., Free Press.

MILLS, CHARLES W. 1956. The power elite. New York, Oxford University Press.

MOORE, HENRY T. 1925. Innate factors in radicalism and conservatism. Journal of Abnormal and Social Psychology 20:234–244.

MORRIS, CHARLES W. 1942. Paths of life; preface to a world religion. New York, Harper and Bros.

MORRIS, CHARLES W. 1956. Varieties of human value. Chicago, University of Chicago Press.

ORTEGA Y GASSET, JOSÉ. 1937. Invertebrate Spain. New York, W. W. Norton.

PEAK, HELEN. 1945. Observations on the characteristics and distribution of German Nazis. Psychological Monographs vol. 59, no. 6, whole no. 276.

RINGER, BENJAMIN B. AND DAVID L. SILLS. 1952–53. Political extremists in Iran. Public Opinion Quarterly 16:689–701.

ROKEACH, MILTON. 1956. Political and religious dogmatism: an alternative to the authoritarian personality. Psychological Monographs vol. 70, no. 18, whole no. 425.

SCHAFFNER, BERTRAM H. 1949. Father land: a study of authoritarianism in the German family. New York, Columbia University Press.

SFORZA, CARLO. 1942. The real Italians: a study in European psychology. New York, Columbia University Press.

SIEGFRIED, ANDRÉ. 1927. America comes of age. New York, Harcourt Brace.

———. 1930. France: a study in nationality. New Haven, Yale University Press.

———. 1951. Approaches to an understanding of modern France. In Modern France, Edward M. Earle, ed. Princeton, Princeton University Press.

SMITH, DAVID H. AND ALEX INKELES. 1966. The OM scale: a comparative socio-psychological measure of individual modernity. Sociometry 29:353–377.

SPRANGER, EDUARD. 1928. Types of men. Tübingen, Max Neimeyer, Verlag-halle.

STOETZEL, JEAN. 1955. Without the chrysanthemum and the sword. New York, Columbia University Press/UNESCO.

STOODLEY, BARTLETT H. 1957. Normative attitudes of Filipino youth compared with German and American youth. American Sociological Review 22:553–561.

STOUFFER, SAMUEL A. 1955. Communism, conformity and civil liberties; a cross section of the nation speaks its mind. Garden City, N.Y., Doubleday.

TOCQUEVILLE, ALEXIS DE. 1947. Democracy in America. New York and London, Oxford University Press.

WALLAS, GRAHAM. 1908. Human nature in politics. London. Selections reprinted in H. Eulau, S. J. Eldersveld, and M. Janowitz, Political behavior. Glencoe, Ill., Free Press, 1956.

WOLFENSTEIN, M. AND N. LEITES. 1950. Movies: a psychological study. Glencoe, Ill., Free Press.

CHAPTER SIX

American Core Value and National Character[1]

Francis L. K. Hsu

In approaching the subject of American national character, students have experienced some unusual difficulties. What they have done so far is either to present pictures of contradictions with little or no attempt to reconcile the opposing elements, or to construct models of what, in their view, ought to be, with little or no attempt to deal with what actually occurs. In this chapter I shall try to show that the difficulties are not insurmountable, that the contradictions, though numerous, are more apparent than real, and that, even the models of what ought to be, though different from reality, can be meaningful once we achieve a proper perspective.

A Picture of Contradictions

After comprehensive sampling of the literature from early times down to 1940, Lee Coleman lists the following as "American traits": "associational activity, democracy and belief and faith in it, belief in the equality of all as a fact and as a right, freedom of the individual in ideal and in fact, disregard of law — direct action, local government, practicality,

---

[1] This chapter is based on a paper presented at the American Psychological Convention, 1959, Cincinnati, Ohio, as part of a symposium under the chairmanship of Dr. Fred J. Goldstein of Los Angeles Psychiatric Service. The author is greatly indebted to Donald T. Campbell, Millard Hoyt, Thomas Gladwin, and Melford Spiro for their valuable criticism.

prosperity and general material well-being, puritanism, emphasis on religion and its great influence in national life, uniformity and conformity" (Coleman 1941:498).

It is clear at once that this list of traits not only fails to give cognizance to such obvious facts as racial and religious prejudice, but the different traits mutually contradict each other at several points. For example, values attached to "local government" and "democracy" are in direct contradiction to that of "disregard of law" leading to "direct action." The beliefs in "equality" and in "freedom" are in direct contradiction to the emphasis on "uniformity and conformity."

Cuber and Harper, writing nearly ten years later in a book entitled *Problems of American Society: Values in Conflict,* have reduced the total number of American values enumerated but not done much else. Their list is as follows: "monogamous marriage, freedom, acquisitiveness, democracy, education, monotheistic religion, freedom and science" (Cuber and Harper 1948:369). Cuber and Harper recognize that some of these values are inconsistent with each other and with social reality. But they attempt to explain such inconsistencies as follows:

> On the surface it might seem relatively easy for a society, and especially for some one person, to discover such inconsistencies as these, evaluate the two positions, choose one, and discard the other. . . . But in practice it seems not to be so easy an undertaking. In the first place, logical inconsistency may constitute social consistency — that is, a person whose values seem inconsistent when analysed by a third party may regard himself to be quite consistent. Both values seem to him to be quite tenable because he can point out the other persons in the society as authority for the rightness of each position (Cuber and Harper 1948:372).

As we shall see later, their explanation contains the germ of truth as to why the individual is not free to act as he sees fit, to make his value orientation more self-consistent, but it has not gone far enough. If every individual adheres to his inconsistent values because he can resort to "other persons in the society as authority for the rightness of each position," then we cannot possibly explain how values in America would ever undergo change, and how some individuals are more affected by the inconsistencies than others, enough for them to espouse certain "causes" and throw their weight behind crusades for emancipation of the slaves or to destroy saloons.

Over the years the analysis of American values has remained stagnant at this level. Thus, in *American Society* Robin Williams again gives us no more than a catalogue of American values as follows: "achievement" and "success," "activity" and "work," "moral orientation," "humanitarian mores," efficiency and practicability, "progress," material comfort, equality, freedom, external conformity, science and secular rationality, nationalism-patriotism, democracy, individual personality, racism and related group-superiority themes (Williams 1951:388–440; 1960:415–470). (The quotation marks applied to seven of these values are Williams'.)

Williams does realize, perhaps more than the other authors, that the values are not of equal importance and that they have to be somehow related and reconciled with each other. Accordingly, in his conclusion on value orientation, he makes a summary classification to emphasize some and to de-emphasize others:

1. Quasi values or *gratifications:* such as material comforts.
2. *Instrumental interests* or means values: such as wealth, power, work, and efficiency.
3. *Formal universalistic values of western tradition:* rationalism, impersonal justice, universalistic ethics, achievement, democracy, equality, freedom, certain religious values, and values of individual personality.
4. *Particularistic, segmental or localistic values:* best exemplified in racist-ethnic superiority doctrines and in certain aspects of nationalism (Williams 1951:441; 1960:468–469).

This classification accomplishes little. It is not simply a question of differences between professed values and the actual reality. Such differences are to be found in any society. More specifically the question is one of unresolved and unaccounted for differences between certain professed values and other professed values. We may reconcile "efficiency" as a value with the continuous blocking of modern improvements in the building trades as a matter of difference between value and reality. But how do we reconcile the "value of individual personality" with the oppressive and increasing demand for "conformity"?

The most glaring contradiction is found between "equality" and "freedom" on the one hand, and "racist-ethnic superiority doctrines and certain aspects of nationalism" on the other. Williams tries to expunge the former by inaccurately classifying the latter as "particularistic, segmented or localistic values."

It is easy to see how Williams errs here. If the belief in racist-ethnic superiority were truly segmental or localistic (by which I think Williams means that it is particular to the South, as do others after him [see Lipset 1963:214–215]), how can we explain the racism that is also prevalent in the North? In fact, it has been aptly observed, and I think with real justification, that the only difference between the South and the North in the matter of racial attitudes is that the South is more open and honest about it, while the North is more covert and hypocritical about it. Of course, this view fails to consider the fact that the local laws by and large still support racism in some Southern states, while their counterparts in the North are more likely to be against it. Besides, practically all the broad legislative and judiciary improvements affecting race relations have originated from the North. These legal changes do not, however, erase the widespread social, economic, and other forms of discrimination which are practiced in the North as well as in the South. The many northern forms of resistance to school integration are only too well known. Furthermore, even if we say that the racist attitude is only characteristic of the South, we must inevitably be confronted with the question: How does the South reconcile its racist attitudes with its professed belief in democracy? Are the North and the South two fundamentally separate cultures?

Some students frankly take the line of least resistance by characterizing the American culture as "Schizoid" (Read Bain 1935:266–276), or inherently "dualistic," that is to say, full of opposites (Harold J. Laski 1948:738). This is the same sort of conclusion reached by Gunnar Myrdal who, after a mammoth investigation of Negro-White relations, left the entire matter as *An American Dilemma* (1944). Apart from presenting many factual details on racial discrimination in this society, Myrdal said nothing more than that there is the problem of a psychological conflict between the democratic ideal of equality, on the one hand, and the existing inequalities in race relations, education, income distribution, health benefits, and so forth, on the other. The few anthropologists who have bothered to study American values have hardly improved on this state of affairs. Thus, Kluckhohn expressed himself in 1941 on this subject:

> While the relative unanimity over some kind of aid to Britain demonstrates that at least in a crisis a nexus of common purposes is still effective, the diagnostic symptom of the sickness of our society is the lack of a unifying system of canons of choice, emotionally believed in as well as intellectually adhered to (Kluckhohn 1941:175).

When the Kluckhohns gave us their more intensive analysis of the American culture six years later (Kluckhohn and Kluckhohn 1947), they offered another list of "orientations" and "suborientations" very much in the manner of Robin Williams' treatment detailed above.

Finally, David Riesman's attempt to characterize the American national character as having changed from inner-direction to other-direction is an unsuccessful way out of this contradiction (Riesman 1950:11–25). Any conclusion that other-direction is the trend toward which this society is moving must be backed by evidence that its opposite is receding. To the contrary, not only ideological emphasis on individual excellence, individual initiative, and individual differences has not abated, but our educational institutions and our social developments are progressively becoming more oriented toward individuation. There are even forecasts that marriage is on the way out because Americans tend to see intimacy betweeen the sexes as a matter exclusively of individual satisfaction (see Kluckhohn and Strodtbeck 1961).

Thus, our understanding of American values is today no better than it was several decades ago. Periodically we note the conflicts and inconsistencies among the different elements, but we leave them exactly where we started.

An American Blind Spot

I have gone to such lengths to come to this futile conclusion because I do not wish to be accused of setting up a nonexistent straw man and then, with the flourish of discovery, knocking him down.

This retarded state of our scientific analysis of value conflicts inherent in American culture is, I believe, due to the fact that many Western and especially American scholars have been too emotionally immersed in the absolute goodness of their own form of society, ethic, thought, and religion that it is hard for them to question them, even in scientific analyses. Consequently, they cannot see anything but the eventual triumph of their cultural ideals such as freedom and equality over realities such as racism and religious intolerance. Some frankly see the former as the basic American truth and the latter as outright deviations which need not even be considered. This attitude is most decidedly characteristic even of eminent scholars such as Henry Steele Commager. In his book *The American Mind* he is most exasperated by the twentieth century manifestations of the American mind in the form of crime, racial and religious bigotry, lawlessness, irreligion, looseness of sex mores, conformity, class formation, and so forth. And he speaks in the following vein:

> All this presented to the student of the American character a most perplexing problem. It was the business of the advertisers to know that character, and their resources enabled them to enlist in its study the aid of the most perspicacious

sociologists and psychologists. Yet if their analysis was correct, the American people were decadent and depraved. *No other evidence supported this conclusion.* Advertisers appealed to fear, snobbery, and self-indulgence, yet no one familiar with the American character would maintain that these were indeed its predominant motivations, and statesmen who knew the American people appealed to higher motives, and not in vain. The problem remained a fascinating one, *for if it was clear that advertisers libeled the American character, it was equally clear that Americans tolerated and even rewarded those who libeled them* (Commager 1944:419; italics mine).

The fact is, while some American politicians appealed to higher motives with success, we can name quite a few others who have with equal success played on their *baser* motives. Furthermore, how could advertisers who successfully induced Americans to buy their wares by exploiting their baser motives have libeled the American character? Is that not known as giving the customer what he wants?

Gordon Allport commits the same error in his book *The Nature of Prejudice.* In its entire 519 pages Allport theorizes about mankind and religion, but his mankind is Western mankind (where he occasionally refers to Negroes and Orientals, he is merely speaking about the different extents to which the different Western groups reject them), and by religion he means Protestantism, Catholicism, and Judaism, with nothing even about Eastern Orthodoxy and one sentence on Islam. Limited by such a culture-bound framework, Allport is not unnaturally inconsistent. In discussing racial prejudice, Allport relies heavily on experimental psychology. There is a great deal of evidence that the more prejudiced personality tends to be one which is more in need of definiteness and more moralistic. For example, "he is uncomfortable with differentiated categories; he prefers them to be monopolistic" (Allport 1954:175, 398–408). Here Allport apparently accepts the conclusion to which his evidence leads him. However, in connection with religious bigotry Allport seems to adopt a different procedure altogether. Here he first admits that religions which claim to possess final truths are bound to lead to conflicts, and that individuals who have no religious affiliations tend to show less prejudice than do church members. But these are, in his words, too "distressing" to him and so demands "closer inspection" (Allport 1954:451).

To the student, what Allport means by "closer inspection" turns out to be a surprise, for Allport departs from the acceptable principle of science by purposely attempting to negate stronger evidences in favor of much flimsier facts. He admits that, quantitatively, the correlation between greater church affiliation and greater prejudice is correct, but he also insists that it is not correct because there are "many cases" where the influence of the church "is in the reverse direction" (Allport 1954:451). In other words, Allport finds the evidences too distressing because they show the Christian churches and the Christian values in an unfavorable light. He simply cannot tolerate the fact that the absolutist Christian faith and the exclusive Christian church membership do lead to greater prejudice. Under the circumstances, Allport has no alternative but to throw over-board the quantitative evidence in favor of some qualitative statements.

Lloyd Warner suffers from a similar difficulty in his book *American Life, Dream and Reality* (1953). He finds the Jonesville *grade school* children's evaluation of one another to be so strongly reflective of social-class values as to blind them to the actual reality. For example, children from the top classes were rated 22 times cleaner than those from the bottom, but in fact, the latter as a whole came to school cleaner and neater than the former. However, he also finds that the Jonesville *high school* students, though following a similar pattern, do not make such categorical and rigid judgments by class values. Warner's explanation of this difference is most revealing:

> Since the older children are presumably more the products of their culture than the younger ones, there appears to be a contradiction here. . . . Actually, the reasons for the differences in judgment help verify our hypothesis. The children in the high school, being products of American society, have learned to be less open and more careful about what they say and how they feel on the tabooed subject of status. *Furthermore, they have learned to use American values of individualism and are able to make clearer discriminations about the worth of an individual than are the younger children* (Warner 1953:182–183; italics mine).

The interesting thing is that Warner's second explanation here not only contradicts the one preceding it but contradicts his entire thesis, which is that social class values strongly influence American behavior and ideas. It is as though this second explanation came out by accident, perhaps a Freudian slip of his research pen, for in sentiments like "the worth of the individual" many Americans find real emotional security.

What we have to see is that in the minds of a majority of our scholars the ideas of democracy and Christianity, with their respective attributes of freedom and equality in one case and of love and mercy in the other, are the overall American values par excellence. They are so consciously upheld that all explanations of American behavior must somehow begin and end with it. Any evidence contrary to this mold is therefore treated as deviation or as "regional phenomena," as "libel," as creating a "schizoid" situation, a "dilemma." This in my view is an American blind spot today. Given this blind spot, our scientists have consistently confused what ought to be with what is. It leads many scholars to explain the kind of American behavior they deem desirable by one theory, and another kind of American behavior, which they abhor and which contradicts the first kind, by another and contradictory theory. Some even misuse the eclectic approach by pleading a multiplicity of correlates or causation in complex human affairs.

The fundamental axiom of science is to explain more and more facts by fewer and fewer theories. Anyone can explain all characteristics of a given situation with as many different theories, but his explanation will not be of value as a piece of work of science. The axiom of explaining more and more facts by fewer and fewer theories is especially crucial if the facts are obviously related, as when they occur in the same organized society and often in the same individuals.

Once this is admitted it becomes obvious that, when confronted with contradictions in the object of his inquiry, the scientist's first duty is, instead of trying to treat them as discrete entities and explaining them with contradictory hypotheses, to explore the possibility of a link between the contradictory phenomena. In doing so the scientist is not presuming that values in any given society must be totally consistent with each other and that all contradictions must be resolved. It is perfectly possible that many societies, being large and complex, have inconsistent or contradictory characteristics. But what our scientists so far would seem to fail or refuse to do is to concede even the possibility of any positive connection between these contradictory characteristics.

Self-Reliance, Fear of Dependency, and Insecurity

What we need to see is that the contradictory American "values" noted by the sociologists, psychologists, and historians are but manifestations of one core value. The American core value in question is *self-reliance*, the most persistent psychological expression of which is the fear of dependence. It can be shown that all of the "values" enumerated thus far, the mutually contradictory ones and the mutually supportive ones, the evil ones as well as the angelic ones, spring or are connected with self-reliance.

American self-reliance is basically the same as English individualism except that the latter is the parent of the former and the former has gone farther than the latter. However, self-reliance possesses no basic characteristics which were not inherent in individualism. Individualism developed in Europe as a demand for political equality. It insists that every individual has inalienable and God-given political rights which other men cannot take away and that every man has the equal right to govern himself or choose his own governors. Self-reliance, on the other hand, has been inseparable in America from the individual's militant insistence on economic, social, and political equality. The result is while a qualified individualism, with a qualified equality, has prevailed in England and the rest of Europe, what has been considered the inalienable right of every American is an unlimited self-reliance and an unlimited equality.

It is not suggested here that all Americans do in fact enjoy the unlimited economic and social equality in which they firmly believe. But it is easy to observe how strongly and widely the belief in them manifests itself. For example, the English have been able to initiate a sort of socialism in reality, as well as in name, but Americans regardless of social security, farm subsidies, welfare, Medicare, and other forms of government planning, intervention, and assistance, are as firmly as ever committed to the idea of free enterprise and deeply intolerant toward other political and social systems. Similarly, the English still tend to respect class-based distinctions in wealth, status, manners, and language, while Americans tend to ridicule aristocratic manners or Oxford speech, and resent status so much that Lloyd Warner, as we noted before, describes it as being a "tabooed" subject in discussing Jonesville high school students. Finally, the English still consider the crown a symbol of all that is best and hereditary, while Americans criticize the personal taste of their highest officials and at least have the common verbal expression that everybody can be president.

This self-reliance is also very different from self-sufficiency. Any Chinese or European village can achieve self-sufficiency as a matter of fact. The average self-sufficient Chinese farmer will have at most only sympathy for other people who are not self-sufficient. But American self-reliance is a militant ideal which parents inculcate in their children and by which they judge the worth of any and all mankind. This is the self-reliance about which Ralph Waldo Emerson wrote so eloquently and convincingly in some immortal pieces. This is also the self-reliance taught in today's American schools. The following is a direct quotation from a statement of "basic beliefs" given to the students by the social science department of one of the nation's best high schools in 1959:

Self-reliance is, as it has always been, the key to individual freedom, and the only real security comes from the ability and the determination to work hard, to plan, and to save for the present and the future.[2]

American self-reliance is then not new. As a concept it is in fact well known and well understood. Yet such is the power of the blind spot that its basic implications and ramifications have so far escaped our scientific attention. How the individualism of Western Europe has been transformed into American self-reliance is a question outside the scope of this paper. It has been dealt with elsewhere (Hsu 1970:120–130). Suffice it to say here that under this ideal every individual is his own master, in control of his own destiny, and will advance and regress in society only according to his own efforts. He may have good or bad breaks, but,

Smile and the world smiles with you,

Cry, and you cry alone.

It is, of course, obvious that not all Americans are self-reliant. Individual variation in temperament, character, and intelligence is found in any society. Furthermore, no ideal manifests itself uniformly in all sections of any society. But a brief comparison will make the point clearer. A man in traditional China where self-reliance was not an ideal may have been unsuccessful in his life. But suppose in his old age his sons were able to provide for him generously. Such a person not only was happy and content about it; he was likely also to beat the drums before all and sundry to let the world know that he had good children who were supporting him in a style to which he had never been accustomed. On the other hand, an American parent who has not been successful in life may derive some benefit from the prosperity of his children, but he certainly will not want anybody to know about it. In fact, he will resent any reference to it. At the first opportunity when it is possible for him to become independent of his children, he will do so.

Therefore, even though we may find many individuals in traditional China and elsewhere who were in fact self-sufficient, and even though we may find individuals in America who are in fact dependent upon others, the important thing is that where self-reliance is not an ideal, it is neither promoted nor a matter of pride, but where it is an ideal, it is both. In American society the fear of dependence is so great that an individual who is not self-reliant is a misfit. "Dependent character" is a highly derogatory term, and a person so described is thought to be in need of psychiatric help.

[2] A mimeographed sheet issued to its pupils by a school in a Chicago suburb in 1959.

However, it is obvious that no individual can be self-reliant. In fact, the very foundation of the human way of life is man's dependence upon his fellow human beings intellectually and technologically as well as socially and emotionally. Individuals may have differing degrees of need for their fellow human beings, but no one can truly say that he needs no one, in this society or any other. It seems that the basic American value orientation of self-reliance, by its denial of the importance of other human beings in one's life, creates contradictions and therefore serious problems for the individual, the most ubiquitous of which is insecurity.

This insecurity presents itself to the individual American in a variety of ways. Its most important ingredient is the lack of permanency both in one's ascribed relationships (such as those of the family into which one is born) and in one's achieved relationships (such as a marital relationship for a woman or a business partnership for a man). Its most vital demand on the individual is a perpetual attempt to compete with his fellow human beings. He has to do this for entry into status-giving groups, or for maintaining his standing in them. In the process he has few alternatives other than submission to the tyranny of organization and conformation to the customs and fads of the peer group which are vital to his climbing and/or status maintenance at any given time and place. In other words, in order to live up to their core value orientation of self-reliance, Americans as a whole have to do much of its opposite. Expressed in the jargon of science, there is a direct relationship between self-reliance and individual freedom on the one hand and submission to organization and conformity on the other (Hsu 1960:151). Exactly the same force of circumstances can be seen to link:

1. Christian love with religious bigotry;
2. Emphasis on science, progress, and humanitarianism with parochialism, group-superiority themes and racism;
3. Puritan ethics with increasing laxity in sex mores;
4. Democratic ideals of equality and freedom with totalitarian tendencies and witch hunting.

These four pairs of contradictions are not exclusive of each other. For example, Christian love is in sharp contrast with racism as with religious bigotry. Similarly emphasis on science, and so forth, is as opposed to totalitarian tendencies and witch-hunting as to parochialism and group superiority themes. In fact, we can contrast the first half of any of the above pairs with the second half of any other.

Christian Love versus Christian Hate

For the purpose of this paper we shall consider some of these contradictions in a composite whole: our emphasis on Christian love, and freedom, equality, and democracy on the one hand, and racism and religious bigotry on the other. This is a contradiction which has tested the energy of some of the best euphemistic orators and the ingenuity of some of the most brilliant scholars, especially in the area of religion. They try to write off the religious wars. They try to forget about the Holy Inquisitions. They try to ignore the hundreds of thousands of witches convicted and burned at the stake. They try to deny any connection between any of these and the Nazi Germany slaughter of the Jews, and especially the anti-Semitism, anti-intellectualism, and racial persecution found here covertly and there openly in the United States. But when some scholars do realize that the past patterns are very much alive at present, though the specific techniques have changed, they tend to make harmless observations of which the following is a typical example:

> Worship in common — the sharing of the symbols of religion — has united human groups in the closest ties known to man, yet religious differences have helped to account for some of the fiercest group antagonisms (Elizabeth K. Nottingham 1954:2).

Robin Williams, who quotes the above passage, goes a little further by suggesting two clues to the riddle as to why some worship in common has united people and some has divided them: (a) Not all conflicts in the name of organized religion are actually "religious" and (b) there may be different degrees of involved commitment actually at work in "nominal religious affiliations" (Williams 1956:14–15). But there is no observable basis for distinction between *true* religious conflict and religious conflicts which are only *nominally* religious. Are theological controversies purely religious or nominally religious? The truth is that, even if the conflict is over nothing but liturgy, or over the question of virgin birth, they are still fought between human beings each with personal, emotional involvements in specific issues.

Williams' second clue is a more sound one. Put differently, this is that the more "involved commitment" actually at work in nominal religious affiliations the more religious dissension and bigotry there will be. Since the stronger one's commitment to an object or issue the more inflexible this commitment becomes, it is natural that more "involved commitment" will lead to more dissension and bigotry. Certain data quoted by Allport, referred to before, directly support this conclusion.[3] It is interesting to note that Williams, after stating this possibility, dismisses it as "extreme." Instead, he collects a conglomeration of twenty divergencies in value — orientations which, he believes but does not demonstrate, are partially the basis of religious conflicts in the United States (Williams 1956:14-17).

It is unnecessary to probe into the reasons why Williams attaches so little significance to his second clue. It is also beyond the scope of this paper to detail the irrelevancy of some of his "divergencies" to this problem on hand. We can, however, indicate how the link between the degree of involved commitment in nominal religious affiliations and the extent of dissension and bigotry is the source of the contradiction: Christian love versus Christian hate. Trained social scientists and other objective observers will readily agree with Williams that religious affiliation in the United States today has become so largely a matter of associational affiliation, and that "the values that inhere in group affiliation and participation" far and above overshadow "the specific values espoused" by the religious body (Williams 1956:17). The overwhelming proof of this is to be found in well-known works such as the Lynds' on "Middle Town" and Lloyd Warner and associates on "Yankee

[3] "Over four hundred students were asked the question, 'To what degree has religion been an influence in your upbringing?' Lumping together those who report that religion was a marked or moderate factor, we find the degree of prejudice far higher than among those who report that religion was a slight or non-existent factor in their training. Other studies reveal that individuals having no religious affiliation show on the average less prejudice than do church members" (Allport 1954:451).

And again, "First, it is well to be clear concerning the existence of certain natural, and perhaps unresolvable, conflicts inherent in various aspects of religion.

"Take first the claim of certain great religions — that each has absolute and final possession of Truth. People who adhere to different absolutes are not likely to find themselves in agreement. The conflict is most acute when missionaries are actively engaged in proselytizing divergent sets of absolutes. Moslem and Christian missionaries in Africa, for example, have long been at odds. Each insists that if its creed were completely realized in practice, it would eliminate all ethnic barriers between men. So it would. But in actuality, the absolutes of any one religion have never yet been accepted by more than a fraction of mankind.

"Catholicism by its very nature must believe that Judaism and Protestantism are in error. And varieties of Judaism and Protestantism feel keenly that other varieties of their own faith are perverse in many points of belief" (Allport 1954:444-445).

City" and "Jonesville,"[4] but particularly in the results of a poll of 100,000 Protestant ministers in all parts of the United States by the *Christian Century* magazine in 1951, to determine the "outstanding" and most "successful" churches. This poll showed twelve to be the chosen ones. One of the twelve was the First Presbyterian Church of Hollywood.

The applauded "qualities" of this church have been analyzed elsewhere (Hsu 1953:273–277 and 1970:270–276). Suffice it to say here that the "successful qualities" of this church seem to be that the "happiness" of the parishioners revolves about the social and material endeavors which rebound to their benefit alone but that the spiritual faith and the quality of the ministers' teachings receive practically no attention.

All of this is understandable once we appreciate the persistent demands that the core American value of self-reliance makes on the individual. The churches must compete and, in order to exist and to be "successful," must satisfy the status quest of their members. To achieve that "success," the churches not only have to conform to the trend toward organization, but they must try to find new ways of increasing their memberships so as to reach greater "successes."

In this psychology we can now find the common ground between religious bigotry and racial prejudice. Western religious dissensions have been associated with many things but their principal and perennial feature has been the search for original purity in ritual and belief. The Reformation was based on it. The entire evolution of Protestantism from the Lutheran church to Quakerism has had it as the central ingredient. The Holy Inquisition was instituted to ferret out impurity in Christian thought and practice. This fervent search for and jealous guard over purity expresses itself in the racial scene as the fear of genetic mixing of races which feeds the segregationist power in the North as well as in the South, no matter what rhetoric or logic is employed. When religious affiliations have become largely social affiliations, this fear of impurity makes religious and racial prejudices undistinguishable. Belief in God is not the question. The point of the greatest importance is affiliation. Consequently the neighborhoods and clubs are as exclusive as the churches and church-related associations, in spite of all protestation of equality, democracy, worth of the individual, Christian love, and humility.

The individual who is enjoined to be self-reliant, unlike one who is

[4]Commenting on religion George C. Homans says: "We are apt to think that the choice of a church among people brought up in the Protestant tradition is a matter of individual conscience. No doubt it is. But it is certainly also true that the membership of churches, in Hilltown as in Boston, tended to correlate roughly with that of certain social groups" (1950:346).

taught to respect authority and external barriers, has no permanent place in his society. Everything is subject to change without notice. He is always anxious to look above for possible openings to climb, but he is at the same time constantly threatened by possible upward encroachment from below. In his continuous effort at status achieving and maintaining, the self-reliant man fears nothing more than contamination by fellow human beings who are deemed inferior to him. This contamination can come about in diverse forms: sharing the same desks at the same schools, being dwellers of the same apartments, worshipping in the same churches, sitting in the same clubs, or being in any situation of free and equal contact.

In this context, as in others, individuals will vary in the extent to which they are pressed by the fear of inferiority. Some will join hate organizations, lynching mobs, and throw stones at Negro residences or paint swastikas on Jewish synagogues. These are *violent acts of prejudice.* Others will do everything they legally or by devious means can do to keep individuals of certain religious, racial, or ethnic groups out of desirable residential areas, preferred occupations, exclusive schools, and social fraternities. These are *active non-violent acts of prejudice.* Still others will quietly refuse to associate with members of religious, racial, or ethnic minorities and teach their children to observe this taboo because one just does not do such things. These are *passive non-violent acts of prejudice.*

Under such circumstances many, perhaps most, individuals find it impossible to act in the same way as they believe, have professed, or were taught. It is not that they love contradiction or that they are, according to their critics, hypocritical. It is simply that they are oppressed by fears for losing status — fears deeply rooted in a relatively free society with a core value of self-reliance. This is also why integration of minorities, be they racial or religious, cannot reach a satisfactory destination either along the line of total assimilation into the majority way of life or along that of pluralism. There is some factual indication that Jewish youngsters who are raised as non-Jews have a much harder time to adjust to their peers in college than those who have been raised consciously and militantly to cultivate their identity in Judaic tradition and church life. In other words, their complete identity and assimilation as Americans is always subject to rejection (Teitelbaum 1953).[5] On the other hand, the rationalization in

[5] This is based on two groups of answers to a questionnaire. The first group of answers was from 230 Northwestern University students in 1951 of whom 210 were undergraduates. A condensed version of the same questionnaire was sent to a random sampling of 730 undergraduates at nine midwestern universities and colleges in 1952–53, from which 325 undergraduates responded. The results, though quantitatively inconclusive, are qualitatively suggestive. First, students of Jewish background experience relatively little anti-Semitism at

support of anti-Oriental legislation was that the Oriental standard of living was too low and that they were incapable of assimilation to the American way of life. The simple fact is that as long as rugged individualism remains the cherished ideal and the principle of self-reliance governs human relations, the West in general and the United States society in particular will not even remotely come close to any solution of its problem of prejudice.

A reverse proof of the hypothesis advanced in this paper is not hard to find. We have only to look at societies where obedience to authority and dependence relationship are encouraged and where the individual is not subject to such pressures coming with self-reliance and, therefore, more sure of his place in society. Individuals in such societies tend to have much less need for competition, status seeking, conformity, and, hence, racial and religious prejudices. For example, religious dissensions, persecutions, and conflicts have always been prominent in the West as they have always been rare in the Orient. In Japan and China, the few occasions on which religious persecutions took place were invariably of short duration, always tied to the insecurity of political rule and never involved masses of the people except as temporary mobs (Hsu 1970:250–252). The case of Hindu-Moslem violence and casteism in India is considered elsewhere (Hsu 1961). The Indian phenomena are not to be confused with their Western counterpart. Physiologically we may develop rashes for a variety of reasons, from food allergies to emotional disturbances. Superficially all rashes look alike, but a competent doctor must separate them in order to prescribe intelligent treatment.

The same reverse proof is also evident in the West. No matter how we look at it, religious dissensions, persecutions, and racial conflicts are today more intense and widespread in Protestant-dominated societies of the West (see Chapter 14) than in their Catholic counterparts. In this dichotomy we are contrasting the United States, Great Britain, Canada, Australia, and

---

the high school level when mixed dates are frequent, but at the university level their social contacts become much less diversified. Second, there is more open identification with Jewish culture and institutions as the generation of Americanization advances. That is to say, the second and third generation American Jews tend to be more openly Jewish than the fresh immigrants or first generation Americans. Coupled with this, Jewish students from families of higher social statuses (such as proprietary and professional) show more open identification than those from families of lower social statuses (such as sales). Third, in spite of these facts, students of Jewish background do not seem to prefer exclusive Jewish friendship and association in college. Fourth, with the term "normal adjustment" meaning acceptance by Gentile students, "the conscious (but not self-conscious) and self-identifying Jews among the students are those most integrated with their own people and the most normally adjusted on the college or university campus" (209). These results correspond amazingly to my personal observations but any final conclusion on the subject must, of course, await further research.

the Union of South Africa as one camp and the Latin American republics as well as Italy, Spain, Portugal, Belgium, and France as the other. What has happened in Protestant-dominated societies is that, by and large, persecution in the form of bloody racial and religious outbreaks has been more driven underground while the manifestations of prejudice have become diffused, one almost may say democratized, if not for the fact that the expression smells of sarcasm. But even in the most advanced Protestant societies, racial and religious violence is always around the corner, ready to erupt now and then, here and there, as indicated by the continuing anti-Negro and anti-Indian outbreaks in England, the recurrent anti-Semitic flare-ups in Europe, and the persistent Black-White hostility in the United States of America and among its armed forces.[6]

Three Uses of Value

It will have been clear to some readers that this analysis of the psychosocial origin of racial and religious prejudices bears some resemblance to that of Kurt Lewin on the problems of the Jews as a minority group in many a western society. But it has significant differences. According to Lewin the most basic problem of the Jews is that of group identity. Often repudiated in the country of his birth and upbringing, yet having no homeland which he can claim as his own, he suffers from "additional uncertainty," thus "giving" him "some quality of abnormality in the opinion of the surrounding groups." He concludes that the establishment of a Jewish homeland in Palestine (which was not yet a reality at the time of his writing) might "affect the situation of Jews everywhere in the direction of greater normality" (Kurt Lewin 1935:175–187).

The Jewish minority certainly shares the central problem, with other minorities, of uncertainty of group identity. But our analysis also shows that the degree of this uncertainty depends, in the first place, on the basic value orientation of the host majority, and, in the second place, on that of the minority groups themselves. There is, for example, every reason to expect the Jewish minority to have far less of a problem of identity in Latin American countries than in North American countries. As far as North America is concerned, the Jews, like other minority groups, will always have the problem of identity whether or not they have a homeland. The Latin American peoples have less of the value orientation of self-reliance and, therefore, the individual has less psychosocial need to reject

[6]The place of Mohammedanism with reference to this analysis will be considered in another publication.

minority groups to maintain his status in society. On the other hand, within the United States, there is good reason to expect the Jewish minority to have a little more of a problem of identity than the Chinese and Japanese minorities even after the establishment of Israel, this despite the fact that the Orientals possess much greater physical distinctiveness than the Jews as a whole from the white majority. For the Chinese and Japanese have stronger ties with their families and wider kin groups than do the Jews, and are, therefore, less self-reliant and less free but more protected from the uncertainty of identity (Hsu 1971).

In this chapter I have not separated the different uses to which the term value may be put. Charles Morris, in a book entitled *Varieties of Human Value,* postulated three such uses: "Operative" values refer to the "actual direction of preferential behavior toward one kind of object rather than another." "Conceived" values refer to the "preferential behavior directed by 'an anticipation or foresight of the outcome' of such behavior," and "involves preference for a symbolically indicated object." He illustrates this meaning of value by the example of the drug addict who firmly believes that it is better not to be a drug addict because "he anticipates the outcome of not using drugs." "Object" values refer not to the behavior preferred in fact (operative value) or as symbolically desired (conceived value) but to what is preferable if the holder of the value is to achieve certain ends or objectives (1956:10–12).

While it is obvious that the three usages of the term "value" are not mutually exclusive and must influence each other, it is equally obvious that they are not hard to distinguish. Applying this scheme to the American scene, we shall realize that self-reliance is an operative value as well as a conceived value. It expresses itself in two directions. In the positive direction it is embodied in the emphasis on freedom, equality in economic and political opportunities for all, Puritan virtues, Christian love, and humanitarianism. These values are far more conceived than operative. On the negative side self-reliance expresses itself as the tendency toward racial prejudice, religious bigotry, laxity in sex mores, and totalitarianism. These values are far more operative than conceived. Values which are more conceived than operative are of great symbolic importance, and will be militantly defended by the people cherishing them. In fact, the less they live up to such conceived values the more they are likely to defend them, because their failures are associated with feelings of guilt. Values which are more operative than conceived are of great practical importance, and will be strenuously pursued by the people needing them. The more they have to act according to such operative values, the less they will admit their reality, since their actions also lead to feelings of guilt. At one extreme we shall find men who will openly fight to guard these operative values most flagrantly. At the other extreme we shall find men who will practice them by devious means. Those who hold on to these operative values openly and those who do so by subterfuge will share one common characteristic: both will deny their actions are motivated by prejudice and Christian hate. They will both insist that their actions are based totally on other reasons. In the South one ubiquitous reason is states' rights. In the North a widespread reason is property value or fear of intermarriage.[7] When the real operative values are divulged accidentally, as it were, by one of those who share them, the reaction of the rest will be resentment against the simpleton who spoke out of turn and angry denial of everything he disclosed. These mechanisms are repeated so often on so many occasions that they need no further illustration or elaboration.

However, the ideas of equality, freedom, and Christian love inevitably affect all Americans because they are values that are conceived more than operative. They might even be described as the conscience of the American society. That is why failure to live according to them or outright opposition to them will both lead to guilt, denial, and subterfuge. These are men and women who champion the cause of the more conceived values just as those who desperately cling to and fight for the more operative values. That is to say, the champions of equality, freedom, and Christian love can consciously use their values as tools for their ends, just as the champions of prejudice, bigotry, and Christian hate can also consciously use their values as tools for their ends.

In the hands of some politicians and all demagogues the relationship between these values and the objects they desire often becomes transparently clear and undisguisedly selfish. It has been suggested that Hitler's hate campaign against the Jews was a major secret of his power. It is not surprising, therefore, to find numerous instances in which politicians and other activists charge each other with wooing liberal votes, Black votes, or conservative votes because of their platforms. But the link between the more conceived American values and the more operative values is the core American value of self-reliance. The supporters of each desire social arrangements in which their own particular nests will be feathered in their own particular ways.

[7] It is interesting that the Kerner Report is mostly descriptive. Where it dwells on the causes of violence it indicates mostly economic or economy-related causes. (See Report of the National Advisory Commission on Civil Disorders, 1968.)

As the emphasis on democratic equality and freedom and Christian love increases with self-reliance, totalitarian racial prejudice and bigotry and Christian hate will also increase with it. When the individual is shorn of all permanent and reliable moorings among his fellowmen, his only security must come from personal success, personal superiority, and personal triumph. Those who are fortunate enough to achieve success, superiority, and triumph will, of course, bask in the sunshine. To them democratic equality and freedom and Christian love are extremely laudable. But success, superiority, and triumph on the part of some must of necessity be based on the failure, inferiority, and defeat on the part of others. For the latter, and even for some of those who are in the process of struggling for success, superiority, and triumph, the resentment against and fear of failure, inferiority, and defeat must be widespread and often unbearable. To them totalitarian prejudice and bigotry and Christian hate can be means to a fleeting security. By pushing others down they at least achieve the illusion of personal success, personal superiority, and personal triumph.[8]

The Problem of Pessimism

If the conclusions of this analysis seem to lend themselves to pessimistic inferences, I wish to assure the readers that this is neither intentional nor desired. But the role of science is that we must contemplate whatever conclusions our evidences lead us to, whether they are pleasant or unpleasant.

In attentuation of certain pessimistic notes in the conclusions reached we need, however, to realize that the contribution of Western self-reliance to human development has been great and that even the chains of conformity and organization have their salutary aspects. What gave the Western man his superiority over the rest of the world during the last 300 years was not his religion or his romanticism but his self-reliance and his competitive organization. It was his self-reliance which led him to discard the shackles of paternal authority, monarchical power, and medieval magic, in favor of wider organizations such as church and state, mercantile fleets, and industrial development. When the West met the East, it was the Western man's well-organized armed might which crushed the East. As late as 1949 one high-ranking United States official attributed civil war-torn China's plight, in a *Harper's* magazine article, to the fact that the

[8]Additional substantiation for this analysis is found in Carl J. Friedrich (ed.), *Totalitarianism*, which contains the results of a conference of scholars in 1953 under the auspices of the American Academy of Arts and Sciences. Its conclusion is that totalitarianism is a new disease peculiar to *modern* culture. *Modern* culture here refers, of course, to Western culture.

Chinese were "organizationally corrupt." It is instructive to note that today, the two giants of the West, the U.S.A. and the U.S.S.R., are still most attractive to the rest of the world for their skill in organization. All over the globe their experts are helping peoples of other nations to organize their educational systems, or their marketing arrangements, or their agricultural practices, or their industrial efforts, or their military capabilities, or their national finances.[9]

The purpose of this paper is neither optimistic nor pessimistic. It is to place the much-lauded American values in their proper genetic perspective. When this is done, we find that the best of America is directly linked with her worst, like Siamese twins. The way out of the worst is not to deny it but to recognize it for what it is.

[9] The problem of why some individuals assume some aspects of the value orientation of their society more than other aspects is outside of the scope of this chapter. That problem is treated intensively in the works of Mering (1961), Kluckhohn and Strodtbeck (1961), and others.

Bibliography

Allport, Gordon. 1954. The nature of prejudice. Cambridge, Mass., Addison-Wesley Publishing Company, Inc.

Bain, Read. 1935. Our schizoid culture. Sociology and Social Research 19:266–276.

Coleman, Lee. 1941. What is American: a study of alleged American traits. Social Forces, Vol. XIX, No. 4.

Commager, Henry Steele. 1950. The American mind. New Haven, Yale University Press.

Cuber, John F. and Robert A. Harper. 1948. Problems of American society: values in conflict. New York, Henry Holt & Co.

Friedrick, Carl J. (ed.). 1954. Totalitarianism. Cambridge, Mass., Harvard University Press.

Homans, George C. 1950. The human group. New York, Harcourt Brace & Co.

Hsu, Francis L. K. 1960. Rugged individualism reconsidered. The Colorado Quarterly 9:145–162.

———. 1961. Clan, caste and club: a comparative study of Chinese, Hindu, and American ways of life. Princeton, N.J., Van Nostrand Co.

———. 1970. Americans and Chinese: two ways of life. New York, Doubleday and Natural History Press.

———. 1971. The challenge of the American dream: the Chinese in the United States. San Francisco, Wadsworth Publishing Co.

KERNER REPORT: REPORT OF THE 1968 NATIONAL ADVISORY COMMISSION ON CIVIL DISORDERS. 1968. New York, Bantam Book edition.

KLUCKHOHN, CLYDE. 1941. The way of life. Kenyon Review, Spring, pp. 160–180.

KLUCKHOHN, CLYDE, AND FLORENCE R. KLUCKHOHN. 1947. American culture: generalized orientation and class pattern, Chapter IX of Conflicts of power in modern culture, 1947 Symposium of Conference in Science, Philosophy and Religion, New York, Harper and Bros.

KLUCKHOHN, FLORENCE AND FRED STRODTBECK. 1961. Variations in value-orientations. Evanston, Ill., Row Peterson and Co.

LASKI, HAROLD J. 1948. The American democracy. New York, The Viking Press.

LEWIN, KURT. 1948. Psycho-sociological problems of a minority group. *In* Character and personality, Vol. III, 1935, 175–187. (Reprinted in Kurt Lewin: Resolving social conflicts, New York, Harper & Bros.)

LIPSET, SEYMOUR M. 1963. The first new nation. New York, Basic Books.

MERING, OTTO VON. 1961. A grammar of human values. Pittsburgh, University of Pittsburgh Press.

MORRIS, CHARLES. 1956. Varieties of human value. Chicago, University of Chicago Press.

MYRDAL, GUNNAR. 1944. An American dilemma. New York, Harper & Bros.

NOTTINGHAM, ELIZABETH K. 1954. Religion and society. New York, Doubleday & Co.

RIESMAN, DAVID. 1950. The lonely crowd. New Haven, Yale University Press.

TEITELBAUM, SAMUEL. 1953. Patterns of adjustment among Jewish students. Northwestern University Ph.D. dissertation.

WARNER, LLOYD. 1953. American life: dream and reality. Chicago, University of Chicago Press.

WILLIAMS, ROBIN M. 1951. American society, a sociological interpretation. New York, Alfred Knopf. (1960, 2nd ed.).

———. 1956. Religion, value-orientations, and intergroup conflict. The Journal of Social Issues 12:14–15.

Methods and Techniques

Two projective instruments, the Rorschach and the Thematic Apperception Test, have practically become standard stock-in-trade for many
anthropologists. Although the popularity of projective testing in anthropological studies seemed to have waned greatly in the late 50's, the
number of relevant works, to judge by the impressive bibliographies
compiled by Spain (Chapter 7 and Appendix), is not inconsiderable. All
sorts of objections and doubts have been raised about their cross-cultural
validity, or their validity as an instrument of studying anything other than
individual differences, or, among psychologists, even their validity for their
original purpose of diagnosing individual maladjustment. But as Spain
points out succinctly, "The novelty of projective tests has long since worn
off. As a result, problems are clearer and the demands for solution are
more insistent than ever." He provides the reader with a highly useful
checklist of problems associated with the use of projective tests under
several headings: those related to conception and design of research and
tests, those related to administration of tests, and those of analysis and
generalization. He does not see most of the problems as unsolvable if the
anthropological user incorporates in his research design a few precautionary steps "in advance" and does not resort to short cuts. In addition he

shows how the psychological anthropologist can reduce error by "understanding of the factors which influence performance on the test" as well as interpretation of the results.

There is one point made by the author with which the editor takes issue. The author rightly notes the pitfall of using Euro-American concepts to understand the behavior of non-Western subjects. But his suggestion that the difficulty can be "circumvented" for the time being by "doing research within a single culture" seems to defeat his purpose. There is no way that an anthropologist, however sophisticated, can unload *all* assumptions of his own culture. A more reasonable research strategy for circumventing the difficulties Spain noted would seem to be systematic comparison between different cultures (see Hsu, *The Study of Literate Civilizations*, 1969).

The bibliography on the use of projective tests Spain assembled, both at the end of the chapter and in the Appendix, is the most comprehensive to date.

The chapter by Watrous and Hsu is an attempt to find a way to utilize some form of TAT on a larger sample than is usually possible in anthropological field work. But its rationale is not merely economy of time and energy. Administering only two TAT cards in a group situation it is hoped that we shall be able to capture more of the shallower psychic materials in personality that are shared with others rather than its deeper and more individualized aspects.

Wallace's chapter is an almost unique contribution in the field of psychological anthropology. "The importance of the organic factors in psychopathology has been largely ignored by anthropological theory," he notes. Yet Wallace does not ignore the importance of society and culture. He tries to blaze the trail toward a biocultural theory of mental illness by integrating the organic and the functional approaches. His primary data concern one of the well-known yet most puzzling of mental illnesses found among Polar Eskimos: *Pibloktoq*, sometimes translated as arctic hysteria. His findings are that *Pibloktoq* is primarily due to calcium deficiency but that both the origin of that deficiency and the Polar Eskimo's response to *Pibloktoq* are cultural. Wallace suggests that while a cultural typology based on differential pathogenicity is not presently possible, an "index of culture" based on "response to mental illness" is well within our grasp. But the core of Wallace's contribution is his sophisticated four stage model integrating organic and functional approaches.

Man's attempt at reading dreams goes back as far as any cultural records, but his scientific understanding of the phenomenon is of very recent origin. Bourguignon's chapter falls into two parts. In the first part she summarizes existing works on what may be termed the anthropology of dreams. These are grouped under five categories: (1) those which present a series of dreams from one or more individuals in particular cultures; (2) those which search for universal subject matter in dreams; (3) those which look for trends in the manifest content of dreams; (4) those which attempt to link dreams with cultural behavior; and (5) those which deal with the use to which dreams are put in particular cultures and cross-culturally the relationship between such uses to other beliefs and institutions. The second part of her chapter is highly original. Here she sees dreams and various kinds of pseudo-perceptions (such as Trance and Possession Trance) as a continuum of psychological dimensions which offers possibilities for greater depth in anthropological investigation.

Campbell, the social psychologist, and Naroll, the anthropologist, are among the foremost methodologists in their respective disciplines. Theirs is the only contribution to this volume which confines itself to the problems of methodology. They show how anthropology has contributed to psychological theory by insisting on cultural relativism and by providing a wider human laboratory for testing psychological theories. However, the authors realize that the testing of psychological theory is only a minor goal of the psychological anthropologist. A more important benefit for him is the improvement of his tools and concepts for methologically more sophisticated field research. The psychological anthropologist (and other anthropologists as well) is asked to pay more heed than he has done so far to such questions as sampling procedure, societal unit definition, data accuracy, causal analysis of correlations, statistical significance, regional variation, and others. In each of these areas the authors have provided a high standard against which the anthropologist can measure his own efforts in the field, in the library, and throughout the process of analysis and search for significance of his results.

In their zeal for methodological neatness perhaps Campbell and Naroll have gone too far on some points. They have probably overdrawn the distinction between what they call the "descriptive-humanistic" and the "abstractive." Strictly speaking, every description is an abstraction and every abstraction must involve some description of the phenomena abstracted. Furthermore there are many studies which are simultaneously descriptive and abstractive.

The other arguable point is their notion that "a comparison of a single pair of natural instances" is scientifically "uninterpretable" and therefore unacceptable. For example, if severe initiation rites are present in one and absent in the other of a pair of societies, and if the student tries to explain this difference by a simple correlation with differences in mother-infant sleeping arrangements, that will indeed leave much to be desired as a scientific exercise. But such a comparison is faulty not because it is limited to two instances, but because the data in question are taken out of their respective multi-dimensional contexts. A more scientifically adequate comparison of the same "pair of natural instances" must include a systematic scrutiny of other aspects of culture associated with each of the "natural instances."

For examples of such multi-dimensional comparisons limited to two or three societies, the reader should consult Francis L. K. Hsu, *Clan, Caste and Club* (Princeton, N.J.: Van Nostrand, 1963) and Francis L. K. Hsu, *Americans and Chinese: Purpose and Fulfillment in Great Civilizations* (New York: Doubleday and Natural History Press, 1970).

CHAPTER SEVEN

On the Use of Projective Tests for Research in Psychological Anthropology[1]

DAVID H. SPAIN

Promises

Projective tests, like prostitutes, have been dismissed by the cynical as illicit or at best mildly seductive, and even then only for the novice. Seen as merely beckoning with sophistication of technique, tempting with promises of insight into the unknown, and titillating with anticipation of satisfaction of desire, they have been heaped with scorn. As with so many things, familiarity seems to have bred contempt. Those who doubt this have only to re-examine the various "Dear Jane letters" on the use of projective tests in non-Western cultures (e.g., Mensh and Henry, 1953; Henry, 1955). In an era of increasing criticism and doubt, what might now be said, if anything, for these oft rejected trollops?

[1] This is a revision of the paper by Bert Kaplan entitled, "Cross-cultural use of projective techniques," which originally appeared in the first edition of this volume. The discerning reader will notice numerous instances throughout this revision (and especially in the sections headed "Performance" and "Problems") which demonstrate my debt to Kaplan's insights. In several places, full sentences and paragraphs have been retained, though often in slightly different contexts or with different emphasis. Acknowledgement is here gratefully given to Professor Kaplan for his permission to use the article in this way. The author would also express his appreciation to John A. Brim, Charles F. Keyes and Oliver Osborne for their valuable comments on an earlier draft of this paper. To L. L. Langness, a special note of appreciation is due for his very insightful comments. As usual, any inadequacies are the responsibility of the author alone.

First, it should be recalled that projective tests were originally developed and used by clinicians. Although neither their goals nor their exclamations about their findings were immodest, it is still basically true that their techniques are not easily transferred to settings outside the clinic, let alone outside the culture in which they were developed. Early anthropological interest came from people who usually were fully apprised of this initial context and were, as a consequence, cautious in adopting them elsewhere. However, there has always been considerable optimism, too. Hallowell, for example, has suggested (1955:63) that Rorschach materials "may be just as significant, at the personality level, in validating the anthropologist's interpretation of the functioning of cultures, as a consideration of cultural data has proved of value to the psychologist in gaining a more comprehensive knowledge of the determinants relevant to the functioning of individuals." For critics, this optimistic statement can be said to contain an ironically insightful (if not prophetic) conditional clause. That is, projective test materials may be just about as useful to anthropologists as cultural data have been for psychologists — not very useful at all. Nevertheless, it must be recognized that the use of these tests by anthropologists need not of necessity be tainted by the supposed shortcomings of our professional cousins.

Second, early anthropological use of projective tests was fostered by the conviction that they provided a means of achieving several traditional — indeed, sacred — anthropological research goals. Thus, projective tests were adopted because they were thought typically to elicit data covering a wide spectrum of human concerns. In using the Rorschach, for example, informants were presented with relatively unstructured but stimulating cues designed to produce responses presumably minimally affected by the ethnographer's concerns. The holistic ideal of anthropology seemed attainable with a technique designed to provide insight into aspects of non-Western personality. Cross-cultural comparison seemed to be facilitated by using projective tests since the "same" stimuli could be presented to all informants. These tests were seen as important links between data and theories concerning the influence of early socialization on adult behavior, the concepts of modal personality, national character and the "character of nationals," and as an index of whether or not personality change was associated with culture change. In short, the promises of projective tests seemed to center on the collection of the previously elusive data which were necessary if we were to help forge a link between those concerned with personality and those concerned with culture.

Performance

Given such promises, one may wonder about our accomplishments.[2] On reviewing anthropological research which utilizes projective tests, one is struck by the strong interest in basic or modal personality. As introduced by Kardiner, Linton and DuBois in the late 1930's, this has been one of the more influential (albeit controversial) theoretical conceptions in psychological anthropology. Following their lead, many anthropologists concerned themselves with describing personality characteristics they found to be prevalent in various non-Western settings. Although they did so in terms of personality traits, structures, and types — concepts which initially had been established through research by psychologists in Euro-American society — the availability of projective tests was a key factor facilitating this inquiry.

After a period of initial enthusiasm, there is today only guarded acceptance of the view that there exists in each culture a core of personality characteristics which are found in *most* of its members. For almost two decades, the existence of this core of homogeneity was regarded by many as virtually axiomatic. It seemed natural to culture and personality workers to *begin* by looking for and describing these typical or modal characteristics. That this aim might prejudge an empirical issue which had not been adequately settled for our own culture, let alone for others supposedly more exotic, did not seem to matter. To be sure, and to their credit, there were some who illuminated the variability that exists *within* societies. They sometimes found it to be embarrassingly large (e.g., DuBois, 1944; Vogt, 1951; Wallace, 1952; Kaplan, 1954; and Inkeles and Levinson, 1954).

In part, modal personality was assumed to exist because two key concepts — culture and personality — were not adequately distinguished. Relatively widely accepted views of the time (e.g., Spiro, 1951; Smith, 1954) held that "culture" and "personality," as abstractions from the same behavior, were arbitrary distinctions. Phrases such as "culture-in-personality" and "personality-in-culture" were widely heard and debated, but the torrent of words only succeeded in obscuring the obvious — if personality is regárded as synonymous with learned cultural behavior, there could be no question about the existence of modal traits since the very

---

[2] We will not attempt here a detailed review of all the anthropological literature which has utilized projective tests. Lindzey (1961) provides an excellent review of the literature prior to 1960. Unfortunately much of what he provides in the way of critical commentary applies to the literature since that time, as well.

concept of culture implied the existence of such uniformities and regularities.

The assessment of personality processes in terms of societal functioning has frequently been a key concern for those interested in the fundamental characteristics of social order and integration. For example, Weber, Parsons, Merton, Fromm, and Riesman have suggested motivational processes of individuals are a key to societal functioning because they have a crucial impact on the initiation of socially required performances. In this connection, Inkeles and Levinson (1954) emphasize the distinction between (1) actual modal personality patterns empirically determined to exist in members of a society, and (2) "socially required" personality patterns needed for optimal societal functioning. The latter consist of the core of motivations which lead individuals to perform the socially necessary roles and act in appropriate ways.

Only recently has the distinction between these two concepts been made systematically. Formerly, in most theoretical schemes, the modal personality model was thought to subsume both the modal patterns *and* the socially appropriate character structure. A number of writers, including Riesman, Parsons, Spiro, Devereux, Singer, and Inkeles (among others) suggest appropriate social behavior is not simply a function of an individual's *total* personality but rather of particular and specific motivational structures. A suggestion made by Parsons and Shils (1951:158) is that from the point of view of society, the crucial matter is "to get the patterns [of behavior] whatever their functional significance to the person . . . it does not matter whether there are important differences among types of personality possessing [the] need-disposition [to behave in the required way] as long as it exists." Thus, from their point of view, it is not necessary to posit modal personality characteristics in order to account for social behavior. Individuals may vary considerably; the important matter is that the jobs get done. Wallace (1961a) argues for a shift in emphasis away from seeking uniformity and towards understanding the "organization of diversity." Thus, the goal of empirical investigation employing these newer schemes is not simply the study of personality for its own sake — i.e., simply describing the distribution and range of human personality. Rather, the problem is to describe the aspects of presonality relevant to understanding the performance of roles.

For some workers, one tack has been to define the problem in terms of the conformity-deviance dimension. For example, Kaplan, Riesman, and others seek to discover the motivational bases which lead to conformative behavior (or in some cases, which lead to deviance from such conformity). They hold that problems of culture change, inadequate role performance and deviance, to note a few of the more common issues, require insight into motivations of the person relative to demands being made on him for social behavior.

In considering what some of these motivations might be, Kaplan (1957, 1961a, 1961b) suggests these bases do not lie in point-for-point isomorphism with specific social requirements and values. For example, he would not see competitive behavior as necessarily supported by motives for competition since these can be understood as being primarily instrumental in nature; i.e., in a means-end relationship to other more generalized motives. He suggests research be focused on those generalized dispositions which articulate the relationship of the person to the social reality in which he acts. Such a reality would be, to a considerable extent, organized in normative terms—i.e., specifying what one should be doing and how. Riesman and Fromm have been concerned with the nature of these generalized dispositions and term them "social character." "Other directedness" is given by Kaplan (1961b) as an example of the kind of generalized disposition he and they are talking about. Riesman's account (1950) of consequences that flow from a society's reliance upon a particular type of motivational orientation is cited, noting that what is at stake is the core and basis of social integration — the essence of social order itself. Clearly, these generalized motives are not viewed as minor aspects of social life. He adds, however, that such descriptions are best understood as empirical matters, which, since they ultimately are related to individual behavior, should be studied at the level of individuals. Although he cites Riesman's *Faces in the Crowd* (1952) as an example of this kind of study, Kaplan does point out that it does not fully meet the goals he has in mind since it is more an illustration of his theory than an analysis of the facts.

Since the enthusiasm of the early 1960's when this view was first being widely discussed, there have been only a few studies which even attempt to consider and reject such a position, let alone undertake to support it through systematic research. In a brief statement of his theoretical position and main hypothesis, LeVine (1966) explicitly considers and rejects the Parsons-Shils-Spiro-Kaplan position in favor of the view put forward by Inkeles (1954, 1959, and 1963). That is, LeVine indicates support for the hypothesis that (p. 12) "specific correspondences between individual motivation and socially structured role requirements [may be] predicted." Though he does not appear to see the views of Kaplan and Inkeles as diametrically opposed, his research strategy is predicated on the analysis of motives which are far less general than those seen as important by Kaplan. In part, this may be due to the clear and utilitarian character of the motive he considers in his analysis (need for achievement), but nevertheless, in considering these more specific motives, LeVine is assuming that there is, in general, an important correspondence between the motives of individuals and the roles they have in society.

The most explicit and extended discussion of the issues raised by Kaplan is that of Phillips (1965:202–8). However, his comments have the appearance of being an after-thought. Since the fieldwork was undertaken several years prior to the publication of the major points in Kaplan's view, this can in no way be taken as a criticism of his work. Moreover, it is not invariably true that such discussions, in order to be meaningful, must of necessity emerge from research for which these concerns were central at the outset. What this does illustrate, if Phillips' efforts may be taken as a representative attempt to deal with Kaplan's views, is that although it may be difficult to develop research which will produce data permitting an adequate test of these issues, it is even more difficult for a discussion based on the results of more general research to do more than stimulate renewed interest in the problems and issues at stake.

Phillips' study is not a general assessment of Thai peasant personality (despite the title of his book) but, rather, is a consideration of dimensions of interpersonal interaction and a "working out [of] the dynamics of social behavior and its meaning to the individual" (1965:208). His data consist (for this report) of "naturalistic" observation of personality, and responses to a lengthy sentence completion test by a sample from a central Thai village.

His discussion of the notion of a generalized motive for conformity and related aspects of Kaplan's hypothesis provides further evidence for what appears to be an important problem in dealing with these issues—i.e., the problems and viewpoints put forward by Kaplan are not readily amenable to rigorous analysis. Perhaps this is because "generalized motivation to conform" is so general it is difficult to operationalize. One of Phillips' major concerns, for example, was to show (on the basis of empirical evidence) that the villagers in his sample have a heightened concern with being "psychologically isolated" (p. 207), and with maintaining their freedom of choice (p. 206). He specifically remarks on the starkness of the contrast between Americans and Thai in regard to their respective needs for conformity, indicating the Thai are noticeably low in this regard (p.

204). They pursue their own goals, "oblivious to the requirements of conformity. . . . " He provocatively suggests (p. 204) Kaplan's formulation may be applicable best to "our own highly complex, functionally specific culture" since conformity seems to be a prerequisite for continuing to operate our society efficiently. He offers the Thai peasant, living in a loosely structured society, with high concerns for individualism and isolation, and with characteristic disinterest for requirements of conformity, as an example which does not fit Kaplan's generalization that such generalized motives for conformity may be expected to be crucial for "any society."

Thailand is not the only society which has been described in such terms. Numerous descriptions of the various northeastern American Indian societies (e.g., among Algonkian peoples) have led to the widely accepted view which holds that in terms of personality, there is a special concern for emotional restraint and inhibition. However, as Leacock (1963:941) points out in a review of another study in this vein (Spindler, 1962), there is insufficient recognition of

> "the fact that there is restraint in some areas, but tremendous latitude for expression in others; that restraint . . . apparently functioned not only to ensure cooperation, but also, paradoxically and most significantly, as one way of not impinging on the freedom of expression, the autonomy, the individuality of others. Further, there has been a stress on 'atomism' and 'individualism' among northeastern Indians, but the manner in which they combine with a fundamental 'collectivism' has been virtually ignored."

It would seem, failing the use of carefully operationalized concepts, one may interpret the role of individualism and related personality characteristics in any number of ways.

If further evidence of the difficulty is needed, we may consider the discussion of "conformity" in American society that is presented in Hsu's comparative analysis of China, India, and the United States (1963:216–24). Recognizing that all societies (if they are to be worthy of the term) may be expected to exhibit some degree of conforming behavior (and Kaplan clearly and explicitly recognizes this obvious fact), Hsu suggests that conformity in America is the result of a fear of inferiority and failure which comes from the highly competitive character of American life. From this and other discussions of conformity, it appears that this concern or motive is indeed generalized in that it can be the basis for self-reliance, social mobility, inner-peace, being full and autonomous, pleasing others, facilitating the smooth functioning of a complex social order, seeking isolation and literal survival. One looks in vain for a study which presents a convincing test of Kaplan's viewpoint. Phillips' data, Hsu's analysis, and Leacock's commentary make it difficult to evaluate the scientific merit of the role of generalized motives for conformity. Thus, it remains for future workers to determine with greater precision the nature and role of such motives, or, if the data point in such a direction, a rejection of this approach in favor of the type exemplified in the research of Inkeles and LeVine. To date, the field has not witnessed a convincing demonstration of the superiority of one view over the other.

Projective Tests

With the great variety of psychological tests, it will facilitate our discussion if we review the basic characteristics of projective tests. The most comprehensive survey of the use of projective tests in cross-cultural research (Lindzey, 1961) reviews the essential, as well as the important but non-essential, aspects of such tests. The term "projective" is used in this context in a way which departs significantly and intentionally from usage in psychoanalytic theory. Rather than a term having to do with individual defense mechanisms and related aspects of the psyche, psychologists (beginning with Frank, 1939) use the term to refer to the tendency for respondents to reveal aspects of their personality when asked to respond to loosely structured stimuli by giving them some structure or order. Thus, minimally, projective tests consist of loosely structured sets of visual and/ or auditory cues to which a person must respond by providing order or structure. In order to meet a number of research goals, such as encouraging a wide range of responses and avoiding the use of cues permitting the subject to become "test-wise" or to fail to "project," the cues are commonly chosen to represent a wide range of interpersonal relationships and/or a wide range of ambiguous objects. In either case, fantasy is encouraged in responses and it is stressed there are no wrong or right answers.

Lindzey (1961) groups the various projective tests into five categories based on the type of response expected: association, construction, completion, choice or ordering, and expression tests. Of the association type, the best known are the Rorschach and word association tests. The latter has undergone a number of variations but these have seldom been used outside either the clinic or Western world (for examples, see DuBois, 1944; Carstairs, 1957). The Rorschach has had a long and turbulent history, especially in its use by anthropologists. One variation, the Cloud Test

(Stern, 1938), has rarely been used in cross-cultural anthropological research. An important and more recent modification, the Holtzman Inkblot Test (Holtzman, 1958 and 1961), has been used in several non-Western settings (e.g., Holtzman, 1965 and 1968; Derogatis, et al., 1968).

Of the construction tests, the Thematic Apperception Test (TAT) is the best known and most widely used. There are also many variations, a number of which have been developed by anthropologists. The Sentence Completion Test (SCT) is the best known of the completion techniques and has been used in a variety of settings with disparate research goals. Thus, Rogers (1969) uses a short, 14 item version of the test as a measure of achievement motivation among Colombian peasants. A more comprehensive analysis using the SCT was made by Phillips (1965). He was seeking the means to achieve a thorough understanding of the personalitites of the Thai villagers who were the subject of his study. However, he also wanted to use a projective test which would have high potential for use by others elsewhere with a minimum of alteration, thereby insuring maximum comparability. The sentence completion test developed by Phillips seems to have met both of these goals. His SCT contained 72 items in each of two versions. In all, 13 personality categories were investigated. As both Rogers and Phillips point out, the test has the advantage of avoiding visual stimuli, thus circumventing problems which arise because of culturally based differences in perception. Moreover, the responses are usually not so voluminous as to unduly hamper analysis (though Phillips does report an average of between 7 and 10 hours of analysis per respondent). The test can be administered with relative ease to large groups of people at the same time (assuming literacy), and is useful in measuring attitudes and other relatively "shallow" aspects of personality — an increasingly popular research goal. However, the test does present some weaknesses, primarily in the difficulty of translating the items and in developing cues which minimize the likelihood of respondents becoming test-wise.

The choice or ordering techniques, including the Szondi and Picture Arrangement tests, for example, typically require subjects to arrange a number of objects, photographs, and the like, into some order. These tests have not been used widely by anthropologists. Of the expressive techniques, the most popular are the various drawing tests, including Draw-a-Person (DAP), House-Tree-Person (HTP), and related variations of these which employ clay or other materials for the creative aspect of the test (for examples of research using these variations, see Ritchie, 1957 and Leininger, 1966). Wayne Dennis (1966) presents an interesting analysis of children's drawings of "a man." The data are from 13 countries and represent more than 25 ethnic and/or socio-economic groups. The focus of the research was to determine whether children, when asked to "draw a man" would draw pictures of men from admired reference groups. If they did, then aspects of the children's values were thought to be indicated and assessable. Moreover, such a finding would counter the prevailing view that children typically drew a picture of the man (or other person) with whom they were most familiar. Dennis concludes that indeed the children in his sample do draw pictures of admired figures and, among other things, he suggests that replications with similar samples done after the passage of a few years should provide a ready index of change in an area important for the analysis of social change and modernization, i.e., images of the ideal man (for commentary in another context on the importance of such images for social change and modernization, see LeVine, 1966). An explicit test of Dennis' modernization hypothesis was made in the Sudan prior to his general consideration of the problem (see Badri and Dennis, 1964). Several research projects have utilized similar expressive techniques among non-Western samples (e.g., Hunkum, 1950; and Melikian and Wahab, 1969, among others).

Other expressive projective tests include various play techniques and certain kinds of role-playing and psychodrama. A study by Landy (1959) incorporated data from doll playing in an analysis of socialization in a Puerto Rican village. Although seeking answers to broader questions related to dramatic social change rather than the more commonly discussed issue in psychological anthropology, Doob (1968) notes the potential of "workshops" and other training groups in effecting and assessing personality change, citing among other studies, a number of such experiments in Nigeria (Nylen, et al., 1961; Seashore, 1965). Lindzey also notes (1961:94) the potential for such techniques in cross-cultural research, citing the work of Stanton, Back, and Litwak (1956).

Since Lindzey's review, a number of other projective tests have been introduced, including the Hand Test, Proverbs Test, Group Personality Projective Test, the Vocational Apperception Test, and many others. Rabin (1968) presents an up-to-date summary of many of these newer tests. The vast majority of these have been developed by social and clinical psychologists, though a few have been introduced by anthropologists. One of the more innovative of these may be briefly mentioned here. LeVine's study of achievement motivation in Nigeria (1966) utilized a construction test which employed auditory rather than visual stimuli. In order to avoid a number of problems which seem to be endemic when using visual cues, he simply asked the respondents to "spend half an hour writing in English a description of the most recent nighttime dream he had had, and the next half hour writing a description of a dream he remembered having had more than once" (1966:51). LeVine views this test as analogous to the blank card of the Murray TAT or to the Open Projective Test (OPT) developed by Forrest and Lee (1962). Whatever its antecedents, it seemed to be successful in eliciting fantasy responses sufficient for an assessment of the need for achievement. A similar application of this technique was made in Bornu, Nigeria, by Spain (1969).

Preferences: the Rorschach

Over the years, users of projective tests have come to rely upon two basic tests and/or their offspring. These are Rorschach's Ink Blot Test (Rorschach) and the Thematic Apperception Test (TAT). Several attempts have been made to compare these tests in terms of utility, cross-cultural validity, and various other criteria. Lindzey (1961:320) notes, for example, that because of differences in the amount of verbal facility required for these tests, one might expect the Rorschach to have an advantage over the heavily verbal TAT. Thus, one could expect to successfully administer the Rorschach to groups varying widely in age, education, or intellectual background and ability (though as we shall see, below, this in no way assures a solution to analytic and interpretive problems). Another supposed advantage of the Rorschach is that it is accompanied by a ready-made and elaborate scoring system, including associated interpretive guidelines. Moreover, Rorschach stimulus material, when compared with the TAT, appears to be less culture-bound, although this point has been debated a number of times (see, for example, the exchange between Adock and Ritchie, 1958; and Clifton, 1959). In a similar vein, Kaplan and Lawless (1965), while finding some expected differences, do find striking similarities from one culture to another in the content of Rorschach populars.

For those interested in modal personality processes, the Rorschach has been particularly easy to use as well as useful in theoretical terms, if for no other reason than because no matter what subjects did with the test, responses could be scored and scores averaged to get measures of central tendency. Unfortunately, this has too often been the only analysis performed and even these more or less uncritically. When averages are not accompanied by measures of variability, as they frequently are not, they are almost useless since they do not give the reader any idea of the distribution of scores around the mean. Measures of variance, however, complicate things because there is no standard criterion which will tell the worker when his group is homogeneous enough to be characterized validly by the mean or mode. It is also of questionable value to pool Rorschach scores of individuals to arrive at a combined psychogram which is then taken to represent the group modal pattern. While the result may be neat and impressive, it often has no relationship to the patterns found in any of the individuals in the group since such patterns are completely synthetic. A further problem is that the large number of scoring categories for the Rorschach (as well as for many other projective tests) leads to the possibility of many different permutations. Wallace (1961b) points out, for example, that even 20 binary indices will yield more than a million types. Thus, an impressive amount of uniformity will have to be present in order to be noticed or else categories defined in more general terms will have to be the focus of the research.

One of the better known attempts to deal critically *and* empirically with the concept of modal personality (Wallace, 1952) used the Rorschach in collecting the data. In his analysis, Wallace arbitrarily but reasonably set a modal range of 2 standard deviations around the mode, defining as members of the modal class those responses which fell within these limits. Further, individuals whose scores fell within these limits on all 21 variables were to be counted as members of the modal group. On this basis, he found 37% of the Tuscarora were in this group while only 5% of the Ojibwa were. The impact of these findings can be seen in some of Wallace's later writings (e.g., 1961a and 1961b) in which, rather than looking for modal personality characteristics (i.e., the "replication of uniformity"), he suggests we be concerned with understanding the diversity of motives which are related and organized through the medium of shared expectations held by the individuals in an orderly society (i.e., the "organization of diversity").

A related issue has been considered by Kaplan (1954) in a study of Rorschach protocols from 170 young men in four cultures (Zuni, Navajo, Spanish American, and Mormon). Making a comparative analysis of 14 variables, he found statistically significant variability from culture to culture for only five of these. However, *within* each of the four groups there was considerable variability. Thus, research designed to measure differences in personality *between* groups was successful in illuminating the magnitude of the *within-group* variability which in fact was greater than the variability between groups. Numerous studies report similar results in that some significant between-group differences are observed, although there are many other differences that are not significant (e.g., Billig, Gellin, and Davidson, 1947 and 1948; Abel and Hsu, 1949; Joseph and Murray, 1951; Straus and Straus, 1956–7; and Hsu, Watrous, and Lord, 1961).

In part because of the nature of the Rorschach test itself (e.g., test pictures, scoring systems, and research designs are relatively difficult to modify), recent anthropological research using this instrument has not changed much in comparison to research using the TAT. However, modest advances have been made in some aspects of research design and implementation (e,g., size and characteristics of samples, methods of data collection, collection of supplementary cultural data, and the significance of theoretical issues). Among the more important recent studies (though not necessarily of equally high quality) are those of Miner and DeVos (1960), Clifton (1961), Spindler (1962), Bricklin and Zeleznik (1963), Wood (1965) and Kaplan and Lawless (1965).

Preferences: the TAT

The use of the TAT and its major variations has increased dramatically in recent years. Various sub-cultures have been studied using this instrument almost exclusively (e.g., a study of the wives of working class men by Rainwater, et al., 1959). Other studies of such sub-cultures have used a variation of the TAT (e.g., Minuchin, et al., 1967, used the Family Interaction Apperception Technique [FIAT]). Several topics of theoretical and practical importance have been investigated with various types of TAT's as the principal data gathering device (e.g., the numerous studies of achievement motivation). A diverse array of non-Western cultures have been studied using this instrument. The samples in these projects have ranged from just a few individuals up to 2,500. This latter study (DeRidder, 1961) utilized a 9 card instrument which, if all were given the entire set, would mean a total of 22,500 fantasy productions!

Many reputed advantages of the Rorschach are, from the viewpoint of some users of the TAT, not advantages at all, especially in non-Western settings. On this basis alone, some have said the TAT is more attractive. Moreover, it has been argued that responses to the TAT are typically more profuse and varied, thus permitting a wider range of inquiries to be made from the same test administration. Further, the tradition of story-telling is itself virtually universal, allowing the user of the TAT to take advantage of this. Certainly one of the more important advantages, if we are to judge by the extent to which the tactic has been employed by anthropologists, is the potential for modifying the original 20 card TAT developed by Murray and his associates. Unfortunately, it may also be true that problems resulting from the development of these permutations may outweigh the gains (Goldstein, 1961; Lesser, 1961; and Rabin, 1961).

Permutations

The number and types of modified TAT's is large and heterogeneous. One of the earliest and perhaps better known variations is the TAT modified for use with American Blacks (Thompson, 1949a and 1949b), though it has been criticized frequently (e.g., Korchin and Mitchell, 1950; Riess, et al., 1950; and Schwartz, et al., 1951). Other well known versions include the Blacky Pictures and the Children's Apperception Test (Blum, 1949; and Bellak, 1954). Those best known to anthropologists are tests developed for use among a variety of non-Western peoples, including a number of African groups (e.g., Lee, 1953; Sherwood, 1957; Biesheuvel, 1958; DeRidder, 1961; Jahoda, 1961; Spain, 1969; Ostheimer, 1969; and Cohen, 1971). Several have been developed for use among North American aboriginals (e.g., Henry, 1947; Alexander and Anderson, 1957; Goldschmidt and Edgerton, 1961; Parker, 1964; and Spindler and Spindler, 1965). A variety were made for use among Pacific peoples (e.g., Gladwin and Sarason, 1953; and Lessa and Spiegelman, 1954), Southeast and South Asia (e.g., Hanks, 1956; Geertz, 1957; Chowdhury, 1960; and Phillips, 1965), and among Orientals (e.g., DeVos and Wagatsuma, 1961; and Caudill, 1962). This list is not exhaustive, nor does it include the numerous modifications made by selecting a few cards from the original TAT (e.g., Caudill, 1949; and Hsu, 1963), or studies using various types of pictures for special purposes in our own culture (e.g., see Atkinson, 1958, for a listing of pictures used to measure achievement, affiliation and power motives).

Clearly, modified TAT's have met with considerable popularity among anthropologists. One of the reasons for this is related to anthropologists' sensitivity to the oft voiced criticism of the original Murray TAT, *viz.*, the stimulus materials have clear Euro-American cultural characteristics and as a result the test takes on an ethnocentric tone when used with subjects from other cultures.[3] Hence, a common goal among those who have

[3] Not all experience with the TAT demonstrates the necessity of modifying the instrument to fit local physical and cultural conditions. Preliminary analysis of a slightly modified Murray TAT used in the New Guinea Highlands indicates the records are insignificantly different from unmodified pictures (James B. Watson, personal communication).

produced modified TAT's has been the development of tests which were appropriate to the culture in which research was underway. Those making such modifications have had a number of other goals which illustrate some of the changing emphases in the field of psychological anthropology.

For example, the TAT designed by Sherwood (1957) was developed, in part, to conform to standards for designing a TAT which had been set forth by Henry (1947), and as such it represents one end of a continuum of styles and goals. The other end of this continuum is exemplified by several sets, including those of Gladwin and Sarason (1953), and Goldschmidt and Edgerton (1961). At various points in between fall most of the others mentioned previously. In terms of style, the key difference between the sets at the ends of the continuum is the amount of shading and/or chiaroscuro in the pictures; i.e., the reality dimension. Another difference (though not necessarily directly related to the reality dimension) is the general content of cues in the set, with the range being broad to narrow.

Sherwood (1957) proposes 13 criteria which he believes should be used in designing and evaluating a test along the lines of the Murray TAT. Six of these are for evaluating cues in each picture, including degree of sharpness of the pictorial image, appropriateness of human figures, physical settings and interpersonal relationships, "incompleteness" of the picture, and "compression" (inclusion of a variety of objects in a single picture). The remaining seven deal with characteristics of the set as a whole. Four of these suggest incorporating a range in number of objects (from few to many), degree of familiarity (from familiar to unfamiliar), emotional tone (from pleasant to unpleasant), and variety and contrast in terms of visual impact (including artistic styles). The other three recommend a number of basic themes which should be included in a set. These include basic family relationships, other important non-familial relationships, and symbolic objects designed to stimulate the respondent's unconscious processes.

The test developed by Goldschmidt and Edgerton was intended as a means of assessing values in a particular culture. Rather than seeking fantasy responses, they were interested in attitudes and related cultural data. To achieve these goals, pictures were drawn using a few well chosen, sharply contrasting, distinct lines. The scenes were specifically designed to be concrete, unambiguous, and culture-specific. The pictures represented visual questions dealing with value conflict. Although criticized by some as posing false dichotomies (e.g., Spindler and Spindler, 1965:322), the utility of their test for their research goals seems to have been given a reasonably rigorous application in the field.

Even a cursory examination of these two sets will verify their marked differences. Although few would question Sherwood's TAT is a full-fledged projective test, several (e.g., Collier, 1967, and Spindler and Spindler, 1965) have described a test such as Goldschmidt and Edgerton's as a "semi-projective technique." Since orthodoxy is not an essential aspect of good scientific research, such a distinction seems of little significance, although the term does reflect noticeable differences in the features of the various modifications of the TAT. Thus, rather than an instrument designed to tap the deeper levels or the full breadth and structure of an individual's personality, these TAT's constitute what some have termed "visual questionnaires" (e.g., Sherwood, 1957:167; Goldschmidt and Edgerton, 1961:28-9; and Caudill, 1962:116).

A serious concern among those who have attempted to modify the TAT has revolved around choosing the appropriate medium. In some cases this issue has been resolved in a manner reflecting a consideration of some theory and a large amount of pragmatism. For example, Spain (1969), working in Bornu, Nigeria, used carefully posed photographs for the pictures in his TAT, in part because it was an obvious way of solving the problem of producing pictures with culturally relevant stimulus material as well as overcoming serious shortcomings in artistic ability (a not insignificant factor, as witness the comments about Lee's TAT by Barnouw, 1963:264-5). The data obtained using this instrument were fully as rich as had been obtained a year earlier by Cohen (1971) working in the same area using a TAT consisting of chiaroscuro drawings.

Ostheimer (1969), reporting on his research in Tanzania which included the use of a modified TAT consisting of 4 pictures (2 photographs taken locally and 2 drawings modified from the Murray series), observed markedly different responses from the same individuals depending upon whether photographs or drawings were used. He found the photographs to be more successful than the drawings which, "though compatible in clothing and race, . . . evoked reactions other than identification with characters in the drawings, including interpretation that people were deformed, starving, evil, or otherwise fantastic" (1969:21).

This is not to say, however, that photographs will always be a preferrable medium for TAT's. Nevertheless, these cases do permit reconsideration of viewpoints expressed by Sherwood (1957:169) and Collier (1967:61-6) about the potential (or rather, the lack of it) of photographs for eliciting appropriate fantasy responses. Neither Sherwood nor Collier regard photographs, because of their "inherent" reality characteristics, as useful *projective* devices. However, an overly literal interpretation of this point of view may be unwarranted if and when proper precautions are taken in appropriate cultural settings. Thus, for example, that Spain was able to elicit fantasy material using a TAT consisting of photographs may have been, in part, due to having used carefully posed, slightly blurred photographs with a sample which, for cultural reasons, did not perceive such pictures as inherently realistic. Moreover, it should be noted that Sherwood's TAT contained a photograph which was apparently no less successful than the drawings in eliciting fantasy material.

Whether photographs or drawings, theoretical concerns have also been an important design factor for those using modified TAT's, though there has been a departure from earlier goals. Several interesting studies exemplify trends in this regard. For example, George and Louise Spindler, in connection with research on acculturation in a community of Blood Indians, were interested in (1965:314) "cataloguing the perceptual and cognitive dimensions most directly related to the economic and social behavior" of the population as it was acculturating to the Western, urban, industrial milieu. In particulary, they were interested in the instrumental activities which were a part of this process, so they developed a new projective test with which to assess them. This instrument, the "Instrumental Activities Inventory" (IAI) is clearly in the tradition of the original TAT, but differs in several important ways. First, it was designed to elicit information concerning cognitive orientations; the "IAI gives us specific, operational perceptions of social reality organized normatively in means-ends relationships" (1965:316). Second, ambiguity, breadth of cues and similar aspects of more standard TAT's (including Sherwood's) were studiously avoided. The pictures are not simple line drawings, there being more than minimal attention to detail, shading and the like, but in general, they were concerned that essential features of the instrumental activity be the single most dominant stimulus. The scenes portrayed ranged from a carpenter and mechanic to formal chief-making and calf roping. In all, there were 24 pictures.

Following Collier (1957), they describe their instrument as a "semiprojective technique" which acts as a "language bridge" for eliciting responses which are not deep aspects of personality (1965:322). Rather than indications about the character and structure of personality, they are concerned with attitudes toward work, possessions, other people, various activities, and a variety of other reality-based situations.

Other workers have had similar research goals but have attempted, with some success, to achieve them through the method of analysis instead of (or in some cases, in addition to) changing the design of the instrument. For example, Caudill's analysis (1962) focused on broad themes reflecting the nature of interpersonal relationships as seen by the respondents; i.e., "the essence of several common emotional patterns among Japanese people" (1962:130).

A number of other studies using somewhat modified TAT's focus on "cultural" variables. For example, in the "Annex" to Hsu's (1963) comparative study of China, India and the United States, there is an analysis of the data from TAT's administered to college students from these three societies. Using cards I and XII BG from the Murray set, Watrous and Hsu focus their analysis for the most part on broad themes concerning the nature of interpersonal relationships and sensitivity to the physical (non-human) environment. Although these broad themes were studied in detail using numerous sub-categories, indices, and word counts of various kinds, and although the subjects' responses were clearly fantasy productions, the materials were analyzed with "minimal emphasis on depth interpretation" (p. 266). No effort was made to analyze the data for basic personality structure or total personality. Rather (p. 270), they were concerned to "observe how certain reactions occurred in integrated clusters, suggesting varying patterns of *cultural behavior* in response to the same picture stimuli" (emphasis supplied).

Moreover, the results of their analysis suggested a number of innovations in the use of projective tests, innovations which have important implications for research design and for data analysis. Noting the observations of Kaplan (1954; 1961b) and Wallace (1952) to the effect that within-group variation in personality may be greater than between-group variation, Watrous and Hsu suggest (p. 309) the use of fewer pictures "may well prove to be a much better aid to the student of man for understanding personality in its *group perspective* than its individual perspective" (emphasis supplied). In addition, they reject a heavily psychometric approach to the analysis of projective material, suggesting that "feeling tone" and other admittedly subjectively derived aspects of the tests may be more revealing. They raise an issue of significant proportions when they suggest that (p. 310) "the broader question . . . is the degree to which quantitative data can validly describe an entity as complex as the human personality." Their answer, it would seem, points in the direction of employing a more subjective interpretation of the responses to fewer stimuli coupled with an objective analysis of major themes, especially when the goal is the assessment of gross differences between groups.

DeVos and Wagatsuma (1961), in a report which they claim is

methodological rather than theoretical, show an interest in assessing the differences in social roles in two Japanese villages. They note (p. 1226) that strictly speaking, the variables considered "were not personality variables, but the relative prevalence of social attitudes within a community."

Another study making much the same point is Parker's (1964). He utilized a TAT consisting of 5 drawings portraying people and situations from both Western and Eskimo society. However, his goal was to obtain data (p. 325) "on selected attitudes" of members of the two Eskimo villages he studied. His analysis contains a number of important theoretical observations, but these are not unrelated to his methodology. He found variation in response by the same individuals to the "same" stimulus material when these were in slightly different contexts. Noting the views of Kaplan (1961a) and others, he indicates they are correct in seeing attitudes and personality characteristics as not fully understandable outside of particular situations; they are "situationally bound." Interpretation of the same data using any of the "trait" theories of personality would lead to the erroneous conclusion that individuals exhibiting such variation in their responses held contradictory attitudes toward the same object. In short, he is making the seemingly obvious but often overlooked point that the "same" object in a different context is not the "same." In regard to a related issue, Parker stresses that an interpretation of such projective test data should not be made without a full assessment of the subjects' roles in society, as well as the general character of the institutional settings for these roles.

Problems

The novelty of projective tests has long since worn off. As a result, problems are clearer and the demands for solution are more insistent than ever. In the present context, isolating a separate section dealing with these problems is most arbitrary since they have been an integral part of our discussion of the history of research using such tests. Moreover, a detailed review of all the problems associated with the use of projective tests would require far more space than is available.[4] In view of this, a checklist of some of the more common problems a number of critics have mentioned from time to time is presented in Table 1.

[4] Again, the reader is directed to the thorough review by Lindzey (1961) of the common problems associated with the use of projective tests. A more recent and equally thorough discussion of these problems may be found in the volume edited by Rabin (1968). Many other writers have furnished items for this list, as well.

TABLE 1: Checklist of Common Problems Associated with the Use of Projective Tests

Problems related to conception and design of research and tests:
  1. TAT's especially but other tests as well are culture-bound, although they are often used in multi-cultural research without testing to see if they are equivalent in all sites.
  2. Projective tests are often designed to assess an individual's entire personality —structure and content—but the actual degree of success often goes unquestioned by the investigator.
  3. Some projective tests are not designed for general personality assessment though they are used as if they had been.
  4. Some research designs are predicated on there being a link between behavior and test response, but this is seldom checked.
  5. New projective tests are not directly comparable to their predecessors though this fact is often not explicitly recognized by test users.
  6. New projective tests and old projective tests in new situations are frequently weakened by the lack of norms although some research designs depend upon the existence of such norms.
  7. In designing projective tests, the use of the same stimulus material is uncritically assumed to yield a test which is the same for all subjects. Though ultimately unavoidable since we will usually use the instrument for more than one subject, the problem becomes crucial when the subjects are from different cultures.
  8. Research designs which rely heavily on projective tests may be weakened because the tests will not yield data of sufficient breadth or depth for making sound conclusions (though conclusions are usually made anyway).
  9. There is a tendency to abuse the potential of wide coverage when using projective tests by simply being satisfied with "merely looking for 'what can be found'" (Henry, 1961:590), rather than asking well formulated research questions and using well designed scoring systems.
  10. Because projective tests are available in prepared packages, they are often used in research without sufficient justification from the standpoint of research design.

Problems related to the administration of tests:
  1. Generally, the researcher records only the strictly verbal responses, ignoring

(for a variety of reasons) the para-linguistic aspects of the response (gesture, emotional tone of voice, facial expression, and the like).

2. Projective tests are deceptively time-consuming to administer well.

3. Responses can be affected by temporary emotional states within an individual, by idiosyncratic response sets, by culturally derived response sets, by intelligence, verbal facility, and a great variety of other relatively invisible states, conditions or situations, all of which will be (or are generally) unknown to the uncritical user.

4. The sex, social class, caste, and other socio-economic and/or subcultural characteristics of the interviewer can have an effect on the response a subject makes (ranging from refusal, to minimal response, to profuse but over-determined response), and this factor is often overlooked in administering the test.

5. Because projective tests are time-consuming to administer and because research designs are not sufficiently thought through, users of projective tests frequently fail to collect adequate ethnographic material.

6. Insufficient attention is given to the numerous problems of obtaining a sample to whom projective tests should be given.

Problems of analysis and generalization:

1. The data are heavily linguistic (usually) and thus require (but seldom or at best an unknown percent receive) careful analysis if one is to avoid making facile translations of responses which are central to the scoring system used and hence, to the variables being measured.

2. Though it may be an advantage that projective tests elicit a wide range of material, the coding schemes used are often crude, narrow, and/or ethnocentric. We may have discovered the Mother-Lode, but we are still using the most primitive of tools to mine our discovery.

3. There is a tendency for users to assume that observed differences in responses, even where sophisticated analytical systems are used, reflect personality differences without considering the import of most of the problems of test conditions, etc. for the character of the responses obtained.

4. Some coding schemes are mystical, others are unreliable, and still others lack adequate measures of validity; some fall short on all three.

5. Adequate normative data are lacking for many tests in Euro-American culture; this is an even greater problem in non-Euro-American cultures.

6. Although projective tests are time-consuming to administer, they produce data that are even more time-consuming to analyze.

7. Often for ostensibly practical limitations imposed by others, research reports frequently fail to publish an adequate sample of the responses to projective tests, thus preventing an independent assessment of the conclusions drawn.

8. Much anthropological usage of projective tests is divorced from concerns linked to psychological theory with the result that the use and interpretation of data is badly skewed and/or wrenched from the appropriate theoretical context.

9. Scoring and interpretation frequently ignores the fact that responses are often produced following instructions calling for heightened use of imagination; thus the exotic response is given special attention by the subject while the "obvious" response may be suppressed as being too unimaginative.

10. There is an all too frequent uncritical acceptance of the "blind analysis" when in fact the original developments in the analysis of such data were predicated on a thorough knowledge of the condition (psychophysical and cultural) of the respondent.

11. Some "blind" analyses are not truly blind; conversely, analyses which make no pretense at being blind do not give full attention to all available information about the culture, the sample, and/or the test conditions.

12. Analysis frequently shifts uncritically back and forth between manifest and latent aspects of the response data.

13. Many scoring systems do not permit an adequate assessment of the meaning of non-response to particular stimulus cues in the tests.

14. Length of response may be the main factor producing variation in scoring results though this is often overlooked in analysis.

15. The terminology of the scoring categories is heavily oriented to the pathological in many widely used tests.

16. With and in spite of samples of unknown representativeness, inferences and generalizations about the entire population are often made on completion of the analysis.

17. There is a tendency for an uncritical acceptance of the assumption that it is essential for the analysis to assess "deep" aspects of personality (assuming for the moment that the tests are even successful in reaching these depths).

18. Authors uncritically accept the notion that projective test material (analysis and samples of the raw data) should be presented separately from the main body of the (usually ethnographic) data.

19. There is a tendency to rely on the extensive use of anecdotal, impressionistic and non-quantified analytical methods with large amounts of projective material.

20. The uncritical assumption that heavily quantified, psychometric analytical techniques somehow produce more *valid* results is too often confused with the gains in *reliability* that such methods actually provide.

21. There is a tendency to ignore the cultural data available in the midst of the personality data in projective test responses.

22. There is a tendency to overlook gross response categories with a concomitant overemphasis on subtle (and often ill-defined) nuances.

23. There is a tendency to overlook the significance of within-group variance in research which has as a primary goal the comparison of differences between groups.

24. All too frequently, there is no attempt made to evaluate the tests' results by any of the available measures of validity.

The list is long (though not definitive) and, in some ways, overwhelming. Few of the problems, however, are the exclusive property of psychological anthropologists using projective tests. In many cases they are generic to research in the social sciences. Frequently, they are deceiving in size in that as listed, they represent the peak of an iceberg of little, interlocking problems and difficulties. Others may be seen as "points to ponder" requiring "only" that the careful investigator consider the relevance of the issue before embarking on research with projective tests. However, most of the problems appear amenable to solution, usually by incorporating *in advance* a few precautionary steps and procedures in the research design. Finally, some of the problems (perhaps most) may be circumvented by avoiding short-cuts and simply doing more, hard work.

There are some problems, however, which pose serious practical and theoretical difficulties for the projective test user. Of these, we will concentrate on a number of problems related broadly to test performance. These occur midway between the conception of research using projective tests and the analysis of data collected. That is, a major concern when conceiving research is that instruments be designed or selected so as to maximize the validity of the data obtained; the analysis, on the other hand, should be oriented toward minimizing the distortion which is inevitable when synthesis and generalization from raw data is attempted. In using projective tests, a clear understanding of the factors which influence performance on the test is essential for successfully meeting either of these basic research goals.

Evidence that there is, from culture to culture and user to user, considerable variability in the way a projective test "works" has been uncovered and received very matter-of-factly by anthropologists. Thus, for example, we have noted almost in passing the contrast between the remarkably sparse Ojibwa Rorschach records and the rich, expressive material in the Hindu records. Similarly, though the variability is even greater, we have accepted as routine the differences in response to the TAT across cultures. We may compare, for example, the sparse records obtained in some research in Thailand (Hanks, 1956) with the fantastically rich material collected in Indonesia (Geertz, 1957) where many individual records ran to more than 50 pages.

A derivative of these observations is the absolutely crucial question of distinguishing those differences in test performance which result from subjects approaching it with differing frameworks, cultural conventions, response sets, and the like, from those which reflect "genuine" differences in personality processes (demonstration of the latter presumably being the nominal research objective). This is especially important in the context of cross-cultural, comparative studies. Although this problem has been raised many times over the years, for most workers it has never been answered satisfactorily.

There seem to be two closely related but distinguishable difficulties here. The first has to do with reasons for differences in "personal permeability" in different societies, and the second with variations in the social contexts in which individuals are willing and able to be personally expressive. Conceptions of self and notions of individuality prevelant in a culture are among the relevant factors for the first problem. For example, in a culture in which there is considerable concern about self and/or where thought about differentiated individuality is stressed, Rorschach materials may be rich and revealing. Hallowell's (1954) analysis of concepts of self and kinds of self-awareness as cultural variables influencing a person's self-image and experience of self is pertinent to this problem and offers worthwhile leads for its solution. The nature of the test, norms and traditions regarding perception, the conditions of the interview situation, the nature of social relationships (especially with strangers), the means and criteria for establishing a relationship of trust, mutuality, and candor are general factors relevant to the second problem.

If we regard personality processes as social action — that is, as being in the realm of what the person is doing rather than as something he has — we are permitted a slightly different orientation to projective data. In such a context, the pattern in a projective test protocol becomes an act, or series of them, which bear explaining. Thus, Kaplan suggests (196lc) action is a function of social reality which is organized around certain normative components coupled with a general motivational orientation relative to this reality. The protocol becomes then a personality pattern which the person establishes for the moment through his action. As a consequence of this view, two kinds of information are essential if we are to understand or explain the data in the protocols: (1) the normative aspects of the situation which define the legitimate expectations that are perceived by the subject; and (2) the motivational orientation which prescribes the position or stance which is taken relative to these expectations. Each response in the projective test can and should be analyzed from both points of view. While the added research burdens are great, the gains should not only be worthwhile (since they involve nothing less than an understanding of the relationship of the actor to the phenomenal reality in which he exists) but also essential (if we are to have a valid synthesis).

As to the relative merits of the Rorschach and the TAT for this problem, it would appear the TAT has important advantages. As the test has been used by Murray and his associates (and by most other psychologists and some anthropologists), a primary concern has been to describe the hierarchy and patterning of motives as well as their relationship to perceived social environment. Since the TAT (in comparison to the Rorschach) elicits stories with a heavy emphasis on actions rather than descriptions of qualities or feelings, this instrument seems well suited to the requirements of the worker in psychological anthropology who subscribes to this view of personality. The Rorschach, on the other hand, ordinarily provides a series of highly condensed and often cryptic visual images from which motivations are at best indirectly inferable. Moreover, these images seem to pertain to the cognitive organization of emotional life of individuals rather than motivational or volitional elements, but as we have seen, users of the TAT have generally had the latter as one of their primary concerns.

A related but more pernicious issue is the problem of perception and the impact of different cultural traditions on this most basic aspect of projective testing. That this should be related to test performance is obvious although it is still not well described or understood. Given the real significance of this factor, it is surprising there is so little in the way of systematic research concerning its effect in general or the consequent implications for test construction and interpretation of data (see above, p. 280, for comments on this problem in connection with developing modified TAT's).

Hallowell (1951 and 1956) was early in expressing a serious concern for this issue in conjunction with the use of projective tests. Although different perceptual styles had been linked to variations in traditions in the visual arts, he suggested that the mere presence or absence of a pictorial art tradition did not in and of itself constitute a basis for predicting the degree of success to expect when using the Rorschach. This general comment remains a useful precaution for anyone about to design and/or use a projective test in any culture; i.e., one should not reject such tests out-of-hand in areas where such traditions are poorly developed, nor should one blithely proceed without due caution even where such traditions are highly developed.

That cultures differ in the way they perceive visual stimuli is an old, time-honored notion in anthropology, dating back at least to observations made by W. H. R. Rivers during the Torres Strait Expedition. More recently, the well-known debate between Herskovits and Campbell was put to a systematic (though not flawless, [Campbell, 1964]) test (Segall, et al., 1956) with a general vindication of the anthropological "perception of perception." Since then, a number of studies have been made, however, which raise issues affecting not only test construction, but more important-ly, the interpretation of data.

A brief article by Kilbride and Robbins (1969:293–301), while adding a number of crucial observations based on their research in Uganda, summarizes the better part of the relatively scanty literature on this problem. In their review, they note that Hudson (1960), using pictures designed specifically to test depth perception in two-dimensional, repre-sentational drawings, established that ability to perceive the "correct" relationship between objects drawn and organized on the basis of Western traditions for indicating depth, was, for his sample, a function of intelli-gence. A subsequent study (Hudson, 1967) broadened these original findings, showing ability to perceive depth in such pictures was also linked to particular cognitive styles and to degree of "cultural isolation." Other studies (e.g., Dawson, 1967a–b; Mundy-Castle, 1966; Heron, 1968; and Iwawaki, 1969) elaborate on these results even further, showing for example that "field dependence" in the responses of subjects is related to variation in childhood experience and education.

On the basis of their Uganda data, Kilbride and Robbins observe that the more acculturated respondents made fewer perceptual errors. They too used the 4 Hudson pictures in their research. Though well designed, it must be remembered these pictures are intended to be a test of depth perception in two-dimensional representational art and not a projective test. As such, they are complex and will pose different (if not more numerous) problems of perception than many if not most of the TAT's in use in non-Western cultures. Nevertheless, it is clear that individuals in different cultures perceive the "same" stimuli differently. Consequently, this must be given full consideration during both the design and analysis stages of research using projective tests of the visual type. This is absolutely essential if a research design calls for comparison of groups which differ dramatically on dimensions which are likely to have an effect on perception and hence test performance (e.g., such factors as intelligence, education, childhood experience, or degree of acculturation).

Ultimately, raising this problem compels us to reconsider several important studies by anthropologists in which just such comparisons are made. Acculturation is a phenomenon which has frequently been investigated through the use of projective tests. Unfortunately, a vital aspect of the research has been the assessment of personality differences between groups differing in degree of Westernization and/or acculturation, but the instruments used to measure the differences have not been shown to be equally sensitive for groups that differ in these ways. We have already cited the study by Kilbride and Robbins in this regard; studies by Hallowell (1942) and the Spindlers (1955) have also shown that expressiveness is associated with acculturation. In a different context, Lerner (1958) indicates that empathy, or the ability to identify with the roles of others, is one of the most important characteristics differentiating modern from traditional individuals. It becomes, then, an ironic fact that as people are more influenced by Western culture, the tests will "work better," but then of course, the possibility of making an acceptable assessment of whether or not personality changes accompany (or precede) culture change becomes ever more remote.

In cross-cultural research with projective tests, we are faced with what seems to be the virtually impossible task of separating out those responses which reflect differences in personality from those reflecting differences in culture. Furthermore, raising this issue brings us face to face again with the dilemma of distinguishing conceptually between "personality" and "culture" — a problem anthropologists have struggled with for years (e.g., compare Spiro's views in 1951 and 1961). It would appear that this issue remains an open one. Though often overlooked, this question must still be dealt with even when we are sampling individuals from the "same culture."

Short of eliminating such research altogether, we are called upon to establish guidelines for reducing to a minimum the possibility that significant portions of projective test data are produced because of "extraneous" factors linked to the test situation and/or subjects rather than the intended "intrinsic" factors of individual personality. Though perhaps unjustified, psychologists seldom face the criticism that the difference in performance by *individuals* is simply a reflection of cultural rather than personality factors. Clearly, since their subjects are never identical, they can never be totally immune from this problem. They circumvent the problem by making the assumption that individuals in their samples are "similar enough," thus allowing the inference that different responses reflect genuine personality differences. For anthropologists, especially those involved in cross-cultural research (including studies of "sub-cultures" of the acculturation type noted earlier), the question then is, "How different can individuals be and still meet the condition of being 'similar enough'?" Confidence in answering this question is a prerequisite for making statements about cross-cultural personality differences which meet reasonable standards of validity. On this basis, Lindzey (1961:238–9) for example, raises doubts about the widely acclaimed study of acculturation and personality change conducted by the Spindlers (1955 and elsewhere). From the Spindler's point of view, however, the variations in response were not seen as simply an artifact of the test's potential bias toward more successful use among westernized subjects. Because of the nature of the problem, it is probably true that in the final analysis the issue can never be resolved to the satisfaction of all.

Prospects

Given that these and related problems are likely to be ever-present in research using projective tests, one may wonder whether any options remain open to those interested in carrying on scientific research using them. Somewhat paradoxically, the nature of the problems as well as the capabilities of anthropological fieldworkers point more to potential improvement than probable impass. As indicated above, some of the solutions are as simple as hard work; others will require some reorientation in research objectives. Here we will briefly consider ways of improving research designs, noting among other things, the advantages of careful hypothesis testing, the necessity of avoiding pseudo cross-cultural designs, and of incorporating validity checks. Further, we will note the usefulness of increasing our concern with the nature of the relationship between personality and social systems. In doing this, we will review a few of the attempts already made to solve some of the problems noted above. Although not all have been successful, we can learn from their efforts.

In many instances, new research strategies have utilized what are probably pseudo-solutions in that they essentially beg the questions raised. For example, we may consider the study by Williams and Williams (1965) which purports to be a cross-cultural study of the Rorschach test situation — a problem frequently noted as one of the most difficult and yet important to solve if we are to sort the cultural from personality factors which determine response. Their discussion also provides insight into the difficulties associated with several of the other above mentioned problems. In addition to biographical records and a full ethnography, their data consist of the Rorschach records from 50 Lebanese Maronite children as well as their responses to a number of other psychological tests.

In regard to the basic problem of distinguishing between the personality and cultural factors which determine response, they suggest that (1965:339) "the impossibility of making this separation is neither cause for despair nor a prerequisite for Rorschach interpretation." They provocatively suggest we need not despair since there is no basis for rejecting out of hand an instrument which supposedly has inherent problems which have not been solved when *not* using the instrument. That is, sifting out culture from personality at the conceptual level is not a problem limited to users of projective tests. Also, they reject strongly psychometric analytic procedures, the use of which they see as implying the unwarranted assumption that variables amenable to quantified analysis are "somehow less affected by the impact of cultural differences on the record obtained." They propose to turn tables on the usual clinical assumption that variation in test perception produces an unknown error. Instead, they intend to use such data as may be available about the subjects' perception of the test as a basis for gaining insight into both personality and culture. Among other things, they note that the test situation was stressful, and their evidence for this is impressive and convincing.

Unfortunately, their conclusions (p. 351), which are intended to "illustrate how very much the personality delineation relies on the qualitative features of the record and the subject's definition of the test situation," do not reach these laudable objectives. Although they recognize (p. 353) other data do not present so bleak a picture of the culture as do the Rorschach data, they do not sufficiently contextualize their interpetations. The interpretive statement most clearly reflecting their recognition of the impact of their subjects' perceptions of the test situation tells us that (p. 353) "The individual villager appears to the poorest advantage when he confronts the unfamiliar and when he does so alone." It is difficult to see how this observation warrants their general observation and conclusion that (p. 353) "a score-bound analysis by itself could have resulted in little more than a few shallow and barren generalizations." Nor, on this basis, does it appear founded that, by combining this with "an assessment of the qualitative features of the protocols and of the subjects' reactions to the testing situation, the yield was considerably richer" (p. 353).

Though their efforts are far from unique, it must be remembered that much of the anthropological literature does not even attempt to deal with the problems which are the focus of the Williams' research. One would hope not, but perhaps this fact is mute testimony to the difficulty of these problems.

From almost the very outset, the broad "net casting" approach has been an integral part of anthropological field research. This is no less true for research in psychological anthropology. In part, such an approach has been justified by noting the complexity of the issues and concepts involved, as well as the huge areas of the world for which relevant data were not available. For a number of good and sufficient reasons, it is obvious that the broad approach can and should not be eliminated from the process of scientific inquiry. However, in the face of the numerous, important problems the use of projective tests seems almost automatically to bring forth, we are obligated to design research which will minimize these problems while maximizing scientific gains. Among other things, such research should be well grounded in appropriate theoretical frameworks and should ultimately focus on the testing of carefully developed hypotheses. This may entail giving higher priority than has heretofore been the case to research on relatively narrowly defined issues. However, the long-range goal still should be the accumulation of numerous well conceived and tightly controlled studies with which to make sound generalizations about the larger issues. Such a strategy is not particularly innovative in the over-all context of the social sciences, though it may represent some newer trends in anthropology.

Cross-cultural research has been the hallmark of many of the high quality contributions by psychological anthropologists. Indeed, much of the early popularity of projective tests was due to the potential seen in these tests for making valid comparative statements about the personality of individuals from different cultures. However, as we have seen, many of the problems now facing us are the result of using projective tests cross-culturally. There is nothing so discouraging, for example, as the colleague using the Rorschach who rushes to compare the per cent M responses given by individuals in his sample with those from another sample distinctive in basic socio-cultural characteristics *if* by so doing it is hoped something more than cultural differences may be assessed. As we have noted, however, much sophisticated research depends upon comparisons of this sort. Other than abandoning these techniques altogether, what are we to do?

In the first place, the fact that projective responses made by individuals from different cultures will vary so greatly points to a need for increased concern with the development of research strategies which reduce such variability while introducing minimal effect on validity. For example, one can in this context see the justification for greater flexibility in the instructions used to explain the purpose and procedures of the test. One can also see the necessity of devoting considerable thought and effort to an assessment of the factors which are likely to have an effect on the formation of response sets (e.g., such factors might include the method of arranging for the interviews, whether payment is to be made for cooperation, whether the interview is to be given privately, the impact of the sex of the interviewer, the time of year, the time of day, etc.).

Investigator and critic alike must remember that short of undertaking dozens of pre-tests under different conditions as a means of establishing local norms for each possible condition, one can probably never be absolutely certain that the most significant factors have been successfully controlled by the design of the research or the choice of the instrument. Moreover even when efforts have been made to optimize data collecting procedures, the investigator would be wise to avoid making hasty conclusions about the actual character of the situation and its impact on the data obtained. For example, Carstairs (1956) collected Rorschach data from two Indian groups (Hindus and Bhils). One group gave outward signs that the test was making them anxious while the other group did not exhibit these tendencies. The projective materials were, however, far richer from the group which seemed more anxious. The investigator is also advised against assuming that failure to make a response indicates the general inability to make it. Characteristics of the test or the administrative conditions may be sufficient to explain the absence of these responses. On the other hand, one should remember the assumption is, in regard to these and other problems thought to introduce bias, that the bias is systematic. Where such an assumption seems unwarranted and/or undemonstrable (where appropriate efforts have been made to do so), the analysis can continue since *random errors* as a result of such problems only *reduce* the possibility predicted, non-random relationships will be observed.

Another suggestion which can help us face these problems is to intensify our efforts in the directions suggested several years ago by Spiro (1961)

and since then by several others (e.g., see Mischel, 1968). Seeing no
grounds for becoming the handmaidens of psychologists and psychological
research (i.e., simply doing their work in exotic places), Spiro called for
increased concern for research which seeks to assess the nature of the
relationship between social systems and personality. As he noted, such a
reorientation is really not new since the pioneers of the field often
exemplified these concerns.[5] However, since this suggestion was made, few
have taken up the challenge (see Aronoff, 1967, for a provocative analysis
in this vein). Further consideration of this issue, in addition to dealing with
a theoretical matter of utmost general importance, may lead to a
resolution of such problems as distinguishing between cultural and personality factors which affect response to projective tests. As we have seen,
many of these problems have been expressed in essentially these terms—
i.e., how does the social structure of a particular group affect the general
parameters of personality, and hence the nature of responses to projective
tests?

Other problems can be avoided if extreme caution is the guiding rule
for those who would undertake truly cross-cultural research using projective tests. For clarity, let it be noted that by "cross-cultural" is not meant,
as so many implicitly seem to assume, simply exotic, non-western research
sites. Research concerned with personality and related issues in psychological anthropology often utilized concepts developed in Euro-American
cultures, and as a result, such research is to a degree "cross-cultural." That
is, we are asking whether these concepts can be used to understand the
behavior of non Euro-American subjects. However, the even more dramatic comparisons inherent in truly cross-cultural research (e.g., using a
concept or instrument developed in Euro-American culture as a means of
comparatively understanding the behavior of individuals from two or
more non Euro-American cultures) raise other, more difficult problems
which, unless solved, should be circumvented by doing research within a
single culture.

A closely related issue, and one of the most common and telling
criticisms addressed to those using projective tests in non-western settings,
has to do with whether or not the data, since they are usually collected

[5]However, numerous contributions have been made by colleagues in other disciplines. In
addition to pioneering efforts by Sorokin (1947) and Gerth and Mills (1953), among many
others, there are the contributions of the Parsons "school" on this issue, including many of
the contributors to the volume edited by Smelser and Smelser (1963), as well as the collection
of papers on the subject by Parsons, himself (1964). Understandably, the use of projective
tests in this research has been minimal.

and presented in terms of Western concepts and scoring categories, are valid. That is, is it correct to assume an "M response is an M response is an M response," when they have been made by individuals from different cultures? Much research is predicated on an affirmative answer to this question — an answer too often only weakly supportable given the designs employed. Unquestionably, there is a need for more, carefully designed research which incorporates adequate tests of validity. The contributors to a symposium on aspects of this problem (see Farberow; Fiske; Henry and Farley; Little; Meehl; and Shneidman; 1959), though not overly optimistic, do offer a few hopeful suggestions to the researcher.

Of the measures of validity, three are of special interest for users of projective tests; these are predictive, concurrent and construct validity (among others, see Lindzey, 1961:314–319, for a more detailed discussion of these). Ideally, all of these tests of validity need to be made when conducting research using any concept; this is no less true for research involving projective tests. Unfortunately, such tests for validity are lacking or unconvincing in much of the anthropological literature. We need, then, research which permits an assessment of whether or not individuals rated in various ways will at some future date actually exhibit behavior thought to be associated with individuals so rated (i.e., a test of predictive validity). We also need research which presents data indicating people rated in terms of various concepts on the basis of behavior will also indicate in their responses to projective tests a tendency to behave in this way (i.e., concurrent validity). Both steps would anticipate the oft voiced criticism that projective test data are insufficiently compared and/or linked to the ethnographic record. Finally, we need research designed to test whether a new test *or* an old test in a new setting produces relationships between variables similar to those observed in earlier research using such tests (i.e., construct validity).

In essence then, our research must grow out of more sophisticated research designs, give greater consideration to an assessment of the relationship between personality and social systems, focus more often on a single culture, and give more systematic attention to the problems of validity. Though such suggestions are singularly uninnovative, they will not, if past experience is any guide, be easily adopted. However, unless we begin to work at meeting these minimal demands, the use of projective tests in psychological anthropology will continue to be plagued, if not by complete failure, then by considerable frustration.

BIBLIOGRAPHY

ABEL, THEODORA M. AND F. L. K. HSU. 1949. Some aspects of personality of Chinese as revealed by the Rorschach test. Journal of Projective Techniques 13:285–301.

ADCOCK, C. J. AND J. E. RITCHIE. 1958. Intercultural use of the Rorschach. American Anthropologist 60:881–92.

ALEXANDER, T. AND R. ANDERSON. 1957. Children in a society under stress. Behavioral Science, 2:46–55.

ARONOFF, JOEL. 1967. Psychological needs and cultural systems: A case study. Princeton, D. Van Nostrand, Co.

ATKINSON, JOHN W. 1958. Motives in fantasy, action and society. Princeton, D. Van Nostrand, Co.

BADRI, M. B. AND W. DENNIS. 1964. Human figure drawings in relation to modernization in the Sudan. Journal of Psychology, 58:421–55.

BARNOUW, VICTOR. 1963. Culture and personality. Homewood, Illinois, Dorsey Press.

BELLAK, LEOPOLD. 1954. The Thematic Apperception Test and the Children's Apperception Test in clinical use. New York, Grune and Stratton.

BIESHEUVEL, S. 1958. Methodology in the study of attitudes of Africans. Journal of Social Psychology, 47:169–184.

BILLIG, O., J. GILLIN, AND W. DAVIDSON. 1947–8. Aspects of personality and culture in a Guatemalan community. Journal of Personality 16:153–187; 326–368.

BLUM, G. S. 1950. The Blacky pictures: Manual of instructions. New York, Psychological Corp.

BRICKLIN, BARRY AND CARTER ZELEZNIK. 1963. A psychological investigation of selected Ethiopian adolescents by means of the Rorschach and other projective tests. Human Organization, 22:291–303.

CAMPBELL, DONALD T. 1964. Distinguishing differences of perception from failures of communication in cross-cultural studies. In F. S. C. Northrop and H. H. Livingston, (eds.), Cross-cultural understanding: Epistemology in anthropology. New York, Harper and Row.

CARSTAIRS, G. M. 1957. The twice-born: A study of a community of high-caste Hindus. London, Hogarth.

CAUDILL, WILLIAM. 1949. Psychological characteristics of acculturated Wisconsin Ojibwa children. American Anthropologist 51:409–427.

———. 1962. Patterns of emotion in modern Japan. In Robert J. Smith and Richard K. Beardsley (eds.), Japanese culture: Its development and characteristics. VFPA #34 (pp. 115–131) Chicago, Aldine Publishing Company.

CHOWDHURY, U. 1960. An Indian modification of the Thematic Apperception Test. Journal of Social Psychology, 51:245–263.

CLIFTON, JAMES A. 1959. On the intercultural use of the Rorschach. American Anthropologist 61:1087–1090.

CLIFTON, JAMES A. AND DAVID LEVINE. 1961. Klamath personalities: Ten Rorschach case studies. Eugene, Department of Anthropology, University of Oregon.

COHEN, RONALD. 1971. Dominance and Defiance: A study of marital instability in an Islamic African society. (Anthropology Study #6. American Anthropology Association.)

COLLIER, JOHN, JR. 1957. Photography in anthropology: A report on two experiments. American Anthropologist 59:843–859.

––––––. 1967. Visual Anthropology: Photography as a research method. New York, Holt, Rinehart and Winston.

DAWSON, J. L. M. 1963. Psychological effects of social change in a West African community. Unpublished doctoral thesis, Oxford University.

––––––. 1967a. Cultural and physiological influences upon spatial-perceptual processes in West Africa. Pt. I. International Journal of Psychology, 2:171–185.

––––––. 1967b. Cultural and physiological influences upon spatial-perceptual processes in West Africa. Pt. II. International Journal of Psychology, 2:171–185.

DENNIS, WAYNE. 1966. Group values through children's drawings. New York, John Wiley & Sons, Inc.

DEREGOWSKI, J. B. 1969. Preference for chain-type drawings in Zambian domestic servants and primary school children. Psychologia Africana, 12:172–80.

DERIDDER, J. C. 1961. The personality of the urban African in South Africa: A Thematic Apperception Test study. New York, Humanities Press.

DEROGATIS, L. R., D. R. GORHAM, AND E. C. MOSELEY. 1968. Structural vs. interpretive ambiguity: A cross-cultural study with the Hotzman Inkblots. Journal of Projective Techniques and Personality Assessment 32:66–73.

DEVOS, GEORGE AND HIROSHI WAGATSUMA. 1961. Value attitudes toward role behavior of women in two Japanese villages. American Anthropologist 63:1204–1230.

DOOB, LEONARD W. 1968. Facilitating rapid change in Africa. In Arnold Rivkin, (ed.), Nations by design: Institution-building in Africa. Garden City, New York, Doubleday & Company, Inc., Anchor Books.

DUBOIS, CORA. 1944. The people of Alor: A socio-psychological study of an East Indian island. Minneapolis, University of Minnesota Press.

FARBEROW, N. L. 1959. Symposium on current aspects of the problem of validity: Validity and methodology in projective tests. Journal of Projective Techniques 23:282–86.

FISKE, D. W. 1959. Symposium on current aspects of the problem of validity: Variability of responses and the stability of scores and interpretations of projective protocols. Journal Projective Techniques 23:263–67.

FORREST, D. W. AND S. G. LEE. 1962. Mechanisms of defense and readiness in perception and recall. Psychological Monographs, 76:1–28.

FRANK, L. K. 1939. Projective methods for the study of personality. Journal of Psychology, 8:389–413.

GEERTZ, H. 1957. Modified TAT's of thirty-three Japanese men and women. *In* B. Kaplan, (ed.), Primary records in culture and personality. Madison, University of Wisconsin Press, vol. 2.

GERTH, HANS AND C. WRIGHT MILLS. 1953. Character and social structure: The psychology of social institutions. New York, Harcourt, Brace & World.

GLADWIN, T. AND S. B. SARASON. 1953. Truk: Man in paradise. New York, Wenner-Gren Foundation.

GOLDSCHMIDT, WALTER AND ROBERT EDGERTON. 1961. A picture technique for the study of values. American Anthropologist 63:26–45.

GOLDSTEIN, FRED J. 1961. Custom-made or store-bought projective techniques: What do they represent? Journal of Projective Techniques, 25:11–20.

HALLOWELL, A. I. 1942. Acculturation processes and personality changes indicated by the Rorschach technique. Rorschach Research Exchange, 6:42–50.

———. 1951a. The use of projective techniques in the study of the sociopsychological aspects of acculturation. Journal of Projective Techniques, 15:27–44.

———. 1951b. Cultural factors in the structuralization of perception. *In* J. H. Rohrer and M. Sherif (eds.), Social psychology at the crossroads. New York, Harper.

———. 1954. The self and its behavioral environment. Explorations, 1:108–65.

———. 1955. Culture and experience. Philadelphia, Universityof Pennsylvania Press.

———. 1956. The Rorschach technique in personality and culture studies. *In* B. Klopfer (ed.), Developments in the Rorschach technique, vol. 2. New York, World Publishing Co., pp. 485–544.

HANKS, L. 1956. Modified TAT's of forty-seven Thai children and adults. *In* B. Kaplan (ed.), Primary records in culture and personality. Madison, University of Wisconsin Press, vol. 1.

HENRY, J., ET AL. 1955. Symposium: Projective testing in ethnography. American Anthropologist 57:245–270.

HENRY, W. E. 1947. The Thematic Apperception Technique in the study of culture-personality relations. Genetic Psychology Monographs, 35:3–135.

Henry, W. E. and J. Farley. 1959. Symposium on current aspects of the problems of validity: A study in validation of the Thematic Apperception Test. Journal of Projective Techniques, 23:273–77.

Heron, Alastair. 1968. Studies of perception and reasoning in Zambian Children. International Journal of Psychology, 3:23–29.

Holtzman, Wayne H. 1958. Holtzman Inkblot Technique. New York, Psychological Corp.

———. 1965. Cross-cultural research on personality development. Human Development, 8:65–86.

———. 1968. Cross-cultural studies in psychology. International Journal of Psychology 3:83–91.

Holtzman, Wayne H., J. S. Thorpe, J. D. Swartz, and E. W. Herron. 1961. Inkblot perception and personality: Holtzman Inkblot Technique. Austin, Texas, University of Texas Press.

Hsu, F. L. K. 1963. Clan, caste and club. Princeton, D. Van Nostrand, Company, Inc.

Hsu, F. L. K., Blanche Watrous and Edith Lord. 1961. Culture pattern and adolescent behavior. International Journal of Social Psychiatry, 7:33–53.

Hudson, W. 1960. Pictorial depth perception in sub-cultural groups in Africa. Journal of Social Psychology, 52:183–208.

———. 1967. The study of the problem of pictorial perception among acculturated groups. International Journal of Psychology, 2:89–107.

Hunkum, V. 1950. Validation of the Goodenough draw-a-man test for African children. Journal of Social Research, 1:52–63.

Husioka, Yosinaru. 1962. Rorschach test in farming villages in North Thailand. (pp. 139–272) In Tatuo Kira and Tadao Umesao (eds.), Nature and Life in Southeast Asia, Vol. II. Kyoto, Japan: Fauna and Flora Research Society.

Inkeles, Alex. 1959. Personality and social structure. In R. K. Merton, L. Broom and L. S. Cottrell, (eds.), Sociology today. New York, Basic Books.

———. 1963. Sociology and psychology. In S. Koch, (ed.), Psychology: Study of a Science, VI. New York, McGraw-Hill.

Inkeles, Alex and D. J. Levinson. 1954. National character: The study of modal personality and sociocultural systems. In G. Lindzey, (ed.), Handbook of social psychology, vol. II, Cambridge, Addison-Wesley.

Iwawaki, Saburo. 1969. Extremity of response among Japanese and American children. Journal of Social Psychiatry, 79:257–9.

Jahoda, Gustav. 1961. Whiteman: A study of attitudes of Africans to Europeans in Ghana before independence. London, Oxford University Press.

JOSEPH, ALICE AND VERONICA F. MURRAY. 1951. Chamorros and Carolinians of Sapian: Personality studies. Cambridge, Harvard University Press.

KAPLAN, BERT. 1954. A study of Rorschach responses in four cultures. Papers of the Peabody Museum of American Archaeology and Ethnology, Harvard University, 42, #2.

————. 1957. Personality and social structure. *In* J. B. Gittler (ed.), Review of Sociology: Analysis of a decade. New York, Wiley and Sons.

————. 1961a. Personality study and culture. *In* Bert Kaplan, (ed.), Studying personality cross-culturally. Evanston, Row, Peterson and Company.

————. 1961b. Editor's epilogue: A final word. *In* Bert Kaplan, (ed.), Studying personality cross-culturally. Evanston, Row, Peterson and Company.

————. 1961c. Cross-cultural use of projective techniques. *In* Psychological anthropology: Approaches to culture and personality, F. L. K. Hsu, (ed.), Homewood, Illinois, Dorsey Press, 1st edition.

KAPLAN, BERT AND RICHARD LAWLESS. 1965. Culture and visual imagery: A comparison of Rorschach responses in eleven societies. (pp. 295–311) *In* M. E. Spiro (ed.), Context and meaning in cultural anthropology. New York, The Free Press.

KILBRIDE, PHILIP L. AND MICHAEL C. ROBBINS. 1969. Pictorial depth perception and acculturation among the Baganda. American Anthropologist 71:293–301.

KORCHIN, S. J., H. E. MITCHELL, AND J. A. MELTZOFF. 1950. A critical evaluation of the Thompson Thematic Apperception Test. Journal of Projective Techniques 14:445–52.

LANDY, DAVID. 1959. Tropical childhood: Cultural transmission and learning in a rural Puerto Rican village. Chapel Hill, University of North Carolina Press.

LEACOCK, ELEANOR. 1963. Review of: Menomini women and culture change by Louise S. Spindler, AAA Memoir #91, 1962. American Anthropologist 65:940–942.

LEE, S. G. 1953. Manual of a Thematic Apperception Test for African subjects. Pietermaritzburg, University of Natal Press.

LEININGER, MADELEINE. 1966. Convergence and divergence of human behavior: An ethnopsychological comparative study of two Gadsup villages in the Eastern Highlands of New Guinea. Unpublished doctoral dissertation, University of Washington.

LERNER, DANIEL. 1958. The passing of traditional society: Modernizing the Middle East. New York, The Free Press.

LESSA, W. A. AND M. SPIEGELMAN. 1954. Ulithian personality as seen through ethnological materials and thematic test analysis. University of California Publications in Culture and Society, 2:243–301.

LESSER, G. S. 1961. Custom-making projective tests for research. Journal of

Projective Techniques, 25:21-31.

LeVine, Robert A. 1966. Dreams and deeds: Achievement motivation in Nigeria. Chicago, University of Chicago Press.

Lindzey, Gardner. 1961. Projective techniques and cross-cultural research. New York, Appleton-Century-Crofts, Inc.

Little, K. B. 1959. Symposium on current aspects of the problem of validity: Problems in the validation of projective techniques. Journal of Projective Techniques, 23:287-90.

McClelland, David C. 1961. The achieving society. Princeton, D. Van Nostrand Co., Inc.

Meehl, P. E. 1959. Symposium on current aspects of the problem of validity: Structured and projective tests: Some common problems in validation. Journal of Projective Techniques, 23:268-72.

Mensh, I. and Henry, J. 1953. Direct observation and psychological tests in anthropological field work. American Anthropologist 55:461-80.

Milikian, Levon H. and A. Zaher Wahab. 1969. First-drawn pictures: A cross-cultural investigation. Journal of Projective Techniques & Personality Assessment 33:539-41.

Miner, H. M. and G. DeVos. 1960. Oasis and casbah: Algerian culture and personality in change. University of Michigan, Museum of Anthropology Papers, No. 15.

Minuchin, Salvador, Braulio Montalvo, Bernard G. Guerney, Jr., Bernice L. Rosman, and Florence Schumer. 1967. Families of the slums: An exploration of their structure and treatment. New York, Basic Books, Inc.

Mischel, Walter. 1968. Personality and assessment. New York, John Wiley & Sons.

Mundy-Castle, A. C. 1966. Pictorial depth perception in Ghanian children. International Journal of Psychology, 1:289-301.

Nylen, Donald, Robert Mitchell, and Thomas Wickers. 1961. Five training institutes in staff development and human relations in West Africa. New York, mimeographed, Ford Foundation.

Ostheimer, John M. 1969. Measuring achievement motivation among the Chagga of Tanzania. Journal of Social Psychology, 78:17-30.

Parker, Seymour. 1964. Ethnic identity and acculturation in two Eskimo villages. American Anthropologist 66:325-340.

Parsons, Talcott. 1964. Social structure and personality. New York, The Free Press.

Parsons, T. and E. A. Shils. 1951. Toward a general theory of action. Cambridge, Harvard University Press.

PHILLIPS, HERBERT P. 1965. Thai peasant personality. Berkeley, University of California Press.

RABIN, A. I. 1961. Devising projective methods for personality research. Journal of Projective Techniques, 25:6–10.

———. 1968. Projective techniques in personality assessment. New York, Springer.

RAINWATER, LEE, RICHARD P. COLEMAN, AND GERALD HANDEL. 1959. Workingman's wife: Her personality, world and life style. New York, Oceana Publishers, Inc.

RITCHIE, JANE. 1957. Childhood in Rakau: The first five years of life. Victoria University Publications in Psychology #10. Wellington, New Zealand, Victoria University College.

———. 1964. Maori families. Victoria University of Wellington Publications in Psychology #18. New Zealand, Department of Psychology, Victoria University.

RIESMAN, DAVID, REUEL DENNY AND NATHAN GLAZER. 1950. The lonely crowd: A study of the changing American character. New Haven, Yale University Press.

RIESMAN, DAVID AND NATHAN GLAZER. 1952. Faces in the crowd: Individual studies in character and politics. New Haven, Yale University Press.

RIESS, B. F., E. K. SCHWARTZ, AND ALICE COTTINGHAM. 1950. An experimental critique of assumptions underlying the Negro version of the TAT. Journal of Abnormal Social Psychology. 45:700–709.

ROGERS, EVERETT M. 1969. Modernization of peasants: The impact of communication. New York, Holt, Rinehart & Winston.

SCHACHTEL, E. G. 1945. Subjective definitions of the Rorschach test situation and their effect on test performance. Psychiatry, 8:419–448.

SCHWARTZ, E. K., B. F. RIESS, AND ALICE COTTINGHAM. 1951. Further critical evaluation of the Negro version of the TAT. Journal of Projective Techniques 15:394–400.

SEASHORE, CHARLES. 1965. An evaluation of staff development and human relations workshop conducted by the Ford Foundation in West Africa 1961–1963. Washington, mimeographed, National Training Laboratories.

SEGALL, MARSHALL H., DONALD T. CAMPBELL, AND MELVILL J. HERSKOVITS. 1966. The influence of culture on visual perception. Indianapolis and New York, The Bobbs-Merrill Company.

SHERWOOD, E. T. 1957. On the designing of TAT pictures, with special reference to a set for an African people assimilating Western culture. Journal of Social Psychology, 45:161–190.

SHNEIDMAN, E. S. 1959. Symposium on current aspects of the problem of validity: Suggestions for the delineation of validation studies. Journal of Projective

Techniques 23:259–62.

SMELSER, NEIL J. AND WILLIAM T. SMELSER (EDS.). 1963. Personality and social systems. New York, John Wiley & Sons.

SMITH, M. B. 1954. Anthropology and psychology. *In* J. Gillin, (ed.), For a science of social man. New York, MacMillan.

SOROKIN, PITIRIM A. 1947. Society, culture and personality. New York, Harper.

SPAIN, DAVID H. 1969. Achievement motivation and modernization in Bornu. Unpublished PhD dissertation, Northwestern University.

SPINDLER, G. D. 1955. Sociocultural and psychological processes in Menomini acculturation. University of California Publications in cultural sociology, 5.

SPINDLER, L. S. 1962. Menomini women and culture change. AAA Memoir #91. Menasha: American Anthropology Association

SPINDLER, GEORGE AND LOUISE SPINDLER. 1965. Researching the perception of cultural alternatives: The instrumental activities inventory. *In* M. E. Spiro, (ed.), Context and meaning in cultural anthropology. New York, The Free Press.

SPIRO, M. E. 1951. Culture and personality: The natural history of a false dichotomy. Psychiatry, 15:19–46.

——. 1961. An overview and suggested reorientation. *In* Psychological Anthropology: Approaches to culture and personality, (1st edition), F. L. K. Hsu, (ed.), Homewood, Illinois, Dorsey Press.

STANTON, H., K. W. BACK AND E. LITWAK. 1956. Role-playing in survey research. American Journal of Sociology, 62:172–176.

STERN, W. 1938. Cloud pictures: A new method for testing imagination. *In* Character and Personality, 6:132–146.

STRAUS, M. A. AND J. H. STRAUS. 1956–7. Personal insecurity and Sinhalese social structure: Rorschach evidence for primary school children. Eastern Anthropologist, v.10, #2.

THOMPSON, C. E. 1949a. The Thompson modification of the Thematic Apperception Test. Journal of Projective Techniques 13:469–78.

——. 1949b. Thompson modification of the Thematic Apperception Test. Cambridge, Harvard University Press.

VOGT, E. Z. 1951. Navaho veterans: A study of changing values. Peabody Museum of Harvard University Papers, Vol. 41.

WALLACE, A. F. C. 1952. The modal personality structure of the Tuscarora Indians as revealed by the Rorschach Test. Bulletin, B. A. E., 150.

——. 1961a. Culture and personality; New York, Random House.

——. 1961b. The psychic unity of human groups. *In* Studying personality cross-culturally, Bert Kaplan, (ed.), Evanston, Illinois, Row, Peterson & Company.

WATROUS, BLANCHE AND F. L. K. HSU. 1963. A Thematic Apperception Test study of Chinese, Hindu, and American college students. *Annex in* Clan, caste, and club by F. L. K. Hsu. Princeton, New Jersey, D. Van Nostrand Company, Inc.

WESLEY, FRANK AND CHADWICK KERR. 1966. Problems in establishing norms for cross-cultural comparisons. International Journal of Psychology, 1:257–262.

WILLIAMS, HERBERT H. AND JUDITH R. WILLIAMS. 1965. The definition of the Rorschach test situation: A cross-cultural illustration. (pp. 338–354) *In* Context and meaning in cultural anthropology, M. E. Spiro, (ed.), New York, The Free Press.

WOOD, WILLIAM W. 1965. Culture and personality aspects of the pentecostal holiness religion. The Hague, Paris, Mouton & Co., Publishers.

CHAPTER EIGHT

An Experiment with Tat*

Blanche Watrous *and* Francis L. K. Hsu

This Thematic Apperception Test study of Chinese, Hindu, and American college students is an exploratory move taken in the hope of finding a scientifically feasible way of utilizing some form of projective test on a considerable scale cross-culturally, as an aid to certain forms of anthropological field work.

I. Data and Approach

The roughly 600 Thematic Apperception Test stories on which this study is based were collected in the autumn and winter of 1961 from about 300 college students[1] in the social sciences[2] by Hsu. They were first subjected to blind analysis[3] and interpretation by Watrous. Her analysis and interpretation form Sections II and III of this article. These are

---

*This was previously published as "Annex" in Francis L. K. Hsu, CLAN, CASTE AND CLUB (Princeton, N.J.: Van Nostrand, 1963), under the title "A Thematic Apperception Test Study of Chinese, Hindu and American College Students."

[1] The following sets of responses were excluded from consideration: two from the Indo-American Society because the subjects were Chinese; two from the Lady Irwin College because the subjects were Ceylonese; and one from Northwestern University because the subject was South African.

[2] Except for those in the Indo-American Society. The Indo-American Society is organized

followed by Hsu's comments and interpretation in the light of Watrous's conclusions, which form Section IV. Section V contains joint remarks in conclusion by both authors. Hsu obtained the Taiwan, Hong Kong, and Hindu fantasies in the course of a field trip to Taiwan, Hong Kong, and India in the winter of 1961. The American students were enrolled in one of his anthropology courses at Northwestern University in the fall of 1961. A few basic points pertaining to the subjects appear in Table A-1.

TABLE A-1   Distribution of the Subjects

Location	No.	Sex M	F	Age Frequency	Group	Education
U.S.A.:	38	14	24	19-24	Northwestern University	Social sciences
China:						
Hong Kong	50	18	32	19-22	Hong Kong University	Social sciences
Taiwan	40	20	20	19-22	Taiwan University	Social sciences
India:						
Calcutta	58	58	0	17-20[a]	Vidyasagar College	Social sciences
Calcutta	52	0	52	18-19	Asutosh College	Social sciences
New Delhi	39	0	39	16-18	Lady Irwin College	Education
Calcutta	26	23	3	15-17	Indo-American Society	Various subjects

a. A few students in the Far Eastern universities omitted their ages.

The average age of the Northwestern students is a few years older than the Hindu students, while the Chinese students fall between the two estimated means. The Indo-American Society students are the youngest in chronological age, the majority being 15 and 16. In certain colleges, from

under the sponsorship and financial support of the USIS to which all interested college or senior high school students are welcome.
[3] "Blind" analysis in the present instance means that Watrous did not see a copy of Hsu's manuscript but does not mean that the interpreter of the test results knows nothing about the three ways of life seen by the collector of the tests. When Oberholzer analyzed the 37 Rorschach test protocols collected by Cora Du Bois, he knew nothing about the Alorese way of life because no writing on it existed before the publication of Du Bois' *The People of Alor* (Minnesota University Press, 1944). Watrous, on the other hand, besides being an American, had certainly read a number of publications on India, China and the United States before she was confronted with these TAT responses. The seven groups of responses were given to Watrous in separate envelopes each bearing the identity of a particular group of responses.

one to three students are considerably older. For example, one North-western graduate student lists his age as 40, three Vidyasagar males give the age of 30, and three Taiwan students list their ages as 28.

To secure a relatively large number of responses from the three cultures it was necessary to shorten the test material. Only Card 1 and Card 12BG in Murray's TAT were used: Card 1 because of its stimulus value in evoking a variety of interpersonal interactions; Card 12BG because of its non-human content and its potential for eliciting associations to the natural environment. An additional factor in this selection relates to the contrasting appraisal of the two pictures by clinicians in the United States. Card 1 is generally considered "the single most valuable picture in the TAT" if attempts were to be made "to make statements about the total personality (Bellak 1954:101)." Conversely, Card 12BG is not considered "too useful in any specific case except in suicidal or very depressed subjects (Abt and Bellack 1950:211)." The possibility that students in other cultures might not react to the stimulus value of these pictures in a manner similar to that of subjects in the United States seemed to merit exploration.

All these tests were administered by Hsu personally in a classroom situation. Except for his own class at Northwestern University, Hsu was in each case introduced by the instructor of the class as a Professor of Anthropology from Northwestern University, U.S.A., who was administer-ing the same psychological test among college students in several parts of the world. The administrator gave the standard instruction provided in Form A of Henry A. Murray's *Thematic Apperception Test Manual* (Murray 1943:3).

After the introduction each subject was given a Thermofax reproduction of Card 1. All were requested to write down their stories on sheets of paper which they had ready. Each student was asked to write on his response sheets his name, age, sex, place of birth, religion, academic status, and in India, his caste. In addition, each student was asked to take from five to ten minutes for each card, to write more than one story for each picture if desired, and to write in any language that he or she felt most comfortable with. He was told that the pictures were not photographs but were simply created by an artist. Some subjects did give more than one story to one card. In the analysis below, varying projections to the same card by one subject are treated as one single story. The last item of instruction was prompted by Hsu's experiences in Taiwan where a few students made the inquiry as to whether they were photographs, and in India where some students asked him, after the testing session was over, what "really" was in the pictures and what he (Hsu) thought was in the pictures. One copy of Card 1 from the Harvard University Press edition of the TAT was put on the blackboard in each session to show the students the original from which the Thermofax versions were reproduced.

In Hong Kong and Taiwan instructions were given in Chinese, the responses were written in Chinese or English and the Chinese responses were translated into English by Hsu. In India instructions were given in English to the Indo-American Society and Lady Irwin College students. In Asutosh and Vidyasagar Colleges instructions were given in English first and then in Bengali (in each case by the instructor of the class). A total of 52 stories were written in Bengali by 23 Asutosh and 6 Vidyasagar students and translated into English by Dr. Moni Nag and Mrs. Uma Guha of the Anthropological Survey of India, Calcutta. But all of the students tested have studied English for at least five years and can speak and read it with varying degrees of proficiency.

After collecting the responses to Card 1, Thermofax reproductions of Card 12BG were then distributed, and responses to them were collected later, with no additional instructions.

The Thematic Apperception Test is assumed to yield data on interpersonal relationships and internalized goals and values, together with attitudes related to self-acceptance or self-awareness. It seems to us possible that, administered to subjects with varying cultural traditions, it might elicit some clues related to modal personalities of the different groups both in their original environment and, in the case of the Far Eastern subjects, under the impact of Western contact.

In general, the contents of the fantasies are analyzed with minimal emphasis on depth interpretation. The interpretation follows well-established lines of reasoning. For example, the introduction of additional figures such as parents, a teacher, or peers into Card 1, which contains only a boy sitting at a table looking at a violin, suggests heightened awareness of the human environment, and a greater need for emotional involvement with other people. Conversely, those subjects who concentrate solely on the character in the picture may be considered less spontaneous, more inhibited in their relationships to other people. Card 12BG is a landscape scene of a rowboat drawn up on the bank of a woodland stream. In the analysis of this picture special attention is focused on the extent to which the subjects are sensitive to the nonhuman environment, and the extent to which they relax with nature. Those who are apparently not threatened by solitude are interpreted as showing attitudes of self-acceptance.

The first category of the projective materials analyzed in both cards is Interpersonal Relationships. With reference to Card 1, this category is then divided into subcategories: Father, Mother, Other Individuals, No Individuals, Dependency, and Resistance (see Table A-2). If a parent or other individual is projected as having died, this person is also scored in the subcategory of appropriate relationship. If "parents" or "family" are seen in the picture, both Father and Mother are scored. The category Dependency is scored only when this behavior is explicitly verbalized; for example, "The boy wanted a violin of his own but his parents were too poor to buy one for him." The category of Resistance includes projection of overt rebellion against parental authority and passive aggressive resistance. As an example of the latter, the boy breaks the violin or notes that the strings are broken.

In terms of plot the manifest content of Card 1 frequently elicits stories of achievement. This category presents scoring difficulties; few subjects in this sample project the degree of positive achievement so readily apparent in the examples of Issei and Nisei stories reported by Caudill and De Vos (1956:1102–1127). In their study "positive achievement" includes clear-cut motivation: "(a) the boy wanted to be a violinist . . . and succeeds by working hard; (b) he is puzzled how to solve the task but keeps working at it; (c) his parents want him to become a violinist and he does so successfully (1956:1108)." In our present study the category Achievement Imagery follows McClelland *et al.* Our Achievement Imagery includes their subcategories "Competition with a Standard of Excellence," "Unique Accomplishment," "Long-Term Achievement," "Long-Term Involvement." Stories fulfilling at least one of McClelland's criteria are scored A.I. Stories which project McClelland's "Doubtful Achievement Imagery" (e.g., a person engaged in a commonplace task) or "Unrelated Imagery" (no reference to accomplishment) are scored as Reverie (McClelland, Atkinson, Clark & Lowell, 1953).

In Card 12BG, Interpersonal Relationships include the subcategories of One Individual, Two Individuals, Two-plus Individuals (any number greater than two) and No Individual (see Table A-3). If the subject projects himself, i.e., the first person singular, verbalizing his affective reaction to the natural environment or solitude, One Individual is scored. One Individual is also scored if the fantasy projects a human character formerly at the scene. (For example, "The fisherman who once owned this boat has moved away.") "People at a picnic," "a party in the wood," "the entire family on an outing" are scored Two-plus Individuals.

TABLE A-2   Responses to TAT Card 1

Subject	Vidyasagar		Asutosh		Lady Irwin		Indo-American		Taiwan		Hong Kong		Evanston	
Number	58	(100%)	52	(100%)	39	(100%)	26	(100%)	40	(100%)	50	(100%)	38	(100%)
Interpersonal Relationships														
Father	3	(6%)	11	(21%)	20	(51%)	9	(35%)	17	(42%)	15	(30%)	19	(50%)
Mother	1	(2%)	10	(19%)	18	(46%)	8	(30%)	12	(30%)	14	(28%)	20	(53%)
Other Persons	13	(24%)	10	(19%)	20	(51%)	18	(69%)	17	(42%)	12	(24%)	29	(76%)
No other human beings	44	(76%)	27	(52%)	10	(26%)	3	(11%)	11	(27%)	27	(54%)	3	(8%)
Dependence	4	(8%)	1	(2%)	7	(18%)	4	(15%)	4	(10%)	4	(8%)	1	(3%)
Resistance	11	(19%)	2	(4%)	10	(26%)	7	(27%)	15	(37%)	15	(30%)	26	(68%)
Fantasy														
Achievement Imagery	14	(24%)	17	(33%)	21	(54%)	22	(85%)	16	(40%)	20	(40%)	20	(53%)
Reverie	44	(76%)	35	(67%)	18	(46%)	4	(15%)	24	(60%)	30	(60%)	18	(47%)
Death	2	(3%)	5	(9%)	7	(18%)	1	(4%)	5	(13%)	1	(2%)	4	(10%)
Blindness	7	(11%)	6	(11%)	7	(18%)	1	(4%)	0	—	1	(2%)	0	—
Brokenness	7	(12%)	1	(2%)	7	(18%)	4	(16%)	3	(8%)	2	(4%)	2	(5%)
Mutability	1	(2%)	7	(13%)	2	((5%)	2	(8%)	0	—	0	—	0	—

TABLE A-3 Responses to TAT Card 12BG

Response	Vidyasagar	Asutosh	Lady Irwin	Indo-American	Taiwan	Hong Kong	Evanston
Number	56 (100%)	50 (100%)	39 (100%)	23 (100%)	40 (100%)	50 (100%)	38 (100%)
Interpersonal Relationships, %							
One individual projected	26	24	15	26	28	29	16
Two individuals projected	4	6	15	4	25	13	34
Two or more individuals projected	42	36	59	67	28	33	34
No human beings projected	27	34	8	0	15	26	10
Sensitivity to Physical Environment, %							
Vivid sensitivity to physical environment	13	26	28	8	13	52	29
Average sensitivity to physical environment	81	54	61	16	55	46	32
No sensitivity to physical environment	5	20	10	67	38	2	39
Plot	13	16	59	74	25	15	32
Reverie	87	84	41	26	75	85	68
Death	11	15	30	17	23	8	10
Mutability	6	20	20	8	0	0	0

The second major category, Sensitivity to the Physical Environment (i.e., nonhuman) is based on numerical count of descriptive adjectives or nouns elaborating the landscape scene. The scale is arbitrarily decided upon as follows: Vivid Sensitivity when seven or more adjectives are used; Average Sensitivity includes at least three descriptive adjectives; No Sensitivity is scored for subjects who exclude any reference to natural scenery description (for example, boys who go on an outing and become involved with robbers, murderers, etc.).

The reaction of the students to Card 12BG (Table A-3) frequently conformed to one of two distinct patterns: either they reacted to the manifest content of the picture stimulus with Reverie-type associations; or apparently threatened by solitude, they produced imaginative plots related to romance or adventure; hence, the categories Reverie and Plot.

The number and kind of picture stimuli used necessarily limited the scope of the blind analysis. As noted above, neither card includes parental figures. When parental figures were "introduced" in the absence of such manifest stimulus, the assumption was made, following Henry, that they may normally be thought of as representing "the subject's need to complete the picture stimulus with figures whom he considers an integral part of the plot as suggested by the actual stimulus picture" (Henry 1956:86–87). Many subjects, however, failed to associate to parental figures, thereby leaving notable lacunae in possible interpretation not only of affective relationships with parents, including patterns of dependency and resistance, but also of possible parental stimulation for achievement. Likewise, without the use of cards which normally elicit heterosexual involvement, sibling rivalry or aggression, interpretation of such behavior is not possible. This analysis is, therefore, not comparable to the intensive studies of modal personality made by such scientists as Wallace (1952), Kaplan (1954), or Gladwin and Sarason (1953), or even the more limited study of Mulligen on Maori adolescents (1957). The limited number of norms available for TAT analysis and current uncertainty as to the meaning of such norms used in cross-cultural studies also preclude subjecting these data to refined statistical methods (Henry 1961:593). No effort is made here to interpret basic personality structure or total personality. It is possible, on the other hand, to observe how certain reactions occurred in integrated clusters, suggesting varying patterns of cultural behavior in response to the same picture stimuli.

A final category concerns fantasies among the Hindus but rare among the Americans or Chinese. This category contains projective materials in which the subjects anthropomorphize fauna, flora, and inanimate things and seem to fail to make absolute distinctions between subject and object. Hsu suggests the category Mutability to describe this behavior, which is used in the analysis of responses to both Cards 1 and 12BG.

II. Analysis of Groups (Watrous)

American (Northwestern University Students). The American students show two distinct trends in their fantasy projections: either they tell one integrated story of approximately 200 words in length, or they project from one to five brief, alternative themes. The two trends are almost equally represented in number with little distinction between the sexes. In general, these young people appear spontaneous, gregarious, energetic, and imaginative, showing strong need for peer acceptance and pronounced rebellion against parental authority. There is little evidence of constraint or caution in a new situation, but at the same time there is fairly striking conflict with respect to feelings and ultimate goals. There is a marked difference between their response to the external environment of people and the external environment of nature (nonhuman); for example, the Americans show limited sensitivity to nature in the manner of Wordsworth or Keats and little of the *Weltschmerz* reaction frequently associated with college students of late adolescent or young adult age. Their perceptual accuracy is sharp, with a need to distinguish between subject and object. They are oriented to action although they do not necessarily project goals related to hard work or sustained effort. Fantasying action is a stronger need than projecting mood. There is little indication from the reactions to the two cards that these young people have been concerned with poverty, illness, and accident or that religious or spiritual feeling is integrated into their personality. For the most part they appear threatened by solitude and show little empathy for reflection and contemplation.

Spontaneity, energy, and ambition are suggested both by the well-integrated stories and by the number of alternative projections. The need to be gregarious and that for peer acceptance are indicated by the fact that 76% of students introduce Others in Card 1 and 68% of them introduce two or more individuals in Card 12BG. In the former group, one-half project fantasies with overt reference to peers. These students are immediately aware of interpersonal relationships with their parents, with one-half of them associating to parents in Card 1. Reactions to parental control are coupled with strong resistance to authority, 68% of them projecting resistance, and at the same time with minimal overt dependency (only

3%). The maternal figure is more often singled out as the object of resistance: "Oh, mother, I've practiced one hour already. Can't I go out and play baseball?" On the other hand, many of the Americans are ambivalent about their resistance: alternative themes are frequently of a reverie type in which the boy "dreams of becoming a great violinist." This readily available defense through fantasy seems to meet two needs of almost equal prominence: for slightly more than one-half the group (53%) fantasy relates in Card 1 to Achievement Imagery; in the remainder fantasy serves as an escape from such projections as in the following: "He is gripping his day dreams as a means of keeping from the act of starting his practicing." Playing the violin, as Henry has observed, is a current middle-class American value which has become a frequent source of conflict between parents and children, especially male children (Henry 1956:147); violin playing by boys is interpreted as a "sissy" activity.

Oral needs with overt associations to food are frequently noted. In particular, family picnics are a common theme in response to Card 12BG. The major emphasis, however, is concerned with interpersonal relationships, in particular resistance to parental authority and involvement with the peer group.

Chinese: University of Hong Kong Students.   The Hong Kong students as contrasted with American students project on the whole shorter stories without alternative plots. They also appear more cautious, more restrained, less spontaneous, and more accepting of self. They are less egocentric, less aggressive, less resistant to authority. Where American students show eagerness to be involved with other people, the Chinese students frequently show lack of intensity in interpersonal relationships. At the same time the Chinese are more sensitive to the external environment of nature, reacting with sensuous imagery to landscape stimuli.

Caution, restraint, and less spontaneity in a new environment are suggested by shorter stories without alternative plots in Card 1. Where 68% of the stories given by American students show resistance to authority, only 30% of the stories given by the Hong Kong students are resistive. The lesser involvement of the Hong Kong students with other people is apparent in the fact that 54% of the Hong Kong stories include no other individual in Card 1 as contrasted with only 8% of the Americans; and 26% of the Hong Kong stories introduce no people to Card 12BG, as contrasted with only 10% of the American stories. The Hong Kong students show minimal interest in peer competition and minimal need for peer acceptance. The outstanding behavior of the Hong Kong students lies in their sensuous, effortless response to the boat scene of Card 12BG: 52% project vivid imagery; 46% show limited responsivity and only 2% are totally indifferent to it. None of the other groups tested reflects this behavior pattern to a comparable degree.

The imagery projected is analogous to the response of the Chinese Hawaiian adolescents to bright color in the Rorschach test, as noted by Hsu, Watrous, and Lord (1961:33–53), where such responses were interpreted as showing more mature emotionality than white Americans of comparable age on the mainland of the United States. With the same comparison in mind, the Hong Kong group's reluctance to project alternative plots, their less vivid imagination suggest that the Hong Kong students, like the Hawaiian Chinese, are less inclined to exploit fantasy defenses in problem-solving than the Americans. Some similarity between the American and Hong Kong students is evident in a limited number of fantasies which are indistinguishable from one group to another on blind analysis. Specifically, sometimes a Hong Kong story in Card 1 involves resistance to parental authority and (more infrequently) a need for peer involvement. Conversely, a relatively small number of American fantasies to Card 12BG include vivid, sensual imagery to the landscape. Achievement Imagery of the Hong Kong students is slightly less prominent (40% of these Chinese as compared with 53% of the Americans project clear-cut motivation in this direction). More significant, however, is the fact that the American students react to Card 1 as if a choice of behavior were possible to them: a choice between practicing and not practicing, a choice between working or engaging in peer-group activity; while the Chinese students are less inclined to show concern with choice, at the same time appearing more thoughtful and meditative.

Chinese: Taiwan University Students. "Robert who has no sunshine," the only Taiwan story with a title, seems to project the prevailing mood of youth in that island at this time. This symbolic vein is echoed in the 12BG story featuring "a couple who took their children into the forest to get cool," but who "forgot a child in the forest." Dysphoric effect with a sense of defeatism and vague, nebulous irritability is fairly characteristic. For example, Resistance in Card 1 is indicated by projecting the boy as being "tired" or "having a headache"; or that "he feels unpleasant," "the teacher scolds," etc. Achievement Imagery is tinged with lack of confidence. "Other people can play; why can't I?" "I cannot learn very well;

the only thing I can do is study the construction in order to mitigate my sorrow." "Why is my sound so ugly?" "The sound is not the kind of sound that will correspond to the strings in my heart. I feel very, very sad." Projections of Death are not infrequent — a parent in Card 1, a child or a lover in 12BG. These young people seem lacking in optimism, uncertain as to ultimate goal, with the "broken string" of the violin speculatively symbolizing their reaction to the future rather than resistance at the moment.

Except for the dysphoria noted above, the Taiwan stories are difficult to classify in terms of a distinct mode. No facet of Taiwan behavior as interpreted from the TAT responses is strikingly different from those of American and Hong Kong youth. For example, like the young people in Hong Kong, the Formosa group are more likely to project meditation than to fantasy action. But like those of the American students the Taiwan stories contain considerably less vivid sensitivity to the natural environment: 13% of the Taiwan stories show vivid sensitivity while 38% show total indifference to this stimulus. (The Hong Kong projections to Card 12BG are 52% vivid imagery, 46% limited sensitivity, and only 2% total indifference.)

The Taiwan projections to Card 1 suggest approximately equal involvement with parents and with other individuals. Resistiveness is fairly prominent although apathetic (37%). In Achievement Imagery and Reverie they have given an identical number of projections with their Hong Kong compatriots. For the most part strong motivation for success is lacking and Achievement Imagery is expressed without much zest or enthusiasm for goal attainment. Many of the projections to Card 1 suggest a feeling only of a task to be performed as summarily as possible.

Projections to Card 12BG are in the main brief, 4 to 6 lines. Of the 25% of Taiwan subjects who project two individuals in this card, 23% perceive them as lovers. The stories lack intensity of emotional involvement. Could it be inferred that neither interpersonal relationships nor the natural environment gratify the emotional needs of these young people? Or could it be said that these students have perhaps lost some of the sense of security provided by the traditional Chinese family constellation and are, consequently, resistive to authority in a passive manner? Or could it be that the current cultural rewards on Taiwan stimulate neither individual initiative nor creative energy in problem-solving?

Hindu: Vidyasagar College Students. The picture stimulus of the boy with the violin elicits from 54 of the 56 Vidyasagar students an identical association — that of "thinking": "A good boy . . . thinks how to play"; "a boy thinks about his future life"; "the boy is thinking about his duty"; "the body is deeply thinking about some tunes to be composed." (Interestingly, of the two young men who do not project "thinking," one perceives the boy as a "European"!) The empathy of these males for reflection in lieu of action or interaction in response to a new situation may also be inferred from their reluctance to associate to other individuals or to project achievement imagery: 73% related only to the boy, with no other individuals; and 69% projected reverie without achievement need. These are the highest percentages in these categories of the seven groups tested. Consistent with the emphasis on "no other individuals," the Vidyasagar males almost completely ignore parental figures, with only one student (2%) associating to the mother and three students (6%) projecting a father figure. Thus, the resistance noted in 19% of the stories is inferred for the most part from the broken strings of the violin and not directly from external authority figures.

The majority of the Card 1 fantasies are brief: four or five lines, with apparent limitations in vocabulary and difficulty with English grammatical constructions. Yet though the administrator of the test (Hsu) specifically asked the students to use their mother tongue if they felt so disposed, only three students elected to do so. This fact, together with the fact that the Card 12BG stories are longer and more spontaneous, suggests that the limiting factor of language difficulty should not be exaggerated. Forty-two percent of the students project two or more individuals to the landscape scene of Card 12BG. As in Card 1, the mental activity is of a musing type, 87% projecting reverie with plot. The small number of students who show no sensitivity to the external environment (5%) is comparable to the Hong Kong group (2%).

The stereotyped fantasies on the whole project minimal influence of Western society and only limited references to Hindu culture. The Hindu reference is apparent in occasional associations to Indian place names and Indian individuals, with the tiger most frequent among animals. The influence of traditional patterns must thus be inferred from the intellectual approach to problem-solving, in particular the emphasis upon thought rather than action, a feeling of reverence when occasional religious associations occur, and, in contrast with the Americans especially, complete unconcern with peer acceptance and approval of others. Marked emotional inhibition is suggested by their fantasies to the two cards. It could be speculated that these students, when contrasted with their exuberant counterparts in the Indo-American Society, whose stories are examined below, are lacking in urbanity and intellectual sophistication. One might surmise that they come quite possibly from a socio-economic status different from that of the members of the Indo-American Society.

To the Western psychologist, their preoccupation with thinking suggests a lack of commitment to action or feeling. One also wonders if the tentative approach of these Vidyasagar students to the test environment is not consistent with their tentative approach to other cultural patterns of the West. They may conform superficially to this alien way of life. Emotionally and intellectually, however, the Vidyasagar are Hindu.

An instructor in an American college, on reading the Vidyasagar fantasies, would assume some collaboration among the students. This impression is based on the fact that two stories are identical and that the projections show a remarkable degree of uniformity (e.g., no plot is found in a majority of the stories; 73% of the projections to Card 1 introduce no other human beings; 54 out of 56 students are preoccupied with thinking). This uniformity is striking even when compared with the other three Indian groups. On the other hand, the projections to Card 12BG show less uniformity and much more spontaneity, 42% of the students introducing two or more individuals to the boat scene. Either the emotional threat of a new situation, i.e., the beginning of a test environment, evokes inhibition as a prevailing personality pattern or the Vidyasagar students are more at ease with a relatively unstructured situation where no definite action involving other human beings is demanded of them.

Hindu: Asutosh College Students. The emotional and intellectual affinity of the Vidyasagar College students with traditional Hindu culture is implicit and only inferred. With Asutosh College students (all girls) this affinity is explicit and verbalized. The command of English in the 29 stories written in the alien language is superior to that of Vidyasagar males. With the greater linguistic fluency, Hindu patterns of thinking and feeling become vibrant and distinctive. The boy perceived by the Asutosh females is the "thinking" boy of the Vidyasagar males, but the Asutosh females project with fluidity of style and traditional Hindu color and intensity of feeling. Thus, the Asutosh boy tries to understand "the essence of the instrument," "to solve by his perception," "to know what the actual thing is," and he "minutely observes the structure." As with Lady Irwin students, to be discussed below, the violin is "the only friend (of the orphan boy), a faithful friend of his life"; "Don't forget me and I shall help you as long as I can." Again contrasted with Vidyasagar, the greater range of

English vocabulary of Asutosh girls is matched by their wider range of imagination. Some of the Asutosh fantasies are similar in culture-hero projection to the stories from the Indo-American Society; others to those from Lady Irwin College. It is doubtful if any of these stories, on blind analysis, would be interpreted as American.

The Hong Kong students react to the external environment with descriptive adjectives. The Asutosh college students, more than any other group, project human emotions into the fauna, the flora, the boat, as if the fauna, the flora, and the boat were integral parts of the society of man and as if the distinction between subject and object were of little moment. "The same pain which is in the mother's breast has also arisen in the mind of the tree by seeing the motherless child"; "but the blossoms of those trees make the small birds happy" (examples of fantasy response to 12BG). Emphasis on trees could be related to current Hindu religious rites. Like Lady Irwin students, the Asutosh girls seem well acquainted with Hindu poverty and death. They are more often dysphoric than consciously optimistic. The dysphoria is, however, accepted as apparently all life experiences of the Asutosh group are accepted — without resistance — and without a seeming awareness of choice in life decisions. With preponderance of reverie over verbalized achievement need (67% as contrasted with 33%) as well as over plot (84% to 16% in 12BG), these young women are less inhibited in self-expression, more congruent with the totality of environmental factors, and more overtly responsive to religious and philosophical stimuli than any of the seven groups in our study. These students react to environmental stress with emotional sensitivy and vivid poetic imagery, with passive acceptance of that which cannot be changed.

The Asutosh students are more similar to the Vidyasagar than to the other groups in their reluctance to introduce additional individuals in their fantasies. For example, 21% associated to a parental figure in Card 1, while 52% introduced no other person. As contrasted with the Americans, no student expressed resistance to parental authority, and as contrasted with 18% of Lady Irwin students, only 2% projected dependency. In the absence of picture stimuli with parental figures, it can only be conjectured that the Asutosh girls accept their parents passively, uncritically, possibly sublimating meaningful interpersonal relationships in their deep involvement with religion.

Hindu: Lady Irwin College Students. Lady Irwin is a female teacher's college. The subjects' interest in the emotional and intellectual welfare of young students is readily apparent in their projections to Card 1. In certain respects the projections of these young ladies appear similar to those of the Americans (for example, 54% A.I. as compared with the Americans' 53%), and their educational philosophy of "understanding the child" is consistent with that taught in American college departments of education. Their environmental settings and place names are, however, frequently British. These students, like the Americans and the Indo-American Society students to be discussed below, tell relatively long stories with rich plots, suggesting vivid fantasy life. Compared with the Indo-American Society students, Lady Irwin girls project slightly higher dependency (18% as compared with 15% of Indo-American Society males), but an almost identical degree of resistance to authority (26% as compared with 27% of the Indo-American males). These projections suggest a greater degree of ambivalence toward patterns of independence and dependence in these two groups, possibly a function of their noticeable westernization. In certain respects, however, striking differences set Lady Irwin students apart from both Americans and Chinese in fantasy projection. These are (*a*) concern with Hindu poverty (30% of Lady Irwin subjects describe this condition in Card 1 as compared with minimal or no concern with it among the non-Indian groups), and (*b*) concern with death or other physical misfortune (18% project death in Card 1 and 25% associate to death in Card 12BG, while 18% project the boy in Card 1 as blind). The latter percentage contrasts sharply with no projection of blindness by United States or Taiwan students, 2% by Hong Kong students. In death projection, the Lady Irwin girls exceed all other Indian and non-Indian groups, though the four Indian groups stand out as a whole noticeably different from the other groups, especially from the Hong Kong Chinese and Americans in response to Card 12BG. In blindness projection to Card 1, not only do the Lady Irwin girls exceed all other groups but the four Indian groups (13%, 11%, 18% and 4%) stand out in conspicuous contrast to the non-Indian groups (2% for Hong Kong students and none for either American or Taiwan students). However, it is probably reasonable to assume that such relatively frequent projections of poverty, death, and blindness reflect at least in part current conditions with which these subjects are acquainted. Misidentification of the violin occurs (projected by 15% of these students as "toy," "book," or "train"), and just as for the Asutosh College group, the violin is projected as having human attributes, for example, as a "friend," by 5% of the group. More frequently (20%) these subjects give human attributes to phenomena of nature: "The leaves of all that tree covered his body and the birds sing a prayer for him." Consistent with this feeling tone, Lady Irwin students verbalize their deep reverence of God: "These forests are God created"; "the father looked around and thanked God for the close of another day." This preponderantly Hindu phenomenon suggests a structuring of reality with different dimensions from that of the Americans and Chinese, a world in which everyday life situations are permeated by intensity of religious feeling.

Hindu: Indo-American Society Students. In sharp contrast with Taiwan youths, the Indo-American Society students (a majority of whom are males) are intensely involved with their fantasy projections, determinedly ambitious, and significantly competitive. Where the Taiwan youths appear defeatist, the Indo-American Society boys are optimistic. In chronological age this group is younger on the average than the other groups tested, and the immature affect of adolescence is occasionally reflected in these students' concern with adventure. Intellectually, however, they appear disciplined, combining their optimism ("dreaming of a bright future"; "though he was young, he was very keen") with realistic formulations of goal attainment ("one had to put forward his best in such cases and go up against any obstacle in the path"; a boy "greatly interested in music and wanted to know everything possible about it"). The goals of these youths suggest both British and traditional Hindu influences: Sir Isaac Newton, James Watt, Krishnon (*sic*), Chander (great writer in Urdu), and Rabindra Nath Tagore are culture heroes.

Many of these boys have recently passed their matriculation examinations—an event which is overtly reflected in their stories projecting competitive situations. In general, these boys are zestful, spontaneous, and spiritually inclined; unlike the American and Taiwan students, religious imagery is frequently projected. In contrast to the Hong Kong youth, the Indo-American Society boys show almost no sensitivity to the natural environment, only 8% projecting vivid sensual responses, 16% average sensitivity, and 67% a total absence of this behavior. The spontaneity of these boys is indicated by their involvement with other individuals and in a concern with their own goals. For example, all of the Indo-American Society boys project people to Card 12BG while 85% show Achievement Imagery in Card 1 — the highest percentages obtained in all the categories among all the groups tested. Achievement Imagery is not, however, consistently related to musical proficiency; many of the boys associate to the violin in Card 1 only peripherally, concentrating rather on mechanical ingenuity and scientific goals. These rather long stories with well-organized plots project the buoyancy, resiliency, and intelligence of emotionally healthy students who seem to have integrated into their personality many of the "ideal" patterns of both Western European culture and the traditional culture of India. These young males are highly motivated to achieve and appear to have the energy and drive traditionally associated with the West. Unlike the Americans, however, need for peer acceptance is not significant. Just as for the Americans, success may be for these youths a mark of masculinity — as exemplified in one of the many projections involving examinations: "[he] should not accept defeat as he was a boy and tried again." It might be speculated that a successful engineer represents optimum achievement for the Indo-American Society males. Conflict of interest seems to be a contributing factor in resistance to parental authority. It occurs with drive for success. In these fantasies resistance is related to the varying goals of child and parent. However, the prevailing Hindu pattern of a thoughtful, contemplative approach to problem-solving is also apparent. For example: "One day James Watt . . . began to think and discovered the truth of the steam engine." The distinction between subject and object, while less nebulous than that of the Lady Irwin and Asutosh College students, is not always clear. This fact can be interpreted from folklore references (the "helpful animal" theme), from anthropomorphizing astronomical bodies ("He, the Sun") and inanimate objects (" . . . waiting for the violin to begin playing by itself") and from such religious projections as "she by the grace of the Almighty changed herself into an old woman and began to preach truth and piety."

III. Group Trends (Watrous)

In evaluating the test results the interpreter lacked the advantage of generally accepted norms for any of the categories used, for the TAT is not usually analyzed in this way. What has been done here is an attempt to analyze the materials in an unconventional manner in order to reveal group trends, if any, without, however, claiming too much for the product.

Despite the internal variations within each of the seven groups analyzed, and despite the differences observed between the two Chinese groups and among the four Indian groups, certain trends may be noted which distinguish, as a whole, the American, Chinese, and Hindu fantasies. The American students as a group focus in their fantasies on resistance to authority, on need for peer acceptance and personal independence, and on the assumption that a choice of decisions in life experiences are available to them. They are spontaneous and imaginative.

Their main approach to problem-solving is through action. They seem to entertain some uncertainty in their attitudes about the self.

The Chinese fantasies convey less spontaneity, less gregariousness and less concern with peer acceptance than do the American responses. They are also generally more thoughtful. The Hong Kong Chinese, of all the groups, appear more relaxed than other groups in attitudes toward the self, whereas the Taiwan Chinese seem to lack direction and optimism.

The Indian fantasies vary most from the other two cultures in a number of ways: in their fuzziness of boundaries between animate and inanimate, and between subject and object, their religious bent, and their tendency to resort to meditation rather than action for problem-solving. Certain basic characteristics seem to separate the Vidyasagar males and the Asutosh College females on the one hand and Lady Irwin College females and Indo-American Society students (mostly males) on the other. The fantasies from the former two groups seem more distinctly Hindu intellectually and emotionally while those from the latter two groups seem to reflect patterns of interpersonal relationships and achievement imageries more in accord with Western personality than the other Indian groups. However, fantasies from all four Indian groups are characterized by meditative trends. Furthermore, the fantasies of Indian females as a whole (the traditional Asutosh girls and the more Western-oriented Lady Irwin girls) are similar in their contrast to those of Indian males. Indian female fantasies convey more passivity and spontaneous projection relating to harmony with the universe as well as more verbalization of traditional Hindu religious stimuli than those of Indian males.

Finally, the same picture stimulus certainly failed to elicit comparable reactions among the different groups. For example, the "middle-class" implications of the boy with the violin in Card 1, so well-known in American responses, are not found in responses by the non-American groups (Henry 1956:147).[4] These groups are simply not sensitive to such implications and they perceive Card I without connecting it with "sissy" behavior — an apparent emotional threat to Americans. They also respond to Card 12BG, which is seldom used by American clinicians, with

---

[4] According to William E. Henry, Card 1 is generally considered "a middle-class picture in that it presents an issue more appropriate to the social definition made by that large group. The struggle with the conflict of free choice and an imposed task is thus one of the basic common themes to this picture. The aura of ambition is, of course, the second, most generally symbolised by stories of the virtuosity of the boy and the potential future musical success" (William E. Henry, "The Analysis of Fantasy").

considerable fluidity and without the usual connotation of depression or suicidal feelings.

IV. Comments and Interpretation (Hsu)

A.   While we began our work on these TAT responses with no idea of relating this Annex to the theme of the book, one cannot but note that the results turn out to be more supportive of its main hypotheses and analytic results than otherwise. The resistance by the Americans to parents and authority, their need for peer group acceptance and hence conformity to its demands, and their approach to problem-solving in terms of action rather than thought or contemplation — these traits apparent in the TAT responses have all been discussed in the book. Their high score in ambition well befits their love of equality, and their spontaneity and desire for choices or alternatives express, on the conscious level, their emphasis on individual freedom. More deeply, the latter may be related to their doubt about self as well as their ambivalence about dependence and independence. Such doubts, in turn, are not unconnected with the need for peer acceptance and conformity noted before.

Watrous is of the opinion that the Chinese responses from Hong Kong are dissimilar from those from Taiwan except that they both are, compared with the American responses, less concerned with peer acceptance and more thoughtful. She is struck by the discordant and aimless note which seems to overshadow the Taiwan responses but which are absent in the Hong Kong responses. This discordant note is indeed noticeable in the outlook of a majority of youths as well as adults to many visitors to Taiwan today and it undoubtedly is related to the difficulties inherent in the political and economic facts of Taiwan today. Apart from the larger picture, individual frustrations are evident. High school graduates find it difficult to enter colleges and universities, college and university graduates find it difficult to seek graduate education or work. The present institutions of higher learning in Taiwan turn out at least 20,000 college graduates every year. Of this total, not many can achieve employment commensurate with their education and only a fraction of those who apply succeed in entering the United States for advanced training. In a certain sense students in crowded Hong Kong share some of these same frustrations but they do not live in a heavily political atmosphere originating from a governmental objective so difficult of attainment; they are free to leave and return to the Colony if they wish; their aspirations are more commensurate with their possible achievements; and above all, more of them are not separated from their families and are not suffering from total lack of contact with their families on the mainland. From this point of view Taiwan students are less "natural" or "ideal" subjects for our TAT study than their Hong Kong counterparts.

Even so, what leads Watrous to see the Taiwan fantasies as being different from the Hong Kong ones is not really so prominently found in her analytic categories as in the feeling tones of the responses. When we ignore the feeling tones of the fantasies we shall note that the two groups of Chinese responses are not only identical in Achievement Imagery and Reverie with reference to Card 1 but also similar in Interpersonal Relationships. In response to Card 1 the fantasies from both Chinese groups show almost equal involvement with parents and with others[5] (in contrast to American fantasies in which involvement with others is greater than involvement with parents); and similar ratios between Dependence and Resistance (about 1:3 in contrast to American fantasies in which the ratio is about 1:20). All of these are in keeping with the Chinese situation-centered way of life in which even the adolescent individual does not have great need for resisting parents; for although the father-son relationship is the center of Chinese social organization, its inclusive and continuous nature enables the individual to involve himself in other relationships without first having to shed his parents. A similar picture obtains in their responses to Card 12BG. In these fantasies the Americans appear to be much more gregarious than both groups of Chinese. The only striking difference between Hong Kong and Taiwan fantasies is that many more of the former than the latter involve no human beings (54% versus 27% in Card 1 and 26% versus 15% in Card 12BG). Even here the two Chinese groups differ from each other far less than they differ as a whole from the Americans (54% and 27% among the two Chinese groups versus 8% among the Americans in Card 1; 26% and 15% versus 10% in Card 12BG). Being usually much more enmeshed in a network of automatic human relation-ships than the Americans, the Chinese do not have as much need as the Americans to work for such relationships. This is, I think, also why, as Watrous observed in her interpretation, the Chinese tend to be more self-accepting than the Americans.

B. To probe into the matter further, I reclassified all the responses into certain broad categories quite different from those employed by Watrous. Some of the conclusions derived from this new classification will be

[5] In the case of Hong Kong the involvement with parents is somewhat greater than with others.

touched upon throughout the rest of my comments but one new category is particularly relevant to the point made here, namely, the Chinese have less need than the Americans to seek human relations and therefore seem more self-accepting. This new category is Enjoyment in Card 12BG defined in terms of expressions of happiness, beauty, excitement, or contentment. The response of each subject is considered as a whole and it is classified only once (or according to the first response in case of alternatives) under the category of Enjoyment if it contains any of the expressions just given but no expression in the opposite direction. When this is done the results obtain that are shown in Table A-4. What we see here are at once the remarkable similarity between the two Chinese groups on the one hand and the remarkable difference between the two Chinese groups and the American group on the other. Though far less concerned with personal enjoyment than the Americans, Chinese can enjoy themselves alone as well as with others; the Americans show a much stronger urge to seek the company of others for the same purpose.

Another kind of response which may be regarded as supportive of the observation that the Chinese are more self-accepting than the Americans is to be found in a category of responses to Card 12BG which I have designated as Noncommittal Description, which is employed for responses lacking any expression of emotional or aesthetic involvement or even curiosity. The percentages of responses fitting this category among the

TABLE A-4   Percentages of Chinese and American Subjects Whose Responses to 12BG are Judged "Enjoyment"[a]

| Nature of Response | *Percentage of Total Number of Subjects of Responses* | | |
	Taiwan	*Hong Kong*	*Evanston*
Enjoyment	17 (43%)	25 (50%)	32 (87%)
NO. OF PERSONS INVOLVED	PERCENTAGE OF ABOVE		
Alone	47%	47%	28%
Two or more person	53%	53%	72%[a]

a. The response of each subject is counted only once according to the prevailing theme. In case a subject gives two or more alternative responses only the theme of the first response is used here and in subsequent tabulations, except where noted. But if all the alternative responses are separately added to the total of each group, these figures for Evanston become even larger, while the Hong Kong figures remain about the same. Taiwan gives no alternative responses to Card 12BG.

three groups are as follows: Taiwan, 20%; Hong Kong, 30%; and Evanston, 8%. The Americans are simply more desirous of external involvement than the Chinese. This conclusion is further augmented by the fact that all Noncommittal responses by the Americans are alternative ones, while the Chinese Noncommittal responses are sole ones.

The similar extent to which the two Chinese groups associate Card 12BG with enjoyment raises the question whether Watrous's observation that the Taiwan group is dysphoric is more apparent than real. My feeling is that it is not, and that one solid piece of evidence for this dysphoria in Taiwan responses is found in the much greater frequency of Death themes among them than among Hong Kong responses to both cards (see Tables A-2 and A-3). Take the Death associations to Card 12BG, for example. Here the percentages for the two Chinese groups and one American group are as follows: Taiwan, 23%; Hong Kong, 8%; and Evanston, 10%. In the case of Taiwan, all Death associations constitute the sole responses, while in the case of Hong Kong three of the four responses making up the 8% total are alternative responses and are, therefore, presumably of lesser importance. Furthermore, the qualities of the Taiwan and Hong Kong Death associations are markedly different. All four Death responses from Hong Kong involve violence. Three of them each involve a murder which is given as an alternative response to another one involving two lovers having a good time. For two subjects the *murder* and the *love* responses are unrelated. But the murder association of one of these subjects involves a man killing an invited "friend" or "a girl or his wife," whom he strangles and whose body he sinks into the bottom of the river by tying a stone to it, while the third subject adds the following line in parentheses after giving one response with two lovers on a picnic and a second with a murderer digging a hole to bury the body: "Hope the lovers would not discover the body!" These and the fact that the remaining one Death response from Hong Kong involves "a young man and his sweetheart" drowned in a storm while rowing in a boat suggest a linkage between romantic rendezvous and sudden violent death in the minds of the Hong Kong youths. But the substances of the Death responses from Taiwan are quite of another hue. To begin with, all except one of the responses associating to death have nothing to do with murder. The characters die of illness, old age, accident, or suicide. The single response involving murder is committed by a man and woman who have to abandon their illegitimate child because the society is against their marriage. In the four romantic responses one involves double suicide because the parents of the couple are against their marriage, a second involves a count who commits suicide because his wife died of illness, and a third involves a pair of sweethearts who grow up together, but unfortunately one dies of an incurable disease, leaving the man broken-hearted and in despair when he surveys the scene. The fourth romantic response goes as follows:[6]

> This is a spot deep in the mountains and thick forest. It is very far from human habitation. Many years ago a pair of lovers came as a result of their rebellion against evil forces of society. They wanted to preserve their pure hearts and sacred love. The two of them discarded their family and society and left in a boat to escape from a sinful city to look for an oasis (t'ao yuan) outside of the human habitation. After many sufferings (of course in their hearts they are extremely blessed) they came to this spot. This was a place of their ideal habitat. Here they have only lovely trees and flowers. The world was theirs. Many years have passed. They have passed away. This morning the first rays of the sun are praying for the events that passed and blessing them.

In comparing the Hong Kong and Taiwan responses associating to Death one is struck by an insistent and insidious pathetic undertone in the latter which is absent in the former. The Hong Kong characters seem to be lively and in full control of their destiny till some unexpected violence extraneous to them stops their lives. The Taiwan characters, on the other hand, are forced to die by society, by natural forces, by sentiment. They are gradually worn down. Their death seems to be an integral part of the life of the victims; it merely, and perhaps unavoidably, unfolds itself at some stage of the human drama. I think it is this contrast which leads Watrous to note the dysphoria in the Taiwan responses.

While this greater prominence of Death associations in Taiwan than in Hong Kong responses may, as Watrous noted, have something to do with the present peculiar circumstances of that island stronghold, we cannot but wonder also about the reason for the intimate linkage between romance and violent death in the Hong Kong but not in the Taiwan responses. I suggest that this difference is at least in part reflective of the fact that the Chinese society in Taiwan shows less Western impact than its counterpart in Hong Kong. Table A-5 presents the picture with some clarity. In Taiwan the traditional Chinese customs are still obvious and strong, though romancing between the sexes does occur among some. If the romance does not meet with the approval of parents and society, not only escape but also drastic measures such as double suicide or infanticide may

---

[6] Unusual grammatical constructions, peculiar uses of words, or errors in spelling, if any, in all fantasies are reproduced in this article as they are given by the subjects.

become necessary. The fact that two of the ten responses connected with love are associated with illness or suicide strengthens this observation. Under the Chinese emphasis on the father-son axis, romantic expressions even between a man and his wife are discouraged rather than encouraged.

TABLE A-5   Responses to 12BG Involving "Lovers" and "Death" From Taiwan, Hong Kong, and Evanston

Behavior or Result	Taiwan	Hong Kong	Evanston
Two lovers enjoying themselves	4 (10%)	2 (4%)	11 (30%)
Two lovers escaping or escaped from society or pursuers (forbidden love)	1 (2.5%)	2 (4%)	None
Love and Death			
Natural death (forbidden love)	1	None	None
Double suicide (forbidden love)	1	None	None
Infanticide	1	None	None
Illness	1	None	None
Suicide due to love	1	None	None
Murder	None	4 (8%)	None
Total	10 (25%)	8 (16%)	11 (30%)
Death not associated with lovers	4 (10%), 2 due to accidents	None	4 (10%), 2 due to accidents and 2 due to senseless murder
Total number of responses or subject (1 reponse = 1 subject)	40	50	37

In Hong Kong, by comparison, Western romancing between boys and girls is probably a somewhat more common occurrence. Though restrictions are still evident, they are far from as severe as the Taiwan subjects see them. Of the two Hong Kong responses in which love is linked with escape, one (subject a male) involves a man and a woman who are eloping because "their family (*sic*) prevented them from getting married," while the other (subject a female) ends in a harmless and even frivolous note. It goes as follows:

> It was a Spring morning. The tress were white with blossoms. There was a gentle mist veiling the woods and the lake. Jonathan and I had a walk in the woods. We just strolled round, silently, breathing in the freshness of the flowers. After half an hour or so, Jonathan suggested that we rented a boat and rowed round the lake. It was not a bad idea and I thought, "How romantic it is to be in a small boat with your beloved on a Spring morning."
>
> We were just about to board on the boat when I caught sight of my stern parents among the blossoming trees. Immediately I pulled Jonathan away and ran in the opposite direction as my parents. Jonathan was greatly puzzled. We went back to the boat-renting service and paid for our one hour "tour" in the boat. That is why you see the boat empty on the bank of the lake. Do you spy my parents, reader?

However, though Love is not clearly linked with Death due to parental or societal opposition, its direct association with Murder in one response and indirect association with Murder in three responses suggests that romance is dangerous. It is as though the Hong Kong youngsters, having been educated in English style schools, consciously consider romance as more or less the acceptable custom but unconsciously they hear a danger note from sanctions rooted in the Chinese traditional way of life. In other words, the father-son axis and its basic attributes, such as opposition to romantic love and suppression of erotic expression between men and women in public, remain strong psychological forces in these students. The only minor point of evidence seemingly contrary to this interpretation is that Taiwan subjects have given more responses containing "two lovers enjoying themselves" than have our Hong Kong subjects. My conjecture is that romancing between two lovers is probably more academic for Taiwan students than for Hong Kong students. It represents something that they would like to do but that most of them have found it impractical to do. This is shown by the fact that of the four Taiwan responses in this category, three are extremely brief and almost noncommittal. The following one is typical:

> This is the season when the flowers are in full bloom. The still surface of the lake reflects the blue sky. A pair of lovers row a boat to the edge of the lake. For certain reasons they both went ashore to take a walk. That is why the boat is left there by itself.

The only one in this group which is longer is a highly impersonal projection. It goes as follows:

> It has been raining for several months. There is no place on earth which is free from water. Everywhere you look you find extensive white water.
> Adam and Eve are riding the ark. They floated everywhere. Weather later on became cleared up. The two of them floated with the ark which stranded on land. Not long after thick bushes and fruit trees grow up in the place where the boat is stranded. This is the Garden of Eden. They are living together happily.

The two Hong Kong responses in this category are by way of contrast much more detailed and intimate. One subject uses the first person singular in her narrative, ending with the sentence: "There, my love and I will spend many an enchanted afternoon, just relaxing and receiving the blessings of Nature, forgetting all the miseries and troubles of the world." The other subject describes two lovers having a "launch (*sic*) picnic down the small stream," "lying on the grass," "playing hide-and-siik (*sic*)," etc.

However, in spite of these differences, the Hong Kong associations to romance still have much in common with their Taiwan counterparts. For example, the Hong Kong association to elopement (12BG) is not a simple elopement as Americans would see it:

> Two people had just left this same boat few minutes ago. They are young man and young woman. They had left their home during the night. They were eloping. They were lovers. Their family prevented them from getting married. Now they running to a place where they could find freedom, then they could do what they wanted. But where was this 'place.' They were not certain. They only ran ahead, until they reached their destination.

American elopers will certainly have more definite ideas as to the location of this "place" where they can "find freedom" and "do what they wanted." The sense of lack of clear destination in this Hong Kong response is another indication of the reality of a norm against romantic love which still prevails generally in the culture. Its prevalence makes the lovers realize that loving each other and running away by themselves are not enough. There are literally forces bigger than both of them. On the other hand the sentiment expressed in this very Hong Kong response may also be connected with the external political and military reality under which the Colony exists today. In this regard another category of responses peculiar to Hong Kong and Taiwan (but absent in those of all other groups tested) seems to provide us with additional support. This consists of responses which have to do with Escape themes — 4(10%) among Taiwan responses[7] and 7(15%) among Hong Kong responses. One response in each of the two groups refers to some ancient event, the Taiwan subject mourning about ancient wars and devastation of human life, while the Hong Kong subject is reminded of a Utopia described by the ancient Chinese scholar T'ao Yuan-ming. The rest of the responses in both groups deal with the flight from danger, hiding from discovery, or avoidance of crowds. This is a theme that is uniformly absent in any other group tested. It certainly is not inappropriate to the psychology of inhabitants on crowded islands with economic uncertainty as well as political and military clouds hanging over them.

However, when the two groups of Chinese responses are compared with the Evanston responses, the contrast is startling. Another look at Table A-5 will show that for the Evanston students "two lovers enjoying themselves" not only forms 30% of the total responses but there is no danger of any sort entailed. There is neither parental opposition nor any question of social disapproval. The American associations to Death simply have nothing to do with romance. Furthermore, the American lovers regard their actions together with a lightheartedness unknown to their Eastern counterparts. To the Hong Kong or Taiwan students, romancing is an extremely serious life-and-death matter. For Evanston students, on the other hand, it may lead to relatively permanent bonds, but frequently it is merely a passing, though enriching, experience as the following Evanston response shows:

> The small boat remained where the two had left it months before. Neither of them would ever forget that lovely early Summer afternoon. They had met quite accidentally. He had just graduated from undergraduate technological school and was pondering his future in the quite isolated solace of the country. He wondered if he would be successful and happy; he wondered if he would really accomplish something or just be another expendable cog in a gigantic masterwork. He was completely absorbed in his own thoughts of himself when he practically stumbled over a young girl, quite attractive, who was obviously upset over something. She too had just finished another year at college and now she was being sent to Europe with her aunt to "broaden her culturally," and the very thought of it brought her near to the point of tears. She desperately wanted to stay near her home, her family and her friends, if only for the short span of the summer months. She was broken hearted and this was the situation when they met, two very unhappy people all wrapped up in themselves. After the awkward embarrassment of this unexpected discovery on the part of each had subsided, they began to walk, quickly at first, hesitantly, two strangers in a world

[7] In addition, one Escape response is found in the Taiwan group as an Alternative.

of quiet and beauty, and for the time being anyway, theirs. And then more and more honestly, it is easier sometimes to be honest with a stranger to a degree that would be impossible with your closest friend, they revealed themselves to each other. They talked. They laughed. They walked. They even found an old boat and they drifted down the creek together to the accompaniment of their secret desires. It was a wonderfully sweet outlook. The afternoon seemed to pass so quickly. They pulled the little boat up on the bank and exchanged farewells. They will probably never meet again. It was a rewarding experience that neither will ever forget.

An examination of the Death associations not connected with love among the three groups is interesting. The Taiwan students obviously have a greater preoccupation with death than the other two groups, but their Death is either caused by love or social pressure or accident — not by murder.[8] The Hong Kong students' Death is all by murder, linked directly or indirectly with romantic love, but not by any other cause. The Evanston students have the least desire to associate to Death. Their Death not only has no connection with romantic love but also tends to be without causation. Two of their four Death responses are attributed to accidents; the other two are uncaused. In one of the latter, the subject says that this picture (12BG) "was taken a few minutes before somebody was murdered." She then goes on to describe how the young victim, a male, was waylaid by a murderer behind the tree, strangled to death after he screamed, thrashed, and struggled. The murderer then buried his victim "in a shallow grave under the rowboat and slipped away, his footprints muffled by the grass." The subject then concludes her story thus:

> It looks like there is a lion or some other member of the cat family to the left and behind the tree which is crouching in the bushes. There are insects around which will dig underneath the ground and devour the body underneath the rowboat.

The other Death response from the Evanston group is a most ingenious construction of a senseless murder:

> The tree in the picture is not an ordinary one; the sap that coarsing through its limps has a strange poisen in its content. It also emits a wonderful smell, fragrant, wonderful, irressatible. people are drawn to this strange tree. In summer one always notices a picnic spread beneath its branches, a person reading, meditating. They come by foot from the neighboring town or by boat up the stream. However, the poisen in the bark will react only with a specific

[8] A single Taiwan response involving killing of an illegitimate child by two lovers "because they cannot marry" is considered capitulation to social pressure.

combination, the true at heart need never fear, even the weak and cowardly are safe, murderers have slept beneath its branches, sucked the fragrant twigs and roots without perishing. The mystery of the tree is a wonder to all, striking at seemingly good people, pillars of their local villages. Last year a handsome young fellow came with his book, rowed upstream in a old row boat, never was seen again alive. Several strollers noticed him earlier that day munching his lunch and engrossed in his book. His disappearance was connected with tree. In his hand was one of the roots of the fragrant tree. The area was shocked, he was such a well-liked fellow. Alas, why was he taken, what is the secret.

In other words, among the three groups, our Evanston students see the least connection between death and life's activities. In terms of the projected data as a whole and in terms of what we have seen of the Chinese and American ways of life presented in the main body of this book, I believe it is an inescapable conclusion that the Taiwan responses are commensurate with the Chinese culture and psychology and the Evanston responses with the American culture and psychology, while the Hong Kong responses represent some sort of intermediary state, a Chinese base with Western incursions.

C. In contrast to the Chinese and American groups, the four Indian groups present certain uniformities not touched upon in Watrous's analysis. Table A-6 shows the percentages of Indian subjects whose responses to 12BG are judged Enjoyment. The figures in it are examined to best advantage if compared with those in Table A-4. One glance will show that the percentage of Indian responses in the Enjoyment category is far smaller than that of either the Chinese or the American fantasies. The

TABLE A-6   Percentages of Indian Subjects Whose Responses to 12BG Are Judged "Enjoyment"

Nature of Response	Vidyasagar	Asutosh	Lady Irwin	Indo-American
Enjoyment	17 (26%)	11 (23%)	7 (21%)	6 (26%)
No. of persons involved:		PERCENTAGE OF ABOVE		
Alone	47%	64%	30%	50%
Two or more persons	30%	27%	57%	33%
Impersonal enjoyment	23%	9%	14%	17%

percentage is lowest in the Lady Irwin responses and highest in the Indo-American responses; but even the Indo-American responses in this category are only about half of the Chinese and about one quarter of the American responses.

In contrast to both the American and the Chinese, three out of four of the Hindu groups associate to Enjoyment Alone more than they do with Two or More Persons. In addition, as Table A-6 shows, there is a kind of Enjoyment response which is highly impersonal that the Indians give but that the Chinese and Americans do not give. Although according to one of Mrs. Watrous's tables (Table A-3), 26% of the Hong Kong and 15% of the Taiwan responses to Card 12BG contain no specific individuals, her basis consists of responses mostly found in my Noncommittal Description category. Some of the Taiwan and Hong Kong Enjoyment responses are also seemingly impersonal, but on closer examination they invariably turn out to have some reference to the person or persons in contrast to their Indian counterparts (four responses from the Vidyasagar group and one response each from the other three Indian groups). The following two examples will convey my meaning:

1. *Response by Vidyasagar Male:* It is a lovely garden and the scenery of the garden is very charming. Snow falling on the trees and grasses. A boat laying under a tree. The snow on the trees and the grasses means that the flowers blooms in beautifully manner and it also seen that snow falls from the trees on the grasses and boat.
2. *Response by Taiwan Male:* This is a beautiful place where hundreds of flowers bloom and cattle drop like snow flurries. A strem runs through the forest. The beautiful scenery is a sight that many people come to enjoy. There is a boat under the tree. To view the scenery from the boat by rowing the boat is a most delightful thing for the heart and the spirit.

Furthermore if we examine all of the Enjoyment responses of the Indian subjects we shall find that at least half of them have an impersonal quality that is absent in the Chinese Enjoyment responses. The following is one from a Vidyasagar male in poetic form which is found in the Two or More Person category in Table A-6.

There was a forest on the bank of a river.

The natural beauty of the forest looks how charming.

If when we go to the forest our mind will also fills up with the beauty of the forest.

And if we has a boat on the particular forest then we could able to fill the beauty of the forest and also we could think about how the natural beauty are!

By the boat we could able to see the hole of the forest and from the boat we could find how river and the forest are!

So the natural beauty are of undescrible.

If among us any one may be poet then his mind will fills up with the beauty of the nature.

The beauty is the undescrible.

Many part of our country describe about the Nature.

An English poet says that we could understand how the natural beauty are when we are in the forest means; returing from the forest we can distinguise the nature from unnatural things.

The Evanston responses contain no impersonal sentiment and only three of them fit the Noncommittal Description category. Two of these are second responses and only one is a first response among three alternatives.

A second peculiarity of the Indian responses to 12BG is the expression of Fear, Danger or Dysphoria in General, although the percentages of Indian responses in this category are not overwhelming. The Indian responses tend toward fear or danger, whereas the few Chinese cases tend toward milder dysphoria. For example, of the two Asutosh responses in this category, one centers upon ferocious animals ready to kill "any man" who "comes to such a place like this," while the other centers upon a girl thinking and being very sad to the point of "dropping tears" about how "she and Dick used to go out on their secret cruise in that boat." The second fantasy ends with the following sentence: " 'The fate of life' she thinks to herself and sighs." One of the three Lady Irwin responses in this category ends with the following sentiment: "The physical appearance is not charming but it looks dull. This photograph shows [as] if no one used to come to this place. It looks very lonely and dangerous as it shows." In contrast the two responses from Taiwan in this category are quite mild. In one the female subject, after describing the scene in noncommital fashion, concludes thus: "It seems that this little boat was used by someone and then discarded." The other subject speaks of 12BG as a forest after rain in one autumn day and ends with the following comment:

This is really a spot of a public park which is not usually discovered by most people. The pond is used for throwing fruit peels by the people who frequent the park, but this spot looks very dirty. It seems that it hasn't been swept for many months.

There are two other responses that border on Dysphoria but not impersonal in the Taiwan group. One concerns a man who rowed a boat which was blown by sudden wind and rain into "this wild island." He is poor and has gone to collect some firewood "so that he can get a fire to warm himself." The other one goes as follows:

> Once I went to the uninhabited place to hunt. I went past many high mountains and rivers. After walking a long way I discovered a small wooden boat in a swamp. I believe that someone has been there before. Probably he also liked the natural life of the primitive times. But I did not find him this time. I feel disappointed.

It is somewhat difficult to put these last two responses in the general Dysphoria category. The single response from the Hong Kong group which expresses general Dysphoria is one which describes the boat as belonging "to the villagers." "They have no pier to tie their boat to and they have to pull it on shore when it is not in use. The picture seems very lonely and deserted."

One of the most unusual themes in the Indian responses is Abandonment. In Table A-7 the designation of this category is Abandonment or Loss of Way. All the Indian responses in this category refer to Abandonment and one case each from Taiwan and Hong Kong refers to Loss of Way. The Taiwan response describes parents going to the woods with their children to escape the heat "during the hottest summer." But when they returned home they "forgot a child in the forest." "The child spent the night in the forest all by himself" is the ending of this response. The response from Hong Kong describes a boy of thirteen and his sister of eleven approaching "the densely forested area" in a boat "without their parents' notice." The boy, "in spite of his sister's opposition," took her into the forest to catch butterflies. The story ends thus:

> At the sight of the butterflies, the girl forgot all about her previous opposition and jumped with delight to help his brother to catch the butterflies. On and on they went, and until evening they were confronted with the problem "which is the way to go back?" With fear they did not know how to get out of the maze. The boat was there quietly and their parents were eager to have their children back.

It should be noted that in the Hong Kong response the children are at fault while the parents eagerly seek their return, but even in the Taiwan case the parents presumably also want their lost child back. In other

TABLE A-7   Other Responses of Indian, Chinese and American Subjects to 12BG, As Percentages of Total Number of Subjects or Responses

Nature of Response	Vidyasagar	Asutosh	Lady Irwin	Indo-American	Taiwan	Hong Kong	Evanston
Fear, Danger or Dysphoria in General	11%	4%	9%	None	5%	2%	None
Abandonment or Loss of Way	15%	11%	6%	4%	2.5%	2%	None
Noncommittal Description	21%	17%	12%	None	13%	20%	None
Death	11%	15%	30%	17%	23%	8%	10%
Lovers	1.5%	4%	9%	None	25%	10%	30%
Alternatives	1.5%	None	None	None	2.5%	8%	29%

a. Evanston students give three such responses, but all of them are alternative responses and therefore not represented here.

words, what is involved in these responses is Loss of Way or separation due to the *accidental* factor but not deliberate or purposeful abandonment. There are a total of seventeen Abandonment or Loss of Way responses from the four Indian groups, with Vidyasagar leading way ahead (10 responses), Asutosh (5 responses) second, Lady Irwin (2 responses) third, and Indo-American Society (1 response) fourth. Fourteen of these are clearly Abandonment while only four are Loss of Way or separation. Three of the latter four end with the return of the lost individual to the group from which he or she was separated earlier, but none of the Abandonment responses develops in this direction. A typical short response in this category is one from a Vidyasagar male, as follows:

> The picture, it appears that it is a garden with a big tree and its side a boat. In the boat a baby is sleeping. The parents of the baby left him in the garden. But the big tree saves the child from the sun rays and rain. The parents of the child had no sympathy and kindness to the child.

A typical longer response is from an Asutosh female, as follows:

> There stands a very large tree. Throughout the ages he has faced events of various kinds, today he is old. He is the protector of all men, animals, birds. The traveller tired of the sun comes and takes rest under his shade. The birds have made their nests in his leaves. They consider that tree as safe shelter. A mother has left her child in that pan. The wailing of the child is piercing his [her] breast. It appears to him that the child's mother has left the child perhaps in great sorrow, great suffering. The same pain which is in mother's breast has also arisen in the mind of the tree by seeing the motherless child.

The expressions "the tree saves the child from the sun rays and rain" and "the same pain which is in mother's breast has also arisen in the mind of the tree by seeing the motherless child" are what Watrous scores as Mutability in her part of the interpretation. They occur often throughout the Indian responses classified under diverse categories but are especially common here. The causes of Abandonment range from unknown ones (as in the second response just given), lack of parental sympathy (as in the first response just given), to fate. A good example of fate as cause for Abandonment is the following given by an Indo-American Society male:

> This picture reminds me of the birth of a very famous poet of Tamil land, namely OVVAIYAR. She was the daughter of a famous sage, and her mother gave birth to her, while she and her husband were travelling through a dense forest. The mother, with her feminine mind, naturally wanted to take the child home. But the sage, who foresaw things, did not approve to it. He said that, the child was going to become a famous poet and moral instructor in the future, and

in spite of the wishes of the mother, left the child in an open basket to float away and reach the hands of a Brahman, who had no child. That Brahman found much spiritual awe in the baby and nursed her. When she became mature, she was forced to marry, but she did not. She, by the grace of the Almighty changed herself to an old woman and began to preach truth and piety. She, however, did not find any new religion.

This power of fate is also apparent in an Asutosh female's response in which a "young couple" was advised by "a Prophet" that "they would have a child which would turn out to be a thief . . . " After the birth of their son "one night they took him in a box and left the child in a forest like place." The child was cared for by some woodcutters and became a big man. But "it so happened that as one day he was going to cut wood he lost his way and he met a gang of robbers who forced him to join their group. Thus he became one of them." Our subject then goes on in the rest of the response to expound on how we have to "bow down to fate."

More than half of the responses in this category from Vidyasagar have adults (or at least grown youngsters) as the abandoned or separated. The following is a good example.

> These is a Tale of a Fisherman.
> Once some fisherman went out for catch fish in a river. They were full of instrument for catch fish. But one of them separate from their companions. He is very thinking. He reach alone in a lonely place of the forest. But he also find that a small river flows behind the dark lonely forest. And he sees a boat beside the jungle. He glad or cheerful to see boat also. But he is unable to go to the boat. He is something fears also.

One of the two responses from Lady Irwin classified in this category might not have been so classified but for the presence in Indian responses of the theme of Abandonment and for the frequency with which plants and other inanimate things are given human or animate attributes. This is a fantasy to 12BG about Abandonment of things:

> Once upon a time the boat which was like a gift to the family who stayed near the forest is now a rotting boat. This is the way one's life is in this world. The things that are near and dear to you vanishes as the days pass by.
> Once upon a time the family was living happily near a forest by the river side. They earned their living by rowing the boat from one side to another or by joy rides. The days past by. They earned quite a lot of money and decided to settle elsewhere. Thus they migrated leaving most of their belongings like the boat and a few extra things. They went with an idea that they would manage with the

money they had. They little knew what was in store for them. Time went by. They little realized that the little things they left behind would give them all that they wanted. The boat was let loose. This boat with no direction found its way into a marshy place where trees and plants were. Thus a thing which was useful has been wasted.

On the other hand the family realised the financial problems and learnt that with little things what people could do.

The gloomy and tragic nature of this fantasy has an obvious affinity with the following response from a Vidyasagar male showing distinct ambivalence toward the scenery in 12BG.

In the deep forest the trees are full of froots and flowers. There is a lake and on the lake there is a boat. But in this deep forest there are no living person. Then I reached at this place and I found the picture. It is so silent that I can not explane. When I reached there I get fear because I am the person who live in the localaty. Although I am afraid but the picture is so beautiful to me that I can not forget it. When a poet sees it once then he must not forget it. I am not a poet minded but I can not forget the seenery.

The importance of responses indicating Abandonment or Loss of Way from the Indian groups is reinforced by the fantasies dealing with Death. Quantitatively all of the Indian groups associate to Death more frequently than do the Hong Kong and Evanston groups. The Lady Irwin group exceeds even Taiwan in this respect. But it is the qualitative picture which truly distinguishes the Indian responses from the non-Indian responses. Table A-8 demonstrates this very well. Of a total of 28 associations to Death only one is caused by "murder" (Indo-American) and one by "suicide" (Lady Irwin). The outstanding cause of Death among the Indian responses is Loss of Way in jungle and/or Eaten by Wild Animals; this and Shipwreck are grouped together and considered of similar psychological significance because they all express a highly fluid relationship between the individual (or a group of individuals) and his (or their) unknown and unfamiliar environment which is full of threat, uncertainty, and death. Furthermore even the only Hindu association to Suicide, as we shall see below, signifies the same thing. For this reason the following War association from an Indo-American male is included in this group:

It was so quiet in the meadow. That was what struck the man first — the silence. After the thunder of the guns and the screams of the dying men and horses the meadow seemed a veritable haven of silence. True, a bird carolled from the large tree standing in the meadow and the stream chuckled its way

TABLE A-8   Activities and Causes in "Death" Associations to 12BG Among Hindus, Chinese and Americans

Death Associations	Vidyasagar	Asutosh	Lady Irwin	Indo-American	Taiwan	Hong Kong	Evanston
Activities Connected with Death							
Unspecified	2	3ᵃ	1		2		
Attachment to boat			1				
Love of dog			1				
Attempt to be like nature			1				
Work to support self		1	1				
Adventure (hunting, butterfly catching, exploring, fishing, enjoying self, hunting treasure, etc.	1			1	2		3
Play (children)	1	2					1
Robber gang	1						
Friendship			1				
Love		1	1		5	4	
Support for family			1				
Bringing aid to mother			1				
Revenge for parents				1			

Roaming alone	1				
Traveling (also sailor on tour)	1	1^b	1		
Summer resort			1		
Causes of Death					
Loss of way	1	5	1		
Eaten by wild animals	2				
Loss of way and eaten by wild animals	3				
Shipwreck	1				
Shipwreck and eaten by wild animals	1		1		
War			1		
Illness		1	1		
Accident		1	2		2
Murder			1	4	2
Infanticide			1		
Old age	1		1		
Suicide		1	2		
Unknown	1	2	1		

a. One response involves a family lost together.
b. "The family members of him were come to search him thy found him died over there and they make his grave over there and come back."

past, but what did this matter, it was peace. It was peace to the man lying at the foot of the tree with his hands clasped tightly over his body.

The old boat which nudged the bank of the stream gently brought back memories to the man. Memories of a childhood spent running barefoot through the woods, of fishing in the stream near his home. Memories of him growing up, going through school and then the most searing memory of all when his father and mother died a result of an enemy shell fired early in this war — this senseless war. He had entered the army for a good reason — revenge. He lay on the turf for a good reason — he was sorely wounded — dying.

But as he lay there he felt no fear and no anger in fact no pain. The peace of the scene had entered into his very soul and when the soul is at peace so is the body. He looked up through the interlaced branches of the tree at the blue sky, he looked down at the stream wending its never ending way and at the trees, at the grass, at everything around it. He heard faintly what sounded like singing — it was a bird chirping in the tree. He felt at peace with the world. He knew that he was dying but there was no regret only a great sense of joy, that he could leave the world at such a beautiful place. And then he was at peace at last.

The similarity between the psychological elements in this battlefield and those inherent in Loss of Way or Shipwreck is obvious. In both, danger and threat are part of an external environment in which the only certainty is that of death.

Among Indian Death associations Unknown Causes are also considerable. Among the non-Indian groups only one Taiwan response fails to give the cause of death, but among the Indian groups four fall into this pattern. Unknown Causes may signify the desire to be noncommittal, but in view of the dominance of Abandonment, Loss of Way, Shipwreck, and Being Eaten by Wild Animals in Indian fantasies, it seems at least arguable that Unknown Causes, too, may be related to the Hindu's diffused outlook and human relationships in which uncertainty outweighs certainty.

The types of activities involved in the Indian associations to Death, as compared with their Chinese and American counterparts, also bear out this conclusion. Of a total of 28 Indian Death associations, only two involve a romantic relationship; two, friendship among men (in one, the friends are a band of robbers); one, love of a boy for his dog; and three, family relationships, making a total of eight. The remaining eighteen involve all sorts of casual relationships from "attachment to boat" and "roaming alone," to "traveling" and various kinds of specified or unspecified adventures. Several points are immediately clear. First, Chinese fantasies of Death are most closely associated with love between a man and a woman; American fantasies of Death are most closely associated with play or adventure activities; and Hindu fantasies of Death are associated with a wide range of activities. If we take Death fantasies as signifying some severe problem and an extreme mode of its solution, then we must see that for the Chinese love of a man and woman is the central problem here, for the Americans individual enjoyments are the central problem here, while for the Hindus many different activities constitute the problem here and therefore the problem is diffused. These differences are of particular interest in connection with Card 12BG which provides stimuli primarily from "nature" and only secondarily "human." It is probable that "nature" evokes in the Hindu minds more human problems of a severe kind than it does either in Chinese or American minds. The Americans do associate Death to nature, but their associations have to do with light-hearted and playful self-enjoyment; and the Chinese also associate Death to nature but their associations are concentrated in close human bondage inherent in love between the sexes and social pressure against deviation. Only the Hindus seem to see a deep intermingling between, or make constant attempts to integrate, eternity and nature and human beings, thus reducing the importance of ties among men. Even the two Indian responses involving "love" between a man and a woman illustrate this observation well. In both of them death comes to the lovers without any reason whatever. It just comes. In one response (from an Asutosh girl) the two lovers, after sitting "in the boat and boating" every evening being happy and full of songs, with "animals like deer and birds coming to them, simply did not return one night." The subject goes on as follows:

> But, what happen then? One day, deer was waiting to hear the song. Birds were ready to fly, but no song was heard. They waited till night, but no sign of their coming. Boat was also there waiting for their arrival but they did not arrive. They all waited for two days and they found them there but dead and they were buried there. How can birds enjoy now? How can deer stay in that place where he was always getting enjoyment? They went away from there. Trees could not do anything but shade away their leaves. Oh! That boat! It was still waiting there. Nature a while is sad and will never be happy anywhere. Nature shows its sign of sorrow and regret for two young lovers.

The response describes how the lovers feel as much as it deals with how the animals and the plants and the boat feel. In the other response (from a Lady Irwin girl) the fantasy begins with Snow White who lives in a "little, cosy village." She is all alone and hates the arrival of Spring every year. She goes out for a change after her work. She is sad when she sees her little boat on the river all empty, "specially when the trees were full of blossoms and water was shining and how nice the body looked if only she had someone to go boating." The subject's fantasy develops as follows:

> Well, all days are not the same. Snow White would also meet someone young and handsome to add joy to her life. One day she did. As she was rowing the boat a stranger asked her to carry him to the other side. This happened every day and they could not stay without each other any more. She came and waited near the boat every day for him and he did always come. But one day he did not. No one knew where he had disappeared to. She cried for him but it was all in vain. But one day a light approached her. She found a young man who asked her to accompany him. He took her to heaven where they both stayed happily. The Spring came every year and found the village very quite without Snow White. The boat still lay there empty. All the charms had left with Snow White.

The final sentences of this response essentially express the same sentiments as does the last half of the first response except that the interrupted love continues in the world of the gods.

By way of contrast, the Chinese responses linking love and death are preoccupied with the lovers' attachment to each other or other people's reaction to them, no human sentiments being attributed to the natural surroundings at all. Even when supernatural overtones are injected into the response, as they are by one Hong Kong female, she dwells on the fears of the living for the "ghosts" of the dead lovers, "since people who meet a violent death haunt the place where they had died."

The widest spread of activities associated with Death is given by the Lady Irwin girls. From this group we have two strongly family-connected responses and one weakly family-connected response, to one from the Indo-American group and none from the other two Indian groups, in addition to one "love" response already discussed above. The two strongly family-connected responses are (1) a girl goes into the woods with a lamp to bring her mother back but she falls into the river and dies, and (2) a poor man, already overburdened with work in support of his family of wife and two little children, injures himself in a flooded river and cannot find his boat in the dark and therefore is drowned. The one weakly family-connected response from a Lady Irwin subject mentions "family members" who bury him in the jungle where he lost his way and died.[9]

[9] The only other references to the family in Death responses are one from the Asutosh group in which "some family" loses its way and dies of starvation and thirst, and one from the Indo-American group in which a son joins the war to revenge the death of his parents in the hands of the enemy.

However, the Lady Irwin group balances itself at the other end of the Hindu scale by non-family-connected activities in association with death. One of these concerns a boy's love of a dog and a second concerns a man who works to support himself. But a third one deals with a girl named Petty. The response begins by stating that "she lived in a hut with her mother near a forest." According to this statement this response should have been classified as one involving family life but as it develops, the family element is completely taken out of the picture by the subject. The response continues with . . . "Petty was a very brave girl and used to go into the forest every·day:" The rest of the fantasy follows.

> One day as she was wandering about she came to a place where the scenery was very beautiful. She discovered a small lake with a small wooden boat in it. She was very happy to find it and danced out of joy. She wondered how that boat came there. She thought the fairies might have left it for her, as she was so fond of all these things.
> Petty used to go there every day and enjoy the fun. One day she fell ill and dreamt that the fairies were carrying her to the fairyland, there she saw many beautiful things, but she cried bitterly, because she could not find her boat there. The fairies said that if she would remember that boat, they will never send her to land. So nobody saw that little girl again in the forest. But voices seemed to be coming from that boat — "Petty, Petty, where are you?"

The response which wrestles hardest with the totality of the problem of integrating man and nature begins by extolling the beauty and wonder of nature and then speaks of a man named Gopal "who was born in the surrounding of nature that is in Kashmir . . . in Kashmir he saw the beauty of nature and became interested in that only." Then:

> During early childhood he appreciated the nature but as he started doing advanced studies he became more and more confused, because it is very difficult to study the complexity of nature.
> Natural beauty can be seen and appreciated but can not be studied. Same proved true in his life also. He became so interested in colourful things that he forgot to see the realities in human life. He be imaginary. A man can never live in the world of dreams. He wanted to create something like nature but failed.
> As he grew older responsibilities of life also came with existence, but he never developed the power of realistic thinking so he tried to get out of that but it was difficult. He was depressed because of nature and ultimately he committed suicide by sailing a boat and while his boat was in the middle, he jumped into the valley and finished his life in nature only.

The rarity of Love in association with Death in Indian responses (as contrasted to its frequency in Chinese responses) seems to suggest that

Love in Indian fantasies has a significance similar to that it has in American fantasies, namely it is of great importance but divorced from Death associations. Actually this is far from being the case. A brief look at Table A-7 shows that, in general, the Hindus associate to Love far less than do the Chinese and the Americans. Only one Vidyasagar response to 12BG concerns Love, which turns out to be a sort of retelling of the famous Indian story of Sakuntala. There are two responses concerning Love in the Asutosh group and three in the Lady Irwin group but none in the Indo-American group. The inescapable conclusion seems to be that the Indians associate to Love least and almost casually, that the Chinese associate to Love considerably more but with trepidation, whereas the Americans associate to Love most and with a sense of boundless enjoyment. The extent and the pattern of association to Love among the three peoples fit well with our data presented in the last column of Table A-7. This column shows the percentages of subjects giving alternative responses to 12BG with reference to the total number of subjects in each of our seven student groups. The Indian subjects give practically no alternative fantasies to 12BG. The more westernized Hong Kong subjects have produced more alternatives than the less westernized Taiwan subjects. The Evanston subjects lead the field, leaving the others far behind. If love between a man and a woman carries the meaning of spontaneity and choice on the part of the individual, then it has very little room in the Hindu world as it is embodied in the Hindu social organization and the Hindu ideal. Alternatives are rare because all existences are preordained by a power that is higher than all and from which there is no escape. Love between a man and a woman as well as the spontaneity and choice which go with it are also out of line with the Chinese way of life as embodied in the Chinese social organization and Chinese ideal. But since their obstacles are human beings who occupy positions of authority within the well-defined limits of the kinship group, there is some room for maneuver. However, being firmly rooted in that group, the Chinese will find attempts to alter the *status quo* painful all around, for their conflict cannot easily be solved by emergence from, or rejection of, the elders. The Chinese world has nurtured in them a continuity and inclusiveness of outlook so that they are likely to be too involved in their elders to relish clear-cut victories over them. This is why the Chinese associations to Love are so intimately connected with their associations to Death. Love between a man and a woman as well as the spontaneity and choice which go with it are for the Americans nearly the be-all and the end-all for the solution of all problems of man, nature and God. This is why Love associations are all Enjoyment and no Death. It is interesting that the only two Evanston responses which mention God are both Love fantasies.

   D.   Some general statements about the responses to 12BG are in order. First, it is obvious that the Evanston students react to 12BG with an overwhelming feeling of Enjoyment in company of other individuals, especially persons of the opposite sex or peers. The Indians on the other hand react to the same stimulus with the least feeling of Enjoyment, tending heavily to be alone and especially to assume the impersonal point of view. The Chinese fall between the two extremes, both with reference to Enjoyment and with reference to the ratio between Enjoyment by Self to Enjoyment with Two or More Others.

   Second, the Hindus as a whole react to 12BG with more negative feelings such as Fear, Abandonment, or Death than do both the Chinese and especially the Americans. The high Taiwan association to Death (which may be related to the peculiar political and military environment of that island) is balaced by the very low Hong Kong association to Death. The importance of Dysphoria, Abandonment and Death in the Hindu responses is further augmented by the fact that an overwhelming majority of the causes of death in Indian Death associations are found in the general category of Loss of Way, Shipwreck and Being Eaten by Wild Animals, responses which indicate highly uncertain or hostile relationships with the external environment.

   Third, the Indian responses to 12BG as a whole suggest the extreme insignificance of the individual vis-à-vis the forces inhabiting the external world. This contrasts sharply with the American responses in which the individual's wishes are paramount. The Chinese responses again fall in between these two extremes. This gradation is particularly evidenced by the insignificance of Love responses among the Indians, the greater importance of Love responses among the Chinese and the even more pronounced importance of such responses among the Americans.

   Watrous proposes in her interpretation (Section III) that the Chinese are more self-accepting than the Americans. This view is largely based on the fact that the Chinese more than the Americans can enjoy themselves without involving peer groups. The reader may receive the impression that the Indians are even more self-accepting than the Chinese since they seem to have even less need for peer involvement. This is not, however, a correct inference. A clearer view of this point will emerge if we turn now briefly to the responses of all three cultural groups to TAT Card 1.

All three conclusions which emerge from the responses to Card 12BG find support through a preliminary examination of the reactions of our subjects to Card 1. A more detailed analysis of these responses will be included in a later publication, so this Annex may not be too bulky and become the tail that wags the dog. But some impressions can be reported here. Among the responses to Card 1, the Evanston students see in the picture principally a problem of resisting parents (with the accent on resisting rather than not resisting) and finding the self through hard work and peer activities; the Hong Kong and Taiwan students see in it principally a matter of following the wishes of the father or mother or both or an older sibling (with resistance to them in a minority of instances) and finding success in hard work and in assistance from persons of superior accomplishments or wisdom; while the Indian students see in it principally meditation by the self, sometimes fantasying success (with least involvement with family members either as particular objects of resistance or of compliance) and of more sadness than enjoyment.

Most of these points can be gleaned from Table A-2 above, in Watrous's section of the analysis. According to that table the fantasies of the two least westernized Indian groups (Vidyasagar and Asutosh) show higher percentages of Reverie and lower percentages of Achievement Imagery than any other group; the Americans show higher percentages of Achievement Imagery and lower percentages of Reverie than all except the two westernized Indian groups (Lady Irwin and Indo-American); while the Hong Kong and Taiwan Chinese fall near the center of the spectrum. With reference to Resistance, the picture is perfectly clear, the Americans falling at one extreme and the Indians at the other extreme, with the Chinese in the middle.

However, two relatively more westernized Indian groups (Lady Irwin and Indo-American) do present us with some seeming difficulties. Contrary to the general observations just made, the Lady Irwin and Indo-American fantasies are higher in Achievement Imagery and lower in Reverie than all other groups of Indian and non-Indian fantasies. Then, in spite of the fact that according to Table A-2, all Indian responses to Card 1 are lower in Resistance, the Lady Irwin and Indo-American groups come very close to the Chinese groups (26% and 27%, versus 37% for Taiwan and 30% for Hong Kong). Even the very traditional Vidyasagar students register numerous Resistance respones (19%). Is there an explanation?

I suggest that there is, and that to find this explanation we must analyze the contents of the Resistance responses. The lower percentage of Resistance responses among all the non-American groups than among the American group may partly be due to the fact that non-Americans do not happen to share what Henry regards as "a current middle-class American value which has become a frequent source of conflict between parents and children" (Henry 1956) (as Watrous noted in her interpretation). But an analysis of the contents of all responses classified in Table A-2 in the Resistance category shows that the psychocultural differences run far deeper. The Evanston Resistance responses are true to our understood American form, namely, plain conflict between specific parental pressure or injuction and rebellion on the part of the child against it. To be sure, there are a number of Resistance responses from the Chinese groups and at least two from the Indian groups which would be difficult to separate from typical American responses. But many of the Chinese and most of the Indian Resistance responses deviate from this form. A majority of the Chinese Resistance responses from Hong Kong conceive the child's problem as due to conflict with his father or mother (often both) in the American form, but a majority from Taiwan see the problem of the child in terms of the adverse circumstances of the family group as a whole. The following two examples illustrate the two Chinese forms:

1. A boy about 10 is forced by his mother to learn the playing of violin. Everytime when he practices, he shows great reluctance. One day, being alone in the room, he is tired of the practice. Having laid the violin on the table, the boy sits down in front of the instrument, looking at it, with his chin in his hands and fingers pressing his temples. There he is thinking about the past famous violin players — why they could play so beautifully and were applaused by generations and their work was thought to be ever-lasting? Why now he has to be scolded and forced to do the same thing. Is it so important to him as to the other musicians? He thinks how delightful he will be if he can have games in the open air with their joyful friends. (Hong Kong.)

2. In a certain place there is a child. He has shown a great inclination toward music ever since he was very little. Especially he is interested in the violin, but his family is very poor. It has no ability to support him to learn the violin. In fact the family cannot even have money enough to buy him a violin. That is why the child feels extremely sad, but Heaven never disappoints a man who is really determined. That is why one day there was a wealthy man who gave him a violin. He feels very happy, but he at the same time is faced with another big problem. He realizes that his talents are limited. At the same time there was no one to instruct him in the art. That is why he is very sad, but eventually he still becomes a very famous violinist. (Taiwan.)

The Hong Kong pattern reminds us, of course, of what was observed earlier: that our Hong Kong students appear to have been more western-ized than our Taiwan subjects; but the Taiwan pattern is understandable in a way of life where the kinship principle of social organization predominates over others. There the ties of birth and marriage are expected to continue indefinitely. In such a culture the individual tends to see his problems as problems of his family group rather than of his own, and their solution cannot, therefore, be his emergence from that group. In other words he is likely to identify his own problems with problems of his family or some extended group.

A majority of the Indian Resistance responses share one characteristic: the boy's problem is that he wants to play the musical instrument (or do something else if the violin is ignored by the subject), but his father or mother (or both or some other family member) do not allow him to do it. This is especially true of Lady Irwin and Indo-American responses among which Resistance, as we noted earlier, is high. The following example is typical of Lady Irwin Resistance responses:

> There was a small boy who loved to play on violin, but his parents did not like this thing so every time he would start to play on it, the mother would come and say stop this nonsense. The father used to say — that this boy is good for nothing. He not at all interested in his studies. What is use of becoming a violinist.
>
> But it was rather difficult to change the boy. Every time he learnt a new tune, or heard a new song, he would practice it on his violin. So one day the father got very angry and turned the boy out of the house. The boy took his violin with him. He was not anxious to meet new adventures in his life. On his way he had many difficulties, roaming here and there. But he did not care for hail or storm — the boy had one aim — he wanted to learn to play more efficiently on violin. Finally on his way he met a group of musicians. They were enjoying a picnic. The boy sat nearby and started playing on his violin. The leader of the group was impressed by his skill. He took the boy with him. There for several years he learnt his skill, and finally became a famous violinist.

Indo-American's Resistance responses are somewhat more varied in content but the Lady Irwin type of response does occur and the father or mother is nevertheless the impediment, as the following response shows:

> There are times in life when every person, of every age, whether man, woman or child, comes across moments of conflict, especially when some decision has to be made. This was one such moment for Thomas. He was ten years old, and the time had come for him to decide what he would do. He was to chose between

becoming a violinist, what his father, a celebrated violinist wanted him to become, or start learning the trumpet, an instrument for which he had a certain fascination. But, there was just one hitch, and that was, that his father, though a celebrated violinist was not so successful in keeping the coffers full, a financial flop, he was unable to pay for the course his son wanted to take, but would easily be able to teach him the violin himself.

Tom sat there looking at the violin. It was an old one of his father's. He picked it up and ran his fingers over the strings, yet undecided because he could not understand why his father was unable to pay for his trumpet lessons.

At last he got up, dusk had fallen long since and as he passed his window, he could see the stars winking at him from there. That did it. He ran out of his room and down the stairs. The stars were twinkling now and would so henceforth too and he would grow up and learn to play the trumpet when he can earn for himself.

Only two responses in the Vidyasagar group are judged Resistant in nature. One of them is given below:

Here is a boy looking over a violine. The violine is an instrument of music but the boy does not know how to handle it. He is thinking, that from such a few strings, how it is possible to got a beautiful harmonic sound. His mind want to know that, who invented this music. Suddenly an idea comes to his mind. He thinks perhaps his father can help him. He wants to learn it clearly. But his father is now at office. He wants to know, what are the things inside it. But his eagerness will come to light, when father will return from house.

My view is that there is a basic difference between seeing the parent as the stipulator of a positive norm (such as studying the violin) and seeing the elder merely as an impediment to a positive goal desired by the child. In the individual's process of growing up, his first experiences with parents are as agents of negative restraints and only later as sources of positive norms. The former are, therefore, more primitive and generalized because they come earlier and they are less specific than the latter.

My major conclusion concerning the Hindu world throughout the book is built on the looseness of the kinship bond, the diluted condition of all human relationships (necessitating caste as a compensatory device against this uncertainty among men) and a diffused world orientation on the part of the individual regulated more by impediment than by suppression or repression. I further postulated that this particular type of orientation is introduced and reinforced in each generation through the greater predominance of the mother-son axis in the nuclear family over the father-son and husband-wife axes. The Indian responses provide us with no specific corroboration of the role of the mother-son axis (though Chinese and American responses are indicative, as we saw above, of the respective importance of the father-son axis in one way of life and husband-wife axis in the other). They do, however, by the fact that the parent figure is fantasied in Card 1 as restraining the child from specific goals rather than pressuring him toward them, strongly suggest relatively diffused interpersonal relationships more characteristic of that between mothers and their children which come earlier to the individual, that of that between fathers and their children, which usually come later. The mother-child relationship is more diffused than the father-child relationship not only because it tends to be established earlier, when the infant is less capable of motivating itself to specific goals, but also the very nature of the mother-child relationship is, as pointed out in Chapter III of the book, more diffused than other relationships.

This diffused outlook is probably at the root of why the Indo-American and Lady Irwin fantasies are so high in Achievement Imagery, not only in sharp contrast to those of the other two Indian groups but also exceeding all non-Indian groups. The characteristic of a diffused outlook is that it is more fluid, and therefore more liable to extremes, than one which is channeled in specific directions. The extreme opposites exhibited in the fantasies of Hindu students may not be unrelated to the fact that Lady Irwin and Indo-American students have been subjected to more Western influences. But such extreme opposites are far from rare in Hindu life; her extremely diverse schools of philosophy and widely contradictory religious beliefs and practices are but two pronounced examples.

From the same standpoint we can also better understand why Resistance responses in the Vidyasagar group (Table A-2) are so high (19%). The Vidyasagar responses that Watrous has classified under the category of Resistance would have been resistive in the context of the American culture but not in that of the Hindu world. The fact is that most of the Vidyasagar responses classified under Resistance are ones in which the boy is seen as being alone and sad vis-à-vis the instrument, either because it is broken or because of other difficulties. In the American cultural context where the nuclear family is close-knit and where, for the child, the hands of his parents are strong and ubiquitous such responses can indeed be legitimately regarded as indicative of Resistance. But in the Hindu cultural context, where neither the nuclear family nor the hands of the parents have comparable importance, such responses are not as reflective of Resistance as they are of the Aloneness. This observation is additionally corroborated (1) by the small number of Enjoyment responses and the preponderance of responses indicating Aloneness, Dysphoria, Abandonment and Loss of Way, etc., to Card 12BG (Tables A-6 and A-7); and (2) by the fact that extraordinarily few Vidyasagar responses to Card 1, in contrast to those of other Indian groups, contain any reference to interpersonal relationships at all (see Table A-2).

V. Concluding Observations (Watrous and Hsu)

In reviewing our separate analyses and interpretations contained in Sections III and IV of this Annex, we have been surprised at the extent to which the projective materials stimulated by two TAT cards turn out to be related to and corroborative of Hsu's hypothesis on the differences between the three worlds. And our surprise is all the greater in view of observations made by several students, among others Kaplan and Wallace, that the intragroup variability in personality seems to be very great and that intergroup differences tend to be much smaller, leading to the conclusion that there is less variability among cultures than was expected (Kaplan 1961:241). We believe that projective studies using the complete Rorschach or full complement of TAT cards may be an impediment rather than an advantage to our understanding of intergroup differences. These tests in full are designed to probe deeply into the psychic structure and content of single individuals which are much less shared by others than those day-to-day levels of personality, necessitated by the identity and role of individuals as participating members of a particular society, in conformity to the normative components of its culture.[10] Our suggestion is, tentative though it must remain, that the use of a few cards, such as TAT 1 and 12BG, may very well prove to be a much better aid to the student of man for understanding personality in its group perspective than its individual perspective. Besides the economy of time and energy, we suggest that this is a technique and approach well worth our consideration and experimentation on purely scientific groups.

Finally, it seems that the numerical count of categories selected for analysis may be considered a reliable index of personality differences only where striking variations in emotional approach occur, for example, the spontaneity of the Americans as contrasted with the diffidence of the

---

[10] After completing this writing, we find that a point similar to this has been made by Goldschmidt and Edgerton ("A Picture Technique for the Study of Values," *American Anthropologist*, Vol. 63 No. 1 (February 1961), pp. 28–29). However, Goldschmidt and Edgerton's remedies are very different from the procedure proposed here.

Indians of Vidyasagar College in response to Card 1; or the impressive resistance of the Northwestern students as contrasted with the low incidence of such projections among the Asutosh group. The feeling tone, which is necessarily subjective in interpretation, is frequently more revealing of at least the emotional trends in the fantasies than the quantitative data. The broader question here is the degree to which quantitative data can validly describe an entity as complex as the human personality. Possibly the answer lies in a more sensitive blending of the objective and the subjective in the interpretation of projective tests as an adjunct to studies in Psychological Anthropology.

BIBLIOGRAPHY

ABT, LAWRENCE AND LEOPOLD BELLAK. 1950. Projective Psychology. New York, Alfred A. Knopf.

BELLAK, LEOPOLD. 1954. The Thematic Apperception Test and the Children's Apperception Test in Clinical Use. New York, Grune and Stratton.

CAUDILL, WILLIAM AND GEORGE DEVOS. 1956. Achievement, Culture and Personality: The Case of the Japanese Americans. American Anthropologist 58:1102–1126.

GLADWIN, THOMAS AND S. B. SARASON. 1953. Truk: Man in Paradise. New York, Viking Fund Publications in Anthropology, No. 20.

HENRY, WILLIAM E. 1956. The Analysis of Fantasy. New York, John Wiley and Sons.

———. 1961. Projective Tests in Cross-Cultural Research. In Bert Kaplan (ed.), Studying Personality Cross-Culturally. Evanston, Row, Peterson and Company.

HSU, FRANCIS L. K., BLANCHE G. WATROUS, AND EDITH M. LORD. 1961. Culture Pattern and Adolescent Behavior. International Journal of Social Psychiatry VII (1): 33–53.

KAPLAN, BERT. 1954. A Study of Rorschach Responses in Four Cultures. Papers of the Peabody Museum of American Archaeology and Ethnology, Harvard University, 42, No. 2.

———. 1961. Cross-Cultural Use of Projective Techniques. In Francis L. K. Hsu (ed.), Psychological Anthropology. Homewood, Ill., Dorsey Press.

MCCLELLAND, DAVID C., J. W. ATKINSON, R. A. CLARK, AND E. L. LOWELL. 1953. The Achievement Motive. New York, Appleton-Century-Crofts.

MULLIGEN, G. D. 1957. Maori Adolescents in Rakan, a TAT Study. Publications in Psychology No. 9, Monographs on Maori Social Life and Personality No. 2. Wellington, New Zealand, Victoria University College.

Murray, Henry A. 1943. Thematic Apperception Test Manual. Cambridge, Mass., Harvard University Press.

Wallace, Anthony F. C. 1952. The Modal Personality Structure of the Tuscarora Indians as Revealed by the Rorschach Test. Bulletin, B.A.E., 150.

CHAPTER NINE

Mental Illness, Biology and Culture

Anthony F. C. Wallace

Introduction

Do different cultures encourage different styles of mental illness? Are there societies in which mental illness is absent, or at least rare in comparison with our own? Have either style or frequency of mental illness, or both, changed during the history of Western civilization? These and similar questions, prompted by practical concern with the mental health of our contemporary world populations, have evoked answers from anthropologists. *Yes,* different cultures do encourage different styles of mental illness, *but* the major categories of mental illness (the organic psychoses, the functional psychoses, the neuroses, the situational reactions, etc.) seem to be universal human afflictions. *No,* there are no societies of whom it can be said with confidence that mental illness is absent or, with certainty, that it is even rare, *but* there are certainly differences in the frequencies of illness and in the readiness of different social systems to recognize what Western psychiatry would call illness as significant disorder. *Yes,* styles and frequencies of various mental illnesses have changed in recent western history (hysteria, for instance, is now a relatively rare diagnosis, and devils and demons have been replaced by radio and radar in paranoid delusions), *but* we do not know all of the reasons for such changes over time nor for the differences between social classes and between regions.

Thus, the relation between culture and mental health remains an intriguing problem for anthropologists, a promising field for research, and perhaps some day a richly rewarding field for application. One of the avenues of research which has been under rapid construction outside of anthropology is biological in concept and method; and since this approach has been relatively unexploited by anthropologists, yet is potentially of great significance for anthropological theory, a considerable part of this chapter will be devoted to considering the ways in which the current cultural-anthropological work in this area can assimilate and exploit what may be regarded, in the context of anthropology, as a physical-anthropological position.

Certain Limitations of Conventional Anthropological Theories of Mental Illness

The culture and personality tradition in anthropology has borrowed its models of personality development, its characterology, and its conceptions of mental illness almost exclusively from a combination of learning, *Gestalt*, and psychoanalytic theories.[1] This is in part a historical accident: these functional approaches were developing most vigorously in American psychology and psychiatry just at the time, in the late 1920's and early 1930's, when cultural anthropologists were first turning their attention seriously to the individual. Anthropologists found these psychologies readily applicable to an understanding of the individual in culture; and the psychologists and psychoanalysts found in cross-cultural materials useful corroborative evidence for their theories. But the more recently developed biological approach, while it has not as yet (anymore than the functional approach) provided a spectrum of "cures" of such refractory disease clusters as schizophrenia and depression, has already yielded a considerable body of knowledge of processes (in this case, of organic

[1] In the last decade, two new schools of thought have become important in clinical psychology and to a lesser extent in psychiatry. The use of the principles of operant conditioning to eliminate unwanted behaviors and encourage desired ones has encouraged the point of view that mental illnesses may be defined as *ad hoc* constellations of learned responses; the symptoms *are* the illness and not motivated but superficial manifestations of a deeper structure. The tradition of Wilhelm Reich, emphasizing states of bodily tension, survives in the work of the Esalen Institute and related groups using T-group techniques and other procedures to release the individual's capacity to sense, to communicate, to feel, and to act. These approaches have not yet heavily influenced anthropology. The latter tradition may conceivably be relevant to the issues discussed in connection with the calcium hypothesis.

mechanisms) which are implicated in one or another type of psychopath-ology. This knowledge should be incorporated without delay, in general outline, into the conceptual armamentarium of every anthropologist concerned not only with mental disease but also with normal personality development and function.

At the present time, anthropological treatments of mental disease topics, particularly by culture and personality scholars, generally depend on a simple paradigm: the symptomatology of the illness under scrutiny is assumed to be motivated behavior expressive of psychological conflicts and to some degree effective in reducing tension and anxiety; the symptoms are "interpreted" in terms of some deductive schema intended to lay bare the (usually assumed to be unconscious) conflict; cultural *Anlagen* in the symptomatic behavior are pointed out; and finally, the source of the conflict is sought in traumatic emotional and/or cognitive dilemmas imposed by the victim's culture. This procedure almost completely neg-lects the victim's body; or, rather, it attributes to the victim's psyche a virtually magical ability to control the state of its body, by uncritically assuming that almost any somatic expression can be satisfactorily ex-plained merely by asserting a plausible concomitant intrapsychic conflict. Even the "psychosomatic" position, it must be emphasized, is not "organ-ic" in the sense indicated above, for it seeks the explanation of both somatic and behavioral disorder in antecedent psychological and cultural rather than in antecedent physiological conditions: thus the ulcer is explained by reference to the autonomic discharge attendant upon intrapsychic conflict, and the existence of intrapsychic conflict is explained by reference to culturally enjoined learning experiences rather than by any neurophysiological process.

Thus, even with regard to syndromes familiar to Western clinicians and conventionally (if not invariably) conceived as functional in etiology, the assumption that biological determinants are negligible is becoming an increasingly hazardous one to make. But the anthropologist is peculiarly vulnerable to criticism when he utilizes the functional paradigm without qualification to explain exotic forms of mental illness, such as the *pibloktoq* of the Polar Eskimo and the *windigo* psychosis of the northern Algonkian hunters. Here, in addition to the difficulties engendered by the fundamen-tal ambiguity of current psychiatric theory over the respective causal roles of psychological and organic factors in clinically familiar syndromes, there are (or ought to be) serious uncertainties introduced by recognition of the extreme climatic, epidemiological (in respect to infectious diseases), and nutritional conditions to which technologically primitive populations are at times exposed (see, for example, Tooth's discussion of the difficulty even psychiatrists experience, when using purely behavioral criteria, in making the differential diagnosis between schizophrenia and certain types of trypanosomiasis in West Africa) (Tooth, 1950).

This paper is not intended, however, as an admonition to anthropologists to abandon an obsolete dogma for the sake of embracing a new scientific faith. Rather, the necessity for incorporating a new viewpoint into an existing tradition is pointed out. That this incorporation will entail modification of some beliefs and procedures may be expected; but the new theoretical position should be a strong synthesis rather than a weak substitute.

The Organic Approach in Psychiatry

The year 1927 may be taken as the beginning of codification of the culture and personality position in anthropology, for in that year Sapir's pioneer paper, "The Unconscious Patterning of Behavior in Society," was published in a symposium on *The Unconscious* (Mandelbaum, 1949). Sapir's paper, probably the first major piece of theoretical writing in the culture and personality tradition, set, or at least prefigured, the frame of reference of later anthropological work in this area. This frame of reference was predominantly psychological rather than biological: it implied that the fundamental, and often unconscious, organizations of individual behavior which are conventionally labeled "personality" are molded, not by physical constitution, but by a combination of cultural milieu and individual experience. The correspondingly functional character of the conventional culture and personality view of mental disorder, as it developed in the next few years in the work of Sapir, Benedict, Mead, and others, can be readily explained by the absence of any substantial competing body of thought; for the biological approach in psychiatry did not even begin to make headway until after 1927.

The most impressive body of psychiatric theory in 1927 was psychoanalytic. This theory, although it gave lip service to biological thinking, and although its builders were well grounded in neurology, was in operation uncompromisingly psychological. Accordingly, the published case histories provided very little information concerning the physiological status of the patients. The analyst sometimes used physical metaphors (like "the economy of psychic energy"), invoked constitutional predispositions, and made assumptions about organically grounded instincts, erogenous body zones, and stages of sexual maturation. Freud, himself a neurologist of distinction, even asserted that behind the analyst stood the man with the syringe. But the psychoanalytic physiology, as it grew beyond Freud's control, was increasingly a pseudophysiology. The Biological man was for all practical purposes constant in the psychoanalytic equation, and "psychological" events (learnings, communications, fantasies, motives, defense mechanisms, etc.) were the variables.

Most of the currently prominent "organic" methods of treatment were developed after psychoanalysis reached its theoretical maturity. In 1927 psychiatry had little else to offer in treatment beyond psychological (including psychoanalytic) methods for the well-to-do and custodial care (eked out by sedatives, hydrotherapy, and work therapy) for the poor. The insulin coma treatment for schizophrenia was introduced about 1930 and metrazol convulsive therapy in 1936; electroshock was not developed until 1938 (and all of these treatments were first publicly described in Europe). Psycho-surgery was seriously developed in Portugal about 1935 and in this country in 1936. Psycho-pharmacology, hitherto a somewhat exotic specialty, began to flourish only during World War II. The use of hypnotic drugs for abreaction of emotional conflict in combat neuroses became prominent during the early years of the war; and the intensive study of the psychotomimetic drugs (principally hallucinogens) and their experimental use for therapeutic purposes has developed chiefly since World War II. The new tranquilizing (or "ataractic") drugs were first offered to the medical profession in 1952, and the energizers (or "psychostimulants") have come even later.

Basic science contributions, apart from psychoanalytic theory, were equally unpromising in 1927. Originally inspired by the discovery of the role of syphilis in paretic psychoses, early speculations about the role of focal infection in the etiology of the other psychoses were failing to find clinical confirmation. Berger's first report on the use of the electroencephalograph (EEG) for recording "brain waves" (electrical potentials originating in the cerebral cortex and in other parts of the brain as well) was not published in Germany until 1929; not until 1935 did American scientists publish confirmatory findings. Clinical chemistry had only in the preceding fifteen years developed the basic techniques for analysis of small samples of blood; prior to World War I, investigations of human metabolic processes had had to depend largely on studies of diet and urine, because the quantities of blood required for chemical analysis were so large as to prohibit their use as routine clinical procedures. The application of these new techniques of blood analysis to problems of psychiatric research, and the biochemical findings based on their use, came almost entirely after

1927. Thus, for instance, endocrinology was still in its infancy in 1927. The importance of the hormones of the adrenal cortex, which play a role in regulating the carbohydrate metabolism and the balance of mineral electrolytes in the body fluids, and which in excess can precipitate psychotic states, was not realized until the late 1920's. Research in that area was so slow in diffusing into other branches of knowledge that as late as 1944, in a widely read two-volume symposium entitled *Personality and the Behavior Disorders* (Hunt, 1944), the adrenal cortex is given one paragraph (and no mention in the index). Selye's first publication on the celebrated stress or general adaptation syndrome concept was first published in *Nature* in 1936 (*vide* Selye, 1956); and the "cortisone psychoses" did not even exist until cortisone was isolated, synthesized, and finally used in the treatment of arthritis about 1945. Franz Kallman's early report on his genetic studies of schizophrenia utilizing pairs of identical twins was published in 1938 (Kallman, 1938). The more modern theories of nerve impulse transmission emerged during and after World War II, some of them stimulated by investigations into the action of the so-called "nerve gases" by the Army Chemical Center.

But there is no reason to continue the demonstration farther. The major point is clear: a large part of the modern knowledge of the physiological parameters of the behavior of the central nervous system in man has been accumulated since the original conceptual structure of the culture and personality viewpoint was built by Sapir, Mead, and other pioneer scholars. Whole literatures, rivaling in size the entire body of culture and personality writings, now exist on such topics as the relation between the adrenal hormones and mental function, the localization of labor in the brain as revealed by electroencephalographic and derivative techniques, and the effects of drugs on mood and cognitive process. And the major portion of all of these fields of knowledge has been contributed well after culture and personality committed itself to a functional approach.

As yet, the various special lines of the new organic approach have not achieved synthesis either among themselves or with the (actually older) psychosocial tradition in psychiatry and the social sciences. Nevertheless, a general philosophy would seem to animate the approach and to determine the nature of any future synthesis with the functional position. This philosophy would seem to reside in four principles:

1. Statements about "behavior," "mind," "personality," "psyche," "mental illness," and other "psychological" entities are statements about physical systems which include brain (for the brain *is* the mind).

2. Any physical disfunction of brain implies some mental disfunction.
3. Some physical disfunctions will produce disorganizations of neural systems most of whose components will remain individually undamaged.
4. Most cases of chronic, and many of acute, behavior disorders (including the functional psychoses) are the symptomatic consequences of chronic, or acute, physical disfunctions of brain.

The reader will note that the organic approach, as thus stated, does not claim that every socially undesirable mental state, attitude, or motive necessarily implies a physical disfunction; thus, hostility, suicide, delusion, antisocial acting out, and so forth, may in principle be produced by brains which function perfectly well but have been subjected to environmental pressures (including faulty communication) to which these "symptoms" are "normal" responses. But the organic approach would differ from the functional approach in claiming that an adequately functioning brain will be able to adapt to, or reduce, environmental pressures, and that *chronic* mental disfunctions are therefore preponderantly the consequence of a chronic physical disfunction which existed prior to, or independently of, the organism's embarrassment by environmental pressures. A radical functional theory, by contrast, would ascribe a far smaller role to organic factors as causal agents in all except the gross and obvious types of organic brain damage; but most functionalists would probably concede that chronic psychogenic stress can on occasion elicit physiological alterations, sometimes irreversible, which aggravate functional mental disorders (just as chronic psychogenic stress can lead to non-mental organic disorders such as duodenal ulcer).

More specifically the organic approach can be divided into such main topical areas as:

1. The study of the anatomy and physiology of the central nervous system (including the autonomic system) considered as an entity.
2. The study of the localization and organization of labor in brain (including the logical structure of nerve nets).
3. The study of nerve and nerve impulse.
4. The study of the relation of metabolic (including digestive, excretory, circulatory, endocrine, and intracellular biochemical) processes to cerebral function.
5. The study of the genetics of mental disorders.
6. The study of the effect of hypoxia, hypoglycemia, and electrolyte imbalance on cerebral function and the various processes responsible for hypoxia, hypoglycemia, and electrolyte imbalance.

7. Psychopharmacology (including the study of tranquilizers, energizers, and psychotomimetic agents).
8. The study of the effect of nutritional variables on cerebral function.
9. The study of the shock therapies (principally insulin coma and electroshock).
10. The search for blood fractions containing suspected psycho-pathogenic concentrations of substances spontaneously produced by the body, particularly certain protein fractions.

The disciplines involved in these and other studies of psychopathology range from mathematical physics and computer design, through such laboratory sciences as physical chemistry, biochemistry, clinical chemistry, physiology, experimental psychology, and neuropsychiatry, to those areas of anthropology and sociology which can contribute data, method, or theory to organically oriented investigations.

A major problem in the organic approach has, of course, been its relative insularity from psychosocial knowledge (this has not been a problem of the functional approach alone). Accordingly a major need of both approaches is a better understanding of how knowledge and speculation concerning the physical aspects of human systems can best be related to knowledge and speculation concerning the psychological and social aspects of these systems. This is imperative because, although cases of mental illness are usually first identified in the community by laymen using social criteria rather than criteria of physical science, and although some part of the total disease process is invariably a function of social system interacting with individual personality, if the development of many of these cases is dependent on organic processes, then very careful analysis must be made of the interaction of social and organic events. And anthropology, by both theory and field investigation, can contribute significantly to the advancement of this kind of analysis.

An Illustrative Problem: Pibloktoq[2]

In its simplest form, the problem faced by anthropological theory in the

[2] The description of the *pibloktoq* syndrome is based on a compilation of published and manuscript descriptions, both specific and generalized, by a variety of observers, from the missionary Hans Egede in 1765 to about 1940. Seventeen photographs of a woman during a *pibloktoq* attack at Etah were taken by Donald MacMillan in June 1914; we were able to use copies of these from the original negatives on file in the Photographic Division of the American Museum of Natural History. I am indebted to Mr. Robert Ackerman, my collaborator in the *pibloktoq* study, who has collected many of the data and contributed heavily to their interpretation; to Dr. Zachary Gussow, who kindly permitted use of his unpublished manuscript on *pibloktoq;* and to Dr. Gilbert Ling, who reviewed the calcium hypothesis and contributed to its refinement.

area of mental illness can be illustrated by the syndrome *pibloktoq* among the Polar Eskimo of the Thule District of northern Greenland. The classic course of the syndrome, as judged from cases described by various travelers in the north (MacMillan, 1934; Peary, 1907; Rasmussen, 1915; Whitney, 1911) and from photographs of one attack (American Museum of Natural History, 1914), is as follows:

1. *Prodrome.* In some cases a period of hours or days is reported during which the victim seems to be mildly irritable or withdrawn.

2. *Excitement.* Suddenly, with little or no warning, the victim becomes wildly excited. He may tear off his clothing, break furniture, shout obscenely, throw objects, eat feces, or perform other irrational acts. Usually he finally leaves shelter and runs frantically onto tundra or ice pack, plunges into snowdrifts, climbs onto icebergs, and may actually place himself in considerable danger, from which pursuing persons usually rescue him, however. Excitement may persist for a few minutes up to about half an hour.

3. *Convulsions and Stupor.* The excitement is succeeded by convulsive seizures in at least some cases, by collapse, and finally by stuporous sleep or coma lasting for up to twelve hours.

4. *Recovery.* Following an attack, the victim behaves perfectly normally; there is amnesia for the experience. Some victims have repeated attacks; others are not known to have had more than one.

The epidemiological parameters seem to be:

1. *Geographical. Pibloktoq* (or, in Danish usage, *perdlerorpoq*) is known to occur among the Polar Eskimo of the Thule District. Whether the same syndrome (whatever it is called) occurs elsewhere is uncertain. Hoygaard, in a dietary and medical study of the Angmagssalik Eskimo in 1936–37, reported that *"Hysterical fits* accompanied by strong mental and physical excitation were frequent, especially in women" (Hoygaard, 1941:72). It does not seem to have been noted in the literature, however, among Candian or Alaskan Eskimo, nor is it certain that it occurs in Asia or northern Europe. Thus we can only say that it *certainly* occurs in northwest Greenland; that it *probably* occurs elsewhere in Greenland; and that it *may* occur anywhere in the world. Whether or not the syndrome is to be considered a uniquely arctic or even Polar Eskimo affliction depends on whether it is a unique disease.

2. *Seasonal.* Reports describe cases occurring at all seasons of the year but cases are said to be fewer in the summer.

3. *Historical.* As might be expected, since the Thule Eskimo were not

visited by white men until 1818, the case notes and descriptions are recent, the best of them dating from the time of Peary's visits to the Polar Eskimo in the first decade of the twentieth century. Detailed accounts have been provided by Peary (1907), MacMillan (1934), Knud and Niels Rasmussen (1915), and Gussow (1960), and others familiar with the Polar Eskimo. It is probable, however, that the disorder is fairly ancient in the area. As early as the mid-eighteenth century, northwest Greenlanders (possibly including the Polar Eskimo) were reported to be peculiarly subject to the "falling sickness." And in the 1850's the crew of Kane's icebound ship, twice wintering north of Thule, were afflicted by a strange "epileptotetanoidal disease" which, in combination with scurvy, killed at least two men, incapacitated others, and rendered their dogs worthless (Kane, 1956). "Epileptotetanoidal" is a reasonably accurate descriptive phrase for *pibloktoq*.

4. *Frequency. Pibloktoq* can apparently reach epidemic proportions: eight of seventeen Eskimo women associated with Peary's 1908 expedition were afflicted during one winter season; other observers have claimed that at certain times cases could be seen almost every day in a single village.

5. *Racial Nonspecificity.* As was noted above, several probable cases of *pibloktoq* among scorbutic whites were observed by Kane and Hayes in the 1850's in the same region.

6. *Possible Species Nonspecificity.* "Fits" among sled dogs, with social withdrawal, snarling, fighting, and convulsive seizures, but usually ending in death, are said to be regarded by Eskimo as the same syndrome and are given the same name, *pibloktoq,* as the human attacks.

The Hysteria Hypothesis.   The major psychological explanation of the *pibloktoq* syndrome has been psychoanalytic. In 1913 A. A. Brill, Freud's self-appointed American apostle, wrote a paper on the subject based on a reading of one of Peary's books and on personal discussion with Donald MacMillan, the naval officer who accompanied Peary (Brill, 1913). Brill considered the syndrome to be classic hysteria major. Following a somewhat simplified Freudian model, he interpreted the seizures as expressions of frustration at lack of love and cited as the type case a female who displayed particularly flamboyant attacks. This attractive young woman had not succeeded in getting a husband because she was a poor seamstress;

she was consequently frustrated in her emotional need for love in all but the most crudely physical sense. More recently, Gussow (1960) has extended Brill's formulation, interpreting the hysterical flight as a seductive maneuver, an "invitation to be pursued," in persons whose chronic insecurities have been mobilized by some precipitating loss or fear of loss, and who seek loving reassurance in a "primitive and infantile, but characteristically Eskimo, manner." Indeed, he feels that such reactions are a manifestation of the basic Eskimo personality. The greater frequency of *pibloktoq* in women he explains culturally as the result of "the socially subservient position of women . . . and their added helplessness in the face of culturally traumatic experiences." The nudity is in part explained by the common tendency of Eskimo to undress indoors and to chill the naked body out of doors after the sweat bath. The glossolalia, mimetic behavior, shouting, weeping, and singing sometimes observed he also explains culturally by pointing out that these behaviors are found in shamanistic performances and religious ceremonies, not only among the Eskimo, but also in Korea. The flight is considered to be a hysterically motivated invitation to be taken care of, rather than a component of an involuntary psychomotor seizure pattern, because no cases of flight have been reported in which the victim was not seen, followed, and rescued. The asserted tendency for *pibloktoq* to occur in winter is illuminated by the observation "that winter, more than other seasons, intensifies Eskimo insecurity — and hence their proneness to derangement — through increased threat of starvation, high rate of accidents, fear of the future, and so forth."

These psychoanalytic and psychocultural explanations, however, are for several reasons not entirely satisfying. Nudity, for instance, is indeed culturally prefigured, since it is the only adequate means of reducing body temperature in persons who have no clothes to wear other than heavy furs in poorly ventilated dwellings where the temperature may rise to over 100° F. But this suggests that the denudation may be merely a response to a sudden somatic sensation of extreme heat. The fact that most reported victims of hysterical flight were rescued from danger without injury may obviously be an artifact of observation: any victims who froze, drowned, lost themselves, were carried away on drifting ice, fell and died alone in the snow, and so on, would by definition be those who were not observed. Furthermore, in at least one case, a rescued woman *was* injured; she suffered a frozen hand and breast, a serious condition in the absence of European medical technology. Two of Kane's men died and the dogs often die. Glossolalia, singing, and so forth are hardly evidence for an influence of *Eskimo* culture on the form of this hysteria, since these behaviors are virtually pandemic. The evidences of extreme physiological stress (blood-shot eyes, flushing of face, foaming at mouth, convulsive movements) and the demented behavior (attempting to walk on the ceiling, eating of feces, and ineffectual destructiveness) are not prefigured in the culture. And finally, the Eskimo are not reported to explain these fits (in contrast to psychotic disorders) by supernatural theories of disease (such as possession, witchcraft, punishment for taboo violation, or soul loss) but seem to regard them as natural ailments experienced by dogs and men alike, comparable perhaps to the common cold, the broken limb, and other ills that the flesh is heir to. This phlegmatic response would not provide very much in the way of reward for a hysterical fit.

The Calcium Deficiency Hypothesis.   An alternative, and in part biological, hypothesis can be suggested which explains *pibloktoq* with at least equal plausibility. Low concentrations of ionized calcium in the blood (hypocalcemia) produce a neuromuscular syndrome known as tetany which is often complicated by emotional and cognitive disorganization. The neurological symptoms of tetany include characteristic muscular spasms of hands, feet, throat, face, and other musculature, and in severe attacks, major convulsive seizures. The tetanic syndrome may be precipitated by trivial stimuli and is usually brief and sporadic rather than continuous (continuous tetany may of course be fatal). Although the information available in the photographs and literature is not sufficient in itself to establish the diagnosis, the symptoms of *pibloktoq* are compatible with the clinical picture of hypocalcemic tetany, and several authorities have suggested the calcium deficiency hypothesis (Hoygaard, 1941:72; Baashuus-Jensen, 1935:344, 388; and Alexander Leighton in a personal communication). Observation and testing in the field would be required to confirm the hypocalcemic hypothesis and to rule out alternative diagnoses (hypoglycemic shock, hysteria, food poisoning, virus, encephalitis, etc.). It is also possible that a tendency toward epilepsy may have been genetically determined by inbreeding in this small isolated group; this is suggested by reports that epilepsy is more common in northern Greenland than elsewhere on the island. The hypocalcemia and epilepsy theories are not mutually exclusive, however, since hypocalcemia probably would tend to precipitate a latent seizure in persons prone to epilepsy. Observation and testing for differential diagnosis would require both the eliciting of neurological signs in victims during attack, or in persons with a history of attacks, and blood tests on victims and on samples of *pibloktoq*-prone and *pibloktoq*-free persons for serum calcium, serum potassium, magnesium, and possibly other constituents.[3]

The plausibility of the calcium deficiency hypothesis is supported not merely by the opinions of certain authorities and by the compatibility of the *pibloktoq* syndrome with the syndrome of hypocalcemic tetany, however. It is also suggested by indirect evidence, both medical and ecological.

Medically, the Eskimo of Greenland (including the Thule District) are characterized by a proneness to hemorrhage and slow coagulation (Hoygaard, 1941:83–85, and Cook, 1894:172). Such a tendency toward bleeding might conceivably be associated with low serum calcium levels (although vitamin K deficiency is more likely to lead to this condition). At Angmagssalik, convulsions in infants, suggestive of hypocalcemic tetany, were reported by Hoygaard to be frequent (Hoygaard, 1941:78, 135), and Bertelsen noted in a medical report on the Greenland Eskimo that there was a high frequency of cramps, especially of the legs, even in adults (Bertelsen, 1940:216). These observations are reminiscent of the account by Kane of the "strange epilepto-tetanoidal disease" which incapacitated his crew north of Smith Sound in the 1850's. He diagnosed two fatal cases of "tetanus" displaying laryngospasm (these could have been actually hypocalcemic tetany going into *status eclampticus*), two fatal cases of the "epilepto-tetanoidal disease," and numerous cases of cramps and muscular pains, sometimes accompanied by "mental symptoms" of disorientation and confusion, both in dogs and man (Kane, 1856).

Ecologically, it may without hesitation be stated that the high arctic environment does not provide rich sources of nutritionally available calcium during all seasons of the year to technologically primitive populations. Hoygaard found that nearly half of the annual calcium intake at Angmagssalik was provided by dried capelin (the bones of dried capelin being edible). When dried capelin was available, the calcium intake was low but above the level asserted by medical authorities to be the minimum for maintenance of health. But without dried capelin (a circumstance which periodically occurred as a result of unavailability of the fish or unsuitability of the weather for drying them), calcium intake dropped well below the minimum (Hoygaard, 1941). Rodahl also found

[3] A graduate student, Edward Foulks, M.D., of the writer's and of his colleague Sol Katz is spending the year 1969–1970 in Alaska in the hope of identifying cases of *pibloktoq* there and if possible determining their etiology. Calcium determinations are being made and other possible mechanisms will be investigated, including untreated *otitis media*, which is said to be rampant in the Alaskan Eskimo population (personal communication from Edward Foulks). *Otitis media* is known to be commonly associated with tetany; it also may, untreated, perforate the skull and produce brain abcesses and destruction of tissue in the temporal lobe.

the dietary of certain Alaskan Eskimo groups to be relatively low in calcium (Rodahl, 1957). At Thule, although no careful dietary studies have been found, it is reported that little fishing is done because fish are sparse and consequently capelin is not caught in substantial quantity. Probably substituting for dried capelin, however, are birds — the "little auks" — which, after storage in seal oil, can be eaten whole, including, apparently, some of the bones (MacMillan, 1918). A further ecological complication may be a product of the high latitude itself. Man requires a certain quantity of vitamin D_3 in order to absorb and utilize dietary calcium efficiently (and possibly also to metabolize carbohydrate efficiently). This vitamin is formed in the human and animal skin when ultraviolet light activates certain cholesterol-containing oils. In the high arctic, however, a combination of low sun angle during summer, a long period of winter darkness, and the need for heavy clothing during most of the year, must prevent the human body from synthesizing much of its own vitamin D_3. Whether sufficient vitamin D_3 can be secured from sea fauna at this latitude is uncertain. Seal oil contains significant quantities of vitamin D_3 but, at Thule, the fish oils rich in vitamin D_3, such as cod liver oil, are probably not a major source of supply because of the aforementioned lightness of fishing in that region. To summarize the ecological problem briefly, even if sufficient vitamin D_3 is available to allow maximum efficiency in calcium absorption and utilization, it is still highly probable that some people, at some seasons of the year, will be unable to secure sufficient dietary calcium to meet published medical standards. If such a low calcium intake were coupled with a high protein and high potassium intake, the neurological consequences would be intensified, and the heavy meat consumption of Polar Eskimo entails a large intake of protein and potassium.

Given, then, a population in which individuals frequently suffer from a nutritionally determined mild hypocalcemia, how does one account for the timing of particular attacks? The mechanism of hyperventilation provides an answer. Prolonged deep breathing tends to deplete the blood of carbon dioxide and thus to alter the acid balance; this in turn reduces the proportion of calcium atoms which are in the ionized state; thus is established a transient hypocalcemia severe enough to produce an attack of tetany. Even mild exercise or emotional stress may be sufficient to produce hyperventilation tetany in persons already low in total calcium.

One fact, however, militates against a simple dietary calcium deficiency hypothesis: the reported extreme rarity of rickets in Eskimo infants and of osteomalacia in Eskimo adults (for example, in pregnant and lactating women) (Bertelsen, 1940). These are diseases in which, as a consequence of inadequate calcium intake or utilization, or both, the bones yield their calcium to the blood and, eventually, to the urine, with the sufferer thus gradually losing calcium from the body at the expense of bony tissue. In temperate latitudes, rickets and osteomalacia are normally forestalled by milk, sunlight, and supplementary vitamin D_3 preparations in cod liver oil and vitamin pills. If one hypothesizes that the Eskimo diet is low in calcium, and perhaps in sun-formed vitamin D_3, how is it that rickets is not evident? The answer to this question requires another hypothesis concerning hormonal function. It would seem that if calcium and/or vitamin D_3 intake is chronically low in the high arctic environment, then the Eskimo physiology must for generations have been forced to "choose" between tetany and rickets — and, unlike more southerly populations, it has "chosen" tetany as the lesser of two evils. (More precisely, of course, it is the environment which has selected the better-fitted physiological alternative.) Rickets and osteomalacia would in a primitive Eskimo economy be fatal because they are physically crippling. Sporadic attacks of tetany, even if occasionally damaging or even fatal, would be by comparison merely an annoyance. Hence the hypocalcemia hypothesis requires the corollary that the Polar and perhaps other Eskimo tend to be mildly hypoparathyroid (or, more exactly, again, that in this cultural-ecological matrix, optimum parathyroid function requires a lower activity than does optimum function under the conditions familiar to European and American medical practice). Such a mild "hypoparathyroidism" would be conceived as a product of natural selection for primitive life in an arctic environment, yielding a type of hormonal balance which retains calcium in the bones even if calcium levels in serum fall occasionally. There is, as a matter of fact, some evidence to support this hypothesis. The doomed medieval Norsemen, not preadapted to high arctic environment, who settled along the west coast of Greenland, and who finally died out were replaced by ricketless Eskimo, *did* suffer from rickets and osteomalacia (Maxwell, 1930:20).

But if we propose a hypocalcemia hypothesis, do we ignore Eskimo culture? Certainly not. Consideration of cultural factors is, in fact, already implicit in the hypothesis as enunciated. This hypothesis rests on the assumption that the subsistence technology is "primitive," that is, in this application of the concept, that manufactured vitamins and imported or specially processed calcium-containing foods are not available and that, to hunters, a strong and undistorted skeletal structure is of greater survival value than freedom from occasional attacks of tetany. These cultural characteristics render the population vulnerable to a local dietary calcium and/or vitamin D_3 shortage and select the nervous and muscular system rather than the skeleton as the target tissue of any calcium and/or vitamin D_3 nutritional deficiency.

But Eskimo culture also functions to minimize, within the limits stated above, the frequency and severity of attacks, *via* the customs of securing, processing, and storing of large quantities of calcium-containing birds (the "little auks"); of obtaining, preserving, and making extensive use of vitamin-D_3-containing seal oils; of stripping and exposing the body to direct sunlight whenever the weather permits; of weaning children late (thus ensuring them maximal calcium intake in mother's milk during the rickets-vulnerable period of infancy); of securing to pregnant women (who are particularly vulnerable to osteomalacia) and children preferred access to fresh and stored foods high in calcium (specifically, the little auks and whatever dried fish are available) by making women and children chiefly responsible for netting the birds and collecting the eggs, and by maintaining standards (to judge from taboos reported from Eskimo groups other than Thule) which have the effect at certain times of substantially restricting the pregnant or lactating mother to the use of dried fish, birds, or other stored foods high in calcium.

It is possible that, apart from its role in etiology, Eskimo custom also affects the details of overt symptomatology. Conceivably the frequently reported impetuous flight from the group during the initial phases of an attack may reflect a personality trait common among Eskimo: withdrawal from, rather than aggression in, a situation when the individual's confidence in his ability to master it has been shaken. Such a tendency may be reflected in the tendency for Eskimo men to abandon kayak hunting if their confidence has once been disturbed ("kayak-phobia")' by the practice of *kiviktoq*, or "going into the mountains" to live a hermit's life, in men and women alike who feel rejected by their communities; by the reported willingness of the aged and infirm to be abandoned to die; and by the anxiousness of Eskimo parents not to disturb the confidence of their children, even when playing dangerously, by frustrating negative commands. Such a psychological interpretation — which is, in a sense, directly contradictory to the hysteria hypothesis — rests on the assumption that any incipient neurological disfunction is susceptible to different interpretations by the victim and his associates and can therefore precipitate different overt responses, depending on particular customs of the individual and group.

And finally, with regard to its handling of cases of *pibloktoq*, Eskimo custom obviously plays a very important role. An attack of *pibloktoq* is not automatically taken as a sign of the individual's general incompetency. The victim is, if necessary, prevented from injuring himself or others; otherwise he is left alone while the attack spends itself. The attack may be the subject of good-humored joking later but is not used to justify restriction of the victim's social participation. There is, in other words, little or no stigma; the attack is treated as an isolated event rather than as a symptom of deeper illness. Such a phlegmatic approach would seem well calculated once again to minimize any damage to the individual's personal confidence and thus would work to forestall the development of chronic psychological invalidism. The impact on chronicity of differential handling of such episodic disorders is well illustrated in the history of American combat psychiatry, which between World War II and the Korean War achieved a 50 per cent reduction in the rate of chronic psychoneurosis developing out of combat breakdown simply by refusing to treat the breakdown as a symptom of illness (Glass, 1953).

Implications of the Alternative Theories. Two alternative armchair theories of *pibloktoq* have been presented. Although the "organic" (hypocalcemia) theory seems preferable, the organic theory is just as much concerned with analysis of cultural factors as is the "psychological" (hysteria) theory. In order to choose between the two, field investigation will be necessary. Such field investigation will have considerable significance for anthropological theories of mental illness (and professional psychiatric theory, for that matter). For not only will it contribute to the solution of a particular — and to some eyes, perhaps, an unnecessarily exotic diagnostic problem, it will also bear on two major theoretical issues.

One of these major issues is the understanding of hysteria itself. As is well known, psychoanalysis was originally conceived as a means for treating hysteria, and upon the analysis of cases diagnosed as hysteria much of its theoretical structure has been erected. Since Freud's time, hysteria has become a rare disorder in most of Europe and America. This may be the consequence of culturally determined changes in modal personality structure in Western countries and in preferences for various styles of psychosomatic expression. It may also be the result of changes in diagnostic practice (it has been suggested, for instance, that "hysteria has vanished right into the diagnosis of epilepsy" (Peterson, 1950)). And it may be the result of culturally determined changes in such matters as style of dress and housing, hours of work, methods of lighting, and diet, which could affect, in particular, calcium intake and utilization in persons vulnerable to tetany and rickets. Certainly rickets has become more rare in precisely those groups once most prone to grand hysteria: the Western European urban populations. But now we are suggesting that at least one type of hysteria (the "grand hysterical attack") may not be purely psychogenic!

Such an implication demands support by way of empirical investigation — an investigation which, in fact, takes up again an abortive line of inquiry into the relationship between tetany and hysteria that began in Europe before the psychoanalytic theories of hysteria swept competing approaches from the field (Barrett, 1919–1920:385–386). It is of more than antiquarian interest to recall that between 1880 and 1895 there was a veritable epidemic of tetany among the working class of Vienna, Paris, and other European cities (Shelling, 1935:115–116). This plague of tetany was, at the time, not understood etiologically, for the role of calcium in tetany had not been established. During the same period, the work of French and Viennese neuropsychiatrists on hysteria was being pursued most intensively, and it culminated, as everyone knows, in Freud and Breuer's *Studies in Hysteria,* which was published in 1895 after a preliminary publication in 1893. This study revealed the psychological connection between the hysterical symptom and traumatic emotional conflict and suggested a technique of "talking" therapy which soon developed into the method of psychoanalysis. We might now ask, however, whether the physiological milieu of hypocalcemia may not have been a conditioning factor in hysteria. The most serious epidemics of rickets and of hypocalcemic tetany — determined by constraints of custom and/or economy on food, dress, interior lighting, working hours, and access to open spaces not only among working people but among all classes in late nineteenth century Europe — came at precisely the same time that hysteria reached its peak as a psychiatric problem. The discovery of the value of sunlight, milk, and vitamin-D_3-containing foods, and the general amelioration of social conditions, during the early twentieth century, was accompanied by a drastic reduction in the frequencies of rickets, of tetany, and of hysteria. Thus we may suggest, as a hypothesis for medicohistorical investigation, that the hysterical attack and perhaps even hysterical conversion will occur most readily in persons with low levels of serum ionized calcium and that chronically low levels may maintain a neurophysiological milieu in which either tetany, hysterical attacks, hypersuggestibility, or hysterical learning of conversion symptoms is sooner or later inevitable, the choice of disorder depending on various conditioning factors of situation, personal history, and biochemical individuality.

Suggesting that the late nineteenth century European hysterias may have been in considerable proportion undiagnosed cases of serum calcium deficiency raises a major issue in psychiatric theory, for psychoanalysis was founded on the analysis of hysterics. In view of this fact, it may be well to evaluate further the culture-historical dimensions of the issue. The late nineteenth century students of hysteria — including Freud — were aware that hysterics might display unusual physiological profiles as well as disordered behavior, and some felt that hereditary predisposition played a role in the pathogenesis of the disease. But these psychiatrists of the 1890's were in somewhat the same position *vis-à-vis* physiological explanations of hysteria as the anthropologists of the 1920's were *vis-à-vis* explanations of psychopathology in general: physiological investigations had not advanced far enough to provide a base for framing testable physiological hypotheses.

Thus the first demonstration that tetany was associated with reduced concentration of calcium in the blood was not made until 1908; hitherto the diagnosis depended on the finding of positive neurological signs. Not until 1921 did the development of micrometric methods of determining quantities of serum calcium make possible widespread testing for serum calcium level (Shelling, 1935:114–116). In certain cases differential diagnosis between hysteria and tetany was extremely difficult, and in fact probably was arbitrary, before the development of the serum calcium and tetany hypothesis and the provision of appropriate methods of clinical chemistry. Consequently, some cases which today would probably be regarded as unequivocally tetany (e.g., the tetanic syndrome following thyroidectomy) were in 1904 diagnosed as mixtures of tetany and hysteria (cf. Curschmann, 1904). Today also we know that hypo- and hypercalcemia may precipitate not only tetany and hysteria but a bewildering mixture of symptoms including those usually classified as schizophrenic and depressive. But it is *impossible* that Freud could have considered the possibility that hysteria, or any other mental disorder, might be a symptomatic consequence of low serum calcium. The cultural milieu in which he worked had not provided him with the concepts or tools by which the question could have been asked or answered. Inasmuch as we cannot return to the nineteenth century to do serum calcium determinations on Freud's original patients, we cannot say what the results would have been, nor can we estimate the impact on the development of psychoanalysis if the findings had been positive. But at least we have still another historical answer to the question "Why has hysteria virtually disappeared in Europe and the United States?" Our (metaphorical) answer is, "It dissolved in bottles of milk and cod-liver oil"—that is to say, the cultural changes associated with an appreciation of the importance of sunlight, vitamin D_3, milk, and various other factors for maintaining proper calcium balance, together with a general improvement of nutritional standards, has virtually eliminated (except in certain rare medical conditions) a total syndrome, one symptom cluster of which was once (and still is) called tetany, and another symptom cluster of which was once (but no longer is) called "grand hysterical attack."

The recent discovery that anxiety attacks (of a severity up to and including the prodromal symptoms of tetany) may be reliably precipitated in persons diagnosed as "anxiety hysterics," and milder symptoms of anxiety in "normal" persons as well, by the simple infusion of sodium lactate, lends further support to the calcium hypothesis, and indeed expands its possible explanatory domain. The neurophysiological effect of increasing the concentration of sodium lactate in blood is to bind calcium to cell membrances, thus producing a functional hypocalcemia; the effect is counteracted by simultaneously infusing calcium. Inasmuch as the neurotic symptoms are commonly understood to be motivated by a desperate urge to reduce anxiety, it would appear that susceptibility to neurosis, as understood psychoanalytically, is perhaps based on a constitutionally and/or nutritionally determined high vulnerability to the excessive binding of calcium ion to a degree associated with the experience of anxiety (Pitts and McClure, 1967). Such an end-mechanism can, of course, be reached by any one or combination of intermediate pathways, such as hyperventilation, hypoparathyroidism, faulty lactate metabolism, and so on.

The need for empirical evidence bearing on the hypotheses outlined above leads immediately to a consideration of the second major issue: the larger theoretical structure which should guide such an investigation. It is evident that even if it is possible to identify a specific physiological variable as the *precipitant* of the overt symptomatology, an adequate explanation of the frequency of the syndrome in the population, its geographical range, its racial and species distribution, its seasonal variation, its history, and the severity and details of form of the symptoms themselves, must depend on evaluating other variables, physiological, psychological, and cultural. It is the interaction of these other variables with the immediately precipitating physiological variable which provides the necessary and sufficient conditions for a type of mental illness to occur in a particular group with a particular frequency. We have already suggested some of these conditions in the *pibloktoq* analysis. Let us now turn our attention to the development of a frame of reference which can guide the refinement of theory and the acquisition of relevant empirical data. We shall begin, in the next section, with a further discussion of a point introduced in the *pibloktoq* analysis: the importance of the "theory of illness" in the formation of a symptomatic structure. And finally we shall attempt to generalize the line of thought represented in the *pibloktoq* analysis, and in the following discussion, into a rough model of a biocultural approach to mental illness.

The Importance of Culturally Institutionalized Theories of Illness as Determinants of Response to Organically Based Psychopathology

Mental illness is an episode in a life program, usually following a more or less extended period of normalcy (as defined by both the person and his community), and terminated either by death or by a return (temporary perhaps) to normalcy. In the biocultural model, a conjunction of pathogenic organic and psychological events is considered to abort a life program normal to the society by crippling the victim's apparatus for cognitive organization. With the onset of the physiologically determined desemantication (reduced cognitive organization capacity) associated with chronic anxiety, the victim is unable to organize his perceptions, his motives, and his actions meaningfully so as to satisfy his own wishes without frustrating those of others or *vice versa*. His more or less desperate efforts reduce the primary anxiety, and to protect himself from the consequences which he expects to follow any drastic reduction of cognitive capacity are apt to be the most conspicuous and serious symptoms of the disorder: withdrawal, aggression, paranoid delusion, and the bizarre use of the familiar mechanisms of defense like repression, sublimation, denial, etc. And simultaneously, the victim's community is responding to this overt symptomatology with its own procedures of withdrawal, aggression, therapy, and so forth.

What will determine the victim's and the community's expectations of consequences and their choices of defensive strategy? Evidently the frequency, duration, and predictability of periods of desemantication, and their commonness in the population, will be data of extreme importance in the evaluation of self by the victim and of victim by the community. If the period of desemantication is relatively brief (not more than a few days), is relatively infrequent (not more than once a month), is predictable (either by a calendrical device or by association with other scheduled events), and is commonly observed to occur in others without dire consequences, then even severe degrees of desemantication with considerable associated inconvenience and discomfort may be tolerated by the personality. Similarly, brief, infrequent, predictable, and common overt disorders may be tolerated by the community. Such situations (to give some familiar examples) are premenstrual tension, drug and alcoholic intoxication, ritually induced dissociation, exhaustion, and the Polar Eskimo *pibloktoq*. The more delayed in the life program, the more frequent, the more prolonged, the less predictable, and the less common the event, the more threatening it will be to the personality and to the community, and the more desperate and (for the victim) the more ill conceived their complementary defensive strategies will become. Where the desemantication is severe and irreversible, as in chronic brain syndromes, the victim may be so preoccupied with maintaining the former sense of competence that even trivial *contretemps* precipitate "catastrophic" reactions (Goldstein, 1940). Schizophrenia and perhaps the affective psychoses (such as involutional melancholia) would appear to have an intermediate status between chronic syndromes and brief episodic attacks. The desemantication is not fully continuous and the victim is consequently able to retain for a considerable period an intermittent normalcy of function, but the episodes are sufficiently frequent, prolonged, and severe to result in an accumulation of permanent defensive strategies which eventually in themselves make adequate social participation almost impossible during the clear periods, and, sometimes, even after the desemantication phase itself has ended.

But it is not merely the timing and conventionality of the disorder which will affect the defensive response of the victim and his community. The personality of the victim and the culture of the group provide models of the experiences and symptoms of the event which assign to them definite meanings and provide recipes for handling the situation. These models are, in the individual's case, a function of the history of his learnings, and in the community's case, a function of other aspects of the culture, its social structure, and its history. They are widely variable in form and are not entirely predictable from a knowledge of the timing and conventionality of the disorder. While the anthropologist may or may not undertake the solution of problems of differential diagnosis and etiology (which, as we observed earlier, unavoidably involve questions of biological as well as psychological dynamics), he can certainly investigate the patient's and the community's theories of illness and its treatment. Thus his most immediately relevant contribution can be an analysis of how, in the society in question, symptomatology and its programming are normally conceptualized. As we have indicated above, whatever its etiology, the course of an illness occurs in a social matrix and is observed both by the victim and his associates. Their conception of what is happening will play an important part in determining what will be their response to the symptoms (see Wallace, 1959a). Thus, even if etiology and the primary symptoms of an illness were, except in an epidemiological inquiry, to be considered as physiological accidents and thus as largely independent of culture, the efforts of the victim and of his fellows to cope with the illness must be recognized as being highly dependent on culture, for these responses to illness are very considerably determined by what may be called the native — and, in particular, the patient's — theory of illness. In short, since the cause of illness even if physiologically initiated is progressively modified by feedback via the victim's and the community's conception of the illness, the victim's personality and the community's culture play a determining role.

Some of the recent literature in social psychiatry has directed attention to theory of illness as a significant variable. Of particular interest are the studies of psychiatric illness in New Haven summarized in Hollingshead and Redlich's book *Social Class and Mental Illness* (1958). These studies demonstrate again not only class differentials in prevalence of certain kinds of treated mental illness (for example, that schizophrenia is about nine times as prevalent in the lowest socioeconomic group as in the highest, even after standardizing for population size), but also class differentials in methods of treatment (that is, that lowest-class schizophrenics receive either organic treatment or no treatment at all, while highest-class schizophrenics receive psychotherapy and/or organic treatment). These differences are doubtless partly a function of differential access to economic resources; but, as Hollingshead and Redlich carefully show, they are also partly a function of differences in the conceptions of illness and of treatment between lower-class and higher-class patients. Specifically, the dissonance between the lower-class patients' and their middle-class physicians' theories of what illness is, how it originates, and how it is cured, interferes with free communication. These differences make mutual acceptance, liking, trust, and intelligent co-operation difficult, and often result in either mutual withdrawal or the patient's refusal to enter into a psychotherapeutic relationship at all.

Other sources have approached the problem of theory of illness from various standpoints. Cannon and others, for instance, have analyzed the phenomenon of "voodoo death" as a type of overresponse to a "realistically" trivial trauma by a victim who is convinced that he will die because he has been bewitched by an enemy or doomed for the infraction of some taboo (Cannon, 1942). Comparable, if less dramatic, studies have revealed that bodily injuries and mental infirmities of one sort or another lead to different responses depending on the culturally defined meaning of the situation. For instance, in their collection of papers reporting on investigations by the National Institute of Mental Health of the impact of mental illness on the family, Clausen and Yarrow describe in some detail the differences in the "meaning" of mental illness to various persons, including the patient, and the effect of these semantic positions in shaping the path to, through, and from the mental hospital (Clausen and Yarrow, 1955). In their study of thirty-three families in which the husband was the patient, they found that nearly half of the husbands were never seen by a psychiatrist before hospitalization was arranged. The difficulty, and usually the reluctance, with which the patient's family came to define his problem as one requiring psychiatric care, and the slowness and uncertainty with which they proceeded to secure that care, meant that "discontinuities of action were frequent, and paths to the hospital were beset with obstacles and traumata for husband and wife" (Clausen and Yarrow, 1955:32). And in our own research at the Eastern Pennsylvania Psychiatric Institute, we have been concerned with the problem of how the patient's theory of the mechanism of hallucination affects his and his fellows' response to that experience. We have worked with cross-cultural materials in the literature and have pointed out, for instance, the contrast between the responses to mescaline intoxication of normal white volunteers and of American Indian religious peyotists (Wallace, 1959b).

A Model for the Analysis of Theories of Mental Illness.   We conceive that among the set (mazeway) of cognitive "maps" which each individual maintains, describing and interpreting the world as he perceives it, is his theory of mental illness. This map gives meaning to experience, by defining the possible states which a person can occupy in a mental health context, and by relating the possible states which the person can occupy to one another *via* various transfer mechanisms, so as to provide the rationale for decision. Such a map can therefore be conceived of as having three aspects: (1) the *states* specified; (2) the *transfer mechanisms* which are conceived to effect change from one state to another; and (3) the *program* of illness and recovery which is described by the whole system. We confine our attention here to the patient's program for the patient himself; his programs for other persons, and the program of others for him, may (or may not) be different. Thus in the following analyses the entity to which each state description refers is constant, being ego, even though ego is variable in the sense of having different properties at different stages of the program, and in the sense of being "now" at one or another of these stages in ego's own (not necessarily correct) opinion. (Interesting possibilities of programs involving multiple referent entities, because of the logical complexities of such schemas, are not considered here.)

Evidently, one can "plug in" on an individual's program at a number of different levels of abstraction. In order to minimize partly the unreliability of reporting which ensues if level of abstraction is left unspecified, we have found it useful to base analysis on five "states," which will constitute stages of every program: "normalcy," "upset," "psychosis," "in treatment," and "innovative personality." These are always to be understood as the subject's concepts of his own possible states and not as the observer's concepts of the subject's condition. The terms are unimportant; they simply label positions in the model. *Normalcy* refers to a state in which the person is performing to his own and others' satisfaction the roles appropriate to his situation in society. *Upset* refers to a state where role performance has been reduced to a level of minimal adequacy, with noticeable personal and/or group discomfort. *Psychosis* is a state where role performance has become so inadequate that in order to reduce personal and group discomfort, some degree of social isolation (either self- or group-imposed) must be instituted. *In treatment* is a state where the person is receiving ministrations from specialists, designed to remove the conditions responsible for personal and group discomfort, and to return the patient to full social participation. *Innovative personality* is a state in which the person is again able to perform roles to his own and group satisfaction, but roles different to a greater or lesser degree from those performed in state N (as the difference approaches insignificance, P approaches N). These five states may be conceived as arranged in a graph whose starting point is N, with "goodness" of state decreasing in order of position to the right of N:

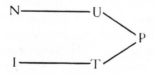

We assume that any individual classification of states will include these five except where concept I is equivalent to N, in which case the graph reduces to:

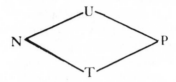

We also assume that between any two states one of four transfer relations may be conceived: no transfer possible (symbolized by open space); one-directional transfer ($\rightarrow$); one-directional transfer ($\leftarrow$); and reversible transfer ($\leftrightarrow$). Definition of the states and of the transfer mechanisms can usually be best represented not on the graph but in appended tables in order to avoid cluttering the graph with written notations. The reader will note that any two states may stand, in relation to one another, as positive and negative goals depending on their relative position on the value dimension. For instance, U may be a negative goal for a person who is in state N, but a positive goal for a person in state P. And finally, depending on the circumstances, additional states may be added to the model if they are part of the subject individual's or culture's phenomenological world.

A given patient's theory of illness can be inferred from several types of behavior:

1. Plain statements (e.g., "It's worrying that makes people lose their minds").
2. Comparative statements (e.g., "Joan was real sick when they brought her in, but now that she's been here awhile, she's quieted down a lot").
3. Differential motor behavior (e.g., avoiding certain patients while socializing with others).
4. Case history material (e.g., information that experiencing hallucinations first convinced the patient that he was seriously ill and required psychiatric help).

These and other data, obtained from tape-recorded interviews with patient and his family and associates, records kept by social workers and therapists, direct observation on the ward, and so on, permit the classification of concepts and beliefs, and the working out of their interrelationships in the subject's mazeway. The investigator must keep constantly in mind that these belief structures can change and (this is often difficult) that it is the subject's (or the community's) belief system, and not the patient's "true" condition as perceived by the clinician, that is being studied. (And if the clinician's belief system is being studied, the validity of the clinician's beliefs is technically irrelevant.) The tediousness of the task should not be underestimated. A satisfactory case history, for instance, covering day-by-day events for months prior to hospitalization, and during the hospital stay itself, requires extensive checking and cross-checking with dozens of sources of information. The process is comparable to the compilation of data for a biography. Discrete items of information, culled from various sources, are ordered first chronologically and then by topic until an internally coherent process appears in which the subject's decisions and attitudes are demonstrably related to his current situation and past experience. Thus one source may reveal that on a certain date the patient, a ritually faithful Catholic, failed to go to Mass; another source may show that the day before, he had an interview with his priest, who counseled him to exercise will power and to cease wallowing in self-pity; a third source reveals that next week the patient went to his family doctor and received a prescription for tranquilizers; and a fourth source finally shows that some time during the week preceding the visit to the priest, the patient experienced a frightening impulse to kill his wife and child. These details fit into the pattern of a process. With increasing fear of losing self-control, the patient, who still regards his "upset" state as one of moral uncertainty, turns to the priest for help; but the priest's advice does not help to resolve the uncertainty, and he redefines his state as an "illness" requiring medical attention.

Illustration: A Zulu Theory of Mental Illness.   Among the Zulu known to Canon Callaway in South Africa, about the middle of the last century, a complex and rather sophisticated theory was held which, in its formal structure, is not dissimilar to some varieties of current psychiatric theory. The structure of this theory is given in the following formula:

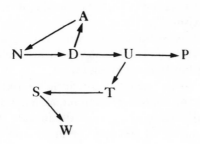

The definition of the states, as given in Callaway's translation of the Zulu text (Callaway, 1931) is as follows:

N: "Robust"; good appetite; not choosy about food.

D: "Delicate, not having any real disease, but delicate."

A: "Ill"; choosy about food; loss of appetite; suffers vague pains; anxious dreams; possessed by spirits of ancestors.

U: "Ill"; choosy about food; loss of appetite; suffers vague pains; anxious dreams; possessed by a class of spirits known as *Amatongo*.

P: "A fool," "unable to understand anythings," "mad," not a "man."

T: Continued ill health, sleeplessness, loss of weight, skin diseases, but hopeful of becoming a shaman.

S: Good physical health; the state of being a shaman or *inyanga*, i.e., one with a "soft head" who, with the help of his familiar spirits among the *Amatongo*, performs the respectable special role of "diviner" (finder of lost objects and physician to possessed persons).

W: "Always out of health," unable to divine, but of unusual wisdom, and able to work.

The transfer operations, to the extent that they are described in Callaway's text are:

N→D: Initial possession by either *Amatongo* or ancestral spirits.

D→A: Completion of possession by ancestral spirits.

A→N: Relinquishment of possession by ancestral spirits after being exorcised by sacrifice of cattle under direction of shamans.

D→U: *Amatongo* increase control over victim but divide into two groups, one group (under influence of medicines and cattle sacrifice exorcism) objecting to complete possession and the other insisting on complete possession.

U→P: Continued "blocking the way" of the *Amatongo* by exorcism and by medicines taken by mouth.

U→T: Patient's family, patient, and community, recognize that *Amatongo* are struggling to possess patient, and terminate medicines and exorcism.

T→S: Patient seeks communication with *Amatongo* in his dreams and singing; community participates in his singing and asks him questions for *Amatongo* to answer.

S→W: A "great doctor" can "lay the spirit" of *Amatongo* to the extent of preventing the patient from remaining a diviner but only at the cost of leaving him chronically in state W.

Notable features of the model are, first, the importance of the differential diagnosis (by a shaman) between possession by the relatively benevolent ancestors and by the dangerous *Amatongo;* and second, the irreversible nature of *Amatongo* possession, which eventuates in a state of dementia unless the victim accepts his fate and undergoes the complete course of training as an *inyanga.*

Application to Clinical Case Material. In the application of the foregoing concepts to clinical case material, it must be borne in mind that the structure and development of a patient's theory of illness may be related to, but is nevertheless distinct from, the structure and development of his conflict structure ("neurosis") and of his therapeutic regime. In one of the two cases which we have analyzed in some detail by the help of the model, we found the model to be helpful in understanding a temporary impasse, with an associated flurry of disturbed behavior, reached at a certain stage in therapy. The crucial problem in treatment, from the therapist's viewpoint, was the patient's unwillingness to accept the presence in himself of hostile feelings toward various close relatives. The therapist defined the goal of treatment (T) as a less repressive personality and he encouraged the patient to assert himself and his needs more freely and to recognize that these needs, and the hostilities generated by their frustration, were not evil but merely human. The patient was stubbornly resistant, not merely because of the psychodynamics of the situation, but also because the therapist was suggesting that he "act out" in somewhat the same way as his own psychotic father had acted out before his hospitalization some years before. The therapist thus was suggesting to the patient a state T which, in the patient's theory of illness, was hard to distinguish from P. The patient's conscious attention was, at this time, centered on a struggle to avoid entering state P; hence the therapist's suggestions were terrifying, not only because they may have aroused unconscious resistance (in the conventional psychodynamic sense), but because they pushed him toward a self-identification with a psychotic father.

The resolution of the impasse was provided by his development of a compromise, which the therapist was willing to accept, between his original theory and the therapist's theory. This compromise took the following form:

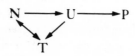

He steadfastly retained the belief that the object of his efforts was a return to his normal, presymptomatic, good-husband-and-father self (N). But he accepted T as a necessary way station on the path to N and as a means of avoiding the alternative state P. His acceptance of the existence and value of T were followed almost immediately by release to the outpatient department.

Application to the Classification of Cultures.   Because of the ubiquity of the major types of mental disease, and because of the uncertainty of etiological understanding, it is hazardous to classify cultures as more or less pathogenic in respect to any particular mental illness or to mental illness in general. In all likelihood, as knowledge of the causes of mental illness is extended, it will become easier to discern the relation between culture and etiology. Thus in the future it may be possible to regard the frequency, distribution, and forms of mental illness in a society as an index of its culture. But at the present time, despite the currency of certain hypotheses based on psychodynamic assumptions about the relation between culture and mental illness, it is not feasible to establish a classification based on demonstrated etiological processes.

It is however reasonable to suggest that cultures may, even on the basis of present knowledge, be classified with respect to such culturally institutionalized responses to various types of mental illness as the society's taxonomy and definitions of mental illness, its theory or theories of illness, and its techniques of therapy and their rationale. Such a classification must, in effect, form a matrix of intersection of a constant typology of mental illness (that is, a typology defined by the investigator and used as a constant referent for controlling cross-cultural comparisons) and of alternatively possible responses available cross-culturally. The types so defined may then be investigated in order to discern whether or not a correlation exists between response type and other aspects of culture. If such correlations can be shown to exist, then at least *response to mental illness* may be considered an index of culture.

Evidently a number of possible schemes, of varying degrees of complexity and abstraction, can be created, based on different constant typologies and different panels of alternative responses. One typological system based on theoretical considerations introduced in the preceding sections will be outlined here. For the constant typology, not Western diagnostic categories, but the two dichotomous dimensions of severity and chronicity will be used (mild versus severe, and intermittent versus continuous). For the response typology, two dichotomous dimensions will be used: episodic versus symptomatic interpretations of illness, and treatment versus extrusion as a method of handling illness. These concepts may be defined further as follows: Mildness and severity refer to the degree of abnormality of the overt behavior itself and not to its duration or frequency of occurrence; intermittency and continuousness refer to halves of a continuum, intermittency being the half in which the disorder can best be characterized as discrete attacks separated by intervals of normalcy, and continuousness as the half in which the disorder can be characterized as a period of uninterrupted disfunction. Episodic interpretations of illness confine attention only to the overt disorder itself and regard it as an isolated episode in an essentially normal life program, whereas symptomatic interpretations construe the overt disorder as a sign of a more serious underlying inadequacy which threatens to recur, possibly in a more undesirable form, on later occasions. Treatment as a method of handling illness implies a policy of attempting to cure, to improve, or to tolerate (even by ignoring the behavior) and make the best use of the victim, in contrast to the method of extrusion, which by such devices as confinement, banishment, or even execution attempts to rid society entirely of an incompatible participant. The suggested dichotomies are, of course, divisions of continua, and the distinctions are easier to make in extreme than in intermediate cases. Thus a series of epileptic attacks is easy to classify in the constant typology as intermittent and severe, and a case of obsessive fear of heights as mild and continuous; but a given schizophrenic psychosis may be neither clearly continuous nor notably severe, yet seem by contrast with epilepsy and the fear of heights to require the continuous and severe classification.

The whole schema may be represented in the following diagram:

	Intermittent	*Continuous*
Mild	Episodic *or* Symptomatic Treatment *or* Extrusion	Episodic *or* Symptomatic Treatment *or* Extrusion
Severe	Episodic *or* Symptomatic Treatment *or* Extrusion	Episodic *or* Symptomatic Treatment *or* Extrusion

Thus any group, with respect to any given syndrome, may be classified as episodic-treatment, episodic-extrusion, symptomatic-treatment, or symptomatic-extrusion, within that cell which characterizes the syndrome on the constant typology. If we consider *pibloktoq*, for instance, we would classify this as intermittent-severe in the constant typology, and the Polar Eskimo handling of it as episodic-treatment in the response typology. The same syndrome in the context of, let us say, an operational wing of the U.S. Strategic Air Command would also be classified as intermittent-severe, but the handling of the condition would be classified as symptomatic-extrusion. And, again, this same intermittent-severe syndrome in the context of a liberal arts college campus would be handled either as episodic-treatment or symptomatic-treatment.

The number of possible cultural patterns established by this paradigm is quite large. Although, with regard to any single syndrome, only four types of response are considered, there are four types of syndrome, with regard to which each of these four possibilities exist. Therefore the number of possible cultural patterns is 4^4 or 256. Furthermore, of course, any *description* of the way in which a society handles mental disorders will make many distinctions, even of a classificatory kind, that cannot be included in a pattern classification scheme. Thus, for instance, with respect to the "treatment" class, it will be noted in any description whether the condition in question is ignored, is recognized but tolerated, or is directly approached by a means of therapy. If therapy is employed, it can be medical (physiological) or psychological; and if psychological, it can be secular or religious, cathartic or repressive, and so on. Rather than attempt to embrace all of the 256 patterns, let alone the further elaborations and refinements desirable for any sort of descriptive account, therefore, it would appear to be useful to note that among the large number of possible patterns, several stand out as stock patterns which may be used for the purpose of seeking to establish whether or not, in principle, correlations may exist between a group's manner of handling behavior disorder and other aspects of its culture.

Four such ideal pattern types are offered below:

	Int.	*Cont.*	*Int.*	*Cont.*	*Int.*	*Cont.*	*Int.*	*Cont.*
Mild	Sy	Sy	Ep	Sy	Sy	Sy	Sy	Sy
	Ex	Ex	Tr	Tr	Tr	Tr	Tr	Tr
Severe	Sy	Sy	Ep	Sy	Sy	Sy	Sy	Sy
	Ex	Ex	Tr	Ex	Ex	Ex	Tr	Tr
	I		II		III		IV	

It is suggested — with the hope not so much that the suggestions will convince as provoke thought and consideration in empirical studies — that these four patterns of institutionalized response to mental illness are associated with definite types of social structures. Pattern I, for instance, would seem to be characteristic of aggressive and power-seeking, self-selected, elite groups generally, whether they be kinship, military, political, economic, or religious. These elite groups extrude (screen out) all persons with visible behavioral anomalies (symptomatic of possible other disabilities as yet unrevealed) in order to maintain a maximally reliable and effective organization. Pattern II would seem to be characteristic of technologically primitive, small communities that recognize disorder as a symptom of a hidden, threatening weakness only when it is continuous, and that will resort to extrusion only when it is both continuous and severe. Pattern III would seem to be characteristic of pre-nineteenth century Western civilization generally: all disorders are symptomatic, and all serious disorders require extrusion. Pattern IV, on the other hand, would seem to characterize the psychodynamic tradition in twentieth century Western psychiatry, and an increasing number of other educated subgroups in Western populations, who regard all disorders as symptomatic, but also consider that all disorders should be treated rather than disposed of by extrusion.

Space does not permit further elaboration of these concepts; but enough has been said, perhaps, to indicate not only the problems in attempting to create a taxonomy of responses to mental illness with cultural index value, but also the possible value of such a taxonomy in establishing relations between responses to mental illness and other aspects of culture. To the extent that these patterns of response have a bearing on the course of various syndromes, whatever their etiology may be, a taxonomy of this kind may additionally have some utility as an evaluative index of social efficiency in handling the problems of mental illness. We may speculate, for instance, that a group whose response to a behavioral disorder is to regard it as symptomatic of an underlying and threatening chronic incompetency, rather than an episode in a normal life program, will induce in the victim a sense of his own inadequacy that is in itself directly pathogenic. We may further speculate that his anxious efforts to defend himself will markedly affect the form and course of the disorder itself. If these defensive efforts are not directed toward the securing of a validly effective therapy, then the pathogenic pressure of the culturally institutionalized definitions of and responses to mental illness will be uncompensated. In such an unhappy case, even if the etiology of the disorder were actually completely organic, the culture would be playing a contributory role in the mental disease process.

Toward a Biocultural Theory of Mental Illness: The Integration of the Organic and Functional Approaches

How can the cultural anthropologist relate his conceptions of the structuring of social behavior to biological theories of mental illness? The model of mental illness advocated in this paper as an answer to this question is essentially homeostatic. A behavior system is considered to be disturbed when an independent variable, organic in nature, passes certain boundary values; and the responses of the various components of this system can be construed as motivated efforts to restore equilibrium. These responses are prescribed by the system itself in its theory of illness. But mere lip service to the ideal of an "interdisciplinary" approach, and pleas for the recognition of the importance of biological or cultural factors, will not solve the scientific problem. Only an approach which considers the *specific nature* of the interaction between biological and cultural (psychosocial) variables can have high predictive value.

The specific nature of this biocultural interaction can best be investigated by conceiving of the total course of the psychotic episode as a single event and then analyzing it into stages. Each stage is defined by a change in one of the major relevant dimensions of the event. A number of plausible programs can be constructed by *a priori* reasoning from different assumptions about the identity of the initial stage. One such program derives from the assumption (not yet justified by empirical findings) that the initial event in the psychotic episode is the occurrence of an organic disfunction in a hitherto intact (even if peculiarly vulnerable) individual.

If one makes this assumption, every episode of serious mental illness can be divided into four stages (exclusive of therapeutic and rehabilitation stages).

In the first stage, the organism is functioning normally.

In the second stage, an intermittent or continuous, of greater or lesser severity, organic interference with normal brain function occurs. Presumably the oft-remarked transcultural invariance of the major clinical entities and the absence of unique ethnic psychoses result because the number of types of organic interference is limited. Many sources of such interferences are known, however: cerebral hypoglycemia or hypoxia, electrolyte disturbances, gross tissue change, hormonal autointoxication, toxic metabolites, drugs, viral invasion, anomalies of enzyme action, and so on. These immediate sources in turn can theoretically depend upon many "final" causes, including prolonged states of psychodynamically and socially determined stress (such as those revealed by psychoanalytic investigations) which may produce temporary, and conceivably sometimes even irreversible, changes in body chemistry. Genetic factors may also be responsible for differential vulnerabilities within a population to the various noxious factors. Thus even from an organismic position one can comfortably look to social and psychological processes as "final" causes, particularly if the differential incidence of disorders rather than the understanding of individual cases is of primary concern. Coincident with the neural dysfunction occurs psychological dysfunction. The quality of this dysfunction is best conceived as a relative difficulty in organizing cognitive content: difficulty in finding the "meaning" of perceptual data, difficulty in maintaining the structure of motives, difficulty in relating affect to "rational" considerations. These difficulties may be metaphorically described as desemantication: the shrinking of the semantic matrix. This kind of dysfunction can vary in severity from an almost imperceptible decrement to a decrement so catastrophic as to approximate decerebration, with attendant loss of perceptual contact with the environment, motor discharge, and release of autonomic functions. At an intermediate level between mild confusion and unconsciousness would seem to fall the experience of meaninglessness, described by some schizophrenics as a sense of unreality, depersonalization, and loss of identity. Desemantication may be briefly episodic, as in hysteriform attacks, or chronic, as (apparently) in schizophrenia. Also coincident with neural and psychological dysfunction is primary behavioral failure attendant upon the desemantication. This is failure as judged by either the victim and members of his group, or both, and may occur in a variety of sectors of life, both interpersonal and technological. While incompetence in interpersonal relations may be the most conspicuous consequence of desemantication in the eyes of the group, technical failures in performing essential routine tasks, such as walking, paddling a kayak, ironing clothes, and preparing food, may come first to the victim's own awareness. Such failures may vary in duration and in the social or individual importance of the area of behavior involved.

If negative self-evaluation by the victim follows the events of the second stage, then the third stage will occur, characterized by anxiety, depression, and other negative affects directed toward the self. All persons constantly monitor and evaluate their competence in attaining their goals, both by self-perception and by perception of others' response to their behavior. A person experiencing desemantication finds the performance of his tasks more difficult and in some instances impossible. If the desemantication is continuous and is relatively severe, he will be unable to deny the reality of his loss of competency. His evaluation of these failures, which is a complex function of his current experience, the responses of others, and past learning, will be less effective than normal precisely because of the desemantication itself. But it will be based, in every instance, in part on concepts available to him from his past learning of the culturally standardized interpretations of the specific experiences and incompetencies which he now recognizes in himself. Thus he may interpret the perplexing voices which he hears as religious revelations, as the delirium accompanying fever, as the result of overwork, as the consequence of emotional conflict, and so forth, depending on the content of the experience, the reactions of others, and the explanations offered by his own cultural background. To the extent that the self-evaluation is negative, he loses confidence in his ability to control his own behavior, to master his environment, and to relate his behavior systematically with others.

The fourth stage is cognitive damage incurred in the course of the victim's defensive response to the negative self-evaluation. The response to his own anxiety and depression is, because of the existence of physiological dysfunction, itself apt to be disorganized. But it is designed to improve the negative self-image and to protect the person from catastrophe, and may in some degree relieve the patient's anxiety and depression, albeit at the cost of cognitive damage in the form of paranoid delusions, self-limiting withdrawal from society, and so on. Part of the response may be "neurotic," in the sense of utilizing such mechanisms of defense as denial, repression, projection, paranoid oversimplification, and so on. Part of it may be impulsive fighting with, or withdrawing from, a now dangerous and exhausting world. Part of it may take the form of seeking help. The style in which the person goes about attempting to defend himself, maintain self-respect, and secure help will of course reflect his cultural learning.

Through the second, third, and fourth stages, the victim's community is also evaluating and responding to him as a "changed person." Even in a homogeneous community, the social evaluation and response may be considerably different from the victim's, both because the victim's desemantication constrains his behavior, and because his motives may be divergent from those of the group. Whether or not his motives diverge from the group will depend considerably on the nature of these beliefs. Thus, for instance, if mental illness as evidenced by hallucination is culturally defined as a degrading condition to which society responds by social extrusion, the victim will be strongly motivated to conceal his condition, to deny it, to withdraw from prying eyes, and to accuse others of conspiracy against him if the charge is made. If, on the other hand, hallucination is a sign of contact — uncomfortable perhaps — with the supernatural world, and is responded to with rituals of intensified social acceptance, the hallucinator's motives will in all likelihood not be directed toward denial, concealment, and defense, but toward maximum publicity.

This model of the process of becoming mentally ill, as an immediate consequence of neurophysiological dysfunction, in a social environment, may be succinctly represented in a paradigm. Such a paradigm, of course, represents only a canonical form or modal type. The symbols are read as follows: "O" represents level of neurophysiological function of brain; "S" represents level of semantic psychological function; "B" represents level of overt behavioral success in achieving goals in social context; "A" represents level of anxiety, depression, and other negative affect directed toward self; and "D" represents the degree of cognitive damage incurred in the course of the defensive responses of the individual to his own negative self-evaluation. The operator $\downarrow$ represents pathological change, and $\wedge$ represents "and."

Stage 0: Eufunction (O,S,B,) $\wedge$ (A) $\wedge$ (D)
 If physiological injury occurs, then
Stage 1: Primary Dysfunction ($\downarrow$ O, $\downarrow$ S, $\downarrow$ B) $\wedge$ (A) $\wedge$ (D)
 If negative self-evaluation occurs, then
Stage 2: Anxiety and Depression ($\downarrow$ O, $\downarrow$ S, $\downarrow$ B) $\wedge$ ($\downarrow$ A) $\wedge$ (D)
 If anxiety and depression are severe and prolonged, then
Stage 3: Cognitive Damage ($\downarrow$ O, $\downarrow$ S, $\downarrow$ B) $\wedge$ ($\downarrow$ A) $\wedge$ ($\downarrow$ D)

Conclusion

The importance of the organic factors in psychopathology has been largely ignored by anthropological theory, which has emphasized psychological factors almost exclusively. If the viewpoint is taken that organic events play a significant role in the etiology of many mental disorders, it is possible to see the role of cultural differences as particularly relevant to etiology *via* their influence in determining the frequency with which the pathogenic organic events occur. From this point of view also, the culturally institutionalized theories of illness and of therapy appear to be extremely important in deciding the nature of the victim's and his group's responses to the disorder. A model of mental illness as a type of event is offered which integrates the organic and psychosocial approaches.

It may be hoped that anthropologists who have occasion to make observations in the field on persons with mental illness will in the future be able to obtain and record more extensive information on the physical status and history of the victims. Data on nutrition, infectious diseases, head injuries, and autonomic symptomatology, both with regard to the individual cases and also with respect to the community as a whole, would be helpful in describing individual cases, in understanding group differences, and in putting the brakes on overly facile attributions of psychopathology to "social structure," "culture," and "basic personality."

BIBLIOGRAPHY

ALLEN, THOMAS E. AND BERTRAND AGUS. 1968. Hyperventilation leading to hallucinations. American Journal of Psychiatry 125:632–637.

AMERICAN MUSEUM OF NATURAL HISTORY, PHOTOGRAPHIC DIVISION.

ARIETI, SILVANO (ED.). 1959. American handbook of psychiatry. 2 vols. New York, Basic Books.

BAASHUUS-JENSEN, J. 1935. Arctic nervous diseases. Veterinary Journal (London) 91:339–350, 379–392.

BARRETT, ALBERT M. 1919–20. Psychosis associated with tetany. American Journal of Insanity 76:373–392.

BELLAK, LEOPOLD (ED.). 1958. Schizophrenia: a review of the syndrome. New York, Logos Press.

BERTELSEN, A. 1940. Gronlandsk medicinsk statistik og nosografi. Meddelelser om Gronland, Bd 117, Nr. 3. Copenhagen.

BEST, CHARLES H. AND NORMAN B. TAYLOR. 1955. The physiological basis of medical practice. 6th ed. Baltimore, Williams and Wilkins.

BRILL, A. A. 1913. Pibloktoq or hysteria among Peary's Eskimos. Journal of Nervous and Mental Disease 40:514–520.

BROWN, E. B., JR. 1953. Physiological effects of hyperventilation. Physiological Reviews 33:445–471.

CALLAWAY, CANON H. 1931. The religion of the Amazulu of South Africa, as told by themselves. In A. L. Kroeber and T. T. Waterman, Source book in anthropology. New York, Harcourt, Brace.

CANNON, WALTER B. 1942. Voodoo death. American Anthropologist 44:169–181.

CLAUSEN, J. A., AND M. R. YARROW. 1955. The impact of mental illness on the family. Journal of Social Issues 11:(4) (whole issue).

Cook, Frederick A. 1894. Medical observations among the Esquimaux. Transactions of the New York Obstetrical Society 1893–1894, pp. 171–174.

Curschmann, Hans. 1904. Tetanie, psuedotetanie und ihre mischformen bei hysterie. Deutsche zeitschrift für nervenheilkunde 27:article 12, 239–268.

Davidson, S., A. P. Meiklejohn, and R. Passmore. 1959. Human nutrition and dietetics. Baltimore, Williams and Wilkins.

Dewan, John G. and William B. Spauling. 1958. The organic psychoses. Toronto, University of Toronto Press.

Duncan, Garfield G. (ed.). 1952. Diseases of metabolism. 3d. ed. Philadelphia, W. B. Saunders.

Fogelson, Raymond D. 1965. Psychological theories of Windigo "psychosis" and a preliminary application of a models approach. *In* Melford E. Spiro, Context and meaning in cultural anthropology. New York, The Free Press.

Freedman, Alfred M. and Harold Kaplan (eds.). 1967. Comprehensive textbook of psychiatry. Baltimore, Williams and Wilkins.

Glass, Albert J. 1953. Psychotherapy in the combat zone. *In* Symposium on Stress. Washington, Walter Reed Army Medical Center.

Goldstein, Kurt. 1940. Human nature. Cambridge, Harvard University Press.

Gussow, Z. 1960. Pibloktoq (hysteria) among the Polar Eskimo: an ethnopsychiatric study. *In* W. Muensterberger, ed., Psychoanalysis and the Social Sciences. New York, International Universities Press.

Hollingshead, A. B. and F. C. Redlich. 1958. Social class and mental illness. New York, Wiley.

Hoskins, R. G. 1946. The biology of schizophrenia. New York, W. W. Norton and Co.

Hoygaard, Arne. 1941. Studies on the nutrition and physio-pathology of Eskimos. Oslo, Skrifter utgitt au Det Norske Videnskaps-Akademi i Oslo, I. Mat.-Naturv. Klasse 1940 No. 9.

Hunt, J. McV. (ed.). 1944. Personality and the behavior disorders. New York, Ronald Press.

Kallman, Franz. 1938. The genetics of schizophrenia. New York, J. J. Augustin.

Kane, E. K. 1856. Arctic explorations: the second Grinnell expedition. Philadelphia, Childs and Peterson.

Kline, Nathan S. 1956. Psychopharmacology. Washington, D. C., American Association for the Advancement of Science.

MacMillan, Donald B. 1918. Food supply of the Smith Sound Eskimos. American Museum Journal 18:161–176.

———. 1934. How Peary reached the pole. Boston, Houghton.

Mandelbaum, David G. 1949. Selected writings of Edward Sapir. Berkeley, University of California Press.

MAXWELL, J. P. 1930. Further studies in osteomalacia. Proceedings of the Royal Society of Medicine 23:639–640.

MERRITT, H. HOUSTON AND CLARENCE C. HARE (EDS.). 1953. Metabolic and toxic diseases of the nervous system. Baltimore, Williams and Wilkins.

MILBANK MEMORIAL FUND. 1952. The biology of mental health and mental disease. New York, Hoeber.

PAGE, JAMES D. (ED.). 1966. Approaches to psychopathology. New York, Columbia University Press.

PARKER, SEYMOUR. 1962. Eskimo psychopathology in the context of Eskimo personality and culture. American Anthropologist 64:76–96.

PAULING, LINUS. 1968. Orthomolecular psychiatry. Science 160:265–271.

PEARY, ROBERT E. 1907. Nearest the pole. New York, Doubleday, Page.

PETERSON, DONALD B., ET AL. 1950. Role of hypnosis in differentiation of epileptic from convulsive-like seizures. American Journal of Psychiatry 107:428–443.

PFEIFFER, JOHN. 1955. The human brain. New York, Harper & Bros.

PITTS, FERRIS N., AND JAMES N. McCLURE, JR. 1967. Lactate metabolism in anxiety neurosis. New England Journal of Medicine 277:1329–1336.

RASMUSSEN, KNUD. 1915. Foran Dagens Oje: Liv I Gronland. Copenhagen.

RESEARCH PUBLICATIONS OF THE ASSOCIATION FOR RESEARCH IN NERVOUS AND MENTAL DISEASE.

RODAHL, K. 1957. Human acclimatization to cold. Arctic Aeromedical Laboratory, Technical Report 57–21.

SARGANT, WILLIAM. 1954. An introduction to physical methods of treatment in psychiatry. Baltimore, Williams and Wilkins.

SELYE, HANS. 1950. The physiology and pathology of exposure to stress. Montreal, Acta.

———. 1956. The stress of life. New York, McGraw-Hill.

SHELLING, D. H. 1935. The parathyroids in health and disease. St. Louis, Mosby.

TOOTH, GEOFFREY. 1950. Studies in mental illness in the Gold Coast. London, H. M. Stationery Office.

WALLACE, ANTHONY F. C. 1959a. Cultural determinants of response to hallucinatory experience. A.M.A. Archives of General Psychiatry 1:58–69.

———. 1959b. The institutionalization of cathartic and control strategies in Iroquois religious psychotherapy. In Marvin Opler, ed., Culture and mental health. New York, MacMillan.

WHITNEY, H. 1911. Hunting with the Eskimos. New York, Century.

WILLIAMS, ROGER J. 1956. Biochemical individuality. New York, Wiley.

YU, PAUL N., BERNARD J. B. YIM, AND C. ALPHEUS STANFIELD. 1959. Hyperventilation syndrome. Archives of Internal Medicine 103:902–913.

CHAPTER TEN

Dreams and Altered States of Consciousness in Anthropological Research*

Erika Bourguignon

Introduction

Dreams and dreaming have been a subject of interest and significance for most human societies, and hundreds of ethnographies contain more or less scattered information on these subjects. Taking ethnographic studies at random, we find references such as the following:

> Horror of death is probably the reason for the great reluctance with which the Nuer discuss dreams, even impersonally and with reference only to stereotyped interpretations, for these only too often are prognostications of death: as when a man dreams of death, or of a fish called *rec ma car* (black fish), or of a turtle walking about which the dreamer fails to catch. (Evans-Pritchard 1956:154, n. 1).

Or again, with reference to the Nyakyusa:

> Proof of the activity and identity of witches is sought first in the dreams of victims and of "the defenders" (*abamanga*) of his (sic) village who are believed to have power to see and fight witches in dreams . . . (Wilson 1963:96).

*Data on altered states of consciousness presented here are part of a larger investigation supported in whole by PHS Research Grant MH 07463 from the National Institute of Mental Health.

Concerning the Alorese, we read:

> At night a household is roused at least once and frequently oftener by some
> member who has dreamed and gets up to replenish the fire and to tell his dream
> to the household. (DuBois 1961: vol. I:45–6).

And among the Saulteaux:

> According to native dogma the ability to conjure is acquired as a "dream
> blessing" during the puberty fast. (Hallowell:1942:19). . . .
> In the last generation, since the practice of puberty fasting has declined,
> native dogma has been elastic enough to sanction dream revelation at *any* time
> as being equally valid with revelations at adolescence itself. (*ibid.:*22).

Reina tells us of the Pokomam that "dreams are held to be real actions
carried out by the soul of the person when it leaves him in sleep at night."
And "dreams are interpreted in reverse." (1966:186). A man who dreamed
that his son had died, was upset about this. The dream was interpreted by
a woman who explained to him:

> Experience has shown that when a person dies in a dream, it actually means
> a long and healthy life. But to dream of a child in a healthy state (*muy galán*),
> on the other hand, is cause for concern. It should be taken as an indication of a
> serious predicament. (Reina, 1966:186).

And finally, we read of the Mestizo peasants of the Colombian village of
Aritama:

> Most people claim to dream frequently and to have occasional nightmares,
> and there is considerable interest in dream interpretation . . . Many lucky or
> unfortunate occurrences in a person's life will be attributed to dreams by
> retrospective interpretation, even if the dream occurred months or years before
> the happening. (Reichel-Dolmatoff, 1961:431).

There are a large number of commonly known dream symbols, which are
the basis for the popular interpretations. About these, the authors say:

> . . . the largest number of symbols refer to the death of relatives. If one accepts
> the view that dreams are frequently a form of wish fulfillment, the emphasis on
> dreams that predict the death of relatives would tend to reflect the high level of
> hostility which prevails in most, if not all, interpersonal relations. It is then also
> significant that to dream of the death of one's mother, or of dead or ill people,
> tombs, and flowers, is interpreted as predicting happiness and that to dream of
> other people's death is said to predict wealth (*ibid.:*433).

These quotations give us a hint of the variety of subject matter and the
variety of research possibilities open to anthropologists with respect to the

topics of dreams and dreaming. They also indicate some of the ambiguities in this area.

We see from our six examples that among some groups, as among the Nuer, there is reluctance to discuss dreams, while among others, such as the Alorese, there is great eagerness to do so. One reason for both the reluctance and the eagerness is found in the use of dreams for purposes of divination, both as foretelling the future, as among the Nuer and as the discovery of hidden facts, as in the identification of witches among the Nyakyusa. In more general terms, Hultkranz (1968) has shown the significance of dream interpretation as a form of divination among North American Indians, as has Favre (1968) for past and present Maya groups. Bastide has presented materials indicating that among ten geographic groupings of Afro-Americans, covering all of the Western hemisphere, dream interpretation is the one universal form of divination (Bastide 1968:423).

However, dreams may not only be considered as providing information, they may also be seen as a medium of action. The Nyakyusa "defenders," for example, actually fight witches in their dreams, while the Saulteaux receive power to carry out a calling. In the case of the Saulteaux, we see an equation between a vision obtained as part of a quest — a fast — and a dream on another occasion. This point is of some importance and we shall return to it presently.

The Pokomam, like the Nyakyusa and the Saulteaux, consider dreams to deal with real actions or experiences of the soul. The Pokomam and the Colombian Mestizos of Aritama interpret dreams in reverse, so that to dream of death is good, while it is bad among the Nuer, as we have seen. The authors of the study of Aritama provide us with a psychoanalytic perspective on such dreams and dream interpretations.

Some Anthropological Studies of Dreams

The anthropological study of dreams has been reviewed a number of times, most notably by Lincoln (1935), Eggan (1961), D'Andrade (1961) and Barnouw (1963) and it is not our intention to do so again. As already mentioned, a vast amount of information concerning dreams and dreaming in particular societies is scattered throughout the ethnographic literature. Yet, while the subjects of dreams and dreaming are touched upon in ethnographies in general, and particularly in those focusing on certain subject matters, such as religion or personality structure, dreams and dreaming have only rarely been the principle targets of major ethnographic or comparative studies. Lincoln's work, which represents the major comparative effort, has not been extended or replicated. Where there has been a concerted effort to study dreams in non-Western societies, this has often been done within a psychoanalytic framework. Thus, we have discussions of dreams, together with other psychologically relevant materials and in some instances, personal documents of various sorts, for the Trobriand Islanders (Malinowski, 1927), the Alorese (DuBois, 1944; Kardiner, 1945), the Trukese (Gladwin and Sarason, 1953), the Kaska (Honigmann, 1961), the Aranda (Róheim, 1947), the Navaho (Kluckhohn and Morgan, 1951) and the Mohave (Devereux, 1957), among others.

Other students have considered dreams in terms of their manifest content, with a view toward the relationship between this content and the culture of the people. Hallowell (1966) viewed the dream world of the Ojibwa as an integral part of their culturally constituted behavioral environment. Bastide has studied the manifest content of the dreams of a sample of Brazilians (1950, 1966) and Eberhard has worked with Chinese dreams (1967, 1968). The most extensive work in the area, however, is the great collection of Hopi dreams by Dorothy Eggan (1952, 1955, 1956, 1957, 1961, 1966) and of the Yir Yoront by Sharp (Schneider and Sharp, 1969).

As of 1961, Eggan had collected 650 Hopi dreams, extending over a period of more than twenty years. Of these, 362 came from the same informant. While Eggan did not publish a statistical analysis of these materials, a major portion of the dreams themselves is available in microcard form (Eggan, 1957). In a lengthy analysis of a series of dreams by several informants, Eggan (1966) shows the relationship of these dreams, and of the problems the individual dreamers were grappling with, to the Hopi water serpent (*Palulukon*) belief and ritual. As a fertility figure, the water serpent is "a *conscious* sexual symbol in the culture" (1966:260, Eggan's italics). But as a deity, he condemns all deviant behavior such as "sexual misconduct, gossip, quarrels and physical aggression." (260–1). His appearance in dreams is interpreted as evidence of the dreamer's transgressions, or those of others appearing in his dream. A bad dream must be confessed. "Hopi rules about dream discussion thus start a frequently successful probing of the dreamer's situation." (261). The manifest content of the dream, the cultural interpretation of dreams and the rules about behavior concerning dreams interact so as to play a decisive role in the problem solving processes through which individuals deal with their life situations. That dreams use symbolic entities of myth and ritual is clearly demonstrated in this study. The use of myth materials in the dreams of Eggan's major informant is presented in an earlier paper (1955), and this is an instance of particular interest, since that informant is a deviant in some ways and used the cultural materials in an idiosyncratic manner. As to the relationship between dream and culture, the individual and the collective, Eggan sums up by saying: " . . . when a Hopi *hikwsi* [psyche] searches through *dimoki* — the "bundle" of his dream thoughts — he finds it richly populated with cultural images that act as a rudder to push a demanding self back into the coercive tide of social process." (1966:263).

Sharp collected 149 dreams (from 43 men and eight women) among the Yir Yoront of Australia during the 1930's. The data and Schneider's analysis have recently been published (Schneider and Sharp, 1969). The manifest content of these dreams was analyzed by Schneider under four headings: sexual intercourse, aggression, death, and dreams of whites and white culture. His initial assumption "that the dreams of a group of dreamers of the same culture and the same society will likely show some clear regularities in manifest content" (1969:14) is indeed borne out. For example, in the dreams of sexual intercourse, the sex partner of the male dreamer is usually of the appropriate social category. However, when she is not, there are specific interruptions impeding intercourse and "the magnitude of the interruption correlates with the strength of the prohibition on sexual relations" (*ibid.:* 51). With respect to aggression, the dreamer is most often the victim (56%) and rarely the actor (19%). The aggression dreams both reflect actual intergroup fighting and the frustration the men experience at the hands of mother's brother and elder brother, who are cast in the role of aggressors in dreams. The death dreams show a matter-of-fact attitude toward the subject, but when it is the dreamer who dies, this is often followed by resurrection, although no actual ideology of resurrection exists among these people. With respect to whites and white culture, the Yir Yoront see themselves quite realistically as "playing subordinate, passive roles" (*ibid.:* 53).

The correspondence between cultural reality and the manifest content of these dreams, taken as a group, is striking.

Since originally studying the Yir Yoront dreams in 1941, Schneider has collected from the literature a total of 1,500 dreams from 75 societies, with major collections from 13 societies. While the analysis of these materials has yet to be published, Schneider suggests the following: "(1) there are certain regularities in the manifest content of groups of dreams regardless of society and culture of the dreamers and (2) there are certain differences between groups of dreams that seem to be a function of the culture of the dreamer" (*ibid.:* 55). These claims are illustrated by the observation that in the groups analyzed, Schneider always finds "a higher proportion of dreams of aggression than of death or coitus" (*ibid.*) with the dreamer more often the victim than the aggressor. Similarly Hall and Domhoff (1963), analyzing the manifest content of dreams of eleven groups, find a consistent difference in the dreams of men and of women, with men always dreaming "more about other men than they do about women, while women dream about men and women in about equal terms" (*ibid.:* 278). In addition to a great variety of U.S. groups, these findings apply to Hopi dreams, provided by Eggan, and to the male Yir Yoront. (The sample of dreams from females being too small for analysis.)

Meggitt (1962) reporting on dreams and dream interpretation among the Mae Enga of New Guinea, suggests that in addition to the manifest content of dreams and their latent (psychoanalytic) content, an intermediary level of symbolization must be recognized, that of the latent content as understood by native dream theory. This is in agreement with Eggan's findings, mentioned above.

The subject of native dream theory may be considered from several points of view: (1) as Meggitt suggests, native theory gives us an indication as to the conscious meaning of a dream for the dreamer aside from its "surface" manifest content, and the presumed latent, unconscious meaning it may carry. As I have suggested on the basis of Haitian data (Bourguignon, 1954) the native theory gives us a clue to the way the dreamer *experiences* his dream, not only to the way in which he interprets it. (2) Native theory gives us an indication of how dreams are *used* in a given society, *e.g.*, with reference to divination, as already indicated above. And (3) in cross-cultural terms, the question arises as to why certain uses of dreams are made in some societies and not in others. This has been treated by D'Andrade (1961) in his cross-cultural study of the "use of dreams to seek and control supernatural powers."

Dream Usages and their Correlates

D'Andrade coded a sample of 64 societies taken from the Human Relation Area Files for use of dreams to seek and control supernatural powers. He found significant differences between those societies that have such use of dreams and those which do not with respect to two variables:

post-marital residence and subsistence economy. Those societies which were found to use dreams to seek and control supernatural powers were more likely to be those where the son resided after marriage in a different village or local group, and least likely to be those where he resided in his parents' household; societies where he resided in the same village or local group were intermediate with respect to their use of dreams. Secondly, societies using dreams in the manner indicated were more likely to live by hunting, gathering and fishing and least likely to have agriculture with animal husbandry. Those having agriculture without animal husbandry were found to be intermediate. Textor, in his *Cross-Cultural Summary* (1968) investigated differences between "societies using dreams to seek and control supernatural powers" and those which do not in regard to a series of societal variables. He reports a total of 24 chi square tests, significant at the .05 level of probability or below, which differentiate these two groups of societies. It should be noted, however, that the samples for these tables vary widely, deriving from overlaps between D'Andrade's sample and those of other investigators. The overall findings suggest that societies with such use of dreams are more likely to have the following characteristics than those without this use: they are located in North America, having non-fixed settlements, with simple agriculture or incipient food production rather than intensive agriculture, having no towns and an average population size smaller than 200, with simple political and jurisdictional hierarchies, without national levels of organization and with class stratification absent. (Additional findings refer to N<37 and are omitted here, although they are coherent with the findings presented above.)

It was D'Andrade's intent to test the hypothesis that "anxiety about being alone and on one's own gives rise to the use of dreams to seek and control supernatural powers" (*op. cit.*:322). Postmarital residence patterns were considered a possible cause of such anxiety. The findings support the hypothesis to the extent that the further sons move away from their parents after marriage, the more likely the society is to have instituted the use of dreams in the manner indicated. Nothing is said in these findings about women's postmarital residential moves, and indeed if a son remains in his natal group, assuming village or band exogamy, his wife will have moved away from hers. As D'Andrade states, in a separate test, no association was found between the distance a woman moves at marriage and the use of dreams. This is interpreted as follows: "Perhaps this is because religion is more frequently a man's affair, or perhaps because women may turn to their spouses in order to relieve the anxiety of loss of parental support in a way men may not" (*ibid.:* 323). As indicated above, in the nature of the case, it would seem impossible for the use of dreams to be linked both to men's and women's patterns of postmarital residence. The hypothesis concerning subsistence economy was derived from the work of Barry, Child and Bacon (1959) showing pressure toward independence, self reliance, and achievement in child rearing among hunting and gathering societies. However D'Andrade states concerning his findings with reference to subsistence economy: "Unfortunately it is not possible to decide whether this association is due to the effect of child rearing, or to the effect of role pressures on adults" (*ibid.:*326).

It should be noted that statistical associations and chi square tests of significant differences do not allow us to test hypotheses concerning causal relations; they allow us only to state the degree of probability with which it can be claimed that associations between traits or differences between groups are not due to chance. In view of the findings made by D'Andrade, and their extension by Textor, it is tempting to suggest that we are dealing here with a causal chain, only certain links of which have been ferreted out by the cross-cultural tests conducted so far. Such a chain might begin with ecological and technological factors, indicated by the data on subsistence economy. These in turn have a bearing on population size and on the tendency to non-fixed settlement noted by Textor, with patterns of political and social organization appropriate to small groups of such types. Postmarital residence rules, on the one hand, and child training practices, on the other, represent appropriate adaptations to such conditions, which, in turn, are mirrored (or projected) in the religious and fantasy life of the people. A similar conceptual scheme is proposed by Beatrice Whiting (1963:5) who moved from ecology to maintenance systems (economy, social structure) to childrearing practices which give rise to child personality, which on the one hand is reflected in child behavior (work, games) and cultural products (fantasy, sayings, recreation, concepts of world) and on the other hand gives rise to adult personality which is inferred from adult behavior (crime rates, suicide rates, leisure time activities, etc.) and from cultural products (religious beliefs, theories of disease, folk tales). It is possible to assign several different positions to dreams and dreaming in such causal chains. It is possible to see the latent content of the dreams as revealing a modal personality type produced by the child training practices of such societies, for example by the pressures toward independence, self reliance and achievement reported by Barry, Child and Bacon (1959) for hunting and gathering societies. It is possible to see the institutionalization of dreaming for certain societal purposes as caused by, or as an expression of, anxiety in the child (as above) or in the young male adult, as at marriage and removal from his natal group, or in the adult as in the anxiety aroused by the pressures to perform in the food quest, in warfare, or in the various other activities for which a dream blessing may be sought. It is possible to view the institutionalization of dreaming either as expressive, as above, or as instrumental in providing certain status holders (*e.g.*, shamans) or validating certain social roles (adulthood, war leadership, etc.) and thus providing a medium of societal articulation. It should be noted that coding a society as having the "use of dreams to seek and control supernatural powers" does not tell us anything about the expected or real incidence of such dreams. It may represent the ideal, and even the exceptional — a statement approaching the status of a myth — rather than a universal experience of all individuals in a given category. In this connection, we may also consider that where such culture pattern dreams were kept secret, no one could really know the incidence of their occurrence. In some societies dream blessing could be acquired by purchase (Benedict, 1923), and in the period of acculturation, at least, they might occasionally be simulated (*e.g.*, Radin, 1926, for the Winnebago). We are therefore on safer ground in operating on a statistical level in viewing such patterns of dreaming as institutionalized attributes of societies, rather than primarily as attributes of individuals and to ask what types of societies are characterized by these patterns, and what functions they may play in the organization and maintenance of such societies.

At our present state of knowledge it seems hazardous to venture further along lines of causal analysis. It should be noted, however, that societies using dreams to seek and control supernatural powers are more likely to be located in North America than elsewhere: It is clear that we are dealing here at least in part with the impact of the vision quest and guardian spirit complex on the data. As such, the role of diffusion must be taken into account as well in order to explain the presence of this particular pattern.

Summary

The materials discussed so far can be classed conveniently under three rubrics:

1. What kinds of dreams do the people report?
2. What cultural uses are made of dreams: interpretations, evaluations, integration into cultural practices of various types?

3. What uses do the anthropologists make of these two types of information, both in dealing with the study of a single culture and for purposes of cross-cultural comparison?

The studies we have referred to may then be grouped somewhat as follows:

1. The actual presentation of a series of dreams from one or more individuals in particular cultures: for example, Lincoln (1935) presents dreams from eight North American Indian groups, Eggan (1957) presents a series of Hopi dreams, Schneider and Sharp (1969) present a series of dreams from the Yir Yoront, and Williams (1957) presents a series of dreams from Maronite Moslems. (These references are cited as examples, and are not meant to be exhaustive in any way.)

2. A search for universal subject matter in dreams. Such dreams were called "type dreams" by Seligman (1923a, 1923b). The most ambitious cross-cultural investigation of this subject was conducted by Lincoln (1935), whose interest with respect to such dreams, like that of his mentor, Seligman, lay in the psychoanalytic symbolism of type dreams and their latent content. As indicated, in spite of the passage of twenty-five years, this work has been neither extended nor replicated.

3. The study of trends — both universal and culturally unique — in the manifest content of dreams. This approach is most clearly represented in the work of Schneider (Schneider and Sharp, 1969) and Hall and Domhoff (1963). Such studies seek to relate the manifest content of dreams both to cultural particulars and social universals. For such analyses, large series of dreams are required.

4. The relationship between dreams and cultural behavior. The relationship between the idiosyncratic dreams of the individual and the broader cultural patterns is quickly seen to be circular in several respects. Dream content is influenced by cultural symbolism and imagery (*e.g.*, Eggan 1955, 1966) and by cultural rules and societal prohibitions (*e.g.*, Schneider and Sharp, 1969). Cultural constitution of the behavioral environment (Hallowell, 1966) is affected and reinforced not only by the manifest content of dreams but also by the cultural rules concerning the interpretation and evaluation of dreams. We must then add under this heading studies of the meaning of dreams as standardized in various cultures (*e.g.*, Bourguignon, 1954; Reichel-Dolmatoff, 1961; Meggitt, 1962; and Reina, 1966).

5. Finally, we come to studies not of specific dreams and their evaluations, but of the use to which dreaming is put in particular cultures
and in interaction with other beliefs and institutions as this is seen in
cross-cultural terms. In the work by D'Andrade (1961) and Textor
(1968) the use of dreams in a certain manner becomes a societal
variable seen in interdependence with other societal variables. This
latter type of study must necessarily operate on a much higher level
of generalization and as such loses much of the refined detail of the
holistic study of individual cultures. However, such cross-cultural
studies make it possible to observe regularities which cannot be more
than suggested on the level of the single culture and single society.
One of the gains we may hope for from such studies, whatever their
current limitations, is that they should be expected to let us perceive
consistent explanations, that is, to allow us to identify "the same
phenomenon" when it occurs again and again and link it with "the
same explanation" rather than to produce unique *ad hoc* explanations
in each instance.

Dreams, Neurophysiology, and Evolution

In quite a different manner from the studies discussed so far, the work
of Kleitman and his associates during the past dozen years represents a
major breakthrough in the study of dreaming (*e.g.*, Kleitman, 1963;
Dement, 1966). As a result of their laboratory studies and those stimulated
by them among other researchers in all parts of the world, we now have
systematic, empirical information concerning a great many aspects of sleep
and dreaming. We now know that there are two alternating forms of sleep,
during one of which, termed REM (Rapid Eye Movement) sleep, or
paradoxical sleep, dreaming occurs.[1] The eye movements apparently quite
literally represent a scanning of the dream images by the dreamer.
Dreaming was found to occur in all subjects studied, even among people
who otherwise never remember dreams. Dreaming occurs several times
each night and has various concomitants, such as changes in EEG, heart
rate, breathing rate, etc.

REM sleep, and thus apparently dreaming, has been observed not only
in human beings (including infants) but in all mammals that have been
studied (dogs, cats, monkeys, sheep) (Dement, 1966:100). Kleitman considers it to be a by-product of physiological processes, saying that

[1] Recent work of several investigators indicates that true nightmares occur in State IV (non-
REM) sleep. What the relationship of this phenomenon to dreaming is, however, remains yet
to be clarified (Broughton, 1968; Fisher, 1970), and will not concern us here.

"dreaming is nothing more than the consequence of repetitive cortical activation or 'paradoxical phase' of periodic variation in sleep EEG patterns" (1963:107). In other words, the activity of dreaming is clearly linked to variations in the physiological aspects of sleep. Whether it may be said to be "nothing more than" is surely a matter of debate. Anthropologists who have followed the lead not only of Freud but also of the peoples they study, assume that the content of dreams (whether "latent" or "manifest") can indeed tell us something about the dreamer and his world and not only about his physiology.

From a psychobiological point of view, it appears clearly established by the work of Kleitman and his associates and other researchers who have studied sleep along similar lines (Bremer, 1966; also, see Kleitman's extensive bibliography), that dreams are a by-product of normal sleep. Dement (1960), impeding REM sleep in his subjects, found increase in irritability, anxiety and appetite and also an increased amount of dreaming when the subjects were permitted to recover from dream deprivation. These experiments led Dement to conclude "that a certain amount of dreaming each night is a necessity,"[2] and that dream deprivation creates a dream deficit which must apparently be made up.

Kleitman has developed an evolutionary theory of sleep, according to which " . . . dreaming and advanced wakefulness is a cortical function." (1963:370). As Hallowell has pointed out, the evolutionary perspective on dreaming which these studies have opened up is of major importance to our understanding of the development of a human mode of adaptation:

> . . . the same condition which made possible the development of a new behavioral plateau, characterized by language and fully developed forms of cultural adaptation, was also that which enabled dreams, visions, and products of imaginative processes to be articulated and thus to assume the social significance which we find in *Homo sapiens* (Hallowell, 1966:269).

and again:

> Unconscious psychological forces, hitherto latent in hominid evolution, but now mediated through dreams, visions and other imaginative processes, intruded themselves upon man, because of his evolving capacity for self-awareness and the knowledge he could acquire of the inner life of other persons. Dream

---

[2] Kleitman does not agree; " . . . dreaming need not have a special function and may be quite meaningless . . . The effects of dreaming curtailment discovered by Dement may be due to interference with an acquired habit" (*op. cit.*:107). He goes on to compare increased dreaming after a period of curtailment with an overindulgence in sweets after a period of curtailed intake of sweets.

experiences could become the object of reflective thought and become socially significant. Varied interpretations of the meaning of dreams could become an integral part of the diversified world views that arose and that became embedded in traditional cultural systems. (*ibid.:*269–70).

It is interesting to note that this awareness of one's dreams, of images and other sensations perceived in sleep, is often not only interpreted but also experienced as the activities of other beings, or as due to the intervention of such other beings, and of some portion of the self over which the dreamer has no control. Yet, as Hallowell points out, in some societies, such as the Papuans mentioned by Devereux (1951:86), individuals do in fact feel responsible for their dream actions. It should be noted that such a view is also recorded in the Old Testament, where Jacob chides Joseph for having been prideful in his dreams concerning his parents and his brothers (Genesis 37:X).

Dreams and Visions

In the passage quoted above, Hallowell speaks of "dreams, visions and products of imaginative processes" (Hallowell 1966:269). In the passage quoted concerning the Saulteaux he speaks of a "'dream blessing' during the puberty fast" (Hallowell 1942:19) and "dream revelation at *any* time" (*ibid.:*22). The Saulteaux puberty fast was a particular instance of the widespread North American pattern of the vision quest (Benedict:1923; Blumensohn:1933), and in any given case we cannot be sure that the vision experienced by the seeker may have been a sleeping dream, a waking hallucination or the product of other "imaginative processes." While we may be able to distinguish dreams from such other hallucinatory processes in the laboratory, the anthropological situation, where we must depend on the self reporting of informants, is rather different. Whether the dreams which occur during REM sleep are distinguished or merged with other vivid hallucinatory experiences will depend in part on cultural dogma. This dogma influences not only the *reporting* of dreams and other pseudo-perceptions, including secondary elaborations, but also, as far as we can tell, the subjective experience of these states. (Bourguignon:1954).

Merriam tells us that among the Flathead Indians songs were acquired in contacts with supernaturals. The occasions for such contacts:

> . . . include the formal vision quest, dreams in an otherwise normal context, surprise encounters at unpredictable times though apparently always when the person or persons sharing the experience are isolated from others, and in what seems to be a relatively extended learning situation (Merriam 1967:7).

Lincoln, in his comparative study, tells us that:

> The dreams and visions of so-called primitive peoples always fall into two distinct classes, the unsought, or spontaneous dream occurring during sleep, here called 'individual' dreams, and the sought or induced 'culture pattern' dreams of special tribal significance (Lincoln, 1935:22).

Lincoln's discussion of dreams then includes both types and as far as the culture pattern dream is concerned he makes no attempt to distinguish between those which, though sought, do in fact occur during sleep and those which are waking hallucinations. The distinction which concerns Lincoln is not between dreams and other forms of pseudo-perception but between the types of meanings culturally assigned to them. These distinctions correspond to the cultural distinctions made by the peoples under study, rather than to distinctions between REM sleep dreams and waking hallucinations which may be of interest in another context, particularly since in Western culture hallucinations are generally thought of in psychopathological terms. Thus, Sullivan tells us that hallucination "is expressive of a dissociated tendency to integrate some particular interpersonal situation" (1947:139). And elsewhere he states that "although hallucinations do not necessarily usher in schizophrenic episodes, they frequently do so" (1953:361). Yet it is clear from ethnographic data, that where visions, or what Lincoln calls culture pattern dreams, are institutionalized, as are the means for obtaining them, this evaluation of hallucination does not hold in quite the same measure as in contemporary Western society where such experiences are unpatterned and feared. We shall return to this point below, with special reference to the contemporary drug cults.

Thus, we may summarize this discussion by stating that a) cultures vary in the importance and types of meanings they assign to dreams and other pseudo-perceptions and b) in subjective reporting and cultural significance dreams are often not distinguishable from other types of pseudo-perceptions. On the other hand, it must also be noted that both in cultural and in psychobiological terms, the several forms of sleep may be considered akin to other states of altered consciousness. Thus, a larger framework for the comparative analysis of dreams and visions may therefore be justified than that which has customarily been employed.

Hallucinatory or visionary states are often reported in the ethnographic literature as "trance," particularly, but not exclusively, when such states are induced by drugs. Sometimes, however, the term is also used as synonymous for such other concepts as "possession" or "possession state." This is the case, for example, in the literature on Bali (Bateson and Mead, 1942; Belo, 1960). Because of the broad scope of these terms it has seemed to me desirable to establish some distinctions (Bourguignon, 1965; 1969). The term "trance" refers to an altered state of consciousness in which contact with self and others is modified in some particular way, ranging from total unconsciousness to a very shallow modification. Trance is observable to the bystander, be he native, anthropologist or clinician. It may be induced in a broad variety of ways, which range from the psychological, such as forms of suggestion or contagion, to the psycho-physiological effects of hallucinogenic drugs. Such states, furthermore, may be given a great variety of interpretations. Among these, two are found very frequently: the idea of a temporary absence of the (or one) soul, which leaves the body and goes on a trip (whether this be in the jargon of the hippy or of the South American shaman), or is abducted, and quite in contrast to this, the idea that the body is activated by one or more possessing spirits for the duration of the trance. In that case, the actions and words of the individual during this state are taken to be those of the spirit, absolving the actor from any responsibility for those actions and words. I have called states of this second type "possession trance," while those which do not involve a belief in possession, being interpreted as soul absence or in some other way, I have referred to as "trance." Parenthetically, a further source of terminological confusion should be mentioned, and that is that the concept of possession is not applied exclusively to states of altered consciousness. For example, it is often applied to cases of physical illness, even sterility. To cite only one instance, such beliefs are found widespread in Ethiopia, as shown in the recent report by Giel, Gezahegn and van Luijk (1968).

Whiting and Child (1953) used both the soul loss concept and the spirit possession concept — without any reference to altered states of consciousness — as explanations of illness linked to dependency. However, at least where altered states of consciousness come into play, the difference between these two kinds of concepts will be seen to be of major significance. The possession concept is also found to refer to situations other than those of illness. For example, among the Shilluk, the king is said to go into a brief state of possession trance during the installation ceremony; however, the spirit, who is believed to take hold of him at that time, is also believed to remain with him permanently, although his presence is then no longer expressed in a dissociated state (Lienhardt, 1954). To sum up, then, we distinguish between Trance and Possession Trance on the one hand, and between Possession Trance and Possession on the other. This latter distinction, however, will not further concern us in the following.

We now know, as we have long suspected, that dreaming is a universal characteristic of mankind, as it is apparently of other mammals. The degree to which aspects of dreaming have been institutionalized, however, varies widely. D'Andrade, as has been mentioned, identified a complex which he refers to as "the use of dreams to seek and control supernatural powers." He found one or more of the four traits composing this complex in 55% of his worldwide sample of 64 societies. We selected a large sample of societies from all parts of the world from Murdock's Ethnographic Atlas (1967). In researching the literature we found some institutionalized form of dissociation in 437 societies, or 89% of the total of 488 for which we were able to obtain data. Of these 38% (186) had Trance, 27% (135) had Possession Trance and 24% (116) had both. Furthermore, there were marked differences in worldwide distribution. Thus, 71% of all North American Indian societies had Trance, 21% had both and a mere 4% had only Possession Trance. In contrast to this, in Sub-Saharan Africa, we found only 16% of our sample societies to have Trance, while 6% had Possession Trance and 20% both forms of institutionalized altered states of consciousness. (For further details, see Bourguignon, ed., n.d., 1968.)

These figures are cited here to indicate that we are dealing, indeed, with phenomena of major ethnographic and theoretical significance. What is the relationship of all this to dreams? Table I shows the overlap between our sample and that of D'Andrade, presenting materials on a total of 54 societies. Table I compares societies where Trance is present with those where it is not with respect to their use of dreams to seek and control supernatural powers. Trance societies are divided into those which have only Trance and those which have both Trance and Possession Trance. Trance Absent societies are divided into those which have Possession Trance and those which have neither.

We expected to find that societies with institutionalized forms of Trance were more likely to be those coded by D'Andrade as having the use of dreams to seek and control supernatural powers than those that do not have institutionalized forms of Trance. Among the reasons for this expectation was a statement by Firth concerning the Tikopia, who have Possession Trance, but not Trance:

TABLE I   Relation of Trance to Use of Dreams to Seek and Control Supernatural Powers

	Total No.	Total %	Trance Present — Trance	Trance Present — Trance/Possession Trance	Total No.	Total %	Trance Absent — Possession Trance	Trance Absent — 0	Total No.	Total %
	54	100			37	100			17	100
Use of Dreams Present	28	52	Paiute a,b,c,d	Semang a,b,c,d	23	62	Ifugao c	Cuna a,b,c	5	29
			Comanche a,b,c,d	Iroquois a,b,c,d			Wolof b			
			Crow a,b,c,d	Jivaro a,b,c,d			Nyakyusa b			
			Ojibwa a,b,c,d	Pukapukans a,b,c			Bemba b			
			Omaha a,b,c,d	Copper Eskimo a,b,c						
			Papago a,b,c,d	Rwala b,d						
			Kaska a,c,d,	Yaruro b,d						
			Chukchee a,b	Kapauku a,b						
			Lapps a,b	Yakut d						
			Mundurucu a	Araucanians b						
			Trobriands c	Azande d						
			Fang a							
	26	48	Karen	Yoruba	14	38	Kurtatchi	Aymara	12	71
Use of Dreams Absent			Callinago	Mataco			Ganda	Min Chia		
			Riffians	Burmese			Tanala	Mossi (Yatenda)		
			Iban	Lepcha			Bhil	Tallensi		
			Tupinambe	Thai			Samoans	Tiv		
				Somali				Nama		
				Ifaluk				Siriono		
				Marquesas						
				Ashanti						

$X^2 = 4.97$ $P < .05$

The theory of spirit-impersonation [possession trance in the terminology of this paper] removes one from the necessity of accepting seriously dream encounters which are undesirable (Firth, 1967:171).

That is, Possession Trance, at least among the Tikopia, is credited with greater authority in matters of supernatural communications than dreams. On the other hand, the private experiences of dreams and hallucinatory trance are so similar as often to be inseparable. They should therefore be expected to be treated similarly. Among the Diegueño Indians, a society which uses dreams as indicated and also Trance, we find that Trance produced by the drug Datura stramonium (*toloache*) authorizes dream communications, as it were. In the words of a Diegueño dream doctor:

> *Toloache* puts you into kind of a dream state of mind that stays with you the rest of your life, and you never forget what you learned. It helps you keep on learning too and gives you real power in everything. Without it you aren't a real doctor. (Toffelmier and Luomala, 1936:201)

Toloache trance is part of the initiation of the dream doctor, and occurs only once. His major curing activity involves his ability to dream successfully, and to interpret his own dreams and those of others.

Our hypothesis of a significant difference with respect to the use of dreams between societies which have Trance and those which do not, is borne out, as shown in Table I. The difference between the Trance Present and Trance Absent societies with respect to their use of dreams is significant at a level of probability of less than .05. We find the use of dreams to seek and control supernatural powers in 62% of the Trance societies. On the other hand, in 71% of those societies where Trance is absent, the use of dreams in this sense is also absent. However, we can push the analysis a bit further and attempt to account for the exceptions to our expected results. Fourteen of the Trance societies do not have the hypothesized use of dreams; 64% of these (9 cases out of 14) are societies that have both Trance and Possession Trance. Only 36% (5 cases) of the exceptions are societies with Trance only. Similarly, 80% of the exceptions (4 out of 5 cases) where Trance is absent, do have Possession Trance. That is, Possession Trance societies are about as likely to use dreams as not to, regardless of whether they also use Trance. A further question we may ask deals with the *kind of use* of dreams that the various types of societies make. With respect to use of dreams to seek and control supernatural powers, D'Andrade coded his sample of societies with respect to the following four traits:

a. Supernaturals appear in dreams and give important powers, aid, ritual, and information.
b. Religious experts (priests, shamans) expected to use their own dreams in performance of their role (*e.g.*, curing, divination).
c. Culture pattern dreams required before some roles may be assumed.
d. Dreams induced by special techniques (*e.g.*, fasting, drugs, sleeping alone, etc.). (D'Andrade, 1961:321).

Table I shows the distribution of these traits. Among the Trance societies six use all four traits, while three of the Trance and Possession Trance societies do. None of the No Trance societies use all four traits, although the Cuna, who do not have either Trance or Possession Trance have three of the four traits, induced dreams being absent. Three traits are also found in one Trance society and two of the Trance/Possession Trance group. Two uses are found among two of the Trance and three of the Trance/Possession Trance group, and the remaining societies only have one trait each. Trait d, which might be expected to have the greatest overlap with Trance, since reports of induced dreams might be interpreted as cases of hallucinatory trance, occurs in 7 of the 12 societies with Trance, but in each case two or more other dream uses are also listed. In the Trance/Possession Trance societies, it occurs in five out of 11 cases. Among the Trance Absent societies it does not occur at all. It is interesting to note, that where Trance is reported we find the greatest variety of dreams use traits, where there is both Trance and Possession Trance, somewhat less, and where there is Possession Trance only, one trait is reported in the four cases that have dream use. All of these refer to specialized roles. The Cuna, that have neither Trance nor Possession Trance have three dream uses and are somewhat of an anomaly. They may well have had Trance at an earlier time.[3]

In summary, then, Trance societies are more likely to be those identified by D'Andrade as using dreams to seek and control supernatural powers than non-Trance societies. Furthermore, our findings concerning Trance societies compared with those having Possession Trance (Bourguignon, 1968), on the whole parallel those of Textor (1968) with reference to dreams: Trance societies are more likely than Possession Trance societies to be found in North America, to be migratory or semi-nomadic (*i.e.*, to have non-fixed settlements); to have smaller local populations (less than 1,000), to have no jurisdictional hierarchy beyond the local level, to lack class stratification of freemen as well as to lack slavery, kin groups are

[3] See review of early sources by Stout (1947:100–102).

more likely to be cognatic, mode of marriage is less likely to be by bride price, cousin marriage is more likely to be non-lateral, and segregation of adolescent boys to be absent, the overall estimated population size is more likely to be below 100,000, family form is more likely to be that of the nuclear family, and monogamy with occasional polygyny is more likely to occur among them than polygyny. (It should be noted however, that when the six major world regions are investigated separately, the findings differ importantly for the above.) The overall picture is one of societies of smaller scale and lesser complexity. On the other hand, societies with Possession Trance tend toward greater scale and greater societal complexity, and those having both Trance and Possession Trance tend to be on the whole intermediate with respect to most of the variables. The same factors which make for a reliance on dreams also appear to be those which make for a reliance on Trance, both, presumably involving a pattern of beliefs in the possibility of direct communication with supernaturals on the part of individuals. In many of these societies, such communications are private, in that the dream or Trance is experienced in isolation. They are almost always private in the sense that the phenomenon is intrapsychic and available to others only through the individual's report. Possession Trance, on the other hand, is generally a matter of public ritual, in which the Possession Trancer acts out the behavior of supernatural entities, and by impersonation, makes a contact between a human group and the supernatural possible.[4] He is often himself amnesic with reference to the events and the contact, which is mediated through him for the group, reaches him only secondarily through the report of others after the termination of his possession trance. Thus, while such a state is a performance, it is not truly an experience for the actor, but rather for the group for whose benefit it is performed. Our justification for differentiating between Trance and Possession Trances, then, rests not only on the differences in conceptualization between these two types of states of altered consciousness, but also in the fact that the different conceptualizations appear to be reflected in the behavior of the actors in the two types of situations.

To discuss REM sleep dreams, Trance and Possession Trance in a common frame of reference, we have placed them along a continuum (Fig. 1), where REM sleep and dreams represent one pole, Possession Trance and impersonations another and Trance with hallucinations (or, in the religious context, visions) a convenient central point. Obviously, no precise meanings are assigned to the distances on the diagram, and the states of

[4] For a discussion of impersonation, comparing the use of masks with that of Possession Trance, see Bourguignon, 1966.

altered consciousness and their behavioral dimensions that are indicated are not meant as an exhaustive inventory. They represent characteristic high points of ritualized forms of altered states of consciousness.[5] Our purpose in this grouping is to permit comparisons along a series of dimensions: psychobiological, interpersonal and reflexive, perceptual and cognitive, and social structural.

The continuum presented in Figure 1 implies a relationship between dreaming and Trance, particularly of the hallucinatory type. Kleitman, thinking apparently primarily of psychopathological hallucinations, says:

> ...granting that dreaming is a hallucinatory experience, it nevertheless possesses the elements of analysis and integration that characterize the levels of waking consciousness. (Kleitman, 1963:106).

This passage seems to suggest that it is legitimate, and indeed appropriate, to discuss dreaming and other types of hallucination, such as visions in a ritual context, within a common framework.[6] In a somewhat similar vein, Wallace (1959:58) defines hallucination as pseudo-perception and includes in his definition dreams and hypnagogic imagery as well as visions. However, our strongest support for the continuum comes from Fischer, who states in a recent paper:

> Since eidetic imagery and entoptic phenomena as well as dreams and hallucinations apparently occur whenever verification, *i.e.*, the motor eating of the sensory pudding, is restricted or blocked, we can redefine hallucinations as *intensely active sensations with blocked peripheral voluntary motor manifestations*. The definition implies that methods or mechanisms which contribute to a sufficient increase in sensory to motor ratio can elicit hallucinations (Fischer, 1969:163).

Thus, in this respect, dreams and hallucinatory states are members of the same group. Fischer has developed his model of an increased sensory to motor ratio in relation to experimental work with psychodysleptic (hallucinogenic) drugs, and has compared these states with the REM dream state at some length (1969:164–6, also Fisher, 1970). In the ritualized Trance states that concern us, too, sensory experiences are reported either during or after the event, but little motor behavior is generally performed during the state. Quite in contrast to this, during Possession Trance there is typically motor behavior of an intensive and often very vigorous kind; for example, not only may there be talking and dancing, eating, drinking and smoking, but there may be jumping and tree climbing, often with considerable degrees of agility and force not available to the individual in

[5] For an inventory of altered states of consciousness, without specific reference to ritualization or institutionalization, see Ludwig (1968).
[6] For further support for this position, see also Hartmann (1967).

SLEEP - TRANCE - POSSESSION TRANCE:

CONTINUUM OF PSYCHOLOGICAL DIMENSIONS

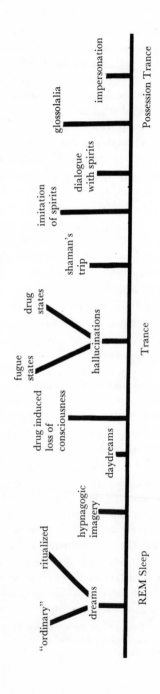

Fig. 1 — ALTERED STATES OF CONSCIOUSNESS

his normal waking state. Whatever the similarities between these two states of altered consciousness, Trance and Possession Trance, the reversal of the sensory to motor ratio seems to distinguish between them as clearly as the differences in conceptualization mentioned earlier. Yet in both dimensions, as indicated in the Figure, there are forms that appear to be intermediary.

Ritual Trance, and Possession Trance as well, have often been interpreted as hypnotic states (Belo, 1960:71; Gill and Brenman, 1961; Wittkower, 1964). In this connection, we may also note Kleitman's comment, summarizing and reviewing a large body of literature on the subject of hypnosis:

> What is known of human and animal hypnosis indicates that it is a state ∪. hyperexcitability which, by appropriate means can be lowered so much as to change into a depression resembling sleep or narcosis. It sometimes passes into real sleep, thus creating confusion concerning the relation of these states to each other. (Kleitman, 1963:338).

In connection with a possible relationship between dreams and hypnosis, one should mention experiments which have attempted to influence the content of dreams by means of post-hypnotic suggestions (Schroetter, 1951; Roffenstein, 1951; Nachmansohn, 1951). It could also be argued that the cultural setting of induced dreams comes close to providing a similar situation. That is, cultural expectation and interpretations serve as strong suggestions to the dreamer in the development of the manifest dream content.

Dreaming occurs during REM sleep, and Kleitman, for one, as we have seen, considers it to be a by-product of this phase of sleep, *i.e.*, it has well established physiological concomitants. The physiological variables associated with hallucinations are less well known. Hallucinations have been produced experimentally by the manipulation of the organism-environment interaction as in situations of sensory deprivation. (Fischer, 1969, however, holds that the source of the hallucinations is motor deprivation, rather than deprivation of sensory in-put.) Henney (1968, n.d.), reviewing the large body of literature devoted to the experimental work in this area, has shown how many of the conditions of the sensory deprivation experiments are duplicated in a ritual retreat among members of a Pentecostal group, the Shakers[7] of the island of St. Vincent in the British West Indies, who experience visions during this period of isolation. Some of the conditions involved are also to be found, for example, in the vision quest of North American Indians (Benedict, 1923; Blumensohn, 1933).

[7] Or Spiritual Baptists

Ingestion of psychoactive drugs is often linked to the production of hallucinations, and here the physiological aspects of the changes in perception and sensations are somewhat better understood (Efron *et al.,* 1967). There is now an extensive comparative literature available, the older as well as the more recent work of anthropologists showing clearly the great importance of cultural structuring in the content and in the social utilization of the vision (Toffelmier and Luomala, 1936; Wallace, 1959; Harner, 1962; La Barre, 1969, among others). The drug cult in the contemporary United States of course has stimulated much publication in this area (Leary, 1968; Blum *et al.,* 1964). It should be noted that there is some evidence which indicates that Possession Trance is significantly less often induced by drugs than Trance (Bourguignon, 1968).

Possession Trance, on the other hand, is probably more frequently induced by psychological contagion, dancing and music (*i.e.,* hyperactivity and hyperventilation) (Field, 1960) and similar factors, rather than drugs or sensory deprivation. Hypnosis, as indicated before, has at times been cited as the principal mechanism of induction (Belo, 1960; Wittkower, 1964). Again, the physiological correlates are not fully understood, and psychopathology, specifically hysteria has frequently been invoked (Dorsainvil, 1931; Devereux, 1956). However, there is now increasing evidence to show the importance of learning in Possession Trance behavior, a fact which cannot be emphasized too strongly (Bourguignon, 1965; Pressel, 1968, n.d.; Goodman, n.d.).

The three forms of altered states of consciousness which concern us here, then, are induced in a variety of ways and, at least in many instances are induced intentionally; yet in spite of this fact of intentional induction, the events themselves, be they dreams, visions or Possession Trances, are not experienced as deriving from the self but are reified through cultural concepts and cultural patterning. Typically, responsibility for the events, whether covert as in dreams and visions, or overt as in the actions of the possession trancer, are assigned to ego alien forces or beings. The self's own strivings, with the help of cultural concepts and expectations, are reified into friendly or hostile supernaturals.

The differences in induction methods are paralleled by other differences between our three types of altered states of consciousness. We have pointed to the sensory to motor ratio, where REM sleep dreams and hallucinatory trance are similar in showing little motor activity in relation to the sensory experience, whereas in Possession Trance, we have little evidence of sensory in-put but much motor activity. An example of an intermediary, somewhat exceptional case is found among the Dard of Northwest

Pakistan. Snoy (1960) has recorded on film the dance of a shaman, in which he acts out the behavior of the spirits that appear to him in his hallucinatory trance. There is motor action and the behavior of the trancer might lead one to believe that possession is involved. Instead, however, we have the mimicking of a visonary experience.

In cultural terms, we may say that where they are ritualized, dreams, Trance and Possession Trance all act as means of contact between humans and supernaturals. All are sources of knowledge, means of divination, media of revelations and as such of culture change. Classically, religious revitalization movements (Wallace, 1956) or charismatic movements (Sundkler, 1961; Burridge, 1960) have their source in revelations of this sort and derive their authority from this type of experience. A particular movement may develop its own theory of dreams, as is shown by Fabian for the Jamaa-Movement of the Congo (Fabian, 1966) involving in this process both tradition and innovation. Again, we may turn to Biblical examples: in Acts XI, for example, we learn of Peter's vision that justified his eating in the company of Gentiles, a vision which provided the authority for a change of existing doctrine and custom. In this instance, as in other historically attested ones, we may ask whether we are dealing with actual experiences, or whether we are dealing with a convention, that provides for innovation if couched in the language of dreams and/or visions.

In this context of communication, dreams and visions, as we have seen, are not always clearly distinguished in the reporting or probably even phenomenologically, in the experiencing. We may expect, however, the content of dreams to be more highly symbolic, more in need of interpretation — and thus possibly allowing for greater individual latitude — and the setting less ritualized than in the case for hallucinatory Trance. On a continuum, dreams are most private, least ritualized, Trance somewhat more amenable to a public, ritualized context, and at the other extreme, Possession Trance virtually requires the public ritual, indeed often a quasi-theatrical setting.

In many respects, dreams, visions and Possession Trance have been seen to function similarly in what we have discussed so far. There is, however, an interesting difference which might well be stressed: while dreams may be induced under specific circumstances (and culture pattern dreams exist in many societies, so that we get a degree of ritualization of dream), the non-ritualized, unpatterned dream is the "normal" dream, both in terms of frequency and in terms of the quality of the experience. On the other hand, non-patterned non-ritualized hallucinatory Trance, or for that matter, Possession Trance (*i.e.*, the belief and/or delusion that one is controlled by someone else) are conceived of as pathological not only in Western society. Unless the trancer can convince others that he has indeed had a supernatural experience, he is a deviant, often one considered to be dangerous (Bourguignon and Haas, 1965).

Not only do dreams, Trance and Possession Trance provide channels of communication with the supernatural, but as Hallowell (1966) has shown for dreams, and specifically for the Saulteaux, they extend the behavioral environment and confirm and verify the beliefs in its constitution, modifying perception and experience. As I have shown elsewhere, specifically for Possession Trance in Haiti (Bourguignon, 1965) but as can be shown for the other forms as well, I believe, these altered states of consciousness that operate in a culturally sanctioned and patterned manner expand the field of experience and of action of the self. Saulteaux dreams and sorcery beliefs are a case in point (Hallowell, 1940) and Wallace (1958) has also made a similar point with respect to Iroquois dreams and dream beliefs.

It is clear from this discussion, that the patterning of behavior in relation to altered states of consciousness provides an area of potential comparative research that has not yet been fully tapped and that may open up in turn newer understandings of psychological functioning. The lack of cultural patterning, of well-defined shared expectations, of social support for the trancer during and after the trance, the lack of positive ritualization, may all be relevant to the apparent pathology, socially and individually, of the current American drug cultists. (Leary, 1968; Blum *et al.*, 1964; Wallace, 1959; LaBarre, 1969).

To sum up: REM sleep, Trance and Possession Trance are altered states of consciousness. They are associated, respectively with dreams, hallucinations and impersonations of supernaturals. They represent three points on a continuum (Figure 1) in which we recognize numerous intermediary steps. The three points, as well as the intermediary ones, have been culturally patterned and ritualized in a very large percentage of human societies now existing and apparently also in the past. These states are both similar and different in a variety of ways. We have briefly compared them with respect to four dimensions:

1. The psychobiological. Here we have mentioned some salient features of these states and, in particular, have discussed methods of induction.
2. Interpersonal and reflexive aspects. This involves the possibility of modifying actions of groups by recourse to these states, as in

innovational movements of the revitalistic or charismatic type. There is also the possibility of alterations in the immediate personal field and the importance to the individual of entering into presumed contact with supernaturals.

3. Perception and cognition. Expectations with respect to altered states of consciousness and experiences during these states contribute to the construction of a cultural universe or behavioral environment and provide channels for the verification of beliefs.

4. The social structural dimension. Societies which utilize dreams to seek and control supernatural powers are similar to those which utilize Trance with respect to a number of societal variables. Those which use Possession Trance tend to be significantly different with respect to these variables, notably variables involving scale and complexity. This finding implies that the phenomena under discussion must be considered not only from the point of view of individual psychological functioning, but also from that of societal functioning.

It may be worth adding here that altered states of consciousness are of particular interest to the anthropologist in that they allow us to approach a highly patterned and very widespread group of phenomena, on a series of levels of investigation. We are able to recognize the autonomy of each level (or dimension) of investigation and find the results to be complementary, thus developing a theory, it may be hoped, which will deepen our understanding of both the individual and the society, without reductionism and without emphasizing one at the expense of the other.

BIBLIOGRAPHY

BARNOUW, VICTOR. 1963. Culture and Personality. Homewood, Ill., Dorsey Press.

BARRY, H., I. CHILD AND M. BACON. 1959. Relation of child training to subsistence economy. American Anthropologist 61:51–63.

BASTIDE, ROGER. 1950. Rêves de noirs. Psyché: Revue internationale des Sciences de l'Homme et de Psychanalyse, 49:802–811.

————. 1966. The sociology of the Dream. *In* The Dream and Human Society. G. E. von Grunebaum, and R. Callois, eds. Berkeley and Los Angeles, University of California Press.

————. 1968. La divination chez les Afro-Américains. *In* La Divination, J. Caquot and M. Leibovici, eds., vol. 2. Paris, Presses universitaires de France.

BATESON, G. AND M. MEAD. 1942. Balinese character: a photographic analysis. Special publications of the New York Academy of Sciences II.

BELO, JANE. 1960. Trance in Bali. New York, Columbia University Press.

BENEDICT, RUTH. 1923. The concept of the guardian spirit in North America. Memoirs of the American Anthropological Association 29.

BLUM, RICHARD, AND ASSOCIATES. 1964. Utopiates: The Uses and Users of LSD-25. Behavioral Science Series: A Publication of the Institute for the Study of Human Problems, Stanford University, New York, Atherton Press.

BLUMENSOHN, JULES. 1933. The Fast Among North American Indians. American Anthropologist 35:451–469.

BOURGUIGNON, ERIKA. 1954. Dreams and dream interpretation in Haiti. American Anthropologist 56:262–268.

――――. 1965. The Self, the Behavioral Environment and the Theory of Spirit Possession. *In* Context and Meaning in Cultural Anthropology, M. E. Spiro, ed., New York, The Free Press.

――――. 1966. Two Forms of Impersonation: Masks and Spirit Possession. Paper Presented to the 75th Annual Meeting of the Ohio Academy of Science, Columbus, Ohio.

――――. 1968. Cross-Cultural Study of Dissociational States. Final Report, Grant No. MH-07463, National Institutes of Health. The Ohio State University Research Foundation, Columbus, Ohio.

――――. ed., n.d. Religion, Altered States of Consciousness and Social Change, Columbus, Ohio, The Ohio State University Press (in press).

BOURGUIGNON, ERIKA AND ADOLF HAAS. 1966. Transcultural Research and Culture-bound Psychiatry. Paper Presented to the Meetings of the Western Division of the American Psychiatric Association, Honolulu, Hawaii.

BREMER, FRÉDÉRIC. 1966. The Neurophysiological Problem of Sleep. *In* G. E. von Grunebaum, and R. Caillois, eds., The Dream and Human Societies, Berkeley and Los Angeles, University of California Press.

BROUGHTON, R. J. 1968. Sleep Disorders: Disorders of Arousal? Science 159:1070–1078.

BURRIDGE, K. 1960. Mambu. A Melanesian Millenium, London.

CAQUOT, J. AND M. LEIBOVICI, EDS. 1968. La Divination. 2 vols. Paris, Presses universitaires de France.

D'ANDRADE, ROY. 1961. Anthropological Studies of Dreams, *In* Psychological Anthropology, F. L. K. Hsu, ed., Homewood, Ill., Dorsey Press.

DEMENT, W. 1960. The effect of dream deprivation, Science 131:1705–1707.

――――. 1966. The Psychophysiology of Dreaming, *In* G. E. von Grunebaum and R. Caillois, eds., The Dream and Human Societies, Berkeley and Los Angeles, University of California Press.

DEVEREUX, GEORGE. 1951. Reality and Dream, New York, International Universities Press.

――――. 1956. Normal and Abnormal: The Key Problem of Psychiatric Anthropology. *In* Some Uses of Anthropology: Theoretical and Applied. J. Casagrande and Th. Gladwin, eds., Anthropological Society of Washington.

————. 1957. Dream learning and individual ritual differences in Mohave shamanism, American Anthropologist 59:177–198.

DORSAINVIL, J. C. 1931. Vodou et Névrose, Port-au-Prince, Haiti.

DU BOIS, CORA. 1944. The People of Alor. Minneapolis, University of Minnesota Press. (reprinted, 1961, Harper Torchbooks, 2 vols.)

EBERHARD, WOLFRAM VON. 1967. Chinesische Träume als soziologisches Quellenmaterial, Sociologus 17:71–88.

————. 1968. Social interaction and social values in Chinese dreams. Journal of Sociology 4:21–44.

EFRON, D. H., BO HOLMSTEDT AND N. S. KLINE. 1967. Ethnopharmacologic Search for Psychoactive Drugs. Public Health Service Publication No. 1645, U.S. Department of Health, Education and Welfare.

EGGAN, DOROTHY. 1949. The significance of dreams for anthropological research, American Anthropologist 51:177–198.

————. 1952. The manifest content of dreams: A challenge to social science, American Anthropologist 54:469–485.

————. 1955. The personal use of myths in dreams, In T. Sebeok, ed., Myth: A Symposium, Journal of American Folklore 68:445–453.

————. 1956. Instruction and affect in Hopi cultural continuity, Southwestern Journal of Anthropology 12:347–370.

————. 1957. Hopi Dreams and a Life History Sketch. In B. Kaplan, ed., Primary Records in Culture and Personality, vol. 2. Madison: The Microcard Foundation.

————. 1961. Dream Analysis, In Studying Personality Cross-Culturally, B. Kaplan, ed., Evanston, Ill., Row, Peterson.

————. 1966. Hopi Dreams in Cultural Perspective, In The Dream and Human Societies, G. E. von Grunebaum and R. Caillois, eds., Berkeley and Los Angeles, University of California Press.

EVANS-PRITCHARD, E. E. 1956. Nuer Religion, London, Oxford University Press.

FABIAN, JOHANNES. 1966. Dream and Charisma. "Theories of Dreams" in the Jamaa-Movement (Congo). Anthropos 61:544–560.

FAVRE, H. 1968. Les pratiques divinatoires des Mayas. In J. Caquot and M. Leibovici, eds., La Divination vol. 2, Paris, Presses universitaires de France.

FIELD, M. J. 1960. Search for Security: An ethno-psychiatric study of rural Ghana. Evanston, Illinois, Northwestern University Press.

FIRTH, RAYMOND. 1967. The Meaning of Dreams. In Tikopia Ritual and Belief. Boston, Beacon Press (orig. 1934 In Essays Presented to C. G. Seligman, E. E. Evans-Pritchard et al., eds., London).

FISCHER, ROLAND. 1969. The Perception-Hallucination Continuum (A Re-Examination), Diseases of the Nervous System 30:161–171.

———. 1970. Prediction and Measurement of Perceptual-Behavioral Change in Drug-Induced Hallucinations. *In* Origin and Mechanisms of Hallucination, W. Keup, ed., New York, Plenum Press.

FISHER, CHARLES, ET. AL. 1970. A Psychophysiological Study of Nightmares, The Journal of the American Psychoanalytic Association 18:747–782.

GLADWIN, TH. AND S. B. SARASON. 1953. Truk: Man in Paradise. Viking Fund Publications in Anthropology No. 20, New York, Wenner-Gren Foundation for Anthropological Research, Inc.

GIEL, R., YOSEPH GEZAHEGN AND J. N. VAN LUIJK. 1968. Faith-Healing and Spirit-Possession in Ghion, Ethiopia. Social Science and Medicine 2:63–79.

GOODMAN, FELICITAS. n.d. Speaking in Tongues. Chicago, The University of Chicago Press (in press).

GRUNEBAUM, G. E. VON AND R. CALLOIS. 1966. The Dream and Human Societies, Berkeley and Los Angeles, University of California Press.

HALL, CALVIN AND BILL DOMHOFF. 1963. A Ubiquitous Sex Difference in Dreams, Journal of Abnormal and Social Psychology 66:278–280.

HALLOWELL, A. I. 1940. Aggression in Saulteaux Society, Psychiatry 3:395–407.

———. 1942. The Role of Conjuring in Saulteaux Society, Publications of the Philadelphia Anthropological Society, Volume II, Philadelphia, University of Pennsylvania Press.

———. 1966. The Role of Dreams in Ojibwa Culture. *In* G. E. von Grunebaum and R. Caillois, eds., The Dream and Human Societies, Berkeley and Los Angeles, The University of California Press.

HARNER, MICHAEL. 1962. Jívaro Souls, American Anthropologist 64:258–272.

HARTMANN, ERNST. 1967. The biology of dreaming, Springfield, Ill., Thomas.

HENNEY, J. H. 1968. "Mourning," A Religious Ritual among the Spiritual Baptists of St. Vincent: An Experience in Sensory Deprivation, Working Paper No. 21, Cross-Cultural Study of Dissociational States, Department of Anthropology, The Ohio State University, Columbus, Ohio.

———. n.d. The Shakers of St. Vincent: A Stable Religion. *In* E. Bourguignon, ed., Religion, Altered States of Consciousness and Social Change, Columbus, Ohio, The State University Press (in press).

HONIGMANN, J. J. 1961. The Interpretation of Dreams in Anthropological Field Work: A Case Study. *In* B. Kaplan, ed., Studying Personality Cross-Culturally, Evanston, Ill., Row, Peterson.

HULTKRANZ, A. 1968. La divination en Amérique du Nord. *In* La Divination, J. Caquot et M. Leibovici, eds., vol. 2, Paris, Presses universitaires de France.

KARDINER, ABRAM. 1945. Psychological Frontiers of Society, New York, Columbia University Press.

KLEITMAN, NATHANIEL. 1963. Sleep and Wakefulness. rev. ed., Chicago, University of Chicago Press.

KLUCKHOHN, CLYDE AND WILLIAM MORGAN. 1951. Some Notes on Navaho Dreams. *In* Essays in honor of Geza Róheim, W. Muensterberger, ed., New York, International Universities Press.

LABARRE, WESTON. 1969. The Peyote Cult. enlarged edition. New York, Schocken Books.

LEARY, TIMOTHY. 1968. The Politics of Ecstasy. New York, G. P. Putnam's Sons.

LIENHARDT, GODFREY. 1954. The Shilluk of the Upper Nile. *In* African Worlds, D. Forde, ed., International African Institute, London, Oxford University Press.

LINCOLN, J. S. 1935. The Dream in Primitive Cultures. Baltimore, The Williams and Wilkins Company.

LUDWIG, ARNOLD. 1968. Altered States of Consciousness. *In* Trance and Possession States, R. Prince, ed., R. M. Bucke Memorial Society, Montreal.

MALINOWSKI, BRONISLAW. 1927. Sex and Repression in Savage Society. London, Kegan Paul.

MEGGITT, M. J. 1962. Dream Interpretation among the Mae Enga of New Guinea. Southwestern Journal of Anthropology 18:216–229.

MERRIAM, A. P. 1967. Ethnomusicology of the Flathead Indians. Viking Fund Publications in Anthropology, No. 44, New York, Wenner-Gren Foundation for Anthropological Research, Inc.

MURDOCK, G. P. 1967. Ethnographic Atlas: A Summary, Ethnology 6, No. 2.

NACHMANSOHN, M. 1951. Concerning experimentally produced dreams. *In* Organization and Pathology of Thought, D. Rapaport, Trans, and ed., New York, Columbia University Press.

PRESSEL, ESTHER. 1968. Structure of Beliefs and Ritual Behavior in Umbanda. Working Paper No. 19, Cross-Cultural Study of Dissociational States, Department of Anthropology, The Ohio State University, Columbus, Ohio.

―――. n.d. Umbanda in Sao Paolo: Religious Innovation in a Developing Society. *In* E. Bourguignon, ed., Religion, Altered States of Consciousness and Social Change, Columbus, Ohio, The Ohio State University Press (in press).

RADIN, PAUL. 1926. Crashing Thunder, The Autobiography of an American Indian. New York, Appleton-Century-Crofts.

RAPAPORT, DAVID, TRANS. AND ED. 1951. Organization and Pathology of Thought. New York, Columbia University Press.

REICHEL-DOLMATOFF, GERARDO AND ALICIA. 1961. The People of Aritama. The Culture and Personality of a Colombian Mestizo Village. Chicago, University of Chicago Press.

REINA, R. E. 1966. The Law of the Saints. Indianapolis and New York, The Bobbs-Merrill Company.

ROFFENSTEIN, GASTON. 1951. Experiments on Symbolization in Dreams. *In* Organization and Pathology of Thought, D. Rapaport, trans. and ed., New York, Columbia University Press.

Róheim, Geza. 1947. Dream analysis and field work in anthroplogy. Psycho-analysis and the Social Sciences 1:87–130.

Schneider, David and Lauriston Sharp. 1969. The Dream Life of a Primitive People: The Dreams of the Yir Yoront of Australia. Anthroplogical Studies, Number 1, Ward Goodenough, ed., American Anthropological Association. Ann Arbor, Michigan, University Microfilms.

Schroetter, Karl. 1951. Experimental Dreams. *In* D. Rapaport, trans. and ed., Organization and Pathology of Thought, New York, Columbia University Press.

Seligman, C. G. 1923a. Type Dreams: A Request. Folklore 34:376–378.

———. 1923b. Note on Dreams. Man 120:186–188.

Snoy, P. 1960. Darden — Nordwestpakistan (Gilgitbezirk). Schamanistischer Tanz. (Film.) Filmbeschreibung. Encyclopaedia Cinematographica.

Stout, D. B. 1947. San Blas Cuna Acculturation: An Introduction. Viking Fund Publications in Anthropology, No. 9. New York, The Viking Fund.

Sullivan, H. S. 1947. Conceptions of Modern Psychiatry, second ed., New York, W. W. Norton Co.

———. 1953. The Interpersonal Theory of Psychiatry, New York, W. W. Norton Co.

Sundkler, B. 1961. Bantu Prophets in South Africa. 2nd ed. London, Oxford University Press.

Textor, R. B. 1967. A Cross-Cultural Summary. New Haven, Conn., HRAF Press.

Toffelmier, G. and K. Luomala. 1936. Dreams and dream interpretation of the Diegueño Indians of Southern California. Psychoanalytic Quarterly 2:195–225.

Wallace, A. F. C. 1951. Cultural Determinants of Response to Hallucinatory Experience, A.M.A. Archives of General Psychiatry 1:58–69.

———. 1956. Revitalization Movements, American Anthropologist 51:264–281.

———. 1958. Dreams and the wishes of the soul: a type of psychoanalytic theory among the seventeenth century Iroquois. American Anthropologist 60:234–248.

Whiting, Beatrice. 1963. Six Cultures. New York and London, John Wiley and Sons.

Whiting, J. W. M. and I. L. Child. 1953. Child Training and Personality: a Cross-Cultural Study. New Haven, Yale University Press.

Williams, Herbert. 1957. Sixteen Autobiographical Dream Series of Moslem Maronite Men and Women. Primary Records in Culture and Personality, vol. 4, B. Kaplan, ed., Madison, Wisconsin, The Microcard Foundation.

Wilson, Monica. 1963. Good Company. A Study of Nyakyusa Age-Villages. Boston, Beacon Press.

Wittkower, E. D. 1964. Spirit Possession in Haitian vodun ceremonies. Acta Psychotherapeutica 12:72–130.

CHAPTER ELEVEN

The Mutual Methodological Relevance of Anthropology and Psychology

Donald T. Campbell *and* Raoul Naroll

Rather than report upon a specific technique, this chapter will deal with some general methodological problems in relating theory to data. Rather than deal directly with an interdisciplinary specialty of Psychological Anthropology, this chapter will emphasize the mutual relevance — at a *methodological* level — of anthropology and psychology. This relevance is believed to hold even when each discipline is focused upon its own pure problems, as well as when they enter into interdisciplinary collaboration. This mutual methodological relevance is emphasized as a mode of contact separate from the inevitable mutual relevance of their substantive theories. The latter, while more important, has also received more repeated attention, and is in any event not the topic treated here.

Anthropology as a Source of Discipline for Psychological Theory

There is no need to reiterate or to document here the tremendous influence which anthropology's culture-personality studies have had upon social psychology since the 1930's. From the tenor of some of the papers of this volume and from other professional stocktakings by anthropologists (for example, Bennett 1946, Kluckhohn 1954b, Honigmann 1954), it can be gathered that many anthropologists feel somewhat uneasy about this very great popularity of what may be a not-too-dependable product; that many might explain the rapid diffusion of this trait complex more as due to the extreme needs of the new converts than to the efficacy of the invention, that is, an acceptance phenomenon more akin to the diffusion of the Ghost Dance Religion than to the spread of the compound bow, barbed fishhook, and better mousetrap. As academic, experimentally oriented, and methodologically anxious social scientists, we, of course, share these misgivings. However, even when in an incomplete and fragmentary form, anthropological evidence has served as a source of discipline, as well as a source of inspiration to psychological theory.

The first, and perhaps still most needed influence is at a very general level. This is the message of cultural relativism (Herskovits 1948). While recognizing that anthropologists themselves are not too happy with this slogan, and that the perspective may not be adequate for anthropology's theoretical purposes, the message it has to offer is still very much needed by academic psychologists. Implicitly, the laboratory psychologist still assumes that his college sophomores provide an adequate base for a general psychology of man. (Such assumptions of universality are automatic for any provincially enculturated ethnocentric.) For social psychology these tendencies have been very substantially curbed through confrontation with the anthropological literature. Continued confrontation, however, will be required to prevent relapse. For the general psychologist, most of the message is yet to be learned (Segall, Campbell and Herskovits 1966).

The message of cultural relativism is very general and nonspecific. Often it is merely a general caution against intemperate generalization. (And often it takes the extreme of a negativistic denial of the possibility of any generalization.) The central purpose of this paper is to call attention to more concrete and specific methodological relevance. As Honigmann (1952, 1954), Whiting (1954, 1968), Child (1954), and Zigler and Child (1969) have pointed out, anthropological evidence has been, and can continue to be, of invaluable service as a crucible in which to put to more rigorous test psychology's tentative theories, enabling one to edit them and select among alternatives in ways which laboratory experiments and correlational studies within our own culture might never make possible.

While this can never be anthropology's central role, what is here argued is that anthropology provides an important part of the scientific apparatus of psychology, particularly for personality theory. This is said within a perspective upon the strategy of science which sees experimentation and the other methods of science as having essentially an editorial function. That is, scientific data serve to choose among, prune out, and in this sense, edit theories. Essential to building a science are such laboratories. Where all are lacking, no science is possible. In the absence of the possibility of experimentation with modes of child rearing and personality formation, a science of personality would be all but impossible were it not for the "laboratory" of crosscultural comparison opened up by the anthropologist.

To illustrate this role, several condensed and oversimplified examples are offered. Note that these are organized around problems in *psychological* theory. (That such problems are not central to anthropology should not distract us from this important service.) Though the "facts" in the illustrations may in fact be controversial, it is hoped that they exemplify the possibility, if not the actuality, of the editing role of anthropological data.

1. Freud validly observed that boys in late Hapsburgian Vienna had hostile feelings toward their fathers. Two possible explanations offered themselves — the hostility could be due to the father's role as the disciplinarian, or to the father's role as the mother's lover. For reasons that can be neglected here (but see Bakan 1958) Freud chose to emphasize the role of the mother's lover. However, working only with his patient population there was no adequate basis for making the choice. The two rival explanations were experimentally confounded, for among the parents of Freud's patients the disciplinarian of little boys was usually the mother's lover. (Remember that in Freud's day it was the *morality* of one's parents more often than their immorality that drove one to choose the analyst's couch over other couches, so that Freud got a biased sample.) Malinowski (1927) studied a society in which these two paternal roles were experimentally disentangled, in which the disciplinarian of young boys and the mother's lover were not one-and-the-same person. And in this society, the boys' hostility was addressed to the disciplinarian, not to the mother's lover. This outcome makes the Oedipal hostility more easily encompassed within the framework of a simple hedonistic learning theory such as that of Thorndike or Hull. While the love-jealousy and the punishment Oedipal theories are no doubt both appropriate to some extent, Malinowski's work helps to integrate personality theory within learning theory and gives us a firmer base upon which to predict the Oedipal complex of the son of a commuting suburban father where the mother is the only source

of discipline.

2. Pettitt's (1946) monograph on educational practices among North American Indian tribes serves the purpose of calling attention to the fact that our theories of learning and cognition predict trouble for the modern emancipated American family. According to learning experiments, conditioned fear and conditioned hostility are the unrational product of temporal contiguity between stimulus and pain, or between stimulus and frustration. And if we go to cognitive psychology, we find that the perception of causality, and with this the phenomenon of blaming, are likewise functions of temporal and spatial contiguity (Heider 1944, Michotte 1946). From these theories it follows that in a society such as intellectual suburbia, where the parents stand alone in representing the restraints which society passes on to children, the parents will become the stimuli for conditioned hostility on the part of the children, the children will perceive the parents as causing, as to blame for, their frustrations. Thus, the conditioning and/or the causal perception processes predict a chronic divisive force within the modern family.

With the inevitable selective process in which, among the countless customs that are tried, some are preserved more readily than others (e.g., Keller 1931, Campbell 1965), one can expect that in stable societies preventive customs will have grown up around this inevitable parental-resentment problem. Pettitt's (1946) analysis spells out the role of shamans and kachina dancers as disciplinarians, of the avunculate, of age grade systems, all as devices serving to deflect the discipline-induced hostility of the child away from the parent, and, thus as preserving intrafamilial solidarity. Reading his monograph gives one both a greater appreciation of the relevance of learning theory for predicting intrafamilial attitudes, and parenthetically a greater sympathy for those unsophisticated parents in our own culture who attempt a similar deflection of childish hostility away from themselves through invoking the sanctions of the policeman, the bogeyman, Santa Claus, or a reified God. (On the other hand, perhaps it is well that in our culture the socialization-induced hostilities are associated with parents, for our occupational structure requires new entrants to the labor force who are willing and eager to leave home permanently. Just such a labor force is lacking in some of the underdeveloped countries, perhaps in part because of the greater "wisdom" of their intrafamilial relationships.)

3. Every practicing psychoanalyst doing therapy with parents has probably recognized that the parent contributes much of the irrational and projected attitudes that comprise the intergenerational Oedipal

interaction — yet this recognition is little represented in the literature, although not totally absent (*e.g.*, Hsu 1940, Wellisch 1954, Bakan 1966). The Herskovitses (1958a, b) have not only called attention to the ubiquity of the theme of the father's hostility toward his first born son in the Oedipus-type myths of Africa and Eurasia, but have in addition hypothesized that this paternal hostility to the newborn represents a reactivation of the father's sibling-rivalry hostility, acquired in his childhood in reaction to a younger sibling who abruptly displaced him in the total attention of the mother. The Herskovitses came to this hypothesis working with the mythology of Dahomey, a polygynous society in which each wife has her own hut, and in which a newborn child is continually with the mother, at work during the day and on the sleeping mat at night, until at around the age of two or three it is displaced by a younger sibling. Corresponding to this familial pattern is a mythology exceptionally full of strife between brothers and between generations, and in which the older brother or the older generation is portrayed as the initiator of the hostility.

Once pointed out, this seems exactly what one would expect from considerations of stimulus equivalence and habit transfer. Certainly in many cultures besides Dahomey (*e.g.*, Levy 1935, Paul 1950, Henry 1944, Spiro 1953) hostility toward younger siblings is among the most characteristic and strongest learnings of childhood. When later as an adult an older sibling is presented with the new stimulus that his own child constitutes, this novel stimulus can be expected to elicit the strongest of the response tendencies learned in the past toward a similar stimulus, that is, the responses learned toward the younger sibling as an infant. The degree of this projected hostility would presumably be correlated with the degree to which the child in its first years had the undivided attention of the mother, and, hence, was the more frustratingly displaced at the end of the infancy period. If initiation rites be taken as symptomatic of the hostility of the older generation toward the younger (as Wellisch 1954 has plausibly interpreted infanticide and the sacrificing of children to be), then one might expect the high correlation between length and degree of infant monopoly of the mother's attention and the hostility of initiation rites, which Whiting and co-workers (1958) report. (Initiation rites could also, on the basis of the same theory, represent the still more direct expression of the hostility of the older already initiated brothers toward the younger.) It can be noted that Dahomey is included in Whiting's sample, and is scored in the very highest category for severity of initiation rites. In Kwoma, the child's displacement may be through the father's return to the sleeping mat, but this is not the pattern in Dahomey. In general, displacement by a younger sibling is probably the more usual mechanism. If the projected sibling hostility is a relevant part of the explanation, then upon examination we should find both actual and mythological sibling strife more prevalent both in cultures with the harsher initiation rites and in the cultures with the longer infant monopoly of the mother's attention in infancy. (See Young 1965 for a social-organizational explanation of these relationships.)

The stimulus equivalence of offspring and younger siblings assumed in this derivation has been confirmed in a study of the types of confusions of names that occur on the part of parents of college students (Campbell, unpublished). When a parent mistakenly calls a child by the name of one of the parent's own siblings, the name of a younger sibling (of the same sex as the child) is most frequently involved. This study cannot, of course, confirm the hostility aspects of the interpretation. Note also that this theory predicts a relative absence of parent-originated hostility for parents who were only children or youngest in their families, except insofar as the newborn is a genuine displacer of the parent in the attentions of the spouse.

4. Freud presented psychology with an insightful, but doubly double-jointed theory relating drive fixation in childhood and adult behavior. On the one hand, the fixation could be produced by overindulgence of the drive in childhood, or by its opposite, underindulgence. As to expression in adult life, fixation could express itself in excessive preoccupation with drive-relevant things or by its opposite, a counterphobic avoidance. Such a prediction is somewhat more specific than no prediction at all, but when combined with the inevitable errors of classification, the polar-cross scatter diagram which it predicts may not be distinguishable from a zero correlation. And whereas on many points, psychoanalysis and hedonistic-associationistic learning theories agree, the learning theories predict most easily a parallelism between conditions of acquisition and those of expression and transfer, rather than compensatory or complementary relationships, since memory but not energy storage is expected to persist. Whiting and Child's (1953) study may be interpreted as confirming those aspects of the Freudian hypothesis which thus agree with the learning theory interpretation. Persons for whom a given drive had been associated with frustration in childhood show phobic reactions regarding it in adult life (negative fixation). And insofar as infantile indulgence and gratification had adult symptoms, those who found a given drive a source of

gratification in childhood sought it out as a source of cure in adult life. Here, again, the result has been in the direction of integrating personality theory with learning theory. Here, again, the anthropological data have been efficacious in selecting among alternative psychological hypotheses. And as Child (1954) shows, insofar as relationships, Freudian or otherwise, have been established between early child training and adult behavior, the confirmations have come primarily from the studies of cross-cultural breadth, rather than from studies making use of the small range of differences within our own culture.

5. Other studies using the cross-cultural method seem to confirm the positive transfer of attitudes between childhood reinforcement conditions and adult personality, the assumptions of stimulus equivalence, transfer, displacement in approach-avoidance conflicts, and so forth. Spiro's (1953, 1958) demonstration of the parallel between infant training by parents and attitudes toward spirits is interpreted as confirmatory in this regard. This may seem contradictory, since in his 1953 paper, Spiro takes his evidence as justifying a choice in favor of a perceptual rather than a learning theory. But behaviorism is silent as to the nature of conscious contents. Hence, evidence regarding conscious contents is not contradictory to learning theory. In particular, evidence regarding "perceptions of" objects cannot be interpreted as corresponding to the stimulus terms of learning theory. Usually a better translation of "perceived as" is "responded to as to." On this ground, learning theory expects the authority symbols of adult life to be responded to as (to be perceived as) were the authority figures of childhood to which the responses (perceptions) were originally learned. For more details on this mode of integrating theoretical terminologies, see Campbell (1963, 1969). For more evidence on the parallels between attitudes toward parents and toward spiritual beings, see Lambert and co-workers (1959).

6. Optical illusions have long been interpreted as atypical exemplifications of normally useful inference processes. Thus the Sander Parallelogram and the Müller-Lyer illusions have been interpreted as due to a probabilistically useful tendency to interpret obtuse and acute angles on the retina (or photograph) as though generated by rectangular objects seen in perspective. But this inference tendency would only be adaptive in a world in which precisely rectangular objects abounded, that is, a "carpentered" world. One can do experiments rearing animals in environments varying widely in frequency of rectangular corners, but for human

beings, one is dependent upon already existing environmental differences. In a study in which some 20 anthropologists collaborated (Segall et al. 1966), there was a general confirmation that these two illusions are strongest in European-style, highly carpentered environments (e.g., Evanston, Illinois). While not all of the subsequent research has been confirmatory, this remains an exciting laboratory for visual research.

The horizontal-vertical illusions have been interpreted as due to a compensation for foreshortening when the vertical lines are interpreted as horizontal lines extending away from the observer. The utility of such a compensatory habit would be maximum on a flat plane. It would be misleading if one lived at the bottom of a well. Segall et al. (1966) found this expectation generally confirmed, albeit with some exceptions. The illusion was maximal among the Australian bushmen and nonexistent among the rainforest Bêté of Africa. Residents of Evanston, Illinois, were intermediate.

In general, the evidence of social anthropology is seen as having a salutary and disciplining effect upon personality psychology, serving, paradoxically, to make personality theory more clearly a part of the learning theory of general psychology.

Some Psychological Comments on Anthropological Method

It is probably true that the testing of psychological theories must remain a very minor part of the research agenda of the anthropologist. In addition, the great difference in task must be recognized between the descriptive, humanistic task of one who seeks to record all aspects of a specific cultural instance and the task of the abstractive and generalizing "scientist" who wants to test the concomitant variation of two isolated factors across instances in general. Cooperation between these orientations is often difficult — but is helped rather than hindered by the explicit recognition of the great difference in goals: Too often those in one camp regard those in the other as the willful practitioners of a wrongheaded approach, implicitly assuming a common goal. Both orientations are represented in the present volume, in some instances both within a single person. The descriptive-humanistic rather than abstractive approach has in the past been typical of much of anthropology. On the other hand, Honigmann (1952), Whiting (1954), and Spiro (1953, 1958) have presented the abstractive, hypothesis-testing commitment. Murray (1949) and Gillin (1954) have called for such an orientation in previous symposia on culture and personality. Our interests are predominantly of this sort, and some of the methodological comments to follow are thus irrelevant to the more typically descriptive anthropological undertaking. Many of these comments come from an interest in a potential psychology of induction (Campbell 1958a, 1959, 1970), and in particular from an application of knowledge about human perception, learning, and biases to the calibration of the human observer as a scientific measuring instrument (for example, Campbell, Hunt and Lewis 1957, 1958, Campbell 1958b, Webb et al. 1966).

Before going into these details, it may be well to note a common cause joining the abstractive-generalizing orientation central to this paper and the descriptive-humanistic orientation as it has been modally represented in anthropological research training. Both stand in opposition to the undisciplined generalizations often found in the more dramatic efforts to interpret man and culture. Both look askance at the sweeping generalizations of a Spencer, a Spengler, a Toynbee, or a Nietzsche when offered as established scientific truth. This common ground is not always noted, and, indeed, each orientation tends to attribute undisciplined generalization to the other.

In the major departments of anthropology of the 1920's and 1930's the theoretical excesses of a previous generation of anthropologists led to an emphasis upon objectivity in field work which was antitheoretical insofar as adherence to theory had in the past served to reduce the objectivity of field work. Herskovits (1960) has called attention to a superior objectivity for the humanistic aspects of anthropological study. Both the descriptive-humanistic orientation and the abstractive, hypothesis-testing orientation wish to avoid self-deception and bias in the data collection process. Both call for reliable, intersubjectively communicable observations. Both are ideally hardheaded, skeptical, modest, and conservative in their orientation to factual knowledge. For these reasons, many of the topics covered in what follows are of joint relevance. This point is made without weakening the appeal for the mutual recognition and respect for a separateness of task and division of labor between the two orientations, both of which are essential in the complete study of man.

The Relation of Intersubjective-Verifiability to Directness of Perception

It goes without saying that a science of either type cannot be built without intersubjective verifiability of observations. Psychological research on the accuracy and person-to-person agreement in independent reporting seems summarizable by the statement that the greater the direct accessibility of the referents to sense perception, the greater the intersubjective verifiability of the observation. The weaker, more intangible, indirect, or abstract the object or attribute, the more the observations are subject to distortion.

It is quite conceivable that there are some aspects of culture, including its overall pattern or ethos, that are so abstract or indirectly inferred that intersubjective verifiability is lost. If this is so, then until corrected, these aspects cannot become a part of science, and we, as scientists, should concentrate on those aspects upon which we can get agreement. Holmes (1957, 1958) has reported a restudy of some of Mead's work on Samoan society, which along with the other restudies of recent years (such as Li An-Che 1937, Bennett 1946, Lewis 1951) supports the methodological expectation of greater verifiability to the more palpable and visible. As far as the great bulk of Mead's ethnology, Holmes confirms her findings, stating "the reliability of Mead's account is remarkably high." While he reports some differences in the description of traditional political systems and other matters, on matters of material culture and observable custom, there is general agreement. This extends also to the observed absence of an adolescent disturbance on the part of the girls, and the easy transition from childhood to adult life. But upon several of the broader aspects of ethos, his findings are in complete disagreement, for example, upon the lack of specialized feeling in human relations, the lack of competitive spirit, the lack of crisis in human relations, and the importance of "Mafaufau," or the gift of wise judgment. In the context of his presentation, one cannot easily interpret these differences as due to culture change in the intervening years, but rather one must interpret them as disagreement in the description of aspects of "the same" culture. If, as Mead has said, "in the matter of ethos, the surest and most perfect instrument of understanding is our own emotional response" (Mead and McGregor 1951:300), and if agreement in such emotional response is lacking, or can be disparaged as merely a shared ethnocentric reaction to a novel culture, then ethos may indeed be beyond the realm of scientific study. This lack of intersubjective verifiability is not inevitable however. Its presence or absence should be studied in Mead's own terms, with the precaution of involving observing anthropologists from different cultures (Campbell 1964, 1970). It is also possible that science can make explicit the existence of abstract general themes in culture through formal combinatorial analysis of more concrete data. Some uses of the cross cultural correlational approach discussed in the final section below can be interpreted in this way, as can more elaborate techniques such as factor analysis (e.g., Sawyer and LeVine 1966), although there are many problems involved. Another quite different and promising approach is that of ethnoscience (Werner and Fenton 1970). Here too intersubjective replicability needs demonstrating.

This emphasis upon the relationship of directness of perception and intersubjective verifiability must not be taken as endorsing an epistemology grounding its claims for certainty upon particulate sense data, or one regarding particulars of any kind as more certainly known than overall patterns. Descriptive humanists such as Mead and Herskovits have a valid criticism of some quantitative social scientists in their emphasis upon the importance of context. The basic perception of even the laboratory instruments in physical science requires both a context of other objects and a temporal background of assumptions and expectations (Campbell 1970). Thus survey-like approaches to specific information in anthropological fieldwork require as a prerequisite an extended acquaintance with the culture (Campbell and LeVine 1970). The emphasis upon the contextual character of knowledge should not, of course, be extended to a denial of the possibility of crosscultural comparison or of identifying corresponding features in dissimilar cultures. To return to perception again, vision would be of little use were it not for the feasibility of, and relative success in, recognizing an object as "the same" in widely differing contexts (Campbell 1970). This is of course a presumptive and problematic process even in visual perception, and specific identifications in crosscultural work are obviously open to challenge (Sears 1961; Norbeck, Walker and Cohen 1962).

One specific implication of this context dependence has been drawn from the crosscultural study of optical illusions. The verification that persons in different cultures had different degrees of these illusions was only possible because a bracketing context of similar perceptions made interpretable a relatively narrow band of different perceptions. Were two cultures to perceive in radically different ways, the differences in perception could not have been distinguished from failures of communication (Campbell 1964).

Adaptation Level and Contrast Effects

In considering the faults of our laboratory experiments in social psychology, we have come up with a list of recurrent flaws, some of which also apply to other types of data collection. One of these has been called infelicitously "instrument decay" (Campbell 1957): When human observers are used as the measuring device their judgmental standards often change in ways that may be misinterpreted as experimental effects. A major source of such "instrument decay" is a set of phenomena in human judgment summarized by Helson (1964) under the concept of "level of adaptation." Its role in social science field work may be illustrated by the anecdote in the following paragraph.

In the last two decades, Russian experts from American universities have been sent on extended visits to the U.S.S.R. In part, they have had different itineraries, some going first to Leningrad, others first to Moscow, and so forth. In comparing notes later they have found themselves in disagreement as to which Russian city (Leningrad or Moscow) was the more drab and which the more lively. These differences in opinion have turned out to be correlated with the differences in itinerary: whichever city one visited first seemed more drab. Against the adaptation level based upon experience with familiar United States cities, the first Russian city seemed drab and cold indeed. But a stay in Russia modified the adaptation level, changed the implicit standard of reference so that the second city was judged against a more lenient standard.[1] Such a process is what would be predicted by extrapolation from laboratory and field studies of the effect of context upon clinical psychology judgments (*e.g.,* Campbell, Hunt and Lewis 1957, 1958, Krantz and Campbell 1961). Of course, other processes were also involved—familiarity with the Russian vernacular, sensitivity to the expressive components of voice tone and gesture, and other skills facilitating warm social contacts were increasing. All such effects were operating, however, to change the calibration of the human observer, and thus to bias his reports in a systematic way.

How can we learn of, and correct, such bias? The anecdote is instructive in this regard. This bias would not have been noted if all of the visitors had had the same itinerary. Their actual pattern constituted a counterbalanced observational schedule, and could have been analyzed as a crossover design (Cochran and Cox 1950) to determine the main effects of firstness versus secondness, of city, and of observer. Essential in the control were multiple observers and multiple sequences.

Today many anthropologists, as in Africa, are combining basic ethnography with acculturation studies, and are faced with the decision as to whether to study first the members of the tribe who remain in the bush, or the members living in the westernized city. Combining the principles of

[1] We are indebted to Professors Deming Brown and Raymond Mack for this information.

adaptation level with other principles of bias, particularly those involving assimilation errors or transfer (see Campbell 1958b for a survey of such biases) some predictions can perhaps be made: (1) If one compares anthropologist's impressions of the indigenous bush culture under the two orders (bush-city versus city-bush), this indigenous culture would probably appear more strange and exotic under the bush-city order. This is because, under that order, the bush culture is perceived with a more divergent adaptation level than that provided when the partially westernized members of the culture have been previously studied in the city. (2) The bush data might be better in detail and intimacy of records for the city-bush order than for the bush-city order. This might be expected insofar as rapport is increased by the familiarity with the culture and the friendship bonds acquired through the city fieldwork with the partially acculturated members of the ethnic group. (3) The observation of "survivals" of the indigenous culture among the westernized urban descendants is no doubt enhanced by detailed knowledge of the relatively untouched bush culture. Thus, such "survivals" might be noted in greater number in the bush-city order. These predictions cannot, of course, be made unequivocally. But whatever the direction predicted, there are adequate grounds to expect the two sequences to produce different results, particularly on those intangible matters most relevant to the culture-personality problem.

The source of error is great enough, and a considerable remedy is near enough at hand, so that we are morally bound to request from our sources of financial support the funds to implement them — particularly since all concerned should now recognize how precious to the social sciences is our rapidly dwindling supply of novel and independent social systems. The cheapest remedy would be to schedule the field work so that it was broken up into several alternating visits to each location, bush and urban, allowing *both* conditions to be recompared several times, and both to be judged against the end-of-field-trip adaptation level. This could probably be accomplished with 10 per cent increases in the travel budgets and 50 per cent increases in the field residence budgets — certainly not impossible to promote once the importance is recognized. A more complete control would double field costs by having the fieldworkers work in pairs, one starting in the bush and one in the city, and trading locations from time to time. This approach would also offer an important control over the "personal equations" or idiosyncratic predilections of the observers, biases of a more permanent and less predictable sort than those due to adaptation level. There would seem no doubt but that this additional cost would be justified. Analogous designs for assessing bias due to the ethnographer's own culture are presented by Campbell (1964).

Adaptation Level and Usable Vocabulary in Cross-Cultural Interviewing

One of the emphases of the present paper is upon the desirability of some studies which collect data on a limited set of topics from many cultural units. This is advocated not as a substitute for the intensive ethnography of single peoples, but rather as a needed additional mode of data collection, particularly for those correlational types of analysis in which dozens of cultures are needed. In such multiple-culture studies the field work would be particularly dependent upon interviews with informants, the anthropologist himself not having time to observe directly all of the customs about which he inquired. In such studies the phenomenon of adaptation level creates for a class of descriptive words "translation" problems over and above the troublesome fact of language differences. That is to say, these adaptation-level problems would remain even if the heterogeneous cultures were to "speak the same language" as the anthropologist.

The words or concepts in question are those used to characterize the tribe as a whole which imply degrees of departure from a usual norm or adaptation level, this norm being itself provided by the average behavior or experience of the tribe itself. Such words are usable to denote individual differences within the tribe, but not to characterize overall attributes of the culture. Thus, for a hypothetical "wholly isolated" tribe, lacking a range of other peoples for comparison, one could not interpret for cross-cultural comparisons answers to questions such as: "Is it hot or cold today?" or "Are your people happy, intelligent, hard-working, strict with children, warm, friendly, prudish, joking, able to endure pain, and so forth?"

Anthropologists, experienced with many cultures and having a common base in European cultures, may be able to make such observations and judgments reliably, particularly if the fluctuations of their own adaptation levels, as described above, be compensated for. But a completely isolated tribe would have no "lingua franca," no inter-tribal measuring stick against which to calibrate their use of the terms. And even though informants might reliably employ the frame of reference provided by the several adjacent tribes, given the ubiquitous tendencies toward regional similarity, this would not entirely eliminate the problem.

For some of these topics, modes of questioning are available which may avoid this problem. Such questioning may make use of internal comparisons within the tribe ("Are the children happier than adults?"). More typically, the problem may be solved by reducing the question to sample behaviors from the implied syndrome, employing terms referring to qualitatively discrete and universal behaviors: "Upon what occasions do women smile and laugh?" "What does a mother do when her child cries?" "What are the times during the day when a man works — or rests?" These suggestions, however, do more to raise the problem than to suggest a solution. (See also Werner and Campbell 1970.)

The Uninterpretability of Comparisons between Only Two Natural Instances

In view of the importance of Malinowski's challenge to the love-jealousy interpretation of the Oedipal conflict, it is unforgivable that his observations have not been replicated. However thorough his field work on other points, his published evidence on this point is very thin indeed. While he alludes to evidence from manifest dream content, of the type that Dorothy Eggan (1952) has discussed, what we need are substantial samples of detailed records of the dreams of boys and girls and men and women.

But while there is a crying need for verifying and extending Malinowski's evidence on Trobriand intrafamilial attitudes, such a replication is of minor importance for testing the Freudian hypothesis. We who are interested in using such data for delineating process rather than exhaustively describing single instances must accept this rule: *A comparison of a single pair of natural objects is nearly uninterpretable.** Between Trobriand and Vienna there are many dimensions of differences which could constitute potential rival explanations and which we have no means of ruling out. For comparisons of this pair, the *ceteris paribus* requirement becomes untenable. But data collection need not stop here. Both the avunculate and the European arrangement are so widely distributed over the world that if testing Oedipal theories were our purpose, we could select a dozen matched pairs of tribes from widely varying culture areas, each pair differing with regard to which male educates and disciplines the boy, but as similar as possible in other respects. Assuming that collections of dreams from boys showed the expected differences between each pair, then the more such pairs we had, the fewer tenable rival hypotheses would be available and, thus, the more certain would be our confirmation.

There is an analogous *ceteris paribus* problem with the use of a single

*See Editor's Introduction to Part II.

measuring instrument. An established difference between two matched populations on a *single* questionnaire item is likewise uninterpretable because there are so many rival hypotheses to explain the difference — the groups may differ because of their reactions to the first word, or to the second word, or to the grammatical features of the wording rather than the semantic features, and so forth. However, if there are multiple indicators which vary in their irrelevant attributes, and if these all agree as to the direction of the difference on the theoretically intended aspects, then the number of tenable rival explanations becomes greatly reduced and the confirmation of theory more nearly certain (Campbell 1957:310, Campbell 1959, Campbell and Fiske 1959, Webb et al. 1966). Doob (1958) has demonstrated the seriousness of this problem in cross-cultural studies, in an important paper which should be read by every graduate student planning to do research on culture and personality. On this point, it has been psychologists studying college sophomores and not anthropologists who have been most guilty of a naive overdependence upon single instruments, and our critical literature on "response sets" (*e.g.*, Cronbach 1946, 1950, Chapman and Bock 1958) shows how misleading this can be.

Hologeistic Studies

By this term, we designate, following Köbben (1952), the dominant method in use for quantitative culture and personality studies. These are the quantitative correlational crosscultural studies based upon ratings and codings of ethnographic prose. (We prefer "hologeistic study" to "cross-cultural survey," since the "survey" connotes public opinion interviews to most social scientists.) For psychological anthropology, the most influential of these studies have been done by Whiting and Child (1953) and their many students and followers. The basic methodology for such studies can be found in Moore (1961) and Otterbein (1969).

These quantitative cross-cultural studies have been the major focus of attack by the descriptive-humanistic anthropologists, an attack long dominant but largely unwritten (however, see Köbben 1952, 1967, Shapera 1953, Lewis 1956). A first general objection has been that *such studies are not anthropology*. This objection can be, of course, an entirely legitimate expression of differences in goals. It may reflect upon the fact that problems of psychological and sociological theory rather than ethnographic description are being worked on. It can express a commitment to anthropology's task, comparable to that of the historian, of documenting in detail the full complexity of single instances. But this objection is usually a concomitant of other objections which reject the studies for the abstract-ing-generalizing purpose also. A second general objection is that *taking fragments of a culture and attempting to interpret them apart from the whole cultural complex is impossible or illegitimate.* Spiro (1958) has cited this widespread objection, and has correctly called it an empirical question to be answered by the final outcomes of trying the approach. Such criticisms might have been right. It might have been that none of the findings would stand up under cross-validation, that no correlational laws relating aspects of cultural phenomena could be established. For a major cluster of relation-ships centering around the evolution of societal complexity, it is already apparent that the critics are wrong. Well cross-validated relationships have been established (Naroll 1970b). For culture and personality, the relationships are not yet as well confirmed, but there have been fewer replication efforts so far. In any event, such laws are not to be ruled out on *a priori* grounds.

From the standpoint of an empirical science of induction (Campbell 1959, 1970), it must be expected that there may be many problem areas in which a science cannot be established. In the terminology of the analysis-of-variance statistics of experimentation, if in a given area one always finds significant highest-order interactions, and never finds signifi-cant main effects or lower-order interactions, then a science probably never can be developed. The healthy infancy of the successful sciences seems to have been predicated upon the stimulating nourishment of crude but effective *ceteris paribus* laws. For example, the force fields of atomic nuclei extend in infinite distance in all directions. However, they decay so rapidly as a function of distance that they can be disregarded in the statement of many crude laws, such as those embodied in Archimedes' mechanics. Were this not so, were Archimedes to have had to limit himself to statements about each particular instance, then physics never could have developed. The critics of the generalizing social scientists are right in cautioning against claiming effective *ceteris paribus* laws when one hasn't got them, but pointing to the obvious idiosyncracy of every person, tribe, or swinging cathedral chandelier provides no *a priori* basis for rejecting the enterprise.

The proponents of hologeistic studies have responded in detail to the more specific criticisms of their method, and have developed methodolog-ical issues of their own. The following eleven problems report on this literature:

1. *Sampling.* What is a representative sample and how may it be drawn?

452   *Methods and Techniques*

What are the respective merits of judgmental sampling and probability sampling? What about "non-responding" tribes, those on which no adequate description exists and — it may also be — whose culture has largely disappeared by now? (See Naroll 1967, Murdock and White 1969, Chaney and Ruiz Revilla 1969, Naroll 1970a, and Naroll and Cohen 1970:Chapter 43.)

The main difficulty today with conducting a strict probability sample of existing societies lies in the fact that most of them have been inadequately described. The number well-enough known to study varies from about 150 to 1000 — depending on the topic of investigation. Since the total number of human societies in existence during the last century is of the order of 4000 to 5000, this problem involves considerable selection bias. Chapter 43 of Naroll and Cohen (1970) discusses at length: (a) some specific systematic errors now known to arise from this selection bias; and (b) some methods for measuring and controlling these biases.

2. *Societal Unit Definition.* What is a tribe, or society? What are we counting in our statistical summaries when we say that so many tribes or societies support a given hypothesis, while so many others tend to discredit it? (See Naroll 1964, Helm 1968, Murdock and White 1969, and Naroll and Cohen 1970:Chapter 39.)

The criteria most frequently used to define societal boundaries have been language, political organization, and territorial occupancy. There has been no agreement among anthropologists on any method of societal unit definition. Two further cross-cultural controls on unit definition inconsistency are possible (Naroll n.d.): (a) *The double-boundary principle.* Although it is often difficult to distinguish two neighboring societies by fixing the location of the boundary between them, it is manifestly easy to draw a world-wide cross-cultural sample of even several hundred varieties such that no two societies in the sample are difficult to distinguish from one another. To do so, it is only required that no two sample members share a common territorial boundary, or speak languages near one another on a linguistic continuum. (b) *An index of ethnic distinctiveness.* Some ethnic units are more sharply defined from their neighbors than others. These differences in our opinion are usually irrelevant to most cross-cultural surveys. Let the differences then be formally measured and this irrelevance formally established by showing the absence of a significant correlation between the index and the variables being investigated.

3. *Data Accuracy.* What errors of fact are found in cross-cultural codings? Such errors may arise in the work of informants, ethnographers or

comparativists. They may be random, and thus measurable by reliability testing, or they may be systematic, and thus measurable by data quality control tests. (See Naroll 1962, Rosenthal 1966, Webb et al. 1966, and Naroll and Cohen 1970:Chapters 8, 10, 44, 45, 46.)

The key point to bear in mind is that random errors differ in their effect on correlations from systematic errors. Random errors tend to lower correlations; systematic errors may tend to raise them. Thus the correlation in Whiting and Child (1953) between witchcraft and weaning may possibly be a mere artifact of the systematic tendencies of ethnographers to underestimate the importance of witchcraft but to overestimate weaning ages. Three characteristics of ethnographers are especially useful data quality control factors: their native language familiarity, the length of their stay among the natives, and the degree of their actual participation in the culture being reported.

4. *Conceptualization, Classification and Coding.* For treatment of such problems in the light of varying cultural contexts, see Ford (1967), Moore (1969), and Naroll and Cohen (1970:Chapters 1, 36, 37, 38).

Twenty years ago, the most commonly heard criticism of cross-cultural surveys was an objection to extracting particular traits from the whole cultural context in which they are imbedded. This criticism is much less heard today. Perhaps more anthropologists now realize that cross-cultural surveys are by their very nature explicit tests of cultural context. They compare particular elements in a culture with other elements in the same culture to see if they indeed are relevant.

5. *Galton's Problem* — the question of the extent to which cross-cultural correlations reflect functional associations on the one hand or cultural diffusion on the other. (See Murdock and White 1969, Schaefer 1969, and Naroll and Cohen 1970:Chapters 47 and 48.)

So far, seven methods of solution to Galton's Problem have been developed. These all depend upon taking geographical propinquity as a measure of diffusion. The cluster method directly tests the hypothesis that functionally linked traits tend to diffuse together and not diffuse separately. New developments include an application of that method to the Geary dyad matrix which hopefully will permit simultaneous measurement not only of all geographical directions but also of all linguistic relationships (Hildreth and Naroll n.d.).

6. *Causal Analysis of Correlations* — the question of discerning causal direction among correlated variables and dealing with the problem of the "lurking variable," the unmeasured unknown which may be producing a

spurious correlation. (See Blalock 1960, 1964, Boudon 1967, Naroll 1969, and Naroll and Cohen 1970:Chapters 4, 5, 6.)

The writers just cited offer methods of strictly limited scope which sometimes in certain circumstances permit inferences about causal sequence. So far not much use has been made in cross-cultural surveys of any method for time-lagging (e.g., Rozelle and Campbell 1969, Pelz and Andrews 1964), but we often have data on culture change among primitive societies. The most useful method of causal direction analysis would seem to involve the establishment of time sequence along with correlation. The cross-lagged correlation would seem to be a useful tool for that purpose, although it has not yet been used in cross-cultural surveys. A study of modernization among under-developed peoples would seem to be a good place to try it.

7. *Paucity of Relevant Data* — how a problem can be investigated if existing literature fails to yield the needed data. For example, how can we compare suicide frequencies among primitive tribes when no accurate statistics are available on suicide rates among them? (See Naroll 1969, Naroll and Cohen 1970:Chapter 1, and Webb et al. 1966.)

Where a variable cannot be directly measured, it must be measured indirectly and the validity of the indicator must be established. Often, however, the mere existence of a strong correlation between indicators itself creates a presumption of their validity. Such a presumption arises when no rival explanation of the correlation is plausible. For example, attention to suicide by ethnographers is highly correlated with divorce rules, marriage negotiation rules, drunken brawling, warfare, homicide frequency and wifebeating (Naroll 1969). None of these correlations makes any sense unless we suppose that ethnographers tend to give more attention to suicide when there is more suicide to attract attention.

Most hologeistic studies limit themselves to data described in published monographs. The topical coverage of these is inevitably uneven, as has been noted, and reflects the anthropological interests of the past since it is no longer fashionable to attempt "general" ethnographies but rather to focus all field work on some specific narrow topic. Thus on some topics of current interest, a hologeistic study would be impossible.

For the most part, this must remain a permanent limitation. However, there have been some efforts to collect new data specifically for cross-cultural comparison (Whiting et al. 1963, Minturn and Lambert 1964, Campbell and LeVine 1970). While these studies have been difficult to carry out and have been limited to very small numbers of cases, we can look to improvements in such methodology.

8. *The "Combing," "Dredging," or "Mudsticking" Problem.* Suppose that like Textor (1967) we have a computer run some 100,000 correlations. Would we not expect 5000 of them to be "statistically significant" at the 5% level by chance alone, even if the data were meaningless garbage, taken say from tables of random numbers? (Strangely enough, as a matter of fact, if the correlations concerned are coefficients of association from four-fold contingency tables and the average sample size is under 50, the answer is *no*. We would expect only about half that many, or 2500.) (See Textor 1967:54–59, Winch and Campbell 1969, and Naroll and Cohen 1970: Chapters 34 and 48.)

The best solution to the problem of group significance is to use the "Whiskers Variable" method of Banks and Textor (1963). A "Whiskers Variable" is a nonsense variable coded from a table of random numbers or from the random numbers generator of a computer. It is important however that the Whiskers Variables keep the numerical distributions of the real variables being compared. Thus, it is not wise to substitute fresh random numbers for the real codings; such random numbers will have the distribution forms of the random numbers source rather than that of the real variables being compared. Better to keep the codings of the real variables but randomly reassign them to cases (Naroll, Bullough and Naroll 1971).

9. *The general problem of Statistical Significance.* Supposing we have a relationship in a cross-cultural study, what is the likelihood that such a relationship is a mere sampling freak? Now since the mathematical model of significance tests prescribes random sampling, some writers (e.g., Young 1965:60) suppose that tests of significance are not applicable where sampling is not random. True, with a non-random sample, a successful significance test does not dispose of the sampling bias problem. But an *un*successful significance test does dispose of the study. In judgmental as compared to random samples, favorable results of significance tests are not equally reassuring; but unfavorable results are equally damning (Winch and Campbell 1969).

10. *Regional Variation.* Do the world-wide results truly reflect world-wide tendencies, or do they instead merely reflect the situation in a particular region? (See Sawyer and LeVine 1966, Driver and Schuessler 1967, and Chaney and Ruiz Revilla 1969.)

There are two ways to cope with the regional variation problem. The better way is to recompute correlations separately for each major continental area. The easier way is simply to correlate each region with each trait being studied. Thus societies may be coded as falling in North

456 *Methods and Techniques*

America or falling outside North America. Then we may see if there is a correlation between North American location and weaning age.

11. *Deviant Case Analysis.* Why exceptions? How can we explain deviant cases, where the association in question is conspicuously absent? (See Köbben 1967.)

We advocate the systematic use of control tests for sampling bias, for unit definition bias, for coding errors, for cultural diffusion, for regional variation. Such tests will go far toward explaining many deviant cases. The use of some method of multivariate analysis like factor analysis will help further. The use of multiple correlation to measure the total variance included in the research design likewise helps understand deviant cases — the higher the multiple correlation, the more likely a single stray unexplained deviant case is due simply to chance. But if there is substantial unexplained variance, deviant case analysis may be a powerful tool in further hypothesis formulation. By studying and seeking to classify unexplained deviant cases, the investigator may be granted the insight to perceive a hitherto unsuspected relationship.

Summary

In the first part of this paper, the role of anthropological data in editing among the competing theories of psychology has been emphasized. Such research can never be central among the anthropologist's tasks, but can be invaluable in the consolidation of psychological theory. Anthropology is in this fashion of great methodological importance to psychology.

In the second part of the paper, the roles are reversed. Since anthropology depends upon enculturated human beings as its measuring instruments, the psychology of bias in human judgment becomes relevant to choices among methodological alternatives open to anthropologists. A final section discusses the methodological issues in quantitative cross-cultural or hologeistic studies.

Bakan, David. 1958. Sigmund Freud and the Jewish mystical tradition. Princeton, Van Nostrand.
———. 1966. The duality of human existence. Chicago, Rand McNally.
Banks, Arthur S. and Robert B. Textor. 1963. A cross-polity survey. Cambridge, M.I.T. Press.

BENNETT, JOHN W. 1946. The interpretation of Pueblo culture. Southwestern Journal of Anthropology 2:361-374.

BLALOCK, HUBERT M., JR. 1960. Correlational analysis and causal inferences. American Anthropologist 62:624–653.

———. 1964. Causal inferences in non-experimental research. Chapel Hill, University of North Carolina Press.

BOUDON, RAYMOND. 1967. L'analyse mathématique des faits sociaux. Paris, Plon.

CAMPBELL, DONALD T. 1955. The informant in quantitative research. American Journal of Sociology 6:339-342.

———. 1957. Factors relevant to the validity of experiments in social settings. Psychological Bulletin 54:297–312.

———. 1958a. Common fate, similarity, and other indices of the status of aggregates of persons as social entities. Behavioral Science 3:14–25.

———. 1958b. Systematic error on the part of human links in communication systems. Information and Control 1:334–369.

———. 1959. Methodological suggestions from a comparative psychology of knowledge processes. Inquiry 2:152–182.

———. 1963. Social attitudes and other acquired behavioral dispositions. *In* Psychology: a study of a science. Vol. 6. Investigations of man as socius: their place in psychology and the social sciences. Sigmund Koch, ed., New York, McGraw Hill.

———. 1964. Distinguishing differences of perception from failures of communication in cross-cultural studies. *In* Cross-cultural understanding: epistemology in anthropology. F. S. C. Northrop and H. H. Livingston, eds., New York, Harper & Row.

———. 1965. Variation and selective retention in sociocultural evolution. *In* Social change in developing areas: a reinterpretation of evolutionary theory. H. R. Barringer, G. I. Blanksten, and R. W. Mack, eds., Cambridge, Mass., Schenkman.

———. 1969. A phenomenology of the other one: corrigible, hypothetical and critical. *In* Human action: conceptual and empirical issues. T. Mischel, ed., New York, Academic Press.

———. 1970. Natural selection as an epistemological model. *In* A handbook of method in cultural anthropology. R. Naroll and R. Cohen, eds., Garden City, New York, The Natural History Press.

CAMPBELL, DONALD T. AND DONALD W. FISKE. 1959. Convergent and discriminant validation by the multitrait-multimethod matrix. Psychological Bulletin 56:81–105.

CAMPBELL, DONALD T., WILLIAM A. HUNT AND NAN A. LEWIS. 1957. The effects of assimilation and contrast in judgments of clinical materials. American Journal of Psychology 70:347–360.

————. 1958. The relative susceptibility of two rating scales to disturbances resulting from shifts in stimulus context. Journal of Applied Psychology 42:213–217.

CAMPBELL, DONALD T. AND ROBERT A. LEVINE. 1970. Field manual anthropology. *In* A handbook of method in cultural anthropology. R. Naroll and R. Cohen, eds., Garden City, New York, The Natural History Press.

CHANEY, RICHARD AND RUIZ REVILLA. 1969. Sampling methods and interpretation of correlation: a computer analysis of seven crosscultural samples. American Anthropologist 71:597–633.

CHAPMAN, LOREN J. AND R. DARRELL BOCK. 1958. Components of variance due to acquiescence and content in the F scale measure of authoritarianism. Psychological Bulletin 55:328–333.

CHILD, IRVIN L. 1954. Socialization. *In* Handbook of social psychology. Gardner Lindzey, ed., Cambridge, Mass., Addison-Wesley.

CHILD, IRVIN L., THOMAS STORM AND JOSEPH VEROFF. 1958. Achievement themes in folk tales related to socialization practice. *In* Motives in fantasy, action, and society. John W. Atkinson, ed., New York, Van Nostrand.

COCHRAN, WILLIAM G. AND GERTRUDE M. COX. 1950. Experimental designs. New York, Wiley.

CRONBACH, LEE J. 1946. Response sets and test validity. Educational and Psychological Measurement 6:475–494.

————. 1950. Further evidence on response sets and test design. Educational and Psychological Measurement 10:3–31.

DOOB, LEONARD W. 1957. An introduction to the psychology of acculturation. Journal of Social Psychology 45:143–160.

————. 1958. The use of different test items in nonliterate societies. Public Opinion Quarterly 21:499–504.

DRIVER, HAROLD E. AND KARL F. SCHUESSLER. 1967. Correlational analysis of Murdock's 1957 ethnographic sample. American Anthropologist 69:332–352.

EGGAN, DOROTHY. 1952. The manifest content of dreams: a challenge to social science. American Anthropologist 54:469–485.

FORD, CLELLAN S. 1967. Cross-cultural approaches: readings on comparative research. New Haven, HRAF Press.

GILLEN, JOHN. 1954. Methods of approach to the study of human behavior. *In* Aspects of culture and personality. Francis L. K. Hsu, ed., New York, Abelard-Schuman.

HEIDER, FRITZ. 1944. Social perception and phenomenal causality. Psychological Review 51:358–374.

HELM, JUNE, ED. 1968. Essays on the problem of tribe. Proceedings of the 1967 annual spring meeting of the American Ethnological Society.

HELSON, HARRY. 1964. Adaptation-level theory. New York, Harper & Row.

HENRY, JULES AND ZUNIA HENRY. 1944. Doll play of Pilage Indian children. Research Monographs No. 4, American Orthopsychiatric Association.

HERSKOVITS, MELVILLE J. 1948. Man and his works. New York, Knopf.

———. 1960. Humanism in anthropological science. VI International Congress of Anthropological and Ethnological Sciences, Paris, August 4, 1960.

HERSKOVITS, MELVILLE J. AND FRANCES S. HERSKOVITS. 1958a. Sibling rivalry, the Oedipus complex. and myth. Journal of American Folklore 7:1–15.

———. 1958b. Dahomean narrative: a cross-cultural analysis. Evanston, Illinois, Northwestern University Press.

HILDRETH, RICHARD AND RAOUL NAROLL. n.d. Galton's problem in cross-national surveys. To appear in a symposium volume edited by Leonard Binder and Sidney Verba reporting the proceedings of the 1970 Social Science Research Council workshop on comparative method.

HOLMES, LOWELL DON. 1957. The restudy of Manu'an culture: a problem in methodology. Unpublished Ph.D. dissertation, Northwestern University.

———. 1958. Ta'u: stability and change in a Samoan village. Wellington, New Zealand, Polynesian Society, Reprint No. 7.

HONIGMANN, JOHN J. 1952. The testing of hypotheses in anthropology. American Anthropologist 54:429–432.

———. 1954 Culture and personality. New York, Harper.

HSU, FRANCIS L. K. 1940. The English wife. Chapter VI, Mother and children, Section 5, A non-Freudian explanation. Unpublished manuscript.

———. 1954. Aspects of culture and personality. New York, Abelard-Schuman.

———. 1969. The Study of Literate Civilizations. N.Y., Holt, Rinehart & Winston.

———. 1970. Americans and Chinese: Purpose and Fulfillment in Great Civilizations. N.Y., Doubleday and Natural History Press.

KELLER, ALBERT GALLOWAY. 1931. Societal evolution (rev. ed.). New Haven, Yale University Press.

KLUCKHOHN, CLYDE. 1954. Southwestern studies of culture and personality. American Anthropologist 56:685–697.

KÖBBEN, ANDRÉ J. F. 1952. New ways of presenting an old idea: the statistical method in social anthropology. Journal of the Royal Anthropological Institute of Great Britain and Ireland 82:129–146. Reprinted in Readings in cross-cultural method. F. Moore, ed., New Haven, HRAF Press.

———. 1967. Why exceptions? The logic of cross-cultural comparisons. Current Anthropology 8:3–34.

KRANTZ, D. L. AND DONALD T. CAMPBELL. 1961. Separating perceptual and linguistic effects of context shifts upon absolute judgments. Journal of Experimental Psychology 62(1):35–42.

LAMBERT, WILLIAM W., LEIGH MINTURN TRIANDIS AND MARGERY WOLF. 1959. Some correlates of beliefs in the malevolence and benevolence of supernatural beings: a cross-cultural study. Journal of Abnormal and Social Psychology 58:162–169.

LASSWELL, HAROLD D. 1931. A hypothesis rooted in the preconceptions of a single civilization tested by Bronislaw Malinowski. *In* Methods in social science. Stuart A. Rice, ed., Chicago, University of Chicago Press.

LEVY, DAVID M. 1935. Sibling rivalry studies in children of primitive groups. American Journal of Orthopsychiatry 9:205–214.

LEWIS, OSCAR. 1951. Life in a Mexican village: Tepoztlan restudied. Urbana, University of Illinois Press.

————. 1956. Comparisons in cultural anthropology. *In* Current anthropology: a supplement to anthropology today. William L. Thomas, ed., Chicago, University of Chicago Press.

LI AN-CHE. 1937. Zuni: some observations and queries. American Anthropologist 39:62–76.

MALINOWSKI, BRONISLAW. 1927. Sex and repression in savage society. London, Humanities Press.

MEAD, MARGARET AND F. M. C. MACGREGOR. 1951. Growth and culture; a photographic study of Balinese childhood. New York, Putnam.

MICHOTTE, A. E. 1946. La perception de la causalite. Louvain, Institute superior de Philosophie, Etudes Psychologiques, Vol. 6. (English translation.)

MINTURN, L. AND W. W. LAMBERT. 1964. Mothers of six cultures: antecedents of child rearing. New York, John Wiley and Sons.

MOORE, FRANK. 1961. Readings in cross-cultural method. New Haven, HRAF Press.

————. 1969. Codes and coding. Behavior Science Notes 4:247–266.

MURDOCK, GEORGE PETER AND DOUGLAS WHITE. 1969. Standard cross-cultural sample. Ethnology 8:329–369.

MURRAY, HENRY A. 1949. Research planning: a few proposals. *In* Culture and personality. S. Stansfeld Sargent and Marian W. Smith, eds., New York, Viking Fund.

NAROLL, RAOUL. 1962. Data quality control. New York, Free Press.

————. 1964. A fifth solution to Galton's problem. American Anthropologist 66:863–867.

————. 1967. The proposed HRAF probability sample, Behavior Science Notes 2:70–80.

————. 1969. Cultural determinants and the concept of the sick society. *In* Changing perspectives in mental illness. Robert B. Edgerton and Stanley C. Plog, eds., New York, Holt, Rinehart and Winston.

————. 1970a. Chaney and Ruiz Revilla: a comment. American Anthropologist 72:1451–1453.

————. 1970b. What have we learned from cross-cultural surveys? American Anthropologist 72:1227–1288.

————. n.d. Mankind, painful progress. New York, Columbia University Press. Forthcoming.

NAROLL, RAOUL, VERN L. BULLOUGH AND FRADA NAROLL. 1971. Military deterrence in history: a pilot cross-historical survey. Albany, State University of New York Press.

NAROLL, RAOUL AND RONALD COHEN, EDS. A handbook in cultural anthropology. New York, Natural History Press.

NORBECK, E., D. E. WALKER AND M. COHEN. 1962. The interpretation of data: puberty rites. American Anthropologist 64:463–483.

OTTERBEIN, KEITH. 1969. Basic steps in conducting a cross-cultural study. Behavior Science Notes 4:221–236.

PAUL, BENJAMIN D. 1950. Symbolic sibling rivalry in a Guatemalan Indian village. American Anthropologist 52:205–217.

PELZ, DONALD C. AND FRANK M. ANDREWS. 1964. Detecting causal priorities in panel study data. American Sociological Review 29:836–848.

PETTITT, GEORGE A. 1946. Primitive education in North America. Berkeley, University of California Press, University of California Publications in American Archaeology and Ethnology Vol. 43, No. 1.

ROSENTHAL, ROBERT. 1966. Experimenter effects in behavioral research. New York, Appleton-Century-Crofts.

ROZELLE, R. M. AND DONALD T. CAMPBELL. 1969. More plausible rival hypothesis in the cross-lagged panel correlation technique. Psychological Bulletin 71:74–80.

SARGENT, S. STANSFELD AND MARIAN W. SMITH. 1949. Culture and personality. New York, Viking Fund.

SAWYER, JACK AND ROBERT A. LEVINE. 1966. Cultural dimensions: a factor analysis of the World Ethnographic Sample. American Anthropologist 68:708–731.

SCHAEFER, JAMES. 1969. Linked pair alignments for the HRAF quality control sample universe. Behavior Science Notes 4:299–320.

SCHAPERA, ISAAC. 1953. Some comments on comparative method in social anthropology. American Anthropologist 55:353–361.

SEARS R. R. 1961. Transcultural variables and conceptual equivalence. *In* Studying personality cross-culturally. B. Kaplan, ed., 445–456. New York, Harper & Row.

SEGALL, MARSHALL H., DONALD T. CAMPBELL, AND MELVILLE J. HERSKOVITS. 1966. The influence of culture on visual perception. Indianapolis, Bobbs Merrill.

SPIRO, MELFORD E. 1953. Ghosts: an anthropological inquiry into learning and perception. Journal of Abnormal and Social Psychology 48:376–382.

SPIRO, MELFORD E. AND ROY G. D'ANDRADE. 1958. A cross-cultural study of some supernatural beliefs. American Anthropologist 60:456–466.

TEXTOR, ROBERT B. 1967. A cross-cultural summary. New Haven, HRAF Press.

WEBB, EUGENE J., DONALD T. CAMPBELL, RICHARD D. SCHWARTZ AND LEE SECHREST. 1966. Unobtrusive measures: nonreactive research in the social sciences. Chicago, Rand McNally.

WELLISCH, E. 1954. Isaac and Oedipus: a study in biblical psychology of the sacrifice of Isaac, the Akedah. London, Routledge and Kegan Paul.

WERNER, OSWALD AND DONALD T. CAMPBELL. 1970. Translating, working through interpreters, and the problem of decentering. *In* A handbook of method in cultural anthropology. R. Naroll and R. Cohen, eds., Garden City, New York, The Natural History Press.

WERNER, OSWALD AND JOANN FENTON. 1970. Method and theory in ethnoscience or ethnoepistemology. *In* A handbook of method in cultural anthropology. R. Naroll and R. Cohen, eds., Garden City, New York, The Natural History Press.

WHITING B. B., I. L. CHILD, W. W. LAMBERT, AND J. W. M. WHITING. 1963. Six cultures: studies of child rearing. New York, John Wiley and Sons.

WHITING, JOHN W. M. 1954. The cross-cultural method. *In* Handbook of social psychology. Gardner Lindzey, ed., Cambridge, Mass., Addison-Wesley.

———. 1959. Sorcery, sin and the superego: a cross-cultural study of some mechanisms of social control. *In* Nebraska symposium on motivation: 1959, Marshall R. Jones, ed., pp. 174–195. Lincoln, University of Nebraska Press, 1959.

———. 1968. Method and problems in cross-cultural research. *In* Handbook of social psychology. 2nd ed. Gardner Lindzey and Elliot Aronson, eds., Cambridge, Mass., Addison-Wesley.

WHITING, JOHN W. M. AND IRVIN L. CHILD. 1953. Child training and personality: a cross-cultural study. New Haven, Yale University Press.

WHITING, JOHN W. M., RICHARD KLUCKHOHN AND ALBERT ANTHONY. 1958. The function of male initiation ceremonies at puberty. *In* Readings in social psychology, 3rd ed. Eleanor E. Maccoby, Theodore M. Newcomb, and Eugene L. Hartley, eds., New York, Holt, Rinehart & Winston.

WINCH, ROBERT F. AND DONALD T. CAMPBELL. 1969. Proof? No. Evidence? Yes. The significance of tests of significance. American Sociologist 4:140–143.

YOUNG, FRANK. 1965. Initiation ceremonies: a cross-cultural study of status dramatization. Indianapolis, Bobbs Merrill.

ZIGLER, EDWARD AND IRVIN CHILD. 1969. Socialization. *In* The handbook of social psychology. G. Lindzey and E. Aronson, eds., 2nd edition, Vol. III, Reading, Mass., Addison-Wesley.

Socialization, Culture and Feedback

If psychological characteristics of the individual, whether identified with his total personality or with the socially functioning part of it, are dependent upon the culturally conditioned child-rearing practices or socialization processes, what are the factors which determine or at least shape the patterns of culture, which in turn condition the child-rearing practices or socialization processes? If human societies are as stable and unchanging as those of ants and bees, the latter type of question, though not wholly irrelevant, would not have been important. But human societies are highly dynamic entities which often undergo changes before our very eyes, just as human individuals in any society are quite capable of, and often given to, deviation from its norm.

The late Jules Henry put it this way: "As I see it, the crucial difference between insect societies and human ones is that whereas the former are organized to achieve homeostasis, the organization of the latter seems always to *guarantee and specifically provide for instability*" ("Homeostasis, Society and Evolution: A Critique." Scientific Monthly, LXXXI, 1955:308). Although this statement suffers from a degree of exaggeration, the truth it contains is undeniable.

Students of psychological anthropology generally see the relationship between the individual and his society and culture as a two-way traffic in spiral progression. The individual's psychological characteristics are results of his socialization processes; but his psychological characteristics are, in turn, at the root of the patterns of culture, in change or in stability, which govern the socialization processes. Some students, however, restrict themselves far more than others in considering what is involved in this spiral progression.

Whiting and Harrington (Chapter 12), and others influenced by the Whiting approach, mainly attempt to link certain specific socialization practices (such as intensity and frequency of punishment) with some limited aspects of the society and culture (such as oral explanations of illness), resulting in the conclusion that "the severity of aggression training (aggression socialization anxiety), which includes the treatment of temper tantrums, physical and verbal aggression, damage to property, and disobedience, is related to explanations for illness involving aggression" (for example, "hostility toward or disobedience to spirits").

From this restricted view Whiting and Harrington regard not only the physical environment (such as climatic conditions) but also man-made conditions (such as social role or size of landholdings) as "extrasystemic causal events." It is also from this restricted viewpoint that they speak of feedback. For example, "in a society which undergoes a change in maintenance systems (due to extrasystemic pressure) like household structure, child training systems may overact to the change. This might create cultural products of exaggerated values to bolster the new order (feedback of cultural product on maintenance system)."

However, the model followed by Whiting and co-workers really does not come to grips with the problem of change except that which is brought about by what they term "extrasystemic causal events." But societies and cultures vary greatly in their stability and rates of change, even without obvious differences in "extrasystemic" causes. Here we must engage in a brief taxonomy of social and cultural change according to the internal or external origin of its impetus:

External Impetus

Natural conditions which favor, limit, or destroy.

Contact with other peoples or isolation from them.

Foreign pressure or conquest.

Internal Impetus

Biological endowment.

Livelihood practice.

Social organization.
Culture pattern.
Pattern of socialization.
Personality characteristics.

External impetuses are forces for change which influence each society and culture from outside. The plague which was said to have helped topple the Roman Empire, the Fertile Crescent which nourished the Mesopotamian civilization, and the extremity of climate under which the Polar Eskimo must eke out an uncertain livelihood, these and many others are varieties of natural conditions which favor, limit or destroy. The hermit kingdom of Bhutan between China and India is still a living example of a society in extreme isolation from the rest of the world; but most peoples of continental Europe have always been in constant contact with each other. Finally there are many tribes of India, such as those in the Nilgiri Hills described by Mandelbaum ("Culture change among the Nilgiri tribes." American Anthropologist, XLIII, 1941:19–26) among which regularized economic transactions take place but each maintains its own way of life. This state of affairs is in sharp contrast to the conditions of existence of peoples under colonial rule throughout the world in which they are at the receiving end of their conquerers' resolute attempts to impose their own customs and religions.

Internal impetuses are forces for change which originate from within each society and culture. The relevance of biological endowment is least understood. Some evidence for genetic differences among different populations does exist. For example, the genetic trait called "sickle cell" is common in some that are subject to endemic malaria, but it is rare or absent in others. The possible relevance of the other five factors listed here has been subjected to far more theorization. Are rural peoples not more conservative and therefore more resistant to change than urban dwellers? Is a society under autocratic rule not more unstable than one organized along democratic lines? Is there not some evidence that a culture with a future orientation is more conducive to change than one emphasizing the past? If children are reared communally, apart from their parents, will it not produce more individuals with altruistic attitudes?

Hsu tackles the spiral progression of personality, society and culture by seeking answers to much larger questions. His methodology is, of necessity, less rigorous than that of Whiting and co-workers. The questions to which he seeks answers are as follows:

1. Even without significant and obvious differences in external pressure,

why have some societies shown a higher degree of internal impetus to change than others?

2. Given similar external pressure, why have some societies responded differently from others?

For Hsu (Chapter 13) the primary forces in social and cultural development are to be found in the pattern of man's relationship with his fellowmen. And of all human relationships, those which characterize the kinship systems come earliest to the individual and are more influential than others. In turn the psychological tendencies nurtured in a majority of the individuals tend to maintain the social and cultural status quo, relentlessly press for alteration of existing arrangements even without external pressure, or move the society and culture toward predictable patterns of response to natural disasters or foreign conquest. Hsu's model in Chapter 13 thus includes all factors considered by Whiting and Harrington (the maintenance systems, the socialization practices, the personality characteristics, and the extrasystemic forces), but it seeks to integrate them into a larger and more comprehensive personality-and-culture whole, which accounts for stability and change without having to shift grounds.

CHAPTER TWELVE

Socialization Process and Personality*

Charles Harrington *and* John W. M. Whiting

1. Introduction and Model

Given the fact that man is not born with a map of his society's acceptable behaviors implanted in his head, students of the socialization process, as it will be described in this chapter, use concepts of personality to show how this knowledge is acquired. Their further commitment is to show how a society induces its members *willingly* to accept these responsibilities. The question becomes one of the integration of society. As Schwartz and Merten (1968:1120) have phrased it: "How does a society make its members feel that the status they eventually must occupy is desirable as well as inevitable?" This study of the socialization process depends on what is being learned as well as how it is being learned. Relevant, then, are accurate descriptions of social structure, the interaction of individuals and groups, variations and cycles within groups, and the choices available to actors at various structural positions. In view of the traditional — and sometimes ritualistic (see Young 1962, 1965, Young

*This is a revision of the 1961 article by John Whiting, "Socialization Process and Personality," which appeared in F. L. K. Hsu, editor, *Psychological Anthropology*, Dorsey Press. The authors would like to thank Mary Fagan for her help with the literature search for the revision and Brian Sutton-Smith for his helpful reading of the revised manuscript.

& Bacdayan 1965) — opposition between the culture-and-personality school on the one hand, and the various structural-functionalist schools on the other, this position may seem surprising. Our position is that the study of socialization is the integrating point of anthropology.[1] The study of socialization process and personality as thus described has been, over the years, a major concern of anthropology, and the literature to be reviewed here is immense, even though we have limited ourselves to work generated by cross-cultural studies as Whiting (1968) defines them.

The term "socialization," to denote the process by which culture is transmitted from one generation to the next, gained favor in the 1930's. One user of the term described the socialization process as "an account of how a new person is added to the group and becomes an adult capable of meeting the traditional expectations of his society." (Dollard 1935). While the term acquired formal acceptance in the 1954 review article by Child, anthropologists in particular have been unhappy with the term's emphasis on social roles and behavior to the exclusion of beliefs, values, and other cognitive aspects of culture. Alternate terms proposed have included "culturalization" (Kluckhohn 1939) and "enculturation" (Herskovits 1948). These terms have not become universally accepted, however, and in this chapter the term "socialization" is often used as a synonym of the term "enculturation" in its broadest sense. This is the sense in which "socialization" is used by Hartley and Hartley, "as learning to be a member of a group. It means perceiving what is considered to be correct and essential in a group, accepting these precepts as right, good and necessary, and learning to behave in congruence with them. This process includes ways of thinking, or feeling as well as ways of behaving, and it covers attitudes towards one's self as well as attitudes and behavior towards other people." (Hartley & Hartley 1952:206).

The anthropologist who studies socialization is not concerned with predicting the individual's idiosyncratic behavior, that is, behavior that does not have meaning for other members of a person's culture. In this sense, his concerns are more general than those, say, of the psychologist. This can also be seen in his use of comparative or cross-cultural studies, which have tended to serve two quite different purposes. Psychologists have tended to view the cross-cultural method as one by which certain assumptions about personality development may be tested. Anthropologists, on the other hand, are more likely to focus on the shared aspects of

[1] The publication in England by the Association of Social Anthropologists of Mayer, 1970, is a welcome expression of interest.

human behavior and to use such studies as *tests of hypotheses concerning the way in which elements of a culture can be integrated by underlying psychological processes.* It is to the latter aim that this chapter is devoted, hoping to demonstrate the usefulness of this approach.

A Conceptual Model. At this point in the chapter a model may help to organize the material. The model explicates the position that the study of the socialization process is the study of the integration of society. An early version of the model illustrated in Figure 1 was developed by Whiting and Child in 1953. The present version is derived from the one used in formulating the more refined hypotheses of the Six Cultures Study (B. Whiting 1963). The examples given here reflect the studies cited in this paper, and are not intended to be exhaustive.

FIGURE 1

MAINTENANCE SYSTEMS (subsistence patterns, economy, residence patterns, household structure, social and political systems and groups)	ADULT PERSONALITY (personality variables and cognitive processes)	ADULT BEHAVIOR CULTURAL PRODUCTS (religion, contents of rituals, values, arts, etc.)
CHILD REARING PRACTICES (time and severity of training, methods, initiation rites, etc.)	CHILD PERSONALITY (personality variables and cognitive processes)	CHILD BEHAVIOR CULTURAL PRODUCTS (views of gods, games, etc.)

Maintenance systems are described by Whiting and Child as the "economic, political, and social organizations of a society surrounding the nourishment, sheltering and protection of its members." From structural anthropology (both the British and American versions) come working models and actual descriptions of maintenance systems. Examples of maintenance systems from the following sections include household composition, sexual division of labor, and residence patterns. Maintenance systems give rise to child training practices.

Child Training Practices, in the broadest sense are what is done to the child to bring about the behavior necessary for social life. In the term child training is implicit some intent on the part of parent or surrogate, and some goal presumably defined by culture. Both the fact that initial child training is done by women, and initiation rites, are examples of child training practices. Child training practices result in personality.

Personality, is the model of what the individual assimilates and of how he organizes what happens to him. In a sense, "personality" may be conceptualized as an individual's adaptation to his socialization. Here the study of socialization depends upon psychological anthropologists and through them, upon the field of psychology itself, so that personality can be expressed in terms of measurable variables. Such a personality variable is sex identity. Personality variables are used to predict the rest of the model.

Adult Behavior is self explanatory. In the studies cited it is exemplified by successful action in the sex roles.

Cultural Products include religion, cultural values, art, games, or any other cultural features not immediately and practically involved in the satisfaction of basic biological needs. In the study of male initiation rites the value of male solidarity would be an example, as well as the symbolic content of the initiation rites themselves.

II. Review of literature testing the model

In the last review of this literature (Whiting 1961), nearly all the studies reported were cross-cultural studies of the Whiting and Child (1953) type. Coders worked with ethnographic data prepared by anthropologists who had no knowledge of the use which would be made of their work. Critics charged that the data were inadequate or were being misused, but the response "they're the best we have" was obvious and sufficed. In the last ten years, spurred by the success of the cross-cultural studies in accounting for behavior, yet troubled by their limitations, students of the cross-cultural method needed new and more relevant data to test their hypotheses. There have been two developments:

1. refinements of cross-cultural techniques. For example, the appearance of the *Six Cultures* type of area study (B. Whiting 1963) in which field teams were sent to six cultures with a unified field guide (Whiting et al. 1966a) of what to research. This method furnished comparable data, specifically oriented to the hypotheses at risk, from

six cultures at one time. These studies are responses to two limitations of the older research (limitations well understood by those carrying out the studies): lack of relevant data and lack of comparable methodology. That they were corrected by those most actively engaged in cross-cultural research reveals the truism that those who carry out cross-cultural research are more aware of its problems and limitations than those who do not (see Whiting 1968). Another refinement of earlier techniques is exemplified by Segall, Campbell and Herskovits (1966) who collected their data from persons already in the field by using standardized instruments. This increased comparability of data at a lower cost than the *Six Cultures* approach, but lacked its contextual detail and hence is suitable to a narrower range of problems.

2. the appearance of within-culture replication of the cross-cultural findings. Given the expense of the *Six Cultures* approach, students of the cross-cultural work have sometimes limited themselves to one culture, and attempted to test the hypotheses demonstrated by cross-cultural work within a particular culture. Monroe followed up his cross-cultural study of the couvade with a study of the couvade in the Black Carib. Harrington followed up his cross-cultural study of adolescent initiation rites and sexual differentiation with a study of errors in sex role learning in teen age boys in the United States. Roberts and Sutton-Smith followed their cross-cultural studies of games by what they termed "sub-system replications" across social class, sex difference, cognitive and personality variables within America (Sutton-Smith, B. & J. M. Roberts, 1963, 1964, 1967). Whiting has recently followed up much of his cross-cultural research with within-culture and within-area studies in Africa.

Although much of the work is still going on, it seems appropriate at this stage to review again the cross-cultural literature and the recent anthropological studies it has generated, in an attempt to assess the utility of this general approach to the study of human behavior. However, some relevant works, not reviewed here, are found in LeVine (1970). We have arbitrarily chosen to order the relevant studies of childhood socialization in terms of the progression from infancy to later childhood, beginning therefore, with those studies related to the treatment of infants.

Infancy. Values, symbols and religious systems have been recognized from Durkheim onward as reflecting social life. Here, the relationship between such systems and child training is explored. For a long time psychologists, particularly those of Freudian persuasion, have assumed that the nature of the gods and their relation to man is a reflection or projection of the child's parental image and, hence, predictable from the relation between parent and child during infancy and early childhood. Several cross-cultural studies have attempted to put this hypothesis to the test (Spiro and D'Andrade 1958; Lambert, Triandis and Wolf 1959; and Whiting 1959a). Each of these studies tends to support the general hypothesis that harsh parental treatment during infancy leads to the cultural belief that the spirit world is harsh and aggressive. Spiro and D'Andrade (1958), using the Whiting and Child (1953) "initial satisfaction of dependence" as a score[2] for estimating the degree to which infants are indulged, found that societies that were judged to be relatively high on the above score tended to believe that the behavior of the gods was contingent upon the behavior of humans and that gods could be controlled by the performance of compulsive rituals.[3] Such societies did *not* propitiate the gods. The authors argue that the adults' treatment of the gods is, therefore, a reflection of an infant's relation to his parents. In other words, infants who are treated indulgently by their parents, that is, whose parents respond to them when they cry or show discomfort, when they grow up feel they can be equally successful in controlling the supernaturals. Lambert, Triandis, and Wolf (1959) used a score taken from Barry, Bacon and Child (1957) for estimating the relation between an infant and his caretakers, consisting of a judgment of the degree to which they treated him harshly or painfully. They found that societies in which infants were treated painfully believed in gods which were judged to be more aggressive than benevolent toward human beings. Again the gods seem to reflect the parental treatment of infants. Finally, Whiting (1959a), using still a different score for infant indulgence, reports a finding consistent with this hypothesis. The score in this study was also from Barry, Bacon, and Child (1957) and was an over-all judgment of the degree to which an infant was indulged by his caretakers.[4] It was reported that societies high in the over-all indulgence of infants tended not to fear ghosts at funerals. The assumption here is that funereal ghosts are, like the gods in the previous studies, a projection of the parental image.

[2] This score includes such items as the encouragement of the infant's dependence, his freedom to be dependent, and the duration of this freedom. For a complete description of this score see Whiting and Child (1953:50, 91).

[3] Unless specified the 5 percent level of confidence or better has been used as a criterion to report a relationship. To simplify presentation P values will not ordinarily be reported.

[4] This score took account of the following items: display of affection, degree of drive reduction, immediacy of drive reduction, constancy of the presence of caretakers, and the absence of pain induced by caretakers.

The next problem is to discover whether or not there is any relationship between social structure of a culture and the degree to which infants are indulged. It was suggested by Murdock and Whiting (1951) that the economic and ceremonial duties of the mother might have some bearing on the amount of time she could spend in caring for her child, and tentative results based on a small number of cases tended to confirm this hypothesis. They report (pp. 33–35) that societies in which mothers have few economic responsibilities and are little involved in the ceremonial life of the tribe tend to be more indulgent with their infants than in societies where mothers have such responsibilities. These results were based on a very small sample of societies and were not statistically significant and, therefore, must be judged as highly tentative. They also reported that there was a tendency for large extended families where there were many hands to care for the infant, to treat him more indulgently. Again this relationship was not strong and reached only the 10 percent level of statistical significance. Murdock (1957), however, has published judgments on the family and household structure for a large number of societies. Using them Whiting (1961) found that the degree of infant indulgence is roughly proportional to the number of adults living in the household. Extended and polygynous families where there are more than two adults living in the household tend to be predominantly indulgent with their infants. Nuclear households with two adults are unpredictable. Finally, in the mother-child household where one woman alone has to care for her children the probability of high indulgence is slight. The percentage of societies with high infant indulgence is as follows: extended, 87%; polygynous, 83%; nuclear, 42%; and mother-child, 25%. The probability that both extended and polygynous households will be high on infant indulgence is statistically significant. Munroe and Munroe (n.d.) investigated whether this effect is present within a single culture as well as across cultures. Working with a small sample (12) in an East African society they visited households and noted 1) whether or not the child was being held by someone and 2) how long it took for someone to comfort him after he started to cry. Using these as measures of indulgence, even with such small numbers, they found that children were significantly more often held and more promptly attended to in large households than in small. More recently, Minturn and Lambert (1964) found for a sample of 76 societies and in an analysis of the *Six Culture* study data that "mothers spend less time with children when other women are available to help." According to the *Six Culture* study data, mothers may become unstable when forced to spend long periods of time without help in caring for their children;

maternal stability also seems definitely related to the number of children she must care for. Since lack of maternal warmth is also associated with responsibility for a large number of children, there may be an interaction of maternal stability and warmth, with optimal conditions for both being a limited number of children to care for and the presence of some help in the household like a grandparent, but not too *many* caretakers, for mothers without privacy in the raising of their children, they found, are relatively muted in their emotional expression to the child when compared with mothers with more privacy.

Before we can accept the thesis that when household arrangements lead to indulgence of infants, then the image of indulgent parents reflected in the nature of the gods — household structure in this way being linked to religious beliefs — we must determine that household structure and the nature of the gods are not related to one another for some other reason. If this latter hypothesis were true, the nature of the gods could be predicted from a knowledge of the household structure, holding child-rearing factors constant. This is not, in fact, the case. The Tenetehara, for example, have extended households but are exceptional in being rated low in the indulgence of infants; their aggressive gods would have to be predicted from their child-rearing rather than from their household arrangements. Conversely, the Chukchee who have mother-child households but are rated high in the indulgence of their children have benevolent gods. Household structure can be shown to be statistically unrelated to the nature of the gods if infant indulgence is not taken into account. Although 87 percent of societies with extended family households have high infant indulgence and 80 percent of the societies with high indulgence are below average on the fear of ghosts at funerals, only 67 percent of the societies having extended families in the sample are below average in fear of ghosts. Thus, it seems that the nature of the gods cannot be predicted from a knowledge of household structure alone. Child rearing with its influence on personality seems to be the prerequisite.

In another study of the treatment of infants, Whiting, Kluckhohn and Anthony (1958) found that in most societies over the world infants sleep in the same bed or on the same sleeping mat with their mothers. Even where an infant has a cradle or cot of his own, this is generally placed next to the mother's bed within easy reach. The sleeping distance between a mother with her nursing infant and her husband, however, is more varied. In slightly over half of the societies of the world the husband sleeps either in a bed in the same room, but at some distance from his wife, or in another room. This may be called an exclusive mother-infant sleeping arrangement. This in turn is related to the presence of polygyny (Whiting 1964). Whiting, Kluckhohn and Anthony hypothesized that such sleeping arrangements would indicate a strong identification of the child with the mother. We shall return to these findings below when we discuss sex role learning through the life cycle.

A series of experiments showing that animals stressed during infancy subsequently grew more rapidly and eventually attained greater skeletal length than an unstressed control group, lead to two cross-cultural studies on a sample of societies in each major area of the world (Landauer and Whiting 1964; Gunders and Whiting 1964). The hypothesis was apparently confirmed. Adult males were on the average two inches taller in societies reporting customary practices relating to infants judged to be stressful than the adult males in societies not having such practices. This association was statistically independent of differences in climate, mode of subsistence, estimated diet, and race. One of the growth-correlated stress-inducers in the cross-cultural studies was vaccination or innoculation for smallpox or other disease, which they believe to cause a stress response through its systematic involvement in immune reactions and their side effects. Subsequently, they studied the relation between infantile immunization and adult stature by reanalyzing data from the Fels and Berkely longitudinal studies of child development (Whiting and Landauer 1968). Again a positive correlation was found between early immunization and terminal stature, this time with parental height controlled statistically.

Turning from biological to socio-cultural consequences of stress in infancy, Ayres has found (1968) a relationship between stress and kinds of music. Infant stress leads to a wider range of styles of singing and polyphony, no stress to monotonic singing. Further cross-cultural research on infancy is indicated since it is now generally conceded that adequate physical growth and psychological development in the earliest months of life profoundly influence subsequent growth and development in later years. For example, malnutrition resulting from disease, an inadequate diet or a combination of the two is thought to interfere with the optimal development of the central nervous system. Similarly, adequate social and physical stimulation in the earliest months is considered to be one crucial element for the development of cognitive and motive abilities in the young child. The definition of these adequate physical and social nutriments remains an unknown not only for the more developed societies, but especially for the developing societies where even the most rudimentary information on these phenomena are frequently lacking.

Early Childhood. Proceeding to the next stage in the life of the child, many cross-cultural studies concern the age at which societies begin the serious training of their children. Age of training has been related to the expression of guilt in cultural products such as religious beliefs, explanations of illness, and folk tales. Whiting and Child (1953), taking as their measure the degree to which a patient was believed to be responsible for causing his own illness (presumably indicating his readiness to accept blame), found that societies with early weaning, early independence training, and early training in modesty with the inhibition of heterosexual play were those that tended to have this kind of explanation of illness. The age of toilet training was not found to be significantly related. Whiting and Child (1953) tentatively explained this relationship by a process of identification. Anticipating Whiting's (1960) status-envy hypothesis, they argued that parents should seem more powerful to a very young child than to an older one who has already learned, to a degree at least, to cope with the environment by himself. Thus, early socialization should produce stronger identification and, hence, guilt over contravening parental values. It is again possible to relate this association to household structure. Whiting (1959a) reports that household structure is a significant determinant of the age of socialization. Nuclear households are earliest for both weaning (median age 2 years) and independence training (median age 2 years 9 months) and mother-child households are the latest.[5] On the average they do not begin to wean their children until they are three years old nor start training them in independence until they are four and one half. Extended and polygynous households fall in between these two extremes for both weaning and independence training.

We have to ask whether nuclear households independently of child rearing are associated with higher guilt scores than mother-child households. This is in fact what is reported by Whiting (1959a); 86 percent of the nuclear households in the sample reported had high scores on patient responsibility for illness, whereas only 14 percent of the mother-child households were high in this regard. Although it is difficult to be sure with the relatively small number of cases on which data are available, it seems that in this instance household structure has some effect independent of child rearing. Whiting (1959a) then showed that age of weaning was correlated with feeling of patient responsibility for illness for monogamous societies but not for polygynous societies, which tended to have a low score on guilt whether weaning was early or late. From this he concluded that,

[5] The age of independence training should not be confused with the degree of infant indulgence referred to above. Mother-child households are both low and late.

while the age of socialization may be a mediating factor between social structure and magical theories of disease, it is clearly not the only one.

By combining the scores for five behavior systems, Whiting and Child (1953) developed an index of over-all socialization anxiety as a measure of severity of childhood socialization. Barry (1957) reports that the decorative art forms of societies that are generally severe in training their children tend to be complex, which supports Ayres' work previously reported for infancy. The game forms are also more complex with severe socialization (Sutton-Smith & Roberts, 1970). Friendly (1956) shows that such societies tended to have ascetic mourning customs. The relation of social institutions such as household structure to over-all socialization anxiety has not as yet been investigated. Fischer (1959), using the Barry (1957) score on complexity of art design and Murdock (1957) scores of complexity of social organization, however, reports that complexity in social structure is reflected in the complexity of decorative art. The presence of status distinctions based on wealth, social class membership, or heredity tends to result in complex designs in contrast to those from societies with no rank distinctions at all, or rank distinctions based on age alone. Sutton-Smith and Roberts (1970) also find that as game types are added, cross-culturally there is an increased severity in socialization as well as complexity of social structure.

Another over-all measure of the severity of socialization in early childhood, "transition anxiety," is provided by Barry, Bacon and Child (1957). This is an estimate of the degree of pressure exerted upon the child during his change of status from infancy to childhood. Whiting and his co-workers (1966b) show transition anxiety to be related to household structure. They report that societies with nuclear households are significantly more severe on this score than are societies with extended family households. It has already been pointed out that societies with nuclear family households begin independence training early. It now seems that they are generally severe as well, suggesting that strong pressures in child rearing toward independence are necessary if a couple are to set up an independent establishment.

Another hypothesis relating to the severity of socialization is Whiting and Child's hypothesis of negative fixation. Estimates of the severity of socialization were made by Whiting and Child (1953) with respect to oral, anal, sexual, aggression, and independence training. The presumed effect of severe training was that of "negative fixation" or the anxious preoccupation with the type of behavior system severely punished. The hypothesis was based upon the presumed effects of intrapsychic conflict rather than on stages of psychosexual development (as oral, anal, genital). They postulated that the conflict induced by the punishment during the socialization process of habits learned in infancy produces a persistent motivation activating behavior in adulthood in some way related to the conflict and presumably functionally defensive in nature.

Explanations for illness and therapeutic techniques were chosen by Whiting and Child (1953) as aspects which might reflect fixation. A content analysis of magical beliefs and practices relating to illness was made for each society with the five behavior systems in mind. Judging the severity of socialization for each system, the following factors were taken into consideration: intensity and frequency of punishment, suddenness of the transition from behavior appropriate to infancy and that to later childhood, and signs of emotional disturbance on the part of the child. In general the fixation hypothesis was supported. The severity of weaning (oral anxiety) was strongly related to "oral explanations for illness." Such oral explanations included the belief that sickness is caused by the ingestion of magically poisoned food or by the verbal spells and incantations of sorcerers. Rosenblatt (1966) found oral anxiety associated with the importance of romantic love as basis for marriage. The severity of aggression training (aggression socialization anxiety), which includes the treatment of temper tantrums, physical and verbal aggression, damage to property, and disobedience, was related to explanations for illness involving aggression. These included hostility toward or disobedience to spirits, poison (if introjected into the patient rather than being ingested), and the use of magical weapons by a sorcerer. The severity of independence training was shown to be related to dependence explanations for illness, a measure which includes the belief that illness could be caused by "soul stealing" or by "spirit possession." The negative fixation hypothesis was not confirmed in the other two systems of behavior. However, there was some indication that relevant avoidance in the anal and sexual behavior systems was used as a therapeutic practice. Societies with severe toilet training tend to have therapeutic practices involving washing or cleansing, the adherence to cleanliness taboos, or the retention of feces, and societies with severe sex training tended to believe that abstention from sexual intercourse by the patient would have a therapeutic effect. In addition, as was reported above, Stephens (1961) found that severe sex training is associated with elaborate menstrual taboos, and Ayres (1954) showed this child-rearing measure to be related to prolonged sex taboos during pregnancy. Each of these may be viewed as an index of negative fixation. Allen (1967) found a strong negative relationship between "ego strength" and childhood socialization anxiety.

The following social structural variables have been reported to be associated with severity of socialization in the various systems. Murdock and Whiting (1951) report that societies with sororal polygyny are significantly less severe in weaning their children than are societies with nonsororal polygny. Monogamous societies, according to their findings, stand between these two extremes and are not significantly different from either. They explained mild weaning in sororal-polygynous societies as a consequence of the cooperation between co-wives who are sisters. The severity of sex training is associated with polygny. Only 15 percent of the societies which are monogamous, or in which not more than 10 percent of the women are polygynously married, are above the median on the severity of sex training, whereas 73 percent of the societies with a higher proportion of polygynous marriages are severe in this regard.

Finally, a strong association between the severity of aggression training and household structure has been reported by Whiting (1959b). Ninety-two percent of the extended families in the sample used are above the median on the punishment for aggression. Nuclear households were least severe in this respect — only 25 percent of the cases being severe. In polygynous and mother-child households, 61 percent were above the median. Whiting et. al. (1966b) in an analysis of the Zuni extended family households suggests that the expression of aggression cannot be tolerated in circumstances where so many people are living in such crowded quarters. Minturn and Lambert tested this hypothesis in 1964 on a sample of 76 societies. They found that "children are severely punished for fighting with each other when many people must share cramped living quarters." No social structural variable has as yet been reported to predict the severity of either toilet training or independence training.

Factor analysis provides another method of estimating the effect of child-rearing practices upon projective systems. Protho (1960) subjected the Whiting and Child (1953) fixation hypothesis to such an analysis. The

[6]It should be noted that the age of socialization was conceptually distinguished from the severity of socialization. Although in general these measures were negatively correlated (Whiting and Child 1953:110), they were empirically distinct as well. In other words, late socialization is not necessarily mild.

first factor, which he called the "aggression-hypochondriasis factor" had high positive loadings for the severity of aggression training and all explanations for illness and the fear of spirits. The third and final factor, "independence-anality," had a high positive loading on the severity and earliness of toilet training, and a strong negative loading on the severity and earliness of independence training. A negative loading dependence-avoidance therapy was the only projective measure which seemed related to this factor.

Cross-cultural studies of the belief in sorcery and witchcraft have generally interpreted this belief in terms of the psychological mechanisms of projection and/or displacement. Two views of this mechanism have been put forth. One, derived essentially from behavior theory, assumes that the fear of sorcerers occurs in societies where the direct expression of aggression is strongly inhibited and, hence, must be either attributed to others or justified by being directed against criminal sorcerers. The other view, derived from psychoanalytic theory, is that belief in sorcery implies the personality variables associated with paranoia — sexual inhibition and latent or overt homosexuality. Whiting and Child (1953) were unable to decide between these two explanations. On the basis of their evidence, sorcery was found to be an important explanation for illness in societies where children were severely socialized with respect either to sex or aggression during childhood. The fact that severity of socialization in these two behavior systems are positively related to one another makes it difficult to disentangle their influence.

Whiting (1959a) presents some evidence in favor of the sex anxiety hypothesis, but the data are not very convincing. The most likely interpretation of the results so far is that there are in effect two kinds of projection, and that the distinction between them may correspond to that proposed to obtain between sorcery and witchcraft, the former being a result of the inhibition of aggression, the latter being associated with conflict in the area of sex. That sorcerers are more often male and witches female is suggestive in this regard. Shirley and Romney (1962) show love magic present with high sexual socialization anxiety (but see Bock 1967).

That aggression may be projected has been shown by Wright (1954) using a content analysis of folktales as an index. He showed that in societies with severe training in the control of aggression during childhood the hero in folktales does *not* direct his aggression toward friends but rather toward strangers or enemies, that a stranger rather than the hero was more likely to be the agent of aggression, and finally that the hero was less likely to be triumphant. Whiting and Child (1953) report a similar finding. Societies with severe aggression training having the belief that spirits can cause illness tend to define the spirits as animal rather than human.

The social structure variables relating to severe socialization for sex and aggression have already been reported—the former is associated with polygyny, the latter with the extended family household. Direct relationships between social structural variables and sorcery beliefs were reported in two studies. Beatrice Whiting (1950), assuming that sorcery functions as a mechanism of social control, showed that a strong belief in sorcery occurs in societies lacking in mechanisms of social control that involve the delegation of authority for the judging and punishing of crime. She also showed that this pattern tended to occur in small rather than in large societies. LeVine (1960a) showed that sorcery tends to occur in societies that maximize jealousy between co-wives. In three East African societies similar in other respects, the preoccupation with sorcery was greatest among the Lup where co-wives lived in adjacent houses and virtually absent among the Kipsigis where the co-wives ordinarily live miles apart. He also reports that, cross-culturally, sorcery is alleged to be a major cause of illness in 93 percent of the societies with polygynous households, 60 percent of the societies with mother-child households, 53 percent of the societies with extended family households, and only 36 percent of the societies with nuclear households. The total pattern for predicting sorcery beliefs thus seems to indicate that such beliefs are held in small societies with no formal systems of social control having either polygynous households and severe sex training or extended family households and severe training in the control of aggression.

Socialization in Later Childhood. An elaborate set of judgments about socialization during later childhood is provided by Barry, Bacon, and Child (1957). These judgments concern the manner in which a child is trained to be obedient, responsible, self-reliant, nurturant, and generally independent, as well as his training for achievement. For each of these behavior systems a separate judgment was made for the general pressure exerted upon the child, the severity of punishment for non-compliance, the performance level demanded, the amount of conflict and the frequency of the response.

Separate judgments on the above scales were made for the treatment of boys and girls by Barry, Bacon, and Child (1957). Significant differences in training were reported. These involved more stress upon nurturance, obedience, and responsibility for the girls and upon achievement and self-reliance for the boys. Although they did not relate these differences to any projective system, they did report that large differences in the training of the sexes occur in societies where large animals are hunted, where grain rather than root crops are grown, where large or milking animals are kept, where fishing is unimportant or absent, where the settlement is nomadic rather than sedentary, and where polygyny is high. They interpreted those results as implying that differential training for boys and girls is required where superior strength and motor skill is involved or where a large family with a high degree of cooperation is required. Munroe, Whiting, and Hally (1969) found that societies that emphasized sex distinctions (in patterns of residence, in kin groups, in kinship terminology, in authority succession, in eating arrangements, and in attendance at birth) less often had institutionalized transvestism. "In general, transvestism *as a social form* is not found in societies that stress sex distinctions of the kind rated." "However, in societies where the sex distinctions are few, the behavior and/or conceptual categories of the individual predisposed to transvestism are already relatively near those of females, so that in becoming a transvestite the individual must change comparatively little ... The degree of change involved probably affects the likelihood that a predisposed individual will become a transvestite and also the probability that the society members will tolerate the change" (Munroe, Whiting, and Hally 1969: 89).

Lambert, Triandis, and Wolf (1959) in the study concerning the nature of the gods, discussed previously, report that the supernaturals are more aggressive in societies which put strong pressure upon the boys for self-reliance and independence. They also report an even stronger relationship in the same direction with a score which combines the pressures exerted in all six systems that is, nurturance, obedience, self-reliance, achievement, responsibility, and general independence. It is interesting that they assume the religious beliefs to be causal in this relationship, rather than a result of the child-training procedures, for they assume that a belief in aggressive gods requires training a child to be independent and self-reliant so that he can cope with a hostile world as an adult.

Bacon, Child, and Barry (1963) show that societies that severely punish their older children for disobedience, irresponsibility, lack of self-reliance, and lack of achievement are high in the frequency of theft. Since they also find that a high frequency of theft is found in societies with low infant indulgence and severe weaning, they interpret these findings as a reaction to emotional deprivation during infancy and childhood. Such anxieties, except for those associated with severe weaning, interestingly enough, are not related to the frequency of personal crime in adults. Child, Bacon and Barry (1965) found low indulgence of dependency and high achievement pressures related to drunkenness and general high alcohol consumption. This supports their dependency anxiety explanation of alcoholism (Barry 1968).

In a fascinating series of studies, the anthropologist John Roberts and the psychologist Brian Sutton-Smith demonstrated a relationship between child training and children's games, using the Barry, Bacon, and Child (1957) scales. Putting games into three categories (games of chance, games of strategy, and games of physical skill) they found that games of chance occur in societies where responsibility is highly rewarded in child training (Roberts and Sutton-Smith 1962 and 1966). Games of chance are seen as providing the player with an expression of conflict of attitudes toward responsibility, and an acting out of irresponsible, chance determined fantasies (compare feeling responsible with blaming failure as 'bad luck'). Games of strategy are found in societies in which emphasis is placed on obedience in child training. Roberts and Sutton-Smith speculate that games of strategy reflect an anxiety about disobedience. Games of strategy enable the child to express aggression and other disobedient acts in play. Games of skill are found in societies in which reward for achievement is high. Such games are "a direct and microcosmic representation of achievement" played by individuals in conflict over achievement. Games then are seen as projections of anxieties engendered by severe socialization practices in child training.

Relationships have also been demonstrated between socialization pressures in later childhood and the basic economic organization. Barry, Child, and Bacon (1959) state, "In considering the relation of economy to adult role, and hence to child training, we felt that perhaps a variable of great significance is the extent to which food is accumulated and must be cared for." (Barry, Child, and Bacon 1959:52). To test this hypothesis they classified societies on the basis of their subsistence activities, categorized according to the degree to which these implied an accumulation of food. Assuming that food "on the hoof" requires the greatest amount of care, societies that were mainly dependent upon animal husbandry were judged to be highest in this respect and hunting and fishing societies were judged to be the lowest. Between these extremes a distinction was made between those societies depending upon agriculture only for subsistence and those depending upon a combination of agriculture, hunting, and fishing with the former assumed to be higher in food accumulation.

Comparing the societies with extreme scores (animal husbandry versus hunting and fishing as the subsistence economy), they showed that societies with a high accumulation of food put strong pressure upon their children to be responsible and obedient and were correspondingly low in stressing achievement, in both boys and girls, independence, in boys, and self-reliance, in girls. They then constructed a general score which they called "pressure toward compliance versus assertion" by adding the scores on obedience and responsibility and subtracting from this sum the combined score on achievement and self-reliance. The striking relationship of this over-all compliance pressure to the degree to which food is accumulated is shown in Table 1.

TABLE 1

Subsistence Economy	% above Median Compliance	N
Animal husbandry	83%	(24)
Agriculture only	93	(15)
Agriculture, hunting & fishing	33	(18)
Hunting & fishing	14	(22)

Relation between pressure toward compliance versus assertiveness as indicated by a subsistence economy scale. Numbers in parentheses represent the number of societies in each category. This table is adapted from Barry, Bacon, and Child (1959: 60).

It should be noted that the sample of societies rated high on the subsistence scale — those with animal husbandry and agriculture — is rather heavily weighted with cases from Africa. Perhaps, then, pressure toward compliance is an African culture trait and the demonstrated association is therefore spurious. With all African cases omitted from the sample, however, the association between subsistence economy and pressure in child training toward compliance is still strong. When this is done, high compliance is represented by the following percentages in order of the degree of accumulation: 70%, 90%, 33%, and 14%. Thus, the relationship, although somewhat less strong, is still substantial. Bacon, Child, and Barry

(1963) indicate that this scale, unlike their earlier scale, is not useful in relating child training to the frequency of theft.

Through the Life Cycle: Sex Role Socialization. Through the study of adolescent male initiation rites and one aspect of behavior, sex role behavior, we hope to show the continuity through the life cycle of the socialization process up to now arbitrarily discussed according to separate phases. Sex role differentiation, or "the division and ascription of statuses with relation to sex," as Linton has phrased it, seems to be found in all social systems. "All societies prescribe different attitudes and activities to men and women" (Linton 1936:116). While societies differ considerably in their definitions of sex roles and the extent to which they differentiate them (see D'Andrade 1966), the cross-cultural study of sex role learning has nevertheless been fruitful.

The relationship of male initiation rites to the socialization of proper sex role behavior has been extensively studied.[7] In their interpretation of male initiation rites, Whiting, Kluckhohn, and Anthony (1958) used the psychological concept of sex identity. Their cross-cultural study established the following:

1. A close relationship between mother and son during infancy as a consequence of either (a) their sleeping together for at least a year to the exclusion of the father, or (b) the mother being prohibited from sexual intercourse for at least a year after the birth of her child, or (c) both of these together, has measurable consequences which are manifested in cultural adjustments at adolescence.

2. These adjustments are either (a) a ceremony of initiation into manhood involving at least one and generally several of the following factors: painful hazing by the males of the society, tests of endurance and manliness, seclusion from women, and genital operations, or (b) a change of residence which involves separation of the boy from his mother and sisters and may also include some formal means for establishing male authority such as receiving instructions from and being required to be respectful to the mother's brother or the members of the men's house.

3. If both the factors specified in (1) are present, the consequences at adolescence tend to be more elaborate and severe than if only one is present (1958: 368–369).

[7] Portions of this section were previously published in Harrington 1970 by Teachers College Press. Permission to reprint is gratefully acknowledged.

The authors offered an interpretation of their findings based upon the personality variable of sex identity. This interpretation was further refined and more completely stated by Burton and Whiting (1961), who viewed the absence of the father as leading to primary cross-sex (feminine) identity in boys. Initiation rites are designed to overcome primary cross-sex identity and substitute male identity and behavior. If the identity conflict were not resolved, boys would retain behaviors inappropriate to the society's adult male role.

Burton and Whiting (1961) distinguish three kinds of identity: "Attributed" (statuses assigned ego by others in his society), "subjective" (statuses ego thinks he fills), and "optative" (statuses which ego wishes to occupy). The aim of socialization is to produce adults whose three identities are congruent. Optative identity is not always a conscious wish, and in fact can be assumed to be either an unconscious wish or a cognitive style; subjective identity, on the other hand, is conscious.

Such use of personality to explain the integration of cultural events does not go unchallanged, however, and while this is true of much of the literature reported above, the initiation rites literature has produced written alternatives. In 1962, Frank Young proposed a theory of initiation rites as an alternative to Whiting's. Young viewed the rites as dramatizations of the male role preparatory to the participation of the initiates in exclusively male societies. Thus, rather than looking to events in the life cycle before age ten and relying upon psychological concepts to explain initiation rites, Young looked to the patterns of association of adult males in the whole society. While Young formulated his "structural" explanation as an alternative to Whiting's, Whiting incorporated Young's position and argued "that both solidarity and male initiation rites are a consequence of conflict in sex identity engendered in infancy" (Whiting 1962:392). Cohen (1964) also has an alternative explanation, but as it does not deal with sex role we do not review it here.

Cross-sex identity, used in reference to males, means that they identify with women, usually the mother. According to Burton and Whiting, the individual forms "primary" or "optative sex identity" in infancy and "secondary" or "subjective sex identity" in childhood, correspond to the status arrangements encountered by him in those respective periods.[8] Primary cross-sex identity is linked to absence of the father as measured by exclusive mother-child sleeping arrangements and long postpartum sex

[8] Here we consider "optative sex identity" equivalent to "primary sex identity" and "subjective sex identity" equivalent to "secondary sex identity."

taboos. Secondary *male* identity, in contrast, is linked to male influence as measured by patrilocality. The definition of father absence for primary cross-sex identity is different from that for secondary because the domain of the child changes. When the child is an infant, his domain is limited largely to where he sleeps, hence the importance of who sleeps with him. As the child grows, his domain enlarges to include the household, and importance shifts from sleeping arrangements to whether the father is present in the household at all to the status males possess (for example, in a patrilocal or matrilocal household).

The relationship of cross-sex identity to behavior depends upon the combination of primary and secondary identities. Primary cross-sex identity may be either reacted against or expressed, depending upon the secondary sex identity. Some societies institutionalize a means for resolving an underlying conflict in sex identities (primary, female; secondary, male) in favor of the secondary sex identity. Circumcision-type initiation rites are an example of this. The ceremonies occur in societies which differentiate boys from girls (Harrington, 1968) and presumably teach boys the appropriate male role. Thus they attempt to insure proper masculine role behavior by making it clear that the boys are now men, and are different from the women who have raised them.

If there is conflict between primary and secondary sex identities without a mechanism to resolve it, the individual reaction to primary feminine identity may be an exaggerated masculinity, through which the boy tries to resolve the conflict (see Munroe, Munroe, and Whiting, 1965). Such hypermasculine traits have been linked to feminine identity by several researchers. B. Whiting (1965) for example, has explained aggression as "protest masculinity," and found it more often in those societies where the father has low salience in infancy but high status later in life. (See her article, 1965, for a summary of the literature on protest masculinity.) If glory in war is taken to be a reasonable index of hypermasculinity or the exaggerated need for men to defend themselves against feminity then it should be found more commonly in societies with an exclusive relationship between a boy and his mother during his infancy combined with a low salience of the father during this period. Such turns out to be true. Polygynous societies in which each child has a mother but at most half a father who often sleeps and eats elsewhere are more likely to value glory in war than do monogamous societies. Exclusive mother-son sleeping arrangements — a more explicit measure of a condition likely to produce cross sex identity — is also significantly associated with the glory in warfare score (Whiting 1969). Whiting, Kluckhohn, and Anthony consider juvenile delinquency in the United States to be another form of exaggerated masculinity:

> It has long been known that there is an association between certain types of juvenile delinquency and broken homes. We would predict that the probability of a boy becoming delinquent in such instances would be highest where the separation of the mother and father occurred during the early infancy of the boy and where she (later) . . . remarried. (1958: 370)

The *macho* complex among Mexican males would be another instance (Lewis 1951). A further case may be that described for Cayman (Howe 1966). Such reactions of exaggerated masculinity typically come about when there is an overlaying of male influence upon a child with primary cross-sex identity. Cultural mechanisms to resolve the conflict, such as circumcision-type initiation rites, are said to make such individual protests superfluous.

Cross-sex identity may be openly expressed if the primary and secondary identifications are both feminine. One institutionalized expression is couvade, a set of practices in which the man shares symptoms of pregnancy and childbirth with his wife (see Munroe, Munroe, and Whiting 1965). Burton and Whiting said that couvade should be a good index of the wish "to act out the feminine role and thus symbolically to be in part a woman" (1961:91). Individual expressions of femininity are also possible. D'Andrade (1962) found that in the United States high feminine identification scores on the Franck Drawing Completion Test was strongly related to father absence during the first two years of life. Carlsmith (1963) as well as Sutton-Smith and Rosenberg (1968) found that father-absent male students had some feminine patterns on scholastic aptitude tests, an individual expression of cognitive cross-sex identity.

The connection between subjective cross-sex identity and overt behavior was specifically tested by Harrington (1970), who studied a group of hospitalized boys in the United States who had shown errors in sex role learning. Harrington found support for Whiting's explanation of male initiation rites in terms of primary and secondary sex identity. Boys with exaggeratedly masculine behavior more often had primary feminine identity and secondary masculine identity, as measured by personality tests, than boys who did not show errors in sex role learning. Boys whose behavior showed errors in the other extreme (behavior inappropriate to the male role) had both primary and secondary feminine identity. Thus the association of measures of primary and secondary sex role identity with the socialization of male role behaviors has been fairly well documented both cross-culturally and by within-culture replications.

Circumcision-type initiation rites are said to be necessary to overcome primary cross-sex identity and inculcate properly male identity and behavior. Recent work in symbolic anthropology, particularly the work of Turner (1969), suggests that from a careful analysis of what goes on within these rituals we may learn more about the dynamics by which they operate. What is particularly needed is a knowledge of what if anything these rituals actually accomplish in terms of socialization. Whiting and John Herzog are currently studying these problems. A recent study of Granzberg's begins to answer this question, not for circumcision-type initiation rites but for rites like those of the Hopi, that emphasize the distinction between the child and adult roles.

Most of the cross-cultural studies of sex role learning reviewed here have been limited to males reflecting a bias to the literature that may be accounted for to some extent by the fact that most of the authors are male. Judith Brown (1963) has redressed this imbalance in part with a study of female initiation rites. She draws three major conclusions. First, female initiation rites occur most often in societies where the girl, as an adult, will not have to leave her parents' domestic unit. Second, those initiation rites that subject the initiated girl to extreme pain are found in societies in which infant and childhood sex identity are in conflict; this establishes a relation between painful female initiation rites and male genital mutilation rites. Third, female rites are found in those societies in which women are important in subsistence activities, thereby (according to Brown) giving her recognition for her contribution to the existence of the society. While much remains to be done on sex role learning by women, the work of Brown and of Barry, Bacon, and Child offers some useful beginnings. We make use of the findings of sex role socialization in the next section as we review the model.

III. Expanding and Revising the Model — Recent Work

In a paper published in 1964, Whiting, in an effort to account for possible affects of physical environments and also for change coming from outside the system, placed the following to the left of the model as illustrated in Figure 1.

These include the cultural as well as physical environment; whatever

Extrasystematic
causal
events

impinges upon the society from outside. This modification has been
interpreted by Harris (1968) as an acknowledgement of the possibility of
techno-environmental determinism. Whiting, however, would include
more than physical environment (see e.g. Whiting, et al.1966b). Whiting's
article of 1964, however, does give impressive evidence of the impact of
environmental factors on the cultural behaviors previously discussed. Since
circumcision initiation rites are found only in societies in Africa and
Oceania, Whiting postulated a possible link between the presence of the
rites and climate. Significant correlations were found between hot, rainy,
tropical climate and the presence of Kwashiorkor, a disease caused by
protein deficiency in infancy. Following our model, the following chain
develops: Low protein availability and the risk of Kwashiorkor were
correlated with an extended postpartum sex taboo to allow the mother
time to nurse the infant through the critical stage before becoming
pregnant again. The post-partum sex taboo was significantly correlated
with the institution of polygyny, providing alternate sexual outlets to the
male. Polygyny, in turn, is associated with mother-child households, child
training by women, resultant cross-sex identity, and where patrilocality is
also present, with initiation rites to resolve the conflict and properly
inculcate male identity.

In addition to the physical environment, there have been studies of the
effects of man made environments. Whiting and Ayres (1968) find forests
necessary but not sufficient for the presence of square houses. Robbins
(1966) demonstrates a relationship between art styles and the shape of
houses. Perhaps the effect of physical environment most studied is on
perception. Work by Segall, Campbell, and Herskovits (1966) has linked
certain attributes of the physical environment to susceptibility to certain
optical illusions. Thus members of cultures whose visual environments are
"uncarpentered," consisting perhaps of flat horizons and round huts, are
less susceptible to optical illusions that depend on assumptions of right
angles for their effect, but more susceptible to illusions that relate to the
perception of the length of a vertical line relative to a horizontal. The
authors conclude:

> Perception is an aspect of human behavior, and as such it is subject to many
> of the same influences that shape other aspects of behavior. In particular, each

individual's experiences combine in a complex fashion to determine his reaction to a given stimulus situation. To the extent that certain classes of experiences are more likely to occur in some cultures than in others, differences in behavior across cultures, including differences in perceptual tendencies, can be great enough even to surpass the ever-present individual differences within cultural groupings.

We have reported here a study that revealed significant differences across cultures in susceptibility to several geometric, or optical illusions. It should be stressed that these differences are not "racial" differences. They are differences produced by the same kinds of factors that are responsible for individual differences in illusion susceptibility, namely, differences in experience. The findings we have reported, and the findings of others we have reviewed, point to the conclusion that to a substantial extent we learn to perceive; that in spite of the phenomenally absolute character of our perceptions, they are determined by perceptual inference habits; and that various inference habits are differentially likely in different societies. For all mankind, the basic process of perception is the same; only the contents differ and these differ only because they reflect different perceptual inference habits. (Segall, Campbell and Herskovits 1966:213–214)

Cultural adjustments to physical environment has also been linked with child raising practices. Berry (1967) reports on the basis of evidence from three societies that scarcity of food leads societies to produce individuals who are independent and self-reliant. Societies in which there is a surplus of food tend to produce more dependent and group-reliant members. The argument is based upon data showing Eskimo to be less susceptible to suggestions about group normalcy (i.e., others see it this way, what do you think?) on a perception test than the Temne. This finding awaits confirmation in a more controlled comparison.

Perception can also be affected by social structure. Recent studies of field dependency made in the United States (Witkin, et al., 1962) offer within-culture evidence that perceptual style correlates with social role. In the field dependency test, in which a vertical line is projected upon a shifting background, women, more often than men, are fooled into thinking that the line is no longer vertical. This susceptibility is paralleled in the woman's role by her greater socio-emotional competence and her greater concern with others' feelings. Further investigations into field dependency cross-culturally, including its associations with behavior and with biology as well seem especially promising. For example, Berry (1966) found field dependency differences between men and women to be culturally determined. Eskimo women are not treated as dependent;

Temne men exercise strong control over their wives. Temne women show strong field dependency when compared with Temne men. Eskimo women show no differences in field dependency with Eskimo men. Socialization into the requirements of a social role, then, can be seen as actually influencing perception which of course thereby reinforces future role learning.

Munroe, Munroe and Daniels (1969), in a replication of an experiment by Bruner and Goodman, have recently been able to show that size of father's landholdings in Kenya was related to the perception by children seven to thirteen years old of the size of a series of coins. The poorer the father, the larger the child reported the size of the coin to be. The explanation given is of a relative deprivation sort: coins are more important to children of poorer parents, and this importance is projected to perception of size. What is important here is not so much the explanation as the further evidence that social role affects perception.

There has been an emphasis in anthropology for some years on devising models relating to cognitive style. Studies of sex role socialization have made use of cognitive sex differences or sex identity. Most recently Whiting (m.s.) has studied these differences in Africa. To test the hypothesis that there are universally similar differences in the cognitive style of males and females, a transcultural test was devised. The test — the *Whiting, Lionells, and Martin Felt Design Test* — was suggested by the Franck test (1946) which showed consistent sex differences in the production of abstract designs. The latter test, since it involved pencil and paper, was found to be inappropriate for people with little or no schooling. The modification involved arranging felt pieces of different shapes on a felt covered board of a contrasting color. Each subject is asked to construct six different designs, each on a board with a different incomplete design as a stimulus. This "felt design test" has been given by Whiting and his co-workers to over 400 subjects varying in age from 6 to 60 from seven communities in Africa. Similar differences were found between the designs constructed by males and females in each of the communities. When the scores were pooled, the largest and most consistent differences were that males more than females made (1) single rather than multiple designs, (2) designs that were built up rather than down from the stimulus, and (3) designs that were symmetrical both vertically and horizontally. It was also discovered that for both males and females the probability of making a "masculine" style design increased with years of schooling. Although this effect of education was striking and highly significant statistically, it did not obscure the sex differences. These were equally strong at each level of education. It is our interpretation that the designs made by men and women reflect the differences in the usual role requirements of men and women. The breadwinning role of the male requires long-term complex plans whereas child care and other female responsibilities, requiring as they do frequent interruptions, are more short-term and repetitive.

Students of the learning process generally make assumptions about the way people think or store what they learn. Research in cognition cross-culturally might help criticize these assumptions. The field as it stands is thoroughly reviewed in Tyler (1969), and the reader is referred to that work to draw his own conclusions about the extent to which cognitive anthropologists have lived up to their task. We feel that too often the findings have not gone beyond cognition to the task of predicting behavior.

Causality and feedback. In postulating that there is a *causal* sequence in illustrating the model in Figure 1, Whiting justifies his logic as follows:

> The correlational method used in cross cultural research cannot, of course, show the direction of causation. It must rest upon other evidence suggesting the relative plausibility of one or the other assumption as to causal direction ... temperature and climate cannot be reasonably assumed to be the effect of a custom. Any association between a climatic variable and a custom can plausibly be interpreted either as an effect of climate upon the custom or as effect of climate upon some other factor associated with such a custom. For example, in this paper it is not plausible to assume that exclusive mother infant sleeping arrangements cause a warm winter, or that a long *post partem* sex taboo caused a rainy tropical climate. Thus, it is the assumption of this paper that ecological variables determine the customs associated with them. (Whiting 1964: 524)

When this review was first published, the flow of causal arrows in this model was essentially from left to right. It will be obvious to the reader that if everything is working properly at any given point there is feedback and support of what has gone before. That is, in the initiation rites literature, the symbols used in the ceremony are a cultural product, yet they are part of the child training initiation rites and their symbolic treatment of male and female reinforces the social structure based upon sex differences, etc. Recent work has focused upon various kinds of feedback. An example of feedback was encountered by Roberts and Sutton-Smith in their work with games. Following our model, in their 1966 article on games of chance they suggest that such games may be played in societies whose situations are not easily controlled by skill or strategy, and where uncertainty exists, "particularly in the areas of environmental setting, food production, social and political interaction, marriage, war and religion." These uncertain conditions lead such societies to emphasize responsibility in child training and generate conflict in the area of sex, aggression, and achievement, since the life situation is one where "favorable and unfavorable outcomes may occur in an uncertain way" (Roberts and Sutton-Smith 1966:143). Games of chance can be viewed as a cultural product, an expression of responses to the passivity of the player's normal life role incompatible with the role of diligent provider. Differential incidence of gambling in our own society emphasizes this point. Thus "antecedent conflicts produced by socialization . . . lead to involvement in models of all sorts, including games. These models represent activities in behavior spheres relevant to the antecedent conflicts" (Roberts, Hoffman and Sutton-Smith 1965: 17). However, in terms of feedback, games also teach. Involvement in games "also results in enculturation or learning which is subsequently useful to the individual and to the larger community or society" (Roberts, Hoffman, and Sutton-Smith 1965:17). Children learn through folklore and games what the culture requires them to know, but will not teach them directly. Referring to what they describe as a conflict-enculturation interpretation, Roberts and Sutton-Smith (1962) argue that

> 1) there is an over all process of cultural patterning whereby society induces conflict in children through its child raising processes; 2) that society seeks through appropriate arrays and varieties of ludic models to provide an assuagement of these conflicts by an adequate representation of their emotional and cognitive polarities in ludic structure; and 3) that through these models society tries to provide a form of buffered learning through which the child can make enculturative step-by-step progress toward adult behavior. (Roberts and Sutton-Smith 1962:183–4)

Each type of game provides information to the child about chance, skill, and/or strategy in assuaging conflict and in learning to handle social life. As Roberts and Sutton-Smith say "between the ages of seven and twelve the child learns, in simple direct form, how to take a chance, how to show skill, and how to deceive" (1962:183). In complex games he learns to combine these skills in circumstances more nearly approaching the conditions of real life. In subsequent studies these authors have demonstrated, for example, that skilled strategy players are more "strategic" in other areas of life (Sutton-Smith & Roberts, 1967). Thus games can be viewed, not only as a projective technique or a cultural product, but also as a child training device. Hence a feedback arrow must be shown in the model, from the products of adults and children to child training.

In addition, Whiting et al. (1966b) have argued that in a society which undergoes a change in maintenance systems like household structure, child training systems may overact to the change. This might create cultural products of exaggerated values to bolster the new order (feedback of cultural product on maintenance system). Values like harmony, achievement, and virtue, however, can be so overdrawn and idealized that living up to them is difficult. Thus, Whiting postulates a cultural defense mechanism to deal with failure to live up to the ideal. Projection of hostile feelings and bad thoughts onto witches or outside the group, and bragging about success even if none exists, are seen as culturally provided defense mechanisms against failure to meet the dominant values. This would be an example of feedback of cultural product upon personality systems.

IV. Looking Ahead to the Next Ten Years

The literature we have reviewed has created a foundation upon which future research must be built. Our problems will be reformulated, our operationalizations will be more refined. The questions we have posed have in no sense been finally answered, but we would expect work to continue, particularly with more within-culture replications of the cross cultural findings. However, any survey of the current anthropological research generated by cross-cultural studies would be remiss if it were not also to offer some idea of new fields in which much new work might be expected in, say, the next ten years.

One such area of considerable promise is the study of political socialization, the learning of political behavior. There has in the last ten years been a dramatic outpouring of studies in political socialization in the fields of political science and psychology (see Adler and Harrington, 1970). But a major fault of this literature is its reliance on the mainstream of white America for its subjects. Even in cross-national studies like Almond and Verba (1963) the data are from societies that have western-style governments. Cross-cultural studies of the kind dealt with in this chapter are absent. LeVine (1960b) showed that among the Gusii, adults subordinate children while the Nuer are much more permissive. This is correlated with the fact that the Gusii have been more compliant to British colonial authority. While LeVine's results are suggestive, his findings await validation in a study of more than two societies. We need to know much more.

Also absent from this literature is the study of the socialization for "local-level politics," an area of study in which anthropologists have a head start. Cross-cultural studies of local politics seem to show that allegiance to national regimes has been the order of study; but what has politics on, for example, an urban ghetto block to do with Senators or Presidents? Studies of subsocieties are rare in the literature; Jaros, Hirsh and Fleron (1968) is a notable exception. There are few studies devoted to black Americans. Books like *Tally's Corner* (Liebow 1969), *Soulside* (Hannerz 1969) and *The Social Order of the Slum* (Suttles 1968) demonstrate the potential richness of anthropological methods and materials in such studies. Blacks are not the only cultural minority who consider themselves outside of the political system of the United States. Many such groups have been studied by anthropologists, yet the specific study of political socialization in such settings as Indian reservations remains to be done. The literature on political socialization also does not deal with "illegitimate" institutions and practices, or with minority elements who stand outside the "political" system though these may have *de facto* authority to rule. There is a rich anthropological literature describing such situations, and we would hope to have an increasing number of studies of how socialization occurs in such settings. Hannerz offers some interesting speculations about sex role learning in an urban slum following the cross-cultural literature outlined above, but what of political socialization in such settings?

Just as we have in this chapter focussed on the role of ritual in sex-role socialization, so in the study of political socialization we need to examine the importance of rituals. Wallace's work on revitalization movements (1962), for example, offers an outline that should be of use in the study of socialization in political movements. Turner (1969) offers an analytic framework which stresses the socialization aspects of the ritual process in social movements by drawing parallels between social movements and rites of passage. Although this paper has concerned itself with answers to static system-maintenance kinds of questions in the studies reviewed of childhood socialization, there is no reason why the concepts of socialization cannot be used to study social change in this way. How does the new order establish and maintain itself? Social movements like Wallace's revitalization movements face the problem of recruitment and resocialization. Williams (1963) has applied Wallace's outline to *Murut* nativistic cults of Borneo. Ladas (1970) has demonstrated the importance in voluntary associations of group support to individual behavior.

The study of such social change movements is a proper study of socialization process and personality, but in considering them our emphasis, at least in part, changes from childhood socialization to socialization in adulthood. We may also wish to turn our attention to changes in individuals across time. For example, Erikson has delineated various stages of life, yet anthropologists covered in this review have focused their attention on the transition from infancy to childhood, childhood to adolescence, and adolescence to adulthood. What of young adult to mature adult, old age, etc.? One of the limitations of the model proposed in this chapter is its emphasis on child training. While some behaviors seem adequately explained by a fixation on childhood as determinant of adult and cultural behaviors, other behaviors may require a recognition of processes of adult socialization. While adult socialization is a topic that has been largely neglected by these cross-cultural anthropologists, Peacock's fine study of the effects on adults of *ludruk* drama in Indonesia begins to redress the balance. He shows how participation in *ludruk* drama stimulates participants to "think, feel, act and judge" in ways conducive to the "modernization of Java" (Peacock 1968:233). Institutions may have their effect on the adult personality as students of the psychiatric hospital such as Goffman (1961) and Caudill (1958) have shown. Harrington and Wilkins (1966) argue that long mental hospital stays can foster dependency. Wing (1962) has shown that the longer a patient has been in a mental hospital the less likely he is to want to leave or have any realistic plans for the future outside. Goffman has called attention to similarities between rites of passage and aspects of total institutions. Such effects on adults of rituals and institutional settings need to be pursued in cross-cultural studies. We know, for example, a great deal about what the kacina cult is supposed to teach children, but what does the adult in the setting learn? While the problem of adult socialization is generally beyond the scope of this review and the model presented here, this paragraph will at least acknowledge its possible significance.

Conclusions

We have reviewed the studies of socialization process and personality that have been generated by cross cultural research in anthropology built around the model in Figure 1. By using the life cycle through adolescence as our organizing principle, we have reviewed studies which use personality to illuminate the integration of societies. Restricting ourselves to a particular set of behaviors, we then reviewed the literature on sex role learning as an illustration of a general model designed to be of assistance to the reader in organizing all the materials presented in this chapter. We traced the development of this kind of anthropological research from its early cross cultural phase in the 50's to its more recent addition of in depth comparative studies of particular cultures. Finally we point out the need for new research in areas that have generally been neglected by cross cultural researchers, but in which we feel they have much to contribute.

In the first version of this chapter in 1961 John Whiting wrote:

> It would seem to this reviewer that the cross cultural study of personality is off to a good start but still has a long way to go. The measurement of child rearing is far from satisfactory partly because ethnographic reports are often inadequate and partly because it is highly unlikely that the variables selected (in the early research) will turn out in the long run to be more than first approximations of the dimensions most crucial . . .

It would seem to us now that the field has moved out of its infancy and into early childhood. Our review of the recent research has shown how the researchers in the field have answered the call raised by Whiting in 1961 for better data and more refined operationalizations. As these trends continue, and as we tackle new and more daring problems, we hope that ten years from now we can report the field as genuinely approaching adulthood. The students of socialization process and personality have consistently increased the number of their methodological options and their refinement. The field began in the 30's with Mead's analysis of New Guinea and Samoa, and Whiting's study of the Kwoma (1941). After the war, unhappy with generalization from one or two cases, the field went broadly comparative, and the full blown cross-cultural survey of the Whiting and Child type appeared and persisted. In the 60's were introduced the *Six Cultures* type of study, where detailed analysis of particular cultures are carried on in comparable ways in more than one culture and the data collectively analyzed, and the Segall, Campbell and Herskovits (1966) type of study where the same pre-constructed instrument was sent to numbers of field workers. We expect to see much more of these types of studies in the future. In addition we have in-depth analyses of particular cultures, but now with tools which enable us to put our analysis of individual cases into a broader comparative framework, and to use the individual cases to test a proposition developed cross-culturally. It is worth noting that, just as Whiting predicted, as we have increased the depth of our analysis of individual cultures we have had to refine our operationalization of variables. For example, Harrington (1970) argues that the operationalization 'father absence' which works cross-culturally above is inadequate to the understanding of the complexities of an individual culture where a better operationalization would be 'father salience'.

In the future we may see the development of more and more anthropological field stations. We have in mind as prototypes such projects as the Harvard Chiappas (Vogt) project, the Harvard (Whiting) field project in East Africa, and the Columbia (Harrington) project in New York City. In such settings students may combine a detailed understanding and analysis of particular cultures with systematic data gathering permitting comparisons across a sample of cultures. Of course this moves anthropology into a team work and division of labor which has not characterized the traditional 'my tribe' approach. As the number of 'tribes' decreases, and the complexity of our problems and methodologies increases, the 'my tribe' approach may be a luxury we can no longer afford.

Interest in our findings in the past ten years has been gratifyingly high in psychology. In the next ten years we expect an increasing interest in our findings by educators, as they realize that these cross-cultural researches of learning form a basis for an anthropology of education. We look forward to reviewing these and other developments ten years from now.

BIBLIOGRAPHY

ADLER, NORMAN AND CHARLES HARRINGTON. 1970. The learning of political behavior. Chicago, Scott, Foresman.

ALLEN, MARTIN J. 1967. Childhood experience and adult personality — A cross-cultural study using the concept of ego strength. Journal of Social Psychology 71:53–68.

ALMOND, GABRIEL A. AND SIDNEY VERBA. 1963. The Civic Culture: Political attitudes and democracy in five nations. Princeton, N.J., Princeton University Press.

AYRES, BARBARA C. 1954. Personality determinants of food and sex taboos during pregnancy. Unpublished doctoral dissertation. Cambridge, Radcliffe College.

————. 1968. Effects of infantile stimulation on musical behavior. Chapter 9 *in* Alan Lomax et al. Folk song style and culture, pp. 211–221. American Association for the Advancement of Science.

BACON, M. K., IRVIN CHILD & HERBERT BARRY. 1963. A cross-cultural study of correlates of crime. Journal of Abnormal and Social Psychology 66:291–300.

BARRY, HERBERT A. 1957. Relationships between child training and the pictorial arts. Journal of Abnormal and Social Psychology 54:380–383.

———. 1968. Sociocultural aspects of alcohol addiction. *In* The addictive states, Association for Research in Nervous or Mental Disease, Vol. XLVI. Baltimore, Williams and Wilkins Co.

BARRY, HERBERT A., M. K. BACON & IRVIN CHILD. 1957. A cross-cultural survey of some sex differences in socialization. Journal of Abnormal and Social Psychology 55:327–332.

BARRY, HERBERT A., I. L. CHILD, & M. K. BACON. 1959. Relation of child training to subsistence economy. American Anthropologist 61:51–63.

BERRY, J. W. 1966. Temne and Eskimo perceptual skills. International Journal of Psychology 1:207–229.

———. 1967. Independence and conformity in subsistence level societies. Journal of Personality and Social Psychology 7:415–418.

BOCK, PHILIP K. 1967. Love magic, menstrual taboos and the facts of geography. American Anthropologist 69:213–217.

BROWN, JUDITH K. 1963. A cross-cultural study of female initiation rites. American Anthropologist 65:837–853.

BURLING, ROBBINS. 1964. Cognition and componential analysis: God's truth or hocus-pocus? American Anthropologist 66:20–28.

BURTON, ROGER AND JOHN W. M. WHITING. 1961. The absent father and cross-sex identity. Merrill-Palmer Quarterly 7:85–95.

CARLSMITH, KAROLYN KUCKENBERG. 1963. Effect of father absence on scholastic aptitude. Doctoral dissertation. Cambridge, Harvard University.

CAUDILL, WILLIAM. 1958. The psychiatric hospital as small society. Cambridge, Harvard University Press.

CHILD, IRVIN. 1954. Socialization. *In* Gardner Lindzey, ed., Handbook of social psychology, pp. 655–692 of Vol. 2. Cambridge: Addison-Wesley.

CHILD, IRVIN, M. K. BACON, & HERBERT BARRY. 1965. A cross-cultural study of drinking. Quarterly Journal of Studies on Alcohol, special supplement 3. pp. 1–111.

COHEN, YEHUDI. 1964. The transition from childhood to adolescence. Chicago: Aldine.

D'ANDRADE, ROY G. 1962. Paternal absence and cross-sex identification. Unpublished Ph.D. dissertation. Cambridge, Harvard University.

———. 1966. Sex differences and cultural institutions. *In* E. Maccoby, ed., The development of sex differences. Stanford: Stanford University Press.

DOLLARD, JOHN. 1935. Criteria for the life history: with analyses of six notable documents. Gloucester, Mass., Smith.

Easton, David. 1965. A systems analysis of political life. New York, Wiley.

Fischer, John L. 1959. Art styles and cultural cognitive maps. Paper presented at American Anthropological Association Annual Meetings, Mexico City, December.

Friendly, Joan P. 1956. A cross-cultural study of ascetic mourning behavior. Senior Honors Thesis. Cambridge, Radcliffe College.

Froman, Lewis A. 1962. People and politics. Englewood Cliffs, New Jersey, Prentice-Hall.

Goffman, Erving. 1961. Asylums. New York, Doubleday.

Granzberg, Gary. 1967. The psychological effects of the Hopi Katina initiation. Doctoral dissertation, Cambridge, Harvard University.

Gunders, S. M. and John W. M. Whiting. 1964. The effects of periodic separation from the mother during infancy upon growth and development. Paper presented at the International Congress of Anthropological and Ethnological Sciences, Moscow.

Hannerz, Ulf. 1969. Soulside. New York, Columbia University Press.

Harrington, Charles. 1968. Sexual differentiation in socialization and some male genital mutilations. American Anthropologist 70:952–956.

———. 1970. Errors in sex-role behavior in teen age boys. New York, Teachers College Press.

Harrington, Charles and M. L. Wilkins. 1966. Treating the social symptoms of mental illness. Hospital and Community Psychiatry 17:136–138.

Harris, Marvin. 1968. The rise of anthropological theory. New York, Crowell.

Hartley, Eugene L. and Ruth E. Hartley. 1952. Fundamentals of social psychology. New York, Knopf.

Herskovits, Melville. 1948. Man and his works: the science of cultural anthropology. New York, Knopf.

Howe, James. 1966. Caymanian drinking behavior. Honors Thesis, Dep't of Anthropology. Cambridge, Harvard University.

Jaros, Dean, Herbert Hirsch & Frederic Fleron, Jr. 1968. The malevolent leader: political socialization in an American subculture. American Political Science Review 62:564–575.

Kluckhohn, Clyde. 1939. Theoretical bases for an empirical method of studying the acquisition of culture by individuals. Man 39:98–105.

Ladas, Alice. 1970. The relationship of information and support to behavior: the La Leche League and breast feeding. Unpublished doctoral thesis. New York, Teachers College-Columbia University.

Lambert, W. W., Leigh Triandis and Margery Wolf. 1959. Some correlates of beliefs in the malevolence and benevolence of supernatural beings: a cross-cultural study. Journal of Abnormal and Social Psychology 58:2.

LANDAUER, T. K. AND JOHN W. M. WHITING. 1964. Infantile stimulation and adult stature of human males. American Anthropologist 66:1007–1028.

LEVINE, ROBERT A. 1960a. Witchcraft and marital relations in East Africa: a controlled comparison. Paper presented at the American Anthropological Association Meeting, Minneapolis, Minnesota.

————. 1960b. The internalization of political values in stateless societies. Human Organization 19:51–58.

————. 1963. Political socialization and culture change. *In* C. Geertz, ed., Old societies and new states, New York, Free Press.

————. 1970. Cross-cultural study in child psychology. *In* Paul H. Mussen (ed.), Carmichael's Manuel of Child Psychology, Vol. II, New York, John Wiley & Sons.

LEWIS, OSCAR. 1951. Life in a Mexican village. Urbana, University of Illinois Press.

LIEBOW, ELIOT. 1969. Tally's corner. Boston, Little, Brown.

LINTON, RALPH. 1936. The study of man. New York, Appleton-Century-Crofts.

MAYER, PHILIP E. D. 1970. Socialization: The approach from social anthropology. London, Tavistock. Association of Social Anthropologists Monograph No. 8.

MINTURN, LEIGH AND WILLIAM LAMBERT. 1964. Mothers of six cultures. New York, Wiley.

MUNROE, R. L., RUTH MUNROE AND ROBERT E. DANIELS. 1969. Effects of status and values on estimation of coin size in two East African societies. Journal of Social Psychology 77.

MUNROE, ROBERT L., RUTH MUNROE AND JOHN W. M. WHITING. 1965. Structure and sentiment: evidence from recent studies of the couvade. Paper read at the American Anthropological Association meeting. Denver, Colorado.

MUNROE, ROBERT L., JOHN W. M. WHITING AND DAVID J. HALLY. 1969. Institutionalized male transvestism and sex distinctions. American Anthropologist 71:87–91.

MUNROE, RUTH H. AND ROBERT L. MUNROE. n.d. Household density and infant care in an East African society. Journal of Social Psychology.

MURDOCK, GEORGE P. 1957. World ethnographic sample. American Anthropologist 59:664–687.

MURDOCK, GEORGE P. AND JOHN W. M. WHITING. 1951. Cultural determination of parental attitudes: the relationship between the social structure, particularly family structure, and parental behavior. *In* Milton J. E. Sean, ed., Problems of infancy and childhood. New York, Josiah Macy Jr. Foundation.

Peacock, James. 1969. Rites of modernization. Chicago, University of Chicago Press.

Prothro, E. Terry. 1960. Patterns of permissiveness among preliterate people. Journal of Abnormal and Social Psychology 61:151–154.

Robbins, M. C. 1966. Material culture and cognition. American Anthropologist 68:745–48.

Roberts, John M. and Brian Sutton-Smith. 1962. Child training and game involvement. Ethnology 1:166–185.

————. 1966. Cross-cultural correlates of games of chance. Behavior Science Notes 3:131–144.

Roberts, John M., H. Hoffman and Brian Sutton-Smith. 1965. Pattern and competence: a consideration of tick tack toe. El Palacio 72:17–30.

Rosenblatt, Paul. 1966. A cross-cultural study of child rearing and romantic love. Journal of Personality and Social Psychology 4:338–343.

Scwartz, Gary and Don Merten. 1968. Social identity and expressive symbols: the meaning of an initiation ritual. American Anthropologist 70:1117–1131.

Segall, Marshall H., Donald T. Campbell and Melville Herskovits. 1966. The influence of culture on visual perception. New York, Bobbs-Merrill.

Shirley, R. W. and A. K. Romney. 1962. Love magic and socialization anxiety. American Anthropologist 64:1028–1031.

Spiro, Melford E. and Roy G. D'Andrade. 1958. A cross-cultural study of some supernatural beliefs. American Anthropologist 60:456–466.

Stephens, William N. 1961. A cross-cultural study of menstrual taboos. Genetic Psychology Monographs 64:385–416.

Suttles, Gerald. 1968. The social order of the slum. Chicago, University of Chicago Press.

Sutton-Smith, B. and J. M. Roberts. 1963. Game involvement in adults. Journal of Social Psychology 60:15–30.

————. 1964. Rubrics of competitive behavior. Journal of Genetic Psychology 105:13–37.

————. 1967. Studies in an elementary game of strategy. Genetic Psychology Monographs 75:3–42.

————. 1970. The cross-cultural and psychological study of games. *In* Gunther Luschen, ed., The cross-cultural analysis of games. Champaign, Ill., Stipes, pp. 100–108.

Sutton-Smith, B. and B. A. Rosenberg. 1968. Father-absence effects on families of different sibling composition. Child Development 39:1213–1222.

Turner, Victor. 1969. The ritual process. Chicago, Aldine.

TYLER, STEPHEN A. 1969. Cognitive anthropology. New York, Holt, Rinehart and Winston.

WALLACE, ANTHONY F. C. 1962. Culture and personality. New York, Random House.

WHITING, BEATRICE. 1950. Paiute Sorcery. New York, Viking Fund Publications in Anthropology #15.

————. 1963. Six cultures. New York, Wiley.

————. 1965. Sex identity conflict and physical violence: a comparative study. American Anthropologist 67, Special publication, pp. 123–140.

WHITING, JOHN W. M. 1941. Becoming a Kwoma. New Haven, Yale.

————. 1959a. Sorcery, sin and the superego: a cross-cultural study of some mechanisms of social control. *In* Symposium on motivation, pp. 174–195. Lincoln, University of Nebraska Press.

————. 1959b. Cultural and sociological influences on development. *In* Maryland child growth and development institute, June 1–5, 1959, pp. 5–9.

————. 1959c. The male and female conscience. Paper presented at American Psychological Association Meeting, Cincinnati, September.

————. 1960. Resource mediation and learning by identification. *In* I. Iscoe and M. Stevenson, eds., Personality development in children. Austin, Texas, University of Texas Press.

————. 1961. Socialization process and personality. *In* F.L.K. Hsu, ed., Psychological anthropology. Homewood, Illinois, Dorsey Press.

————. 1962. Comment. American Journal of Sociology 67:391–393.

————. 1964. Effects of climate on certain cultural practices. *In* Ward H. Goodenough, ed., Explorations in cultural anthropology, pp. 511–544. New York, McGraw Hill.

————. 1968. Methods and problems in cross-cultural research. *In* Gardner Lindzey, ed., Handbook of social psychology, 2nd edition Cambridge, Addison-Wesley.

————. 1969. The place of aggression in social interaction. Paper presented at the Annual Meeting of the American Anthropological Association, New Orleans, La., November.

————. Unpub. man. Masculine and feminine cognitive styles.

WHITING, JOHN W. M. ET AL. 1966a. Field guide for the study of socialization. New York, Wiley.

WHITING, JOHN W. M. ET AL. 1966b. The learning of values. *In* E. Z. Vogt and E. M. Albert, eds., People of rimrock: a study of values in five cultures. Cambridge, Harvard University Press.

WHITING, JOHN W. M. AND BARBARA C. AYRES. 1968. Inferences from the shape of dwellings. *In* K. C. Chang, ed., Settlement archeology. National Press Books.

WHITING, JOHN W. M. AND IRVIN CHILD. 1953. Child training and personality. New Haven, Yale University Press.

WHITING, JOHN W. M., RICHARD KLUCKHOHN AND ALBERT S. ANTHONY. 1958. The function of male initiation ceremonies at puberty. *In* E. E. Maccoby, T. Newcomb & E. Hartley, eds., Readings in social psychology, pp. 359–370. New York: Henry Holt.

WHITING, JOHN W. M. AND T. K. LANDAUER. 1968. Infantile immunization and adult stature. Child Development 39:59–67.

WILLIAMS, THOMAS RHYS. 1963. The form of a North Borneo nativistic behavior. American Anthropologist 65:543–51.

WING, J. K. 1962. Institutionalism in mental hospitals. British Journal of Social and Clinical Psychology 37:1–26.

WITKIN, H. A., R. B. DYK, H. F. FATERSON, D. R. GOODENOUGH & S. A. KARP. 1962. Psychological differentiation. London, Wiley.

WRIGHT, GEORGE O. 1954. Projection and displacement: a cross-cultural study of folk tale aggression. Journal of Abnormal and Social Psychology 49:523–528.

YOUNG, FRANK. 1962. The function of male initiation ceremonies: a cross-cultural test of an alternative hypothesis. American Journal of Sociology 67:379–391.

———. 1965. Initiation ceremonies: a cross-cultural study of status dramatization. New York, Bobbs-Merrill.

YOUNG, FRANK AND A. A. BACDAYAN. 1965. Menstrual taboos and social rigidity. Ethnology 4:225–240.

CHAPTER THIRTEEN

Kinship and Ways of Life: An Exploration[1,2]

Francis L. K. Hsu

To the individual in all societies the importance of other human beings, as compared with that of nonhuman elements in his environment, is supreme. This factor can even overshadow his basic desire for self-preservation, for it is not hard to find individuals in any culture who will give their lives because of their parents, spouses, tribe, or nation. Not only that, but most cultures have more or less elaborate moral codes governing or inducing such behavior. Whether the custom is head-hunting or potlatch, whether the economic activity is agriculture, nomadism, or mechanized industries, and whatever the individual's status or interest, the prime mover of the individual's behavior lies in the nature of his relationship with other members of his society. The extent to which he will

[1] In preparing this chapter, I am particularly indebted to Dr. Paul J. Bohannan for reading the entire manuscript and making many valuable comments and suggestions, especially with reference to the relationship between kinship structure and kinship content. I am also indebted to Dr. G. P. Murdock for his constructive comments when the basic ideas of the paper were first presented at the annual American Anthropological Association meetings at Tucson, Arizona, in 1953, and to Drs. W. R. Bascom and Fred Eggan for reading the early version of the manuscript and materially helping its birth.

[2] The first edition of this chapter was reprinted in *Social and Cultural Foundations of Guidance: A Source Book*, edited by Esther M. Lloyd-Jones and Norah Rosenau (1968). Pp. 226–257.

exert himself is in direct ratio to the degree to which he feels he has attained a proper place among his fellow men. That is to say, he tends to experience a greater urge to strive toward improvement of his position if he pictures himself to be in a wrong or lower place from where he ought to be, whereas he tends to be more satisfied with the status quo if he feels the reverse. The specific methods he resorts to are, of course, as varied as they are culturally given, but the basic objects he strives for may be summarized into three categories: sociability, security, and status. The meanings of these basic social needs of the individual, and how they compare with needs postulated by other scholars, have been discussed elsewhere (Hsu 1963, 149–154). Suffice it to point out here that whether the individual has achieved his proper place among his fellow human beings is measured by two interrelated yardsticks: on the one hand, by what Mead, Sullivan, and others, describe as the *attitudes toward himself* (M. H. Kuhn 1954:43); on the other hand, the *attitudes toward him* on the part of those fellow men to whom he is bound or with whom he is identified.

Thus, whether the individual attempts to improve himself by getting married, by conquest of air and sea, by acquisition of wealth, or by elaboration of the imaginary, his primary concern is his place among fellow men. The place of the individual among his fellow men refers, of course, not only to the present. It could be keyed to the past, so that this concern is chiefly centered in his elders and, by extension, his departed ancestral spirits; or it could be keyed to the future, so that this concern is primarily aimed at his descendants, and, by extension, those yet to be born; or it could be keyed to both past and future.[3]

Nor is the place of the individual among his fellow men static. It is subject to the changing circumstances in which the individual finds himself. For example, in spite of the most serene childhood experiences, a majority of individuals will not feel secure when faced by later economic, social, or political uncertainty. Regardless of early histories, a majority of human beings in any crowd escaping from a fire will become panicky and trample one another.

The relative importance of early versus later experiences is immaterial to the arguments of this chapter. The crucial point here is the importance of kinship as the primary web of relationships connecting every new-born individual with his fellow men and, through them, with the overall pattern of thought and action prevailing in the society of which he forms a part.

[3] A more precise formulation and development of this theory of man is found in Hsu 1971a.

The connection between a kinship system and the overall pattern of thought and action of a people may be seen from two angles. On the one hand, some kinship systems enable the individuals reared in them to achieve their appropriate places with greater ease than do other kinship systems. The inference is that the individuals who grow up and live in the former type of kinship systems may be expected to bestir themselves far less than those who grow up and live in the latter type of kinship systems. Hence, the societies with the former type of kinship systems are likely to be less dynamic than those with the latter type.

On the other hand, the individual can be expected to strive more not only when his self-attitude is higher than accorded it by his fellow human beings but also when the people related to him cause him to feel that he has some chance of success and much to gain after his success. Conversely, he is unlikely to strive very hard when the people related to him give him reason to believe that he has little chance of success or little to gain even with success. Therefore, the individual's tendency to adventure, conquest, and expansion no less than his tenacity to face terrible disasters like epidemic, drought, or foreign conquest depends greatly, in the first place, on whether or not his society demands such heroic actions on his part in order for him to keep his membership in it as a self-respecting man, and in the second place, on whether or not his group provides him with psychosocial support for prolonged efforts and concerted action.

This hypothesis makes no assumption on the uniformity of behavior in any society. A few individuals may be aggressive where most others in the same society are docile; a few may fight a last-ditch battle where most others have given up; but the behavior of the majority is strongly affected by the forces just described.

The Hypothesis. However, results of kinship studies so far would seem to show that varieties of kinship have no connection with the diverse life ways of different societies. This conclusion is unavoidable when we note that the Eskimo "type" of "kinship organization" is also characteristic of the highly industrialized Yankees of New England, the peasant Ruthenians of eastern Europe, the simple agriculturalists of Taos Pueblo in the southwestern United States, and the Andamese pygmies of the tropical forest as well as many others (Murdock 1949: 226–228); and that the Dakota type of kinship organization is also characteristic of such diverse peoples as the Fijians, the Tallensi, the Manchus, and the Chinese (Murdock 1949: 236–238). For in spite of the similarity or even the identity of the kinship structures in question, the ways of life[4] of the diverse societies in which they are found bear no resemblance one to another.

What has happened is that most students of kinship from Murdock (1949), Spoehr (1940), and Goldschmidt (1948) to Lévi-Strauss (1949, 1963), Eggan (1950), Leach (1951), and Needham (1962) have concentrated on certain aspects of kinship structure. They attempt to answer in one way or another the following types of question: What factors are correlated with the development of kinship groups such as clan, phratry, dual organization, or their shift from one emphasis to another? What factors affect the change of kinship usages such as relationship terms, mother-in-law avoidance, and forms of marriage? But there has been little or no serious attempt to deal with kinship *content* which can go far to help us with another type of question: What effects do certain types of kinship organization have on the pattern of thought and behavior of individuals reared in them?

The psychoanalysts who contributed to our discipline were not totally uninterested in this question [Freud (1918, 1938), Kardiner (1945), and Erikson (1950)]. Some psychological anthropologists sought answers bearing on this question chiefly by way of child-rearing practices [e.g., Gorer (1948), Gorer and Rickman (1962); also see Harrington and Whiting in Chapter 12 of this book]. Even some traditional students of kinship have sporadically touched on it. For example, it may have been implicit in parts of works by Eggan when he spoke of the "sociological correlates" of the kinship systems of the Western Pueblo (1950:292). It had been skirted by Malinowski when he attempted to show the effect of matrilineal inheritance in the Trobriand Islands on the nature of father-son relationship (1929, 1933), and by Fortune (whatever we think of his conclusions) when he related the Dobuan world view with their kinship usage of alternative residences (1932). The only more extensive examination of this question is a work of Firth (1951), but this volume, though sometimes stimulating and insightful, comes to little more than the general observation that human behavior is intimately intertwined with social organization.

However, armed with an untenable antithesis between psychological

---

[4]The term "way of life" will be used throughout this chapter to denote the characteristic manner in which the people of a given society look at things and express their outlook in concrete actions. It is, therefore, the same as "national character," a term used in Chapters 6 and 7, except that "national character," by custom is applicable to large and literate societies, while "way of life" here applies to all societies. For a fuller exposition of what the "way of life" means, see Hsu 1970:1–11.

and sociological explanations, students of kinship have not only seen no necessary connection between their work and psychological anthropology, but often reacted to the latter with frank hostility. Psychological anthropologists, on their part, have since become much more restricted themselves to the one-sided goal of ascertaining the so-called "determinants of personality" (see Harris 1968, Honigmann 1967).

The task of a systematic exploration of the exact relationship between kinship variation and specific ways of life in different societies remains to be attempted. This line of inquiry seems imperative if the study of kinship is to attain a truly significant place in the total perspective of the science of man. For if kinship is the web through which human beings are woven together from birth to death, it most certainly must, a priori, be related not only to matters such as kinship terms or mother-in-law avoidance but also to the formation, organization, and operation of the most essential patterns of thought and behavior.

The purpose of this chapter is to show that a very real correlation exists between kinship and ways of life. This hypothesis is based on three interrelated propositions:

1. The failure to perceive this correlation thus far is due to concentration on structure to the neglect of content,
2. kinship structure is less clearly related to the thought and action patterns of the individual than kinship content, and
3. kinship content is, in the last analysis, rooted in kinship structure.

Kinship Structure and Kinship Content Differentiated. Kinship *structure* describes those features which govern the formal patterns of arrangement among individuals standing in reciprocal categories of kinship. It comprehends rules of descent, residence, inheritance, in-law avoidances, conjugal or joint families, and so forth. Kinship *content* pertains to the characteristics which govern the tenacity, intensity, or quality of interaction among individuals related through kinship. It has to do with the feelings of individuals toward each other in kinship, and the extent to which each member of the group allows others to enter into and share his private life. In its more permanent outward crystallization, it is embodied in such values as individualism or mutual dependence, romantic love or parental arrangement in marriage, emphasis on youth or on old age, and the importance of ancestors.

To illustrate, a new-born infant may have early in his life only his parents or mother and mother's brothers plus a few siblings and an occasional contact with others; or he may have early in his life relatives including not only his parents or mother and mother's brothers as well as siblings, but also a vast array of other relatives and nonrelatives. These are matters of kinship structure. They spell the differences between the conjugal family and some larger unit, or between patrilocal or matrilocal residences.

However, two infants who have the same number and kind of individuals in their respective lives may be affected differently because these individuals may act as though they each possess them and can order their lives separately; or these individuals may act as though they are mere spectators and that their own mothers are the real powers that lay down all laws. These are matters of kinship content. They underlie the difference between mutual dependence and individualism, both terms to be explained below.

A fuller discussion of the differences between structure and content is found in another publication (Hsu 1959). What needs to be pointed out here, however, is that the content of a kinship system is to a great extent determined by the emphasis given one or another particular primary dyad in the kinship structure.

Eight basic dyads are to be found in every nuclear kinship setting. They are those of husband-wife, father-son, mother-son, mother-daughter, father-daughter, sister-sister, brother-brother, and brother-sister. No matter how much more extensive the kinship system is, the relationships between more remotely situated individuals in it (designated in this chapter as secondary dyads) are, with few exceptions, extensions of one or another of these primary dyads. However, these eight primary dyads are not given the same emphasis in different kinship systems. Furthermore, when a kinship system gives emphasis to one of these dyads, it does so not only by reducing the importance of other dyads but also by modifying their content, so that the resulting kinship systems vary greatly in attributes and in their influences on the individuals reared in them.

To pursue this hypothesis I propose to examine, in the balance of this chapter, four types of kinship systems, each dominated by one structural dyad, and see how they may be related to many outstanding characteristics in thought and behavior among the peoples living in them. The hypothesis presupposes that each structural dyad possesses inherent and distinctive attributes. When one dyad is elevated over other dyads in a given kinship system, the attributes of the dominating dyad tend to modify, eliminate, or at least reduce the importance of the attributes of other structural dyads. The hypothesis further states that the total effect of the dominance of the attributes of one structural dyad leads to a particular kind of kinship content which in turn strongly conditions the pattern of thought and behavior of the individual reared in the kinship system and in the society at large. The four types of kinship content and their structural connections are given below.[5]

A. Mutual dependence among members of kin and community, which is rooted in the emphasis on father-son dyad at the expense of all other dyads.

B. Self-reliance on the part of the individual which is rooted in the supremacy of husband-wife at the expense of all other dyads.

C. Supernatural reliance which is found where the mother-son dyad tends to have more primary importance over other dyads.

D. Mutual dependence seriously undercut by rivalry which coexists with the emphasis on brother-brother dyad and practically no worship of the ancestors.

It is understood, of course, that no typology covers all the facts or puts all of them into perfectly neat compartments (Steward 1954). First, every typology is a matter of abstraction, and the level of abstraction determines what facts must be included and what must be excluded. Second, even the facts covered by any one statement are never as uniform as the statement would indicate. Consider such an observation as "American society is founded on the ideas of equality, freedom, and fair play." Surely any reader can find many historical and contemporary facts as well as the outlook of individual Americans which obviously negate the high-sounding principles. Yet, to conclude that the American society is not founded on these ideas is to be blind to the fundamental trend of development of American society and culture and, therefore, to be very wide of the mark. Even a statement such as "Universal education prevails in American society" is not without exception. In World War II, at least two percent of American males were rejected because of illiteracy. Yet, no one can dispute the fact that universal education is firmly established in this society both as a matter of conviction and as a matter of practice. Third, every type enumerated below contains internal variations which, in more elaborate treatments, may merit description as subtypes. Finally, these four types by no means exhaust all the kinship possibilities on a world wide scale. Instead, they must be considered as forming the beginning in our effort to chart the larger picture.

[5] A fuller statement of this hypothesis is found in Hsu 1965, 1966. An extensive and critical examination of this hypothesis by fourteen anthropologists and three sociologists is found in Hsu (ed.) 1971a.

With these qualifications in mind, let us then examine in some detail the characteristics of behavior in the four types of societies that are associated with the four different kinds of kinship content.[6]

Type A Societies

Included in this group are those of a majority of the Oriental peoples, including Chinese, Japanese, Koreans, Siamese, and others, but excluding the major inhabitants of India — the Hindus and Moslems.

Kinship. The structural characteristics of these kinship systems are simple: they are patrilineal, patrilocal, and by and large patriarchal. The basic unit in which the infant finds himself is generally the patrilineal extended family. Among the lower classes this unit is smaller, approximating the individual family of parents and unmarried children, but in higher classes, it is sometimes enormous. However, even among the poor, the child's grandparents and in-laws are likely to be much in evidence.

The dyad most elevated is that of the father-son. All other relationships are either extensions of this central axis, or are subordinated to and modified by it. The boldest example of this type is found among the Chinese and the weakest among the Siamese. The first attribute of the father-son dyad is inclusiveness. There is only one father but there are usually many sons. In fact, even when there is only one son the parents as a rule hope for more. Its second attribute is continuity. Every father-son dyad is a link in an endless chain of father-son dyads. For every father is a son and every son, in the normal course of events, will be a father.[7]

The overall kinship content correlated with the emphasis on the father-son dyad is mutual dependence. Enmeshed in a network of continuous relationships, the individual is conditioned to orient himself lineally, and, in a secondary way, laterally within a well-defined group; he is naturally the product of his forebears before him as he automatically anticipates

[6] The sequence of A, B, C, and D given the four types of society discussed in this chapter has no ranking significance. It really follows the sequence of my academic acquaintance with these societies. I began my studies of the Chinese culture as a student in 1934; then came my introduction to English culture in 1937; this was followed by my residence and work in the United States since 1944; and a period of 18 months' field work in India from 1955 to 1957. Since the First Edition of the book I spent 1964–1965 in Japan. I now have examined the Japanese kinship system and found it to be a significant variant of the Type A and exhibits many characteristic differences from it. The results of that examination are found in a publication in Japanese (Hsu 1971b) and in a forthcoming book, *Iemoto: The Heart of Japan* (in preparation). My serious reading and reflection on Africa had only begun in 1959.

[7] In the fuller statement of the hypothesis (Hsu 1965) we noted two more attributes of the father-son dyad: authority and asexuality. But for the purpose of this chapter, these will not be discussed.

being the progenitor of his descendants yet to come. His place in that line is specific and inalienable. Superficially the relationship seems to be one-sided, namely, sons owe much more to their fathers than their fathers do to them. The obligations are actually quite mutual. The son owes his father all services as desired, unquestioned obedience, extreme respect, and complete support in life as in death. But the father owes to the son marital arrangement, protection, and all his inheritance. (In Japan the inheritance rules are governed by unigeniture.)[8] The ideal son is sensitive to every whim on the part of his father. The father's every wish is his command. But the ideal father takes every precaution to see that his sons are well married, well educated, well connected, and well provided for. Death and torture are often endured willingly by sons and fathers in fulfilling some of these obligations. The mother, by virtue of her marriage to the father, her assumption of his clan membership, and the biological relationship with the son, is an integral part of this core relationship: whatever is due to the father is equally due to the mother, except that she is not expected to have the means to support her son.

Starting from this basic father-son dyad, similar relationships extend both vertically and horizontally. Vertically each father-son dyad is a necessary link in a chain connecting one's lineal forebears, living or dead, with one's lineal descendants already born or yet to be born. Horizontally it is the model against which are measured one's attitudes, duties, and obligations toward all agnatic male kinsmen and their wives in the ascending or the descending generations.

In this web of kinship the individual has no freedom; he is hedged in on all sides. But freedom is the wrong word, being of non-Chinese origin. The question does not come up. Instead the individual has little fear of being left out, for he can count on help from all sides just as he is expected to give help. This is at the root of the well-known Oriental nepotism, except in Japan (Hsu 1954). Symptomatic of this solidarity is the fact that ancestor worship, going back for many generations, is the rule among them. The living descendants have the duty of providing for the ancestors who have departed and of glorifying them. In turn, the departed members of the family as a matter of course look after the interests of the living descendants. So great is this sense of solidarity that, unlike the ancestor cult found in any other part of the world, these peoples generally do not believe that the departed ancestors will do them harm as spirits. Ancestral

[8] That is one source of difference between Japanese kinship and culture.

spirits are not prayed to for forgiveness during emergencies such as sickness, floods, or epidemics.

The great importance given to the father-son dyad reduces, modifies, or dominates all other relationships, including that between husband and wife. Indeed, the married woman's primary duties are not those to her husband but to her husband's parents or her sons. Similarly the married man's duties to his parents and to his sons take precedence over those to others. For this reason romantic love as an ideal is absent and public expressions of intimacy, whether by a man and his wife before his parents or by a man and his wife before their children, are taboo. A son can be required by parents to divorce his wife if she fails to please them, just as he is duty-bound to take a concubine if his wife fails to provide a son. The need for vertical continuity and horizontal solidarity within the kinship group practically eliminates individual privacy. Consequently, children are raised to enter into the adult world as soon as they are physically and mentally capable of doing so. In fact, mutual dependence requires that children share the vicissitudes of the adult world from infancy onward. Discipline (punishment, reward, rules) tends to be inconsistent for it is never exclusively in the hands of mother or parents. For not only grandparents, but in-laws, neighbors, and friends can actively interfere with discipline.

The clan is seen as an extension of the father-son dyad to all male agnates. Clan is usually present among most of these peoples.[9] This clan is not a mere device to regulate marriage. It is usually an organized body which controls the members' behavior, settles their disputes, and defends them against outside oppressors or enemies. So strong is the patrilineal emphasis in the clan that all women married into it assume its identity, a trait not found elsewhere so far except among the Gusii of Kenya (Mayer 1949).

General Characteristics.   People living in this type of kinship pattern will be satisfied with the status quo and are conservative. There is no urge within the society toward fission. On the contrary, there are deep-seated centripetal tendencies. Since the place of the individual in the web of kinship is inalienable and perpetual, his need for striving to prove himself is not great. And since the individual's growing up experiences are multiple-centered, he tends to view the world not in absolute terms of black and white but in a relativistic fashion with many compromises.

[9] Japan has *dōzoku* but not clan (Hsu 1971b).

Consequently, there are fewer chances for men to be pulled asunder by abstract issues or by the desire for all or none. Even faced with famine, they tend to tighten their belts and eat less instead of moving to new lands. The small minority who do emigrate tend to make up an elaborate duplication of the way of life that they knew before, and/or maintain their solidarity with the home society and/or return physically to the home society at some later date (Hsu 1968, 1970:288–289). With few exceptions, they wish to die at the place of their birth and to be buried in their ancestral graveyard. Most of them do so.

From this point of view we may see the relation between language and culture in a new light. Some scholars have tended, even before Whorf published his well known thesis, to conclude that the Chinese had not developed science because Chinese thought would have been incongruous with Western logic based upon Indo-European grammar (Granet 1934 and Chang 1952). Our analysis here makes it clear that the Chinese lack an interest in abstraction because their anchorage in the web of human relations foredoomed the sustained development of any scientific spirit and inquiry, in spite of an early history of science and invention. Elsewhere I have already detailed this point (Hsu 1970:367–369). What we need to point out here is that the Chinese language, especially the written version, instead of being the cause of Chinese lack of science, was probably shaped by the same restraining forces which limited the development of Chinese science. Chinese is the only completely non-alphabetical language in the modern world; it is more difficult to learn and use than the alphabetical ones. What is more, while Japan, Korea, and Annam of Indo-China (until the French conquest) each has its own separate set of alphabets, all have tenaciously retained the Chinese characters which they borrowed before they acquired their alphabets, to be concurrently used with their own alphabetically derived words, even though this is not only unnecessary, but also a source of great inconvenience. Their conservatism is, therefore, great. A final fact indicating that language does not limit the development of science is that Japan, after her Meiji Restoration which propelled her to a position of world prominence, did not even attempt to eliminate the parallel use of Chinese language. After World War II the teaching of Chinese in Japanese schools was temporarily suspended on order of General MacArthur, but was resumed after the end of the American occupation. Nowadays, most but not all writers of Japanese restrict themselves to 1850 Chinese characters (known as *tōyō kanji* or "Chinese characters in everyday use").

Their literature is voluminous. And their art works, especially those of China and Japan, are regarded as among the best in the world. But because of the individual's security and submersion among fellow human beings, their literature and art delve very little into the unseen. Their music is characterized by melodious elaboration of a simple nature, albeit they have many more kinds of musical instruments than most nonliterate peoples. Yet no matter how many instruments are played together, the result is unison, not harmony of different chords or melodies. The music is often functional, to be played on social, ceremonial and religious occasions and is at best tied to acting such as in opera.

Central Government. These peoples tend to develop overall national states with centralized governments. Submission to parental authority and to long lines of ancestors and continuity with the past in general are consistent with acquiescence to political authority. Rank is ubiquitous and consciously acknowledged by the highly placed as well as by those inferior in situation, much as that which prevails in the kinship organization. The ruler therefore, will be frankly autocratic but not authoritarian. His autocracy is expressed in his unconcealed claim to superiority over his subjects. He and his subjects both admit that his decrees are, at least in theory, absolute. He maintains his unabashed ranking distinctions by his almost complete separation from his subjects. He tends to have no direct contact with his subjects, either bodily or even by sight. In fact, a majority of Orientals have been traditionally forbidden to possess a likeness of their ruler.

But the ruler cannot be authoritarian for two reasons. First, because of the attributes of continuity and inclusiveness, the ruler's power, however absolute, is invariably hampered by his parents, wives, concubines, or parents of his wives or concubines, or eunuchs and their parents, or powerful ministers or their relatives, or the ruler's relatives' relatives. The ruler cannot deal with these and other related individuals effectively even if he objects to what they do because, in a framework of mutual dependence, he is consciously dependent upon them as much as they are upon him.

The other reason why the ruler cannot be authoritarian is that while the ruler-subject relationship is a projection of the basic kinship model, there is one difference. The latter lies in the fact that, in the normal course of events, the primary circle of security of the common man is with his parents and other relatives. The ruler in such a situation does not easily achieve the sort of determined and vehement following often achieved by many of his counterparts in Type B societies (Western) because the individual is not at liberty to do so. Consequently, the function of the Oriental ruler is to maintain, by and large, the status quo. (Even Japan is no real exception, to be noted below.) He is less the leader of the people than the keeper of the existing tradition and arbitrator of the social order. He cannot arouse his subjects easily to march with him because their support of him lacks the necessary zeal.

This lack of zeal explains why, unless a ruler is grossly incompetent or has behaved contrary to the established customs and ways of the people, he would have no trouble with the problem of dissension. Even when an established reign has tumbled and when many warlords are fighting for supremacy, some new dynastic founder tends to emerge with relative ease within a short period of time. The lack of positive zeal for the leader and the need for preserving the kinship group taught Oriental lords to fight no battle of desperation unless there was absolutely no escape from death. As soon as one faction looked like a winner, the inclination of the other contenders was to jump on the bandwagon and find themselves a comfortable but secondary place through subordination. This picture holds true even if the new ruler happens to be an alien. Unless the changes imposed by the alien ruler touch the fundamentals, peoples of this type are not likely to resist subordination by violence. In fact, being relativistic in their view of life, they will not be ashamed to adjust by passive acquiescence to, and even by a degree of active cooperation with, the enemy. They may try with amazing speed even to assume the external patterns of action of the conqueror.

These are perhaps some of the reasons why Oriental states usually were able to maintain unity for longer periods of time than those of the West. The idea of an opposition as a normal feature to check on the dominant power is unknown in Oriental tradition. But for the same reason the unity of Oriental states was generally without the kind of active solidarity and feverish strength characteristic of their counterparts in the West. For the real solidarity lay in the kinship organization, so that changes in the wider political overlordship did not concern the individual except when the new ruler actively interfered too much with the individual's private life and relations. Therefore, when faced with modern Western states, the Oriental political organizations generally appeared to be powerless.

Religion. Polytheistic. The core is usually ancestor worship. But, in addition, there are a multitude of personified gods. They have a large number of gods. They will borrow "gods" from other peoples freely so long as these gods can coexist with each other and with previously established gods. The deities may be arranged hierarchically, and there may be one supreme deity over all others. However, there is no idea that one god only is true and others are false or that all deities are diverse expressions of the same supreme being. This is perfectly in harmony with their relativistic view of life based on the fact that all males, and even females, will in due course achieve their greatness in a continuum along the father-son axis of long lines of ancestors and descendants. Their lack of concern for the unseen and the abstract manifests itself clearly. The gods are worshipped by the people expressly for solutions to specific problems such as disease, longevity, fertility, epidemics, and so forth. Their good will is maintained through offerings, sacrifices, verbal exaltation, recitation of portions of scriptures by the devotees themselves or hired priests, or good deeds among men. Their religious dogma, in spite of their long written histories and literacy, tends to be simple and matter-of-fact, similar to those found among non-literate peoples, and usually offers common sense solutions to their problems. Some of their faiths may have a systematic theology running into volumes. But the latter concern only a minority of the believers. Hence, followers of all cults tend to mix with each other in rituals and beliefs. In fact it is usually difficult to describe them as followers of any particular cult. Religious "persecution" may flare up on rare occasions with sudden impact of a foreign cult, but such persecution is inevitably tied up with political insecurity or economic distress and is neither long lasting nor widespread. For they have no idea of an all-or-none struggle between "good" and "evil." They know no religious wars. Some of them may be "converted" to monotheistic faiths, but few of the converts exhibit anything approaching the religious fervor and devotion of many of their Western brethren. For they have no missionary zeal and are not interested in converting nonbelievers. In keeping with the pattern of mutual dependence, merits and demerits are transferable along kinship lines. Individuals could soar to fame or fortune by virtue of the deeds of their ancestors or descendants, or their souls could be rescued from hell by such relatives.

Impetus to Change. The individual tends to be highly competitive for traditional goals. A man can, and is in fact encouraged to, exhibit initiative in getting up more costly and pompous funerals for his parents, or in going to some extreme to please his parents in filial piety, to glorify his ancestry, or, in Japan, to show devotion to the emperor. But he is unlikely to exercise his imagination by doing things which are not traditionally given, such as for a scholar to go into business. Internal impetus to change within these societies is generally lacking. For the individual can, in the main, reach his proper station among fellow men through the kinship framework. But forces limiting change have a snowballing effect, thereby escalating tradition. Thus, a tradition, whether it be footbinding or contempt for soldiers, tends to become stronger and even goes to extremes as time goes on. Footbinding in China began as a frivolity among some court dancers who wrapped their bare feet with white satin to please the emperor. By the late nineteenth century, many women deformed their feet into such small points that they could hardly walk. The higher the social class, the greater the competitive tendency and the smaller the feet. Footbinding was abolished in China only under Western impact.

Most individuals are automatically assured of honorable places in the social organization, in life as well as after death. Ancestor worship provides a complete continuity between the dead and the living, the past and the present. Therefore, while the tendency to excel in glorification of the lineage and ancestry is great, the tendency to preserve everything traditional, from duties and obligations to mores and customs, is also great. The very close and permanent human ties serve as a drag on initiative so that people are prevented from venturing out into untrodden paths, intellectually, emotionally, and physically. The social organization is such as softly but unremittingly to nip in the bud a majority if not all internal efforts to change the scheme of things. There is a general lack of interest in association other than those based on kinship, marriage, locality, and occupation. For the vast majority there are not even age groups or hunting organizations and rarely any sort of sport which requires competition between two organized bodies. Overthrow of the ruling dynasty occurred (except Japan), but revolution was unknown before impact of the West. Since they have little urge to elaborate the unseen, their utopias, never numerous, tend to be close copies of the actual worlds in which they live, minus such disturbing elements as war, banditry, and dishonesty. There may be different indigenous philosophies, but these have never become bases for contending factions in any irreconcilable way for the simple reason that the majority of peoples in this type of society have a tendency not to get actively involved in ideologies which are abstract and remote from the immediately apprehended reality.

Over long periods of time there seem to be only two conditions which are the mainsprings for change in these societies. One condition is the increase of population which precipitates some inevitable expansion, even though the people entertain no great dream about new frontiers. But, as pointed out before, the expansion is slow and is not accompanied by any noticeable desire to cultural, political, or economic independence of the newly acquired territory. The other condition for change is external pressure or invasion. Such societies have successfully withstood external forces, military, or cultural, by their basic cohesion. But they may be overrun, although they seem to have the ability to modify ultimately the alien forces in their midst, and they usually recover by achieving new syntheses between their traditional and the alien elements. They tend to render the alien-imposed programs ineffective not by armed opposition (though this occasionally occurs) but chiefly by emasculating them through unobtrusive persistence. The strength of their way of life lies in its permanent solidarity between the dead, the living, and the unborn. This kinship relationship provides the individual with great resilience toward environmental problems so that he is not easily given to despair or loss of heart.

In the process of their persistence, they cannot but change a little. For everything in the universe changes in time. But such changes, especially the more spectacular and speedier ones, do not easily take deep root. It has been said that while China had successfully absorbed her foreign conquerors in the past, she may not be able to do it with Western powers. This remains to be seen. From this analysis, it seems certain that neither China nor Japan will be basically threatened or altered very easily by the West, even though the West, including the Communist West, certainly has caused them great disturbances.[10]

No society in this type is likely either to die out physically through conquest or loss of resources or even to lose the continuation of its way of life such as is found in many parts of the nonliterate world or the West.

Type B Societies

Type B includes the societies of a majority of the Western peoples — Europeans and the peoples in societies of European origin throughout the world.

Kinship. The kinship structure of these peoples is usually patrilineal, patrilocal or neolocal, and in many instances, nominally patriarchal. The

[10] For an assessment of how much change has occurred in China since 1949 see Ho and Tsou (eds.) 1968. For an interpretation of the difficulties encountered by the new Chinese government vis-à-vis the Chinese type of kinship system see Hsu 1968.

basic unit in which the infant finds himself is the individual family, consisting of parents and unmarried children. In some parts of Europe, especially in premodern times, the joint family prevailed more than the individual family, and even in modern times some of these peoples have more affines living under the same roof than others. Among the lower and upper classes, the number of children is generally larger, while among the middle classes, the trend is in reverse.

The structural relationship most elevated is that of the husband-wife dyad. All other relationships are either subordinated to this central dyad or are patterned after and modified by it. The strongest example of this type is found among modern Americans of the United States, and the weakest, among the eastern Europeans.

Unlike those of the father-son dyad, the attributes of the husband-wife dyad are exclusiveness and discontinuity.[11] It is discontinuous over the generations because each husband-wife dyad is ended when one or both of the partners die. It is exclusive of other individuals because each husband-wife dyad is not only complete by itself but is intolerant of intrusion by a third party. It must, therefore, insist on monogamy as an absolute *ideal*. Among the peoples constituting Type B there is, of course, variation in the nature of the husband-wife dyad. In Eastern Europe the husband-wife dyad unquestionably is husband-dominated, and in the United States the wife so equals her husband in nearly every way that it gives the impression of being wife-dominated. But whichever case we refer to, the central and dominating position of the husband-wife dyad over all others in this type of kinship system is obvious. In contrast to Type A societies, the husband-wife union is the only relationship which is expressly and elaborately sanctioned, guaranteed and safeguarded by the church as well as by the law. It is so elevated above all other relationships and so freed from their encumbrances, that it is glorified by, and only supposed to be founded, on romantic love, an expression which embodies unaccountableness of the choice, exclusive possession between the partners of each other, freedom from interference by other human beings, and complete lack of definite links with other dyads whether they be parent-child or fraternal. In Type A societies the father-son dyad symbolizes all that is "forever." In Type B the husband-wife dyad is the only relationship which is "forever."

Given this central emphasis it is easy to see how the other relationships in this type of system are either subordinate or thoroughly unimportant. The parent-child dyad is important only before the son or daughter

[11] Two other attributes not discussed here are volition and sexuality (Hsu 1965).

reaches majority. Even during this period, once the parental consent for marriage is given the parents no longer have control over anything. Support of children by parents is limited by the same factor. Support of parents by children is, even where the law insists on it, highly conditional and no child has to keep a parent under the same roof with his or her spouse. Generally speaking, parents have complete freedom in bequest.

Polygamy of any variety is incongruous with the emphasis on husband-wife dyad. Mistresses and gigolos may be kept on the side by men and women who have the means. They may be connived by the public and in the church, but these relationships have never been made truly *legitimate* as they have in Types A, C, and D societies. Divorce rested at first with the church and has gradually been shifted into the hands of the two married partners, but at no time has it been a matter of the authority of the parents. Sibling relationships, uncle-niece relationships, uncle-nephew relationships, mother-in-law and daughter-in-law relationships are all reduced more or less to matters of friendship. If the parties concerned like each other, they may develop very great solidarity with each other. But if they do not happen to enjoy the sight of each other, one can die without knowing where the other lives. They have no definite legal or social obligations to each other. Their economic relationship is limited to voluntary gift making or certain claims on assets left by the intestate dead. This is the only type of kinship system in which all sorts of public display of erotic expressions between lovers and between spouses is encouraged, pictorialized, glorified as though they should be separated from physical sex, and played up so that they can almost stop traffic in the busiest thoroughfare.

While dominance by the father-son dyad leads naturally to the social importance of extended relationships along the male line and the formation of the clan, the emphasis on husband-wife dyad cuts each married couple adrift to itself. The family starts with a man and a woman. They beget children and the family may be enlarged to a size of ten or even fifteen or more, but as the youngsters are married and move away, the family shrinks back to where it began. In contrast to the child in Type A, that in Type B grows up under the monolithic hands of the parents, usually the mother. Right and wrong, reward and punishment, tend to be absolute and clear cut. Before reaching majority, children are the exclusive charge of the parents. Any interference in discipline of the child from any source (even grandparents) is resented unless the parents ask for it. At the same time the value of individual privacy leads the parents to foster in their children a childhood world of their own, divorced from that of their elders. The tendency is to make this childhood as simple as possible, as consistent as possible, as angelic as possible, so that the little ones will be free from adult anxieties or frustrations. Since parents tend not to divulge their own affairs to their children and since children's activities have little or no reference to the adult world (such as making a living), the youngsters are likely to be unaware of the inconsistencies in adult life, in which honor and dishonesty, triumph and tragedy may occur simultaneously or intermixed, sometimes without rhyme or reason. On the contrary, the children tend to be conditioned to a black or white picture of life, in which all good men are rewarded and all bad ones punished.

The overall kinship content most commensurate with the emphasis on husband-wife dyad is individualism or self-reliance. Having to seek a mate on his or her own merits or demerits, and having to establish and nurture such a new relationship by cutting himself adrift from those who have been so dear and so close, the individual is conditioned to think in terms of the first person singular, here and now; his own rights, his own pleasures, and his own privacy; his own status, and his own chances for advancement or danger of regression. For he is trained to regard the human world around him as impermanent. He has no inalienable place in the scheme of things except that scheme he himself initiates and constructs.

Here one must enter a note of caution about the use of the term "individualism." This term has been used so loosely to to describe the pattern of behavior of many nonliterate societies (see, for example, Mead 1937) that it has lost all significance. Individualism is neither the same as individual differences nor as self-interest or egotism. Individual differences exist in all societies, as demonstrated by Gillin years ago (1939) and reiterated by Hart more recently (1954). Self-interest is never absent even among peoples who are said to value "giving for the sake of giving" (Hsu 1954), and the pattern of self-interest can certainly vary in degree from society to society. But individualism is that conception of each human being as unique and as possessing God-given rights which cannot be taken away from him by men, society, or tradition. To express this uniqueness he must have freedom and, to safeguard his right, his due is equality. Individualism so defined was only initiated and exemplified by Occidental peoples of our Type B and was unknown among all other peoples before the impact of the West. Self-reliance is the American variety of individualism where it has reached its widest and most extreme expression so far

(Hsu 1970:120–130).

The peculiarity of this kinship content is the primary emphasis given to the uniqueness of the individual rather than relationships between individuals, and to the likes and aspirations of the individual rather than the duties and obligations of one individual to another — for parents and children tend to be equal before the law and certainly before the supernatural. There is, therefore, an inherent tendency to conflict between the generations not known in other types of kinship systems. On the one hand parents view their children as their exclusive possession, since they are given unbridled authority to order the youngsters' lives. On the other hand, privacy and self-reliance keep parents and children apart even before the latter reaches majority in ownership of property, correspondence, relationship with friends, romance, and in the choice of life partners. Therefore, parents often find it hard to let their children go their own way as the youngsters advance in age, while children often find it necessary to reject their parents as the most important sign of maturity and independence. As a result the parent-child tie is not only terminated legally upon the youngster's reaching majority, it may be socially and psychologically broken long before.

Ancestor "worship" even when present is never more than the mere pride in a distinguished genealogy and is never calculated to benefit the dead. In fact, death severs the relationship among men, for the spirits of the dead have no more interest in the living, while the living remember the dead only if there is individual affection. Clan is generally not an active organization, and wherever present, as in Scotland or Ireland today, of little more than nominal value.

General Characteristics. The emphasis on the uniqueness and independence of each individual cannot but encourage creativity (that is, change and deviation from the established norms) in general. Given a blackest black or whitest white pattern of approach, these cannot but cause those who desire change to champion their ends as absolute and with finality. Such individuals at once threaten those who do not see eye to eye with them and who are committed to other positions with equal absoluteness and finality.

There is an eternal struggle. Those who desire to change what has so far been held as true will be vehement about their intentions and often violent in their techniques. Others who think they have the truth already will inevitably feel compelled to defend themselves as vehemently and violently. Consequently, in this type of society, we obtain ultraconservatives and ultraradicals, arch-racists and arch-lovers-of-all-mankind, extreme isolationists and extreme one-worlders, each, being armed by the absolute truth, bent on a showdown with and complete conquest of the "enemy." The net result is a type of society full of exuberance. It is characterized, on the one hand, by convulsions, purges, and revolutions, and, on the other, by initiative, emigration, science and technology, idealism, and search for new frontiers. Even without significant internal turmoil, the tendency of the individual in this type of society is centrifugal. Many of them cannot wait to move out to somewhere else or to move up the social or economic ladder. In any event, the desire to change may come about as a means of climbing the social ladder or be precipitated by the need to better the older generation or by the differences of opinion within the primary group. And when there is significant failure in the natural resources, such as the failure of Irish potatoes in the late eighteenth century, or when there is a significant strife between those who entertain different beliefs, such as that which underlay the tensions between the early American pioneers and their other Anglican brethren, emigration tends to be on a large scale. Moses led the Jews out of Egypt, and the White Russians dispersed all over the world after 1917. It is interesting to note that even where there was still an unlimited frontier nearer to home, a considerable number of Southerners moved from the United States to Brazil and elsewhere as a result of the Civil War.

When peoples from this type of society move to a new area, their intrinsic tendency is to set up a new society that is independent from their old. This tendency is founded on two factors. One is that, lacking permanent kinship ties, they will as a whole have little urge to return to their home society. Second, they are likely to be fired by an idealism that is not often present among peoples from societies of other types. Children who are raised apart from the vicissitudes of adult life tend to be freer with their imagination. But since the children are at the same time under the complete control of their parents, they are likely often to use their fantasy world as a reaction against the elders. Personal independence is often inextricably interwoven with the idea of doing something different. This was why all the independent immigrant republics were formed by Westerners, from Australia to the New World. Conversely, no Chinese immigrant groups in historical times and no Japanese colonizers in modern times have ever even suggested a separatist movement from their respective home countries (except for one Chinese group in Borneo for a few years). Under conquest, people of this type of society will tend to resist with violence either in open rebellion or in underground movement. Many of them would rather die than conform to the new rule. And the population is likely to be sharply divided between those who accommodate to the conquerors and those who do not. The ultimate result is likely to be either that the conquerors are overthrown by force or that the resistors are overcome and driven out by force. This does not mean that the ways of life of the conquerors or the conquered will not in the end become intermixed, but there will be persistent efforts to root out the suppressed elements.

They all have alphabetical languages of probably the same origin. Their written languages have changed from society to society and from period to period. Both of these changes tend to be much more pronounced than with the Oriental peoples belonging to Type A. The archaic form of Chinese writing found inscribed on oracle bones 3,700 years ago has more in common with modern Chinese writing than does Latin with French or even Chaucerian English with modern English.

Part of the reason may, of course, be that the Indo-European written languages are phonemic while the Chinese written language is ideographic, but that is certainly not the whole story. As we noted earlier, the Japanese and Koreans are unwilling to give up the more inconvenient Chinese ideographs even after adoption of the alphabet. The conservatism of Japanese and Koreans with reference to their written languages is obviously based on other reasons than the relative ease with which their written languages can or cannot change.

Their literature is more voluminous than that found in Type A societies in spite of the fact that they came upon printing much later than the Chinese. Their literature is infinitely richer in the imaginative and emotional qualities than the Orientals or non-literate peoples, but not peoples of Type C such as the Hindus. Their art is great for the same reason. Since the uniqueness of the individual is best displayed in creativity, art for art's sake has developed to an extent unknown elsewhere. Their music is truly one of the greatest gifts bestowed upon mankind; even the great music of the Hindus cannot surpass it. They have developed harmony in music systematically and intensively; they have a wider variety of instruments, more precise instruments, and instruments which are capable of covering a wider musical range than all other peoples except, perhaps, the Hindus. Unlike the peoples of Type A, they have much music that is played simply as music, not as accompaniment to some thematic plot or dance. Thanks to the attributes of discontinuity and exclusiveness, which feed the urge to explore the unseen and the unknown, these peoples have advanced science both qualitatively and quantitatively to a height undreamed of by the rest of the world.

Central Government. These peoples tend to develop national states whether in modern or premodern times. These states tend to be either extremely authoritarian or pronouncedly democratic. In both forms, the rulers feel compelled to make personal appearances before the people for the purpose of solidarity, since the people, having no mooring in their primary groups, are always in search of wider circles of solidarity. Because of the tendency toward extremes, both the authoritarian and the democratic rulers have to be heavily guarded. The techniques are somewhat different, but allegiance to the system as well as allegiance to the leader is important in both. Both types of government will be heavily organized and in both the primary relationships of man are of far less importance than either the impersonal law or the impersonal state. Universal military service and later universal education tend to be the rule and not the exception. In these and other ways, the state tends to enter into the private lives of the average individuals whether they like it or not. This type of society gives rise to modern nationalism which underlies its strong solidarity at given points of time, especially in the face of dangerous enemies, either human or natural. But in the long run, the organizations of such societies tend to be unstable or undergo rapid changes because they are subject constantly to attack from within, either by recognized opposition or by unrecognized foes, and to threat from without by other societies similarly constituted. This is, perhaps, one of the reasons why Europe was never united under one government, while large societies like China were marked by long periods of peace under one ruler interspersed only by short periods of interdynastic chaos.

Religion. The monolithic family constellation and attributes of exclusiveness and discontinuity are concordant with a monotheistic view of the supernatural. Even before Christianity came into being, disputes over gods and efforts to suppress creeds other than those adhered to by the ruler were not unfamiliar in Rome and in the Middle East. We mentioned the fact that there is as a rule no ancestor worship. When and if more than one supernatural being is believed in, the tendency is for the ones other than God to be regarded as parts of God's expression, and prayer to them is only justified on the ground that they will intercede with God for the benefit of the believer. On the other hand, though believing in the same God, they will be irretrievably and continuously divided as to faith. The extent to which the church is divided tends to go hand in hand with the development of individualism. New sects and denominations will appear even when no theological differences exist. This greater tendency on the part of the freer branches of the church to subdivide is closely related to the sharper division among men under stronger individualism. Thus in Catholicism and Eastern Orthodoxy, prevalent in southern Europe, eastern Europe, and Latin America, the clerical hierarchy is important while in the Protestantism prevailing in northern Europe and North America, it becomes less important or of no consequence as far as the relationship of the worshipper and his God is concerned. Then, as we move from Catholicism to Protestantism the other-worldly punishment goes from being somewhat relative to irretrievable. In the Catholic purgatory the soul still has hope since the good works of his kinsmen as well as his own devotion can raise him, but when the Protestants removed the belief in purgatory they severed all permanent relationships between the individual and his kin.

Lacking any permanent relationship among men, the individualist has to compensate it with attachment to some other objects: faith, creed, dogma, and so forth. He tends, therefore, to be hostile toward, or persecute, those who do not share his faith or his version of the fundamentally same faith. Since polytheists will not fight about or for their supernaturals, the monotheists will inevitably have their most trouble with other monotheists. They must missionize the nonbelievers as well as other monotheists, for the individualists must "advance" personally as a way to salvation or they will surely lag far behind or even be engulfed by the others. To buttress themselves they must have not only systematic theology but many techniques in organization and indoctrination. They need more and more interpretation and reinterpretation of the theology, but in spite of such theological erudition, the core of the dogma tends to remain unchanged and uncompromising, thus requiring more theology in turn as objective circumstances change.

Religious prejudice, ranging all the way from outright persecution, inquisition, and burning of heretics to occupational and social discrimination, is common. The religious wars of the world were practically all fought by monotheists. Even when religion is not the outstanding issue, the monotheists cannot but inject religious elements into any struggle that each group makes with another. While both parties in a combat may worship the same god, each will consider its own war a struggle of the good against the evil. An eternal struggle is inherent in monotheism. Their religious men may preach dependence upon God, but the worshippers usually waste no time doing it themselves.

Impetus to Change. Over any period of time, this type of society tends to propel itself toward incessant change. There will be, as pointed out above, extreme conservatives and extreme radicals. But since those who do not wish to change do not hesitate to force a showdown with those who desire extremely to change, the result is usually a major or minor explosion. And when the remains of an explosion are gathered and reintegrated together, they are never the same as before. In any case, the average individual in this type of society is encouraged to show initiative or he will lose his self-respect. This is the psychological background of free enterprise as a way of life. This is the reason why associations of all descriptions, based on both abstract and concrete goals, are countless (Hsu 1963). This is the crucial force giving societies of this type a degree of internal impetus to change undreamed of by all other types.

In one sense, the technological development and changes are most noticeable and are usually described as being most characteristic of this type of society. But changes in other areas of life are no less colossal. Thus, in religion, this type of society has changed from early polytheism to Catholicism, and from Catholicism to Protestantism; or from polytheism to Mohammedanism and then branching out into such creeds as Bahaism. The family has changed from being extremely authoritarian in form through being equalitarian to that of America in which the family ties even between parents and children are based on ideals of friendship. There are drastic changes in laws, in the treatment of criminals, and so forth. Most prominent of all are the revolutions which are unique to this type of society. The revolutions, though primarily directed to a change in the form of government, always have had much wider effects, partly because Western forms of government affect the people's way of life much more than do the Oriental ones, and partly because each revolution is always based on some ideology which envisages a new society that it hopes to realize. Utopias are numerous and most of them are very different in form from existing reality.

Such societies tend to develop strong internal solidarity to withstand external pressure, military or cultural. But because of their strong solidarity and the solidarity of those who hope to conquer or are opposed to them, the resulting conflagration and destruction are sometimes irreparable. In addition to the more severe nature of the explosion, many, perhaps most, individuals in this type of society tend to be brittle psychologically and lack elasticity to deal with ambiguity, having been trained in a kinship pattern to insist on all or none, black or white, completely right or completely wrong. They will be hilarious in their triumphs and extremely depressed in their failures. They may go on to greater achievements and greater glories, but they may also sicken at heart and die out, in the Toynbeean sense.

Type C Societies

Societies in this group include those of the Hindus in India and possibly the Moslems of this subcontinent as well.

Kinship. The center of the kinship structure of the Hindus is the joint family ideal like that in China and Japan. It is patrilineal, patrilocal, and generally patriarchal. It has a nominal "clan" (*gotra,* etc.)[12] that is mainly a negative means of regulating marriage, but is not organized as a whole and not based on blood (genetic) relationships.

In one respect the kinship pattern is similar to that in Type A. Children tend to live in the adult world and are actively initiated into adult roles as soon as they are physically and mentally capable of doing so without waiting for the official age of majority (Mandelbaum 1949 and Murphy 1953). But the most important structural relationship is that of mother-son. The mother-son dyad distinguishes itself from both the father-son and husband-wife dyads by several attributes. Like the father-son dyad but not the husband-wife dyad, it is inclusive. There is usually more than one son, and there is the perpetual desire on the part of the parents for more than one son. In the Orient and in India, high infant mortality is especially conducive to the usually conscious feeling that there is security in numbers. Unlike the father-son dyad, but like the husband-wife dyad, the mother-son dyad is discontinuous. No mother is a son and no son is a mother. The mother-son dyad is not, therefore, a link in a chain of a continuous mother-son line.

A third attribute of the mother-son dyad makes it totally dissimilar to both of the other dyads. It is more one-sidedly dependent, and more all-inclusively so, than either of the other two. I term it unilateral depend-

---

[12] Berreman, in his work in Sirkanda, speaks of a "clan" other than *gotra* (Berreman 1963:183–191). But this is hardly defensible "since villagers themselves do not recognize the clan as a group" (Berreman 1963:184).

ence. Related to unilateral dependence is a fourth attribute, diffuseness[13]. An infant after birth is undifferentiated in its reaction to its surroundings, whether human, animal, or material. Watson, reporting the studies of Bridges, states that the emotional differentiations in the infant begin at about three weeks of age "when distress characterized by muscular tension, trembling, crying, and checked breathing can be distinguished from excitement" in general (Watson 1959:199–201). The mother-son relationship begins essentially with complete emotional and physical dependence on the part of the son upon the mother. As the infant grows in years he learns more and more to differentiate between persons, things, and ideas, as well as between different persons, different things, and different ideas. Paralleling with these processes the infant experiences another: while external stimuli are undifferentiated, all things are translatable into all things. But with differentiation of them into categories, he finds that some categories are translatable, or more nearly so, into each other while others are absolutely immutable into each other. For example, a toy dog and a toy duck are far more easily translatable into each other, from the point of view of the child, while a toy dog and an actual dog are far less translatable into each other. For some time a toy dog and an actual dog may be the same to a child, but as he matures, he is going to perceive a greater immutability between inanimate and animate things. Similarly, as he grows in his power of perception he is likely to become aware of the differences between a toy dog and a toy duck even though this pair will remain more translatable into each other than the other pair. At first baby sitters are usually translatable into each other. As the child is more used to one baby sitter than another, he may develop a higher degree of preference for one over the other, thus developing a feeling that some baby sitters are not translatable into others. But in the majority of cases, the younger the infant the more dependent he is upon his mother, since she is the answer to all his troubles and needs, and the more all categories of stimuli which come to him are translatable into each other (or undifferentiable).

In a kinship system where the father-son dyad is dominant (Type A) the son does not come into close relationship with the father at first,[14] but is

[13] One other attribute of this kinship type, libidinality, is discussed elsewhere (Hsu 1965, 1971a).

[14] The picture may be different in societies where the custom of *couvade* prevails. But what is said here certainly applies to the Type A peoples specified in this chapter.

more likely to do so from one year of age or when he is weaned upon the birth of the next sibling. In a husband-wife dominated system (Type B) the son may come into close relationship with both parents at the same time, though his relationship with the mother is likely to be more intense at first. His possibly close contacts with both parents from the beginning of life may enable him to have from the start a greater experience of differentiated stimuli than in the case of the father-son dyad. In a mother-son dominated system (Type C), since the son retains a close contact with the mother until he is much older than in those of Types A and B, the individual is conditioned to retain more of the thought pattern of mutability between all categories of stimuli than would be the case in the other two types of kinship system.

The overall kinship content correlated with the dominance of the mother-son dyad is what may be described as supernatural dependence. The most basic quality of the content of supernatural dependence is that, instead of solving life's problems by self-reliance, external safeguards, and conquests as in Type B, and instead of looking to mutual dependence with other human beings as in the case of Type A, the individual is encouraged to seek supernatural help either by passivity or by active elaboration of rituals to control or at least influence the gods. Passivity often leads to reduction and even the elimination of many or all of the individual's desires and wants. (Popularly this pattern has been associated with Buddhism. What is less well known is that Buddhism is merely a protestant movement of Hinduism and that self-negation has always been part of the essence of traditional Hinduism as well.)

The importance of the mother-son dyad in Hindu India is not rooted in the cultural design. It is not the traditional ideal. Wherever mentioned in Hindu scriptures, the father-son and mother-son relationships are given nearly equal importance, with a slight edge in favor of the former. However, the actual pattern of life in the Hindu kinship system is such as to produce the unintended effect of increasing the importance of the mother-son dyad and of decreasing the importance of the father-son dyad.

The Hindu culture, even more so than the cultures in Type A, is male-oriented. For example, where the Hindu scriptures and ritual practices are concerned, the males are the primary beneficiaries or sufferers. Females are mentioned sometimes. They may suffer in the other world as a result of certain things; but if and when they benefit somewhere, such benefit primarily comes through men. Otherwise they seem to have the role of accumulating spiritual merits for men. They observe fasting days for their husbands and sons; they practice austerities so that their deceased husbands can fare better in the nether world; and they jump on their husbands' funeral pyres so that all members of their husbands' families in many generations can go straight up to heaven. They have no part in the major rituals of any worship. They cannot wear the sacred thread except in a modified form among smaller protestant sects such as Lingayats.

The clearest statement of the male-oriented nature of Hindu culture is to be found in the four states (*ashramas*) of life which every individual should *ideally* pass through: *brahmacharya* (studentship), *grhastha* (life of a married man), *vanaprastha* (life of disinterested hermit, in which familial ties and social relations are renounced) and *samnyasa* (life of the ascetic). I am not aware of any Hindu scripture or even its modern expositions which attempts to apply this or any similar scheme to women. It is simply designed for men.

Despite the male-centered nature of Hindu kinship and culture, the mother-son dyad exerts far greater influences on the Hindu individual for a variety of reasons. In the first place, the Hindu household is one in which adult males and females are much more segregated from each other than in Type A and Type B societies. The higher the caste and the socio-economic status, the closer the family tends to approximate complete segregation. Male children, before puberty or adolescence, tend, therefore, to be under the protective and guiding hands more of females such as mothers and grandmothers than of males such as fathers and grandfathers. This seems not only to be true of individuals like Indrasingh, who grew up in his mother's village because his father passed away when he was fifteen months old, as reported by Gitel Steed (1950 and 1955) but also of numerous other Hindu men in general (see also Minturn and Hitchcock 1963). G. Morris Carstairs (1957) has the following to say:

> Although it is particularly through his participation in the adult male world of caste and family discussion that a child receives the imprint of his community's values, the process has begun even before this, during his earliest years when he spent more time in the women's side of the household than in the men's. Brahmans commonly mentioned that it was their mother, or their grandmother, who first impressed upon them the need to bathe if they touched a low-caste person, until the response became second nature to them. It is women, also who give a boy his early toilet training.... From his mother and his substitute mothers, a boy also learns how and what to eat, how to dress, what constitutes good manners and what is to be avoided as indecent or shameful.
>
> From his mother, grandmothers and aunts a child learns the concrete details

of religious observance at all the multitude of holy days in the calendar. . . . A part of the experience of every child in Deali is to be taken by his mother to a bhopa when he is sick. . . .

The child's sources of verbal instruction can now be viewed as a series of concentric circles, the innermost representing the women's world; then that of the extended family in which his father, if he himself is a younger son, may seem to play a minor part. (Carstairs 1957:148–149).

In the second place, the relationship between Hindu fathers and their sons is less close than that between their Oriental or Occidental counterparts. Mrs. Murphy observes in her chapter on "Roots of Tolerance and Tensions in Indian Child Development" that Hindu children "are carried easily, first in cradled arms which do not grasp them possessively . . . later they straddle a hip of a sister or a brother, father or mother, balancing comfortably" (Murphy 1953:49). In different parts of India, from Punjab to Cape Comorin, Bengal to U.P., a child may be carried in this way most frequently by a mother, or sister, less frequently by a young brother, but rarely by a father. I think part of the reason is the Hindu male's strong aversion against pollution by the bodily functions of infants and children. But another part of the reason is that the Hindu father is also likely to be more preoccupied with some aspect of the ritual activities, such as pilgrimage, designed to bring him closer to his deities or the Truth.

It is not implied that all Hindus live strictly according to the injunctions of the ancient scriptures, any more than all Americans live strictly according to the spirit of the Declaration of Independence and the Christian concept of universal love or turning the other cheek. But many Americans have undoubtedly been motivated by the high principles which form part of their heritage. Likewise, it is among Hindus, and not among Japanese, Chinese, or Germans, that we find hundreds of thousands of devout human beings carrying out various forms of asceticism or doing penance up in the Himalayas and other centers of pilgrimage; and we find also the great popularity of such leaders as Gandhi with his supernatural-centered philosophy and ascetic practices. Furthermore, Hindu children in their home environments are taught much more about the importance of the great ultimate than the children in other societies (Mukerji 1923 and Chaudhuri 1951). Therefore, even though many Hindu fathers do not leave their homes to become hermits and ascetics as they grow older, most of them cannot but in many ways be affected by or attracted to their religious ideal and practices especially away from home.

It is a well-known fact that, even without the Hindu's supernatural orientation, older individuals in any culture tend to gravitate more toward religion than younger ones. As the Hindu ages, he is more likely to devote much time and attention to pilgrimages and, if he can read, scriptures. Furthermore, my personal observation and Steed's show it is not at all necessary to be aged for the Hindu to turn to seclusion and gods. Indrasingh, whom we met in a previous paragraph, a man 26 years old with two wives but no children, turned from opium smoking, one form of institutionalized retreat, to "goddess-worship which will change a man's present and future." Yet, "by other members of Kasandra society, Indrasingh's reactions were not regarded as socially deviant" (Steed 1955:141–143). I have seen again and again where men with children conducted themselves in a way quite similar to what Indrasingh did.

Whatever the cause, the lack of close relationship between the Hindu father and son is also documented by other students (see Carstairs 1957:67–70). Dube's description of a Hyderabad village confirms Carstairs' findings except that it is more cursory (Dube 1955:148–150).[15]

One other fact is worth noting. While the father-son dyad in Type A societies is, as in the Hindu scene, also marked by greater formality than the mother-son dyad, it is far more continuous in nature than the latter. The Hindu father-son dyad does not seem to go much beyond life since ancestor worship is of no great importance. The overall tendency of the people is to look to the ultimate station of reaching oneness with the universe through religious devotion rather than the maintenance of entities of individual ancestors and lineages. Thus, while each father-son dyad in the Chinese kinship system is one link in a perpetual line of ancestors and descendants fortified by an organized clan, the Hindu father-son dyad has no such significance and is not so fortified. In fact, many ancestral spirits "torment the household" in which they had lived and have to be continuously propitiated by worshipping rites (Berreman 1963:110–111). The Hindus tend to keep no genealogical records except in Rajasthan and, as we noted earlier, have no organized clan,[16] though the recognized circles of relatives are greater than in Type B. At the same time the absence of individualism does not encourage the Hindu children to any great desire for independence from their parents which, under the circumstances, means their mothers more than their fathers. Hindu

---

[15] Though some field workers report that this occurs not during the youngster's early childhood but later (see Mandelbaum 1970:58–63).

[16] This fact is more extensively documented and discussed in Hsu, *Clan, Caste and Club* (1963).

mothers, in contrast to American mothers, do not have to worry about resentment on the part of their grown sons, because Hindu sons, in contrast to American sons, do not have to regard acceptance of their mothers' affection and control as signs of immaturity or weakness. The result is a closer mother-son tie than is found in either of the other two types of kinship systems analyzed before.

It is, of course, difficult to determine whether the kinship content of supernatural dependence or the structural elevation of mother-son dyad came first. That is not a scientifically profitable question to be dealt with. But given the cultural tradition of supernatural dependence, the strong influence of mother-son dyad generates the appropriate psychological material in the individual for it. Ramakrishna, the greatest Hindu saint in modern times, asked: "Why does the God lover find such pleasure in addressing the deity as Mother?"

And he answered himself: "Because the child is more free with its mother, and consequently she is dearer to the child than anyone else" (Muller 1938:No. 89).

Sister Nivedita, one of Ramakrishna's European disciples, nee M. E. Noble, who was a pillar of the Vedanta movement after the death of the master, experienced the following episode and sentiment:

> Shortly after her arrival in Calcutta, she heard a cry in a quiet lane. Following her ears, she traced it to a little Hindu girl who lay in her mother's arms dying. The end came soon, and for a while the mother wept inconsolably. After a while she fell back into Sister Nivedita's arms and turning to her said: "Oh, what shall I do? Where is my child now?" "I have always regarded that as the moment when I found the key," says Sister Nivedita. "Filled with a sudden pity, not so much for the bereaved woman as for those to whom the use of some particular language of the Infinite is a question of morality, I leaned forward. 'Hush, mother,' I said, 'Your child is with the Great Mother. She is with Kali.' And for a moment, with memory stilled, we were enfolded together, Eastern and Western, in the unfathomable depth of consolation of the World Heart." (Nivedita 1904:17ff.)

These narrations, used by Ernest A. Payne in his book on *The Saktas* (1933:128–129) as evidence for the psychological foundation of Mother Goddess worship are, from what we know of child development today, actually at the psychological root of all religions, whether the deities in question are male or female. Undoubtedly Mother Goddess worship is one of the most prevalent forms of worship in India, but there is no need to restrict our consideration of it. The complete dependence of the child upon the mother is a universal human fact. To the child, the mother is the magical source of all power, gratification, and punishment. This is the psychology that makes the widespread appeal of the creation story in Genesis or other forms possible. In Type A societies this mother dependence is soon tempered by the authority of the father and later altered by the individual's integration into a network of human relationships, with specific duties, responsibilities, and privileges with reference to ascendants including deceased ancestors and descendants both born and unborn. The adult individual's place in the scheme of things is measured by concrete points of reference, and no longer submerged under the unexplainable power of the mother. In Type B societies growing up means independence not only from the mother but also from the father, self-reliance in food and sex quest, and ability to make decisions and bear consequences. It is not surprising to find that Type A peoples are close only to their ancestral spirits and make offerings to other gods primarily for ulterior motives, while Type B peoples believe that God only helps him who helps himself.

The preponderance of the mother-child relationship of Type C peoples generates the psychological material which feeds a cultural orientation of supernatural dependence, continued and elaborated generation after generation. The difference between supernatural dependence and self-reliance is obvious, but the difference between supernatural dependence and mutual dependence is less obvious but equally significant. For one thing, in contrast to mutual dependence, it is one-sided. The worshipper-dependent expects much more from the gods than they give to the gods, just as the child does with the mother. For another thing, it is all demanding and, therefore, the objective realities tend to be less differentiated and more mutable. The worshipper-dependent expects simple boons to solve all problems however difficult, just as the child demands of his mother. And finally, unlike mutual dependence, it is loaded with diffused sexuality.[17] Type A peoples relegate sex into a few social compartments and see sex as having no relevance to their relationship with the supernatural. Type B peoples repress sex so that they must have a God-child who is born without sex. Type C peoples neither relegate sex into separate compartments nor eradicate it. As a whole, they approach the supernatural through sexuality, an element which is at times blatant, and at other times thinly veiled, but at all times more or less present (Hsu 1971a:439–476). When demands or supplications fail, the strongest step on the part of the worshipper-dependent is extreme passivity, fasting, absten-

---

[17]This attribute is now designated libidinality and is one of the two other attributes of mother-son dominated kinship systems extensively dealt with elsewhere (Hsu 1963, 1965).

tion, and other forms of austerity, just as many a child can, or thinks he can, bring his mother to her knees by refusing to eat or to get up. The Hindu approach to the supernatural, from complicated ritualism to extreme forms of Samadhi, will be touched on below. The Hindu way in penance and austerity to achieve power has been made famous by Gandhi in India's long history of struggle against British colonialism, but also by the martyrs and would-be martyrs in many an internal struggle (for example, the struggle for linguistic states) since Independence.

General Characteristics.   There will be more emigration from this type of society than from those of Type A because the peoples will not only be propelled by hunger, but also motivated by pilgrimage. However, Type C peoples disperse less easily than Type B because their societies have no inherent tendency to explosion as have their Western counterparts. When peoples from this type of society move to a new area, they tend not to set up a new society that is completely independent from their old one. To that extent they are like Type A peoples such as the Chinese and the Japanese. On the other hand, there is also no such great urge as exhibited by the Chinese and the Japanese to return to their homeland for retirement or death. Under conquest peoples in this type of society tend to act like those of Type A, except that, because of the centrifugal tendencies inherent in their supernatural orientation, the conquerors will find them more difficult to administer than Type A peoples.

At home they will show more dissatisfaction with the status quo than the Chinese or Japanese, and will be more vociferous about their dissatisfaction. This is in tune with a centrifugal outlook. Most religions embody contradictions, but they see little or no necessity to reconcile highly obvious incongruities in their religious beliefs as well as in their secular life which is governed by religion. Hence, historical changes in their society due to internal impetus are as insignificant as among Type A peoples.

Their art and literature tend to be richer than that found in Type A such as China or Japan with reference to the imaginative and emotive qualities, but poorer than that of the Occidental societies in the logical and rationalistic qualities. Their music is neither Oriental nor Occidental, being based on the most refined and complicated rhythmic patterns and tonal elaborations the world has ever seen. Interest in the unknown and unseen, which is a form of discontinuity (from reality), is essential for the development of pure music, unrelated to concrete human plots. Hindu music must be regarded as one of the two (along with Western) great musical traditions of human history. Supernatural dependence imbues nearly all Hindu music with religious significance, like Hindu art and literature. This is in sharp contrast to its Chinese counterpart in which the role of religion is negligible to non-existent. However, since the Hindu interest in the unseen is so strongly tied to the supernatural, and so permeated with unilateral dependence, it led to few theoretical and practical contributions in science.

Central Government. These peoples tend to develop multiple national states. In essence, the states are not authoritarian or democratic as in the West, but are autocratic as among Type A peoples. Political and other relationships are secured either by exaggerated external signs of differentiation between those who are in power or superior and those who are not or inferior (caste is an example), or on the basis of brutal power (conquest) or by supernatural qualities (magic or austerity). The rule of man in the name of the supernatural overshadows the impersonal laws of the state. Universal education and universal military service were unknown before contact with the West, but there tends to be more direct interaction between the ruler and the people than in Type A societies. The discontinuity of the primary grouping and the supernatural orientation propel the individual toward wider alliances. Therefore, political leaders in India can exert a greater active influence over their followers than can their counterparts in Type A societies. In spite of and probably also because of this, the stability of the central authority is always in question. The diffuse outlook and the many diverse issues, objects, and personalities enjoying great separate public enthusiasms tend to make large and tight organization difficult. Hence, their written languages tend to change much more in time and space than do those of their Chinese or Japanese counterpart.

Religion. Since they are supernatural-oriented and diffuse in their efforts in seeking help, their gods multiply much more freely than in Type A societies. The Hindus have more gods than any other known people on earth. Yet, there is also an opposite tendency to view the multitude of gods as diverse expressions or part and parcel of the same Supreme Being.

Hindus, more than the Chinese and Japanese, are occasionally divided somewhat in religion. There is, however, no irreconcilable schism among the believers. In fact, even those who call themselves Vaishnavats (worshippers of Vishnu) or Saivats (worshippers of Shiva) tend not to neglect, and certainly not to be contemptuous toward, other gods.

Theology is more important than in Type A societies but much less important than in Type B societies. The central dogma is always obscure. Where clarified, it comes to no more than the negative ideas of "action

with nonattachment," or extreme "devotional love." Theological literature increases largely through the increase of rituals and to a lesser extent
through protestant movements. But religious truths tend to be relative, so
that the elite and the common man are understood to possess different
grades of knowledge about God and different experiences with Him, which
are considered equally valid. There will be far more reform or protestant
movements in Hinduism than in the religion of the Chinese and the
Japanese, but such protestant movements do not seem to succeed in really
dividing the believers. This is why the remnants of Buddhism in India
were merely absorbed by Hinduism instead of existing as a rival creed.
Jainism, Sikkhism, and so forth remained in India but have become caste
groups in the same Hindu fold. Contrary to popular misconception, riots
between the Hindus and Moslems are of post-British origin and very
recent. It is a well-known fact that Hindus and Moslems lived and still live
peacefully in close proximity in the villages (Murphy 1953). The Hindus
are probably as difficult to convert to any monotheistic belief as peoples of
Type A, except for specific reasons of social and economic improvement.
One of the basic reasons for Hindu conversion to Mohammedanism was
the lowly position of the Untouchables who hoped to better themselves.

Over and above these general characteristics, the Hindu approach to
religion, like that of the Chinese and Westerners, reflects even more clearly
the basic content in the Hindu kinship system. The Type A peoples, with
the dominance of the father-son dyad and their permanent web of vertical
and horizontal kinship relationships, need their gods and goddesses for
functional and utilitarian purposes. They cannot get excited about their
supernaturals unless the latter can satisfy their materialistic requests. Type
B peoples, with the dominance of the husband-wife dyad and their
impermanent human relationships, in the long run need their gods to be
masculine, stern, single-minded, and exclusive, though this stress on
masculinity applies more to Western Protestants than Western Catholics.

The gods of Type C peoples, though represented bisexually, are
basically more feminine than masculine. No other people worship as many
female deities as the Hindus. Not only did recent popular revolutionary
writers like Bankim Chandra Chatterjee sing of India's aspirations to
Mother and not only do modern Indians refer to Bharat Mata (Mother
India), but also the mother goddess in the form of Kali, Durga, Radha,
Sita, Parvati, Chumundeshvari, or the wife of Ramakrishna, founder of
the modern Protestant movement bearing his name, is worshipped in
every part of India. Moreover, in Indian popular mythology the gods

sometimes change themselves into females for sexual purposes.

One famous tale concerns Vishnu and Shiva, who were so intoxicated by the scenery they saw together that Vishnu changed himself into a female so that the two could have a sexual union on the spot to enjoy themselves. Today, there are temples in West and South India in which are worshipped gods each representing half of one and half of the other sex, or half Vishnu and half Shiva. Finally, the Hindu devotee's approach to the supernatural is predominantly what, for want of a better term, may be described as "feminine."

I am aware that Margaret Mead in her classic work on *Sex and Temperament* has stressed the notion that cross-culturally, psychological characteristics are not peculiar to either sex. Whether we call the Hindu devotee's approach "feminine" or not is immaterial. What is relevant is that this approach is characterized by traits which traditionally in the West have been subsumed under the term "femininity." I mention this term here to help me clarify my position on the subject. Like other peoples, the Hindus resort to all sorts of rituals to coerce or channelize many gods and spirits according to their wishes, but one age-old and most widespread Hindu approach to the supernatural is austerity (fasting, abstention, suffering, and so forth) to get what one wants. This method is so frequently used in Indian mythology, history, and contemporary worship, not only by men to coerce gods, but also by one god to coerce other gods, that it is sheer redundancy to mention it more than in passing.

The more modern version of the same approach is represented by the Bhakti movement begun by Chaitanya of Bengal about 250 years ago, the central theme of which is to love God (the Lord Krishna) as though the worshipper is the God's illicit sweetheart (Radha). In South India an outstanding devotee using this approach would be Kshetranja, the composer and performer of God-love songs and dances. Foreign visitors and observers have often been so shocked by the proliferation of sexual representation in Hindu temples that they project into it much that is profane, but non-Hindus and some modern Hindus, scholars, and others, have understandably been defensive about this by trying to explain the sexual elements away from them altogether. What we can say is that the Hindu attitude is characterized by passivity, submissiveness, diffuse eroticism which, if not feminine in character, is certainly different from that found among Type A and Type B peoples.[18]

Prejudice.   The attributes of exclusiveness and discontinuity of Type B

[18] For a fuller discussion of diffuseness in sexuality in Hindu religion see Hsu 1963.

seem to be related to the greatest exhibition of prejudice, in contrast to those of inclusiveness and continuity in the kinship system of Type A, which seem to be related to the least exhibition of prejudice. The contrast in prejudice has been more fully dealt with in a previous chapter (Chapter 7, American Core Values and National Character). The Hindu kinship system, being dominated by the mother-son dyad, occupies in this regard an intermediary position. It is more inclusive than that of Type B but less so than that of Type A; it is more continuous than that of Type B but less so than that of Type A. This would seem to be commensurate with the fact that prejudice, though strongly present in the form of caste, untouchability, and Hindu-Moslem riot, is without finality. That is to say, there are obvious and above-board mechanisms for crossing the caste lines or for raising the statuses of entire castes. For example, even the extremists in casteism accept the premise that the lower castes and higher castes are one in the reincarnation scheme. That is why some Untouchables or Sudras can become holy men whom even the higher caste people may worship. Then, the caste of meritorious individuals had often been changed by edicts of kings and princes. Finally, the place of entire low castes, such as the Reddy of Andbra and Kayastha of Bengal, were raised by reason of their numbers of occupation. The entire question of caste in India is treated in a separate publication (Hsu 1963) and need not be detailed here. There is some witchhunting in Type C societies but it is moderate, like that in nonliterate societies of Type D.[19]

Impetus to Change.   To the extent that there is more internal dissatisfaction with the status quo in such societies than in Types A and D, there should have been more internal tendency toward change. But this pressure for change is greatly undercut by the diffuseness of its direction and objectives. Over a long period of time, there tend to be changes in appearance but not in substance. This is probably a partial explanation for the fact that of all the large status-oriented societies of the East and West, only India built up a total caste system,[20] the numerous princely states, and the highly differentiated nature of the endogamic circles within each caste. The Hindu caste system is an accommodation between the two opposites: change and no change (Hsu 1963). There have always been many centrifugal tendencies but there have never been any revolutions

[19]The complex psychocultural basis of caste in India is treated intensively in *Clan, Caste and Club*, Hsu (1963).

[20]Japan has a partial caste system, in which only the *Eta* are totally separated from the rest of the society. For differences among Hindu, Japanese, and the United States societies with reference to caste, see Hsu 1971b.

and/or utopias which aimed at achieving a new way of life on this earth. These types of societies are less likely to die out than the Western variety, either from loss of resources or from external conquest. The peoples of this type of societies have a similar ability to endure suffering as those of Type A, even though they may appear more unhappy about it because of their tendency to voice their dissatisfaction with the status quo. The peoples in this type of societies are somewhat more likely to take to changes than their brethren in Type A, once they are under the pressure of, and given direction by, the West, though the permanency of the new changes is questionable.

Type D Societies

Type D societies are to be found among the majority of the Africans south of the Sahara.

Kinship. The kinship structures are varied and the basic unit in which the infant finds himself may be large or small. There is no ideal of individualism or supernatural dependence as a road to personal salvation. The structural element in systems of kinship which seems to have a great deal of dominance over others is the brother-brother dyad, across lines of descent, inheritance, and succession.

Similar to the father-son and mother-son dyads, the brother-brother relationship is inclusive. But similar to the husband-wife and mother-son dyads, it is discontinuous. There is always more than one brother, but the brothers of each generation have no intrinsic relationship with the brothers of another generation. To the extent that the individual tends to be oriented little toward the past and the future but much toward the present, the brother-brother dyad is similar to the husband-wife dyad. And to the extent that the individual is conditioned to be mutually dependent among the peers, the brother-brother dyad is similar to the father-son dyad. But the feature which distinguishes the brother-brother relationship from all other dyads, including the husband-wife dyad, is its inherent competitiveness but especially rivalry. Where there is acknowledged unequalness between the parties of a relationship, there is little potential source of competitiveness. This is the situation of the father-son and mother-son dyads. The father and the son or the mother and the son are not equal. In the husband-wife dyad the relationship may be equal in conception but never really equal in reality, for men and women are different and they are bound to perform different roles and have different affective ties with their children, however such differences are minimized by cultural factors. The brother-brother dyad is one in which the parties to the relationship are more equal and more similar than the parties to any of the other three dyads and, therefore, more competitive but especially rivalrous with each other. Competitiveness is milder than rivalry. In the former the opponents seek a common objective, while in the latter they seek mutual replacement or even destruction.

The overall kinship content correlated with the brother-brother relationship is fraternal equivalence. But before I go into the characteristics of fraternal equivalence I must enter a word of caution for my readers.

In the analysis of the African situation I am on far less certain ground than in what has gone before. My views on the previous systems are based on my own field observations as well as extensive acquaintance with works of my colleagues. I have had no field experience in Africa, having visited parts of it for only short periods of time, and my acquaintance with anthropological works on Africa is far more limited. Nevertheless, what I have read so far has emboldened me to make this exploration, following the same trend of analysis which I have pursued so far, and to hope that the results will stimulate further works in this direction.

In analyzing Types A, B, and C peoples, I have first examined the characteristics of a particular structural relationship which dominates the kinship system; then proceeded to relate those characteristics to the overall kinship content; and finally extended the latter characteristics to the attitudes and ideas underlying the wider culture as a whole. In analyzing Africa I shall reverse the first two, by discussing first content of the kinship system and then stating my case for expecting the dominance of the particular structural dyad in question.

Like Type A and Type C societies, Type D peoples raise their children to enter into adult worlds as soon as they are physically and mentally capable of doing so. They do not attribute great value to individual privacy. These two facts favor a community of interest between the generations. But in spite of such resemblances to Type A societies, the kinship situation is one in which the ties between generations are overshadowed by those between males of the same generation.

First, the claims to dependence between parents and their children seem to require constant reiteration or open gestures to meet with satisfaction. The fear against overclaim and against nonfulfillment of expected claims is indicated by the almost univeral belief in sorcery or witchcraft among close family members, especially between parents and children (between mother's brother and sister's son in matrilineal systems), and between other individuals, who are related as seniors and juniors, but almost none between brothers and others, who are related as equals (Middleton and Winter 1963).

Secondly, though some African societies — Dahomey, Yoruba, many Bantu tribes, and others — maintain rites designed to deal with the dead, they and their ancestral spirits do not have unquestioned reliance upon one another. The living may regard the dead as possible sources of benevolence but more constantly suspect them as possible sources of harm; while the dead always enforce their demand on the living for sacrifices and offerings by means of disasters such as epidemics and personal accidents imposed on their descendants (see *e.g.,* LeVine 1966 and Middleton 1960). More recent work involving other African societies (Gusii and Lugbara) has lent further support to this observation (Tatje and Hsu 1969).

Thirdly, in many instances the African word translated into English as ancestors simply means spirit or god. In most cases there is a tendency for ancestral spirits to lose their identity and connection with their own descendants, so that ancestral spirits are simply one of the several mechanisms (equally important) for human beings to reach the supernatural, or the connection with the past is simply a means for vindicating the status of the present.

Fourthly, strong age-grading customs prevail in most parts of Africa except among people like Dahomean and Bantu of North Kavirondo (Wagner 1949) so that the youngsters, after reaching a certain age, leave their parental houses for their own separate quarters and/or by the well-known phenomenon of secret societies in which members maintain strong bonds outside of kinship. The children may or may not be directly dependent upon initiatory rites, but such rites are undoubtedly as important in Africa as they are insignificant in Asia. The relationship among the youngsters so separated from their parents may range from that of intimate friends, such as the "best friend" institution in Dahomey (Herskovits 1938a), to what has been described as a kind of "communist" order such as found among the Umbundu (Childs 1949:114–115). Among the Nyakyusa of Nyasaland the age set has become more highly institutionalized than perhaps among all other peoples. The boy of Nyakyusa progressively severs his ties with his natal family long before he is ready to marry and have children of his own. He is then enmeshed in an age set which forms the basis of his own social structure for the rest of his life (Wilson 1951).[21]

Fifth, although parents and other elders can exercise an authoritative hand over members of the younger generation, the latter seem to exhibit much more independence of thought and action than in Type A societies. In some African societies the pattern is even described as "respect" for the personality of the children (Childs 1949:120–121). In practically all known African societies the young tend to have to work for the establishment of their own homes and their own marriages, as well as to exercise rather decisive influences over the choice of their own spouses. In addition there is much evidence indicating a linkage in the marriage payments and obligations between brothers and sisters (Radcliffe-Brown 1950:52–53).

Sixth, while the institution of blood-brotherhood (that is, a group of unrelated men usually of similar age swearing themselves into a brotherhood by rites involving letting or exchanging of blood) is found sporadically in diverse parts of the world including Europe and Asia, its prevalence in Africa south of the Sahara and outside of Ethiopia is well known. It is said that a blood brother is a "much better friend than a real brother" (Tegnaeus 1952:13ff.).

Finally, while the problem of royal succession is nowhere on earth near a perfect solution, it seems to assume extraordinary proportions in many parts of Africa. Tor Irstam of the Ethnographical Museum of Sweden has made a study of the sacral kingship in Africa in which he surveys many traits (he calls them "institutions") connected with the coronation, life, and death of the king in 103 tribes from existing ethnographic reports. Four of the traits are particularly relevant to the question of succession: (1) "The announcement of the king's death was followed by a period of anarchy"; (2) "the king's death was kept secret for a certain time"; (3) "the king's brothers were killed"; and (4) "the king was challenged to a 'ritual combat'" (Irstam 1944:78–166).

We must, of course, exercise much caution in ascertaining the meanings given to each fact by the particular people among whom it occurs. Thus, among the Ganda the king's ritual combat sometimes led to actual fighting which was "continued until only one of the rival princes was left alive," but among the Nyoro, as far as the ethnographer was able to

---

[21] In a comprehensive treatise on age groups all over the world, Eisenstadt's examples from the "Primitive" and "Semihistorical" societies are all taken from Africa (over 40 tribes and groups of tribes) except for ancient Sparta, five of the Plains Indians groups in North America, Irish peasants, some tribes in India, and some vague allusions to ancient Inca and Aztec empires (Eisenstadt 1956).

determine, "only actual fighting for the throne occurred" (Irstam 1944:62). Again, the custom of the newly crowned king going into a certain period of solitude was practiced "to avoid his brothers' envy and conspiring" but the same sentiment was not reported for the other tribes with a similar custom. For this reason, this last-mentioned usage is not included in our list of traits considered as supporting our contention that the problem of royal succession seems extraordinarily severe, and that the magnitude of this problem is related to the importance of the kinship content of fraternal equivalence which undermines the vertical continuity.

From Irstam's study we have 62 tribes (or over 60 percent of his total) in which at least one of the four traits or customs indicating succession difficulties was found. Trait No. 2 ("The king's death was kept secret for a certain time") was found among the largest number of tribes, 32. Trait No. 1 ("The announcement of the king's death was followed by a period of anarchy") was found among the second largest number of tribes, 19. The other two traits are found among 7 (Trait No. 3) and 10 (Trait No. 4) tribes, respectively. From the logical point of view the four traits are obviously interrelated. The fraternal contention for the throne will lead to suppression of the news of the king's death, which when released leads to a period of anarchy, and for both of which the killing of the king's brothers seems to be a reasonable solution. The ritual combat to which the king is challenged could be considered a formalized version of the actual fight which frequently occurs among the contenders.

A tabulation of the occurrence of these traits shows a high degree of correlation among them and indeed supports this thesis. The correlation is less pronounced between Trait No. 2 and others (out of 51, 19 are correlated with one or more other traits) than between Trait No. 1 and others (out of 19, 17 are so correlated). (See the table on p. 552.)

It is on the basis of the foregoing facts that I expect the dominance of the brother-brother dyad in a majority of African kinship structures over other dyads. I frankly admit that I have as yet insufficient direct data except in a few African societies, such as the Kyakyusa age-set villages already referred to (Radcliffe-Brown and Forde, eds., 1950:111–138). However, I feel strongly that if future students of African tribes will explore this hypothesis, their chances of being rewarded are likely to be good. Furthermore, the theory of tribal and lineage segmentation developed by Africanists like Evans-Pritchard and Fortes in which the peoples are said to live in "ordered anarchy" (Evans-Pritchard 1940b:181) and in which corresponding segments oppose each other, suggests that horizontal or fraternal solidarity and opposition are actually far more important in African kinship system than are parent-child and other relationships.

Distribution of Traits among Tribes*

Trait or Trait Combination	Tribe	Total Number of Tribes in Category
No. 1	Kabinda, Ha	2
Nos. 1 & 2	Dahomey, Konde, Kuba, Luba, Lunda, Mbundu, Nyamwezi, Pare, Shambala	9
Nos. 1 & 3	Wydah (Wadai) (?)	1
Nos. 1, 2 & 3	Abyssinia	1
Nos. 1, 2, & 4	Congo, Loango, Ruanda, Shilluk	4
Nos. 1, 2, 3 & 4	Ganda, Nyoro	2
No. 2	Ashante, Bena, Camba, Comendi, Daka, Djaga, Gbande, Gissi, Gogo, Hona, Igara, Yoruba, Jukun, Kam, Kanakuru, Kimbu, Konongo, Kpelle, Mbum, Ngoni, Safwa, Sango, Saramo, Shona, Soga, Sove, Temne, Tikai, Toma, Vende, Zeguha, Zulu	32
Nos. 2 & 3	Kaffitsho	1
Nos. 2 & 4	Tonga, Nkole	2
No. 3	Limmu, Koki, Benin	3
Nos. 3 & 4	Rundi	1
No. 4	Umundri, Moossi, Ziba, Toro	4
	Total	62

*Greater statistical sophistication is not attempted at this stage of the analysis. This must be done later when more precise data become available.

Since the first publication of this analysis in 1961, more intensive data on the problem of succession in Bornu, a West African kingdom, have become available (Cohen 1966, 1967, 1971). They bear out the extraordinary succession difficulties outlined by earlier authors, notwithstanding the prolonged existence of the Kanuri Kingdom in time. Furthermore, according to Cohen, in no African society is there a regularization of succession (personal communication). The political instability of newly independent African nations in the last two decades, from Nigeria, the Congo, to Uganda, seems further to be symptomatic of the problem discussed here.

General Characteristics.   In contrast to Type B societies the individual here will have less urge to leave home because there is no need to prove his worth elsewhere. But in contrast to Type A societies the individual here will also be more easily forced to do so by nature (population pressure, epidemics, and so forth), or by human enemies (war, conquest, and so forth), because of lack of strong anchorage with the past. The overall kinship content of fraternal equivalence makes possible larger expansion of human relationships than in Type A. That is to say, whereas in Type A societies the individual is encouraged to think lineally and to regard himself as a link in an endless chain connecting the past with the future, in Type D societies he is encouraged to think horizontally and to gravitate toward contemporaries far and near. But the relationships thus formed may be less stable than in Type A societies. Therefore, once forced to move they tend to be more ready than Type A peoples to give up much of the past and make *new* adjustments on *new* bases. Some of them, like the Masai, might resist innovation in their modes of livelihood but some have gone from dry cultivation of rice to wet cultivation of rice (Linton 1939). Others might start with a well-defined monarchial system and disintegrate into a context of contending nobles, none of whom has any central authority (Evans-Pritchard 1940a:51–61). In Southern Rhodesia, there are ruins of one or more rock cultures of perhaps only 1,500 or 1,000 years ago, or less, which are probably ancestral to the cultures of some of the modern Bantu groups (such as Ba Vanda) but with which the latter today claim no psychocultural affiliation (Caton-Thompson 1931). On the other hand, in the nonliterate world, Africa is one of the continents where trade contacts, team work, and group dances (ritual and otherwise) were most extensive and impressive. The magnitude of their messianic-movements against conquest and oppression, within or without the Christian Church, in Africa or in the New World (Herskovits 1938b), is without parallel among other peoples in similar circumstances.

Compared with Type A peoples, they have less determination to resist external cultural pressures or to absorb the invaders and to restore their past glory; but compared with other nonliterate peoples they are much more indomitable because of their tendency to group themselves horizontally. They do not easily give up the struggle for political independence. However, their fraternal solidarity is undermined by much opposition which some psychoanalysts could easily see as sibling rivalry. The Type B peoples form many effective nonkinship groups to revolt against the past. Type A peoples form few effective nonkinship groups because they have solidarity with the past. But the most important attributes of Type D peoples' kinship content is rooted in the fact that the brother-brother dyad is discontinuous with both past and future at the same time that it is internally rivalrous. The difficulties of the horizontal groupings of Type D peoples are due, outside of foreign domination, primarily to the fact that they are their own worst enemies.

As a rule they have no written languages even though they must have at one time or another come into contact with either the Egyptian hieroglyphics or the Indo-European alphabets. My inference is that the assumption of a written language, even though its elements may have been borrowed, as were those of a majority of mankind who have written languages, depends upon a strong need for a wide circle of communication and for a permanent preservation of the relationships with the past, and requires a concerted and continuous group exertion. Most peoples of Type D obviously did not feel the need and were not willing or prepared to make the necessary efforts.

Central Government. Though some of these peoples have developed centralized national states, or at any rate some forms of externally recognized chieftainship, the political domains are not likely to reach the extent of some of those found among Types A or B, nor are they likely to be as stable. We have already related the succession difficulties of African chieftainship. A reverse support for this thesis is seen in the degree of correlation in Africa between more centralized political organizations under autocratic kings or chiefs, and a somewhat more well-defined ancestor cult in Africa. A preliminary survey, without meaning to be exhaustive, shows the correlation to hold in the following African tribes: Bemba, Lozi, Ngoni, Nyakyusa (Colson and Gluckman 1951:1–93, 164–291), Dahomey (Herskovits 1938a), Kikuyu (Kenyatta 1939), Yoruba (Bascom 1944), Tanala (Linton 1933), Jukun (Meek 1931), Shilluk (Hofmayr 1925 and Seligman 1932), Baganda (Roscoe 1911), Fanti (Christensen 1954), Kgatla (Schapera 1941), Ankole, Zulu, and Mgwato (Fortes and Evans-Pritchard (ed.) 1940:25–82, 121–164).

The following African tribes seem to have little belief in ancestral spirits coupled with unclear, vague or lack of centralized tribal organization: Tonga, Yao, Shona tribes (Colson and Gluckman 1951:94–163, 292–395), Lang (Driberg 1923), and Anuak (Evans-Pritchard 1940a).[22] The few

[22] A well-defined ancestor cult includes the following basic elements: a. the belief in the existence of ancestral spirits; b. the belief that all ancestral spirits are interested only in their own living descendants and can affect their welfare; c. shrines, sacred places or tombs where offerings and sacrifices are made to the ancestors regularly or on special occasions from facts already noted. Ancestor cult in most African societies cannot be described as well-defined. The usual African pattern is that only a few of the ancestors are remembered and made offerings to, that the ancestral spirits so honored tend to be merged with other gods, and, therefore, not necessarily worshipped only by their own descendants because the spirits' interest is wider and more vague.

tribes known to me in which this correlation does not seem to obtain are Tallensi (Fortes and Evans-Pritchard 1940:239–271), and several tribes composing the Bantu Kavirondo (Fortes and Evans-Pritchard 1940:197–236, and Wagner 1949:277–288), which have a somewhat more well defined ancestor cult but no centralized tribal organization. The clearest negative cases are those of the Nuer and the Tiv who have no belief in ancestral spirits and no centralized tribal organization of any kind (Evans-Pritchard 1940; Fortes and Evans-Pritchard 1940:272–296; and Laura and Paul Bohannan 1953).[23]

The reason for this correlation between more centralized political authority and better-defined ancestor cult has already been suggested with reference to Type A peoples: submission to parental authority and to long lines of ancestors and continuity with the past in general pave the way to ties with the wider government.

In line with the fact that the kinship content is fraternal equivalence, the centralized governments tend to be somewhat "democratic." The word "democratic" is used to denote the fact that, while at any given time the ruler of such a government may have the power of life and death over his subjects, he tends to remain in touch or in direct contact with them and to be at their mercy. In Type A societies, the ruler will not be in any close contact with the people and there tends to be no occasion on which the

[23] Both Fortes and Evans-Pritchard speak elaborately of political organization when in fact only some kinship or lineage system prevails. This problem has been dealt with elsewhere (Hsu 1959).

One group, the Ngoni, has a centralized political organization but about whom the ethnographer reports no present evidence of ancestor cult (Colson and Gluckman 1951:194–252). Judging by the case of Nupi (and probably that of Kede, a formerly independent group within the Nupi kingdom) who have well-defined political organization but are presently Moslems (Fortes and Evans-Pritchard 1940:165–195, and Nadel 1947), complete absence of ancestor cult among the Ngoni is inconclusive. For the Nupi, though converted to Islam, hold to their mythical ancestor-king, Tsoede, as of basic importance to whom annual sacrifices are made, recite long lists of illustrious ancestors of noblemen at public functions, and consider the Tsoede's grave and relics as the most sacred treasures they possess (Nadel 1947:66–67, 72, 85, 130, and so forth). In addition, we find: "We shall see that the ruling house of Nupe crystallized in three dynasties, which trace their descent from different sons of the founder of the ruling house, and divide between them the rights and duties vested in the ruling house. The ancestors of the three dynasties lived only two or three generations back; but already certain religious observances (prayers on their grave) mark them off from all subsequent royal ancestors. In this rigidly defined system of reckoning descent in the father's line back to these almost sanctified 'first ancestors' and in the relationship with one another which is in the nature of mutual obligations for the sake of the larger unit, the royal house itself, the three dynasties correspond, from kinship point of view, to incipient "clans" — the only analogy to clan structure which we find in Nupe" (Nadel 1947:33). It is probably, therefore, not unreasonable to suggest that in pre-Islam days the Nupi did have some sort of ancestor cult.

people can as a matter of convention turn out to see the ruler in person. In Type B societies, the people demand to see the ruler in person, whether upon his return from the Crusades or from the victory at Verdun, essentially to admire him as a hero for what he has done, for his shining armor, or for his stately bearing and good looks. The modern Western tendency of criticizing their heads of states for poor taste or calling them by shortened names like "Ike" or "Jack" is but a variety of the same underlying attitude. The ruler-subject relationship in Type D societies differs from either in some respects but combines both in other ways. Here the ruler can and must maintain direct contact with his subjects under specified conditions. In order to maintain his power among psychological equals he must awe and exact obedience from them. His person is surrounded with taboos and restrictions, and as a rule his subjects treat him with great ceremony often including prostration before him so as to avoid his sight (Bascom 1951; Gluckman, 1951; Herskovits 1938a:Vol. II; Meek 1931; Oberg 1940; and others).[24]

The other feature in which the ruler-subject relationship in Type D societies distinguishes itself is that the ruler always seems to be very much at the mercy of his subjects, or at any rate many of them. The despotic position of the rulers of Lozi (Gluckman 1951) or Dahomey (Herskovits 1938, Vol. 2:22–48) may appear absolute enough. But in most Type D societies the power of the ruler is basically diffused, residing in the hands of his chief councils, ministers, Queen Mother, lesser dignitaries, and even the commoners. In 50 percent of the 103 African tribes surveyed by Irstam, the king was killed under various stipulations (1944:146). Even where the custom of killing the physically weakening king does not prevail, the ruler is likely to be subject to election and deposition by the courtiers and/or by many of the people (Fortes and Evans-Pritchard 1940; Colson and Gluckman 1951; and Bascom personal communication). The fact is that if a considerable number of the people are opposed to the ruler in a Type D society, or even show no interest in him, there is very little that such a man can do to force the obedience of the people. He will simply be unable to find instruments for the implementation or enforce-

---

[24] The King of Ife in Yorubaland makes, for example, according to W. R. Bascom, two public appearances before his subjects every year. One is for the worship of the Deity Orishanla and the other for the worship of two other deities. On the first occasion no subject is allowed to see him. Everybody is required to go home and lock their windows and doors, and if caught peeking, will be beaten. On the second occasion the King appears with great fanfare and the whole town turns out prostrating before him. At all other times the king is not even supposed to leave the palace (personal communication).

ment of his rule. The rulers in Types A and B, though limited by their subjects in the long run, are much more secure, and, therefore, more absolute in their rule at any given point of time.

Religion. The beliefs in Type D societies will range from simple animism to personified gods. Their religious mythology tends to be matter of fact, which offers common sense answers to problems of origin or of daily life. Their supernatural beings, often mixed with ancestral spirits, are valued more or less for concrete ends. There is no missionary zeal or movement. There is no systematic theology as the West knows it. Jealousy between rival priests is reported, but religious strife on theological or denominational basis cannot be expected. Like Type A peoples they do not fight religious wars. New gods are introduced as in Types A and C societies, but having little feeling for vertical continuity with the past or with the unfathomable Ultimate Reality, gods are much more replaceable than in Types A and C societies. In fact, Africa is the only continent outside Europe in which entire societies such as the Basuku simply gave up their own gods wholesale and without a struggle in favor of the missionary's holy water (Igor Kopytoff 1960).

Prejudice. There tends to be no racial or religious prejudice of the Western kind, except that learned from their present or former colonial masters. Rivalry and strife among medicine men or priests, or between different ethnic or linguistic groups, will occur as it will wherever there is conflict or practical interests. African societies believe in witches and conduct witch hunts. But what has so far escaped the attention of students who have made specific contributions on the subject (Evans-Pritchard 1937; Kluckhohn 1944) and the students who contributed to one special number of *Africa* (1935, Vol. VIII, No. 4) is that witch hunting in all nonliterate and Type A and C societies is relativistic while its counterpart in the West is absolutistic. For example, Western "witches," convicted or suspected, were rarely spared, while "witches" in all other societies can be freed from such punishment by material compensation from their families. In nonliterate societies there are always counterwitchcraft measures or white magics which are essentially the same sort of acts as those employed (alleged or actual) by the witches or the sorcerers, but which are greatly valued by the people (Wolfe 1954:853–856). Possessors of such counter-witchcraft measures may even achieve positions of influence (Browne 1929; Hogbin 1934:216; Firth 1954:103 and 113–115). The question has been dealt with elsewhere (Hsu 1960).

Impetus to Change. Because the individual can more or less reach his proper station among fellow men through the kinship framework, there is, as in Type A, little internal impetus to change. But since the solidarity within the kinship groups is far less than that in Type A, there is not the same centripetal force to resist deviation. In fact, there is evidence that a daring member of the society, if he is really determined, can actually break some of the traditional rules by personal initiative. Witness the way in which incest taboos can be and are actually broken in spite of the threat of death penalty, which is rarely carried out to the extent that they are formally threatened (Hsu 1940). But although they tend to have more *nonkinship* groupings than in Type A societies, such as age-set villages and secret societies, which seriously claim the individual's allegiance and attention, such ties remain concrete but not idealistic in nature. Therefore, customs, whether considered by the West as good or evil, tend to perpetuate themselves since no individuals or groups will take it upon themselves to eradicate them. Too, although they have many more revolts against their rulers than would be the case among Type A societies, they also know no such thing as revolution of an internal origin, which aims at not only changing the ruler but also the social order. Having no written languages, their opportunities for accumulation of knowledge and ideas from the past and for stimulation within the society are much more limited than among Type A, B, and C peoples. This fact actually gives such societies, in spite of their greater instability, fewer internal chances for cultural evolution than Type A societies.

Concluding Remarks

This chapter is no more than what its title suggests: an exploration. It is offered in the spirit of a Chinese proverb: "Throw the bricks to lead in the jade." More recent works on this hypothesis by other scholars have considerably advanced its utility (Tatje and Hsu 1969, Hsu (ed.) 1971a). In spite of the latter certain precautions must be kept in mind. In the first place, there are, of course, many facts which cannot be squeezed into the categories postulated, although as pointed out before, no scientific classification covers all the facts. In the second place, many differences do exist within each of the types postulated. Take prejudice, for example. Obviously, not all societies in Type B are equally prejudiced. The pattern of variation in prejudice coincides roughly with that of variation in individualism. In Europe, racial prejudice is more pronounced in Britain and Germany, where individualism is stronger, than in Spain and Italy where it is weaker. This difference becomes magnified when European peoples settle in colonies. As a matter of fact, there is almost a complete dichotomy with Protestant colonies, including the United States, Canada (the word "colony" is applied to these independent countries in a historical and cultural sense), Union of South Africa, East Africa, and Australia, showing more racial prejudice than Catholic colonies from French Equatorial Africa, Portuguese East Africa, to Mexico and all South American republics.[25]

The diversity in patterns of life among nonliterate tribes, even of one in sub-Sahara Africa, is both great and obvious.

The relationship between kinship structure, kinship content, and way of life postulated in this chapter must be seen as circular or spiral, with all variables boosting or limiting each other in time, rather than in the manner of a straight line, with one variable being the ultimate cause of another. The circular or spiral relationship in the four types of societies may be crudely represented in the following diagrams.

The peoples belonging to each of the four types of kinship systems presented here enjoy some obvious advantages and suffer from some obvious drawbacks. Continuity in Type A is an advantage because it provides the individual with psychological security, but it can be a drawback because it restrains the individual's initiative. With reference to the discontinuity of Type B, the order of advantage versus disadvantage is exactly the reverse. Type C peoples may be more diffused in outlook than others but among them we find more individuals reaching great heights of spirituality than among others. Type D peoples may fight more among themselves, but their kinship content is the only one of the four which seems truly consistent with universal brotherhood of man.

Finally, the kinship structure and content of a people obviously form only one of the variables, though a most important one, affecting its development. The physical facts of size of population and ecology may have a great deal to do with it. Firth's description of Tikopian family, clan, and ancestor cult (Firth 1936) bears great resemblance to what we find in

[25] New Zealand is a possible exception so far. There the relationship between the Protestant whites and the Maoris shows greater harmony than that between the indigenous populations and white settlers elsewhere. There are some peculiar but complex reasons for this which are not as yet systematically explored. One of these reasons is that the Europeans never scored decisive victories over the Maoris in battle. Another reason is that Maori values seem to have a great deal of affinity toward other nonwhites, the significance of the nature of their relationship with the Maoris remains inconclusive. According to recent reports, the situation in Angola seems to be one other exception. But the usual defect in such reports is their failure to distinguish politically and militarily oppressive actions from the continued and tenacious prejudice in day-to-day life. A truer picture must await more intensive researches.

China (Tatje and Hsu 1969 and Rohlen 1971), but factors other than kinship (for example, life on isolated islands as compared with that on a vast continent) obviously have some important bearing on why the

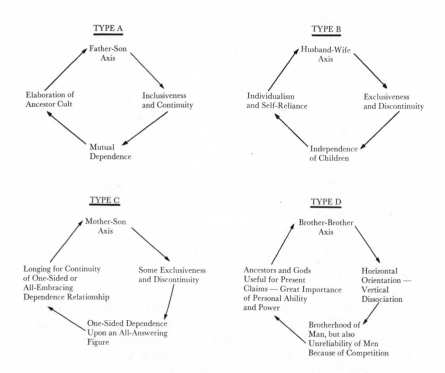

TYPE A

Father-Son
Axis

Elaboration of
Ancestor Cult

Inclusiveness
and Continuity

Mutual
Dependence

TYPE B

Husband-Wife
Axis

Individualism
and Self-Reliance

Exclusiveness
and Discontinuity

Independence
of Children

TYPE C

Mother-Son
Axis

Longing for Continuity
of One-Sided or
All-Embracing
Dependence Relationship

Some Exclusiveness
and Discontinuity

One-Sided Dependence
Upon an All-Answering
Figure

TYPE D

Brother-Brother
Axis

Ancestors and Gods
Useful for Present
Claims — Great Importance
of Personal Ability
and Power

Horizontal
Orientation —
Vertical
Dissociation

Brotherhood of
Man, but also
Unreliability of Men
Because of Competition

Tikopia did not develop vast empires such as those of the Chinese. Other important factors in the development of peoples are the presence or absence of external threats of conquest, of inter-tribal or international communication and stimulation, and perhaps even climatic conditions and biological compositions.

The error of some students lies in their attempt to produce final explanations for all by one factor. But the error of some others lies in reluctance to explore any hypothesis to its logical conclusion for fear of the accusation of being one-sided. Neither of these approaches, if carried to the extreme, is likely to be fruitful in the long run.

What I have tried to do in this chapter is probably to raise many more questions to be settled by further research than I have answered. My purpose is to show that the patterns of kinship content, which have been neglected in systematic kinship studies, are demonstrably rooted in those of kinship structures, and that both have strong bearing on the patterns of behavior and of culture in different societies. In the preliminary results, I plead guilty to having lumped numerous peoples together whom many will certainly regard as being incongruous. But I am no more guilty than the zoologist who puts fish, chickens, crocodiles, monkeys, and humans together into the single category of vertebrata and attributes to all of them a number of common characteristics. If differences alone are stressed, I am positive that no two human societies are identical. For that matter we can go further and note that no two individuals are completely alike. At a certain level, it is important to ascertain the exact cultural differences between two particular tribes just as at a certain other level it is relevant to see the mental differences between two individual leaders. But before those who are interested in diamonds attempt to ascertain the differences between diamonds and pebbles, they must first make sure that they know what separates, on the one hand, the diamonds and pebbles (which are both stones), and, on the other, cabbages and turnips (which are both vegetables).

BIBLIOGRAPHY

AFRICA. 1935. Vol. VIII, No. 4.

BASCOM, W. R. 1944. The sociological role of the Yoruba cult-group. American Anthropological Association, Memoir, 63.

————. 1951. Social status, wealth and individual differences among the Yoruba. American Anthropologist (Part I) 53:490–505.

BERREMAN, GERALD D. 1963. Hindus of the Himalayas. Berkeley, California University Press.

BOHANNAN, LAURA AND PAUL. 1953. The Tiv of Central Nigeria. Ethnographic Survey Series, International African Institute, London.

BROWNE, C. R. 1929. Maori witchery. London, J. M. Dent and Sons, Ltd.

CARSTAIRS, G. MORRIS. 1957. The twice born. London, The Hogarth Press.

CATON-THOMPSON, G. 1931. The Zimbabwe culture ruins and reactions. London, Oxford University Press.

CHANG, TUNG-SUN. 1952. A Chinese philosopher's theory of knowledge. Yenching Journal of Social Studies, I.

CHAUDHURI, NIRAD C. 1951. The autobiography of an unknown Indian. New York, Macmillan Co.

CHILDS, GLADWYN M. 1949. Umbundu kinship and character. London, Oxford University Press.

CHRISTENSEN, J. B. 1954. Double descent among the Fanti. New Haven, Human Relations Area Files.

COHEN, RONALD. 1966. The dynamics of feudalism in Bornu. Boston University Publications in African History, Vol. II.

———. 1967. The Kanuri of Bornu. New York, Holt, Rinehart and Winston.

———. 1971. Dominance and defiance: marital stability in a Sudamic emirate. Washington, D.C., American Anthropological Association.

COLSON, E. AND M. GLUCKMAN (ED.). 1951. Seven tribes of British Central Africa. London, Oxford University Press.

DRIBERG, J. H. 1923. The Lango, London, T. F. Unwin, Ltd.

DUBE, C. S. 1955. Indian village. Ithaca, New York, Cornell University Press.

EGGAN, FRED. 1950. Social organization of the western Pueblos. Chicago, University of Chicago Press.

EISENSTADT, S. N. 1956. From generation to generation: age groups and social structure. Glencoe, Ill., The Free Press.

ERIKSON, ERIK. 1950. Childhood and Society. New York, Norton.

EVANS-PRITCHARD, E. E. 1937. Witchcraft, oracles and magic among the Azande. London, Oxford University Press.

———. 1940a. The political system of the Anuak of the Anglo-Egyptian Sudan. London, P. Lund, Humphries & Co., Ltd.

———. 1940b. The Nuer. London, Oxford University Press.

FIRTH, R. 1936. We the Tikopia. London, Routledge & Kegan Paul.

———. 1951. Elements of social organization, London, Watts & Co.

———. 1954. The sociology of 'magic' in Tikopia, Sociologus, 14, 2, New Series, 97–116.

FORTES, M. AND E. E. EVANS-PRITCHARD. 1940. African political systems. London, Oxford University Press.

FORTUNE, R. 1932. Sorcerers of Dobu. London, G. Routledge & Sons, Ltd.

FREUD, SIGMOND. 1918. Totem and Taboo. London, Routledge and Kegan Paul.

———. 1938. Civilization and Its Discontents. London, Hogart Press.

GILLIN, J. 1939. Personality in pre-literate societies. American Sociological Review 4:681–702.

GLUCKMAN, MAX. 1951. The Lozi of Barotzeland. *In* Colson and Gluckman, Seven Tribes of British Central Africa, pp. 1–93. London, Oxford University Press.

GOLDSCHMIDT, WALTER. 1948. Social organization in native California and the origin of clans. American Anthropologist 50:444–456.

GORER, GEOFFREY. 1948. The American People. New York, W. W. Norton and Company.

GORER, G. AND J. RICKMAN. 1962. The People of Great Russia. London, Cresset.

GRANET, MARCEL. 1934. La pensee Chinoise. Paris, La Renaissance du Livre.

HARRIS, MARVIN. 1968. The Rise of Anthropological Theory. New York, Thomas Crowell.

HART, C. W. M. 1954. The sons of Turimpi. American Anthropologist 56:242–261.

HERSKOVITS, M. J. 1938a. Dahomey, 2 Vols. New York, J. J. Augustin.

———. 1938b. Acculturation. New York, J. J. Augustin.

HOFMAYR, WILHELM. 1925. Die Schilluk. Vienna, St. Gabriel, Modling bei Wien. Admistration des Anthropos.

HOGBIN, IAN H. 1934. Law and order in Polynesia. New York, Harcourt Brace & Co.

HONIGMANN, JOHN. 1967. Personality in Culture. New York, Harper and Row.

HSU, FRANCIS L. K. 1940. The problem of incest tabu in a North China village. American Anthropologist 42:122–135.

———. 1943. Incentives to work in primitive communities. American Sociological Review 8:638–642.

———. 1953. Americans and Chinese: two ways of life. New York, Abelard-Schuman.

———. 1954. Cultural factors. *In* Williamson and Buttrick (ed.), Economic Development. New York, Prentice-Hall.

———. 1959. Structure, function, content and process. American Anthropologist (Part I) 61:790–805.

———. 1960. ʼA neglected aspect of witchcraft studies. Journal of American Folklore 73:287. ·

———. 1963. Clan, caste and club: a comparative study of Chinese, Hindu and American ways of life. Princeton, Van Nostrand and Co.

———. 1965. The effect of dominant kinship relationships on kin and non-kin behavior: A hypothesis. American Anthropologist 67:638–61.

———. 1966. Dominant kin relationships and dominant ideas. Brief Communications. American Anthropologist 68:997–1004.

————. 1968. Chinese Kinship and Chinese Behavior in Ping-ti Ho and Tang Tsou (eds.), China in Crisis, Vol. 1: China's Heritage and the Communist Political System, pp. 579–608. Chicago, University of Chicago Press.

————. 1970. American and Chinese: Purpose and Fulfillment in Great Civilizations. Revised and enlarged edition of Americans and Chinese: Two Ways of Life, 1953. New York, Natural History Press. (Division of Doubleday).

————. 1971a. Kinship and Culture (ed. and contributor). Results of a symposium on Hsu's hypothesis. Chicago, Aldine.

————. 1971b. Japanese kinship and Iemoto, three new chapters in the Japanese translation of Clan, caste and club: Hikaku Bunmei Shakai Ron, Tokyo Baifukan.

————. In Preparation. Iemoto: The Heart of Japan.

Ho, Ping-Ti and Tang Tsou (eds.). 1968. China in Crisis. Chicago, University of Chicago Press.

Irstam, Tor. 1944. The King of Ganda, studies in the institutions of sacral kingship in Africa. Stockholm, The Ethnological Museum of Sweden, New Series, Publication 8.

Kardiner, Abram. 1945. Psychological Frontiers of Society. New York, Columbia University Press.

Kenyatta, J. 1939. Facing Mount Kenya. London, Routledge & Kegan Paul.

Kluckhohn, C. 1944. Navaho witchcraft. Cambridge, Peabody Museum Papers, XXII, 2.

Kopytoff, Igor. 1960. Suku religion: A study in internally induced reinterpretation. Evanston, Ill., Northwestern University doctoral dissertation.

Kuhn, Manford H. 1954. Factors in personality: socio-cultural determinants as seen through the Amish. *In* Francis L. K. Hsu (ed.), Aspects of Culture and Personality, pp. 43–45. New York, Abelard-Schuman.

Leach, E. R. 1951. The structural implications of matrilateral cross-cousin marriage. Journal of Royal Anthropological Institute of Great Britain (Part I and II) 81:23–55.

LeVine, Robert. 1966. Dreams and Deeds: Achievement Motivation in Nigeria. Chicago, University of Chicago Press.

Lévi-Strauss, Claude. 1949. Les structures elementaires de la parente. Paris, Presses Universitaires de France.

————. 1963. Structural Anthropology. New York, Basic Books.

Lintcn, R. 1933. Tanala, a hill tribe of Madagascar. Chicago Field Museum Series, XXII.

————. 1939. *In* A. Kardiner, The individual and his society. New York, Columbia Univeristy Press.

————. 1940. A neglected aspect of social organization. American Journal of Sociology 45:870–866.

————. 1945. The Comanche. *In* A. Kardiner, The psychological frontiers of society, pp. 47–48. New York, Columbia University Press.

————. 1955. The tree of culture. New York, Alfred Knopf.

LLOYD-JONES, ESTHER AND NORAH ROSENAU (EDS). 1968. Social and Cultural Foundations of Guidance. New York, Holt, Rinehart and Winston.

MALINOWSKI, B. 1929. Sexual life of savages. 2 vols., London, G. Routledge & Sons, Ltd.

————. 1933. Sex and repression in a savage society. London, G. Routledge & Sons, Ltd.

MANDELBAUM, DAVID G. 1949. The family in India. *In* R. N. Ashen, ed., The family, its function and destiny. New York, Harper Bros.

————. 1970. Society in India. Vol. 1. Continuity and change. Berkeley, Los Angeles, London, University of California Press.

MAYER, PHILIP. 1949. Lineage principle in Gusii society, Memorandum XXIV, International African Institute, London.

MEAD, MARGARET (ED.). 1937. Cooperation and competition among primitive peoples. New York, McGraw Hill Book Co., Inc.

————. 1939. Coming of age in Samoa. *In* From the South Seas. New York, Morrow & Co.

MEEK, C. K. 1931. A Sudanese kingdom. London, Kegan Paul, Trench, Trubner & Co., Ltd.

MIDDLETON, JOHN. 1960. Lugbara religion: ritual and authority among an Eastern African People. London, Routledge & Kegan Paul.

MIDDLETON, JOHN AND E. H. WINTER. 1963. Witchcraft and Sorcery in East Africa. New York, Praeger.

MINTURN, LEIGH AND JOHN T. HITCHCOCK. 1963. The Rajputs of Khalapur, India. *In* Beatrice B. Whiting (ed.), Six Cultures: Studies of Child Rearing. New York, John Wiley & Sons, pp. 203–361.

MUKERJI, D. GOPAL. 1923. Case and outcaste. New York.

MULLER, F. MAX. 1938. Ramakrishna, his life and sayings. London.

MURDOCK, GEORGE PETER. 1949. Social structure. New York, Macmillan & Co.

MURPHY, GARDNER. 1953. In the minds of men. New York, Basic Books, Inc.

MURPHY, LOIS B. 1953. Roots of tolerance and tensions in child development, chap. IV, *In* Gardner Murphy: In the minds of men. New York, Basic Books, Inc.

NADEL, S. F. 1947. The Nupa. London, Oxford University Press.

Needham, Rodney. 1962. Structure and sentiment. Chicago, University of Chicago Press.

Nivedita, Sister (Miss M. E. Noble). 1904. The web of Indian life. London & Bombay, Longmans, Green & Co.

Oberg, K. 1940. The Kingdom of Ankole in Uganda. *In* Fortes and Evans-Pritchard, eds., African political systems. London, Oxford University Press.

Payne, Ernest A. 1933. The Saktas. Calcutta & London, Oxford University Press.

Radcliffe-Brown, A. R. 1950. Introduction. *In* African systems of kinship and marriage, edited by A. R. Radcliffe-Brown and Daryll Forde, pp. 1–85. London, Oxford University Press.

Radcliffe-Brown, A. R. and Daryll Forde, (ed.). 1950. African systems of kinship and marriage. London, Oxford University Press.

Rohlen, Thomas P. 1971. Father-son dominance: Tikopia and China. *In* Francis L. K. Hsu (ed.), Kinship and culture, pp. 144–157. Chicago, Aldine Publishing Co.

Roscoe, J. 1911. The Baganda. London, MacMillan & Co. Ltd.

Schapera, I. 1941. Married life in an African tribe. New York, Sheridan House.

Seligman, C. G. and B. Z. 1932. Pagan tribes of the Nilotic Sudan. London, G. Routledge & Sons, Ltd.

Spoehr, Alexander. 1940. Changing kinship systems. Anthropological Series. Field Museum of Natural History, vol. 33, No. 4.

Steed, Gitel P. 1950. Life history documents, I (Indrasingh). New York, Columbia University Research in Contemporary India Project (hectographed).

———. 1955. Personality formation in a Hindu village in Gujarat. *In* McKim Marriott (ed.): Village India, pp. 102–144. Chicago, University of Chicago Press.

Steward, Julian. 1954. Types of types. Discussion of Ford, The type concept revisited. American Anthropologist 56:42–54, 55–57.

———. 1955. Theory of Cultural change. Urbana, University of Illinois Press.

Tatje, Terrence and Francis L. K. Hsu. 1969. Variations in ancestor worship beliefs and their relation to kinship. Southwestern Journal of Anthropology, Vol. 25, pp. 153–172.

Tegnaeus, Harry. 1952. Blood brothers. Stockholm, The Ethnological Museum of Sweden, New Series, Publication 10.

Wagner, G. 1949. The Bantu of North Kavirondo. London, Oxford University Press.

Watson, R. I. 1959. Psychology of the child. New York, John Wiley & Sons.

WILSON, MONICA. 1951. Good Company: a study of Nyakyusa villages. London, Oxford University Press.

WOLFE, ALVIN W. 1954. The institution of demba among the Ngonje Ngombe. Zaire (Belgian Congo Review) 8:843–856.

INTRODUCTION TO PART IV

Assessment

In this final section Spiro gives us his view of the whole field of psychological anthropology. He touches on some of the chapters of this book which have gone before but he also takes into consideration other works not specifically dealt with by the contributors to this volume. The reader will note that in certain areas Spiro does not agree with those of some of his colleagues. To take but a few examples: He opines that anthropology cannot claim to be a synthetic science of man because "vast dimensions of human behavior and experience," from "British folklore, American politics, Greek archaeology" to "Chinese economy," do not "come within our purview." But quite a few anthropologists specialize wholly or partially in "national character" studies of large and literate societies.

Then the term "primitive," which Spiro uses liberally and which the other contributors use only rarely or not at all, is meeting with increasing disfavor among anthropologists. Apart from other considerations, such as the fact that in our fast-changing world most former colonies now enjoy equal diplomatic relationship with the great powers, there are grave doubts, from the purely scientific point of view, concerning the lumping together of diverse peoples, from Australia and Polynesia to Africa and the

Americas, into this one category. It is not defensible no matter how it is defined, for it covers too much diversity. It confuses rather than clarifies. Dichotomizing the world's peoples into primitive and civilized categories is as useful for understanding human behavior as separating them into Heathens and Christians. (For an intensive examination of the question see Francis L. K. Hsu, "Rethinking the Concept 'Primitive,'" *Current Anthropology* 5 (1964):169–178.)

Spiro's principal thesis begins with a very important observation which differs from the Editor's only in emphasis. The Editor's view is that psychological anthropology must deal with "the origin of psychological characteristics as they are molded by the patterns of child rearing, social institutions, and ideologies but also account for the origin, development and change in these child-rearing practices, institutions, and ideologies" (Introduction). Spiro insists that the more important of the two tasks for anthropologists is the "maintenance of social systems" and "the problem of their internal change." Parts of Chapter 12 and most of Chapter 13 of this book are also devoted to the problem of how personality characteristics influence the course of society and culture.

Spiro's central contribution in this chapter is his analysis of how personality dynamics operate toward the maintenance and change of social systems. There are at least three situations, according to him, in which the potential conflict between personal desires and cultural norms is not resolved and the motivation for noncompliance with cultural norms is stronger than the motivation for compliance. He then proceeds to examine these in detail and how such conflicts and their eventual resolution in each of the three situations — psychologically, structurally and culturally induced — enable the social systems to persist or to change.

However, two points should be noted. First, although Spiro set out to consider the role of personality dynamics in the maintenance and change of social and cultural systems, he has not given *change* attention equal to that he gave to *maintenance*. He alludes to how "frustrated drives provide an important motivational basis for the disruption of social systems" but does not go far beyond that. What we must realize is that a structural situation in many societies which appears to the Western observer to be frustrating may not have been frustrating to the peoples involved at all. On the other hand, frustrations, even though felt more or less intensely, may lead to opposite solutions in different cultures. For example, the presence of the ideology of equality and freedom has made the lack of opportunity for advancement frustrating. Its presence will certainly induce expressions of the frustration and solutions to it different from those where it is absent. This is true in slave-owner and peasant-landlord situations, no less than in caste and male-female situations.

The other point concerns the extent to which the psychological anthropologist can rely on psychoanalytic concepts and mechanisms. Spiro stresses the overwhelming importance of the dynamics of personality in understanding society and culture. In his brief new Introduction (1971) to the chapter he reiterates the conviction in even stronger terms. But various universal mechanisms of ego defense, including repression, aggression, sublimation, displacement, though they may "contribute importantly to the maintenance of social systems . . . by resolving the conflict between cultural norms and personal drives in ways which are satisfactory to both personality and society" (p. 596) do not account for how different social systems are maintained differently, or even how different sectors within the same system function differently.

For example, Spiro points to structural exclusion of American Blacks from certain favored roles as cause for drive frustration on the part of Blacks, which in turn leads to non-compliance with cultural norms. But what has led to non-compliance with cultural norms on the part of many White Americans in support of the structurally excluded Blacks, especially among Whites in a position to achieve the same favored roles from which the Blacks have been excluded?

Cross-culturally the contrast is even clearer. Chinese women have had to submit to footbinding for nearly ten centuries. It was a painful process and permanent disability which every woman had to endure from girlhood on. But there were no Chinese Florence Nightingales or Carrie Nations to organize and protest against this atrocity and to my knowledge only three Chinese male scholars ever wrote in its disapproval. In the end it was the arrival of Western missionaries and the transplantation of Western ideas by Chinese returned students which brought about its abolition. Why did the Chinese in both favored and disfavored positions acquiesce in such a role structure which must (or at least could) have been so drive frustrating to their mothers, sisters, wives or selves?

The answer to such questions obviously cannot be found in some universal drives, their frustration, and their resolutions. Instead they must be sought in the different ways societies and cultures have nurtured the individuals in their expectations and in their approaches to their relations with men, gods, and things. This brings us to the distinction between internal impetus and external impetus to change which the Editor discussed in the Introduction to Part III and in Chapter 13. There are obviously societies which train their members to seek continuity with standards and practices handed down from the past, in contrast to others which encourage their members to seek discontinuity from such standards and practices in the name of creativity or freedom. These and other messages are transmitted from generation to generation first through the kinship situation — that primary agency of human development. What we need, in addition to Spiro's brilliant analysis given here, is a new look at different kinship systems (see Francis L. K. Hsu [ed.], *Kinship and Culture*, Chicago: Aldine Publishing Co., 1971) and a new look at personality dynamics (see Francis L. K. Hsu, "Psychosocial Homeostasis and *Jen:* New Concept for Advancing Psychological Anthropology." *American Anthropologist* 73:23–44). It should be noted that these new views on kinship and on personality dynamics do not repudiate Freudian or psychoanalytic approaches, but seek either to confine them to their proper places or to extend them beyond that which their exponents are ready to grant.

CHAPTER FOURTEEN

An Overview and a Suggested Reorientation

MELFORD E. SPIRO

The Emergence of Culture and Personality

An examination of textbooks in general anthropology, of symposia such as *Anthropology Today*, of compendia such as the recently inaugurated *Annual Review of Anthropology*, of the classification of book reviews in the *American Anthropologist*, or of much of the empirical and theoretical work which is labeled as "culture-and-personality" — an examination of all of these yields the unambiguous impression that for most anthropologists culture-and-personality is a substantive field within the larger domain of anthropological science.* Since anthropology as a collective enterprise auda-

---

*Except for some minor changes, indicated in the text by brackets, and except for those few explanatory footnotes marked by letters rather than numbers, the present chapter is a reprinting of the one prepared for the first edition of this book. Although Professor Hsu asked me to revise this chapter for the new volume, it became apparent, when I reread the chapter, that any attempted revision would require wholesale rewriting — in effect, a new chapter — and however desirable that endeavor would be, it was not possible to undertake such a major task in time to meet the projected production schedule.

Needless to say, the reprinting of a chapter written more than a decade ago has a number of disadvantages: more recent research findings and newer theoretical advances are not included, bibliographic references are dated and more appropriate ones are omitted, and changes in the author's views are not indicated (cf. Spiro 1968a). Despite these disadvantages, I was not unwilling to reprint this chapter because although I would have preferred to

ciously pursues an imperialistic course consistent with its etymological meaning — I say, "collective," because with Kroeber's demise no single anthropologist pursues the study of man in all its dimensions — we easily and naturally slice up our field into *physical* anthropology, *linguistic* anthropology, *cultural* anthropology, *social* anthropology, *historical* anthropology, and finally — in the case of culture-and-personality — *psychological* anthropology. When we are challenged by some of our academic colleagues to explain the meaning of "anthropology" in each of the above expressions, we are often embarrassed in our attempts to provide a satisfactory response because, of course, other sciences are centrally concerned with man's soma, his society, his psyche, and so forth. We sometimes attempt to explain "anthropology" in these expressions — and at the same time to justify our imperialism — by claiming that "anthropology" connotes a concern for all of these dimensions of man's existence in a synthetic or holistic manner.

Unfortunately this claim cannot be seriously defended. There are vast dimensions of human behavior and experience with which we have little or no concern. Seldom, for example, do British folklore, American politics, Greek archaeology, Chinese economy — to take but a few examples — come within our purview. On the other hand, we do study Navaho folklore, Nuer politics, Iroquois archaeology, and Samoan economy. In short, not Man, but primitive man, has been our concern.[a] It must be admitted, of course, that in some important instances, the development of theoretical models and analytic schemes has proceeded without special concern for the uniquely primitive. But when this has occurred, progress has been made by eschewing the holistic approach. Thus in those fields

[a] In the ten years since this essay was written, a growing number of anthropologists have been working in modern societies (cf. Hsu 1969) and, indeed, the field in Urban Anthropology has become a recognized specialty in the anthropological profession.

express them with greater clarity and felicity, its main ideas continue (in the main) to represent my present views. Indeed, these ideas have since been incorporated in a number of empirical inquiries which may be found in the expanded bibliography (cf. Spiro 1965, 1966, 1967, 1968a, 1968b, 1971).

In reflecting upon the research operations and theoretical formulations that have occured over the past decade, I am even more convinced that any important advance in the understanding of society and culture requires that greater attention be given to the dynamics of personality. If I were writing this chapter today, I would not only make this point more forcibly than I did a decade ago, but I would underscore other increasing convictions. First, psychoanalytic personality theory is the only one adequate thus far to cope with the enormous complexities of the human psyche. Second, without an understanding of these complexities, we shall make little advance toward a deepening understanding of society and culture in their relationship to human nature and behavior.

where advance has been most spectacular, such as population genetics or structural linguistics, the anthropologist has become indistinguishable from his nonanthropological colleagues working in these vineyards.

These comments concerning the anthropological concern with primitive peoples[b] are not intended as a criticism, but rather as a characterization of the nature of our discipline, which in turn provides the historical context within which culture-and-personality studies developed. These studies emerged, I believe it is fair to say, as a result of a serious crisis with which anthropology was confronted beginning, roughly, about 1920. One might almost characterize this crisis, as Erik Erikson characterizes the typical adolescent crisis, as one of "identity."

When anthropology first arose as a separate discipline, its primary concern was with the origin, evolution, and distribution of man and his cultures. Holding this aim as its charter, armed with the older comparative method as its main research tool, and accepting as a methodological premise the approximate equation of primitive and prehistoric peoples, its rationale for the study of primitive peoples was axiomatic. With the growth and development, however, of American anthropology and its disparagement of both the aims and methods of the various evolutionary schools, the rationale for the focus on primitive peoples lost much of its force. If, according to the American school, the study of American or Australian aborigines could shed little light on the origin and evolution of culture, what interest, for other than an antiquarian curiosity, could aboriginal peoples have for modern science? And if, in accordance with the emerging conception of cultural relativism, the cultures of aboriginal peoples (like our own culture) were to be viewed as so many variants of a universal culture pattern, rather than as different stages in an evolutionary scheme or as different points on some scale — of progress, or development, or complexity, or any other measure — why bother to study them? To provide further documentation for the thesis of variability and of relativism? But were anthropologists then to become like those, of whom Pierce (1935:233) complained, who

> . . . seem to love to argue a point after all the world is fully convinced of it. But no further advance can be made. When doubt ceases, mental action on a subject comes to an end; and, if it did go on, it would be without a purpose.

[b] As I am using the term, "primitive peoples" live in relative isolation from the main currents of world trade and international politics, and are characterized by the following configurations of variables: small scale societies, non-industrialized economics, kinship-based polities, and non-literate cultures.

In general, American anthropologists justified their preoccupation with primitive cultures by arguing that ethnographic facts — when they were all in — would constitute vital data for the reconstruction of culture history, and, perhaps, provide the evidence for an inductive construction of cultural "laws" (presumably, laws of change, invention, diffusion, and so forth). Hence, like the older evolutionists — but for different reasons — anthropologists continued to collect ethnographic facts. They differed from the evolutionists in that their facts were collected at first hand in the field, rather than from the reports of missionaries and travelers. They differed too in their antitheoretical bias. Since science was "objective," ethnographic science was to be descriptive, assiduously avoiding all theoretical entanglements; and the immediate if not the ultimate aim of ethnographic research was to be the meticulous observation, collection, and classification of facts — in the spirit of Ranke's historiography: *wie es eigentlich gewessen ist.* Only after this essentially descriptive task was performed in a fairly large number of societies could the anthropologist (if he were so inclined) attempt to discover cultural laws. And even then, as Boas (1936:257) cautioned, "cultural phenomena are of such complexity that it seems doubtful . . . whether valid cultural laws can be found."

This approach to the study of primitive peoples — the approach of radical empiricism — which, I believe, represented a serious attempt to solve our identity crisis, had at least two important consequences for anthropological theorizing. On the one hand, it led to the proliferation of speculative, nontestable theory. On the other, it led to an extreme skepticism concerning the possibility of any theory. As one wit put it, it led to the generalization that the only valid anthropological generalization is the generalization that there are no valid generalizations.

That a method which insisted on the divorce of theory and data should have resulted in a proliferation of speculation was, though ironical, inescapable. If theoretical generalizations are to emerge *from* research, they must be used *in* research. And if theory is divorced from research, it necessarily leads an independent existence, neither affecting the nature of inquiry, nor being affected by the results of inquiry. Removed in effect from any empirical context, it remains in the realm of speculation — and of fruitless controversy. This state of affairs can cease only when theory exists in a correlative relationship with fact, when, that is, it generates hypotheses to be tested in inquiry. Only then are its concepts formulated operationally and its predicted consequences confirmed or disconfirmed empirically. But the method of radical empiricism precluded the empirical resolution of theoretical controversy. Since theory was not employed in research, facts adduced for the support of theories were, at best, illustrative; and equally good illustrations could be found for almost any theory and its antithesis.

Facts can become data only when they are used as evidence for the testing of scientific hypotheses, only when, that is, they are expected to solve theoretical problems. For it is a theory, in the form of a hypothesis to be tested, that determines which facts out of a potentially infinite number are to be collected — those facts, namely, which are believed to constitute evidence for the inquiry at hand. Dewey (1938:497) put it much better when he observed that:

> All competent and authentic inquiry demands that out of the complex welter of existential and potentially observable and recordable material, certain material be selected and weighed *as* data or the "facts of the case." This process is one of adjudgment, of appraisal or evaluation ... An idea of an end *to be* reached, and end-in-view, is logically indispensable in discrimination of existential material as the evidential and testing facts of the case. Without it, there is no guide for observation; without it, one can have no conception of what one should look for or even is looking for. One "fact" would be just as good as another — that is, good for nothing in control of inquiry and formation and in settlement of a problem.

That the method of radical empiricism should have led, too, to scientific agnosticism is not at all surprising, Cultural phenomena are indeed complex, as Boas rightly cautioned; but this method could hardly have decreased the impression of their complexity. The fact is, of course, that the phenomenal world — the physical no less than the cultural — is always complex; it is, as William James put it, a "booming, buzzing, confusion." Hence, it is at least arguable that the order and simplicity now perceived to characterize the physical world are conceptual rather than phenomenal, and that the absence of order and of simplicity that seems to characterize the cultural world may similarly be conceptual rather than phenomenal. For we anthropologists are no exception to a universal law of perception: *viz.,* that any stimulus field becomes a perceptually meaningful field only when it is structured. But having decided to collect all the ethnographic facts, and to collect them as objectively as possible — that is, without explicit theory — anthropology was confronted with an enormous corpus of unstructured ethnographic material. And, as in any other unstructured situation, the resultant perception was one of enormous complexity.[1]

It is against this background and within this context that culture-and-personality studies emerged.[2] In an era of radical empiricism and scientific agnosticism, it is probably inevitable that the desire of some scholars for a different methodological charter and a satisfying theoretical orientation should lead to new approaches. For anthropologists this desire was satisfied in two quite dissimilar ways and by two seemingly dissimilar schools: the British school of social anthropology and the American school of culture-and-personality.[c] Despite the important differences that divided these

[1] In this connection the following statements, one by an eminent physical, and the other by an eminent social, anthropologist, are relevant. In an article on social structure Lévi-Strauss (1953:549) observes: "Surprisingly enough, it is at the very moment when anthropology finds itself closer than ever to the long-awaited goal of becoming a true science that the ground seems to fail where it was expected to be the firmest: the facts themselves are lacking, either not numerous enough or not collected under conditions insuring their comparability." Washburn, writing in the same volume (1953:714–715) on physical anthropology, states: "After more than a century of intensive fact-finding there is less agreement among informed scientists on the evolution of man to other primates than there was in the latter part of the nineteenth century."

[2] Since these studies have historical roots both in eighteenth century thought and in nineteenth century scholarship, I do not mean to imply that culture-and-personality represented an unprecedented innovation. Indeed, in addition to its deeper historical roots, it will be remembered that Edward Sapir, Ruth Benedict, and Margaret Mead were all students of Franz Boas, whose psychological interests are well known. But continuity is not identity, and these three pioneers are sufficiently distinct from their intellectual predecessors to warrant our reference to their work as a "new approach."

[c] Although the present volume is entitled "psychological anthropology," I prefer the traditional "culture-and-personality" to designate the concerns of this chapter, at least, and of those problems discussed in this volume that are of interest to me. It is becoming increasingly fashionable in academic psychology to dismiss the personality concept as too vague or too holistic for rigorous scientific investigation, and if by "scientific" is meant "experimental" — in the laboratory sense of "experimental" — this is probably a reasonable position. In the same manner, and possibly as a reflection of these trends in academic psychology, much of the current work in "psychological anthropology" has little concern for "personality" viewed as a dynamic, holistic, system. "Culture-and-personality," with all of its difficulties, has the advantage of stressing the continuing importance of the concept of personality for the social and behavioral sciences.

A second reason for preferring this older term is that "psychological anthropology" has tended increasingly to become little more than cross-cultural psychology, the autonomy of culture, as a holistic system, being as rapidly lost in the process as the concept of personality. For me the basic problems concerning the relationship between the (analytically) autonomous systems of culture, society, and personality — the classical problems of the culture-and-personality school — are still to be solved, and the retention of the older title serves to emphasize their importance.

schools, it should be observed that they also had much in common. First, in contrast to the earlier historical schools, both displayed almost systematic indifference to problems of a historical nature. This is not to say, as is sometimes charged, that they dismissed historical variables as irrelevant, but rather that they viewed the task of anthropology as something other than historical reconstruction. Second, in contrast to an older trait-list approach, both emphasized the primacy of context, pattern, configuration, and structure. Third, instead of a descriptivist approach, both were theoretically oriented. Primitive societies were to be studied for the light they could shed on theoretical issues: in the one case — and here they differed — sociological, in the other, psychological. The one was interested in the forms of society, the other in the dynamics of behavior. And this difference in turn led to still another fundamental difference. The one either dismissed culture as irrelevant to its interests (for example, Radcliffe-Brown), or else concentrated on an examination of its properties (for example, Malinowski); the other viewed it as of crucial importance, but as an independent rather than as a dependent variable. That is, its interest was in demonstrating the importance of culture as an efficient cause in the development of personality and in the patterning of behavior. In any event, both innovations — social anthropology and culture-and-personality — represented important attempts to salvage anthropology as a theoretically informed discipline, concerned with discovering laws or principles that would explain classes of phenomena, whether these phenomenal classes be social, cultural, behavioral, or psychological.

For culture-and-personality, the phenomenal class to be explained was personality and its cross-cultural variability. This school, like the older historical schools, was deeply interested in culture — and, like the older schools, it conceived of culture as a holistic concept, including social structure, material goods, social norms, values and ideas, and so forth; in short, the "man-made part of the environment." But this school, as has already been stated, was interested in culture as an independent, rather than as a dependent, variable. Instead of asking — as did older schools — what historical, environmental, or biological variable(s) produced certain cultural variables or even a total culture, culture-and-personality asked what cultural variables produced certain personality variables or a total personality. Culture-and-personality, focusing on personality but stemming from general anthropology, was concerned with demonstrating that almost all behavior was cross-culturally variable rather than constant; that this variability was a function (primarily) of environment rather than biology (race); that the crucial environmental variable was culture; and that culture was learned rather than innate.

The Copernican revolution in anthropology which was sponsored by culture-and-personality did not consist (as the threadbare cliché has it) in the promotion of the study of the individual, in contrast to social or cultural anthropology which studied the group (as if it were possible to do either without the other!). It consisted, rather, in the change from the traditional focus on culture as *explanandum* to culture as *explanans,* and in the substitution of personality as *explanandum.* Indeed even a cursory examination of the early literature of culture-and-personality will reveal how false is the claim that culture-and-personality was — or is — a "study of the individual in culture." Although some autobiographies were collected, the autobiography was exploited to the end of discovering not individual differences, but cultural influences on the individual. The "individual" was of concern not in those characteristics which differentiated him from other individuals in his group — not, that is, as an idiosyncratic person — but as a social person, as an example of a culturally molded psychological or personality type. The question to be examined was how this individual, viewed as a prototypical Hopi or Samoan or Alorese acquired a Hopi, rather than an Alorese or Samoan personality. Culture-and-personality students became, in short, the personality psychologists of primitive societies — comparative human psychologists — attending always to the crucial importance of culture for personality: its development, its structure, and its functions. And since there were many new theories to be tested, culture-and-personality studies were, from their inception, strongly theoretical — if not always systematic — in orientation.

Nevertheless, and despite its theoretical emphasis, culture-and-personality did not — and in some quarters does not, even today — receive an entirely favorable reception even among theoretically oriented anthropologists. Many — perhaps most — of the pioneering articles in culture-and-personality were published in nonanthropological journals — sometimes, to be sure, because psychologists replaced anthropologists as the reference group of certain members of this school, but more frequently because their work did not receive the imprimatur of anthropology. In general, those anthropologists who were dissatisfied with the older intellectual styles in anthropology turned, not to culture-and-personality, but to British social anthropology for new directions. Despite some of the dramatic changes introduced by this school, it was not the *terra incognita* of culture-and-personality. Kinship and economics, divination and totemism, government and law — rather than shame and guilt, projection and displacement, hostility and repression — continued to comprise its basic vocabulary. In short, if British structuralism[3] constituted a revolution in anthropology, it was certainly not Copernican; for however radical its departure from the more conventional anthropological tradition, British structuralism remained, like the latter, a social science. Culture-and-personality, on the other hand, entered anthropology — and was eventually legitimized — as its behavioral science branch. Its unique contribution to the understanding of behavior was the culture concept of traditional anthropology. By conceiving of culture.as an efficient cause which could not only, like other putative efficient causes, explain behavior but which could also, unlike some other putative causes, explain its cross-cultural variability, culture-and-personality not only commanded serious — if not always respectful — attention among the other behavioral sciences, but it also provided the anthropological concern for primitive peoples with triumphant vindication. Instead of satisfying essentially exotic, quixotic, or romantic curiosity, anthropology — according to the more partisan supporters of culture-and-personality — was pursuing a scientific enterprise of the first magnitude: it was engaged, almost uniquely, in an "experimental" study of human behavior. Whereas the other behavioral sciences were studying the same highly restricted sample of behavior drawn from an atypical segment of the total universe of behavioral samples, the study of primitive peoples allowed anthropology to sample the total universe. Since anthropology had already shown that behavioral differences within the class of primitive societies were even greater than the differences between primitive societies as a class and nonprimitive societies as a class, primitive societies could acquire new interest for the behavioral sciences not because they were alike but because they differed. Since all societies were members of the same universe, each society — including primitive — represented a variation on the same human theme.

With this new rationale and this new approach, the study of primitive peoples, for many anthropologists who had viewed the more traditional approach as having entered an intellectual *cul-de-sac,* received new and

[3] Here, and elsewhere in this chapter, the term "social anthropology" is not intended to be synonymous with British social anthropology: the latter is to the former what the part is to the whole. I use the term "British structuralism" or "pure structuralism" to refer to that school within social anthropology which views the discovery of "structural principles" as its major analytic task, and which systematically excludes psychological variables from its modes of analysis.

important justification. Primitive peoples, it was claimed, were important, not because they could contribute to an understanding of a separate class of behavior, the class of *primitive* behavior, but because they could contribute to the understanding of a larger behavioral class, the class of *human* behavior. From this point of view, each primitive society was thought to constitute, as it were, a natural laboratory for the study of different dimensions of behavior. And since these laboratories seemed to be the special preserve of anthropologists, they alone, it was alleged, were able to study the complete content, and to test the full limits, of human behavioral variability.

Toward a Reorientation of Culture-and-Personality

It is not my task to evaluate this charter, or to assess the culture-and-personality studies which have been conducted in many parts of the world within its provisions: the latter task is admirably accomplished in other chapters in this volume. I am concerned rather with assessing the future contribution which such studies may make to the furtherance of the theoretical aims of anthropological science. It is, of course, both difficult and hazardous to draw hard and fast distinctions among the various sciences; and it is even more hazardous to fix the frontiers of any discipline and, thus, to declare as alien all research concerns that fall beyond those frontiers. I do not intend to do either. At the same time, within the present system of scientific specialization it is obvious that anthropology and sociology have been traditionally concerned with the analysis of cultural and social systems, while other disciplines (personality psychology, psychiatry, and so forth) are centrally concerned with personality. I would suggest that anthropology, including culture-and-personality, persist in its traditional concern — not because I believe that cultural or social systems are of greater scientific interest or importance than personality systems, but because the theoretical problems which they pose are still for the most part unsolved; and if anthropologists (as well as sociologists) eschew them, they may never be solved. Hence, I am suggesting that, as anthropologists, the important task for culture-and-personality theorists today is the analysis of sociocultural systems rather than personality systems. [This does not mean, as we shall see below, that personality systems are to play a less important role in our studies — if anything, their role is to be more important — but rather a different one.]

This suggested reorientation of the focus of culture and personality is not intended to imply that our past efforts have been wasted, misguided, or misdirected. Quite the contrary! I believe they were crucially important and highly desirable, both for anthropology as well as for personality psychology. Their importance for the latter discipline has been marked. The relevance of sociocultural variables in the process of personality development and formation, though acknowledged in part prior to the work of culture-and-personality, was seldom incorporated systematically into personality theory. This is no longer the case. Most personality theorists — from psychoanalytic, to stimulus-response — are now systematically aware of the relevance of sociocultural variables for personality development and persistence. This is not to say that culture-and-personality was solely responsible for this change. Many currents in the social, behavioral, and psychiatric sciences contributed to this growing awareness of the importance of sociocultural variables. (Indeed, it is possible, as Wallace implies in his chapter in this volume, that the importance of sociocultural determinants has been exaggerated, and that it might be well to take another look at genetic and other biological variables.) Nevertheless, the documentation of the importance of cultural determinants in personality formation was a major — though not exclusive — intellectual achievement of culture-and-personality studies, and it represents the major contribution of anthropology to personality theory.

The importance of culture-and-personality has been, if anything, even more important for anthropology than for psychology. By focusing on personality dynamics and on social behavior (rather than on culture traits or social structure) these studies have impressed upon some anthropologists, at least, the realization that cultures and/or social systems do not lead an independent existence of their own; that their operation and maintenance are dependent to a marked degree on their internalization (either as cognitive or as affective variables) within the personalities of the members of society; and that for many — but by no means for all — problems of both structure and process, a studied indifference to the psychological dimensions of behavior can only lead to truncated, if not false, theories.

Indeed it is precisely because it has been so successful that I am suggesting a reorientation of culture-and-personality. Having succeeded in its attempts to induce personality psychology to incorporate sociocultural concepts within its conceptual apparatus, and having succeeded in legitimizing the use of personality concepts by anthropology, it might be argued that its original mission has come to its end. For if, on the one hand, the study of personality is *not* the focal concern of anthropology, I can see no grounds for pursuing something which others can do better than we; or are we content to become for personality theory what medieval philosophy was for theology, its handmaiden? — in this case, a handmaiden in exotic places. If, on the other hand, the study of culture and of social systems *is* the focal concern of anthropology, I can see no grounds for abandoning this concern to other anthropologists whose conceptual apparatus does not systematically include what for us is a key concept: the concept of personality.

For those *au courant* with the literature of culture-and-personality (if only from having read the previous chapters in this volume), this suggestion for a reorientation of the focus of our interest will not be received as a new or original suggestion. Much of the research and theory in culture-and-personality, even that of its pioneers — Mead, Hallowell, Henry, Kluckhohn, and others — exemplifies the approach which is proposed in this chapter. This proposal, therefore, is intended not as a radical departure from, but rather as a strengthening of, a trend which already has distinguished practitioners. But this trend must be broadened as well as strengthened. Because, as comparative personality theorists, we have been primarily concerned with explaining personality, our studies have in general focused on those aspects of social systems and culture which putatively are determinants of personality. And since, in the main, our theories have stressed the primacy of primary groups and the crucial importance of the socialization system, we have tended to ignore other social groups and other systems. In saying this I am not concerned here with evaluating the validity of our theories concerning the importance of primary groups or of socialization, but rather with explaining the relative neglect of other systems — political systems, as Inkeles rightly observes in his chapter in this volume, are a notable case in point — in culture-and-personality studies.

It is at least debatable, of course, that even as comparative personality theorists we have been negligent in our relative neglect of other systems; perhaps political systems, for example, are important determinants of personality formation. If this is so, our theories of personality development must be revised. But this is not the brunt of this discussion. Even if it were established that political and other institutions have no bearing on personality formation, my proposal for a reorientation of culture-and-personality would nevertheless demand that these institutions, instead of personality as such, become our major concern.

In suggesting that we abandon the Copernican revolution of culture-

and-personality, I do not intend to imply that we abandon our concern for personality. On the contrary! The introduction of personality concepts has been our unique contribution to anthropology, and the retention of personality as a crucial variable is our very *raison d'être.* My suggestion implies, rather, that its conceptual status be changed from *explanandum* to *explanans,* from a concept to be explained to an explanatory concept. Hence, though we would share a common focal concern — social system and culture — with our fellow social anthropologists, we would differ from them in our emphasis on personality and personality-derived concepts as our central analytical tools.

Restricting the discussion to social systems, I think it can be shown that current anthropological theories of social systems which explicitly preclude personality concepts from the domain of anthropological modes of explanation — pure structural theories — frequently fail to deal adequately either with the problem of the maintenance or persistence of social systems, or with the problem of their internal change. With respect to change, the strategy of pure structural analysis almost necessarily precludes the possibility of dealing with internally derived sociocultural change. The analysis of social structure is, of course, the first task in the analysis of social and cultural systems, and any theorist — psychological and antipsychological alike — must derive his structural variables by abstraction from the behavior of psychobiological organisms. The pure structuralist differs from other theorists, however, in insisting that these structural variables are the only legitimate data for anthropological analysis, and in denying other variables which can be derived from the behavior of these psychobiological organisms the status of legitimate anthropological concern. Since psychological variables are *not* structural variables, they are relegated to the psychologists. Having thus excluded the very variables which comprise a constant and persistent source of internal (in contrast to external) change — the needs and drives of the psychobiological organisms whose frustrations exert a continuous innovative strain — pure structural theories must necessarily adopt models of stable equilibrium, models which are almost inherently incapable of dealing with internally derived change.

Yet personality variables are as important for the maintenance of social systems as for their change. Without the use of personality concepts, attempts fully to explain the operation of these systems, either in terms of efficient causes or in terms of functional consequences, are seldom convincing. (Indeed the frequent recourse to psychological explanation, albeit in disguised form, at crucial points in many "antipsychological" structural analyses attests to the validity of this thesis.) Thus, although no one could take issue with Radcliffe-Brown's assertion (1950:82) that "the social function of any feature of a system is its relation to the structure and its continuance and stability, not its relation to the biological needs of individuals," — although no one could take issue with this assertion (because, of course, no one would commit the semantic fallacy of confusing *social* with *biological* functions), and although we might even concede that our task as social anthropologists is the discovery of social rather than biological functions, we might still want to ask whether in some instances at least an understanding of the biological functions of some structural unit may not be necessary for an understanding of its social functions. Or are we to say that the satisfaction of biological needs or their frustration have no consequences — even crucially important consequences — for the operation of a social system? If a negative answer to this question is the obviously correct answer, it is certainly not obvious to me.

Similarly although we might agree with Firth (1956:224) that in studying religious ritual the anthropologist "is concerned primarily with the kinds of social relations that are produced or maintained, rather than with the inner state as such of the participants," we would ask whether it is at all possible to understand the nature of a "social relation" without having some understanding of the "inner state" of the participants? Whether, indeed, the different "kinds" of social relations are not, among other things, a function of different "kinds" of "inner states."

Theories which attempt to explain the operation of social institutions, either in terms of their efficient causes or of their functional (particularly their latent) consequences, must necessarily include personality variables as explanatory concepts because, as I have attempted to show elsewhere (Spiro 1961), these institutions provide culturally approved and/or prescribed means for the satisfaction of personality needs, and these, in turn, provide the motivational bases for the performance of the roles which comprise these institutions. Hence, if the *social* function of personality — it has others — consists in the contribution it makes to the maintenance or persistence of a society, and if the *psychological* function of social systems — they have others — consists in the contribution they make to the maintenance of personality, the unique task of culture and personality, as a theory of social systems, is to explain their operation in terms of personality dynamics, and to explain their social (not merely their psychological) functions by reference to their capacity for the gratification and frustration of personality needs.

This is, however, a most difficult task. Human social systems are necessarily culturally constituted systems; and although culture may be viewed, in evolutionary perspective, as man's unique and crucial mechanism for adapting to nature and adjusting to other men, it is at the same time a new environment to which man must adapt and adjust. In short, culture is both an instrument and an object; it contributes to social adaptation and adjustment and at the same time it constitutes an object for adjustment. Hence, any analysis of human, that is, culturally constituted, social systems must explain how man adapts to the demands of culture — with all the conflict attendant upon the process — at the same time that he uses culture for the purpose of adaptation. Analyses which ignore or are unacquainted with the dynamics of behavior — including such unconscious mechanisms as psychological defenses — cannot perform this task satisfactorily. This is the thesis to be examined in the next section.

Culture-and-Personality Theory and the Operation of Social Systems[4]

On the basis of our present knowledge, it is probably safe to compile at least a partial list of both personal and social functional requirements. In this short compass we shall be concerned merely with those which are germane to the relatively narrow focus of this discussion — some of the problems posed by cultural conformity and social control. With respect to the functional requirements of personal adjustment and integration, at least the following must be mentioned: (a) the gratification of drives, both acquired and innate; (b) their gratification by means which comply with cultural norms; (c) their gratification by means that preclude pain for the actor, whether imposed by others (in the form of social sanctions) or by the self (in the form of shame or of moral anxiety). These functional requirements are fulfilled by the organization and operation of personality. Similarly, the functional requirements for the adaptation and integration of society include at least the following: (a) the gratification of the drives of its members; (b) the performance of those tasks which achieve commonly accepted group ends; (c) the protection of its members from aggression and other socially disruptive acts. For the most part these

---

[4] Isolated paragraphs, scattered in various parts of this section, have been taken from Spiro 1960.

functional requirements are fulfilled by the organization and operation of social systems.

If social systems be conceived as configurations of reciprocal roles which are shared by the members of a group in virtue of their inheritance from a prior generation — innovations do not become part of a social system until or unless they are accepted, that is shared, and thereafter transmitted to succeeding generations — then, in the most inclusive comparison of societies, from insect to human, we can distinguish three broad types of social systems. First, there are those whose constituent roles are inherited but not learned. These, of course, are the insect social systems whose shared roles are inherited through some process of biological determination, either by genetic inheritance or by postpartum nutrition. The persistence of these systems poses no special problem for the theorist of insect social systems: a worker ant must do whatever it is that worker ants *do* do; her status is defined by her role, and her role is determined by her nature. Second, there are social systems whose constituent roles are inherited, at least to some extent, through learning. These are the mammalian, and especially the primate, social systems. Third, there are social systems whose roles are not only inherited through learning, but whose roles are *prescribed*. These are human social systems.

Whereas the second type of social systems is found in those biological species characterized by a relatively small degree of plasticity, and, hence, by a relatively narrow range of behavioral variability, the third type is found in a species — *homo sapiens* — which exhibits an enormous degree of plasticity and, hence, a broad range of behavioral variability. Thus, holding the physical environment constant, all societies within the same infrahuman mammalian species have, more or less, the same social system; and within each society the system persists with little change over time. This homogeneity in space and time suggests that although many, if not all, of the social roles in these societies are learned, the behavioral repertoire of the typical member of these societies is not significantly broader than the learned behavior patterns that comprise this group's social system. Hence, in these societies what any member has learned to do in order to satisfy his needs is little different from what he is able to do and it, therefore, corresponds (more or less) to what he would like to do.

For the human species, even when the environment is held constant, different societies have different social systems and, for any society, social systems change over time. Since, therefore, the actual range of behavioral variability within the species is much broader than the permitted range of variability within any society of the species — since, that is, humans are capable of doing many things in addition to those they are expected to do — it is obvious that for human societies it is not sufficient that social roles be inherited, shared, and learned; they must also be *prescribed*. Hence, if human social systems differ from those of other mammals in that only the former are cultural, the crucial difference between cultural and noncultural systems is not — as we anthropologists have always, and I now believe wrongly, maintained — a difference between learned and nonlearned systems. Recent work in comparative animal sociology (Beach and Janes 1954; Schneirla 1950; Carpenter 1958) shows convincingly that learning is an important mechanism in the social behavior not only of man, but of all social mammals. With Hallowell (1960), Parsons (1951), and others, I believe that the distinctive feature of culture resides, rather, in its normative or prescriptive dimension.[5]

This prescriptive, or normative, dimension of culturally constituted social systems is for human societies what narrow plasticity and biological determination are, respectively, for mammalian and insect societies: it reduces the range of intragroup behavioral variability and, thus, helps make social order possible. Without this technique for reducing the range of potential variability inherent in any status, the long-range adaptive value of flexibility — which is made possible by wide plasticity — would have had to be sacrificed for the short-run superiority of social order achieved through narrow plasticity. Hence, the invention of culture allowed man to achieve both flexibility and order; in short, *almost* to have his cake and to eat it too. Almost, but not quite; for since what a person *must* learn to do in order to participate in his social system is not the same as what he *can* learn to do, it may conflict with what he would *like* to do.

This is, however, not the only conflict which may exist between personal

[5] In a previous publication (Spiro 1951) I argued that culture and personality were interchangeable concepts, since culture, if it had any ontological status, was internalized by the individual. This extreme position was adopted in opposition to various superorganicist theories which seemed to postulate a reified entity, culture, which was empirically as well as analytically divorced from its "carriers," and was assigned an independent existence in its own ontological realm. It has long been obvious to me that this extreme position is no more tenable than the position it had attempted to counter. In the first place, although it may be cognized, culture need not be internalized; and even when internalized, it comprises only one dimension of the personality: the superego. I would now argue, in agreement with the Parsonian tripartite classification, that culture consists, among other things, of the norms which govern social relationships; that these norms are to be distinguished analytically from that system of social relationships which may be termed the social system of a society; and that both are to be distinguished from personality, by which I understand the motivational system (including internalized norms) that characterizes individuals. It is obvious, from this classification, that much so-called "culture and personality research" is really concerned with social systems rather than with culture, or with culture rather than with personality.

desires and cultural norms. Cultural norms may be proscriptive as well as prescriptive. The former not only function to reduce the range of potential variability in a society, but also to preclude the expression of those activities which are, or are deemed to be, socially disruptive. In short, in human societies *par excellence* there exists, potentially, persistent conflict between cultural norms and personal desires. But since cultural conformity — whether in the form of the performance of socially prescribed tasks or in the form of the inhibition of socially prohibited acts — is a functional requirement of society,[6] this conflict must be resolved in such a way as to achieve compliance with the cultural norms. On the other hand, since the gratification of drives is a functional requirement for personal adjustment, this conflict must be resolved in such a way as to permit at least a minimum degree of drive gratification. In short, the conflict must be resolved so as to satisfy the functional requirements of the individual and of society simultaneously. How can this be done?

If it be granted that behavior is motivated, it is obvious that the mere learning of the cultural norms is not sufficient to induce compliance. For if behavior is motivated, cultural conformity can be achieved only if, in addition to the learning of the norms, the motivation for compliance with their demands is stronger than the motivation for the performance of competing behavior patterns that comprise the behavioral repertoire of the actors. With respect to the performance of social roles (compliance with prescriptive norms) there is one obvious way in which this can be achieved. If motivated behavior is goal-oriented behavior, and if we conceive of goals as objects, events, or conditions which gratify drives, the performance of roles can be ensured if, in the first place, the goals which are achieved by their performance are cathected by and, hence, serve to gratify personality drives, and if, secondly, the roles are perceived to be efficient means for their achievement. When this occurs, not only are the functional requirements of individual and society satisfied simultaneously, but the functional requirement of each is satisfied by an attribute of the other; that is, personality drives serve to instigate the performance of social roles, and the performance of roles serves to gratify personality drives.

There are, as far as I can tell, only two types of objects, conditions, and events which can become cathected as goals for the gratification of drives,

---

[6] It is not the maintenance of *the* social system, but of *a* social system that is a functional requirement. It is not cultural change but *anomie* that is dysfunctional, so that new roles may fulfill the functional requirements just as well if not better than the old ones. But change in a social system does not alter the problem with which we are concerned: potential conflict between compliance with the new norms and gratification of drives.

and which, therefore, can serve to instigate the performance of roles which attain them. These are (a) the functions which comprise the culturally defined *raison d'être* of a status, and also (b) those social rewards, or incentives,[7] which societies offer to the occupants of statuses. To use the esteem drive as an example, those individuals for whom the culturally prescribed functions of health or economic productivity are cathected as goals for the gratification of this drive will be motivated, respectively, to occupy the statuses of doctor or entrepreneur. Frequently, however, a status is occupied, even though its social function is not cathected, because of the cathexis of those rewards which societies offer to the occupants of the status. Thus, the statuses of doctor and entrepreneur may be occupied because of the incentives provided by a prestigeful title or a high income. If, then, occupants of a status perform its prescribed role in order to obtain either or both of these goals, the motivation for their performance may be termed "function oriented" and "incentive oriented" respectively.[8]

To summarize, if the culture of a society provides goals which gratify drives, and if its social system consists of roles whose performance is instrumental in achieving these goals, the functional requirements both for successful personal adjustment as well as for social adaptation and integration are satisfied. Although potential conflict between personal desires and cultural norms is frequently resolved in this way, there are at least three situations — psychologically, structurally, and culturally in- duced — in which this type of resolution is not achieved, in which, on the contrary, the motivation for noncompliance with cultural norms is strong- er than the motivation for compliance. In each of these situations other means for ensuring cultural conformity — means which are usually re- ferred to as "techniques of social control" — are required. We may begin with the least disruptive of these situations, that which is psychologically induced.

Although the performance of social roles may attain drive-gratifying goals, some of their constituent norms may be sufficiently irksome to lead to a psychologically induced preference for noncompliance with these norms. Thus, a teacher may prefer not to comply with a five-day teaching schedule, although in general he is otherwise content with his role. Compliance with norms of this type must be achieved by some technique other than function-oriented or incentive-oriented role motivation.

---

[7] "Social rewards" is used instead of the conventional "positive sanctions."

[8] This is a deliberate oversimplification. It is obvious that role performance is almost always motivated by a congeries of conscious and unconscious needs (*cf.* Spiro 1961).

A second situation of potential violation of norms obtains even though the performance of roles is an efficient means for the attainment of drive-gratifying goals, because the social structure prevents certain social strata from occupying the statuses in which these roles are performed, so that drive gratification requires other — perhaps proscribed — means for the attainment of the goals. Hence, unlike the first situation in which cultural conformity (compliance with prescriptive norms), however irksome, produces drive gratification, the second situation is one in which cultural conformity (compliance with proscriptive norms) leads to drive frustration. Thus, if Negroes are prevented from occupying those achieved economic statuses in which role performance attains prestige-gratifying goals, they may acquire a structurally induced motivation for proscribed techniques of gratification. I say "may" because often, as we shall see below, a frustrated drive is free to seek gratification by other approved techniques, as well as by those which are proscribed. Only if these alternative means are not attempted or, if attempted, prove to be unsuccessful, can it be predicted that the frustration of the drive will become a powerful basis for the motivation of proscribed behavior. And in order to preclude these proscribed motives from seeking overt expression, techniques of social control are required.[d]

The third basis for nonconformity — one which is culturally induced — obtains when a drive can find no sanctioned means of gratification because the drive itself is culturally disapproved. This is almost universally true with respect to such interpersonal drives as hostility and dependency. That any expression of these drives should be deemed socially undesirable is not difficult to understand. Although the minimal satisfaction of a child's initial dependency is a necessary condition for the survival of society, the persistence of childhood dependency into adulthood is sufficient condition of its extinction. Similarly uncontrolled aggression against the in-group would ultimately eventuate in a Hobbesian state of war of all against all. Culturally viewed, these drives are therefore entirely different from, for example, the esteem drive. Although cultural norms may differ concerning the desirability of the latter drive — cross-culturally the norms may vary

[d] Clearly, the above analysis obtains primarily when those in the lower social strata have culturally induced expectations concerning both the possibility and desirability of social mobility as a means of drive gratification. Building on such expectations, the Civil Rights Movement in America can be viewed as one which, rejecting "proscribed techniques," attempted to achieve the satisfaction of the needs and desires of Negroes through *social* change, while the black revolution is now attempting to achieve this end by means of *structural* change.

from permission to encouragement to applause — there is no society to my knowledge in which every undisguised expression of this drive is prohibited. And in those societies in which this drive is widely frustrated, it is not because the drive itself is deemed undesirable, but because, as we have seen, the social roles by which it may be gratified are not available to large segments of the population. Hence, where a conflict exists between the esteem drive and proscriptive norms, the conflict is between cultural norms and certain [but not all] of the motives for the gratification of the drive, rather than between cultural norms and the drive itself. In the case of hostility and dependency, however, there is a conflict between the cultural norms and drives themselves because, since they are socially disruptive, all motives for their gratification are proscribed. But since these are powerful drives, techniques of social control are required to prevent their overt expression.

In sum, the psychologically induced bases for nonconformity require techniques of social control to ensure the performance of socially required tasks, while the structurally and culturally induced bases for nonconformity require techniques of social control to protect society from socially disruptive activities.

It would seem that there are two techniques of social control — provided by the social system — which may be employed for the fulfillment of these functional requirements of society. One technique consists of social sanctions, that is, socially administered punishments,[9] which induce the members of society to perform prescribed activities or to suppress (or inhibit) proscribed activities. If these sanctions — which consist either of physical or emotional punishment (prison terms or public censure, for example), and which may be administered either by constituted authority (natural or supernatural) or by peers — are cathected as negative goals (because their imposition frustrates important drives), the resultant motivation to comply with cultural norms may be termed "sanction oriented."

But social sanctions may not be sufficient to ensure compliance with all cultural norms for the obvious reason that many activities occur at times and in places which are temporarily inaccessible either to authority figures (super alters) or to peers (alter egos). If the social system, through its socialization institutions, produces personalities in which the norms themselves are cathected as goals — personalities, that is, that have acquired a superego — cultural conformity may be achieved by what may be termed "norm-oriented" motivation. In this technique of social control — one

[9] "Social sanctions" is used here in place of the traditional, "negative social sanction."

whose universality is still a matter of dispute among anthropologists (Spiro 1961) — compliance with cultural norms itself becomes a goal (which gratifies the drive of self-esteem). In short, norm-oriented motivation differs from the other motivational bases for cultural conformity in that the norms are internalized as ends as well as means. By providing these techniques of social control, social systems satisfy two functional requirements of society: they assure the performance of those tasks which achieve commonly accepted group ends, and they protect society from socially disruptive activities.

Although they arrive by somewhat different routes, most theories of social systems — psychologically oriented and antipsychological, alike — converge at this point. That is, almost all theorists agree that the potential conflict between the normative demands of cultural systems and the personal desires of psychobiological systems presents all societies with one of their crucial maintenance problems. Almost all theorists agree, too, that this potential conflict is resolved by various techniques of conflict resolution that are built into the very fabric of the social system: on the one hand, by socialization mechanisms which, at least to some extent, create personalities whose desires are consistent with cultural norms; on the other hand, by techniques of social control which serve to preclude the expression of those desires that remain in conflict with cultural norms. Thus, by these (and other) maintenance mechanisms, the potentially disruptive forces inherent in any society are contained.

Yet it is precisely at this point of convergence that psychologically and nonpsychologically oriented theorists diverge most dramatically. The typical pure structural theorist would now conclude that with the resolution of conflict equilibrium is achieved, and society can now go about its business. For the culture-and-personality theorist, on the other hand, it is only at this point that the problem of social control becomes truly vexatious. For though the techniques of social control described above are adequate to handle what are termed the psychologically induced bases for nonconformity, they are most definitely inadequate to handle, except temporarily, the structurally and culturally induced bases for nonconformity. That is, the desire to achieve goals by means less onerous than those culturally prescribed (psychologically induced nonconformity) can easily be held in check by ordinary techniques of social control because the culturally prescribed means of attaining cathected goals, however sufficient or irksome, do in fact lead to drive gratification. This is not true of the other two bases for nonconformity. Although forbidden motives (proscribed means for gratifying the sanctioned esteem drive, for example, and all means for gratifying the forbidden hostility or dependency drives) may be *inhibited* by the fear of superego or of social sanction punishment, the drives which activate these motives are not *extinguished*. On the contrary, they persist and they continue to demand gratification. Hence, although the expression of the forbidden motive may be effectively contained by techniques of social control, the conflict between cultural norms and personal drives remains unresolved. In short, although they may satisfy a functional requirement of society by discouraging the expression of forbidden motives, techniques of social control may prevent the satisfaction of a functional requirement of personal adjustment when, as in the case of culturally and structurally induced forbidden motives, they not only contain the expression of forbidden motives, but they also prevent the gratification of personal drives. And since these drives demand gratification, they must either be gratified by some approved technique whose existence eludes the conceptual framework of pure structural analysis, or else their continued frustration will lead either to serious dysfunctional consequences for personality — which, in turn, is bound to have serious dysfunctional consequences for society — or to the breakdown of social control (that is, the motives for noncompliance will be stronger than those for compliance).

To summarize, techniques of social control serve to contain the expression of socially disruptive motives without producing ill effects on personal adjustment or social integration if the drives which instigate the performance of the motives are gratified in other ways — ways which the more conventional anthropological theories have not systematically explored because of their exclusion of personality variables from their conceptual formulations. Culture-and-personality theory, cognizant of the importance of frustrated drives, and realizing that these drives must be handled in some way, can make a unique contribution to the analysis of social system by an investigation of this problem. Not only unique, but important! For however these drives are handled, their expression has important consequences for the maintenance, change, or disruption of social systems. Here we can offer only some preliminary suggestions.

Frustrated drives, in the first place, provide one motivational source for social-cultural change. Thus, in the case of structurally induced drive frustration, the frustrated drive, which cannot be gratified by the performance of social roles, is free to seek gratification, as we have already indicated, by other approved means. For example, individuals whose esteem drive is frustrated may seek satisfaction in the invention or borrowing of new means for the achievement of blocked goals, means which, though not proscribed, are different from the prescribed roles. Should these instrumental innovations, however bizarre, fall within the limits of variability permitted by the cultural norms, they are socially acceptable; and should they be broadly imitated by others, they become the basis of cumulation and/or change in the social system. If, on the other hand, new means are not available or if they do not succeed in attaining the blocked goals, the pain of drive frustration may.lead to a substitution of new goals for the gratification of the drive (nativistic and utopian movements provide extreme examples). Sometimes this may be achieved by the conversion of the norms themselves into goals. If, for example, the sanctioned norms are conceived to have been instituted by the gods, compliance with the norms may become the goal whereby esteem is gratified. This is frequently the stance taken by movements of religious protest and sectarianism.

Secondly, frustrated drives provide an important motivational basis for the disruption of social systems. Thus, from the data now available there is abundant reason to believe that frustrated drives — whether culturally or structurally induced — constitute at least one important motivational basis for delinquency, crime, and political revolution. And such frustration must surely be a powerful basis for the *anomie* that is said to characterize certain sectors of industrial society, as well as for the frequently observed disruptive consequences of acculturation.

Our concern in this discussion is with the persistence of social systems. And here it would appear that the most important means by which forbidden motives are handled consist of the various mechanisms of ego defense described in the personality literature. These mechanisms have been viewed by personality theorists as techniques for defending the ego against pain — the pain of shame, of moral anxiety, of guilt, and of social sanctions. For the social system theorist, however, their significance resides in their social functions. That is, by resolving the conflict between cultural norms and personal drives in ways which are satisfactory to both personality and society, they not only protect the ego from the pain of inner conflict, but they may also — as we shall see — contribute important-ly to the maintenance of social systems. Among the various types of defense, three are of special importance to us here because of the additional light they may shed on this thesis. These are repression, displacement, and sublimation.

Repression — the rendering of the awareness of a drive or of its frustration unconscious — although an important means of ensuring cultural conformity is, at best, an unsatisfactory defense mechanism. The persistence of an unconscious, because forbidden, motive may, for example, lead to guilt and depression. Moreover, the energy required for persistent repression may result in continuous enervation and fatigue. Or, perhaps, the motive may break through the repressive forces only to find expression in some hysterical symptom. Alternatively, as in the case of unconscious hostility, it may be turned against the self and result in suicide. Depression, hysteria, and so forth, are unlikely candidates for indices of good mental health; and, should they become widespread, they would hardly (except in certain special circumstances) provide the psychological basis for a viable social system. In brief, a successful defense mechanism must not only protect the individual from the inner conflict and pain produced by the motive in question, but it must also allow him to gratify it in some form. But is this possible for such drives as hostility and dependency, all of whose motives are prohibited?

The answer is, of course, that althouth proscribed drives are not permitted direct gratification, they may be gratified in disguised ways. Thus, since it is the meaning of a motive, rather than the motive itself, that renders it acceptable or unacceptable, a change in any of its four dimensions — the drive, or its goal, the act, or its agent — may sufficiently alter its meaning so that it may re-enter consciousness and, in its disguised form, seek gratification. Each of these dimensional distortions produces each of the well-known defense mechanisms which need not be described here.[c] Although these mechanisms may resolve inner conflict (between norm and desire) and promote drive gratification, not all of their expressions are equally desirable, either for the individual or for society. Indeed, using the latter qualification as a criterion, we can distinguish three types of defenses: (a) those that are *culturally prohibited*, and socially and psychologically disruptive; (b) those that are *culturally approved*, and socially and psychologically integrative; (c) those that are *culturally constituted*, and socially and psychologically integrative.

[c] What, perhaps, should be described here is, however, the way in which defense mechanisms are produced by a change in one (or more) of the dimensions of a motive. If, for example, ego (agent) is hostile toward (drive), and wishes to harm (act), alter$_1$ (goal), then (1) a substitution of alter$_2$ for alter$_1$ characterizes the defense of displacement, (2) the reversal of agent and goal, so that alter becomes the putative agent and ego the putative goal characterizes the defense of projection, (3) the conversion of drive and act into their opposites, so that hostility becomes love and harm becomes protection, characterizes the defense of reaction formation, and so on.

Let us begin with the first type. If the distortion of a forbidden aggressive motive, for example, should lead to paranoid projection and therefore to acting-out behavior, on the one hand, or to its displacement onto other members of the in-group, on the other, the defensive behavior (in-group aggression) encounters the same cultural disapproval and meets the same social sanction as the original motive. The resolution of inner conflict is achieved at the price of mental illness and/or social punishment for the individual, or of the breakdown of social control for society. This is hardly a satisfactory type of defense.

The second type of defense does not require the payment of such a high price. In any society, everyone uses defenses of this type all the time, and they serve them, their society, and their social system very well. Thus, for example, the kicking of a tree instead of attacking a kinsman; the killing of animals for sport, instead of assassinating a chief; the temporary dependence upon a wife during illness, instead of the permanent dependence upon mother — these and scores of other defenses are used by individuals in all societies. They protect individuals from inner conflict and, at the same time, permit them to satisfy, albeit in a disguised form, forbidden needs; they achieve compliance with cultural prohibitions and thereby protect society from the expression of forbidden motives. Their importance both for the student of personality and for the student of social systems cannot be overestimated. For the latter they provide an important conceptual tool for the analysis of cultural conformity. They enable him to understand how techniques of social control can frustrate proscribed motives without producing dysfunctional consequences for the members of society or for their social system.

But defense mechanisms are of even greater importance to the social system theorist than has thus far been suggested; and this brings us to our third type of defenses. Defense mechanisms, like other behavior patterns, are both idiosyncratic and culturally patterned. That is, some defense mechanisms — the ones to which we have already alluded — are developed by the individual through his own personality resources; others are developed by groups of individuals, and even by an entire society by means of resources which are provided by their social system or their culture. In short, if social systems and cultures are analyzed by an array of conceptual tools — psychological as well as structural — it would appear that many of their component parts (values, norms, beliefs, roles, and so forth) are used by the typical member of society as the bases for defense mechanisms. Indeed, their use as important ingredients of defense mechanisms may sometimes be their crucially important (latent) function. These mechanisms of defense, to be described below, which are based on beliefs, practices, and roles, and other constituent parts of cultural or social systems, comprise that type which I have termed "culturally constituted," in contrast to the other two types which consist of privately constituted defense mechanisms. The analysis of these culturally constituted mechanisms is, in my opinion, one of the vital tasks of culture-and-personality as a theory of social systems. Although this task has still to be undertaken, I should like to suggest a preliminary classification of culturally constituted defenses.

One type of culturally constituted defense is the functional equivalent for society of the private defense of expression. Like repression — but by other means to be explained below — it serves to preclude the expression of socially disruptive motives. A second type — analogous to displacement — utilizes materials from the social or cultural system for the distortion of a forbidden motive and, hence, its disguised gratification. Both of these types are essentially techniques of social control; they serve, that is, to contain the potential expression of disruptive motives. A third type — analogous to sublimation — not only serves to contain socially disruptive motives, but it uses these very motives as an important basis for the performance of social roles. This type, in short, not only protects society from the expression of proscribed motives, it also provides an important motivational basis for the performance of prescribed roles. Space permits only a brief description of each of these types. We shall begin with the first.

I would suggest that various types of avoidance behavior, based on avoidance taboos, may be viewed as culturally constituted defenses which serve to prevent the expression of forbidden motives. These are the functional equivalents of the private defense of repression. This suggestion has been made by Freud (1919, ch. 1) and Murdock (1949:273) with respect to sexual avoidance, when they observe that patterned avoidance of relatives of opposite sex — mother-in-law and son-in-law, for example — is a means of preventing incest. Similarly, other motives which are deemed socially disruptive — aggression against a same-sex in-law, for example — may be denied expression by separating (physically or emotionally) the motivated individual from the source of temptation. Other customs may have the same function. For example, the couvade — shorn of its cultural elaborations — has the objective consequence of separating a father from his offspring for a certain period after its birth. If we assume that fathers are initially hostile to their offspring of either sex (because they are competitors for his wife's affection, nurturance, and so forth), either repression of the hostility or institutionalized avoidance (or some third functional equivalent) would serve to preclude the overt expression of the motive. To be sure, since avoidance behavior serves only to contain the motive rather than to gratify the drive, we would expect to find other means of disguised or symbolic gratifications — either in private or cultural fantasy (religion, myth, and so forth) or in one of the other culturally constituted defenses.

The differences between this type of analysis and a typical "structural" analysis of the Radcliffe-Brown type — in which in-law avoidance is interpreted as symbolic expression of friendship (1952:92), and postpartum fatherhood rituals as symbolic expression of paternal concern (1952:150) — are threefold. First, hypotheses of the former type are deduced from fairly well established, empirically grounded, principles of behavior, while those of the latter type are based on certain assumptions concerning human nature — in this case, the necessity to symbolize certain types of interpersonal relationships — whose validity is merely assumed. (Both types, be it noted, are "psychological.") Second, hypotheses of the first type are based on a functionalist conception of social systems which views them as (in the long run) instrumental to a variety of personal and social adaptive and integrative ends, while those of the latter type view them as essentially serving the one end of maintaining the social structure. Third, and most important, hypotheses of the first type are empirically testable: they can be confirmed or disconfirmed. Those of the latter type are essentially nontestable. What kinds of empirical data could either confirm or disconfirm the hypothesis that sentiments of friendship between in-laws must be institutionalized and symbolically expressed, and that avoidance does in fact constitute such an expression?

The second type of culturally constituted defense uses materials provided by the social or cultural systems, not for the containment of forbidden motives, but for their distortion and, hence, for their disguised gratification. This type, which is most frequently exemplified by culturally constituted displacement mechanisms has a number of subtypes. Thus social systems which include headhunting raids permit the displacement of aggression from in-group to out-group. Similarly, cultural systems that postulate the existence of malevolent supernaturals permit the projection and displacement of aggression from in-group to out-group. In both these subtypes, a forbidden motive (in-group aggression) is allowed disguised gratification by a cognitive distortion of either its object and/or its agent — a distortion which is based on culturally constituted beliefs or behavior patterns. By allowing for the disguised and culturally approved gratification of a forbidden motive, this defense reduces the probability of its undisguised gratification, and thus protects society from its disruptive consequences. "Rituals of rebellion," as Gluckman terms them, exemplify still a third subtype of culturally constituted displacement mechanisms. Here again, it is instructive to contrast a psychologically oriented analysis with a nonpsychologically oriented analysis. According to Gluckman (1956:ch.5) these rituals, in which the politically subservient symbolically rebel against authority figures, strengthen rather than weaken loyalty to the political order, because "they assert acceptance of common goals despite these hostilities." Viewed as a culturally constituted defense, however, the performance of these rituals would be said to achieve this end *because of,* rather than *despite,* "these hostilities." This seemingly trivial substitution of adverbs contains an entirely different mode of explanation.

In Gluckman's structuralist point of view, these rituals are essentially expressive; their performance "asserts" or symbolizes a state of affairs which exists prior to their performance — the acceptance of common goals. From a culture-and-personality point of view these rituals are essentially instrumental; their performance is a means for the attainment and/or persistence of a state of affairs — the acceptance of common goals. Gluckman's mode of analysis is, of course, paradigmatic of almost all structural analyses — at least those that derive from Radcliffe-Brown: practice *a* symbolizes the solidarity of the lineage, practice *b* reflects the structure of the clan, practice *c* symbolizes both the conjunctive and disjunctive dimensions inherent in a social relationship, and so forth. But even if it were granted that certain practices are symbolic, for example, of solidarity, why, it may be asked, is it necessary or important either from a social system point of view or from a personality point of view to symbolize that which, *ex hypothesi,* exists prior to its symbolization? Thus, in the case at hand, if rituals of rebellion merely express a state of affairs — the acceptance of common goals — which already exists, then, from a social system point of view, what possible functions can these rituals have? Certainly not the strengthening of the political order since, so it is argued, the acceptance of the political order exists prior to their performance. And, even if it be argued that they have some function of which we are not aware, we still have the problem, from a personality point of view, of accounting for their motivation. That their performance is highly motivated is an obvious conclusion from Professor Gluckman's graphic descriptions. Yet, unless we postulate some personality "need" to symbolize political loyalty, we are at a loss to account for their motivation. And even if we were to grant the existence of such a dubious need, we would ask why this need is symbolized in this peculiar form.

If, on the other hand, these rituals be viewed as culturally constituted displacement mechanisms, their motivation is explicable in terms of personality theory, and their functions become explicable in terms of the functional requirements of any society. For since, as Gluckman describes very clearly, those who are politically subservient are hostile to those who hold political power, and since the expression of this hostility in acts of aggression is in conflict with norms which prohibit such expression, we may conclude that (*a*) the performance of these rituals is motivated by hostility to authority; (*b*) their performance serves the personal function of gratifying the hostility drive — in a socially approved and nondisruptive (symbolic) manner; (*c*) in serving this personal function, these rituals serve the adaptive social function of preserving political order because by gratifying this hostility drive in a symbolic manner, their performance reduces the probability of its gratification in ways (such as revolution) that would be disruptive of this order; and (*d*) by serving this personal function, these rituals also serve the integrative social function of strengthening political loyalty because in draining off these hostile emotions, their performance permits the commitment to "common goals" to reassert itself over those emotional forces which militate against this commitment.

It may be noted that in the first two subtypes of culturally constituted displacement mechanisms, a forbidden motive finds disguised gratification through a distorted expression of the motive; in this third subtype, a forbidden motive finds direct gratification through a symbolic (ritualized) expression of the motive.

The third type of culturally constituted defense — that which is analogous to the private defense of sublimation — is even more important than the first two. For in this type, society is not only protected from the possible dysfunctional consequences of socially disruptive drives, but these very potentially disruptive drives are used as the motivational bases for the performance of social roles. This may be illustrated by a brief examination of a universally prohibited drive — dependence — and its vicissitudes on the atoll of Ifaluk. The Ifaluk, like all people, must express and gratify their dependency drive in a disguised manner; and, in my opinion, the disguise by which they express this drive takes the form of obedience and subservience *to* their chiefs, while the disguise by which they gratify the drive takes the form of affection and food *from* their chiefs.

The desire for love from the chiefs and the fear of its loss is in Ifaluk the primary basis for chiefly authority and, hence, for cultural conformity. Indeed, if love from the chiefs were not of primary importance for the Ifaluk, it would be difficult to understand how their authority could persist. For Ifaluk chiefs can neither reward nor punish; they possess neither punitive sanctions nor the means to implement them. Since they possess no means of enforcing their authority, it must be delegated to them; and the primary basis for its delegation seems to reside in almost magical significance for emotional well-being with which their love, expressed in praise and in kindly understanding, is invested by the people. The Ifaluk say that if the chiefs "talk good," the people will live long, but if they "talk bad," the people will perish. In the former instance the people, as they say, are *eratu dipei* — that is, their stomachs are "good"; in the latter, they are *engau dipei*, their stomachs are "bad." In short, in this society, in which food — from the earliest age and in almost all anxiety-producing contexts — is used for comfort and nurturance, the kind talk of these chiefs who — as it is said in pidgin, are "all same pappa this place" — is symbolic of nurturance, their harsh talk of its withdrawal.

This symbolism of good stomachs and bad stomachs provides a possible explanation for the otherwise inexplicable, but ubiquitous, Ifaluk ritual of food distribution. At the completion of almost any collective activity — and in Ifaluk they are frequent — the chiefs distribute food and tobacco. Since, except for a small quantity of tobacco, both the food and the tobacco distributed by the chiefs has been offered to them by the people, and since the amount received by any one household is of the same quantity and quality as they had brought, and since in any event the economic value of a few coconuts, a taro pudding, and a few ounces of tobacco is negligible, the eagerness and expectancy with which the Ifaluk await its distribution is manifestly inexplicable. Indeed, for the Ifaluk themselves the entire ritual is inexplicable. To an inquiry into its meaning, the Ifaluk retort with *musuwe, musuwe* ("before, before"); that is, "this is a tradition, and we cannot know why we perform it." But if food is a symbol of nurturance (as it is in Ifaluk), and if the chiefs are perceived by the Ifaluk as nurturant parent figures (as I believe them to be), their eager and expectant attitudes may be explained in terms of the meaning of the ritual as an instrument for the gratification of their dependency drive. (This ritual, of course, has other functions as well.)

Since the chiefs gratify the Ifaluk dependency drive, by providing them with love and nurturance, the expectation of gratifying this potentially dysfunctional drive becomes an important motivational basis for obeying the chiefs, which in effect ensures the maintenance of the political system and the body of cultural norms which it supports. This function of Ifaluk chieftainship was cogently articulated by the paramount chief:

> The chiefs are like fathers here. Just as an empty canoe is tossed about by the waves and finally sinks, so, too, a society without chiefs is tossed about by conflict and strife and is destroyed. If a father asks his son not to behave badly the latter may not obey him since he may not respect him highly. But all people obey the words of the chiefs, since they are feared and respected by all. The chiefs' duty is to see that the people behave well. The chiefs must constantly tell the people to be good, or else the society, like the canoe, would be destroyed.

Notice, then, the important functions, both personal and social, that are served by this type of culturally constituted defense mechanism. By utilizing elements of the social system as a means for disguising and thereby gratifying a forbidden drive (*a*) this type — like the second type — permits the members of society to resolve conflict between a cultural norm and a forbidden drive in a way that precludes psychotic distortion of the drive; (*b*) it protects them from punitive sanctions or punitive superego, since the disguised drive is gratified in socially prescribed activities; (*c*) society is protected from the socially disruptive influence of the direct gratification of the forbidden drive; (*d*) finally — and this function is served only by the third type — a potentially disruptive drive is transmuted into a powerful force for the maintenance of the social system.

Conclusion

I have suggested that, rather than persist as a distinctive sub-discipline within the total range of the anthropological sciences, culture-and-personality conceive of itself as part of that subdiscipline — social anthropology — which is concerned with the analysis of social and cultural systems. Thus the contributions of culture-and-personality theory can be combined with the important contributions of structural theory (notably those of British social anthropology) and of role theory (notably those of American sociology and social psychology) to advance our understanding of human society and culture. As a partner in this venture, culture-and-personality can make (indeed, has made) a unique contribution.

Rooted as it is in an instrumental approach to behavior, culture-and-personality necessarily looks at social systems from the perspective of ends to be achieved, functions to be served, and requirements to be satisfied. Given this perspective, its important theoretical goal is to discover the ways in which personality systems enable social and cultural systems to serve their social functions. These functions, it is obvious, are not served by the mere *existence* of these systems, but by their *operation*. And their operation is, in the last analysis, a motivational problem. Hence, culture-and-personality — always mindful that human behavior is the empirical datum from which all systems, all structures, and all sociocultural variables are ultimately abstracted — insists that the operation of social and cultural systems cannot be understood without reference to the empirically demonstrable or inferential needs whose expected gratifications constitute the motivational basis for human behavior, and which, therefore, comprise the immediate antecedent conditions for the operation of these systems. Hence, if the gratification of needs constitutes the personal function of social and cultural systems, their social functions cannot be served unless their personal functions are served. In short, although social and cultural systems develop — through a process of adaptive selection — as a response to various functional requirements of human social life, they persist because of their ability to satisfy the functional requirements of human personal life.

Despite the importance of motivation in the operation of social and cultural systems, an understanding of their operation could proceed without the benefit of culture-and-personality analysis if culture and personality always existed in a one-to-one relationship so that conformity with cultural norms always gratified personal needs, and personal needs were always gratified by means of culturally prescribed or approved behavior. If this were the case, motivation could be taken for granted by the social anthropologist; and though the social functions of these systems could be served only if their personal functions were served, the anthropologist would not require an understanding of the latter in order to understand the former. But conformity with cultural norms — alas — does not always gratify needs. Conformity often leads to the frustration of needs; and it is because of this frequent conflict between need gratification and cultural conformity that an understanding of personality dynamics is crucial for an understanding of cultural conformity, social control, and the operation of social systems. For, although social sanctions and superegos may, as control mechanisms, induce conformity, they do not extinguish culturally proscribed desires and, hence, they do not reduce intrapersonal conflict (between cultural norm and personal desire). It is one of the tasks of culture-and-personality to discover how this intrapersonal conflict is resolved in such a way that functional requirements both of the individual and of social life are satisfied simultaneously. The analysis of culturally constituted defense mechanisms offers one such avenue of investigation.

Bibliography

BEACH, FRANK AND E. JANES. 1954. Effects of early experience upon the behavior of animals. Psychological Bulletin 51:239-263.

BOAS, FRANZ. 1938. Race, language and culture. Boston, Heath.

CARPENTER, C. R. 1958. Naturalistic behavior of the non-human primates. Handbuch der Zoologie. Berlin, Walter de Gruyter.

DEWEY, JOHN. 1938. Logic: the theory of inquiry. New York, Holt.

FIRTH, RAYMOND. 1951. Elements of social organization. London, Watts.

FREUD, SIGMUND. 1919. Totem and taboo. New York, Moffat, Yard.

GLUCKMAN, MAX. 1956. Custom and conflict in Africa. Glencoe, Free Press.

HALLOWELL, A. IRVING. 1960. Self, society, and culture in phylogenetic perspective. *In* the evolution of man. Sol Tax, ed. Chicago, University of Chicago Press.

HSU, FRANCIS L. K. 1969. The study of literate civilizations. New York, Holt, Rinehart & Winston.

LÉVI-STRAUSS, CLAUDE. 1953. Social structure. *In* Anthropology today. A. L. Kroeber, ed. Chicago, University of Chicago Press.

MURDOCK, GEORGE PETER. 1949. Social structure. New York, Macmillan.

PARSONS, TALCOTT. 1951. The social system. Glencoe, Free Press.

PIERCE, CHARLES. 1935. Collected papers Vol. 5. P. Weiss and C. Hartshorne, eds. Cambridge, Harvard University Press.

RADCLIFFE-BROWN, A. R. 1950. Introduction. *In* African systems of kinship and marriage. A. R. Radcliffe-Brown and Daryll Forde, eds. London, Oxford University Press.

SCHNEIRLA, T. C. 1950. A consideration of some problems in the ontogeny of family life and social adjustment in various infrahuman animals. *In* Problems of infancy and childhood. M. Senn, ed. New York, Josiah Macy Fd.

SPIRO, MELFORD E. 1951. Culture and personality, the natural history of a false dichotomy. Psychiatry 14:19-46.

———. 1959. Culture heritage, personal tensions, and mental illness in a South Sea culture. *In* Culture and mental health. M. K. Opler, ed. New York, Macmillan.

———. 1960. Social control, socialization, and the theory of social systems. Presented at the Berkeley Conference on Personality Development in Childhood.

———. 1961. Social systems, personality, and functional analysis. *In* Studying personality cross-culturally. Bert Kaplan, ed. Evanston, Rowe-Peterson.

———. 1965. Religious systems as culturally constituted defense mechanisms. *In* Context and meaning in cultural anthropology. Melford Spiro, ed. Glencoe, Free Press.

———. 1966. Buddhism and economic saving in Burma. American Anthropologist 68:1163–1173.

———. 1967. Burmese supernaturalism: a study in the explanation and resolution of suffering. Englewood Cliffs, N.J., Prentice-Hall.

———. 1968a. Culture and personality. International Encyclopedia of the Social Sciences.

———. 1968b. Politics and factionalism in Upper Burma. *In* Local level politics. Marc Swartz, ed. Chicago, Aldine.

———. 1971. Buddhism & society. New York, Harper & Row.

WASHBURN, S. L. 1953. The strategy of physical anthropology. *In* Anthropology today. A. L. Kroeber, ed. Chicago, University of Chicago Press.

A Supplementary Bibliography on Projective Testing

compiled by DAVID H. SPAIN

The items in this bibliography have been divided into three broad, somewhat overlapping categories: (1) theoretical and general works; (2) aspects of test evaluation, analysis, and the assessment of technical problems; and (3) cross-cultural and (primarily) non-western applications of projective techniques. As is well known, many descriptive applications have also contributed to the theory and method of projective testing. Moreover, many of the publications designed to evaluate and improve methods of administration and other technical matters have also contributed numerous important descriptive observations. Nevertheless, for purposes of economy, each reference, including those which clearly touched on more than one of the major categories of the bibliography, was only listed once.

The items in the bibliography cover most intensively the period from 1960–1969, though many are from an earlier period and a few are more recent. All of the sources are in English, reflecting not so much the realities of scholarship as the limitations of time. Because of space limitations, the plethora of short (frequently single page) articles were excluded from this bibliography. This is not to say short articles are less useful than longer ones; often the contrary is the case. In some instances, these articles may have touched on matters of considerable importance, but as a rule of thumb, eliminating these seemed wiser than eliminating others of greater detail or scope. Readers interested in locating these and additional references are invited to consult *Psychological Abstracts*.

Items which were thought likely to be included in the references for other papers in this volume were purposely excluded from this bibliography. Though omissions (especially in the "applications" section) may have resulted from this procedure, reasons of economy made them unavoidable. Finally, this is a selected bibliography; that is, it is not comprehensive. Hopefully however, there will be ample stimulus for thought in the range of items included. It is also to be hoped anthropologists particularly will pick up the challenge put forward by the colleagues in other disciplines cited here.

I. Theoretical and General Works (including new tests, and scoring).

ABEL, T. M. 1948. The Rorschach test in the study of culture. Rorschach Res. Exch., 2:79–93.

ALLEN, ROBERT M. 1966. Student's Rorschach manual: An introduction to administering, scoring and interpreting Rorschach's psychodiagnostic inkblot test. New York, Inter. Univ. Press.

ANASTASI, ANNE. 1961. Psychological testing. New York, Macmillan.

ATTKISSON, C. C., L. HANDLER, AND R. R. SHRADER. 1969. The use of figure drawings to assess religious values. Jour. of Psychol., 71:27–31.

BECK, SAMUEL J. 1968. Reality, Rorschach and perceptual theory. In A. I. Rabin, (ed.), Projective testing in personality assessment. New York, Springer.

BELLAK, LEOPOLD. 1947. Bellak TAT Blank: For recording and analyzing Thematic Apperception Test stories. New York: The Psych. Corp.

BORGATTA, EDGAR F. AND H. J. MAYER. 1961. Make a Sentence Test: An approach to objective scoring of sentence completions. Genet. Psychol. Mono., 63:3–65.

BRICKLIN, BARRY, Z. A. PIOTROWSKI, AND E. E. WAGNER. 1962. The Hand test. Springfield, Thomas.

CALDWELL, W. E. AND C. MATTOON. 1966. The Somato-Chroma apperception test: A quantitative projective technique. Jour. of Gen. Psych., 74:253–272.

CAMPBELL, D. T. 1957. A typology of tests, projective and otherwise. J. Consult. Psychol., 21:207–210.

CAMPOS, LEONARD P. 1968. Other projective techniques. In A. I. Rabin (ed.), Projective testing in personality assessment., pp. 461–520. New York, Springer.

CASSEL, R. N. AND T. C. KAHN. 1961. The Group personality projective test (GPPT). Psychol. Rep., 8:23–41.

CHATTERJU, B. B. AND N. K. SHRIMALI. 1958. Story completion test as a projective technique. U. Rajputana Stud., 2:121–142.

COHEN, YEHUDI A. 1961. Social structure and personality: A casebook. New York, Holt, Rinehart and Winston, Inc.

COLEMAN, JOHN C. 1969. The levels hypothesis: A re-examination and reorientation. Journ. Proj. Tech. and Pers. Assess., 33:118–122.

CREMSHAW, DAVID A., ET AL. 1968. The use of projective methods in research: 1947–1965. Jour. of Proj. Tech. and Pers. Assess., 32:3–9.

CRONBACH, LEE J. 1960. Essentials of psychological testing. New York: Harper.

DASTON, PAUL G. 1968. Word associations and sentence completion techniques. *In* A. I. Rabin (ed.), Projective testing in personality assessment. New York, Springer.

DAVID, HENRY P. AND J. C. BRENGELMANN. 1960. Perspectives in personality research. New York, Springer.

DAVID, HENRY P. AND WILLIAM RABINOWITZ. 1960. Brief projective methods in personality assessment. *In* Henry P. David and J. C. Brengelmann (ed.), Perspectives in personality research. New York, Springer.

DRAGUNS, JURIS G., E. MARIE HOLEY AND LESLIE PHILLIPS. 1967. Studies of Rorschach content: A review of the research literature: I. Traditional content categories. Jour. of Proj. Tech. and Pers. Assess., 31(1): 3–32.

————. 1967. Studies of Rorschach content: A review of the research literature: II. Non-traditional cases of content indicators. Jour. of Proj. Tech. and Pers. Assess., 31(2): 3–38.

————. 1968. Studies of Rorschach content: A review of research literature: III. Theoretical formulations. Jour. of Proj. Tech. and Pers. Assess., 32: 16–32.

FARBEROW, NORMAN L. (ED.). 1968. Symposium: Consensus Rorschachs in the study of problem behavior. Jour. of Proj. Tech. and Pers. Assess. 32:326–357.

FEIN, LEAH G. 1960. The three-dimensional personality test. New York, Internat'l Univ. Press.

FINE, R. 1955. A scoring scheme and manual for the TAT and other verbal projective techniques. J. Proj. Tech., 19:306–309.

FISKE, DONALD W. AND PAMELA H. PEARSON. 1970. Theory and techniques of personality measurement. *In* Paul H. Mussen and Mark R. Rosenzweig, (eds.), Annual Review of Psychology, v. 21. Palo Alto, Annual Review, Inc.

FRANK, L. K. 1948. Projective methods. Springfield, Thomas.

————. 1960. Toward a projective psychology. J. Proj. Tech., 24:246–253.

FRIED, JACOB. 1954. Picture testing: An aid to ethnological field work. AA:56:95–97.

FRIJDA, N. AND G. JAHODA. 1966. On the scope and methods of cross-cultural research. Internat'l Journal of Psychology, 1:109–127.

FULKERSON, SAMUEL C. 1965. Some implications of the new cognitive theory for projective tests. Jour. of Consult. Psych., 29:191–197.

GOLDBERG, P. A. 1965. A review of sentence completion methods in personality assessment. Jour. of Proj. Tech. and Pers. Assess., 29:12–45.

GOODENOUGH, FLORENCE L. 1946. Semantic choice and personality structure. Science, 104:451–456.

GRANT, G. V. AND SCHEPERS, J. M. 1969. An exploratory factor analysis of five new cognitive tests for African mineworkers. Psychologia Africana, 12:181–192.

HANDLER, L. AND J. REYHER. 1965. Figure drawing anxiety indexes: A review of the literature. Jour. Proj. Tech. and Pers. Assess., 29: 305–313.

HAMMER, EMANUEL F. 1968. Projective drawings. *In* A. I. Rabin (ed.), Projective testing in personality assessment. New York, Springer.

HARROWER, MOLLY. 1968. Appraising personality: An introduction to the projective techniques. New York, Simon and Schuster.

HAWORTH, MARY R. 1966. The CAT: Facts about fantasy. New York, Grune and Stratton.

———. 1968. Symposium: The children's Apperception test: Its use in developmental assessments of normal children. Jour. Proj. Tech. and Pers. Assess., 32:405–427.

———. 1968. Doll play and puppetry. *In* A. I. Rabin (ed), Projective testing in personality assessment. New York: Springer.

HENRY, J. AND M. E. SPIRO. 1953. Psychological techniques: Projective tests in field work. *In* A. L. Kroeber (ed.), Anthropology today. Chicago: University of Chicago Press., pp. 417–429.

HENRY, W. E. 1947. The thematic apperception technique in the study of culture-personality relations. Genet. Psychol. Monogr., 35:3–135.

———. 1961. Projective tests in cross-cultural research. *In* B. Kaplan, ed. Studying personality cross-culturally. Evanston, Row, Peterson; pp. 587–596.

HIRT, MICHAEL (ED.). 1962. Rorschach science: Readings in theory and method. New York, Free Press.

HOLZBERG, JULES D. 1968. Psychological theory and projective techniques. *In* A. I. Rabin, (ed.), Projective testing in personality assessment. New York, Springer.

HUNDLEBY, J. D.; K. PAWLIK, R. B. CATTELL. 1965. Personality factors in objective test devices: A critical integration of a quarter century in research. San Diego, Knapp.

HURLEY, J. R. 1955. The Iowa Picture interpretation test: A multiple-choice variation of the TAT. Jour. of Consul. Psych., 19:372–376.

JENSEN, A. R. 1964. The Rorschach technique: A re-evaluation. Acta Psych., 22:60–77.

JOHNSON, A. W., JR. AND R. H. DANA. 1965. Color on the TAT. Jour. Proj. Tech. and Pers. Assess., 29:178–182.

KAGAN, JEROME AND GERALD S. LESSER (EDS.). 1961. Contemporary issues on thematic apperceptive methods. Springfield, Thomas.

KAPLAN, BERT. 1963. Projective techniques and the theory of action. Merrill-Palmer Quart., 9:3–10.

KLOPFER, W. G. 1968. Current status of the Rorschach test. *In* P. McReynolds, (ed.), Advances in Psychological Assessment. Palo Alto, Science and Behavior Books.

KLOPFER, B. AND D. M. KELLY. 1942. The Rorschach technique. New York, Harcourt, Brace and World.

KODAMA, HABUKU. 1957. Personality tests in Japan. Psychologia, 1:92–103.

LANSKY, LEONARD M. 1968. Story completion methods. *In* A. I. Rabin, (ed.), Projective testing in personality assessment. New York, Springer.

LEVINE, DAVID. 1968. Why and when to test: The social context of psychological testing. *In* A. I. Rabin, (ed.), Projective testing in personality assessment. New York, Springer.

LEVY, SIDNEY. 1952. Sentence completion and word association tests. *In* Progress in Clinical Psychology, V. I., section I: Daniel Bro···⁻r and Lawrence Edwin Abt (eds.), New York, Grune & Stratton.

LINDZEY, GARDNER AND SHIRLEY H. HEINEMAN. 1955. Thematic apperception test: Individual and group administration. Jour. of Personality, 24:34–55.

LOVELAND, N., L. WYNNE AND M. SINGER. 1963. The Family Rorschach: A new method for studying family interaction. Family Process, 2:187–215.

LYNN, DAVID B. 1959. Structured doll play test (SDP): A projective test for use with children. Denver, Test developments.

MACHOVER, K. 1949. Personality projection in the drawings of the human figure. Springfield, Thomas.

MAHER, B. A. (ED.). 1964. Progress in experimental personality research. New York, Academic Press.

MESSICK, SAMUEL AND JOHN ROSS (EDS.). 1962. Measurement in personality and cognition. New York, Wiley.

MEYER, N. N. 1963. Family relations test. Jour. Proj. Tech. and Pers. Assess., 27: 309–314.

MILLON, THEODORE (ED.). 1968. Approaches to personality. New York, Pitman.

MILLS, DAVID H. 1965. The research use of projective techniques: A seventeen year survey. Jour. Proj. Tech. and Pers. Assess., 29:513–515.

MISCHEL, W. 1968. Personality and Assessment. New York, Wiley.

MURRAY, H. A. 1938. Explorations in personality. New York, Oxford.

MURSTEIN, BERNARD I. 1963. Theory and research in projective techniques (emphasizing the TAT). New York, John Wiley and Sons.

———. 1965. Handbook of Projective Techniques, New York/London, Basic Books, Inc.

NAWAS, MIKE. 1965. Objective scoring of the TAT: Further validation. Jour. Proj. Techs. and Pers. Assess., 29: 456–460.

NEURINGER, CHARLES. 1967. Art and Science in projective techniques. Jour. of Consult. Psych. 31:85–88.

———. 1968. A variety of thematic methods. *In* A. I. Rabin (ed.), Projective testing in personality assessment. New York, Springer.

PAREEK, UDAI AND S. N. CHATTOPATHYAY. 1965. A projective technique to measure change—proneness of farmers. Jour. of Soc. Sciences, 4:1–14.

———. 1965. Measuring level-of-aspiration of farmers through a projective technique. Indian Jour. of Soc. Work, 25:363–373.

PHATAH, P. 1961. Comparative study of revised draw-a-man scale (Harris) and Phatak draw-a-man scale for Indian children. Psychol. Stud., Mysore, 6:12–17.

PRZEWORSKI, ADAM AND HENRY TEUNE. 1966–67. Equivalence in cross-national research. Public opinion Quarterly, 30:551–568.

PSYCHOL. BULL. SUPPLEMENT. 1954. Technical recommendations for psychological tests and diagnostic techniques. 51, 2, part 2, 1–38.

RABIN, A. I. (ED.). 1968. Projective technique in personality assessment: A modern introduction. New York, Springer.

———. 1968. Adapting and devising projective methods for special purposes. *In* A. I. Rabin, (ed.), Projective testing in personality assessment. New York, Springer.

———. 1968. Projective methods: An historical introduction. *In* A. I. Rabin (ed.), Projective testing in personality assessment. New York, Springer.

RABIN, ALBERT I. AND MARY R. HAWORTH (EDS.). 1960. Projective techniques with children. New York, Grune and Stratton.

RAO, S. K. RAMACHANDRA. 1962. Studies with thematic apperception test. Trans. Atl.-India ment. health., pp. 40–70.

RICCIUTTI, HENRY. 1962. Development and application of projective techniques of personality. Rev. Educ. Res., 32:64–77.

ROBINSON, SANDRA A. 1968. The development of a female form of the Blacky pictures. Jour. of Proj. Tech. and Pers. Assess., 32:74–80.

ROSENBERG, JERRY M. 1962. Ethnodrama as a research method in anthropology. Group Psychother., 15:236–243.

ROSENWALD, GEORGE C. 1968. The thematic apperception test. *In* A. I. Rabin, (ed.)., Projective testing in personality assessment. New York, Springer.

SARGENT, HELEN D. 1953. The Insight Test. New York, Grune and Stratton.

SATZ, P. AND L. T. CARROLL. 1962. Utilization of the proverbs test as a projective instrument: An objective approach through language behavior. Jour. Gen. Psychol., 67: 205–213.

SCHACHTEL, ERNEST G. 1966. Experiential Foundations of Rorschach's test. New York/London, Basic Books, Inc.

SCHAIL, K. WARNER. 1963. The color pyramid test: A nonverbal technique for personality assessment. Psychol. Bulletin, 60:530–547.

SHERWOOD, J. J. 1966. Self-report and projective measures of achievement and affiliation. Jour. of Consulting Psychol. 30:329–337.

SHNEIDMAN, EDWIN S. 1949. Make-a-picture-story ('MAPS') test. New York, The Psychological Corp.

STRAUS, MURRAY A. 1969. Family measurement techniques: Abstracts of published instruments, 1935–1965. Minneapolis, University of Minn. Press.

SCHWARTZ, J. D. AND W. H. HOLTZMAN. 1963. Group method of administration for the Holtzman inkblot technique. Jour. of Clinical Psychol., 19:433–441.

SZALAY, L. B. AND J. E. BRENT. 1967. The analysis of cultural meanings through free verbal associations. Jour. of Soc. Psych., 72:161–187.

TAKOLA, MARTTI. 1964. Studies of the Wartegg drawings completion test. Annales Academial Scientiarum Fennicae, 131:1–112.

TAULBEE, EARL S. AND DAVID E. STENMARK. 1968. The blacky pictures test: A comprehensive annotated and indexed bibliography (1949–1967). Jour. Proj. Tech. & Pers. Assess., 32:102–137.

TERHUNE, KENNETH W. 1969. A note on thematic apperception scoring of needs for achievement, affiliation, and power. Jour. Proj. Tech. and Pers. Assess., 33:364–370.

TSERJI, S., H. FUJI AND K. ONO. 1965. Studies on the scenario-test. Japanese Jour. of Psych., 35:297–305. [a verbal TAT].

ULETT, GEORGE. 1960. Rorschach introductory manual (3rd ed.). St. Louis, Bartgett.

VAN KREVELEN, D. AM. 1961. Introduction to the book catalogue test. Acta-paedopsychiat., 28: 49–59.

VAN LENNEP, D. J. 1948. Four-picture test. The Hague, Martinus Nijhoff.

VERNON, P. E. 1964. Personality assessment: A critical survey. New York, Wiley.

WALLACE, JOHN AND LEE SECHREST. 1963. Frequency hypothesis and content analysis of projective techniques. Journal Consult. Psychol., 27:287–293.

WHITLA, D. K. (ED.). 1968. Handbook of measurement and assessment in behavioral sciences. Reading, Addison-Wesley.

WITKIN, H. A. 1967. A cognitive-style approach to cross-cultural research. Inter. Jour. of Psych. 2:233–250.

Wohl, J. 1963. Traditional and contemporary views of psychological testing. Jour. Proj. Tech. & Pers. Assess., 27:359–365.

Zubin, Joseph, Leonard D. Eron, and Florence Schumer. 1965. An experimental approach to projective techniques. New York, John Wiley & Sons, Inc.

Zulliger, Hans. 1956. The Behn-Rorschach test. Bern, Switzerland, Hans Huber.

II. Aspects of Test Evaluation, Analysis, and the Assessment of Technical Problems

Alzobaie, A. J. 1965. The validity of the Goodenough draw-a-man test in Iraq. Jour. of Experimental Educ., 33:331–335.

Amir, Y., R. Kohm-Raz, and G. Rabinotwitz. 1966. The effect of non-personality factors in ink-blot responses in a cross-cultural study. Jour. of Proj. Tech. and Pers. Assess., 30:247–249.

Bagh, D. 1958. An experimental study of Rorschach characteristics of different cultural groups of rural Bengal. Indian Jour. of Psychol. 33:55–66.

Berg, A. I. 1967. Response set in personality assessment. Chicago, Aldine.

Berrien, F. Kenneth. 1967. Methodological and related problems in cross-cultural research. Inter. Jour. of Psych., 2:33–43.

Block, J. 1965. The challenge of response sets. New York, Appleton-Century-Crofts.

Bradsfield, Robert H. 1964. The predictive validity of children's drawings. Cal. Jour. of Ed. Research, 15:166–174.

Broen, W. E., Jr. and R. D. Wirst. 1958. Varieties of response sets. Jour. Consult. Psychol., 22:237–240.

Brunswik, E. 1956. Perception and the representative design of psychological experiments. Berkeley, U. Calif. Press.

Caudill, W. 1955. Comment on J. Henry. Projective testing in ethnography. AA 57:250–253.

Cowan, Gloria and Faye J. Goldberg. 1967. Need achievement as a function of the race and sex of figures of selected TAT cards. Jour. of Pers. and Soc. Psych., 5:245–249.

Dana, R. H. 1962. The validation of projective tests. Jour. Proj. Tech., 26:182–186.

Dana, R. H. and D. J. Mueller. 1961. Congruent validation of a TAT score: Perceptual organization. Jour. of Psych. Studies., 12:150–157.

Dennis, W. 1951. Cultural and developmental factors in perception. In Perception: an approach to personality, R. R. Blake and G. V. Ramsey, eds. New York, Ronald Press.

Deregowski, Jan B. 1968. Pictorial recognition in subjects from a relatively pictureless environment. African Social Research, 5:356–364.

ERVIN, SUSAN M. 1964. Language and TAT content in French-English bilinguals. Jour. of Abnorm. Soc. Psychol., 68:500–507.

FISKE, D. W. 1955. Comment on J. Henry, Projective testing in ethnography. AA 57:258–259.

GHOSH, MOLINA. 1962. Influence of the presence of foreign elements in moving TAT pictures in the contents of stories given by Indian subjects. Shiska, 14:98–102.

GOLDFRIED, M. R. 1966. A suggested approach to evaluation of projective techniques. Psych. Reports, 18:111–114.

GOLDFRIED, MARVIN R. AND MELVIN ZAX. 1965. The stimulus value of the TAT. Jour. Proj. Tech. and Pers. Assess., 29:46–57.

GORDON, LEONARD V. AND AKIO KIKUCHI. 1966. American personality tests in cross-cultural research: A caution. Jour. of Soc. Psych., 69:179–183.

GORHAM, D. R. 1967. Validity and reliability studies of a computer-based scoring system for inkblot responses. Jour. of Consult. Psych., 31:65–70.

GRANICK, S. AND NORMA A. SCHEFLEN. 1958. Approaches to reliability of projective tests with special reference to the Blacky pictures test. J. Consult. Psychol., 22:137–141.

GROVES, M. H. AND P. A. PETERSON. 1968. Effectiveness of projective techniques as established by the objective agreement of therapists with diagnosticians. Proc. Am. Psychol. Ass'n.

HALLOWELL, A. I. 1955. Comment on J. Henry, Projective testing in ethnography. AA 57:262–264.

HAMMER, MAX AND A. M. KAPLAN. 1966. The reliability of children's human figure drawings. Jour. of Clinical Psych., 22:316–319.

HAUCK, P. A. 1955. Ute Rorschach performances and some notes on field problems and methods. U. of Utah Anthropological Papers, No. 23.

HAVIGHURST, R. J., M. K. GUNTHER, AND I. E. PRATT. 1946. Environment and the draw-a-man test: The performance of Indian children, J. Abnorma. Soc. Psychol., 41:50–63.

HONIGMANN, J. J. 1955. Comment on J. Henry projective testing in ethnography. AA 57:253–256.

HONIGMANN, J. J. AND R. N. CARRERA. 1957. Cross-cultural use of Machover's figure drawing test. Americ. Anthrop., 59:650–654.

HUDSON, B. B., M. K. BARAKAT AND R. LA FORGE. 1959. Problems and methods of cross-cultural research. Jour. Soc. Issues, 15:5–19.

HUNT, R. G. AND M. E. SMITH. 1966. Cultural symbols and response to thematic test materials. Jour. of Proj. Tech. and Pers. Assess., 30:587–590.

ICHIMURA, JUN. 1966. Ten year follow-up study on the early prediction of juvenile delinquency by means of the Rorschach test. Japanese Psych. Res., 8:151–160.

JACOBY, JACOB. 1967. The construct of abnormality: Some cross-cultural considerations. Jour. of Exper. Res. in Person., 2:1–15.

KAPLAN, B., M. RIEKERS-OVSIANKINA, A. JOSEPH. 1956. An attempt to sort
Rorschach records from four cultures. J. Proj. Tech. 20:172–180.

KAPLAN, MARTIN F. 1969. The ambiguity of TAT ambiguity. Jour. of Proj. Tech.
and Pers. Assess., 33:25–29.

KARON, BERTRAM P. 1968. Problems of validities. *In* A. I. Rabin, (ed.), Projective
testing in personality assessment. New York, Springer.

KENNY, D. T. AND S. W. KENNY. 1953. Ambiguity of pictures and extent of
personality factors in fantasy responses. Jour. of Proj. Techs., 14:445–452.

KLEIN, G. S., ET AL. 1951. The effect of personal values on perception: An
experimental critique. Psych. Rev., 58:96–112.

LANGNESS, L. L. AND LESLIE Y. RABKIN. 1964. Culture contact stress: Bena Bena
attitudes and feelings as expressed in TAT responses and 'unguarded moments'.
Paper presented to the First International Congress of Social Psychiatry,
London.

LANTZ, HERMAN. 1948. Rorschach testing in pre-literate cultures. Am. Jour. of
Orthopsychiatry, XVIII, 287–291.

LEWIS, LAURA H. 1968. Acquiescence response set: Construct or artifact? Jour. of
Proj. Tech. & Pers. Assess., 32:578–584.

MAHER, BRENDAN A., NORMAN WATT, AND DONALD T. CAMPBELL. 1960. Comparative validity of two projective and two structured attitude tests in a prison
population. J. Applied Psychol., 44:284–288.

MARWIT, S. J. AND J. E. MARCIA. 1967. Tester bias and response to projective
instruments. Jour. of Consult. Psychol., 31:253–258.

MASLING, JOSEPH M. 1960. The influence of situational and interpersonal variables
in projective testing. Psych. Bull., 57:65–85.

MAUSNER, BERNARD. 1961. Situational effects on a projective test. Jour. Applied
Psychol., 45:186–192.

McGEE, R. K. 1962. The relationship between response style and personality
variables: I. The measurement of response acquiescence. Jour. Abnorm. Soc.
Psychol., 64:229–233.

McGUIRL, D. AND C. S. MOSS. 1962. An indirect validation study of the draw-a-
person test through the cartoons of William Steig. Jour. Proj. Tech., 26:88–95.

MOLE, R. P. 1962. Further evidence of seasonal influences on tree drawings. Jour.
of Clinical Psych., 18:109.

MORGENSEN, ALAN, OJERTRUD FENGER AND BERT LANGE. 1961. Rorschach on 122
ten-year old Danish Children: A standardizational and structural study. (in 3
parts) Psycho. Res. Rep., Risskov.

MUKERJI, K. AND P. K. MAJUMTAR. 1968. A comparison of direct and projective
method of personality assessment. Manas: A Jour. of Sci. Psych., 15:19–24.

MURSTEIN, B. I. 1958. Non-projective determinants of perception on the TAT. Jour. of Consult. Psychol., 22:195–198.

———. 1964. A normative study of TAT ambiguity. Jour. of Proj. Tech. and Pers. Assess., 28:210–218.

———. 1965. New thoughts about ambiguity and the TAT. Jour. of Proj. Tech. and Pers. Assess., 29:219–225.

NADEL, S. F. 1955. Comment on J. Henry, Projective testing in ethnography. AA 57:247–250.

PAREEK, UDAI. 1960. An investigation of the validity of the Indian adaptation of the Rosenzweig picture-frustration study (children's form). Indian Jour. Psychol., 35:71–80.

PHAREX, E. JERRY, L. M. STEWART AND J. M. FOSTER. 1960. Instruction variation and Rorschach performance. J. Proj. Tech. 24:20–31.

PRESS, IRWIN. 1967. Maya aging: Cross-cultural projective technique and the dilemma of interpretation. Psychiatry 30:197–202.

RAO, S. K. RAMACHANDRA AND T. RAMADEVI. 1958a. Situational analysis of TAT responses. J. of All-India Inst. of Mental Health, 1:18–25.

———. 1958b. An experiment in the analysis of TAT responses. J. of All-India Inst. of Mental Health, 1:42–50.

RIVERS, W. H. R. 1901. Vision. *In* A. C. Haddon (ed.), Reports of the Cambridge anthropol. expedition to Torres Straits. Vol. II, Part I, New York, Cambridge.

ROER, L. G. 1965. The great response-style myth. Psychol. Bulletin, 63:129–156.

ROTHSCHILD, B. H. 1964. Response style: A basis for Rorschach construct validity. Jour. Proj. Test and Pers. Assess., 20:474–483.

RUNDQUIST, E. A. 1966. Item and response characteristics in attitude and personality measurement: A reaction to L. G. Rorer's "The great response-style myth". Psychological Bulletin, 66:166–177.

SCHWARTZ, P. A. 1963. Adapting tests to the cultural setting. Educ. and Psych. Measurement, 23:673–686.

SHAPIRO, M. B. 1960. The rotation of drawings by illiterate Africans. Jour. Soc. Psych., 52:17–30.

SHIPMAN, W. G. 1964. TAT validity: Congruence with an inventory. Jour. of Proj. Tech. and Pers. Assess., 28:227–232.

SMITH, MARSHALL S. 1968. The computer and TAT. Jour. of School Psych., 3:206–214.

SOLKOFF, NORMAN. 1960. Effects of a variation in instructions on responses to TAT cards. J. Proj. Tech., 24:67–70.

SPINDLER, G. D. 1955. Comment on J. Henry, Projective testing in ethnography. AA 57:259–262.

SPIRO, M. F. 1955. Comment on J. Henry, Projective testing in ethnography. AA 57:256–258.

THOMAS, R. MURRAY AND ANWAR SJAH. 1961. The draw-a-man test in Indonesia. Jour. Educ. Psychol., 52:232–235.

VERNOOR, PHILIP E. 1967. Abilities and educational attainments in an East African environment. Jour. of Special Education, 1:335–345.

WEISSKOPF, EDITH A. 1950. An experimental study of the effect of brightness and ambiguity on projection in the Thematic Apperception Test. Jour. of Psychol., 29:407–416.

WILLITS, FERN K., H. W. WILLITS. 1963. A study of image projection obtained by a pictorial testing technique. Rural Sociology, 28:186–193.

ZAX, MELVIN, GEORGE STRICKER AND J. H. WEISS. 1960. Some effects of non-personality factors on Rorschach performance. J. Proj. Tech., 24:83–93.

ZAX, M. AND S. TAKAHASHI. 1967. Cultural influence on response style: Comparisons of Japanese and American college students. Jour. of Soc. Psych., 71:3–10.

ZELIN, N. AND L. SECHRIST. 1963. The validity of "mother" and "father" cards on the Rorschach. Jour. Proj. Tech., 27:114–121.

III. Cross-cultural and (primarily) Non-Western Applications of Projective Techniques

ABEL, T. M., J. BELO, AND M. WOLFENSTEIN. 1954. An analysis of French projective tests. *In* R. Metraux and M. Meade, (eds.). Themes in French culture: a preface to a study of French community. Hoover Inst. Studies, Stanford, Stanford U. Press., 109–118.

ABEL, T. M. AND R. A. CALABRESI. 1951. The people as seen from their Rorschach tests. *In* O. Lewis (ed.), Life in a Mexican Village: Tepotzlan, restudied. Urbana, Univ. of Illinois Press.

ABEL, T. M. AND RHODA METRAUX. 1959. Sex differences in a Negro peasant community: Montserrat, B.W.I. Jour. Proj. Tech., 23:127–133.

ANASTASI, ANNE AND P. P. FOLEY, JR. 1936. An analysis of spontaneous drawings by children in different cultures. J. Appl. Psychol. 20:689–726.

———. 1938. A study of animal drawings by Indian children of the North Pacific Coast. J. Soc. Psychology, 9:363–374.

BANFIELD, EDWARD C. 1967. The moral basis of a backward society. New York, Free Press.

BARNOUW, VICTOR. 1950. Acculturation and personality among the Wisconsin Chippewa. AAA Memoir, #72.

BLEULER, M. AND BLEULER, R. 1935. Rorschach's Ink-Blot test and Racial Psychology: Mental Peculiarities of Moroccans. Character and Personality, 4:97–114.

BOGGS, S. 1958. Culture change and the personality of Ojibwa children. AA 60:47–58.

BOURGUIGNON, E. E. & E. W. NETT. 1955. Rorschach populars in a sample of Haitian protocols. Jour. Proj. Tech., 19:117–124.

BOYER, L. B., U. KLOPFER, F. B. BRAWER AND H. KAWAI. 1964a. Comparisons of the shamans and pseudoshamans of the Apaches of the Mescalero Indian Reservation: A Rorschach study. Jour. of Proj. Tech. and Pers. Assess., 28:173–180.

———. 1964b. Apache age groups. Jour. of Proj. Tech. and Pers. Assess., 28:397–402.

BOYER, L. BRYCE, R. M. BOYER, B. KLOPFER AND S. B. SCHEIVER. 1968. Apache "learners" and "nonlearners": II Quantitative Rorschach signs of influential adults. Jour. Proj. Tech. and Pers. Assess., 32:146–159.

BRICKLIN, BARRY AND CARTER ZELEZNIK. 1963. A psychological investigation of selected Ethiopian adolescents by means of the Rorschach and other projective tests. Human Organization., 22:291–303.

CALLEY, MALCOLM J. C. 1965. God's People: West Indian Pentecostal sects in England. London & New York: Oxford Univ. Press.

CAUDILL, WILLIAM. 1958. The psychiatric hospital as a small society. Cambridge, Harvard University Press.

CAUDILL, W., & DEVOS G. 1956. Achievement culture and personality: the case of the Japanese Americans. AA 58: 1102–1126.

COOK, P. H. 1942. The application of the Rorschach Test to a Samoan group. Rorschach Res. Exchange, VI, 52–60.

DENNIS, WAYNE. 1960. The human figure drawings of Bedouins. Journal of Soc. Psych., 52:209–219.

———. 1966. Goodenough scores, art experience and modernization. Jour. of Soc. Psych., 68:211–228.

DEVOS, GEORGE AND HORACE MINER. 1958. Algerian culture and personality in change. Sociometry, 21:255–268.

DREGER, RALPH M. 1966. Just how far can social change change personality? Jour. of Psychology, 64:167–191.

DUIJKER, H. C. J. AND N. H. FRIJDA. 1961. National character and national stereotypes: A trend report prepared for the International Union of Scientific Philosophy. New York, The Humanities Press.

EDGERTON, ROBERT B. 1965. "Cultural" vs. "Ecological" factors in the expression of values, attitudes, and personality characteristics. AA 67:442–447.

FISHER, SEYMOUR AND RHODA LEE FISHER. 1960. A projective test analysis of ethnic subculture themes in families. Jour. Proj. Tech., 24:366–367.

GUTMANN, DAVID. 1966. Mayan aging: A comparative TAT study. Psychiatry, 29:246–259.

HALLOWELL, A. I. 1941a. The Rorschach method as an aid in the study of personalities in primitive societies. Character and Personality, IX, 235–245.

———. 1941b. The Rorschach Test as a tool for investigating cultural variables and individual differences in the study of personality in primitive societies. Rorschach Res. Exchange, V, 31–34.

———. 1945a. The Rorschach technique in the study of personality and culture. AA 47:195–210.

———. 1945b. "Popular" responses and cultural differences: An analysis based on frequencies in a group of American Indian subjects. Rorschach Res. Exch., 9, 153–168.

———. 1946. Some psychological characteristics of Northwestern Woodland Indians. *In* Frederick Johnson, (ed.)., Man in Northeastern North American, v.III of the Papers of the R. S. Peabody Foundation for Archaeology.

———. 1949. Psychosexual adjustment, personality and the good life in a nonliterate culture. *In* P.H. Hoch & J. Zubin (eds.), Psychosexual development in health and disease, pp. 102–123. New York, Grune & Stratton.

HAVIGHURST, R. J. & B. L. NEUGARTEN. 1955. American Indian and white children: A sociopsychological investigation. Chicago, U. of Chicago Press.

HENRY, J. & ZUNIA HENRY. 1944. The doll play of Pilaga Indian children, Am. J. Orthopsychiat., Research Monogr., No. 4.

JOSEPH, ALICE, ROSAMUND B. SPICER, AND JANE CHESKY. 1949. The desert people: A study of the Papago Indians. Chicago: Univ. of Chicago Press.

JOSHI, VIDYA. 1965. Personality profiles in industrial and preindustrial cultures: A TAT study. Jour. of Soc. Psych., 66:101–111.

JULKA, GULSHAN. 1962. The Rorschach responses of Bhil children. U. Rajasthan Stud. in Educ., 5:21–42.

KLOPFER, BRUNO AND BRYCE L. BOYER. 1961. Notes on the personality structure of a North American Indian shaman: Rorschach interpretation. Jour Proj. Tech., 25:170–178.

KLUCKHOHN, CLYDE AND J. C. ROSENZWEIG. 1949. Two Navajo children over a five year period. Am. Jour. of Orthopsychiatry, XIX, 266–278.

LEIGHTON, D. AND C. KLUCKHOHN. 1948. The children of the people. Cambridge, Harvard Univ. Press.

LEWIS, OSCAR. 1951. Life in a Mexican village. Urbana, Univ. of Illinois Press.

MACGREGOR, GORDON. 1946. Warriors without weapons. Chicago, Univ. of Chicago Press.

MEAD, M. 1949. The Mountain Arapesh V: The record of Unabelin with Rorschach analysis. Anthrop. Papers Am. Museum Nat. Hist., V. 41, pt. 3.

MELIKIAN, LEVON H. 1964. The use of selected TAT cards among Arab university students: A cross-cultural study. Jour. of Soc. Psychol., 62:3–19.

MORSBACH, HELMUT. 1969. A cross-cultural study of achievement values in two South African groups. Jour. of Soc. Psych., 79:267–268.

PRESTON, CAROLINE E. 1964. Psychological testing with Northwest Coast Alaskan Eskimos. Genetic Psychology Monographs, 69:323–419.

RABIN, A. I. 1959. Comparison of American and Israeli children by means of a sentence completion technique. Jour. Soc. Psychol., 49:3–12.

RABIN, A. I. AND JOSEFINA A. LINNACO. 1959. Sexual differentiation of American and Filipino children as reflected in the Draw-A-Person test. Jour. Soc. Psychol., 50:207–211.

REBONSDIN, ROLAND AND JOEL W. GOLDSTEIN. 1966. Achievement motivation in Navaho [sic] and white students. AA 68:740–745.

ROSS, ALAN O. AND E. M. BRUNER. 1963. Family interaction at two levels of acculturation in Sumatra. Amer. Jour. of Orthopsychiatry, 33:51–59.

SCHACHTEL, ANNA H., JULES HENRY AND ZUNIA HENRY. 1942. Rorschach analysis of Pilaga Indian children. Am. Jour. of Orthopsychiatry, XII, 679–712.

SINGER, JEROME L. 1968. Research applications of projective methods. *In* A. I. Rabin (ed.), Projective testing in personality assessment. New York, Springer.

SPINDLER, G. D. & LOUISE J. SPINDLER. 1957. American Indian personality types and their sociocultural roots. Ann. Amer. Acad. Pol. Soc. Sci., 311:147–157.

STRAUS, M. A. 1957. Anal and oral frustration in relation to Sinhalese personality. Sociometry, 20:21–31.

SYDIAHA, D. AND J. REMPEL. 1964. Motivational and attitudinal characteristics of Indian school children as measured by the thematic apperception test. Canadian psych., 3:139–148.

THOMPSON, LAURA AND ALICE JOSEPH. 1955. The Hopi way. Chicago, Univ. of Chicago Press.

WEINBERG, RITA M. 1968. Personality characteristics of African children: A projective analysis. Jour. of Genetic Psychology, 113:65–77.

YANG, K. S., M. Y. TZUO, AND C. Y. WU. 1963. Rorschach responses of normal Chinese adults. Jour. Soc. Psychol. 60:175–186.

Abate, Mario, 27
Abel, Theodora M., 217, 279
Aberle, David, 1, 144
Abt, Lawrence, 311
Ackerman, Robert, 370n
Adair, J., 136
Adcock, C. J., 277
Adler, Norman, 497
Adorno, T. W., 217
Ahlshwede, Gordon, 71n
Ainsworth, Leonard H., 110
Ainsworth, Mary D. Salter, 75, 76, 77
    77n, 79, 110
Albert, E. M., 142, 143n
Albino, R. C., 79
Alexander, T., 280
Allen, Martin J., 481
Allport, Gordon, 220, 231, 246, 247,
    253n
Almond, Gabriel A., 204, 208, 224, 225
Anderson, Frank, 454
Anderson, R., 280
Anthony, Albert, 476, 487, 490
Aristotle, 207, 208, 211, 229
Aronoff, Joel, 298
Asch, S. E., 84
Atkinson, John, 40, 232n, 280, 313
Aubert, Villem, 222
Ausubel, David, 183, 189
Ayres, Barbara C., 477, 479, 492

Baashus-Jensen, J., 374
Babcock, Charlotte, 48
Bacdayan, A. A., 470
Back, K. W., 276
Bacon, Margaret K., 75, 83, 88, 190n,
    410, 474, 479, 483, 484, 485, 486, 491
Badri, M. B., 276
Bain, Read, 244
Bakan, David, 437, 439
Banks, Arthur S., 455
Barnett, Homer B., 179, 180
Barnouw, Victor, 13, 14, 141, 282, 405
Barrett, Albert M., 380
Barry, Herbert III, 75, 82, 88, 190n,
    410, 474, 479, 483, 484, 485, 486,
    491
Bascom, W. R., 554, 556, 556n
Bastide, Roger, 405, 406

Bateson, Gregory, 172, 173, 188, 189,
    417
Bauer, Raymond A., 210n
Bayley, Nancy, 77n
Beach, Frank, 589
Beaglehole, Ernest, 170, 180, 181, 182,
    183, 184, 185, 186, 189
Beaglehole, Pearl, 180, 183
Bear, Roberta Mayer, 98
Beier, H., 129, 215
Bellah, Robert N., 39, 53
Bellak, Leopold, 280, 311
Belo, J., 417, 425, 426
Bender, L., 177
Benedict, Ruth, 22, 24, 27, 28, 39, 125,
    126, 127, 131, 139, 147, 172, 203, 205,
    209n, 210, 213, 366, 411, 415, 425,
    578n
Bennett, John, 21n, 24, 43, 44, 127, 435,
    444
Berndt, R. M. and C. H., 170
Berrien, F. K., 27
Berry, J. W., 84, 85, 91, 92, 93, 110, 493
Bertelsen, A., 375, 377
Beveridge, W. M., 93
Biesheuvel, S., 77, 78, 82, 280
Billig, O., 141, 279
Blalock, H. M., Jr., 454
Bleuler, M. and R., 216
Blood, Robert O., 43
Blum, G. S., 280, 426, 428
Blumensohn, Jules, 415, 425
Boas, Franz, 124, 125, 209n, 211, 576,
    578n
Bock, R. Darrell, 450, 482
Bogardus, E. E., 12, 14
Bohannan, Laura, 99
Bohannan, Paul J., 99, 509n
Boudon, Raymond, 454
Bourguignon, Erika E., 12, 265, 408,
    412, 415, 421, 422n, 426, 428
Bremer, Frédéric, 414
Brickner, Richard M., 205
Brill, A. A., 372, 373
Brim, John A., 267n
Brogan, D. W., 201, 203
Broughton, R. F., 413n
Brown, Deming, 446n
Brown, Judith, 491

Browne, C. R., 557
Bruner, Edward M., 95
Bruner, Jerome, 86, 87, 88, 89, 101, 494
Buchanan, W., 221
Bullough, Vern, 455
Burg, Moses, 44
Burridge, Knelmo, 176, 427
Burrows, Edwin G., 179
Burton, Roger V., 89, 488, 490
Burton-Bradley, B. G., 176

Caldarola, Carl, 43
Callaway, Canon H., 389, 390
Campbell, Donald T., 12, 90, 241n,
    265, 292, 436, 438, 440, 441, 443,
    444, 445, 446, 447, 448, 449, 450,
    451, 454, 455, 473, 492, 493, 500
Canon, Walter B., 386
Cantril, H., 221, 225
Carlsmith, Karolyn Kuckenberg, 490
Carothers, J. C., 71n, 72n, 74
Carstairs, G. M., 217, 297, 537, 538
Casler, L., 77
Caton-Thompson, G., 553
Cattell, R. B., 7, 15
Caudill, William, 21n, 24, 28, 36, 37,
    39, 40, 43, 47, 48, 109, 280, 282, 284,
    313, 499
Chaitanya, 545
Chaney, Richard, 452, 455
Chapin, F. S., 129
Chapman, Loren J., 450
Chatterjee, Bankim Chandra, 325, 544
Chauduri, Nirad C., 538
Chesky, J., 136
Child, Irvin L., 75, 83, 88, 141, 190n,
    400, 417, 436, 440, 441, 450, 453,
    471, 472, 474, 474n, 478, 479, 480,
    482, 483, 484, 485, 486, 591
Childs, Gladwyn M., 549, 550
Chowdhury, U., 280
Christensen, J. B., 554
Clark, R. A., 313
Clausen, J. A., 386
Clifton, James A., 277, 279
Clignet, Remi, 101
Cochran, William G., 446
Codere, H., 127
Cohen, M., 445
Cohen, Ronald, 12, 280, 282, 452, 453,
    454, 455, 488, 553

Cole, M., 87, 88, 101n
Coleman, Lee, 227, 241, 242
Collier, John, Jr., 136, 282, 283
Colson, E., 554, 555n, 556
Commager, Henry Steele, 201, 245,
    246n
Cook, P. H., 186, 375
Cornell, John B., 46, 47
Cox, Gertrude M., 446
Cronback, Lee J., 450
Cuber, John F., 242, 242n
Curschmann, Hans, 381

D'Andrade, Roy G., 12, 87, 405, 408
    409, 410, 413, 418, 421, 474, 487, 490
Daniels, Robert E., 95, 99, 495
Davidson, W., 141, 279
Dawson, J. L. M., 92, 93, 292
Dean, R. F. A., 77, 78, 79, 81
Dement, William, 413, 414
Dennis, W., 276
DeRidder, J. C., 279, 280
Derogatis, L. R., 275
DeTocqueville, Alexis, 201, 228, 228n,
    229, 230, 234n
Devereux, George, 123, 270, 406, 415,
    426
De Vox, George, 1, 13, 17, 18, 21n, 25,
    32, 36, 37, 41, 43, 44, 45, 46, 47, 48,
    49, 110, 284, 313
Dewey, John, 577
Dicks, Henry V., 214, 215, 217, 219, 233
Doi, Takeo, 28, 37, 39, 43, 44, 51
Dollard, J., 174, 470
Domhoff, Bill, 408, 412
Donaghue, John D., 46
Doob, Leonard W., 73, 74, 75, 82, 83,
    97, 98, 100, 102, 276
Dore, Ronald, 37, 43
Dorsainvil, J. C., 426
Driver, Harold E., 111, 455
Dube, C. S., 539
DuBois, Cora, 144, 172, 178, 183, 184,
    269, 274, 310n, 404, 406
Durkheim, Emil, 473
Dyk, Walter, 123

Earle, M. F., 183
Eberhard, Wolfram von, 406
Edgerton, Robert, 72, 93, 94, 102, 103,
    111, 280, 281, 282, 359n

Eggan, Dorothy, 405, 406, 407, 408, 412, 449
Eggan, Fred, 509n, 512
Eguchi, Keika, 6
Eisenstadt, S. N., 201n, 550n
Elkind, David, 87
Emerson, Ralph Waldo, 249
Erikson, Erik H., 8, 10, 131n, 158, 233, 499, 512, 575
Evans, Judith, 74, 87, 88
Evans-Pritchard, E. E., 5, 15, 211, 551, 553, 554, 555, 555n, 557
Eysenck, H. J. 218

Fabian, Johannes, 427
Fagan, Mary, 469n
Fallers, L. A., 108
Fallers, M. C., 108
Farber, M. L., 142
Farberow, N. L., 299
Farley, J., 299
Favre, H., 405
Fernandez, James W., 100
Fenton, JoAnn, 455
Ferguson, F., 149n
Field, M. J., 104, 105, 426
Firth, Raymond, 5, 187, 418, 420, 447, 559, 586
Fischer, John L., 179, 413n, 423, 425, 479
Fleron, Frederick Jr., 498
Flint, Carol, 71n
Force, Maryanne, 179
Ford, C. S., 124, 453
Forde, Daryll, 551
Forrest, D. W., 277
Forster, E. B., 102
Fortes, Meyer, 5, 82, 108, 211, 551, 554, 555, 555n
Fortune, Reo F., 174
Foulks, Edward, 375n
Fox, Lorene K., 82
Frager, Robert, 27
Frank, L. K., 274
Frazer, Sir James G., 170
Freedman, Daniel G., 78n
Freud, Sigmund, 10, 11, 170, 171, 172, 187, 367, 372, 379, 380, 381, 414, 437, 512, 599
Friedrick, Carl J., 260
Friendly, Joan P., 479

Fromm, Erich, 10, 212, 217, 270, 271
Fujioka, Y., 27, 31
Fukazu, Chikako, 36

Gallimore, Ronald, 187, 189
Gay, J. H., 87, 88, 101n
Geber, Marcelle, 75, 76, 77, 78, 79, 80, 81
Geertz, H., 280, 290
Gerth, Hans, 298n
Gezahegn, Yoseph, 417
Giel, R., 417
Gillespie, James M., 220, 231
Gillin, John, 3, 15, 141, 442, 527
Gjessing, G., 127
Gladwin, Thomas, 1, 17, 18, 132, 156, 167n, 174, 176, 177, 178, 179, 189, 241n, 280, 281, 316, 406
Glass, Albert J., 379
Glasse, Robert M., 176
Glick, Leonard, 176, 189
Gluckman, Max, 5, 554, 555n, 556, 601, 602
Goffman, Erving, 499
Goldfrank, E. S., 130, 131, 140, 147
Goldman, 11, 142
Goldschmidt, Walter, 72, 93, 280, 281, 282, 359n, 512
Goldstein, Curt, 384
Goldstein, Fred J., 241n, 280
Goodenough, D., 12
Goodman, Mary Ellen, 36, 426, 494
Goody, Jack, 101
Gopal, 351
Gorer, Geoffrey, 21n, 34, 201, 210, 210n, 213, 512
Gough, Harrison G., 43
Granet, Marcel, 519
Graves, D. T., 150, 158
Greenfield, Patricia Marks, 86, 88, 89, 101
Guha, Uma, 312
Gulick, J., 156
Gurin, Gerald, 232n
Gussow, Z., 370n, 372, 373

Haddon, A. C., 170
Hagen, E. E., 41
Hall, Calvin, 408, 412
Hallowell, Irving A., 123, 128, 129, 130, 143, 147, 190n, 268, 290, 291, 293, 404, 406, 412, 414, 415, 428, 584, 589

Hally, David J., 484
Hamaguchi, Esyun, 21n
Hanfmann, Eugenia, 129, 215
Hanks, Lucien, Jr., 280, 290
Hannerz, Ulf, 498
Hanson, C., 150, 152
Harada, Atsuka, 36
Hare, Paul A., 96, 100
Hare, Rachel T., 96, 100
Haring, D. G., 50, 141, 210n
Harner, Michael, 426
Harper, Robert A., 242n
Harrington, Charles, 466, 468, 473, 489,
   490, 497, 499, 500, 501, 512
Harris, Marvin, 190, 513
Hart, C. W. M., 3, 15, 527
Hartley, Eugene L., 470
Hartley, Ruth E., 470
Hartmann, Ernst, 423n
Havighurst, R. J., 136, 139
Hayashi, T., 39
Hearnshaw, F. J. C., 203
Heider, Fritz, 438
Helson, Harry, 446
Henney, J. H., 425
Henry, Jules, 266, 439, 466, 584
Henry, W. E., 178, 280, 286, 299, 316,
   318, 327, 327n, 355
Heron, Alastair, 292
Herskovits, Frances S., 292
Herskovits, Melville J., 3, 15, 90, 97, 436,
   439, 443, 445, 470, 473, 492, 493, 500,
   549, 553, 554, 556
Herz, Frederick, 202
Herzog, John, 491
Hildreth, Richard, 453
Hippler, Arthur A., 110
Hirsh, Herbert, 498
Hitler, Adolf, 205, 212, 233, 259
Hoffman, H., 496
Hofmayr, Wilhelm, 554
Hogbin, Ian H., 557
Hollingshead, A. B., 385
Holmberg, Alan R., 141
Holmes, Lowell Don, 444
Holtzman, Wayne H., 275
Holzinger, C. H., 156
Homans, George C., 254n
Honigmann, I., 1, 15, 140, 149, 149n,
   150
Honigmann, John J., 13, 18, 123, 132,

141, 144, 149, 149n, 150, 153, 210,
   210n, 406, 435, 436, 442, 513
Hook, Sidney, 228, 228n, 229, 230
Horkheimer, Max, 217
Horney, Karen, 10, 132
Horton, Robin, 101, 103, 104
Hoshino, Akira, 27, 34
Howard, Alan, 186, 189
Howard, Irwin, 169n
Hoygaard, Arne, 374, 375
Hoyt, Hillard, 241
Hsiao, H., 62
Hsu, Francis L. K., 11, 14, 15, 18, 73,
   101, 204, 204n, 210, 217, 222, 224n,
   250, 251, 254, 256, 258, 264, 266, 273,
   274, 280, 284, 309, 309n, 310, 310n,
   311, 319, 328, 359, 439, 467, 468,
   469n, 514, 515n, 516n, 517, 518n, 519,
   524n, 525n, 527, 528, 533, 539n, 541,
   541n, 545n, 546, 549, 555n, 557, 558,
   560, 570, 572, 573n, 574
Hudson, W., 97, 292
Hughes, Charles, 102, 105, 106, 109, 111
Hull, C., 174, 175, 188, 437
Hultkranz, A., 405
Hunkum, V., 276
Hunt, J. McV., 98, 368
Hunt, William A., 446
Hyman, Herbert, 233

Iga, Mamorv, 42, 44, 46
Imanishi, K., 31
Inkeles, Alex, 1, 18, 129, 202, 215, 225,
   269, 270, 271, 274, 584
Irstam, Tor, 550, 551
Irvine, S. H., 74
Ishida, Eiichiro, 27, 51
Ishiguro, Taigi, 35, 37
Iwawaki, Saburo, 292
Izumi, Seiichi, 23, 31, 49

Jaensch, Erich R., 205
Jahoda, Gustav, 91, 93, 280
Jahoda, M., 87, 88, 89
James, B., 123, 129
James, William, 577
Janes, E., 589
Janowitz, Morris, 217, 218
Jaros, Dean, 498
Jelliffe, D. B., 73
Jessor, L., 150, 158

Jessor, R., 150, 158
Johnson, Erwin, 43
Johnson, R. T., 187
Jones, Ernest, 171
Joseph, Alice, 136, 137, 176, 177, 279

Kagan, Jerome, 87
Kali, 540, 544
Kallman, Franz, 368
Kane, E. K., 372, 375
Kaplan, Bert, 1, 3, 8, 15, 49, 267, 269, 270, 271, 272, 273, 274, 277, 278, 279, 284, 285, 290, 316, 359
Kardiner, Abram, 10, 131, 132, 144, 172, 183, 184, 185, 186, 188, 269, 406, 410, 512
Kato, Hidetoshi, 28, 29
Kato, Seiichi, 43
Katz, Sol, 375n
Kawashima, T., 24
Kaye, Barrington, 78, 82
Keats, John, 317
Kecskemeti, Paul, 231
Keller, Albert G., 438
Kenyatta, J., 554
Keyes, Charles, F., 267n
Kiev, Ari, 103
Kiefer, C. W., 40, 43, 44
Kilbride, Philip L., 97, 292, 293
Kiste, Robert C., 180
Kitano, Harry H. L., 36
Klein, Nancy H., 101, 102
Kleitman, N., 413, 414, 414n, 415, 423, 425
Klineberg, Otto, 12, 15, 174, 202
Klingelhofer, E. L., 109
Kluckhohn, Clyde, 4, 15, 121, 124, 136, 141, 142, 156, 157, 210n, 244, 244n, 406, 435, 470, 557, 584
Kluckhohn, F., 12, 142, 245, 261n
Kluckhohn, Richard, 476, 487, 490
Knudson, K. E., 180
Kobben, Andre J., 450, 456
Kodama, Habuku, 31, 36
Konishi, T., 27
Kopytoff, Igor, 557
Kornhauser, Arthur, 218
Korchin, S. J., 280
Krantz, D. L., 446
Krishna, 325, 545
Kroeber, A. L., 3, 15, 129, 574

Kuhn, Manford, H., 510
Kuper, Hilda, 100n

LaBarre, Weston, 22, 34, 171, 426, 428
Lambo, Adeoye, 102, 103, 105, 106, 109, 111
Lambert, William W., 72, 83, 441, 454, 474, 475, 481, 489
Ladas, Alice, 498
Landaver, T. K., 477
Landes, R. 128
Landy, David, 276
Lane, R. E., 218
Langness, L. L., 167n, 176, 267n
Lanham, Betty, 34, 36, 37
Lantis, M., 147, 148, 149
Larson, Eric H., 180
Laski, Harold J., 244
Lasswell, Harold, 207, 211, 212, 228n, 229
Lawless, Richard, 277, 279
Lawrence, Peter, 176
Laye, Camara, 82
Leach, E. R., 512
Leacock, Eleanor, 273, 274
Leary, Timothy, 426, 428
Lebra, William P., 51
Lee, Dorothy M., 172, 189
Lee, S. G., 95, 96, 107, 277, 282
Leighton, Alexander, H., 10, 47, 102, 105, 106, 109, 111, 123, 374,
Leighton, Dorothea C., 102, 105, 106, 109, 111, 123, 136
Leininger, Madeline, 176, 275
Lemert, E. M., 150
Lemkin, S., 87
Lerner, Daniel, 224, 224n, 225, 293
Lessa, W. A., 171, 176, 178, 280
Lesser, G. S., 280
LeVine, B., 1
LeVine, David, 82
LeVine, Robert A., 17, 18, 71n, 74, 82, 96, 99, 100, 101, 102, 110, 223, 271, 272, 274, 276, 277, 445, 454, 455, 473, 483, 497, 549
Levinson, D. J., 201n, 202, 218, 222n, 234, 269, 270
Lévi-Strauss, Claude, 512, 578
Levy, David M., 214, 439
Levy, Robert F., 169, 179, 182, 186, 187, 191

Lewin, Kurt, 8, 257
Lieber, Michael D., 180
Liebow, Eliot, 198
Lienhardt, G., 418
Lifton, R. J., 44
Lincoln, Jackson S., 405, 412, 416
Lindesmith, A. R., 142
Lindzey, Gardner, 269n, 274, 276, 277, 285n, 299
Ling, Gilbert, 370n
Linton, Ralph, 8, 15, 18, 131, 180, 183, 210, 233, 487, 553, 554
Lipset, S. M., 209, 234, 243
Little, K. B., 299
Litwak, E., 276
Lloyd, Barbara B., 89
Lloyd, P., 100n, 101
Lloyd-Jones, Esther M., 509n
Lofland, J., 153n
Lord, Edith, 319
Lowell, E. L., 313
Ludwig, Arnold, 423n
Lundsgaard, Henry P., 180
Luomala, K., 420, 426
Lurie, Walter A., 207
Lynd, Robert and Helen, 253n
Lystad, M. H., 98

MacArthur, General Douglas, 519
MacGregor, G., 136, 131n, 444
Mack, Raymond, 446n
Macklin, David B., 102, 105, 106, 109, 111
MacMillan, Donald B., 370n, 371, 372, 376
Mahoney, Francis B., 179
Malinowski, B., 5, 18, 171, 183, 187, 189, 406, 437, 449, 512, 579
Mandelbaum, D. G., 366, 467, 534, 539n
Maretzki, T. W., 50, 169n
Maritain, Jacques, 228, 229
Marvick, D., 217, 218
Maruyama, M., 39
Masland, R. L., 174
Maslow, A. H., 123
Masserman, Jules, 11, 15
Maxwell, J. P., 377
Mayer, Philip, 470
McClelland, David, 40, 41, 97, 98, 100, 231, 233, 313

McClosky, Herbert, 218
McClure, James J. Jr., 382
McDougall, W., 170
McGranahan, D. V., 219
McKiever, B. L., 97
Mead, Margaret, 18, 123, 124, 125, 156, 172, 180, 181, 184, 186, 187, 188, 189, 209, 210, 213, 366, 368, 417, 444, 445, 510, 527, 545, 578n, 584
Meek, C. K., 554, 556
Meggars, Betty J., 140, 141
Meggitt, Mervyn, 176, 408, 412
Meehl, P. E., 299
Melikian, 305
Mensh, I., 267
Merriam, Charles E., 211, 415
Mering, Otto Von, 261n
Merton, Don, 469
Merton, Robert, 270
Michels, Robert, 209
Michotte, A. E., 438
Middleton, John, 97, 549
Migliorino, Guiseppi, 110
Miller, Neal E., 174
Mills, C. Wright, 209, 298n
Minami, Hiroshi, 28
Miner, Horace, 100n, 279
Minturn, Leigh, 72, 83, 454, 475, 481, 537
Minuchin, Salvador, 279
Mischel, Walter, 298
Mitchell, H. E., 45, 280
Miyake, Kazuo, 36
Miyawaki, Jiro, 36
Moloney, J. C., 50
Molymeaux, Lambert, 99
Moore, Charles A., 21n
Moore, Frank, 450, 453
Moore, Henry T., 211
Morgenthaler, Fritz, 102
Morioka, Kiyomi, 36
Morris, Charles, 221, 222, 258
Moses, 529
Mowrer, O. H., 4
Muensterberger, W., 10
Mukerji, D. Gopal, 538
Muller, F. Max, 540
Mulligan, D. G., 183, 316
Mundy-Castle, Acastair C., 97, 292
Murakami, Taiji, 43

Muramatsu, Tsuneo, 25, 31
Munroe, Robert L., 75, 87, 95, 99, 475, 484, 489, 490, 494
Munroe, Ruth H., 75, 89, 95, 99, 475, 489, 490, 494
Murdock, George P., 111, 452, 453, 479, 481, 509n, 511, 512, 599
Murphy, Gardner, 534
Murphy, John M., 102, 105, 106, 109, 111
Murphy, Lois B., 538, 544
Murray, Henry A., 4, 141, 210n, 280, 284, 291, 311, 442
Murray, Veronica F., 176, 177, 279
Myers, C. J., 170
Myrdal, Gunnar, 244

Nachmansohn, M., 425
Nadel, S. F., 6, 15, 92, 97, 108, 175, 555n
Nag, Moni, 312
Nagai, Michio, 24
Nagashima, N., 23
Nakamo, Takashi, 43
Naroll, Raoul, 12, 13, 265, 451, 452, 453, 454, 455
Needham, Rodney, 512
Nerlove, Sara B., 89, 99
Neugarten, B., 136, 139
Newman, Philip, 176
Newton, Isaac, 325
Nivedita, Sister, 540
Niwa, Yoshiko, 36
Niyekawa-Howard, Agnes, M., 44, 50
Norbeck, Edward, 1, 17, 18, 21n, 34, 38, 48, 51, 56n, 97, 445
Norbeck, Margaret, 13, 34
Northrop, F. S. C., 142
Nottingham, Elizabeth K., 252n
Nylen, Donald, 276

Oberg, K., 556
O'Hara, John, 155n
Olver, Rose, 86
Oliver, Douglas, 169, 187
Oliver, Symmes C., 99
Opler, Marvin K., 3, 49
Orlansky, H., 142
Ortigues, Edmund, 104
Ortigues, Marie-Cecile, 104

Ortega y Gasset, José, 205
Osborne, Oliver, 266n
Ostheimer, John M., 99, 280, 282
Otterbein, Keith, 450
Otterberg, Simon, 97
Ovvaiyar, 343
Owen, Constance P., 100, 101, 102

Parin, Paul, 104
Parin-Matthey, Goldy, 104
Parker, Seymour, 285, 380
Parman, Susan, 56n
Parsons, T., 270, 271, 298n, 589
Paul, Benjamin D., 439
Payne, Ernest A., 540
Payne, R. W., 217
Peacock, James, 499
Peary, Robert E., 371, 372
Pelz, Donald C., 454
Peterson, Donald B., 380
Peterson, Donald R., 110
Pettitt, George A., 438
Phillips, Herbert P., 272, 274, 275
Piaget, J., 85, 88, 89, 188
Pierce, Charles, 575
Pitts, Ferris N., 382
Plath, David W., 36
Plato, 202, 207, 208, 211
Porteus, S. D., 173, 174, 182, 189
Powdermaker, H., 98, 101
Pressel, Esther, 426
Price-Williams, D. R., 86, 88
Prince, R., 105
Prinsloo, T., 97
Prothro, E. Terry, 481

Rabin, A. I., 276, 280, 285n
Radcliffe-Brown, A. R., 171, 550, 551, 579, 586, 600
Radin, P., 123, 411
Rainwater, Lee, 279
Ramakrishna, 540
Rasmussen, Knud, 371, 372
Rasmussen, Niels, 372
Raum, O. F., 82
Read, K. E., 175
Read, Margaret, 82
Reader, D. H., 97
Reay, Marie, 175
Redlich, F. C., 385

Reich, Wilhelm, 364n
Reina, R. E., 404, 412
Reichel-Dolmatoff, Gerardo and Alicia,
  404, 412
Reuilla, Ruiz, 452, 455
Richards, Audrey I., 72
Rickman, John, 512
Riesman, David, 245, 270, 271
Riess, B. F., 280
Ringer, Benjamin B., 218
Ritchie, James E., 183, 185
Ritchie, Jane, 183, 275, 277
Ritchie, J. F., 18
Rivers, W. H. R., 5, 90, 170, 172, 292
Robbins, Michael C., 97, 292, 293, 492
Roberts, B., 473
Roberts, John M., 473, 479, 485, 496
Rodahl, K., 375, 376
Roffenstein, Gaston, 425
Rogers, Everett M., 275
Róheim, Géza, 10, 15, 142, 170, 171,
  187, 406
Rohlen, Thomas P., 560
Rokeach, Milton, 218
Rokkan, Stein, 222n
Romney, A. K., 482
Roscoe, J., 554
Rosenau, Norah, 509n
Rosenberg, B. A., 490
Rosenblatt, Paul, 480
Rosenthal, Robert, 453
Rozelle, R. M., 454

Sapin, David H., 12, 263, 264, 266, 299
Sapir, E., 121, 124, 125, 140, 180, 366,
  368, 578n
Sarason, Seymour B., 174, 177, 280, 281,
  316, 406
Savage, Charles, 105
Sawyer, Jack, 445, 455
Scarr, Harry A., 28
Schaefer, James, 453
Schaffner, Bertram H., 219
Schapera, I., 450, 555
Schneider, David, 210n, 406, 407, 408,
  412
Schneirla, T. C., 589
Schroetter, Karl, 425
Schwartz, E. K., 280
Schwartz, Gary, 469
Schwimmer, Eric, G., 180

Scotch, Norman A., 100
Scott, R. B., 77
Sears, Walter E., 445
Seashore, Charles, 276
Segall, Marshall H., 87, 88, 90, 292, 436,
  442, 473, 492, 493, 500
Seligman, C. G., 170, 172, 412, 554
Selye, Hans, 368
Sera, Masatoshi, 26
Serpell, R., 88
Sforza, Carlo, 205
Sharp, R. L., 406, 407, 412
Shelling, D. H., 380, 381
Sherwood, E. T., 280, 281, 282, 283
Shils, E. A., 270, 271
Shirley, R. W., 482
Shimada, Kazuo, 21n
Shiva, 545
Shneidman, E. S., 299
Siegel, Bernard, 159n
Siegfried, Andre, 203, 204
Sielkema, Mildred, 34
Silberman, Bernard, 21n
Sills, David L., 218
Simmons, Leo, 82, 124
Sinclair, Alex, 175
Smelser, William T., 298n
Smelser, Neil J., 298n
Smith, Allan H., 50
Smith, David H., 225
Smith, M. B., 269
Smith, Robertson, 170
Smith, Robert J., 46, 49
Smith, T. C., 50, 53
Snoy, P., 427
Sofue, Takeo, 21n, 22, 27, 31, 33, 34, 36,
  44
Sorokin, Pitirim A., 298n
Spengler, O., 126, 127
Spicer, R. B., 136
Spiegelman, M., 178, 280
Spillius, James, 187
Spindler, G. D., 129, 142, 143, 157, 280,
  281, 282, 283, 293, 294
Spindler, L. S., 129, 144, 144n, 145, 157,
  273, 279, 280, 281, 282, 283, 293, 294
Spiro, Melford E., 1, 12, 176, 179, 190,
  241n, 269, 270, 271, 297, 439, 441,
  442, 451, 474, 569, 570, 571, 573n,
  574n, 587n, 589n, 591n
Spoehr, Alexander, 512

Spranger, Eduard, 207
Stalin, Joseph, 209
Staniford, P. S., 49
Stanton, H., 276
Steed, Gitel P., 537, 539
Stern, W., 275
Steward, Julian, 515
Stoetzel, Jean, 24, 220
Stoodley, Bartlett H., 220
Stout, D. B., 421n
Straus, J. H., 279
Straus, M. A., 279
Stouffer, Samuel A., 209
Strauss, A. L., 142
Strodbeck, Fred, 245, 261n
Strong, E. K., 47
Suchman, Rosslyn Gaines, 87
Sue, Hiroko, 36
Sundkler, B., 427
Sullivan, H. S., 416, 510
Suttles, Gerald, 498
Sutton-Smith, Brian, 469n, 473, 479,
    485, 490, 496
Swartz, Marc, 179

Tagnaeus, Harry, 550
Tagore, Rabindranath, 325
Takahashi, Keiko, 36
Tanaka, Kunio, 36
T'ao Yuan-Ming, 336
Tatje, Terrence, 549, 558, 560
Taylor, C. R. H., 169
Teitelbaum, Samuel, 255
Textor, R. B., 409, 410, 413, 455
Thomas, A., 207
Thompson, C. E., 280
Thompson, L., 136, 137, 157
Thompson, V. J., 79
Thorndike, T. T., 437
Tiara, Koji, 43
Toffelmier, G., 420, 426
Tonkinson, Robert, 180
Torrance, E. P., 187
Tooth, Geoffrey, 102, 366
Triandis, Leigh, 474, 484
Tsou, Tang, 524
Tsukishima, Kenzo, 26
Tsumori, Makaot, 36
Tsuru, Hiroshi, 36
Tuden, A., 78
Turner, Victor, 498

Tyler, Stephen A., 495

Underwood, F., 140

Valentine, C. A., 169, 176, 189
Vanden, Berghe, P. L., 100n
Van Luijk, J. N., 417
Verba, Sidney, 224, 225, 497
Veroff, Joseph, 232n
Vinacke, W. Edgar, 169n
Vishnu, 545
Vogel, Ezra F., 36, 37, 43, 44
Voget, F. W., 147
Vogt, E. Z., 142, 143n, 269, 501

Wagatsuma, Hiroshi, 21n, 22, 27, 32, 36,
    41, 43, 44, 46, 51, 284
Wagner, G., 549
Wahab, Zaher, 277
Waitz, Theodore, 209
Walker, D. E., 445
Wallace, A. F. C., 1, 12, 13, 130, 141,
    142, 144, 145, 146, 147, 155, 190,
    190n, 278, 284, 316, 359, 385, 386,
    423, 426, 427, 428, 498
Wallas, Graham, 211
Warner, W. Lloyd, 170, 247, 247n, 249
Washburn, S. L., 578n
Watrous, Blanche, 264, 279, 284, 309,
    310, 310n, 319, 326, 329, 331, 338,
    343, 354, 355, 359
Watson, James B., 175, 176, 281n
Watt, Ian, 101
Watson, R. I., 535
Watt, James, 325, 326
Weber, Max, 39, 53, 100, 270
Webb, Eugene, 443, 450, 453, 454
Weinstein, Helen, 36, 37, 40, 109
Weinberg, S. K., 141
Wellisch, E., 439
Werner, Oswald, 445, 449
West, James, 183
Whitaker, S., 217
White, Douglas, 452, 453
White, G. M., 180
White, Leslie A., 3, 15
Whiting, Beatrice B., 1, 72, 74, 84, 84n,
    410, 417, 436, 439, 440, 472, 483, 489
Whiting, John W. M., 12, 72, 74, 75, 84,
    89, 141, 174, 175, 188, 190n, 442, 450,
    454, 466, 468, 469n, 470, 471, 472,

473, 474, 474n, 475, 476, 477, 478, 479, 480, 481, 482, 483, 484, 487, 488, 489, 490, 491, 492, 494, 495, 497, 500, 501, 512
Whitney, Harry, 371
Wickert, Frederic R., 73
Wilbur, G. B., 10, 15
Wilkins, M. L., 499
Williams, Herbert H., 294, 296, 412
Williams, Judith R., 77, 294, 296
Williams, J. S., 183
Williams, Robin M., 242, 243, 243n, 244, 252, 253
Wilson, Monica, 403, 550
Winch, Robert F., 455
Wing, J. K., 499
Winter, Edward, 99, 549
Witkin, H. A., 493
Witthoft, J., 123

Wittkower, E. D., 425, 426
Wolf, Margery, 474, 484
Wolfe, Alvin, A., 557
Wolfenstein, M., 156
Wordsworth, William, 317
Worsley, Peter, 176
Wright, George O., 482

Yamamoto, Tatsuro, 21n
Yamane, Tsuneo, 43
Yamaochi, K., 39
Yarrow, M. R., 386
Yoda, Akira, 36
Young, Frank W., 190n, 440, 455, 469, 488

Znaniecki, Florian, 207
Zigler, Edward, 436

Abortions
  among Ila women, 78
Abstraction
  among Kraska, 133; among
  Moroccans, 216; and distortion,
  444; and Piaget, 85; as description,
  265; levels of, 387; little Chinese
  interest in, 519
Abstractive-generalization approach
  to research, 442, 443
Acculturation, 110, 143;
  among American Indians, 95, 123,
  144, 146; among Japanese, 53, 54,
  55; among Maori, 183; detriments
  of, 144; dreams and, 411; studies
  of 96, 98-99, 446
Achievement motivation, 50, 90, 496;
  among American Indians, 123; among
  Colombian peasants, 275; among
  Issei, 48; among Nisei, 47; and
  games of chance, 485; and politics,
  207-08; as an American value, 243;
  in Japan, 39-40, 52-53, 55; in
  Nigeria, 96, 276; of Americans,
  Japanese, Germans, 228; pressures
  toward, 410
Adaption level
  discussion of, 445-49
Adolescence, 100;
  among Efik, 82; and European
  imitation, 98; and identity, 575;
  and Mead, 189; and sex identity,
  487; disturbance of female during,
  444; dreams during, 404; explained
  behavior of, 88; in Africa, 81-89;
  sexual impulse in Hopi during, 139
Adulthood
  among Hopi, 138, 140; and its
  relationship to dreams, 410; as
  relates to political beliefs, 233;
  behavior during, 185, 440; gratification in, 440; in American
  parents, 250
Africa
  agricultural societies of, 83, 84;
  bush culture of, 446-47; city
  dwellers in, 72; depression in,
  104-05; discussion of, 71-111;

farmers of, 93-94; kinship structure
  of, 547-58; on subsistence scale,
  486; sex differences in, 494
Age roles
  and effects on dreams, 95;
  seniority among Yoruba, 89
Aggression, See also Hostility
  among Eskimos, 149; among Hopi,
  139; among Menomini, 144;
  among Tuscarora, 145; as "protest
  masculinity", 496; as symptom of
  mental disorder, 383; control of,
  482; cultural expectations producing, 89; dreams of, 407-08; in
  Kasla Indians, 133; in Teton
  Dakota, 130; inhibitions of, 128,
  282; in spirit world, 474; power
  and, 395; socialized forms of, 466,
  480; tolerance of, 101; toward
  siblings, 80; verbal forms of, 50
Agricultural societies
  "compliance" in, 83-84; hoe farming
  in, 93-94; subsistence level of, 486;
  success of farming in, 182; use of
  dreams in, 409
Ainu, 45
Aitutaki
  culture of, 180-82
Akan
  mental illness among, 104-05
Alcoholism, 242;
  and community response, 384;
  anxiety of, 485; in Tahiti, 187;
  of American Indians, 146, 149-50
Algonkian
  mental illness among, 365; personality of, 273; studies of, 156
Alienation
  among Japanese youth, 44; and
  extremists traits, 226; and
  politics, 208, 218, 219; demands
  of, 190; of political and social
  forms, 225
Allport-Vernon Scale of Values, 207, 222
Alorese
  dreams of the, 404-06
Altered states of Consciousness, 403;
  discussion of, 418-29

Amami Oshima, 50
Amatongo
 as spirits, 390-91
American character, 241;
 and foreign policy, 204; and
 inner-directed, 245; and obedience,
 220; and outer-directed, 245, 271; as
 compared to English, 249; as democratic, 226-31; as expressed by
 advertisers, 245; as "Schizoid",
 244-45; discussion of, 221-61;
 of auto workers, 218;
 relationship to government, 224
American Indians, 157;
 acculturation of, 95, 146; and
 political socialization, 498;
 and Trance, 418; compared with
 Spanish and Anglos, 150-55;
 discussion of, 159; divination
 among, 405; education among,
 438; emotions among, 128; personality effect by Euro-Canadian
 culture, 129; peyotists among, 386;
 "psychological homogeneity" of,
 18; study of children of, 136;
 vision quest of, 425
American Japanese, *See also* Nisei
 personality traits of, 47, 54;
 psychological traits of, 44
American Life, Dream, and Reality, 247
American Mind, The, 245
American School of Culture-and-
  Personality
 discussion of, 578-79
American Society, 242
An American Dilemma, 244
Ancestors, 539;
 cults of, 73, 204, 555, 555n;
 of Kachinas, 138; spirits of, 390-91,
 517, 518, 549; worship of, 521,
 523, 528, 549
Andamese pygmies
 kinship system of, 511
Anglo-Americans
 discussion of, 152-55; norms of, 151
Animal husbandry
 agriculture with, 409; dependence
 upon, 485-86; in Africa, 83, 84;
 subsistence of, 486
Animistic thinking, 88;

among Ghanaian school children,
 88-89; among Hopi, 139; in
 Africa, 557; Mead's work on, 189
Anlagen
 cultural, 365
Anomie
 among workers, 218; and extremists,
 226; and frustration, 596; and
 politics, 208
Anthropology
 and behavior, 581; and boundaries
 between fields of study, 1-2; and
 psychological theory, 438-442;
 and social events, 370; and
 socialization, 470
Anti-Semitism
 in United States, 252, 255n-256n
Anxiety
 about obedience, 485; and culture,
 184-85; and dream deprivation,
 414; as socialized behavior, 466;
 attacks of, 382; dreams causing,
 411; during infancy and childhood,
 479; in American Indians, 149; of
 being alone, 409; oral, 480; of
 physical and verbal forms of, 480;
 reduction of, 365, 383; toward self,
 397-99; "transition", 497
Apache
 lack of study on, 156
Arabs
 acculturation of, 49, 224
Aranda
 dreams of the, 406; totemism and
 conflict among, 170
Archaeology, 1
Art
 for art's sake, 530; of China and
 Japan, 520; of the Hindu, 542-43
Arts and crafts
 of American Indians, 137; of
 Eskimos, 92
Atimeland, 183
Ashanti, 98;
 and mental illness, 104, 105;
 naming of, 89
Assimilation
 of American Indians, 137; of Jews,
 255; of Menomini, 144; of
 Orientals, 256

Australia, *See also* Aranda
  aborigines, 170, 575; religious
  persecution in, 256
*Australian Totemism: a Psycho-
  analytical Study in Anthropology,*
  171
Authoritarianism
  and extremism, 226; and foreign
  affairs, 218; character traits of, 219
Authority
  acceptance of, 88; and mental health,
  44; and pastoralists, 94; and
  tyranny, 230; anti—, 520; attitude
  towards, 232; compliance with,
  85; constituted, 231; in American
  character, 255, 256; in Germany,
  212; in personality, 208, 217; in
  state and family, 213; lack of male
  type of, 157, 487; Oriental
  parents as, 520; orientation toward,
  229; paternal, 260
Autocracy
  among Hindu rulers, 543; among
  Oriental rulers, 520; in Russia, 208

Bali, 173
Bamileke, 99
Bantu, 82;
  death rites of, 549; language of, 94;
  valuation of land by, 111
Becoming a Kwoma, 174
Behavior
  alcoholic, 146; and cross-sexual
  identity, 489; and primitive people,
  582; and social rules, 470; and
  social systems, 587-88; and values,
  258; anti-social, 369; as cross-
  cultural variable, 580; as goal-
  oriented, 590; as motivated by
  others, 509; avoidance form of,
  599; competitive, 271; conformative, 271; deviant, 406, 488;
  emotional determinants of, 184;
  infant imitation of adult forms of,
  80; in altered states of consciousness, 425-28; in children and
  adults, 440; learned cultural, 269;
  motivated, 365; national character
  of, 203; neurotic, 146; of adults,
  472; of Americans, 247; of central
  nervous system, 368; of infant dur-

ing weaning, 80, 109; of Nisei, 47;
  of prophets, 146; of Russians, 215;
  overdetermined nature of, 131;
  overt, 490; paranoid, 205, 219;
  patterns of, 93; "person-defining
  value" of, 121, 124; personal outcomes of, 153; political forms of,
  218; problems in Hopi boys with,
  137; social, psychological in
  nature, 5, 272; suppression of,
  130; versus beliefs, 420
Behaviorial science
  in Japan, 22
Belgium
  religious persecution in, 257
Bender-Gestalt Test, 177
Bété, 442;
  perceptual skills of, 91
Bhutan
  hermit kingdom of, 467
Bigotry, *See also* Prejudice, Racial
    prejudice
  and Christianity, 259-60; religious
  form of, 253-54
Biological characteristics
  and race, 204-05
Biomgbo
  definition of, 103
Birth, *See also* Infancy, Weaning
  among Hopi, 137
Blackey Pictures, 280
Blacks, *See also* Negroes
  and frustration, 571; and political
  socialization, 498; and TAT
  results, 280; and revolution, 592n;
  votes of, 259
Brahmacharya, 537
Brain, *See also* Mind
  electrical potentials of, 367;
  physical dysfunction of, 368-69
Brazilians
  dreams of, 406
Bridewealth, 73
British School of Social Anthropology
  British structuralism, 581;
  discussion of, 577-78
Buddhism, 536, 544
Buffalo
  importance of, 130
Bush culture
  of Africa, 447

Bushmen, 441;
of Kalahari Desert of South Africa, 173; perception of, 91

Calcium deficiency
and *pibloktoq,* 374-79
Canada, 122;
religious persecution in, 256
Canadian Indians, 150
Cannibalism, 170
Caretakers, of infants
and relation to infant, 474; helping mothers, 476; in Africa, 74-76
Carolinian
on Saipan, 177
Caste
extremists for, 546; hierarchy of, 537; status of, 546; Untouchables, 544
Catholicism, 246, 532-33
Catholic Church, 144
Caucasian Americans
children of, 47; infants of, 77n
Central nervous system
and malnutrition, 477; dysfunction of, 368-69
Ceremonies
among Hopi, 137; "naven" among Iatmul, 172
Chaga, 75;
discipline among, 82
Chamorro
on Saipan, 177
Character traits
influencing politics, 235
Chemistry
body, 397; clinical, 367; study of, 370
Cherokee, 156
Chi Square Tests, 409, 410
Chiefs, *See also* Rulers, Kings
of the American Indians, 130-31
Child Development
among Okinawans, 50; and stress, 477; theories of, 124
Child training, *See* Child-rearing
Child Training and Personality: A Cross-Cultural Study, 141
Childhood, 18;
among Ekif, Ngoni, 82; among Maori, 185-86; among Yoruba, 109;

characteristic of Hopi during, 85; cognitive development during, 85; drive fixation in, 440; early years of, 477; emotional deprivation of, 485; experiences of, 292, 293; gratification in, 441; in Africa, 72, 81-89; in brother-brother dyads (Africa), 549-50; in father-son dyads (Orient), 518; in husband-wife dyads (West), 526-27; in mother-son dyads (Hindu), 537-38; personality during, 131, 132, 140; responsibility for siblings during, 185; sexual identity in, 488; socialization anxiety of, 481; socialization in late years of, 483
Children
testing of, 276
Children's Apperception Test, 280
Child-rearing
among Eskimos, Nunivak, 148; among Hawaiians, 186; among Ifaluk, 179; among Kibei and Nisei, 49; among Okinawans, 50; among Pedi, 82; among Temne and Mende, 92; and belief in gods, 476; and dependency, 38, 40; by social class, 35; culturally-conditioned trends in, 465; dreams effected by, 410; experimentation with, 437; in Japan, 34; learning methods of, 36; parental attitudes toward, 36; permissiveness, during, 37; practices, during, 481; regional variations of, 38; related to adult behavior, 36-37; related to mental health, 44; relation of variables to, 2; Ryukyuan practices of, 50
China, 273;
religious persecution in, 256; war-torn country of, 260-61; TAT tests in, 284
Chinese, 204;
and abstraction, 519; and group identity, 258; and Rorschach tests, 217; dreams of, 406, father-son dyad among, 516; frustration among, 571; kinship system of the, 511; relationship to government of, 224; self-sufficiency in, 249

Chinese-Americans
  and acculturation, 54; and
  infancy, 78n
Chinese-Hawaiians, 186
Christianity
  and American Indians, 131; and
  democracy, 228n, 247; church of,
  247; forms of love in, 251-52,
  259-60; forms of hate in, 252,
  259-60; missionaries, 253n
Chrysantheum and the Sword, The,
  22, 24, 25, 39, 203
Church
  prejudice and affiliation with, 252-53
CIMA (Coordinated Investigation of
  Micronesian Anthropology), 176
Circumcision rites, 489, 490, 491;
  in Africa, 73, 487, 492; in Oceania,
  492
Citizenship
  in a democracy, 227, 231
Clan, 528, *See also* Kin group;
  nominal for Hindus, 534, 538; to
  control behavior, 518
Climate, 228;
  and customs, 495; and initiation rites,
  492; as it effects Polar Eskimos, 467
Cloud-test
  274-75
Cognition, 51, 173, 180;
  development of, 189; effect of drugs
  on, 368; organization of, 181, 383;
  process of, 182; theories of, 438
Cognitive development, 189, 92;
  disorders of, 374; in children, 85,
  86, 87; part language plays in, 88;
  part school plays in, 88
Collective consciousness, 10
Colonialism, 73
Colombia
  peasants in, 275
Comanche, 132, 156
Coming of Age in Samoa, 125, 180
Committee on Human Development, 78
Common Interest Associations, 55
Community, 151, 398;
  attitudes toward, 230; reactions to
  mental illness by, 383-85
Competitiveness
  among Africans, 548; among

Japanese, 50; among Kwakiuth,
  126; among Orientals, 522; lack
  of, 444; organization of, 260
Concept formation
  among Wolof, 86-88
Concubine, 518
Conflict
  approach and avoidance, 441; emotional forms of, 398; in sex
  identity, 482, 488, 489, 491;
  intra-psychic, 365, 480; of Hindu-
  Moslem, 256; of male identity,
  492; psychological, 122-23;
  religious, 252-53, 256
Conflict and Dream, 172
Conformity, 245, 251, 605-06;
  among Americans and Japanese, 27;
  among Africans, 72; among
  Eskimos, 84-85, 153; among Temne
  of Sierra Leone, 84-85; among Thai
  and Americans, 272-73; in
  American society, 242, 243, 273
Conjugal family, 514
Consciousness
  of Kalabari, 104
Conservatism, 218-19, 226;
  in patrilineal clans, 518; votes, 259
Conservation
  among children, 86, 88
Crime
  among Koreans, 45; and Americans,
  245; in Japan, 42, 44; judging
  and punishing of, 483
Cross-culture, 141;
  and acculturation, 54-55; and
  cognitive style, 92; comparison
  of, 437, 441; comparison of mental
  illness in, 392; comparison of sex
  roles, 487; correlational approach,
  444; in Africa, 72; intelligence
  tests, 174; measurements of intelligence, 181; methodology of, 158;
  of dreams, 408, 410, 411; personality study, 187; research on, 293,
  296, 495; research on mental
  illness, 386; research tests, 81, 142,
  274; sorcery, 483; studies of, 450,
  470-71, 472-73, 477, 497; study
  of optical illusion, 445; study of
  personality, 500; studies of local

politics, 498; surveys, 83; use of
tests, 267
Cross-Cultural Summary, 409
Cross-sexual identity, 488-89;
and behavior, 489; and exaggerated
masculinity, 490; and femininity,
490; mother-son relationship
causes, 489
Cultural anthropology, 125;
definition of, 5
Cultural Anthropology and Psychiatry,
124-25
Cultural relativism, 436
Culture, 122, 225;
and dreams, 406, 407, 412, 416;
as a holistic concept, 450-56,
578n, 579; as "learned", 580; as it
explains behavior, 581; concept of,
124, 270; fieldwork on, 445; forces
for change of, 467; function of,
268; mental illness of a, 392; of
Africa, 72, 73, 121; of Eskimos,
377; origin and evolution of, 575;
pressure of, 181; spiral progression
of, 466; stability of, 466; white
dreams of, 407
Culture and Ecology Project in East
Africa, 72, 93, 95
Culture-and-personality, 1-2, 90, 121,
123, 126, 131; and cognition, 190;
and politics, 211; behavior of, 3;
characteristics of society and, 6;
criticism of research into, 52;
definition of, 2; discussion of,
578-79; in Africa, 72; in Japan,
33, 42, 46, 50, 51, 53, 56; in
Oceania, 187; in Polynesia, 181;
influence on social psychology, 435;
natural group differences of, 3;
of Pueblo, 127; reorientation of,
582-86; research into, 176, 180;
school of thought, 470; shared
behavior, 6; social psychological
differences of, 3, 4; studies of, 135,
368; theoretical writings on, 366;
traditions of, 260
Culture, Genuine and Spurious, 124
Culturology
transcending personalities, 3
Cuna
and Trances, 421

Custer's Massacre, 130
Cybernetics, 173

Dahomey
death rites of, 549; initiation rites
among, 439
Dard, 426-27
Death 127, 408;
and love, 337; and TAT responses,
331-59; dreams of, 407; Eskimos
belief in, 149; horror of, 403;
Japanese concern about, 32;
Pueblo Indians view of, 125;
ritual of, 549
Defense mechanisms
and psychoanalytic theory, 131;
importance of, 596-602; use of, 383
Democracy
and personal beliefs, 230; and
personality, 227; and racism, 244,
252; and religion, 244, 252; and
tyranny, 230; as a political form,
208; belief in, 241; English tradition of, 225; in Africa, 555;
philosophy of, 229; preserving of,
233; qualities of, 228; stability of
a, 234; United States tradition
of, 225
Democratic character, 218, 226-31
Dependency
American fear of, 248-51; among
father-son relationship, 516; among
Japanese, 37-38, 40, 50, 55; among
Kraska Indians, 133; between
parents and children, 548; of
Hindu child on mother, 540-41;
of Ifaluk, 603
Depression, 597;
among Nisei, 48-49; and physiological
dysfunctions, 364, 397-98; in
Africa, 102-03, 104-05
Descriptive-humanistic approach
to research, 442, 443, 450
Desemantication, 383-84;
and mental illness, 397-98
Deviancy, 428;
among American Indians, 149,
150-52; and behavior, 406, 408;
hatred of, 226; individual vs.
group, 42, 55; relationship of
"anomie" to, 153, 154

Dictatorship, 208, 227
Diegueño Indians
  and dreams, 420
Dignity
  toward others, 229; toward self,
  228-29
Discipline, 210, 437;
  among Eskimos and Temne, 92;
  among Orientals, 518
Displacement
  as mechanism, 482, 596, 598-99, 602
Disease, 370, 400;
  as it effects mentals health, 367, 397;
  epilepsy among Eskimos, 374;
  Kwashiorkor, 492; malnutrition
  resulting from, 477; theories of, 410
Divination
  dreams used for, 405, 408, 427, 581
Draw-a-Person (DAP)), 275
Dream interpretation, 405, 415
Dreams, *See also* Dreaming
  among Alorese, 404-06; among
  Nigerians (Ibo, Yóruba, Hausa),
  96; among Zulu, 95, 390; and
  character traits, 421; and sleep,
  413; and spirit impersonation, 420;
  and supernatural, and visions,
  415-429; as experiences of the soul,
  405; blessings of, 411; "Culture
  Pattern", 416; indicative of
  violence, 133; "individual", 416;
  in non-Western studies, 406;
  "latent" and "manifest", 414;
  manifest content of, 449; motivating nature of, 131; of North
  Americans, 411; reading of,
  264-65; sexual interpretation of,
  134, 172, 176; summary of
  research on, 412; symbols of, 404;
  use of, 413
Dreamer
  as aggressor, 407; culture of, 408;
  experiences the dreams as, 408;
  problems of the, 406
Dreaming, *See also* Dreams
  and REM sleep, 425; and Trance,
  423; and witches, 403;
  as cortical activity, 414; as
  discussed by ethnographers, 405;
  as hallucinatory experience, 423;
  institutionization of, 410-11;

  meaning of, 414n; research on, 413
  universal characteristics of, 418
Drugs, *See also* Hallucinogens
  addicted to, 258; and community
  acceptance, 384; and hippies, 417;
  and mental dysfunction, 396;
  Datura, 420; effects of, 368;
  experiments with, 423; induced
  states with, 416; inducing dreams
  with, 421; inducing Possession
  Trance, 426; opium, 539;
  psychiatric use of, 367;
  psychoactivity and, 425
Dyads
  brother-brother, 547-48; definition of,
  514; father-son, 516-24; husband-
  wife, 524-34; mother-son, 534-47

Eastern Orthodoxy, 246, 532
Ecology
  and personality, 137; and psychological variables, 90, 110; dreams
  affected by, 410; effecting Eskimos,
  92-93, 375-76; "human", 190
Economy
  and socialization pressures, 485;
  as it effects dreams, 410, 499;
  exploitation by, 93; high accumulation of, 83; of Polynesia,
  Melanesia, Micronesia, 168;
  resources of American Indians, 152;
  subsistence levels of, 486
Economic development, 581;
  achievement motivations effecting,
  97; in Japan, 41; in Asian countries, 53
Economic institutions, 203;
  as cause for violence, 259
Education, 41, 97, 100;
  among American Indians, 438; and
  democratic system, 234; and
  "field dependence", 292; and test
  performance, 293; as American
  value, 242; as political determinant,
  225; level of parents', 77; of Kibei,
  49; of Zulu, 98; universal concept
  of, 515
Educators, 71
Efir
  childhood and adolescence, 82
Ego, 184, 387; *See also* Superego

among Japanese, 32; and alien forces, 426; and status, 488; as defense against pain, 596; defense mechanism for, 219; egocentricity among Kraska Indians, 132, 134; Eskimos' repression of, 147-48; strength of, 481

Eidos, 188, 189; definition of, 172

Electroencephalograph (EEG) and dreams, 414; findings of, 367, 368

Electrolyte imbalance, 369, 396

Elite groups, 395

Emotions, 97, 134; *See also* Guilt among American Indians, 125, 128, 133, 157, 273; among Japanese, 28-30; between mother and child, 78-79; channeling of, 231; deprivation of, 485; dilemma of, 365; disorder of, 374; disturbance of, 480; larger community as a source of, 138; of Amami Oshima islanders, 50; of Russians, 215; response to, 444; withdrawal from, 139

Emotional Reponse Test, 136

Empathy, 293

Endocrinology, 368

England democratic tradition of, 225; government of, 227; individualism in, 248; prejudice in, 257; socialism in, 249

Englishmen, Frenchmen, Spaniards, 203

Environment and behavior, 588-89; anxiety producing, 177; as "carpentered", 90-91; as "extra-systematic causal events", 466; as man-made, 492; cultural and physical, 491-92; of Oceania, 167; pressures from, 369; relationship to, 145; social and political, 225; TAT and sensitivity to, 316

Equality and Christianity, 259, 260; as American trait, 241, 243; between sexes, 525, 547; conflicts due to, 244; in economic and political opportunities, 258

Esalen Institute, 364n

Escape from Freedom, 212

Eskimos and climate, 467; and group normalcy, 493; arts and crafts of, 92; culture of, 377-79; discipline among, 92; hysteria among, 371; kinship system of, 511; language of, 91; mental illness among, 264, 365; myths and personality of, 147-49; perception of, 84-85, 91; *pibloktoq,* 370-83, 384, 393-94; socialization practices of, 92

Ethnocentrism, 55

Ethnography, 94, 109, 141, 172, 446; and dreams, 405; literature of, 71; of Kwoma, 174; of New Guinea Highlands, 168; of single peoples, 446; "new", 189

Ethnology, 1, 121; Japanese Society of Ethnology, 22

Ethos, 188, 189, 444

Etiology, 385, 392, 395

European-Americans, 130; behavior of, 298; "individual-centered", 204; neonates of, 78

European children precocity of, 79

European infants as compared with African, 78

Ewe, 99

Existentialism in Japan, 29

Exogamy, 409; taboo of, 171

Extrasystemic causal events, 466, 468

Extremism and change, 533; in Americans, 529; propensity toward, 234; traits of, 226-27

F scale, 217, 218, 222, 232

Faces in the Crowd, 271

Family relations among Hopi, 138; among Tahitians, 187; authoritarian types of, 232; between parent and child, 474; changes in, 533; devisive forces in, 438; dyads in, 514-561 *passim;* extended and polygynous, 475; filial obligations, 48, 49, 53; filial piety of Chinese, 204; in Africa,

72, 101; in Japan, 32, 35, 36, 38,
43, 251; infant dependency on
mother, 12, 37; instability of, 106;
mother-son, 40-41; political
systems and, 213
Fantasy, 274, 367;
among college students, 316-25;
among Hindu, Americans, 316;
among Chinese, 326-27; and TAT,
312; gratification in, 600; life of
people, 410; responses to, 281
Farmers
of Africa, 93-94
Farming, *See also* Agricultural societies
Fascism, 219, 271n
Father, 213, 487
absence of, 488-89, 490; Hindu
relationships with hostility to
newborn, 536-39; low salience in
infancy, 489
Females, 100;
and witchcraft, 480; as agents of
socialization, 137; crying among,
107; in myths, 147; personalities of, 172; sexual
distinction, 484; stability of roles
as, 106
Femininity, 489;
and cross-sex identity, 490; individual
expressions of, 490; of Hindu
gods, 544
Fertility
symbols of, 406
Field theory, 8
Fijians, 187;
kinship system of, 511
Filipinos, 54
Fishing societies, 182;
and food accumulation, 485-86;
assertion in, 83; Baffin Eskimos,
84; use of dreams in, 409
Fixation, 440
Flathead Indians
songs and supernatural of, 415
Folklore, *See also* Folktales, 189;
African, 73; American Indians, 123;
learning through, 496
folkgeist, 203
Folktales, *See also* Folklore, 482-83;
about food, 99; and dreams, 410
Fon, 75

Food
among Zulu, 390; accumulation of,
485; anxiety in, 411; calcium
contained in, 377; concern for, 99;
distribution as ritual, 603; production of, 409, 496; scarcity effecting
personality, 493; sparsity of and
anxiety of, 141
France
literature of, 73; national character
of, 205; psychocultural research,
73; religious persecution in, 257;
studies of, 73
Franck Drawing Completion Test
as related to father absence, 490
Freedom
American beliefs in, 242, 243, 245,
252, 258, 259, 260; among
Orientals, 517; and individualism,
527; of choice, 272
Free enterprise, 249, 533
Freudian, 372;
and behavior, 441; and individuality,
104; and learning theory, 440; and
personality dynamics, 8, 572;
Orthodox, 189; psychologists
as, 473
Friendship, 203, 229
Frustration, *See also* Gratification
and "anomie", 596; expression of,
570-71; of drives, 595-96

Galton's Problem, 453
Games
and feedback, 497; children's, 410,
485; learning through, 496; of
chance, 485, 495-96
Ganda, 78;
adults, 87; compared with Western
infants, 77; indulgence of infants
among, 77; influence of household
members in, 76; kings ritual combat among, 550; precocity of infant
in, 76; relationship of mother to
child in, 75; religion among, 100;
weaning, 79, 80-81
Genetics, 78;
of mental disorder, 396; of
schizophrenia, 368; traits of, 467
German character, 205, 228;
and its propensity toward authori-

tarian government, 212, 233; and
Nazism, 214-15, 219, 228
Germany
government of 213, 227, 233, 367
*Germany the Aggressor Throughout
the Ages,* 203
Gestalt psychology, 126, 364
Gesell Tests, 77;
developmental test items, 80;
Ghana, 78, 93;
animistic thinking, 88, 93; child
training practices in, 82
Ghosts
belief in, 168, 179; fear of 474, 476
God, 230, 234n, 249, 438, 541, 544;
Hindu, 540; in monotheistic religions,
531-33; Krishna, 545
Gods
aggressiveness of, 476; belief in, 474;
benevolent, 476; nature of, 474, 476,
484; Oriental, 521-22; reflecting
parents, 474; replacement of, 577
Governing of Man, The, 47
Government
African, 553; American, 530; authoritarian, 227, 233; dictatorial and
totalitarian, 227; Hindu, 543; Oriental, 520; self—, 230; socialist, 249;
types of, 208-09, 227
Gratification, 587, *See also* Frustration
as motivation for behavior, 590-602;
for Ifaluk, 604; in infants and adults,
440
Great Britain
religious persecution in, 256
Greenland
Eskimos in, 371
Grhastha, 537
Gregoria, The Hand Trembler, 123
Group Personality Projective Test, 276
Guilt, 226, 259, 581; *See also* Emotions
among Africans, 105; among American Indians, 150; among Eskimos,
148-49; among Japanese, 40-41, 44,
52-53; as related to households, 478
Gusii, 84, 497;
mothers of, 83; patrilineal emphasis,
518; population growth, 99; relationship of mother-child, 74; sexual
differences among, 89

Hallucinations
and dreams, 416, 423; and sensory
deprivation, 425-26; and society, 398-
99; and Trance, 422; as pseudo-perception, 423; experience with, 415;
mechanisms of, 386
Hallucinogens, 367; *See also* Drugs
experimental work with, 423;
physiological effects of, 417
Hand Test, 276
Handbook of Social-Psychology, 202
Harvard Values Project, 142
Hawaiians, 180, 186
Hausa, 87;
success among, 96
Health, 137;
among Eskimos, 375-77; and nutrition, 73, 80, 370, 400; benefits of,
244; malnutrition, 73, 477
Hebe, 94
Hedonistic learning theory, 437, 440
Herding societies
compliance in, 83
Heredity, 187
Hindus
kinship structure, 534-47
Hologistic study, 450-56; *See also*
Cross-culture
of anthropology, 238
Hopi, 121;
culture of, 124, 135-140, 156; dreams
of the, 406, 408, 412; initiation rites
of the, 491
Holy Inquisition, 252, 254
Homosexuality, 170, 482
Hostility, 148, 581; *See also* Aggression
and "liberals", 219; and physical
dysfunction, 369; between generations, 439; between sexes, 176;
between siblings, 439, 440; in-group,
179; projection of, 226; to authority,
231, 602; toward beliefs, 532; toward
children, 439; toward fathers, 437;
toward parents, 438, 440; toward self,
597; toward spirits, 466, 480
Households
and aggressive training, 481;
extended, 476; Hindu, 537; mother-
child, 476, 478, 492; nuclear, 478-79,
483; polygynous, 478, 483; studies of,
475-76

House-Tree-Person (HTP), 275
Humanitarianism, 258
Human Relations Research Group, 25
Hunting societies
  among Eskimos, 91, 148; and food,
  485-86; assertion in, 83; of Plains
  and Pueblo Indians, 125; of Teton
  Dakotas, 130; use of dreams in, 409
Hypnosis
  and dreams, 425; and sleep, 425
Hypoglycemia, 369, 396
Hypoxia, 369, 396
Hysteria, 371, 379-83; *See also Pibloktoq*
  among Eskimos, 372-74; and mental
  health, 597

Iatmul
  of New Guinea, 172-73
Ibo
  achievement of individuals, 96; religion of, 100; status mobility of, 96
Id
  among Eskimos, 148
Idakho, 82
Identity, 8;
  and adolescents, 575; "attributed",
  "subjective", "optative", 488-91
Ideologies, 230
Ila of Zambia
  married women, 78
Illness, 478
  and therapeutic techniques, 480;
  sorcery causing, 482; spirits causing,
  483
Illusion susceptibility, *See also*
  Perception
  in African societies, 90-91
Incest
  taboo of, 171
Independence, 94, 135, 410, 484;
  See also Self-reliance
  among Tuscarora, 145; from
  children, 250; Ganda mothers, 80;
  of child from mother during
  weaning, 80; of children in Africa,
  550; self-centered, 132
India, 74, 273;
  casteism in, 256; TAT tests in, 284
Indian, Eastern
  anti-feeling in England, 257;
  Rorschach tests on, 297

Indian Education Research Project, 135
Indian Reorganization Policy, 137
Individualism
  among Thai and American Indians,
  273; in England, 248-49; of children,
  247; of Western Europe, 250;
  "rugged", 256
Individuality
  American orientation toward, 224,
  245; among American college
  students, 220; among Ibo, Yorba,
  Hausa, 96; among Lovedu, 82;
  among Temne, and Eskimos, 84;
  and autonomy, 44; belief in, 241;
  cultures expressed through, 3-4; in
  Africa, 72
Individual and His Society, The, 131,
  183,
Individuals
  and society and culture, 466;
  anthropological attention to, 364;
  centrifugal tendency of, 528;
  cultural influence on, 580; dreams
  of, 416; freedom of, 242; psychological characteristics of, 465;
  test performance by, 294; uniqueness
  of, 528; worth of, 228-29
Indonesia, 290
Industrialization
  in democratic systems, 234;
  in Japan, 53
Infancy
  and mother influencing sex roles,
  487; and relationship to systems,
  473; convulsions in, 375; dependency
  on mother during, 74-75, 476; emotional deprivation during, 485;
  in Africa, 74-81; immunization of,
  477; indulgency during, 75, 79
  474-75, 485; motor prococity
  during, 77; precocity in, 77;
  rickets in, 376; sex identity in,
  488; treatment during, 474
Infants
  desire for, 107; Ganda, 76-77;
  indulgent care of, 135; Maori
  rejection of, 182-83; mortality of,
  534; Negro, 77; Puerto Rican,
  78; tests for, 81
Inferiority complex
  among Americans, 255; among
  Eskimos, 148

Inhibition, 273
Initiation rites
  and child training, 495; and
  climate, 492; child dependency on,
  549; for females, 491; harshness of,
  440; into Kachina cult, 238; male,
  73, 89, 490, 491; symptomatic of
  hostility, 439
Innovative personality
  definition of, 387
Insecurity, 248
Institute for the Study of Child
  Rearing in Japan, 36
Instrument decay
  definition of, 446
Instrumental Activities Inventory
  (IAI), 283
Integration, 244;
  of minorities, 255
Intelligence
  and personality, 173; and test
  performance, 293; functions of, 292;
  of Eskimos, 149
Interaction
  as different from personality-
  culture, 3
Interpersonal relations, 141;
  and interaction, 272; and national
  character, 204; as revealed by TAT,
  312-13; incompetence in, 397
Interpretation of Dreams, The, 170
Intersubjective verifiability and
  perception, 443-45
in treatment
  definition of, 387
Introjection
  as psychological mechanism, 53, 55
Iran
  compared with Turks, 224;
  extremists in, 218
Iraqw, 99
Iroquois, 156
Issei, 46, 47;
  and TAT, 313; comparison of Nisei,
  Kibei with, 49; maladjustment to
  American culture, 47
Islam, 246
Italy
  government of, 227; national
  character of, 206, 225; religious
  persecution in, 257

Jainism, 544
Jamaica
  "John Crow" song of, 3
Japan
  and language, 519; discussion of,
  21-56; government of, 227; religious
  persecution in, 256; rural residents
  of, 31, 33, 52; student uprising in,
  37-39
Japan's Invisible Race, 46
*Japanese; An Empirical Study of
  Culture and Personality, The,* 26
Japanese
  character of, 17, 21, 24, 25, 26, 186,
  213, 220-21, 228; child training of,
  22; descendants, 46; emotions of,
  28; inferiority complex of, 51;
  language, 52, 59; personality, 22;
  social roles, 285; students of, 222;
  villages of, 258
Japanese Society of Social Psychology,
  22
Jews, 252;
  Hitler's campaign against, 259;
  identification with, 256n; problems
  of group identity among, 257-58;
  raised as non-Jews, 255
Judaism, 246, 253n
Justice
  among Ghanian school children,
  88-89
Juvenile delinquency, 42, 43;
  among Japanese, 44-45; among
  Koreans, 45; in broken homes, 490;
  cultural expectations produce, 89;
  in subsaharan Africa, 85, 110

Kalabari Ijaw
  personality of, 103
Kalenjin, 111;
  language of, 94
Kamba, 82, 94
Kaska
  alcoholism among, 149; dominant
  motivations of, 132-35; dreams
  of, 406
Kerner Report, 259n
Kibei
  definition, 49
Kikuyu, 99
Kings, *See also* Rulers, Chiefs

chieftainship, 554; death of, 551;
in Africa, 550-51; killings of, 556
Kin groups, 55, 512
preserving Oriental, 521
Kinship, 73, 204, 484, 581
connecting people, 510; systems of,
468; questions about, 512; and
"ways of life", 513
Kinship content
definition of, 513; example of, 514;
"mutual dependence", 516-24;
"rivalry", 547-48; "self-reliance",
524-34; "supernatural", 544-47
Kinship structure
definition of, 513; example of, 514;
of Africans, 547-58; of Hindu,
534-47; of Orientals, 516-24; of
Western society, 524-34
Kinship system, 511;
content of, 514; emphasis on dyads,
514-58
Kipsigis
population growth among, 99;
religion of, 100
Kiva
religious structure of, 138
Kohs Blocks
used among Hausa schoolchildren,
87
Koreans, 45
Kowhai, 180
Kpelle of Liberia, 87, 101
Kwakiutl
Dionysian life of, 126, 127
Kwoma
child's displacement among, 439;
personality development, 174-75

Lac du Flambeau, 128, 129, 130
Language
African, 73, 554; alphabetical, 530;
and culture, 519; Chinese, 519;
descriptive 214; differences of, 448;
Eskimo, 91; Indo-European, 531; in
infants, 77; Japanese, 519; Kalenjin
and Bantu, 94-95; Kpelle compared to English, 87; Menomini,
143; school, part of, 88; unalpha-
betized, 519; written form of, 88;
written Hindu, 543; written
Western, 530
Latin America, 233;

Jews in, 257; religious persecution
in, 257
Laws, 19, 581;
among American Indians, 131; cultural, 576; disregard of, 240;
familist system of, 204; racial, 244
Learning theory
and personality, 441;
hedonistic, 437-440; in America, 438
Liberalism
in politics, 218-19, 226; voting, 259
Law and Order, 210
Lebanese Maronites
Rorschach records of, 295
Life histories
of American Indians, 124; Sun
Chief, 124
Linguistics
comparative, 167
Literature
Hindu, 542-43; of Orientals, 520;
of Western societies, 530
Literacy
in Africa, 101
Logoli
household, 75, 87; population
growth, 99; religion, 100
Love, 247;
Christian, 251; lack of, 372;
need for, 373; romantic, 518, 525
Lovedu
cultural traits of, 82
Lovers
and death, 337; response to
TAT on, 331-37
Luo
education of, 98
Lup, 483

Macho, 490
Mae Enga
dreams of, 408
Magic, 148;
beliefs in, 480; medieval, 260
Maintenance system, 410, 466, 468, 497
definition of, 471
Males
and Hindu culture, 536-37; and
sorcery, 482; dreams of, 94;
hostility toward women, 100;
initiation rites of, 487; identity
and behavior of, 491; instability of

roles of, 106; myth creators, 147;
personalities of, 172
Malnutrition, *See* Health
Manchos
kinship system of, 511
Manus, 172;
children of, 188
Maori, 185; *See also* Rakau
and Protestants, 559n;
personality of, 180-83
Maronite Moslem
dreams of, 412
Marriage, *See also,* Monogamy,
Polygamy
African, 78, 101; American
monogamy, 242, 251; and romantic
love, 32-33, 480; arranged, 43;
consent for, 526; in Iatmul, 173,
210; interracial, 259; mode of, 422;
polygamous and monogamous, 481,
525, 526; premarital behavior, 134;
reluctance for, 134; role changes, 138
Masculinity
exaggerated, 489-90
Matrilocal relationships, 514
Maturation, 185
Maya, 405
Media
in Japan, 28; in United States, 28
Medicare, 249
Meiji Restoration, 519
Melanesia
cultural contact in, 169; discussion
of, 170-76; economy of, 168;
research in, 167
Memory, 440
Men, *See also* Males, Masculinity
dreams of, 408; sex role of, 487
Mende
spatial-perceptual skills of, 92
Menomini
culture among, 142-44
Mental health, 175, 368; *See also*
Mental Illness
as related to child rearing, 44;
culture and, 43-45; 364
Mental illness, 13, 364n; *See also*
Neurosis, Psychiatric disorders
among non-Western peoples, 179,
187; among Okinawans, 50; among
Polar Eskimos, 370; among Zulu, 389;

biocultural theory of, 264; causes of,
392; chronic, 369; compared with
Europeans, 102, 103; cultural determinants of, 363, 395, 396;
effect of socio-cultural change on,
108; hospitals, 499; in Africa, 71,
73; interpretations of, 393; paranoid,
398, 482; process of becoming, 399;
theory of, 383, 386, 387-88, 391,
399-400; treatment of, 393-94
Mercy, 247
Messianic movement, 146
Mestizo
dreams of the, 404, 405
Metabolism, 367;
and its relationship to cerebral function, 369; calcium deficiency, 374;
carbohydrates and, 368; affecting
mental health, 396
Methodology, 436, 473
Mexico, 74, 228;
macho in, 490
Micronesia, 17;
and Polynesia, 169; discussion of,
176-80; economy of, 168
Midewesin ceremony, 129
Middle East, 224
Migration
of Japanese, 49; rural, 43, 54
Migratory labor, 100
Military power, 220
Mind, 368, *See also* Brain
Mind in Sleep, The, 172
Mine workers
in Africa, 72
Minority groups
in United States, 45; status of,
56; stress on, 49
Missionaries, 71, 122, 128;
Christian, 532; Moslem and
Christian, 253n
Modal personality, 226;
and culture, 223; and politics, 224;
as revealed in dreams, 410; concept
of, 268; definition of, 144-45;
differing types of, 212; of adults,
205; of groups, 30; of Maori, 183;
pattern of, 215; processes of, 277-78
Modernization, 276; *See also*
Industrialization
in Japan, 38, 39, 41, 53; in

Polynesia, 191; social disintegration
caused by, 106
Mohammedanism, 544
Mohave
dreams of the, 406
Monarchy, 208
Monogamy, *See also* Marriage
as an *ideal*, 525; as it effects sexual
identity, 488-89; in North America,
422; in society, 481
Moral Ideology Test, 136
Mormon
Rorschach protocols among, 278
Moroccans
character of, 216
Mothers, 79;
and abortions, 78; and anxiety-free
pregnancy, 78; and child, 439, 475,
487; and expectation toward
infants, 80; and relationship to
infants, 74-76, 80; and son relationship, 489, 535-38; ceremonial
duties of, 475; Gusti, 83; Hindu,
540; male identification with, 488;
need for privacy by, 476; Oriental
father-son relationship and, 517;
stability of, 475-76; surrogate, 185
Mother Goddess
Hindu worship of, 540
Motivation, 271, 367; *See also* Achievement Motivation
for compliance, 520, 591; for non-
compliance, 570; individual and
role, 271; of behavior, 590
Muller-Lyer Illusion, 90-91, 441
Mundugumor, 172
Music
among Western societies, 530;
and stress, 477; Hindu, 542-43;
of China and Japan, 520; singing,
478
Myth
as dream content, 407; ideals and,
411; Oedipus-type, 439
Mythology
of Dahomey, 439; of Indian gods,
545n; of Nunvak Eskimos, 147-49;
relationship of men and women to,
147; religious, 557

National Institute of Statistical
Research (Committee for the Study
of National Character), 26
National character, 201;
as action, 203; as institutional pattern, 203; as racial psychology,
204-06; culture theme of, 203;
definition of, 202, 224; discussion
of, 200-35; measurement of, 206;
pliability of, 221; relationship of
government to, 213, 227; studies of,
216, 223, 569
Nationalism, 243, 531
Native Dream Theory, 408
Nature of Prejudice, The, 246
Navajo, 156;
acceptance of white values, 143;
dreams of the, 406; Rorschach
protocols among, 278; values of
men, 142
Naven, 172, 189
Nazis
and other Germans, 214, 219-20;
character of, 210, 214
Negative fixation
and frustration, 440; and
socialization, 479-80
Negroes, 45, 244; *See also* Blacks
and prejudice, 246, 255, 257; and
white relations, 257; infants of, 77;
gratification for, 592, 592n
Nepotism
Oriental, 517
Neurosis, *See also* Mental Illness
among American Indians, 146;
combat, 367; withdrawal caused
by, 398
New Guinea, 167, 168;
personality in, 172; TAT in, 175
New Guinea Highlands, 17, 168
New Zealand, 167, 168
Ngoni
childhood, 82
Nigeria
achievement motivation in, 276-77,
282
Nightmares, 404, 413n
Nisei, 46; *See also* American-Japanese
and TAT, 313; behavior of children
motivation, 47; depression among,
47-48; maladjustment, 47
Normalcy
definition of, 387
North, the, 244, 259

North American Stirling County
    Study, 106, 107
Norway
    college students of, 222
Nuclear Family, 423, 475;
    among Americans, 525
Nuer, 403;
    as compared with Gusii, 82; dreams
    of, 405; permissiveness among, 497
Nupe, 93;
    female dominance of, 97
Nutrition, *See* Health
Nyakyusa
    dreams of, 403; witches among, 405

Obedience, 483;
    children, 88; child-training, 83
    expectations of Gusii mothers, 83;
    to authority, 219-20; to political
    leaders, 226
Occupational group, 33;
    group dependency, 38; Japan
    (comparisons), 31;
Oedipus complex, 131, 171, 438-49,
    449;
    hedonistic learning theory of, 437
Ojibwa
    accultural among, 143, 156; dreams
    of, 406; personalities of, 128; psycho-
    logical features of, 129-30;
    Rorschach among, 289
Okinawa, 75
Okinawans, 50, 51
Open Projective Test, 277
Operant conditioning, 364n
Operationalizing, 85
Opportunity
    possibilities for, 153
Optical Illusions, 443, 445, 493
Orientals, 246, 258, 280;
    Kinship structure of, 516-21;
    standard of living of, 256
Oyabun-Kobun, 45

Papago, 156
Paranoia, *See* Mental illness
Parents
    as stimuli for hostility, 438; child's
    relationship with, 474; hostility
    towards, 440

Pariah status, 56
Parliaments, 210
Pastoralism, 73, 93, 94
Paternalism, 38;
    in Japan, 43
Patriarchal
    among Hindus, 534; among
    Orientals, 516; nominally among
    Western European peoples, 524
Patrilineal
    among Hindus, 534; among
    Orientals, 516; among Western
    European peoples, 524; emphasis of,
    518
Patrilocal, 514;
    among Hindus, 534; among Orien-
    tals, 516; among Western European
    peoples, 524
Patriotism, *See* Nationalism
Patterns of Culture, 125, 158, 172,
    209n;
    criticisms of, 126-28, 158
Pedi
    cultural traits of, 82
People of Alor, The, 184
Perception
    and spatial skills, 91-92, 93, 110;
    and thought, 182; as effected by
    social structure, 493-94; causal, 438;
    coin-size estimation, 95; cultural
    differences of, 91, 275; effect of, 293;
    effect of physical environment on, 90,
    492; in Africa, 72; learned, 441;
    loss of, 397; of projective tests, 295;
    of self and others, 397; organization
    of, 383; *perception* of —, 292; physi-
    ological aspects of, 426; pseudo —,
    265, 415, 416, 423; visual illusion,
    90-91; universal law of, 577
Performance tests
    discussion of, 269-77
Personality, 173, 186, 216, 217, 274;
    analysis of, 231; and F scale, 25; and
    its cross-cultural variability, 579;
    and political systems, 210, 232-33,
    234; and Rorschach, 25; and social
    systems, 8, 124, 127, 294; and TAT,
    25; as result of child training, 472;
    as it reveals emotions, 144; as social
    action, 290-91; assessment of, 178;

authoritarian, 219, 230; changing of,
268; comparing Indians, Spanish,
and Anglo people with regard to,
153; components of, 4; cultural
milieu and individual experience as,
366; definition of, 7; democratic,
229; development of, 175, 583; differences of, 145; group, 223, 232;
"ideal", 82, 125; individual, 370;
measurement of, 207; "models" in
Oceania, 169; of aborigines, 130; of
American Indians, 122-23, 128,
132-33; of Eskimos, 149; of Germans,
214; of Hopi, 140; of Japanese, 54;
of Kalabari, 103; of Russians, 215;
patterns of, 223; structure of, 405;
tests of, 222; theory of, 436; to explain cultural events, 488; research
on, 90; variable of sexual identity,
488; variables of, 24, 93
Personality and the Behavior Disorders,
368
Peyotists, 143, 386
Philippines, 74;
anti-democratic learnings in, 220
Physical anthropology, 1, 168
Physiology
and dreams, 413; study of, 370;
variables of, 382
Pibloktoq, 13, 365, 383;
and community acceptance, 384; as
arctic hysteria, 264; discussion of,
370-79
Plains Indians, 127;
Dionysian life of, 125-26
Pluralism, 255
Pokoman
dreams of the, 404
Pokot, 94
Politicians, 259;
American, 246
Politics, 203, 207; *See also* Systems
African, 211; alienation from, 225;
and culture, 224-25; definition of,
208-09; of Germany, 214; of Soviet
Russia, 215; participation in, 226;
personality and, 218, 222
Polygamy, 526, *See also* Marriage
Polygyny, 73, 422, 484, 492; *See also*
Marriage

as it effects sexual identity, 448-89;
sororal, 481
Polynesia, 167, 168, 169;
discussion of, 180-89
Population
elements of, 216; growth among
Iraqw, 99; Oriental increase of, 524;
pressures of, 100; size of, 410; study
of, 168; traits of national, 232
Porteus Maze Test, 177, 183;
discussion of, 173-74
Portugal
religious persecution in, 257
Possession
among Tikopia, 420; and dreams,
418-29
Possession Trance
discussion of, 418-29
Post-marital residence
as it effects dreams, 409-10
Poverty, 42, 190;
as cause of personality traits, 123;
part of social disintegration, 106
Precocity
African vs. European infants, 78;
among Ganda infants, 76; at birth,
78; motoe, 77, 78n
Pregnancy
in Africa, 78
Prejudice, 545; *See also* Bigotry,
Racism, Religious persecution
active and passive acts of, 255;
"blackbirding", 169; racial and
religious, 242, 252, 253n, 255, 257,
258, 259, 532; solution to problem
of, 256, 257; toward "witches", 577
Primitive people, 569;
and behavior, 582; definition of, 575
Problem situation tests
in Peru, 49
*Problems of American Society: Values
in Conflict,* 242
Projection
and hostility, 581; and paranoia, 570;
mechanism of, 53, 54, 55, 184
Prophets, 146
Prostitution, 44, 45
Protestanism, 246, 253n; *See also,*
Religion
religious persecution by, 256-57

Protestant ethic, 39, 41, 53, 100
Proverbs Test, 276
Psyche, 365, 368
  energy of the, 366; of the Hopi, 407
Psychiatric disorders, 210;
  in Africa, 105-06
Psychiatric research, 366-67
Psychiatrists, 71, 102
Psychiatry, organic
  discussion of, 366-70; Western, 395
Psychoanalysis, 367, 382;
  learning theories of, 440; of dreams,
  412; theory of, 171
Psychoanalysts, 364, 438;
  and kinship, 512
Psychoanalytic theory
  and mental illness, 364; and personality, 211, 574; and politics, 211,
  214; use of, 131-32
Psychodrama, 276
Psychological anthropology, 131, 145,
    158, 170, 175, 186, 190, 574, 578n;
  and kinship, 512; and personality,
  121-22; and "primitive people", 209;
  and psychic materials, 10; cross-
  cultural in approach, 12; difference
  between social psychology, 11-13;
  discussion of, 578; emphasis on natural group differences, 11; field of,
  570; hostility towards, 513; research
  in, 296; students of, 465
Psychological characteristics, 89
Psychological Frontiers of Society, The,
  132
Psychological testing, *See* Projective
  Tests, Rorschach, TAT
Psychologists, 124, 246, 248, 364, 436;
  in European-American society, 269
Psychology, 368, 369, 440;
  clinical, 364n; experimental, 370;
  group, 10; induction, 443; of mobs,
  10; of racism, 204-06; taboo in
  Africa, 72; theory of, 437
Psychology of the Japanese, 28
Psychopathology, 176, 400;
  organic features of, 399; studies of,
  370, 381, 383
Psychopathology and Politics, 211
Psycho-pharmacology, 367, 370
Psychosexual development
  oral, anal, genital, 480

Psychosis, *See also* Mental illness
  among Africans, 102-08; among
  Eskimos and Algonkian, 365; among
  Japanese, 43; and primitives, 172;
  caused by fluid imbalance, 368; "cor-
  tisone", 368; definition of, 387; in
  Micronesia, 177; paretic, 367;
  windigo, 365
Psychosocial Homeostasis, 11
Psychosomatic, 365
Psycho-surgery, 367
Psychotherapy, 385
Puberty
  among Hopi, 138; feast rites of, 404,
  415
Puerto Ricans
  infants of 77n; socialization among,
  276
Pueblo, *See also* Zuni
  Apollonian life of, 125, 127; kinship
  system of, 511, 512
Pukapuka, 180
Punishment, 466;
  administered, 593; among Guisii
  mothers, 83; among Lovedu, 82;
  among Tuscarora, 145; for boys, 84;
  frequency of, 480; of older children,
  484; of Pedi children, 82
Puritanism, 242, 251, 258

Quakerism, 254

Racism, 46, 56; *See also* Prejudice
  and Americans, 242, 243-44, 245;
  and Christianity, 260; and contradictions, 252; and psychology, 246; and
  religious bigotry, 254; and self-
  reliance, 258; in Europe, 253n, 558
Radical empiricism, 577, 578
Rakau, 180, 183; *See also* Maori
Rapid Eye Movement (REM), 422,
  425-26, 428;
  during sleep, 413-16
Rarotonge, 180
Rationality, 224
Reading
  in Africa, 101
Reality
  among Japanese, 31; denial of, 149;
  discontinuity with, 542; of Eskimos,
  147; social, 271

Rejection
in Eskimos, 149, 378
Religion, 171, 245, 253, 405; *See also*
Protestantism, Catholicism,
Christian
among Indians, 131, 132; and prejudice, 246, 252-59 *passim;* as a man's
affair, 409; as cultural product, 472;
belief in, 476; church affiliation in
United States, 19; Confuscius, 39;
emphasis on, 227, 242; governing
secular life, 542; heritage of, 224; in
Africa, 72, 577; in Melanesia, 176;
life of, 410; missionaries, 100; monotheistic, 242, 531-33; "Old-line
Protestant", 152; polytheistic, 521-22,
543; revelations of, 398; worship of,
252
Religious persecution, 256-57, *See also*
Prejudice
Repression, *See also* Defense mechanism
as defense mechanism, 581, 596, 597;
of Eskimos, 147, 149
Reservations, Indian, 122, 123
Revolution
among Blacks, 592n; among Orientals, 523; among Westerners, 533
Rituals, 148, 406;
as dream content, 407; control of
gods by, 474; death, 549; of food
distribution, 603; of king, 550-51;
of rebellion, 601; religious, 586
Ritual Trance, 425
Role-playing, 276
Rorschach test, 25, 295; *See also* Projective tests
and acculturation, 47; and American
Indian, 129-30, 139, 141, 144-45;
and Eskimos, 149; and Japanese-
Americans, 49; and modal pattern,
215; and Moroccans, 216, 217; and
psychoanalytic theory, 131; as
methodological aid, 136; as projective
instrument, 263, 274; discussion of,
296-98; in Africa, 94; in Japan, 30,
31; in Oceania, 177, 178-79, 182,
183; interpretation of, 268, 274; of
Ojibwa, 289, versus TAT, 277-79;
280, 291
Rote leaning, 182
Rulers, *See also* Chiefs, Kings

authoritarian, 531; autocratic, 520;
democratic, 531; in Africa, 556; incompetence of, 521; of Ifaluk, 603,
604
Russia
government of, 227; national character of, 213; refugees of, 215
Ruthenians
kinship system, 511
Ryukyu Islands, 50

Saktas, The, 540
Samoa, 172, 444
Samnyasa, 537
Sander Parallelogram, 441
Saulteaux, 415, 428;
and puberty rites of, 404; dreams
of the, 404, 405
Schizmogenesis
definition of, 172-73, 188
Schizophrenia, 364;
and behavior, 107; and desemanti-
cism, 384-85, 397; and dreams, 416;
genetic study of, 368; in West Africa,
366
Scholastic Aptitude Tests
490
School, 88, 101, 109, 122, 247
Security, 510
Self-evaluation
negative, 397
Self-denial
in Japan, 53
Self-identity, 44, 258
Self-preservation, 509
Self-reliance, *See also* Independence
among Americans, 248-49, 254-56,
527; among Hopi, 139; among Latin
Americans, 257; among Plains Indians, 125; and food scarcity, 493;
as a militant ideal, 249-51; as values,
258-260, 273, 410; in children, 483;
test of, 486
Self-sufficiency, 249, 250
Sensory development, 78
Sentence Completion Test (SCT),
33, 275
Sex and Repression in Savage Society,
171
Sex and Temperament, 545
Sex distinctions
emphasis on, 484

Sex roles
  among Zulu, 95; antagonism between,
  97; cross-cultural comparisons of,
  487; differences among Gusii, 89;
  equality between, 525, 547; in Africa,
  494; learning of, 491; reversal of, 97;
  socialization of, 487, 494; training
  of, 484
Sexual behavior
  among Kaska Indians, 134; anal,
  480; avoidance of, 599; constriction
  of, 134; deviant, 406; dreams of,
  406-08; imitation of, 82; in Africa,
  72; intercourse and, 487; laxity in,
  258; mores of, 245; pre-marital, 134,
  147; preoccupation with, 149, 170;
  training, 480-81
Sexual identity, 487-91
Shakers
  visions among, 425
Shaman, 417;
  among Zulu, 390; and dreams, 421;
  as disciplinarian, 438; as status holders, 411; dance of a, 427; performances by, 373
Shame, *See also* Emotions
  in American Indian, 150; in Japanese, 54-55
Shilluk
  "possession" of, 417
Shiva, 543, 545
Siblings, 527, 538;
  displaced by, 439-40; rivalry, 185,
  553
Sikkhism, 544
Sioux, 121, 158
Siriono, 141
Six-Cultures Study, 72, 74, 83, 471,
  472-73, 475
Sleep
  and dreaming, 413; and hypnosis,
  425; evolutionary theory of, 414
Smoke From Their Fires, 124
Social anthropology
  American definition, 5; British defini-
  tion, 5; interpersonal mechanisms of,
  5
Social Change in the South Pacific, 182
Social Class and Mental Illness, 385
Social disintegration, 106-07
Social Order of Slums, The, 498

Social psychology
  and culture-and-personality, 3; and
  psychological anthropology, 11-13;
  from Western data, 12; in Japan, 22;
  methodology of, 435-36
Social security, 249
Socialism
  in England, 249
Socialization, 50, 465, 469;
  age of, 478-79; aim of, 488; among
  American Indians, 151; and adult
  role expectations, 82; and initiation
  rites, 491; as integration of society,
  471; definition of, 470; in Africa,
  44, 48, 75, 84; in India, 27; in Japan,
  27, 33, 35; in later childhood, 483;
  in Puerto Rico, 276; political, 497-98;
  pressures of, 485; of male role, 491;
  of sex roles, 487; responsibility and
  obedience to, 83; severity of, 482;
  spiral progression of, 466
Society
  African, 83, 85, 675; art forms of,
  479; authoritarian, 19; democratic,
  19; human, 465, 589; insect, 465;
  interests of members of, 234; matrilineal, 171; monogamous, 478, 480,
  489; patriarchal, 516, 524, 534; patrilineal, 516, 518, 524, 534; patrilocal,
  514, 516, 524, 534; polygynous, 439,
  479, 489; Polynesian, 180; restraints
  of, 438; stability of, 438; "Trance
  Present" and "Trance Absent" forms
  of, 420
*Society, Personality, and Deviant
  Behavior,* 150, 158
Sociocultural change, 97, 98, 106, 210;
  affects on mental disorder, 99, 108;
  and Japanese personality, 54
Sociologists, 246, 248
Sociology, 370
Son of Old Man Hat, 137
Sorcerer, 480; *See also* Witches
Sorcerer of Dobu, 172
Sorcery, 157, 168, 428; *See also*
  Witchcraft
  and social control, 482; among
  family members, 548-49; as result of
  inhibition of aggression, 482; beliefs
  in, 483; in Africa, 557
Soulside, 498

Source traits
definition of, 7
South, the, 244, 259
South America, 228
South American Japanese
personality traits, 46, 49, 54
Spain
national character of, 205; religious
persecution in, 257
Spanish-Americans
discussion of, 150-55; Rorschach
protocols among, 278
Spirits, *See also* Supernatural
possession by, 480; world of, 474
Status, 249, 469, 510
and ego, 488; and goals, 591; fear of
losing, 255; presence of, 479
Stress
acculturative, 183; among American
Indians, 146; animals under, 477;
and music, 477; emotional, 376; infants under, 477; intra-psychic, 49;
physiological, 374; psychological, 53;
socially determined, 397
Students, college
anti-Semitism among, 257; in Africa,
72; personalities of, 220, 222; results
of projective tests given to, 316-53
Students, high school
anti-Semitism among, 256n; in
America, 87, 247, 249
Submission, 149
Suburbia
intellectual, 438
Success
American value of, 228, 254, 260;
among African tribes, 96; chances
for, 511; for Nisei, 48; motivation for,
53
Sun Chief
American Indian leader, 124
Supernatural, *See also* Spirits, Sorcerers,
Sorcery
as kinship structure, 540-44; communication with, 420, 422; experience of the, 428; forces of, 106-07;
friendly or hostile, 426; Hindu belief
in, 538-39; orientation to, 542;
possession, 117; use of dreams and,
408-411, 422
Superorganic
Kroeber's concept of, 3

Surface traits
definition of, 7
Swazi, 75
Sweden, 227
Switzerland, 222
Sublimation, 596, 598-99, 602; *See also*
Defense mechanisms
Systems
age grade, 438; behavior, 479, 483;
cultural, 514, 589; kinship, 511;
personality, 582, 585-88; political,
208-09, 226-27, 232-35; projective,
185; religious, 473; Russian, 215;
social, 570, 583, 592, 596, 597
Szonoi and Picture Test, 275

T-groups, 364n
Taboos
avoidance, 599; cleanliness, 480;
incest, 558; menstrual, 480; of intimacy among Orientals, 518; on
rulers, 556; sex ("post-partum"),
492, 495
Tahitian, 187
Tally's Corner, 498
Tallensi, 82, 108, 511
Tanzania
testing in, 282
Tchambuli, 172
"teme"
definition of, 103, 104
Temne
and group normalcy, 493; cultural
traits of, 84; discipline, 92, 93; men
and women, 493; perception, 91;
socialization, 92
Tenetehara
extended households of, 476
Tension, 365
Tepoztlan, 141
Tetany, 380, 381, 382
Teton Dakota
inter-personal behavior, 130
Thai
peasant personality, 272-73; 275
Thailand, 273, 290
Theft, 484-85
Thematic Apperception Test (TAT),
32-33, 49, 95, 96, 136, 175, 176,
178-79, 215, 232, 263, 264, 275
and Death responses, 331-38; and

enjoyment, 338; and Love responses, 331-38; data yield, 312-17; examples of results of, 317-26; vs. Rorschach, 277, 279-85, 286, 289, 291, 292
Therapy
electric, 367; hydro and work, 367; shock, 370, 392
Thonga, 75
Tikopia
Possession Trance among, 420
Tiv
conservation study of the, 86, 88; males, 88
Toilet training, 35, 537;
differences in Japan and United States, 34; severity of, 480, 482
Tokugawa Religion, 53
Tokugawa, 50
Tokushu Burakumin
Japanese minority group, 45, 46
Tonga, 180
Totalitarianism, 227, 258
Totemism
among Aborigines, 170; among Aranda, 171, 581
Totem and Taboo, 170, 171
Torres Straits, 5, 170;
Expedition, 292
Traditions, 125;
impervious to change among Orientals, 522; Western, 292
Trance, 418-29;
and "possession", 417; definition of, 416-17; hallucinatory, 427; "toloache", 420
Transfer
habit, 439, 447
Transvestism, 484
Trobriands, 5, 171, 172
dreams of the, 406; father-son relationship, 512; intrafamilial attitudes, 449
Treaties
violence resulting from, 130
Trypanosomiasis
in West Africa, 366
Turkana, 75
Turks
compared with Iran, 224
Tuscarora, 144-45
Typology, 515

Uganda
perceptive tests in, 292
Unconscious
of Kalabari, 103; psychological forces of, 414; Tuscarora, 145
Unconscious, The, 366
Union of South Africa
religious persecution in, 257
UNESCO, 221
United States, 74, 122, 273;
anti-semitism in, 252; democratic tradition of, 225; government of, 227; Indian Education Research Project, 128; Office of Indian Affairs, 136; national character of, 213, 217-18; religious persecution in, 256; TAT tests in, 284
Urban ecology, 42
Urbanization, 42-43, 190, 234;
effect of cognitive growth, 88; effect on population, 100
Urban residents, 31;
in Japan, 52
U.S.S.R.
organization of, 271, 446
Utilitarianism, 133
Utopias
belief in, 547

Values, 18, 230, 231, 235;
American, 242, 243; behavior to exclusion of, 470; Christian, 247; idealized, 497; of group affiliations, 253; *operative, conceived, object,* 258-59
Vanaprastha, 537
Varieties of Human Value, 258
Vedanta, 540
Verbalization, 81
Vishnu, 543, 545
Visions, 425, 426, 427, 445, *See also* Hallucinations
Vocational Apperception Test, 276
Vocational Aspirations
American-Japanese 36, 48
Voodoo death, 386
Vote, 218, 259
Volksgeist, 124

War, 132, 146;
anxiety, 411; as national character,

203; between American Indians and Euro-Americans, 130; intelligence during, 184; religious, 532

Way of life, 512n, *See also* National character
and kinship, 513

Weaning, 34, 478, 536;
among Ganda and Zulu, 79; among Hopi, 137; among Yorubu, 101; behavior during, 80; late, 378; prevailing experience, 81; relationship to personality, 142; severity of, 480, 481; traumatic character of, 74
Weimar republic, 208

Welfare, 249;
Indian problem of, 136

Western culture
influence in Africa, 98, 246; Japanese assimilation of, 53; kinship structures of, 524-34; perceptions, 90; religious persecution in, 256; superiority of, 260; tradition of, 292; norms of, 81

Westernization, 101, 293;
and mental illness, 102

Whiting, Lionells and Martin Felt Design Test
results of, 494

Windigo, 365, *See also* Psychosis

Witches, *See also* Sorcerers
belief in, 557; hunts in Africa, 557; identification of, 405; in dreams, 403

Witchcraft, 73, 97, 105, 374; *See also* Sorcery
and family member, 548-49; associated with sex conflict, 482

Without the Chrysanthemum and the Sword, 24

Wolof
concept formation among, 86, 87, 88

Women, *See also* Females
and socio-emotional competence, 493; anxiety in, 409-10; dissatisfaction with roles, 133; dreams of, 94, 408; Eskimo, 493; expanded roles, 100; importance in subsistence activities, 491; Lovedu, 82; male identification with, 488; sex roles of, 487; subserviance of, 373; Temne, 493

Work, 139

World War I, 208;
investigations of metabolism before, 367

World War II, 26, 30, 42, 47, 50;
cultural change in Japan after, 54; economic collapse of Japan in, 53; illiteracy in, 515; "nerve gas" after, 368; psychiatry during, 367; research about, 215; research after, 216

Yankees
kinship system, 511

Yir Yoront
dreams of the 406, 407, 412; male dreams of, 408

Yoruba, 92, 105, 109;
death rites, 549; families, 101; mental illness, 152; religion, 100; success among, 96

Yurok, 158

Zuni, *See also* Pueblo
Rorschach protocols among, 278

Zulu, 389-90;
education, 98, 100; relationship of mother to infants, 74; weaning, 79, 80-81